WRISTWATCH ANNUAL
2018

THE CATALOG

of

PRODUCERS, PRICES, MODELS,

and

SPECIFICATIONS

BY PETER BRAUN

WITH MARTON RADKAI

ABBEVILLE PRESS PUBLISHERS

New York London

info@cwjbrands.com, 954-279-1220

Dear Reader, several years ago, I was told that the druids of yore used to hang themselves upside down in order to get a new perspective on the world. Whether this is true or not, I'd prefer not wasting time finding out, because as the old saying goes: *Se non è vero, è ben trovato* . . .

It seems that the watch industry may have been trying this exercise in order to get out of its recent crisis, which lasted about two years. In Switzerland, export figures finally started climbing again in 2017, reaching 2011 levels in June. In contrast to the 2009 crisis, which was basically financial—the sudden evaporation of lots of fictitious cash—this one was mostly structural, it seems, with overproduction leading to saturated markets, retailers sitting on large stocks of material, and, as a corollary, the gray market swelling to uncomfortable proportions.

The industry reacted first with battle cries and positive thinking. And then prices started coming down a bit, particularly on newer models to move merchandise, doors were closed, while online portals opened to facilitate and enlarge consumer access. China's economy stabilized, as well, which helped.

Tweaking sales and production strategies is fine and good, but the industry is ultimately about product and marketing emotion. And so an odd shift happened. In early 2016, the organizers of the SIHH, essentially a Richemont Group trade fair, decided to invite a group of independents and small brands to its hallowed halls. The "Carrée des Horlogers" included such radicals as MB&F, Urwerk, HYT, Hautlence, and others. And it created enough buzz to call for a repeat performance a year later, in January 2017, when the list was lengthened with such names as Romain Jerome, Peter Speake-Marin, MCT, and the Grönefelds. Besides bringing these small companies in from their temporary exhibition rooms in the suites of Geneva's luxury hotels, where they drew clientele away from the fair, the Carrée seems to be a tacit acknowledgment of what many experts in the field have been saying for years: These are the watchmakers pushing the envelope and opening up new spaces, creating watches unconstrained by market demands, and, above all, drawing lots of attention. They are simply very exciting, and could whet the appetite of newbies, while serving as object lessons to newer collectors and aficionados still afraid to buy outside the box.

Baselworld followed suit in 2017, relocating the small maverick brands from their windy "palace" on the green adjacent to the fair buildings, to the second floor of the main hall. It was a bit out of reach, but it did conjure the image of a fountainhead allowing creative juices to trickle down to the big brands below.

LETTER TO THE READER

Many serious trade journalists I spoke with said: "Finally!" Indeed, the smaller firms are like expert commandos who slip into the future and make way for the infantry. Even the marketing managers, CEOs, and other leaders of the larger houses would agree, though not necessarily in public.

And that is the industry turning upside down and looking at the world a little differently.

As a window on the watch industry, *Wristwatch Annual* continues to give space to those other, alternative watchmakers as well as the established brands. For a focused look on the independent scene, we always rely on Beth Doerr's unique expertise (page 12). Many of the extremely original—and at times young—brands are back in again with new material, like Artya, Azimuth, MB&F, Louis Moinet, Manufacture Royale. Three mavericks need special mention, as their vision of the watch is not ultra-modern, but rather ultra-classical: Julien Fleury from La Chaux-de-Fonds with his remarkable duManège brand, Raffaello Radicchi and the *manufacture* Schwarz Etienne, and finally Laurent Ferrier, whose complicated watches reflect Zen-like simplicity and beauty. Czapek & Cie. has also found place in these pages, a company reviving the legacy of Patek's first business partner, Frantiszek Czapek. While not necessarily "small," let me give a special mention to Fabergé, whose watch department under the leadership of Aurélie Picaud, has managed to create a stunning portfolio within very few years.

American brands are always welcome, naturally, and this year Deep Blue, a specialist in divers' watches, is back to accompany Detroit, Hager, RGM, and others.

With watchmaking, the devil is often in the details. To oil a watch, you can't just reach for the WD-40. Five different lubricants are used in some mechanisms, and applying the wrong one, or the wrong amount, can mean a watch will suddenly start acting up. Bill Yao and Lee Dowell look into this technology on page 42. As for design, having glimpsed Itay Noy's Open Mind watch in 2016, I decided this year to explore skulls and watches and found a huge trove of remarkable work (page 20). Finally, this: If you spot a multi-axis tourbillon, maybe coupled with a resounding minute repeater, or some other extreme complication, chances are Pierre-Laurent Favre had his virtuosic fingers in it. This outstanding watchmaker works with major brands, but always in the background. Literally in secret.

By the way: Any prices mentioned in the book are subject to change.

To close, a few notes of thanks. First to the contributors mentioned above, who offer their unique expertise. Thanks, too, to Ginny Carroll for excellent proofing and steering production of the book. Any errors are, regretfully, mine. Finally, a mention of our advertisers, who make *Wristwatch Annual* possible, and to you, the reader, who has purchased this book. We live in a somewhat frenetic age of online evanescence, but the book you have in your hand will last a long time. Your contribution helps us maintain our independence and publish this yearly, durable tribute to beautiful timepieces. Please enjoy it.

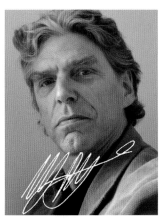

Marton Radkai

This year's *Wristwatch Annual* cover showcases Bovet's extremely complicated Recital 20 Asterium, a watch that expresses the passage of time by the movement of heavenly bodies. The main dial of blue sapphire represents a night sky with luminescent constellations and twenty-four hours. The equation of time and precision moon phase appear on a separate subdial, retrograde minutes and the ten-day power reserve indicator on another. The tourbillon, with seconds, at 6 o'clock is visible from both sides of the watch. The case back is dedicated to a full annual calendar showing equinoxes, seasons, and signs of the zodiac. The 46-millimeter watch comes in red gold, white gold, or platinum with an alligator strap and gold buckle.

FUNCTIONS

Hours	Precision Moon Phase Indicator
Retrograde Minutes	Season
Seconds on Tourbillon	Solstice and Equinox Indicator
Annual Calendar	Astrological Zodiac Indicator
Night Sky	Power Reserve Indicator
Equation of Time	

THE INDEPENDENT SCENE 2017

ELIZABETH DOERR

In spite of hard times in the industry, the independent watchmakers seemed to have made advances in 2017. Baselworld created the buzzing new Les Ateliers hall just for them, while the SIHH's Carré des Horlogers will jump to a record 16 independent brands and creators in 2018.

The heart piece of the independent scene remains the A.H.C.I. (Académie Horlogère des Créateurs Indépendents/Horological Academy of Independent Creators), a group of independent creators founded in 1985. The way of these individualistic watchmaker-inventors is indeed anachronistic, and though the products that emerge may not be everyone's cup of tea all of the time, they do attract the attention of collectors of rare taste who follow not only the horological escapades of these 30-odd extraordinary men of varying age and nationality, but also the passion and personality that go into each extremely limited timepiece.

FROM THE EAST

Self-taught Japanese horological virtuoso **Hajime Asaoka** has been associated with the A.H.C.I. for several years, but it is his appropriately named **Chronograph** that is now catapulting him into the limelight of the select circle of connoisseurs who appreciate high-quality work by independent watchmakers. After working for years developing multiple tourbillon movements as well as Tsunami, a time-only movement with a massive 16 mm balance wheel, Asaoka turned his sights on the column wheel chronograph. Chronograph is based on the Tsunami movement with its oversized balance wheel even though much of the new caliber needed to be redesigned for new hand locations and to make space for the chronograph mechanism. Asaoka's main goal—aside from creating his own example of the beloved complication—was to place the chronograph mechanism on full view on the dial side of the 38 mm stainless steel case, a size that perfectly complements today's vintage tendencies.

Crypto-steampunk chronograph by Hajime Asaoka with the mechanism in full view on the dial.

The intricate Moscow Comptus Clock by Konstantin Chaykin.

Chaykin's Joker displays hilarious time.

Beat Haldimann keeps the dials free for his striking blue.

Konstantin Chaykin, now president of the A.H.C.I., resides in Moscow. But that does not stop him from creating some of the world's best and most complicated timepieces. The **Moscow Comptus Clock** with 26 indications springs to mind as a recent attest of his patient genius. However, it is 2017's **Joker** that has brought him a great deal of attention: an ETA-driven wristwatch with an inventive and funky clown face whose eyes and mouth move along with the displays. "Mr. Chaykin, don't be so serious!" reads the accompanying press release—and the fun countenance certainly showed the serious watchmaker's lighter side while attracting lots of publicity.

SWITZERLAND

There was no shortage of independent Swiss creations in 2017 either, both inside and outside the A.H.C.I. **Romain Gauthier** introduced his first automatic wristwatch and, as one might expect, it is anything but ordinary despite the fact that it was conceived as a daily wearer. This 39.5 mm timepiece available in a variety of variations inside red gold or platinum cases boasts a visible movement wound by a 22-karat gold micro rotor. The name **Insight Micro-Rotor** evokes the fact that the inner workings of the mechanics are fully on view. Rarely does the fan of good watchmaking actually get to see the rotor at work when the watch is on the wrist; Gauthier has designed an impeccably finished watch whose style is efficient and elegant at the same time. But we expect no less of this brilliant engineer.

Beat Haldimann is known for his elegant style of complicated watchmaking that is firmly rooted in the principles of creative, philosophically inclined haute horlogerie. Therefore, encasing his work in stainless steel has not yet been an option; however, 2017 sees the first watches by Haldimann housed in 39 and 42 mm steel cases. The second surprise is the rich blue dials becoming the faces of the new **H11** and **H12** models, which only differ from each other in

Romain Gauthier opens a view onto the microrotor.

M1-Woodward chronograph. Swiss caliber ETA 7750 automatic mechanical movement. 44mm case with deployment clasp. Designed and Assembled in Detroit.

Exclusively available at **detroitwatchco.com**

M1 Exhibition Back   M1 Blue Dial   M1 Caseback

DETROIT WATCH COMPANY®

the absence or addition of a second hand, exhibiting a startling sheen and frosted effect obtained by using a silver dial blank and silver powder. Turning these watches over, one is rewarded with an even more spectacular view: a hand-frosted manually wound movement highlighting the central position of the balance with a proprietary shock absorber. Haldimann's own modified escapement is not visible.

Manufacture Royale introduced its ninth manufacture movement within an all-new timepiece called **ADN** (the French word for "DNA"). The 67-part 46 mm case's well-rounded curves, now resembling something from the steampunk era, are available in stainless steel, DLC-coated stainless steel and forged carbon, or pink gold and forged carbon. Caliber MR09 continues the micro brand's recent quest for transparency with a barely-there skeletonized movement that includes a flying tourbillon as well as jump hours and a crown-operated second time zone capable of displaying every time zone, even those 30 or 15 minutes off the GMT reference. Translating haute horlogerie into something wearable, understandable, and yet unique for the average city-dwelling watch wearer, **Louis Moinet**'s answer to the "urban watch" is the new **Metropolis**. "It combines ergonomics with design and function with style. We've broken free of neoclas-sical conventions and adopted a committed, contemporary approach that's unlike anything we've done before," explains CEO Jean-Marie Schaller. Putting openworked elements in different places (hour markers, dial, lugs, vertical bridges) provides a rather three-dimensional character to the watch available in a 43.2 mm stainless steel or red gold case; the complicated case alone comprises 55 components. Both versions, limited to just 60 pieces, are powered by manually wound manufacture Calibre LM45.

Czapek & Cie., the product of three impassioned watch industry professionals, has mastered the art of great quality and fair pricing as the new unisex-sized **33s** model

The purely modern ADN (meaning DNA) of Manufacture Royale.

Louis Moinet's urban and urbane Metropolis.

Czapek & Cie.'s revival of their namesake's masterpiece

Advanced winding technology, for your fine watches.

SIENA SERIES 1 | 2 | 3

demonstrates beyond the shadow of a doubt: grand feu enamel dial, manufacture movement, 38.5 mm red gold or stainless steel case, and blued white gold fleur-de-lys hands harmoniously combine to make one stunner of a watch. "Aside from collectors, it's women today who are increasingly in love with fine watchmaking," says Xavier de Roquemaurel, brand CEO. "They also want to enjoy that discreet beauty of the Quai des Bergues collection, and we are thrilled to see that it is just as popular with women as men."

TWO "NEWCOMERS"

Two newcomers (though not really) have also made something of a splash in the independent scene in 2017. **James C. Pellaton**'s name has been resurrected from the annals of horological history by Michel Dawalibi, an independent watchmaker based in Le Locle. Dawalibi created the 44 × 14.85 mm red or white gold **Royal Marine Chronometer** fully in the style of his historical hero, having used the basic architecture of the historical

Pellaton tourbillon movements and expanding on the style and design for a modern wristwatch. **Montandon & Co.**'s **Windward** emerged from founder Daniel Montandon's history designing racing catamarans and rigging and structural components for ships as well as the numerous patents he holds for his work on various projects. The manufacture movement powering the 44 × 11 mm watch available in bronze or white gold made by Swiss independent watchmaker David Candaux contains an automatic flying tourbillon that resides in an oculus in the movement, making it visible from the front or the rear.

GERMANY

Marco Lang and his boutique brand **Lang & Heyne**, at home in the cradle of Saxon watchmaking, Dresden, returned in 2017 with an absolutely stunning rectangular watch with a new shaped caliber: Georg measures 40 × 32 mm and is as svelte as can be at 9.4 mm in height, thanks to the superbly finished, manual winding Caliber VIII.

Lang & Heyne's classic face (above) belies the modern design of the Caliber VIII (below).

Its beauty is enhanced by a simple enamel dial as the cherry on top.

But that's not all the A.H.C.I. has coming from Dresden: The organization's newest member, **Kim Djapri**, also hails from the Saxon capital. Djapri, who got his start at Lang & Heyne, announced his own boutique watch brand, **Bélier**, in 2016. This year his fabulous fully handmade watch, **Reverse**, is available in a new color scheme that lends it a completely new look. The 46.6 mm Reverse represents a reflection of a classic movement with everything placed as if the watch were looking at itself in a mirror. The time on the dial runs counterclockwise, and the numbers are arranged likewise. This superbly finished timepiece is chock full of delicious details, but my favorite is perhaps the small engraving on the back of the movement that proudly declares it is "made with passion."

Elizabeth Doerr is a freelance journalist specializing in watches and was senior editor of Wristwatch Annual *until the 2010 edition. She is now the editor in chief of* Quill & Pad, *an online magazine that "keeps a watch on time" (http://quillandpad.com).*

Mirrored time from Bélier's Reverse

The James C. Pellaton Royal Marine Chronometer improving on a venerable mechanism.

Montandon's sailing past is suggested on the dial of the Windward.

LIFE AND DEATH WATCH

MARTON RADKAI

Once an element of the subculture, the skull has undergone a process of gentrification. As a decorative element, it can be found all over the place and may have lost its power to surprise because of it, like punk music. But its ties to watchmaking are older and deeper.

Not too long ago, the skull moved from being a societal symbol of danger, fear, and death, to being a popular decorative element printed on clothing, from caps to socks. Suddenly, it served as inspiration to make handbags, shoes, shot glasses, dessert spoons, lighters, sugar cubes—in short any daily object or accessory. Today, anyone from beefy bikers to maturing teenagers, from regular folk to pale goths, from serious women in business to TGIF-celebrating stockbrockers, from connected Millennials to disconnected New Agers, from real toughs to wannabe bruisers—literally everyone seems perfectly comfortable wearing or carrying a skull somewhere.

The man many consider responsible for the demotion of the skull from threatening to mainstream banal was the baddest boy of bad-boy fashion, Alexander McQueen. He shook up the catwalk during his brief and meteoric career that ended in his suicide in February 2010. However, the popularity of the skull, and by extension skeletons, could not have happened were it not for the fact that the skull as an image is deeply ingrained in human culture. Culture explorer David Colman wrote in the *New York Times* in 2006: "[A]s consumers young and old tire of being marketed to, the skull appears to offer a kind of antidote: an ultimate unbrand, one that belongs to no one. Curiously, then, what began as an outlaw anti-logo may as

well be viewed as the death rattle of an underground aesthetic."

Eleven years later, that "unbrand" is, ironically, alive and kicking. And while it may have lost all semblance of creepiness or danger, there are some segments where it can still generate an emotional response and offer some food for thought. That is, as a decorative element in watchmaking. The reason for this may be the intimate relationship that each of us has with time ticking away and what it really means. When you look at your traditional watch—in other words, not a digital clock—it will tell you not the time, but how much time you have left for an activity, Ronnie Bernheim, CEO of Mondaine (now Lumondi), once told me.

Skulls are ubiquitous, from clothes to kitchen.

STURMANSKIE
THE FIRST IN SPACE

Only one watch company holds the distinction of being the first watch in space - Sturmanskie

It is rare when the phrase "own a piece of history" has real meaning. In the case of the Sturmanskie Yuri Gagarin commemorative edition it is not hyperbole.

Inspired by the original watch Gagarin wore during his historic 1961 flight, the watch is the only timepiece in the world authorized to use Gagarin's likeness. Hand assembled in Moscow, the watch uses the same Poljot movement as the original and truly brings the history of space travel to your wrist.

The spooky cranium, with hollowed eyes, bared or absent teeth, and a hint of a nose bone, has indeed remained one of the most durable representations of death and, dialectically, of youth and the passage of time. In a seventeenth-century *vanitas* still life, a skull will sit, dark and brooding, next to a beautiful bouquet of effusively colorful flowers; though motionless, it will represent something dynamic, the inexorable passage of time. If it could speak, it would be saying that the flowers will wilt, and that, in turn, tells us that each breath we take, each beat of the heart is one less in a lifetime. By extension it is whispering "*Carpe diem*, seize the day, live now." Our watches are in fact saying the same thing.

TOUCHSTONES FOR THE WRIST

Skulls and watchmakers have history going back to the sixteenth century. These memento mori were serious objects to remind people of their mortality. Today's skull watches, on the other hand, are different. The skulls appear mostly on the dial either lacquered or as an applique. They are meant to generate a response from the beholder, of course, but they may not consciously at least lead to thoughts about one's fragility. They are, in short, often entertainment. **Franck Dubarry**'s Revolution Fileteado displays a scary skull grinning from just below the center of the dial with effusive floral elements in fileteado style that extends to the similarly engraved case. At 6 o'clock, a stray heart reminds one of the intimate connection between love and death, a subject that will reappear below.

Integration of the skull in the natural structure of the watch is another popular approach. On their **TNT Royal Retro**, Pierre DeRoche shaped the main bridge on the dial as a skull and crossbones holding the disparate parts of the complex movement together, in particular the six little retrograde hands that sweep away time in a gentle ballet of ten-second dead beats. Another brand, HYT, used the natural shape of its glass capillary tubing carrying the fluid marker to produce a skull shape. The two miniature bellows at 6 o'clock look eerily like a set of clenched teeth. Seconds tick in the left eye, the power reserve is shown in the right one. The designers of the watch had a field day with luminescent components. It's quite the nighttime talking piece, with glaring red eyes and, in one version, a wild Maori tattoo on the "dial."

A third idea worth mentioning was presented in 2014 by the German independent Stefan Kudoke. The **Real Skeleton** is a pun: a skeletonized Unitas movement

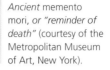

Ancient memento mori, *or "reminder of death"* (courtesy of the Metropolitan Museum of Art, New York).

Right: Austrian Artist Leo Zogmayer's Now Watch tells us to seize the moment (courtesy of Leo Zogmayer, jetzt-uhr.com). Below: The dial as canvas on Dubarry's Revolution Fileteado. Bottom: Skull integration on the TNT Royal Retro Pierre DeRoche (left) and the HYT Skull Red Eye (right).

Stefan Kudoke's spooky watch with gilt bones and skull with diamond-studded eye cavities.

A cranial tourbillon drives the skull-themed Christophe Claret X-TREM-1-StingHD.

with bridges and plates shaped like bones and plated in rose gold. On the dial, two long bones point to the time, while a skull, with eyes of diamonds, stares intently at the viewer. It was inspired from an early seventeenth-century skull, a time when death was having a field day due to epidemics and religious wars.

The Kudoke watch connects quickly with the viewer, partly because it was all made by hand with very rudimentary tools, giving it a very artistic feel, almost improvised. Christophe Claret, on the other hand, sober, silent, stringently technical, took a different path. The new StingHD collaboration on the **X-TREM-1** has two skulls. One appears on the sapphire crystal when you blow on it. The other is always present, a skull with fiery ruby eyes that turns slowly and hypnotically on the tourbillon cage. It is just a small decorative element, but it inexorably draws attention to the tourbillon as a core driver of the movement. If the watch were a human being, it could serve as the first (root) chakra, the place where the Kundalini resides and Lord Ganesha presides, the deity that helps overcome physical and spiritual obstacles.

LOVE OF LIFE AND DEATH

In 2013, independent watchmaker Hajime Asaoka released a darkly humorous tourbillon with a handful of stylized skulls floating on the dial. They looked a little like Munch's *The Scream* and had flowers in their eye sockets. The hour hand was a straight dagger, but the minute hand a squiggle that made reading the time quickly rather difficult. Point is, you can't really say when your exact time has come. But there is no dickering with Death. Red Gothic lettering on the dial says: "Death takes no bribe."

Asaoka's black humor finds some refutation in a number of watches that purport to actually defy death and express a desire to be genuinely resilient. This is the domain of the military, where soldiers of all stamp and political persuasion have used skulls on clothing, patches, or flags to terrify their enemies—often civilians caught in the conflict—or to express their willingness to fight unto death. American parachutists during World War II wore a patch with a skull and crossbones bearing the inscription "Death From Above." It appeared on the iconic **Bell & Ross Skull** in 2009, a watch that has reappeared in several iterations, recently with flames engraved on the trademark case. The skull itself is highly realistic and is coated with Superluminova, making it glow eerily at night.

GREUBEL FORSEY
ART of INVENTION

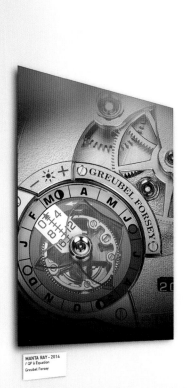

MANTA RAY - 2014
/ QP à Équation
Greubel Forsey

QP À ÉQUATION

White gold case - Millésimé

While soldiers are compelled to defy death, others choose to do so for whatever reason. Bikers hurtling along the asphalt-covered battlegrounds of the open road take a certain odd pride in riding the thin line between life and death on their machines. The **Bolt-68** series by Bomberg was tailor-made for bikers or those who need to wear some mettle-toughening iconography. The pieces are attractive and harmonious, but may lack the cragginess demanded by adult hellions of the road. For that, one must turn to the in-your-face skull watch experience, designed by the master of hyperbole and out-of-the-case thinking, Yvan Arpa. When I asked him about skulls in his collection, he rummaged around in a drawer and pulled out the **Raging Skulls**: a watch encased in a 3D skull and held onto the wrist with a bracelet of skulls and bullets. On the bezel, a crown of barbed wire, suggesting pain and suffering, perhaps a metaphor for life. "That's not for the faint of heart," I suggested. "No," he answered, digging around a bit in another drawer and pulling out a minimalistic black watch with a gentle skull in shimmering rainbows made of mother-of-pearl. Both watches, seen side by side, create two different emotions, demonstrating why skulls are so popular.

TILL DEATH US DO PART

The one force that can overcome death is love, so maintained the romantics throughout literary history. In Speake-Marin's motto, "Fight, Love and Persevere," we can almost sense the skull and the heart as appropriate symbols. The warrior, poet, and devoted lover all meet in those three words. Early on in his career, Speake-Marin turned to the skull motif, and the **Crazy Skulls** launched in January 2017 appears as an apotheosis of his work. The timepiece itself is a minute repeater carillon with a tourbillon at 6 o'clock. What makes this a bravura piece, however, is the fact that the tourbillon is invisible at first. All one sees is two skulls and between them a heart ("united in love even after death . . ."). Activating the minute repeater separates them to reveal the tourbillon and the end of time, no less, as the large Roman XII splits in two. After the peal of the bells, the skulls and heart and Roman XII resume their original spot.

THE CULTURE OF DEATH

The attitude toward death and the skull varies from one culture to the next. Europeans tend to see death with a varying mix of seriousness, pathos, and stoicism. One thinks of those drinking songs by the eighteenth-century Swedish poet Michael Bellmann that speak of jealous lovers losing out to their rivals when the Grim Reaper comes a-visiting. One also finds more active celebrations in the "Danse Macabre" art form, which depicted rowdy postmortem dances by the departed. But the idea of death as a liberation

The Speake-Marin Crazy Skulls repeater summons love, death, and time.

ArtyA's Raging Skulls (above) contrast with a more poetic mother-of-pearl design (below).

Bell & Ross's skull evolution borrows from a World War II paratrooper badge.

MTM ⊕ 3·GER

Gray 3-Ger with saphire
ball-bearings

S P E C I A L O P S W A T C H . C O M
Designed, engineered and hand-assembled in the US

The MTM Special Ops line of tactical time pieces is sold exclusively through **MTM**
Toll Free · 1 800 284 9487   International · 1 213 741 0808   1225 South Grand Ave Los Angeles CA 90015

The famous Mexican skull on the Angelus Calavera Tourbillon.

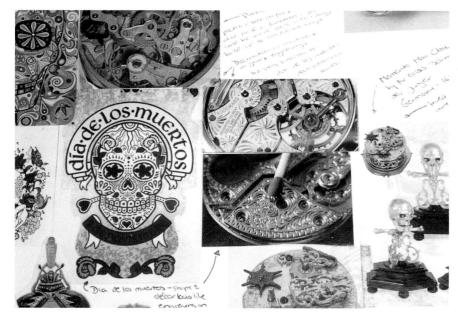

from the constraints of three-dimensional life is strongest in those cultures where animism still holds sway. Latin America is a good example, with Mexico in the lead for freely mixing Christianity with older spirituality. "The Mexican," wrote author Octavio Paz, "is familiar with death, jokes about it, caresses it, sleeps with it, celebrates it. He looks at it face to face, with impatience, disdain or irony." Death in the country is personified as *Santa Calavera*, literally the holy skull, a woman often garishly dressed. (As a chatty aside, the word *calavera* is related to Calvary, the Golgotha, where Jesus was crucified.)

Many brands have fallen under the spell of *la Santa Calavera*. A somewhat angry-looking Ms. Calavera in bright colors appears on the eponymous watch by the recently revived brand Angelus. Exactly why the motif was chosen is not clear, barring the fact that it is an eyecatcher. At any rate, the execution, so to speak, is outstanding.

The prize for the greatest skull watches celebrating Mexico, however, must go to Fiona Krüger, a Scottish designer and artist. She admits she knew next to nothing about watches until, while studying art in Lausanne, she visited the Patek Philippe Museum in Geneva. "That is where I realized that watches did not need to be round or square," she says. "But as an artist, I needed a concept, and the idea of the watch and mortality seemed logical." Krüger, a small, intense woman with piercing blue eyes, did some research and found that Mary, Queen of Scots had owned a skull pocket watch, a typical sixteenth-century *memento mori*. This revelation combined with three influential years she had spent in Mexico as a child. She set about finding the people and suppliers who could help her project along. Besides the creative challenges, she also had to break through a number of ceilings: She is a non-Swiss, very young, female watch designer.

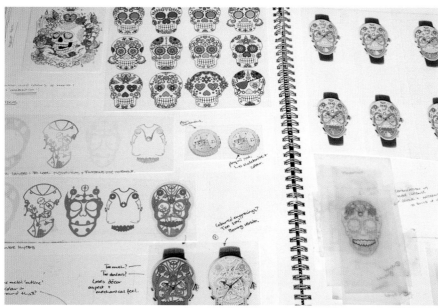

The creative world of Fiona Krüger, unique mistress of the skull watch: from sketch to product.

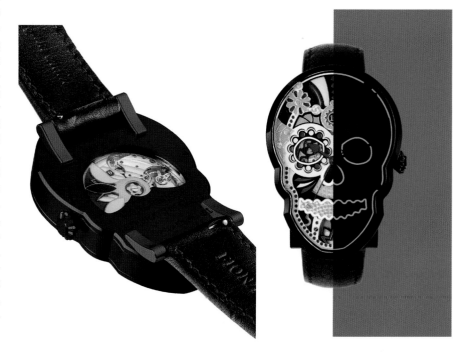

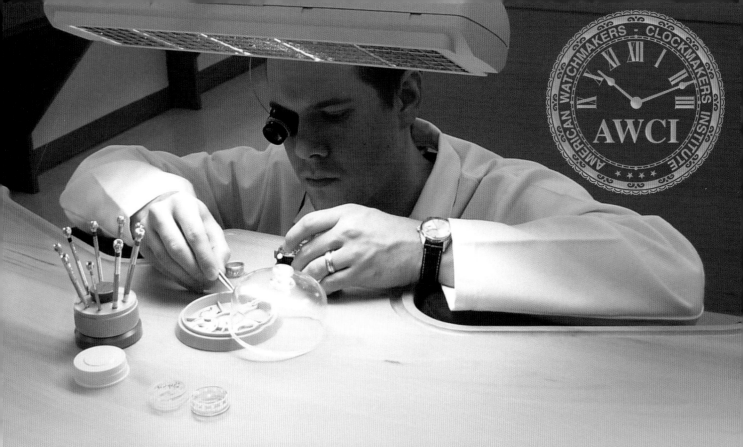

Krüger's skull-shaped watches are meticulously prepared. She always draws a pattern first on paper, so each watch's evolution can be traced in her notebooks. The Mexican-inspired timepieces are called Celebration. The vivid colors are carefully chosen, as each one has a certain symbolic meaning. Krüger also uses Superluminova with great care to highlight the key elements of the face, the mouth, nose, lips, and the outline of the skull along the bezel.

Krüger was amazed by the success of her concepts, which she had put online. She was already getting orders before completing a single watch. She continued to make new skulls using more traditional watchmaking techniques, such as guilloché. Thanks to her unique timepieces, Fiona Krüger has established herself as an outstanding watch-artist. Her talent caught the eye of Fabergé, for which she created an on-dial seaside image of rubies and diamonds for the Libertine III (see page 147).

Itay Noy (above) provides food for thought with his Open Mind (left).

THE MIND AT WORK

When I set out to write about skulls and watches, I hardly thought the subject was so vast and profound. Countless brands have used the motif, some as a banal fashion statement, some as a political statement, others because it has meanings that go beyond just being edgy. Corum has exploited skulls to great effect in its Bubbles, which include an array of skulls, from one wearing a pirate's bandana (see page 128), to the terrifying Voodoo figure Baron Samedi, a skull in a top hat who invites the dead to go to hell.

All skull watches seek to create a visceral response, but emotions are fluid and cannot really explain the durable attraction of the skull. When Israeli watch designer Itay Noy decided to make a skull watch, the Open Mind, he scanned a host of types with his mind's eye, from medieval skulls to Harley-Davidson. His first sketch was too scary, according to his young son, so he made it, as he describes it, "more medical." It jibed well with his other idea: "I thought of the movement, and the ticking of the watch was like a brain thinking." This is typical Noy, whose watches give time and act as food for thought at the same time. The Open Mind features a skull with an opening over the oscillating balance wheel, ticking away relentlessly, driving any number of gearwheels and regulating the wild impulsion from the mainspring. It has become the brain of the watch, rather than the heart, the traditional metaphor for the balance.

Noy's watch is remarkably successful. Several surgeons purchased one, but, interestingly, the first customer was a female judge, which makes sense in a serendipitous way. It suggests that there may be another meaning to the skull than just *carpe diem*. Indeed, for alchemists of yore, it was a "receptacle used in the process of transmutation," according to J. E. Cirlot's *A Dictionary of Symbols*. For most of us, the skull, as the home of our brain, is where we consider, deliberate, and transform information. In Norse mythology, the world is made of the giant Ymir's body, and the skull became the sky, itself a universal symbol of a power greater than the individual, a god, a mysterious force, or simply the collective human experience. This greater connection may account for the long partnership of the skull and the watch. The myriad crania combined with the passage of time are somehow a reminder of the evolution of human consciousness. They are fun, brittle, sexy, iconoclastic, but they are also serious matter.

The Voodoo guide in the afterlife, Baron Samedi, on a Corum Bubble.

IT'S COMPLICATED

MARTON RADKAI

Big watch brands like to boast of their technical prowess. It's undoubtedly true. But when they encounter a challenge that's a bit more than they can handle effectively, or if they have no development and manufacturing capacities, they find watchmakers like Pierre-Laurent Favre.

I t's somewhat ironic that the key figures of the watch industry, the hands-on watchmakers, are not the ones the public sees most often. Ambassadors, PR and marketing staff, even the CEOs are usually on the front line facing finicky consumers and talking up their products. The watchmakers themselves, the individuals who design, make, and assemble the parts to manufacture the watches, stay in the shadows. Some have made a business of this. Stealthily, these so-called *motoristes*, literally engine makers, work away at some of the most spectacular pieces to hit the markets.

Even among this discreet crowd, Pierre Favre stands out as a modicum of understatement and calm. When I went to visit him, I could barely even find his company, MHC, which is tucked away chameleonically in a residential block in Geneva's Eaux-Vives district.

"He's very, very modest," says Yvan Arpa, founder and CEO of ArtyA, and a longtime client. "He's also an outstandingly talented watchmaker." It may be an understatement. Favre, a small man with—like many watchmakers—a calm and deliberate energy, insists early on in our meeting that he must protect the confidentiality of his clients. Because of this, wandering around his offices has a surreal quality. In every work space, I spot some of the most common names in the industry. In one in/out tray, wrapped in protective foil, a watch covered in baguette-cut stones waits to be shipped, apparently. Pierre Favre picks it up with a resolute hand and, with typical modesty, comments not on the engine inside, which is his creation, but on the outstanding stone setting, another Geneva specialty.

Each watchmaker at MHC works on a watch from beginning to end.

Traditional tools are required for the handcrafting work.

AVANTGARДE

EMOTION • INNOVATION • PROVOCATION

Babylonian Hand winding. Hand engraved movement. Three levels open dial with MOP ring. Blued hands. Stainless steel. 5 ATM. 500 pcs limited Edition.

LITTLE *Treasury* **JEWELERS**

2506 New Market Lane
Gambrills, MD 21054
410-721-7100
www.littletreasury.com

ALEXANDER SHOROKHOFF
UHRENMANUFAKTUR
GERMANY

WWW.ALEXANDER-SHOROKHOFF.DE

On another table, in the more technical side of the business, a few watches await by the witschi, a machine that will test for accuracy in six positions, and an indispensable tool of the trade. At first glance, it hardly looks like a watch, just a movement encased in some transparent box. A closer glance reveals a case machined out of sapphire crystal, a very difficult process due to the extreme brittleness of the material. "It's a monster project with a gossamer movement," says Favre, suppressing his pride. He holds it like a bird that has fallen from its nest.

The brands that have approached MHC would probably not suffer any adverse consumer reactions were it known that their highly complicated watches were developed and built in part under the direction of a man with nearly forty years' experience in the business, including three major industry crises.

SALT OF THE RIGHT EARTH

Pierre-Laurent Favre was born in watch country, the canton of Neuchâtel, and into a watchmaking family. As a child, his grandfather took him along to his work at the old Angelus factory in Le Locle. That put him on the scent. As a teenager, he attended the watchmaking school of Geneva. It was the beginning of the quartz crisis, and the teachers were convinced that watchmaking in Switzerland was a dead craft. "I was in a class of five students, so we learned a great deal, we could ask all the questions we wanted," he recalls.

Crisis or not, barely out of school, he was recruited by Patek Philippe and tasked with working on complications for wristwatches.

He stayed with the company for twenty-five years. But as it happens, around those middling years of a man's life, he began thinking about the rest of his professional career. With four children to support, jumping into the unknown would not be an easy move. "I realized that I could make an entire watch, so why not do it for other brands that did not have the capacity to build such watches." Not many were actually doing contract manufacturing, it was 2005, money was flowing, and so he joined the famous BNB Concept, which made complicated movements for high-end brands, notably Hublot.

CRASH AND BOUNCE

The hyperbolization of luxury watches in the late aughts came to an abrupt end with the crash of 2008–2009. Brands had

Pride of place: Favre's own "school watch."

MHC only does very advanced complications, like tourbillons and minute repeaters.

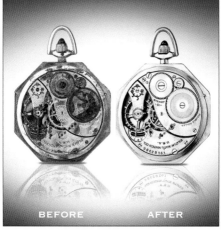

Right: Protecting every part from dust.

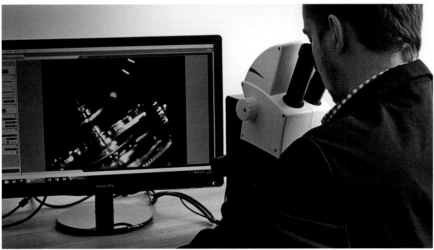

Left: CAD means shorter design times.
Below: The tiny, complex setting lever spring waiting for beveling.

been spending huge sums on extravagant watches, and suddenly the money dried up. This put paid to the meteoric rise of BNB Concept, leaving many of its customers high and dry. With a family to feed and a professional life to shape, Favre decided to found MCH, which would pick up where BNB left off and could contribute to the defunct company's after-sales service. "It was on my fiftieth birthday, and I thought, if I start when things are difficult, when things get better it will all seem easy," says Favre.

It was a time of negotiations with former BNB Concept clients and hunting for new ones. He decided to start with a small team: himself, a designer, and a watchmaker. At Baselworld 2010, he was approached by Michel Pitteloud, CEO of Graff, who was planning a watch division for the company. Could he do a minute repeater in less than a year? "I said 'Of course,' and even he recognized that it was a mission impossible,"

Favre recalls. "We started work, doing the machining wherever we could." In 2011, they delivered and were hired again for another round of watchmaking for Graff.

Fast growth was not the strategy. Instead, Pierre Favre decided that fascinating projects were most important, especially those involving tourbillons—single, dual-axis, or triple-axis ones—and minute repeaters, stuff he had profound experience with.

TICKING ALONG

Today, the company has 18 employees, including seven full-fledged watchmakers. In many larger *manufactures*, they would work on pieces sequentially. Favre and the watchmakers prefer having a single piece to work on from soup to nuts. "You can then trace a watch back to its maker, and it's a guarantee of higher quality because each has a feeling of responsibility for his piece," says Favre. One worker is building a triple-

axis tourbillon, another is doing something with tweezers on pieces too small to see with the naked eye. Along the window is a third workstation, where a woman is manipulating a setting lever spring. She has a special task: ensuring the perfect finishing of the movements—chamfering, flank drawing, polishing—which is such an important and time-consuming aspect of a perfect watch.

With a small team, organization is key. That job goes to Cindy Cart, who devised an ordering and storage system for the myriad components and spare parts that boggles the mind. Colored boxes are stacked in shelves (the colors are in fact irrelevant, I learn later) over narrow numbered drawers containing meticulously marked envelopes, each with components from the MHC portfolio. "It's great, it allows us to react very quickly to customer requests," Favre points out.

WILLIAM HENRY

One watch personality who does not mind having his name connected with Pierre Favre is Yvan Arpa. The two men have known each other for a long time, and the mutual respect is palpable. "If I go to a company with a complicated project, they look a bit sheepish, then hem and haw," says Arpa. "Favre says, great, what a fantastic idea. He understands things quickly, he has empathy!" Until recently, the ArtyA offices were nearby, and Arpa would show up to brainstorm with the design team. "Everything starts on a blank piece of paper," Favre says with a smile. "Then Yvan keeps adding things, so there are not many limits. We're not afraid of these projects, we step back, take a look, begin designing, and soon we find solutions."

On the day of my visit, work was being done on ArtyA's phenomenally complicated Three Gongs Minute Repeater, Regulator, and Double Axis Tourbillon. The watch has a minute, quarter hour, and hour repeater on two gongs, and a third dedicated one to inform the user that the repeater is running. "The most difficult part was to combine the two complications, and then to integrate the hammers and three gongs into such confined space," says Favre.

The ArtyA watch appears on a computer screen. It's like an MRI of the piece. The inside is a thicket of gearwheels, cams, and components with odd shapes, none of which are without a vital function. Running around the edge is the third gong. But while CAD can speed up certain processes, it is not a replacement for the expert eye of the watchmaker. "If we had a forty-five-degree axis tourbillon cage, we could have had fewer gearwheels," Favre says, pointing at the lower section of the plan. "It would have used less energy." These are the challenges.

A SOLID POSITION

As a movement maker, Favre and his team touch on three areas of watchmaking. The first is design, involving engineering, creation, and finding solutions. "It's very mathematical." The next area is micromechanics, where the designs are implemented and, at times, changed if a better solution can be found. The third area is actual watchmaking, assembly, finishing, testing. In contrast to large *manufactures*, however, all three areas work closely together and support each other.

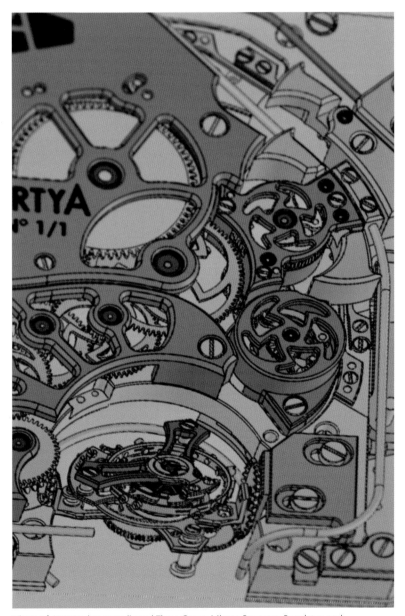

Views of Artya's ultra-complicated Three Gongs Minute Repeater, Regulator, and Double Axis Tourbillon.

TIME TONE
2017 COLLECTION

From his vantage point at the heart of the industry, Favre has insights into the evolution of watchmaking. The past two years have seen the industry in a crisis, his third, and he is quick to point out that it is structural rather than financial: Markets are saturated and retailers can't move the product. This has brought about a pressure on prices, and therefore a greater demand for lots of bang for fewer bucks. This can be frustrating for *motoristes*, who, by nature, are perfectionists.

And Favre has noticed other changes as well. People are not only going for the big names but also following their emotions and seeking out less standard, not to say unique, pieces. This is why he is not worried about the current crisis, though he does feel for his industry. "Every day we can work on projects together with the madcap gang I have here," he says. "We all have a great time working on novelties." He has done all the "guitars" for ArtyA, to mention one major and unique project.

Working directly with collectors, however, is not for him. "It would put me in direct competition with my clients," he says. "That is why Christophe Claret decided to found his own brand . . . Never had the desire to make a watch . . ." Besides, he adds, doing one thing all the time would not be nearly as exciting. It's a view I have often heard from dyed-in-the-wool *motoristes*. The world wants to rationalize and simplify. In watchmaking that is anathema. Complications are the way to go.

Each part at MHC has to be made from scratch.

Organization is everything: Pierre-Laurent Favre and MHC's spare parts storage.

M
duManège

La Chaux-de-Fonds

Heritage Red Gold 18 carat
«Grand Feu» Ivory enameled dial

Public price: 9 996 USD (without local VAT)

www.dumanege.ch

WATCH TECH

THE RIGHT STUFF: LUBRICANTS

BILL YAO and LEE DOWELL

Making watches is delicate business. A real watchmaker needs to be versed in many esoteric sciences. And when all has been assembled, the timepiece needs to be oiled. Even
that is a science in itself, one that can make or break the movement.

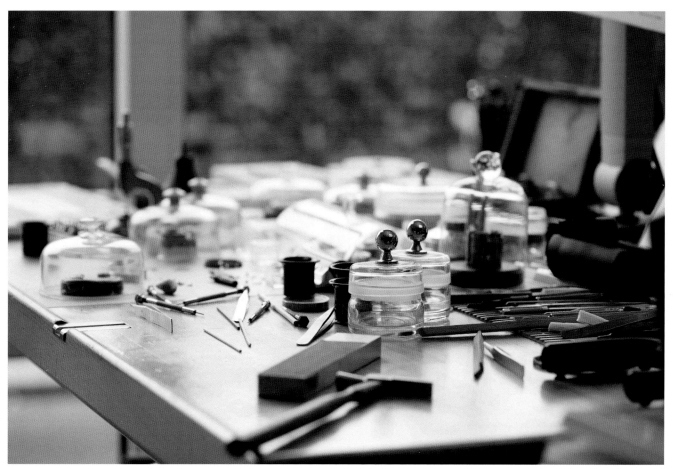

Watchmaker's workbench, or alchemist's lair?

Watch oils are a largely ignored aspect of watchmaking and to hear the recent develop-ments in watchmaking it seems they are the buzz kill at every party. In fact, so much so that enormous efforts and resources are being allocated to banish them from watchmaking altogether. The heroes of watchmaking are the gears, the guilloché on the dials, blued hands, and German silver plates. Those are the things that collectors and customers can see and appreciate. But deep inside the engine, invisible to the naked eye, are the real heroes of the craft: watch lubricants. Yes, that is a plural, because lubricating a watch is not quite as simple as giving your old Dodge Dart a quick lube job at Jiffy's. And in spite of the money dedicated to getting rid of them, the technology of lubricants has continued to march on. Experimenting with silicon certainly helped, but it was not a panacea. The history and use of oils is more nuanced and deserves to be celebrated, and its history explored.

HAGER

*The Hager Diplomat Strikes a note
of elegance all its own and was made
for the man who knows the value of time...*

Now comes the hard part...which Hager?

SLICK AND SLICKER

There are two basic types of lubricants used in watchmaking: oils and greases. Selecting one or the other depends primarily on the surfaces to be protected. Generally speaking, grease is used where the aim is reduction of friction between two metal surfaces, such as the keyless works (winding mechanisms). Oils are used when the surfaces to be protected are metal and a jewel. Wherever you see a "ruby" in your watch, you'll see a small depression at the top, enough to receive a tiny drop of oil.

Greases and oils can be refined from organic, synthetic, and petroleum sources. Modern lubricants for watchmaking are either synthetic or petroleum based. However, at the turn of the twentieth century most watchmaking lubricants were derived from animal sources such as whales and cattle hooves. The transition from organic oils to synthetic and petroleum-based lubricants would appear to have been perfectly logical, but there were trade-offs. Synthetics generally do not oxidize and can keep watches working for longer periods between ser-

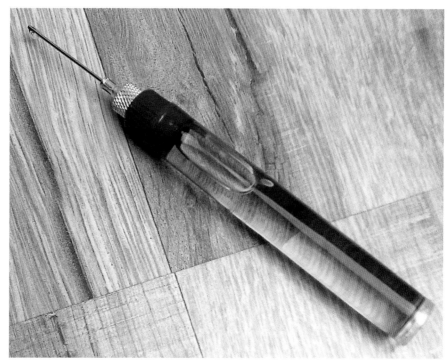

Prefilled oil delivery system.

Set of oil dippers for different viscosities.

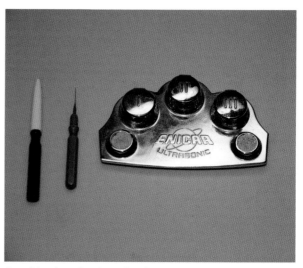

A traditional watchmaker's oil and grease reservoir.

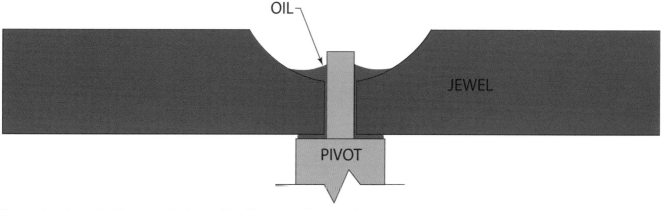

Cross-section of a jewel holding a pivot: Getting the right oil level is crucial (courtesy of American Watch and Clock Institute).

ESSENTIAL GEAR.

F-22 Raptor™ Chronograph 9241.M: 44mm, titanium case, screw down crown & case back, antireflective sapphire crystal, bidirectional rotating bezel with black aluminum slide rule ring, dial ring with tachymetric scale, solid link titanium bracelet with security clasp, water resistant to 200 meters, and Luminox self-powered illumination. Swiss Made.
Preferred timepiece of Military and Commercial Pilots

®**ALWAYS VISIBLE**
Constant Glow for up to 25 Years.

Shop Online
Shop.Luminox.com

The *LOCKHEED MARTIN* Collection

Oil is too high on the pivot, working surface is dry (courtesy of American Watch and Clock Institute).

Too much oil can leak and leave traces.

Oil splash leaves the pivot dry (courtesy of American Watch and Clock Institute).

Winding and time-setting mechanism under the dial needs grease.

vices. They are also odorless. In addition, producing organic oils with consistent performance characteristics was exceptionally difficult. The properties of an animal-based oil would depend upon factors such as age of the animal at slaughter, its diet (especially if wild), the season in which the animal was harvested, and its overall health. The problem, of course, is that the watch mechanism is extremely delicate and finicky.

The drawback of synthetic lubricants is actually a factor of their strength. It is very difficult to tell when synthetic and inorganic lubricants have dried out and/or spread out. Their longevity can also mean that customers wait too long between services, and that

means replacing more components rather than just cleaning and relubricating the timepiece. By contrast, organic oils tend to break down and gum up as they oxidize, which will indicate a need for a service while minimizing damage to physical components. This is a classic engineering problem. Making an element of a machine more durable pushes the point of failure to another part of the system. In the final calculation one has to balance benefits against the consequences of a new and inevitable point of failure.

DRIPS AND DROPS

What makes an oil suitable for watchmaking? Why not just use corn oil? After all,

oil is oil, right? It's more complicated than that. . . . There are three main qualities that have to be considered when selecting an oil suitable for watchmaking. The first two are the oil's environmental stability and mechanical performance. The property that usually gets the most attention is the length of time it takes for the oils to dry out or oxidize. Other considerations include the oils' sensitivity to light and their stability over a range of temperatures. A more arcane consideration, before the widespread adoption of nonorganic oils, was whether or not the oil possessed qualities such as acidity, which would damage metal components over time. It is one of

the reasons why olive oil is not suitable for watchmaking.

When it comes to mechanical qualities, the property that preoccupies the minds of new watch owners most is whether they have to actively manage the viscosity of the oils, in other words, whether or not the oils will stay in place. Indeed, must you wear the watch or keep it running to make sure the oils are evenly distributed? The answer is to wind the watch every now and then to keep the lubrication in its place.

Naturally, an oil's ability to reduce friction is the reason why oils are used in watchmaking in the first place. Less obvious is an oil's ability to resist pressure and its capacity to receive, store, and dissipate heat. Finally, the purity and consistency of an oil source are important for its ability to perform as expected. While this was more of a consideration in the past, it does enter the modern debate between justifying the extra cost to use industry-specific lubricants and using seemingly interchangeable generic alternatives that will save customers money on a service.

ON THE WORKBENCH

The extreme care given to movement assembly, an activity that must be done by hand, is very important. Vital, then, is how the movement is lubricated by the watchmaker. Selecting the correct type of lubricant for each key point in a movement and applying it in the ideal amount is essential to making watches work and perform at their best. Most manufactures specify particular lubricants for each application and some go so far as to develop their own lubricants to suit their needs. Rolex in particular has developed several proprietary lubricants for their movements.

Aside from manufacturer specifications and preferences, there are heuristics that guide a watchmaker's selections. The size of the movement and hence the size of the components are one consideration. Generally speaking, because of the heavier loads, larger movements and larger components require thicker oils and greases. For example, chronometer grade movements generally have heavier balances and therefore require thicker oils than non-chronometer grade movements of similar sizes.

Another factor is frequency. Higher-frequency movements, 28,800 vph and higher, are much more sensitive to cleanliness and reliant on lubricants than watches with a lower operating frequency. Low-beat movements—for example, 18,800 vph—can, while not recommended, run "dry." Since most modern watches are high-beat,

purity of the oils as well as the quality and fastidiousness of the watchmaker are critical.

DEVILISH DETAILS

It should be noted that applying the correct oil incorrectly or in the incorrect amounts can lead to problems. If applied incorrectly the oil or grease can migrate to other points in the movement, contaminating the lubricants in neighboring areas and reducing their effectiveness. In the case of overoiling, the excess oil can overwhelm the capillary action of the oil, causing it to migrate away from its intended location and, ironically, leaving that area underlubricated. That is why owners of watches should always have them serviced by a qualified watchmaker. This maximizes intervals between servicing, and can minimize long-term cost of ownership by minimizing the number of components that need to be replaced. Besides maintaining the watch's accuracy, of course.

Given the difficulties and the skill required to lubricate movements, it can seem very attractive to minimize or even avoid the use of liquid lubricants altogether. While simultaneously developing better lubricants, the watch industry has made some strides in reducing the use of them. First

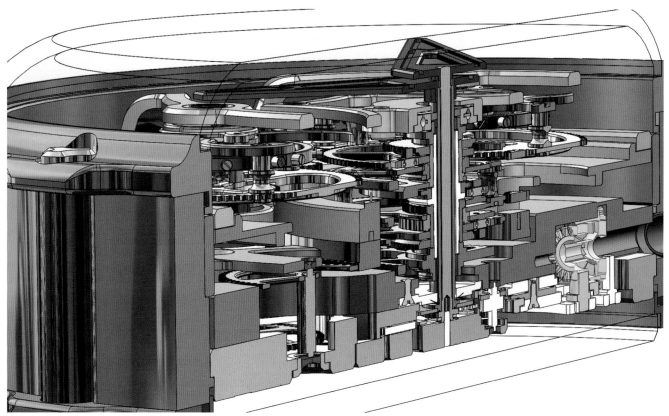

The complex inner workings of a watch, here the Tourbillon of Tourbillons by Antoine Preziuso

employed by Ulysse Nardin in 2001, silicon in the escapement has been a major milestone in simplifying the lubrication of one of the hardest-working sections in a watch movement. This innovation has since been adopted by companies including Patek Philippe, Breguet, and Audemars Piguet. Using a combination of high-tech materials and coatings, watches like the Cartier ID Two and Panerai LAB-ID have done one better by featuring a movement that doesn't require any lubrication at all. These are fascinating developments, but it remains to be seen how serviceable these types of movements will be in the future. It is certainly possible that one will end up with a Theseus paradox if it is found that silicon components, DLC coatings, or ceramics require that you replace the movement rather than service it. If that is the trade-off for long service intervals, collectors will have to ask themselves if eliminating lubricants is really what they desire.

Bill Yao is founder and CEO of Mk II Watches; Lee Dowell is a SAWTA-certified watchmaker and founder of Schmutz Watches).

Too much oil can run off the pinion and contaminate other components (courtesy of American Watch and Clock Institute).

A. LANGE & SÖHNE

Lange Uhren GmbH
Ferdinand-A.-Lange-Platz 1
D-01768 Glashütte
Germany

Tel.:
+49-35053-44-0

Fax:
+49-35053-44-5999

E-mail:
info@lange-soehne.com

Website:
www.lange-soehne.com

Founded:
1990

Number of employees:
500 employees, almost half of whom are
watchmakers

U.S. distributor:
A. Lange & Söhne
645 Fifth Avenue
New York, NY 10022
800-408-8147

Most important collections/price range:
Lange 1 / $34,700 to $332,500; Saxonia /
$14,800 to $62,100; 1815 / $24,800 to
$234,600; Richard Lange / $32,500 to
$230,400; Zeitwerk / $76,200 to $118,700

In summer 2015, A. Lange & Söhne inaugurated a new *manufacture* in Glashütte. It was a big enough event for German chancellor Angela Merkel to attend. And why not? Lange, as it is known for short, exemplifies the steady, careful, and effective way Germans do business. The story is one for the books.

On December 7, 1990, on the exact day 145 years after the firm was founded by his great-grandfather Ferdinand Adolph Lange, Walter Lange re-registered the brand A. Lange & Söhne in its old hometown of Glashütte. Ferdinand Adolph had originally launched the company as a way to provide work to the local population. And shortly after German reunification in 1990, that is exactly what Glashütte needed as well.

The company quickly regained its outstanding reputation as a robust innovator and manufacturer of classically beautiful watches. A. Lange & Söhne uses only mechanical, manually wound *manufacture* calibers or automatic winders finished according to the highest Glashütte standards. The movements are decorated and assembled by hand with the fine adjustment done in five positions. The typical three-quarter plate and all the structural parts of the movement are made of undecorated German silver; the balance cock is engraved freehand. The movements combine equal parts traditional elements and patented innovations, like the Lange large date, the SAX-O-MAT with an automatic "zero reset" for the seconds hand, or the patented constant force escapement (Lange 31, Lange Zeitwerk).

The entry-level family is the Saxonia, while the Lange 1, introduced in 1994, is considered the company leader. Among the leading novelties of 2017 are the Tourbograph "Pour le Mérite," combining a flyback chronograph, perpetual calendar, and a tourbillon, and the perpetual calendar in the 1815 line.

The company's reputation was further enhanced by the 2015 visit from Chancellor Merkel. It was a particularly nice capstone for the work of Walter Lange, who died in January 2017, after a life of outstanding entrepreneurship.

Lange 1

Reference number: 191.039
Movement: manually wound, Lange Caliber L121.1; ø 30.6 mm, height 5.7 mm; 43 jewels; 21,600 vph; swan-neck fine adjustment, hand-engraved balance cock, 8 screw-mounted gold chatons, parts finished and assembled by hand; 72-hour power reserve
Functions: hours, minutes, subsidiary seconds; power reserve indicator; large date
Case: white gold, ø 38.5 mm, height 9.8 mm; sapphire crystal; transparent case back; water-resistant to 3 atm
Band: reptile skin, buckle
Price: $34,700
Variations: yellow gold ($34,700); pink gold ($34,700); platinum ($49,500)

Lange 1 Moon Phase

Reference number: 192.029
Movement: manually wound, Lange Caliber L121.3; ø 30.6 mm, height 6.3 mm; 47 jewels; 21,600 vph; 8 screw-mounted gold chatons, swan-neck fine adjustment, hand-engraved balance cock, parts finished and assembled by hand; 72-hour power reserve
Functions: hours, minutes, subsidiary seconds; power reserve indicator; large date, moon phase
Case: white gold, ø 38.5 mm, height 10.2 mm; sapphire crystal; transparent case back; water-resistant to 3 atm
Band: reptile skin, buckle
Price: $40,900
Variations: red gold ($40,900); platinum ($54,700)

Grosse Lange 1

Reference number: 117.028
Movement: manually wound, Lange Caliber L095.2; ø 34.1 mm, height 4.7 mm; 42 jewels; 21,600 vph; 7 screw-mounted gold chatons, swan-neck fine adjustment, hand-engraved balance cock, parts finished and assembled by hand; 72-hour power reserve
Functions: hours, minutes, subsidiary seconds; power reserve indicator; large date
Case: white gold, ø 40.9 mm, height 8.8 mm; sapphire crystal; transparent case back; water-resistant to 3 atm
Band: reptile skin, buckle
Price: $41,500
Variations: yellow or red gold with light dial ($41,500); platinum (on request)

Lange 1 Timezone

Reference number: 116.032
Movement: manually wound, Lange Caliber L031.1; ø 34.1 mm, height 6.65 mm; 54 jewels; 21,600 vph; hand-engraved balance cock, 4 screw-mounted gold chatons; 72-hour power reserve
Functions: hours, minutes, subsidiary seconds; 2nd time zone; large date; power reserve indicator; day/night indicator for both time zones
Case: pink gold, ø 41.9 mm, height 11 mm; sapphire crystal; transparent case back; pusher-driven bezel with city names
Band: reptile skin, buckle
Price: $49,400
Variations: white gold ($51,800); platinum ($64,300)

Lange 1 Daymatic

Reference number: 320.032
Movement: automatic, Lange Caliber L021.1; ø 31.6 mm, height 6.1 mm; 67 jewels; 21,600 vph; hand-engraved balance cock, 7 screw-mounted gold chatons, central rotor with platinum weight; 50-hour power reserve
Functions: hours, minutes, subsidiary seconds; large date; weekday (retrograde)
Case: pink gold, ø 39.5 mm, height 10.4 mm; sapphire crystal; transparent case back; water-resistant to 3 atm
Band: reptile skin, buckle
Price: $43,200
Variations: platinum (on request); yellow gold (on request)

Small Lange 1 Moon Phase

Reference number: 182.030
Movement: manually wound, Lange Caliber L121.2; ø 30.6 mm, height 6 mm; 44 jewels; 21,600 vph; 8 screw-mounted gold chatons, swan-neck fine adjustment, hand-engraved balance cock, parts finished and assembled by hand; 72-hour power reserve
Functions: hours, minutes, subsidiary seconds; power reserve indicator; large date, moon phase
Case: pink gold, ø 36.8 mm, height 9.5 mm; sapphire crystal; transparent case back; water-resistant to 3 atm
Band: reptile skin, buckle
Remarks: guilloché dial
Price: $39,500

Lange 1 Tourbillon Perpetual Calendar

Reference number: 720.032F
Movement: automatic, Lange Caliber L082.1; ø 34.1 mm, height 7.8 mm; 76 jewels; 21,600 vph; 1-minute tourbillon with stop function on movement side, off-center balance, 6 screw-mounted gold chatons, hand-engraved intermediate wheel cock and tourbillon cock, rotor with platinum oscillating weight; 50-hour power reserve
Functions: hours, minutes, subsidiary seconds; day/night indicator; perpetual calendar with large date, weekday, month, moon phase, leap year on movement side
Case: pink gold, ø 41.9 mm, height 12.2 mm; sapphire crystal; transparent case back; water-resistant to 3 atm
Band: reptile skin, folding clasp
Price: $332,500
Variations: white gold ($332,500)

Saxonia Thin

Reference number: 211.027
Movement: manually wound, Lange Caliber L093.1; ø 28 mm, height 2.9 mm; 21 jewels; 21,600 vph; hand-engraved balance cock, screw balance, 3 gold chatons; swan-neck fine adjustment; 72-hour power reserve
Functions: hours, minutes
Case: white gold, ø 40 mm, height 5.9 mm; sapphire crystal; transparent case back; water-resistant to 3 atm
Band: reptile skin, buckle
Price: $24,500
Variations: pink gold ($24,500); 37-mm case ($14,800)

Saxonia

Reference number: 219.047
Movement: manually wound, Lange Caliber L941.1; ø 25.6 mm, height 3.2 mm; 21 jewels; 21,600 vph; 4 gold chatons, screw balance, swan-neck fine adjustment, hand-engraved balance cock; 45-hour power reserve
Functions: hours, minutes, subsidiary seconds
Case: white gold, ø 35 mm, height 7.3 mm; sapphire crystal; transparent case back
Band: reptile skin, buckle
Remarks: mother-of-pearl dial
Price: $16,100
Variations: red gold ($16,100)

Saxonia Moonphase
Reference number: 384.032
Movement: automatic, Lange Caliber L086.5;
ø 30.4 mm, height 5.2 mm; 40 jewels; 21,600 vph;
hand-engraved balance cock, screw balance, swan-
neck fine adjustment; 72-hour power reserve
Functions: hours, minutes, subsidiary seconds; large
date, moon phase
Case: pink gold, ø 40 mm, height 9.8 mm; sapphire
crystal; transparent case back; water-resistant to
3 atm
Band: reptile skin, buckle
Price: $29,000
Variations: white gold ($29,000)

Langematik Perpetual
Reference number: 310.026
Movement: automatic, Lange Caliber L922.1;
ø SAX-O-MAT; ø 30.4 mm, height 5.7 mm; 43 jewels;
21,600 vph; rotor with platinum oscillating weight;
hand-setting mechanism with "zero-reset," main pusher
for synchronous correction of all calendar functions, plus
3 individual pushers; 46-hour power reserve
Functions: hours, minutes, subsidiary seconds;
additional 24-hour display; perpetual calendar with
large date, weekday, month, moon phase, leap year
Case: white gold, ø 38.5 mm, height 10.2 mm; sapphire
crystal; transparent case back; water-resistant to 3 atm
Band: reptile skin, buckle
Price: $83,000
Variations: red gold ($83,000); platinum (on request)

1815 UP/DOWN
Reference number: 234.032
Movement: manually wound, Lange Caliber
L051.2; ø 30.6 mm, height 4.6 mm; 29 jewels;
21,600 vph; three-quarter plate, 7 screw-mounted
gold chatons, screw balance, hand-engraved balance
cock, parts finished and assembled by hand; 55-hour
power reserve
Functions: hours, minutes, subsidiary seconds;
power reserve indicator
Case: red gold, ø 39 mm, height 8.9 mm; sapphire
crystal; transparent case back; water-resistant to 3 atm
Band: reptile skin, buckle
Price: $29,400
Variations: yellow gold (on request); white gold
($29,400)

1815 Annual Calendar
Reference number: 238.026
Movement: manually wound, Lange Caliber
L051.3; ø 30.6 mm, height 5.7 mm; 26 jewels;
21,600 vph; 3 screw-mounted gold chatons, hand-
engraved balance cock, parts finished and assembled
by hand; 72-hour power reserve
Functions: hours, minutes, subsidiary seconds;
annual calendar with date, weekday, month, moon
phase
Case: white gold, ø 40 mm, height 10.1 mm;
sapphire crystal; transparent case back; water-
resistant to 3 atm
Band: reptile skin, buckle
Price: $36,600
Variations: red gold ($36,600)

Tourbograph Perpetual "Pour le Mérite"
Reference number: 706.025F
Movement: manually wound, Lange Caliber
L133.1; ø 32 mm, height 10.9 mm; 52 jewels;
21,600 vph; 1-minute tourbillon chain and fusée
transmission; 6 screw-mounted gold chatons
including 2 diamond capstones, screw balance;
36-hour power reserve
Functions: hours, minutes, subsidiary seconds; split-
seconds chronograph; perpetual calendar with date,
weekday, month, moon phase, leap year
Case: platinum, ø 43 mm, height 16.6 mm; sapphire
crystal; transparent case back; water-resistant to 3 atm
Band: reptile skin, folding clasp
Price: 480,000 euros; limited to 50 pieces

Richard Lange
Reference number: 232.032
Movement: manually wound, Lange Caliber
L041.2; ø 30.6 mm, height 6 mm; 26 jewels;
21,600 vph; hand-engraved balance cock, 2 screw-
mounted gold chatons, finished and assembled by
hand; in-house balance spring with patent-pending
anchoring clip; 38-hour power reserve
Functions: hours, minutes, sweep seconds
Case: platinum, ø 40.5 mm, height 10.5 mm;
sapphire crystal; transparent case back; water-
resistant to 3 atm
Band: reptile skin, buckle
Price: on request
Variations: pink gold

Richard Lange Perpetual Calendar "Terraluna"

Reference number: 180.032
Movement: manually wound, Lange Caliber L096.1; ø 37.3 mm, height 11.1 mm; 80 jewels; 21,600 vph; three-quarter plate, double spring barrel, constant force escapement, intermediate winding spring, screw balance, 1 screw-down gold chaton, hand-engraved balance cock; 336-hour power reserve
Functions: hours, minutes, subsidiary seconds; power reserve indicator; perpetual calendar with large date, weekday, month, leap year, orbital moon phase with day/night display on back
Case: pink gold, ø 45.5 mm, height 16.5 mm; sapphire crystal; transparent back; water-resistant to 3 atm
Band: reptile skin, folding clasp
Price: $229,200

Datograph UP/DOWN

Reference number: 405.031
Movement: manually wound, Lange Caliber L951.6; ø 30.6 mm, height 7.9 mm; 46 jewels; 18,000 vph; 4 screw-mounted gold chatons; 60-hour power reserve
Functions: hours, minutes, subsidiary seconds; flyback chronograph with precisely jumping minute counter; power reserve indicator; large date
Case: platinum, ø 41 mm, height 13.1 mm; sapphire crystal; transparent case back; water-resistant to 3 atm
Band: reptile skin, buckle
Price: $90,700
Variations: pink gold ($70,500)

Datograph Perpetual

Reference number: 410.038
Movement: manually wound, Lange Caliber L952.1; ø 32 mm, height 8 mm; 45 jewels; 18,000 vph; column wheel control of chronograph functions; 4 screw-in gold chatons
Functions: hours, minutes, subsidiary seconds; added 24-hour display; day/night indicator; flyback chronograph; perpetual calendar with weekday, month, moon phase, leap year
Case: white gold, ø 41 mm, height 13.5 mm; sapphire crystal; transparent case back; water-resistant to 3 atm
Band: reptile skin, buckle
Price: $136,600
Variations: pink gold ($136,600)

Zeitwerk

Reference number: 140.029
Movement: manually wound, Lange Caliber L043.1; ø 33.6 mm, height 9.3 mm; 66 jewels; 18,000 vph; hand-engraved balance cock; 2 screw-mounted gold chatons; continuous drive through constant force escapement; 36-hour power reserve
Functions: hours and minutes (digital, jumping), subsidiary seconds; power reserve indicator
Case: white gold, ø 41.9 mm, height 12.6 mm; sapphire crystal; transparent case back; water-resistant to 3 atm
Band: reptile skin, buckle
Price: $76,200
Variations: pink gold ($76,200)

Tempo Decimal Strike

Reference number: 143.050
Movement: manually wound, Lange Caliber L043.7; ø 36 mm, height 10 mm; 78 jewels; 18,000 vph; three-quarter plate, 2 screw-mounted gold chatons; continuous drive through constant force escapement (remontoir); 36-hour power reserve
Functions: hours and minutes (digital, jumping), subsidiary seconds; power reserve display, automatic 10-minute chimes
Case: "honey gold," ø 44.2 mm, height 13.1 mm; sapphire crystal; transparent case back; water-resistant to 3 atm
Band: reptile skin, buckle
Price: $125,600; limited to 100 pieces

Lange 31

Reference number: 130.039
Movement: manually wound, Lange Caliber L034.1; ø 37.3 mm, height 9.6 mm; 62 jewels; 21,600 vph; double spring barrel, 3 screw-mounted gold chatons, constant force escapement (remontoir), power reserve with switch-off mechanism; 744-hour power reserve
Functions: hours, minutes, subsidiary seconds; power reserve indicator; large date
Case: white gold, ø 45.9 mm, height 15.9 mm; sapphire crystal; transparent case back; water-resistant to 3 atm
Band: reptile skin, folding clasp
Remarks: comes with winding key
Price: $140,500; limited to 100 pieces
Variations: red gold (on request); platinum (on request)

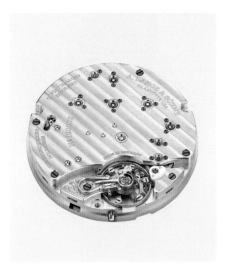

Caliber L121.3

Manually wound; stop-seconds mechanism, 8 screw-mounted gold chatons, swan-neck fine adjustment; double spring barrel, 72-hour power reserve
Functions: hours, minutes, subsidiary seconds; power reserve indicator; moon phase, day/night indicator
Diameter: 30.6 mm
Height: 6.3 mm
Jewels: 47
Balance: glucydur with eccentric regulating cams
Frequency: 21,600 vph
Balance spring: in-house manufacture
Shock protection: Kif
Remarks: parts finished and assembled by hand, hand-engraved balance cock

Caliber L031.1

Manually wound; stop-seconds mechanism; double spring barrel, 72-hour power reserve
Functions: hours, minutes, subsidiary seconds; 2nd time zone (world time display with city reference ring); power reserve display, day/night indicator for both time zones; large date
Diameter: 34.1 mm
Height: 6.7 mm
Jewels: 54, including 4 screwed-mounted gold chatons
Balance: glucydur with weighted screws
Frequency: 21,600 vph
Balance spring: Nivarox 1 with special terminal curve and swan-neck fine adjustment
Shock protection: Kif

Caliber L082.1

Automatic; 1-minute tourbillon with stop-second; 1-way gold rotor with platinum mass; single barrel, 50-hour power reserve
Functions: hours, minutes, subsidiary seconds; day/night; perpetual calendar, large date, weekday, month, moon phase, leap year
Diameter: 34.1 mm
Height: 7.8 mm
Jewels: 76, including 6 screw-mounted golden chatons and 1 diamond counter-bearing
Balance: glucydur, eccentric regulating cams
Frequency: 21,600 vph
Balance spring: in-house manufacture
Shock protection: Kif

Caliber L085.1 SAX-O-MAT

Automatic; bidirectional, finely embossed 21-karat gold and platinum three-quarter rotor, zero reset hand adjustment, stop-seconds mechanism; complete or individual calendar correction; single spring barrel, 46-hour power reserve
Functions: hours, minutes, subsidiary seconds; full calendar with large date, weekday, month, moon phase
Diameter: 30.4 mm
Height: 5.4 mm
Jewels: 43
Balance: glucydur with weighted screws
Frequency: 21,600 vph
Balance spring: Nivarox 1 with special terminal curve and swan-neck fine adjustment
Shock protection: Kif

Caliber L133.1

Manually wound; chain and fusée drive, 1-minute tourbillon; 2 diamond capstones, column wheel control of chronograph functions, German silver mainplate and bridges; single spring barrel, 36-hour power reserve
Functions: hours, minutes, subsidiary seconds; split-seconds chronograph; perpetual calendar with date, weekday, month, moon phase, leap year
Diameter: 32 mm
Height: 10.9 mm
Jewels: 52, including 6 screwed-mounted gold chatons
Balance: glucydur with weighted screws
Balance spring: in-house manufacture
Remarks: hand-engraved balance cock and chronograph bridges

Caliber L096.1

Manually wound; constant force escapement with intermediate winding spring, stop-seconds; double spring barrel, 336-hour power reserve
Functions: hours, minutes, subsidiary seconds; power reserve indicator; perpetual calendar with date, weekday, month, leap year; orbital moon phase with day/night display on case back
Diameter: 37.3 mm
Height: 11.1 mm
Jewels: 80
Balance: glucydur with weighted screws
Frequency: 21,600 vph
Balance spring: in-house manufacture
Shock protection: Kif

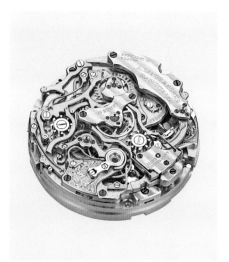

Caliber L101.1

Manually wound; swan-neck fine adjustment, German silver mainplate and bridges; single spring barrel, 42-hour power reserve
Functions: hours, minutes, subsidiary seconds; power reserve indicator; split-seconds chronograph; perpetual calendar with date, weekday, month, moon phase, leap year
Diameter: 32.6 mm
Height: 9.1 mm
Jewels: 43, including 4 screwed-mounted gold chatons
Balance: glucydur with weighted screws
Frequency: 21,600 vph
Shock protection: Kif
Remarks: mostly decorated and assembled by hand, hand-engraved chronograph bridges

Caliber L951.6

Manually wound; stop-seconds mechanism, jumping minute counter; single spring barrel, 60-hour power reserve
Functions: hours, minutes, subsidiary seconds; power reserve indicator; flyback chronograph; large date
Diameter: 30.6 mm
Height: 7.9 mm
Jewels: 46
Balance: glucydur with weighted screws
Frequency: 18,000 vph
Balance spring: in-house manufacture
Shock protection: Incabloc
Remarks: three-quarter plate of untreated German silver, manufactured according to highest quality criteria

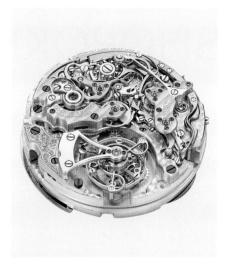

Caliber 952.2

Manually wound; 1-minute tourbillon; single spring barrel, 50-hour power reserve
Functions: hours, minutes, subsidiary seconds; day/night indicator, power reserve indicator; flyback chronograph with precisely jumping minute counter; perpetual calendar with large date, weekday, month, moon phase, leap year
Diameter: 32.6 mm;
Height: 9 mm
Jewels: 58, including 5 screw-mounted gold chatons, 1 diamond end stone
Balance: glucydur with weighted screws
Frequency: 18,000 vph
Balance spring: in-house manufacture

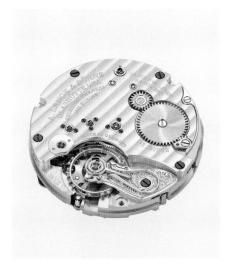

Caliber L051.3

Manually wound; swan-neck fine adjustment, stop-seconds, German silver mainplate and bridges; single spring barrel, 72-hour power reserve
Functions: hours, minutes, subsidiary seconds; annual calendar with date, weekday, month, moon phase
Diameter: 30.6 mm
Height: 5.7 mm
Jewels: 26, including 3 screwed-mounted gold chatons
Balance: glucydur with weighted screws
Frequency: 21,600 vph
Balance spring: in-house manufacture
Remarks: parts finished and assembled by hand, hand-engraved balance cock

Caliber L043.7

Manually wound; jumping minute, continuous drive through constant force escapement (remontoir), stop-seconds system; single spring barrel, 36-hour power reserve
Functions: hours and minutes (digital, jumping), subsidiary seconds; power reserve display, acoustic signal every 10 minutes and on the hour (switch-off mechanism)
Diameter: 36 mm
Height: 10 mm
Jewels: 78
Balance: glucydur with eccentric regulating cams
Frequency: 18,000 vph
Balance spring: in-house spring clamp (patent pending)
Shock protection: Incabloc

Caliber L034.1

Manually wound; key winding with torque limiter, constant force escapement (remontoir), stop-seconds mechanism; two winding springs, each 1.85 m. long (approx. 6 ft.); double spring barrel, 744-hour (31-day) power reserve with switch-off mechanism
Functions: hours, minutes, subsidiary seconds; power reserve indicator; large date
Diameter: 37.3 mm
Height: 9.6 mm
Jewels: 62
Balance: glucydur with weighted screws
Frequency: 21,600 vph
Balance spring: Nivarox 1 with special terminal curve and swan-neck fine adjustment
Shock protection: Kif

ALEXANDER SHOROKHOFF

The ultimate goal for the watch connoisseur may be realizing one's own ideas for timepieces. In the first stages of his life, Alexander Shorokhoff, born in Moscow in 1960, was an engineer and then an architect with his own construction company. These turned out to be an excellent platform to begin expanding into the field of fine timepieces. In 1992, shortly after the demise of the Soviet Union, Shorokhoff founded a distribution company in Germany to market Russia's own Poljot watches. This gave him the insight and practice needed to launch phase two of his plan: establishing his own manufacturing facilities for an independent watch brand under his own name.

At Shorokhoff Watches, three main creative lines are bundled under the general concept "Art on the Wrist": Heritage, Avantgarde, and Vintage. The three lines share a design with a distinctly artistic orientation. They all focus on technical quality, sophisticated hand-engraving, and the cultural backdrop. "We consider watches not only as timekeepers, but also as works of art," says Alexander Shorokhoff. It's a statement that can be seen in the watches. The brand is at home in the world of international and Russian art and culture. Each dial is designed down to the smallest detail. The engraving and finishing of the movements is unique as well.

All of them are taken apart in Alzenau, reworked, and then reassembled with great care, which is why the brand has stamped each watch with "Handmade in Germany." Some of the modules used in these timepieces have been developed by the company itself. Before a watch leaves the *manufacture,* it is subjected to strict quality control. The timepiece's functionality must be given the cleanest bill of health before it can be sent out to jewelers around the world.

Alexander Shorokhoff
Uhrenmanufaktur
Hanauer Strasse 25
63755 Alzenau
Germany

Tel.:
+49-6023-919-93

Fax:
+49-6023-919-949

E-mail:
info@alexander-shorokhoff.de

Website:
www.alexander-shorokhoff.de

Founded:
2003

Number of employees:
15

Annual production:
approx. 900 watches

Distribution:
About Time Luxury Group
210 Bellevue Avenue
Newport, RI 02840
401-846-0598

Most important collections/price range
Heritage / approx. $4,500; Avantgarde / approx. $1,500

Vintage 5
Reference number: AS.V5-C
Movement: automatic, Poljot Caliber 2416; ø 24.6 mm, height 4.55 mm; 29 jewels; 18,000 vph; hand-engraved and finished movement; 36-hour power reserve
Functions: hours, minutes, sweep seconds; date
Case: stainless steel, ø 40 mm, height 10.1 mm; sapphire crystal; transparent case back; water-resistant to 5 atm
Band: calfskin, buckle
Price: $1,750; limited to 35 pieces
Variations: stainless steel Milanese bracelet; silver-colored dial (limited to 35 pieces)

Babylonian I
Reference number: AS.BYL01
Movement: manually wound, Caliber 2609.AS (base Poljot 2609); ø 25.6 mm, height 4.05 mm; 17 jewels; 21,600 vph; finely finished movement; 42-hour power reserve
Functions: hours, minutes, sweep seconds
Case: stainless steel, ø 46.5 mm, height 11.5 mm; sapphire crystal; transparent case back; water-resistant to 5 atm
Band: ostrich leather, buckle
Price: $2,835; limited to 500 pieces

Regulator R02
Reference number: AS.R02-1
Movement: manually wound, Caliber 3105.AS (base Poljot 3105); ø 31 mm, height 5.38 mm; 23 jewels; 21,600 vph; hand-engraved and finished movement; 40-hour power reserve
Functions: hours (off-center), minutes, subsidiary seconds; date
Case: stainless steel, ø 43.5 mm, height 11.55 mm; sapphire crystal; transparent case back; water-resistant to 5 atm
Band: calfskin, buckle
Remarks: partially skeletonized dial
Price: $2,400; limited to 98 pieces
Variations: stainless steel Milanese bracelet; various dial colors

Crossing

Reference number: AS.JH01-4
Movement: automatic, Dubois Dépraz Caliber 14400A; 25 jewels; 28,800 vph; blued screws, hand-engraved rotor; 40-hour power reserve
Functions: hours (digital, jumping), minutes (off-center), subsidiary seconds
Case: stainless steel, ø 43.5 mm, height 11.3 mm; sapphire crystal; transparent case back; water-resistant to 5 atm
Band: reptile skin, buckle
Price: $4,650; limited to 25 pieces
Variations: various dials; stainless steel Milanese bracelet

Winter

Reference number: AS.LA-WIN-3
Movement: automatic, Caliber 2824.AS (base ETA 2824-2); ø 25.6 mm, height 4.6 mm; 25 jewels; 28,800 vph; hand-engraved rotor; 38-hour power reserve
Functions: hours, minutes, sweep seconds; date
Case: stainless steel, ø 39 mm, height 10.6 mm; sapphire crystal; transparent case back; water-resistant to 5 atm
Band: galuchat, buckle
Remarks: handmade dial set with diamond dust
Price: $1,850

Miss Avantgarde Diamant

Reference number: AS.AVG02-WGG-D
Movement: automatic, ETA Caliber 2824-2; ø 25.6 mm, height 4.6 mm; 25 jewels; 28,800 vph; hand-engraved rotor, blued screws; 39-hour power reserve
Functions: hours, minutes, sweep seconds; date
Case: white gold, ø 39 mm, height 12.75 mm; bezel set with diamonds; sapphire crystal; transparent case back
Band: galuchat, buckle
Price: $9,790; limited to 20 pieces
Variations: various strap colors

Chrono-Regulator CR02

Reference number: AS.CR02-1
Movement: manually wound, Caliber 31679. AS (base Poljot 3133); ø 31 mm, height 7.35 mm; 23 jewels; 21,600 vph; blued screws, skeletonized, hand-engraved and finished movement; 42-hour power reserve
Functions: hours (off-center), minutes, subsidiary seconds; chronograph; date
Case: stainless steel, ø 43.5 mm, height 13.65 mm; sapphire crystal; transparent case back; water-resistant to 5 atm
Band: reptile skin, buckle
Remarks: partially skeletonized dial
Price: $7,100; limited to 68 pieces

Fedor Dostoevsky Chronograph

Reference number: AS.FD41
Movement: manually wound, Soprod Caliber 7750SORM-3H; ø 30 mm, height 7.9 mm; 25 jewels; 28,800 vph; blued screws, hand-engraved and finished movement; 50-hour power reserve
Functions: hours, minutes, subsidiary seconds; power reserve indicator; chronograph; date
Case: stainless steel, 43 × 43 mm; height 14.2 mm; sapphire crystal; transparent case back; water-resistant to 3 atm
Band: reptile skin, buckle
Price: $9,700

Regulator R01

Reference number: AS.R01-3
Movement: manually wound, Caliber 3104.AS (base Poljot 3104); ø 31 mm, height 5.38 mm; 17 jewels; 21,600 vph; blued screws, hand-engraved and finished movement; 42-hour power reserve
Functions: hours (off-center), minutes, subsidiary seconds; date
Case: stainless steel, ø 43.5 mm, height 11.55 mm; sapphire crystal; transparent case back; water-resistant to 5 atm
Band: calfskin, buckle
Price: $1,400
Variations: folding clasp; stainless steel Milanese bracelet

ALPINA

The brand Alpina essentially grew out of a confederation of watchmakers known as the Alpina Union Horlogère, founded by Gottlieb Hauser. The group expanded quickly to reach beyond Swiss borders into Germany, where it opened a factory in Glashütte. For a while in the 1930s, it even merged with Gruen, one of the most important watch companies in the United States.

After World War II, the Allied Forces decreed that the name Alpina could no longer be used in Germany, and so that branch was renamed "Dugena" for Deutsche Uhrmacher-Genossenschaft Alpina, or the German Watchmaker Cooperative Alpina.

Today, Geneva-based Alpina is no longer associated with that watchmaker cooperative of yore. Now a sister brand of Frédérique Constant, it has a decidedly modern collection enhanced with a series of movements designed, built, and assembled in-house: the Tourbillon AL-980, the World Timer AL-718, the Automatic Regulator AL-950, the Small Date Automatic AL-710, and more recently the Flyback-Chronograph Automatic AL-760, which features the patented "Direct-Flyback" technology. Owners Peter and Aletta Stas have built up an outstanding business over the years, and in 2016 they sold it to Citizen Group, but continue managing the brands until 2020.

Alpina likes to call itself the inventor of the modern sports watch. Its iconic Block-Uhr of 1933 and the Alpina 4 of 1938, with an in-house automatic movement, set the pace of all sports watches, with a waterproof stainless steel case, an antimagnetic system, and shock absorbers. But beyond a target group engaged in water and air sports, the brand is now looking at the twenty-first-century hipsters whose life is electronic. The Horological Smartwatch, equipped with a quartz movement, connects with mobile phones and other electronic devices and can display the data on an analog dial.

Alpina Watch International SA
Route de la Galaise, 8
CH-1228 Plan-les-Ouates, Geneva
Switzerland

Tel.:
+41-0-22-860-87-40

Fax:
+41-0-22-860-04-64

E-mail:
info@alpina-watches.com

Website:
www.alpina-watches.com

Founded:
1883

Number of employees:
100

Annual production:
10,000 watches

U.S. distributor:
Alpina Frederique Constant USA Inc
954-312-3600
sales@usa.frederique-constant.com

Most important collections/price range:
Alpiner 4 / from approx. $1,395; Seastrong Diver / from approx. $995; Smartwatch / from approx. $595 to 795; Startimer Pilot / from approx. $595 to $2,095

Startimer Pilot Automatic

Reference number: AL-525G4TS6
Movement: automatic, Caliber AL-525 (base Sellita SW200-1); ø 25.6 mm, height 4.6 mm; 26 jewels; 28,800 vph; 38-hour power reserve
Functions: hours, minutes sweep seconds; date
Case: titanium-colored stainless steel, ø 44 mm, height 10.7 mm; sapphire crystal; screw-in crown; water-resistant to 10 atm
Band: calfskin, buckle
Price: $1,050

Startimer Pilot Quartz

Reference number: AL-240S4S6B
Movement: quartz, AL-240
Functions: hours, minutes, sweep seconds; date
Case: stainless steel, ø 42 mm, height 9.4 mm; sapphire crystal; water-resistant to 10 atm
Band: stainless steel, folding clasp
Price: $695

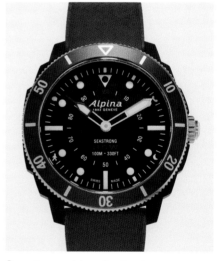

Seastrong Horological Smartwatch

Reference number: AL-282LBGR4V6
Movement: quartz, MMT-282-1
Functions: hours, minutes; connected hands, electronic motion detection (activity tracker) and sleep monitoring, smart alarm function (crown-controlled), active alerts, dynamic coach, worldtimer, cloud storage, collection, notifications (e-mail, call, messages from up to 18 phone apps)
Case: stainless steel, fiberglass, ø 44 mm, height 10.2 mm; unidirectional stainless steel bezel with 0-60 scale; sapphire crystal; water-resistant to 10 atm
Band: rubber, buckle
Price: $595

Startimer Pilot Quartz GMT

Reference number: AL-247B4S6
Movement: quartz, AL-247
Functions: hours, minutes; additional 24-hour indicator (second time zone/GMT); date
Case: stainless steel, ø 42 mm, height 9.4 mm; sapphire crystal; water-resistant to 10 atm
Band: cordura, buckle
Price: $595

Seastrong Diver Heritage

Reference number: AL-525S4H6
Movement: automatic, Caliber AL-525 (Basis Sellita SW200-1); ø 25.6 mm, height 4.6 mm; 26 jewels; 28,800 vph; 38-hour power reserve;
Functions: hours, minutes, sweep seconds; date
Case: stainless steel, ø 42 mm, height 12.03 mm; crown-adjustable inner bezel with 0-60 scale; sapphire crystal; transparent case back; screw-in crown; water-resistant to 30 atm
Band: calfskin, buckle
Price: $1,695

Startimer Pilot Quartz Big Date Chronograph

Reference number: AL-372BMLY4FBS6
Movement: quartz, AL-372
Functions: hours, minutes, subsidiary seconds; chronograph; large date
Case: stainless steel with black PVD coating, ø 44 mm, height 12.4 mm; sapphire crystal; screw-in crown; water-resistant to 10 atm
Band: cordura, buckle
Price: $995

Startimer Pilot Automatic Chronograph

Reference number: AL-725N4S6
Movement: automatic, Alpina Caliber AL-725; ø 30.4 mm, height 7.8 mm; 26 jewels; 28,800 vph; 46-hour power reserve
Functions: hours, minutes, chronograph, date
Case: stainless steel, ø 44 mm, height 14.6 mm; sapphire crystal; screw-in crown; water-resistant to 10 atm
Band: calfskin, buckle
Price: $1,995

Alpiner 4 Automatic

Reference number: AL-525BS5AQ6B
Movement: automatic, Caliber AL-525 (base Sellita SW200-1); ø 25.6 mm, height 4.6 mm; 26 jewels; 28,800 vph; 38-hour power reserve
Functions: hours, minutes, sweep seconds; date; antimagnetic
Case: stainless steel, ø 44 mm, height 13.2 mm; sapphire crystal; screw-in crown; water-resistant to 10 atm
Band: stainless steel, folding clasp
Price: $1,495

Seastrong Diver 300 Automatic

Reference number: AL-525LBN4V6B
Movement: automatic, Caliber AL-525 (base Sellita SW200-1); ø 25.6 mm, height 4.6 mm; 26 jewels; 28,800 vph; 38-hour power reserve
Functions: hours, minutes, sweep seconds; date
Case: stainless steel, ø 44 mm, height 13.06 mm; unidirectional bezel with 60-minute divisions; sapphire crystal; screw-in crown; water-resistant to 30 atm
Band: stainless steel, folding clasp
Price: $1,495

AQUADIVE

According to Laver's Law, a style that shows up again at the fifty-year mark is "quaint." So much for the outward impact, maybe. But what about the intrinsic long-term personal and ephemeral value, the sometimes collective memories associated with a particular moment in our lives? Today, the very sight of a watch from times past might bring forth images of a different era, much like hearing the songs of Procol Harum or touching Naugahyde in an old Dodge Dart. Nostalgia is a powerful impulse, especially in an era like ours, which appears enamored by its own frenetic pace and refuses categorically to stop and reflect.

So when a group of watch experts decided to revive an iconic watch of the sixties and seventies, they were bound to strike a positive note. In its day, the Aquadive was considered a solidly built and reliable piece of equipment seriously coveted by professional divers. It might still be around had it not been put out to pasture during the quartz revolution.

In its twenty-first-century incarnation, the Aquadive bears many hallmarks of the original. The look is unmistakable: the charmingly awkward hands, the puffy cushion case, the sheer stability it exudes. In fact, some of the components, like the 200 NOS case and sapphire crystal, are leftovers from the old stock. The Swiss-made automatic movements and the gaskets, of course, are new.

Modern technologies, like DLC, and advances in CNC machining have transformed the older concepts. And to ensure reliability, the watches are assembled in Switzerland. The top of the current line is the Bathyscaphe series, machined from a block of stainless steel, and featuring new shock absorbers and an automatic helium release valve.

AQUADIVE USA
P.O. Box 113
Wicomico, VA 23184

Tel.:
888-397-9363

E-mail:
info@aquadive.com

Website:
www.aquadive.com

Founded:
1962

Number of employees:
18

Distribution:
Retail and direct online sales

Most important collections/price range:
Bathyscaphe / $1,290 to $3,990, NOS Model 77

Bathyscaphe 100
Reference number: 1002.11.36211
Movement: automatic, ETA Caliber 2836-2; ø 25.6 mm, height 4.6 mm; 25 jewels; 28,800 vph; 42-hour power reserve; regulated in 5 positions
Functions: hours, minutes, sweep seconds; date
Case: stainless steel, ø 43 mm, height 14 mm; unidirectional bezel with 60-minute divisions; antimagnetic soft iron inner case; sapphire crystal; screw-in crown; automatic helium release valve; water-resistant to 100 atm
Band: Isofrane, buckle
Price: $1,690; limited to 500 pieces
Variations: mesh bracelet ($1,890); gun metal DLC-coated version ($1,890)

Bathyscaphe 300
Reference number: 3002.11.36211
Movement: automatic, ETA Caliber 2824-2; ø 25.6 mm, height 4.6 mm; 25 jewels; 28,800 vph; 42-hour power reserve; regulated in 5 positions
Functions: hours, minutes, sweep seconds; date
Case: stainless steel, ø 47 mm, height 14 mm; unidirectional bezel with 60-minute divisions; sapphire crystal; screw-in crown; automatic helium release valve; water-resistant to 300 atm
Band: Isofrane rubber, buckle
Price: $2,490

Bathyscaphe 100
Reference number: 1002.11.36212
Movement: automatic, ETA Caliber 2836-2; ø 25.6 mm, height 4.6 mm; 25 jewels; 28,800 vph; 42-hour power reserve; regulated in 5 positions
Functions: hours, minutes, sweep seconds; date
Case: stainless steel, ø 43 mm, height 14 mm; unidirectional bezel with 60-minute divisions; antimagnetic soft iron inner case; sapphire crystal; screw-in crown; automatic helium release valve; water-resistant to 100 atm
Band: Isofrane, buckle
Price: $1,690; limited to 500 pieces
Variations: mesh bracelet ($1,890); gun metal DLC-coated version ($1,890)

Aquadive Model 77

Reference number: 771.12.365112
Movement: automatic, ETA Caliber 2836-2;
ø 25.6 mm, height 4.6 mm; 25 jewels; 28,800 vph;
42-hour power reserve; regulated in 5 positions
Functions: hours, minutes, sweep seconds; date
Case: stainless steel, 41 × 51 mm, height 16 mm;
unidirectional bezel with 60-minute divisions;
sapphire crystal; screw-in crown; automatic helium
release valve; water-resistant to 100 atm
Band: rubber, buckle
Price: $1,290; limited to supply of old stock parts
Variations: mesh bracelet ($1,390); overhauled
NOS Anton Schild movement ($1,390)

Bathyscaphe 100 Bronze

Reference number: 1006.13.365311
Movement: automatic, ETA Caliber 2836-2;
ø 25.6 mm, height 4.6 mm; 25 jewels; 28,800 vph;
42-hour power reserve; regulated in 5 positions
Functions: hours, minutes, sweep seconds; date
Case: German bronze alloy, ø 43 mm, height
15 mm; unidirectional bezel with 60-minute
divisions; sapphire crystal; screw-in crown; automatic
helium release valve; water-resistant to 100 atm
Band: Isofrane, buckle
Price: $1,690; limited to 100 pieces

Bathysphere 100 GMT

Reference number: 1001.13.935113
Movement: automatic, ETA Caliber 2893-2;
ø 25.6 mm, height 4.2 mm; 21 jewels; 28,800 vph;
42-hour power reserve; regulated in 5 positions
Functions: hours, minutes, sweep seconds; date,
GMT hand for 24 hours indication
Case: stainless steel case, ø 43 mm, height 15 mm;
unidirectional bezel with 60-minute divisions;
sapphire crystal; screw-in crown; automatic helium
release valve; water-resistant to 100 atm
Band: Isofrane, buckle
Price: $1,990; limited to 300 pieces
Variations: mesh bracelet ($2,150); DLC-coated
gun metal ($2,090); 2 additional dial colors

Bathysphere 500

Reference number: 5001.14.VMF.5112
Movement: automatic, decorated In House Caliber,
Geneva stripes, VMF; ø 25.6 mm, height 3.7 mm;
28 jewels; 28,800 vph; 50-hour power reserve;
regulated in 5 positions
Functions: hours, minutes, sweep seconds; date
Case: stainless steel, ø 42 mm, height 11 mm;
unidirectional bezel with 60-minute divisions;
sapphire crystal; see-through case back, screw-in
crown; water-resistant to 500 atm
Band: Isofrane, buckle
Price: $2,990
Variations: stainless steel link bracelet or mesh
bracelet

Bathyscaphe 300 DLC

Reference number: 3002.11.36211
Movement: automatic, ETA Caliber 2824-2;
ø 25.6 mm, height 4.6 mm; 25 jewels; 28,800 vph;
42-hour power reserve; regulated in 5 positions
Functions: hours, minutes, sweep seconds; date
Case: DLC steel, ø 47 mm, height 14 mm;
unidirectional bezel with 60-minute divisions;
sapphire crystal; screw-in crown; automatic helium
release valve; water-resistant to 300 atm
Band: Isofrane rubber, buckle
Price: $2,490

Aquadive Model 50 Depth Gauge New Old Stock

Reference number: 1976.50
Movement: quartz, depth gauge
Functions: hours, minutes, seconds; depth gauge
Case: stainless steel, ø 47 mm, height 17 mm;
unidirectional bezel with 60-minute divisions; mineral
crystal; screw-in crown; water-resistant to 20 atm.
Band: Isofrane rubber, buckle
Price: $4,490

ARISTO

"If you lie down with dogs, . . ." goes the old saying. And if you work closely with watchmakers . . . you may catch their more beneficial bug and become one yourself. That at any rate is what happened to the watch case and metal bracelet manufacturer Vollmer, Ltd, established in Pforzheim, Germany, by Ernst Vollmer in 1922. Third-generation president Hansjörg Vollmer decided he was interested in producing watches as well.

Vollmer, who studied business in Stuttgart, had the experience, but also the connections with manufacturers in Switzerland. He speaks French fluently, another asset. He acquired Aristo and in 1998 launched a series of pilot watches housed in sturdy titanium cases with bold onion crowns and secured with Vollmer's own light and comfortable titanium bracelets. Bit by bit, thanks to affordable prices and no-nonsense design—reviving some classic dials from World War II—Vollmer's watches caught hold. The collection grew with limited editions and a few chronometers.

In October 2005, Vollmer GmbH and Aristo Watches finally consolidated for a bigger impact. Besides their own lines, they produce quartz watches, automatics, and chronographs under the names Messerschmitt and Aristella. The Aristo brand has been trademarked worldwide and is sold mainly in Europe, North America, and Asia. The collection is divided up into Classic, Design, and Sports, with the mechanical segment further split based on elements Land, Water, and Air. The timepieces range from quality wristwatches with historical movements from older Swiss production to attractive ladies' watches or replicas of classic military watches, all assembled in Pforzheim. The company also has an established name as a manufacturer of classic pilot watches. Aristo took another step toward the higher end of the market by launching the "Erbprinz" series, named after the street where the company also has a workshop for manufacturing metal bracelets.

Aristo Vollmer GmbH
Erbprinzenstr. 36
D-75175 Pforzheim
Germany

Tel.:
+49-7231-17031

Fax:
+49-7231-17033

E-mail:
info@aristo-vollmer.de

Website:
www.aristo-vollmer.de

Founded:
1907/1998

Number of employees:
16

Annual production:
8,000 watches and 10,000 bracelets

Distribution:
retail

U.S. distributor:
Long Island Watch, Marc Frankel
273 Walt Whitman Road, Suite 217
Huntington Station, NY 11746
631-470-0762; 888-673-1129 (fax)
www.longislandwatch.com

Most important collections/price range:
Aristo watches starting at $400 up to Vollmer watches at $1,900; Erbprinz watches up to $1,000

Classic Chronograph "De Luxe"
Reference number: 4H86BM
Movement: automatic, ETA Caliber 7750; ø 30 mm, height 7.9 mm; 25 jewels; 28,800 vph; 42-hour power reserve
Functions: hours, minutes, subsidiary seconds; chronograph; date, weekday
Case: stainless steel, ø 44 mm, height 14.5 mm; sapphire crystal; transparent case back; water-resistant to 5 atm
Band: stainless steel Milanese mesh, folding clasp
Price: $1,390

Titanium U-Boot Watch
Reference number: 5H92TiB
Movement: automatic, Caliber Aristomatic (base Sellita SW200-1); ø 25.6 mm, height 4.6 mm; 26 jewels; 28,800 vph; 38-hour power reserve
Functions: hours, minutes, sweep seconds; date
Case: titanium, ø 38.5 mm, height 10 mm; sapphire crystal; water-resistant to 10 atm
Band: titanium, folding clasp
Price: $650
Variations: textile strap ($565)

Titanium Carbon Chronograph
Reference number: 5H99
Movement: automatic, ETA Caliber 7750; ø 30 mm, height 7.9 mm; 25 jewels; 28,800 vph; 42-hour power reserve
Functions: hours, minutes, subsidiary seconds; chronograph; date, weekday
Case: titanium, ø 40.5 mm, height 15.5 mm; mineral glass; transparent case back; water-resistant to 5 atm
Band: carbon fiber, folding clasp
Price: $1,490
Variations: sapphire crystal ($1,590)

Blue 47 "Beobachter"

Reference number: 3H159
Movement: automatic, Caliber Aristomatic (base Sellita SW200-1); ø 25.6 mm, height 4.6 mm; 26 jewels; 28,800 vph; 38-hour power reserve
Functions: hours, minutes, sweep seconds; date
Case: stainless steel, ø 47 mm, height 11.4 mm; mineral glass; water-resistant to 5 atm
Band: calfskin, buckle
Price: $550
Variations: "Pilot" and "Navigator" models

Vintage Flieger Chronograph

Reference number: 7H186
Movement: automatic, ETA Caliber 7750; ø 30 mm, height 7.9 mm; 25 jewels; 28,800 vph; 42-hour power reserve
Functions: hours, minutes, subsidiary seconds; chronograph; date, weekday
Case: stainless steel, ø 44 mm, height 14.5 mm; sapphire crystal; transparent case back; water-resistant to 5 atm
Band: calfskin, buckle
Price: $1,550

Vintage 47 "Pilot"

Reference number: 7H98
Movement: automatic, ETA Caliber 2824-2; ø 25.6 mm, height 4.6 mm; 25 jewels; 28,800 vph; 38-hour power reserve
Functions: hours, minutes, sweep seconds
Case: stainless steel, ø 47 mm, height 11 mm; sapphire crystal; water-resistant to 5 atm
Band: calfskin, buckle
Remarks: comes with second calfskin strap
Price: $950
Variations: "Pilot" and "Navigator" models

Erbprinz "Black Forest"

Reference number: BFR2
Movement: manually wound, Ronda Caliber 4135; ø 19.4 mm; 17 jewels; 21,600 vph; 42-hour power reserve
Functions: hours, minutes, sweep seconds; date
Case: stainless steel, rose gold PVD coating, 26 × 40 mm, height 9.9 mm; sapphire crystal; water-resistant to 5 atm
Band: calfskin, buckle
Price: $495
Variations: Arabic numerals; stainless steel without PVD coating

Erbprinz "Karlsruhe"

Reference number: K1
Movement: automatic, Caliber Aristomatic (base Sellita SW200); ø 25.6 mm, height 4.6 mm; 26 jewels; 28,800 vph; 38-hour power reserve
Functions: hours, minutes, sweep seconds; date
Case: stainless steel, ø 41 mm, height 11 mm; mineral glass; water-resistant to 5 atm
Band: stainless steel Milanese mesh, folding clasp
Price: $650
Variations: calfskin strap ($590)

Erbprinz "Goldstadt 250"

Reference number: GS-1
Movement: automatic, Caliber Aristomatic (base Sellita SW200-1); ø 25.6 mm, height 4.6 mm; 26 jewels; 28,800 vph; 38-hour power reserve
Functions: Hours, minutes, sweep seconds; date
Case: stainless steel, ø 43. mm, height 14.5 mm; bezel with rose gold PVD treatment; sapphire crystal; transparent case back; water-resistant to 5 atm
Band: stainless steel Milanese mesh, folding clasp
Remarks: guilloché dial
Price: $995; limited to 100 units for 250th anniversary of "Golden City of Pforzheim"

ARMIN STROM

For more than thirty years, Armin Strom's name was associated mainly with the art of skeletonizing. But this "grandmaster of skeletonizers" then decided to entrust his life's work to the next generation, which turned out to be the Swiss industrialist and art patron Willy Michel.

Michel had the wherewithal to expand the one-man show into a full-blown *manufacture* able to conceive, design, and produce its own mechanical movements. The endeavor attracted Claude Geisler, a very skilled designer, and Michel's own son, Serge, who became business manager. When this triumvirate joined forces, it was able to come up with a technically fascinating movement at the quaint little *manufacture* in the Biel suburb of Bözingen within a brief period of time.

The new movement went on to grow into a family of ten, which forms the backbone of a new collection, including a tourbillon with microrotor—no mean feat for a small firm. The ARF15 caliber of the Mirrored Force Resonance, for example, features two balance wheels placed close enough to influence each other (resonance) and give the movement greater stability. The two oscillating systems are connected by a clutch spring.

This essential portfolio has given the *manufacture* the industrial autonomy to implement its projects quickly and independently. Armin Strom has additionally created an online configurator (on its homepage), giving fans and collectors the opportunity to personalize their watches. All components can be selected individually and combined, from the dial, hands, and finishing to the straps. The finished product can be picked up at a local dealership or at the manufacturer in Biel/Bienne, including a tour of the place.

Armin Strom AG
Bözingenstrasse 46
CH-2502 Biel/Bienne
Switzerland

Tel.:
+41-32-343-3344

Fax:
+41-32-343-3340

E-mail:
info@arminstrom.com

Website:
www.arminstrom.com

Founded:
1967

Number of employees:
22

Annual production:
approx. 600 watches

U.S. distributor:
Contact main office for information on U.S. distribution

Most important collections/price range:
Offers an online configurator for individual design using six in-house movements (manual, power reserve, automatic with or without date, tourbillon, and skeletons): $9,900 to $100,000 plus.

Mirrored Force Resonance Fire

Reference number: RG15-RF.5N
Movement: manually wound, Caliber ARF15; ø 36.6 mm, height 7.7 mm; 43 jewels; 25,200 vph; two separate regulating systems connected by a resonance clutch spring and mutually stabilize each other; finely finished movement; 48-hour power reserve
Functions: hours, minutes (off-center), two subsidiary seconds
Case: rose gold, ø 43.4 mm, height 13 mm; sapphire crystal; transparent case back; water-resistant to 5 atm
Band: reptile skin, buckle
Price: $67,100; limited to 50 pieces
Variation: stainless steel ($54,100)

Gravity Earth

Reference number: ST13-GE.90
Movement: automatic, Caliber AMR13; ø 36.6 mm, height 6 mm; 32 jewels; 18,000 vph; screw balance with gold weight screws, Breguet hairspring; microrotor visible on dial side; 120-hour power reserve
Functions: hours, minutes, subsidiary seconds
Case: stainless steel with black PVD coating, ø 43.4 mm, height 13 mm; sapphire crystal; transparent case back; water-resistant to 5 atm
Band: reptile skin, buckle
Remarks: additional rubber bracelet
Price: $12,900

Gravity Date Air

Reference number: TI14-DA.50
Movement: automatic, Caliber ADD14; ø 36.6 mm, height 6 mm; 30 jewels; 18,000 vph; screw balance with 18 gold weight screws; Breguet spring; microrotor; 120-hour power reserve
Functions: hours, minutes, subsidiary seconds; additional 24-hour display with day/night indicator; date
Case: titanium, ø 43.4 mm, height 13 mm; sapphire crystal; transparent back; water-resistant to 5 atm
Band: reptile skin, buckle
Remarks: additional rubber bracelet
Price: $19,300

Skeleton Pure Water

Reference number: ST15-PW.05
Movement: manually wound, Caliber ARM09-S;
ø 36.6 mm, height 6.2 mm; 34 jewels; 18,000 vph;
2 spring barrels, screw balance with gold weight
screws, Breguet spring, crown wheels on dial side;
skeletonized wheels/spring barrel bridges, base plate
with blue PVD coating; 168-hour power reserve
Functions: hours, minutes, subsidiary seconds;
power reserve indicator
Case: titanium, ø 43.4 mm, height 13 mm; sapphire
crystal; transparent back; water-resistant to 5 atm
Band: reptile skin, buckle
Remarks: additional rubber bracelet
Price: $30,000

Tourbillon Skeleton Earth

Reference number: ST15-TE.90
Movement: manually wound, Caliber ATC11-S;
ø 36.6 mm, height 6.2 mm; 24 jewels; 18,000 vph;
1-minute tourbillon, double spring barrel,
skeletonized platinum, wheels and bridges, Breguet
hair spring, screw balance with gold weight screws,
crown wheels visible on the dial; 240-hour power
reserve
Functions: hours, minutes, subsidiary seconds
Case: stainless steel with black PVD coating,
ø 43.4 mm, height 13 mm; sapphire crystal;
transparent case back; water-resistant to 5 atm
Band: reptile skin, double folding clasp
Remarks: additional rubber bracelet
Price: $81,500

Edge Double Barrel

Reference number: RG16-EB.5N
Movement: manually wound, Caliber ARM16;
ø 36.6 mm, height 7.7 mm; 34 jewels; 18,000 vph;
double spring barrel, winding wheels visible on dial
side; 192-hour power reserve
Functions: hours, minutes, subsidiary seconds;
power reserve indicator
Case: rose gold, ø 46.8 mm, height 13.2 mm;
sapphire crystal; transparent case back; water-
resistant to 5 atm
Band: reptile skin, buckle
Remarks: additional rubber bracelet
Price: $36,900
Variations: stainless steel ($24,900)

Caliber ATC11-S

Manually wound; 1-minute tourbillon, gold escape
wheel and pallet lever with hardened functional
surfaces, fully skeletonized movement, mainplate
with black PVD coating; double mainspring barrel;
240-hour power reserve
Functions: hours, minutes, subsidiary seconds
Diameter: 36.6 mm
Height: 6.2 mm
Jewels: 24
Balance: screw balance with variable inertia
Frequency: 18,000 vph
Balance spring: Breguet hairspring
Shock protection: Incabloc
Remarks: finely finished movement

Caliber ARF15

Manually wound; 25,200 vph; two separate
regulating systems connected by a resonance clutch
spring and mutually stabilize each other; single
spring barrel, 48-hour power reserve
Functions: hours, minutes (off-center), two
independent symmetrically mirrored subsidiary
seconds
Diameter: 36.6 mm
Height: 7.7 mm
Jewels: 43
Balance: two balance wheels oscillating in opposite
directions on a single hairspring
Frequency: 25,200 vph
Remarks: 226 components; fine hand-decorated
movement

Caliber ARM16

Manually wound; gold escape wheel and pallet
lever with hardened functional surfaces; double
mainspring barrel, 192-hour power reserve
Functions: hours, minutes, subsidiary seconds;
power reserve indicator
Diameter: 36.6 mm
Height: 7.7 mm
Jewels: 34
Balance: screw balance with variable inertia
Frequency: 18,000 vph
Balance spring: Breguet hairspring
Remarks: finely finished movement

ARNOLD & SON

John Arnold holds a special place among the British watchmakers of the eighteenth and nineteenth centuries because he was the first to organize the production of his chronometers along industrial lines. He developed his own standards and employed numerous watchmakers. During his lifetime, he is said to have manufactured around 5,000 marine chronometers, which he sold at reasonable prices to the Royal Navy and the West Indies merchant fleet. Arnold chronometers were packed in the trunks of some of the greatest explorers, from John Franklin and Ernest Shackleton to Captain Cook and Dr. Livingstone.

As Arnold & Son was once synonymous with precision timekeeping on the high seas, it stands to reason, then, that the modern brand should also focus its design policies on the interplay of time and geography as well as the basic functions of navigation. Independence from The British Masters Group has meant that the venerable English chronometer brand has been reorienting itself, setting its sights on classic, elegant watchmaking. With the expertise of watch manufacturer La Joux-Perret behind it (and the expertise housed in the building behind the complex on the main road between La Chaux-de-Fonds and Le Locle), it has been able to implement a number of new ideas.

There are two main lines: The Royal Collection celebrates John Arnold's art, with luxuriously designed models inspired from past creations with delicate complications, tourbillons or world-time displays, or unadorned manual windings featuring the new Caliber A&S 1001 by La Joux-Perret. The Instrument Collection is dedicated to exploring the seven seas and offers a sober look reflecting old-fashioned meters. Typically, these timepieces combine two displays on a single dial: a chronograph with jumping seconds, for example, between the off-center displays of time and the date hand or separate escapements driving a dual time display—left, the sidereal time; right, the solar time; and between the two, the difference. Perhaps the most remarkable timepiece in the collection is the skeletonized Time Pyramid with a dual power reserve, a crown between the lugs, and an overall modern look.

Arnold & Son
38, boulevard des Eplatures
CH-2300 La Chaux-de-Fonds
Switzerland

Tel.:
+41-32-967-9797

Fax:
+41-32-968-0755

E-mail:
info@arnoldandson.com

Website:
www.arnoldandson.com

Founded:
1995

Number of employees:
approx. 30

U.S. distributor:
Arnold & Son USA
510 West 6th Street, Suite 309
Los Angeles, CA 90014
213-622-1133

Most important collections/price range:
Nebula, DBG, DBS, Golden Wheel, HMS, TB88, TBR, TE8 (Tourbillon), Time Pyramid, UTTE / from approx. $10,000 to $325,000

Nebula

Reference number: 1NEAS.B01A.D134A
Movement: manually wound, Arnold & Son Caliber 5101; ø 31.5 mm, height 4.04 mm; 24 jewels; 21,600 vph; skeletonized and finely finished movement; 90-hour power reserve
Functions: hours, minutes, subsidiary seconds
Case: stainless steel, ø 41.5 mm, height 8.73 mm; sapphire crystal; transparent case back; water-resistant to 3 atm
Band: reptile skin, buckle
Remarks: skeletonized dial
Price: $14,500
Variations: pink gold ($25,950)

Tourbillon Chronometer No. 36

Reference number: 1ETAR.G01A.C112A
Movement: manually wound, Arnold & Son Caliber 8600; ø 37.8 mm, height 5.9 mm; 33 jewels; 28,800 vph; 1-minute tourbillon; mainplate and bridges of pink gold–plated German silver; 90-hour power reserve; COSC-certified chronometer
Functions: hours, minutes, subsidiary seconds
Case: pink gold, ø 46 mm, height 12.66 mm; sapphire crystal; transparent case back; water-resistant to 3 atm
Band: reptile skin, buckle
Price: $56,550; limited to 28 pieces

HM Double Hemisphere Perpetual Moon

Reference number: 1GLAR.U03A.C122A
Movement: manually wound, Arnold & Son Caliber 1512; ø 34 mm, height 5.35 mm; 27 jewels; 21,600 vph; astronomically accurate moon phase display for 122 years; 90-hour power reserve
Functions: hours, minutes; double moon phase
Case: pink gold, ø 42 mm, height 11.43 mm; sapphire crystal; transparent case back; water-resistant to 3 atm
Band: reptile skin, buckle
Remarks: two hand-engraved three-dimensional moon disks
Price: $31,000

Tourbillon Chronometer No. 36

Reference number: 1ETAS.G01A.C112S
Movement: manually wound, Arnold & Son Caliber 8600; ø 37.8 mm, height 5.9 mm; 33 jewels; 28,800 vph; 1-minute tourbillon; mainplate and bridges of pink gold–plated German silver; 90-hour power reserve; COSC-certified chronometer
Functions: hours, minutes, subsidiary seconds
Case: stainless steel, ø 46 mm, height 12.66 mm; sapphire crystal; transparent case back; water-resistant to 3 atm
Band: reptile skin, buckle
Price: $39,995; limited to 28 pieces

Eight-Day Royal Navy

Reference number: 1EDAS.U01A.D136A
Movement: manually wound, Arnold & Son Caliber 1016; ø 33 mm, height 4.7 mm; 33 jewels; 21,600 vph; 192-hour power reserve
Functions: hours, minutes, subsidiary seconds; power reserve indicator; date
Case: stainless steel, ø 43 mm, height 10.7 mm; sapphire crystal; transparent case back; water-resistant to 3 atm
Band: reptile skin, buckle
Price: $12,950
Variations: black or silver-white dial

HM Perpetual Moon

Reference number: 1GLAR.I01A.C122A
Movement: manually wound, Arnold & Son Caliber 1512; ø 34 mm, height 5.35 mm; 27 jewels; 21,600 vph; astronomically accurate moon phase display for 122 years; 90-hour power reserve
Functions: hours, minutes; moon phase
Case: pink gold, ø 42 mm, height 11.43 mm; sapphire crystal; transparent case back; water-resistant to 3 atm
Band: reptile skin, buckle
Remarks: hand-engraved three-dimensional moon disks
Price: $29,950
Variations: blue guilloché dial ($29,950); stainless steel with black dial ($16,300); stainless steel with blue guilloché dial ($16,950)

DSTB

Reference number: 1ATAS.U01A.C121S
Movement: automatic, Arnold & Son Caliber 6003; ø 38 mm, height 7.39 mm; 32 jewels; 28,800 vph; true beat second escapement visible on dial side; finely finished movement; 45-hour power reserve
Functions: hours, minutes (off-center), subsidiary seconds (true beat)
Case: stainless steel, ø 43.5 mm, height 13 mm; sapphire crystal; transparent case back; water-resistant to 3 atm
Band: reptile skin, buckle
Price: $29,995
Variations: black dial ($31,950); pink gold with anthracite dial ($48,550)

DBG Skeleton

Reference number: 1DGAP.S10A.C120P
Movement: manually wound, Arnold & Son Caliber 1309; ø 35 mm, height 3.9 mm; 42 jewels; 21,600 vph; double spring barrel, two independent gear trains and escapement systems; skeletonized movement; 40-hour power reserve
Functions: hours, minutes (two symmetrical movements, two time zones), sweep seconds; day/night indicator (per time zone)
Case: rose gold, ø 44 mm, height 9.89 mm; sapphire crystal; transparent case back; water-resistant to 3 atm
Band: reptile skin, buckle
Price: $38,850; limited to 30 pieces

Time Pyramid

Reference number: 1TPAR.S01A.C125A
Movement: manually wound, Arnold & Son Caliber 1615; ø 37 mm, height 4.4 mm; 27 jewels; 21,600 vph; skeletonized movement; double spring barrel, 90-hour power reserve
Functions: hours, minutes, subsidiary seconds; double power reserve display
Case: pink gold, ø 44.6 mm, height 10 mm; sapphire crystal; transparent case back; water-resistant to 3 atm
Band: reptile skin, buckle
Remarks: symmetrical, pyramid-shaped movement structure inspired from table clocks by John and Roger Arnold
Price: $43,200
Variations: stainless steel ($31,900); Time Pyramid Guilloché in gold with guilloché case back ($46,950)

ARTYA

Shaking up the staid atmosphere of watchmaking can be achieved many ways. The conservative approach is to make some small engineering advance and then talk loudly of tradition and innovation. Yvan Arpa, founder of ArtyA watches, enjoys "putting his boot in the anthill," in his own words.

This refreshingly candid personality arrived at watchmaking because, after spending his *Wanderjahre* crossing Papua New Guinea on foot and practicing Thai boxing in its native land, any corporate mugginess back home did not quite cut it for him. Instead he turned the obscure brand Romain Jerome into the talk of the industry with novel material choices: "I looked for antimatter to gentrify common matter," he reflects, "like the rust: proof of the passage of time and the sworn enemy of watchmaking."

Leaving Romain Jerome liberated Arpa from brand constraints. He founded ArtyA, where he could get his "monster" off the slab as it were, with a divine spark. "I had worked with water, rust, dust, and other elements, and then I really caught fire," says Arpa. From cases hit with an electrical arc to cut-up Euro bills, Artya's watches hit nerves and drew a gamut of emotional responses. That's his aim, to surprise and amaze. His dials shake up the owner, and are often genuinely unique. They can include real butterfly wings, exquisite engravings by Bram Ramon, or mysterious mother-of-pearl crafting—for 2017, he even revived the snipped money idea, this time with dollars. He never shuns a crazy idea, like the Son of Sounds, with their guitar-shaped case and chrono pushers designed like guitar pegs—Alice Cooper owns one, obviously.

Arpa wants us not only to wear a watch, but to reflect on aspects of our world and society, the meaning of money, bullets, skulls, our love-hate relationship with electronics, the passage of time, love and violence, the beauty of nature frozen in death, and the significance of music. His provocations, though, do not arise from a sophomoric need to be contrarian, but rather from his long and rich experience of an industry that tends to play it safe. No wonder Samsung recruited him to design their Gear 3 hybrid pocket watch.

Luxury Artpieces SA
Route de Thonon 146
CH-1222 Vésenaz
Switzerland

Tel.:
+41-22-752-4940

Website:
www.artya.com

Founded:
2010

Number of employees:
12

Annual production:
at least 365 (one a day)

U.S. distributor:
Contact headquarters for all enquiries.

Most important collections/price range:
Son of a Gun / $8,800 to $167,000; Son of Art / $3,800 to $21,000; Son of Earth / $4,300 to $183,000; Son of Love / $4,300 to $54,500; Son of Sound / $4,300 to $22,110; Son of Gears / $6,550 to $16,550

Dollar for Dollar

Movement: automatic, Swiss-made A82 Caliber, modified in-house; ø 25.6 mm, height 4.4 mm; 25 jewels; 46-hour power reserve
Functions: hours, minutes, seconds
Case: stainless steel with lateral ArtyOr inserts; ø 44 mm, height 11.3 mm; triple antireflection sapphire crystal; screw-down engraved case; water-resistant to 5 atm back
Band: calfskin, buckle
Remarks: dial hand decorated with snippets of real dollar bill by artist D. Arpa-Cirpka
Price: $5,900; unique piece

Son of Earth Butterfly "Delicacy"

Movement: automatic, Swiss-made A82 Caliber, modified in-house; ø 25.6 mm, height 4.4 mm; 25 jewels; 46-hour power reserve
Functions: hours, minutes, seconds
Case: stainless steel with chocolate PVD treatment and lateral ArtyOr inserts; ø 44 mm, height 11.3 mm; sapphire crystal with triple antireflection; screw-down engraved case back; water-resistant to 5 atm
Band: reptile skin, buckle
Remarks: dial decorated with genuine iridescent butterfly wings and gold leaf by artist D. Arpa-Cirpka
Price: $7,900; unique piece

Son of Sea Tourbillon

Movement: manually wound ArtyA; 33 mm, height 12 mm; 19 jewels; 21,600 vph; flying tourbillon; 100-hour power reserve
Functions: hours, minutes
Case: stainless steel with exclusive blue carbon fiber lateral inserts, ø 44 mm, height 18 mm; screw-down engraved case back; water-resistant to 3 atm
Band: reptile skin, buckle
Remarks: dial decorated with natural seabeds, butterfly wings, pigments, gold leaf, by artist D. Arpa-Cirpka
Price: $137,000; unique piece

Artya 3 Gongs Minute Repeater, Regulator, and Double Axis Tourbillon

Movement: manually wound, by MHC, design by ArtyA; ø 13.2 mm, height 6.6 mm; 21,600 vph; 46 jewels; double axis tourbillon, 30-second in one direction and 60-second in other; minute repeater; 64-hour power reserve
Functions: hours (off-center), sweep minutes, seconds on tourbillon
Case: titanium and ArtyOr with PVD treatment, ø 64.6 × 47.3 mm, height 18.1 mm; sapphire crystal; transparent case back; water-resistant to 5 atm
Band: reptile skin, buckle
Remarks: special gongs, customizable
Price: $480,000; unique piece

Golden Dragon Tourbillon

Movement: manually wound, ArtyA; 33 mm, height 12 mm; 19 jewels; 21,600 vph; flying tourbillon; 100-hour power reserve
Functions: hours, minutes, seconds (on tourbillon cage)
Case: stainless steel with lateral PVD-treated inserts, ø 44 mm, height 18 mm; transparent engraved and screw-down case back; water-resistant to 3 atm
Band: reptile skin, buckle
Remarks: hand-engraved and chiseled dial and bezel in titanium with gold inlays by Bram Ramon
Price: $170,000; unique piece

Shining Star Tourbillon

Movement: manually wound, ArtyA (MHC engineering); 33 mm, height 12 mm; 19 jewels; 21,600 vph; flying tourbillon; 100-hour power reserve; dial set with diamonds
Functions: hours, minutes, seconds (on tourbillon cage)
Case: stainless steel, ø 37 × 49 mm, height 15 mm; screw-down transparent engraved case back; protected against humidity and dust, but not water-resistant
Band: reptile skin, buckle
Remarks: hand-engraved and chiseled dial and bezel in titanium with gold inlays by Bram Ramon
Price: $185,000; unique piece

Son of a Gun "Target"

Movement: automatic, Swiss-made A17 Caliber, modified in-house; 17.6 mm, height 4.8 mm; 19 jewels; rotor with cut-off rounds; 52-hour power reserve
Functions: hours, minutes, seconds
Case: stainless steel with PVD treatment, 47 mm, height 12 mm; target engraved on bezel; screw-down transparent engraved case back; water-resistant to 3 atm
Band: reptile skin, buckle
Remarks: dial with engraved target
Price: $7,900; limited to 99 pieces

Son of Gun Russian Roulette "Glasnost"

Movement: manually wound, ArtyA patent; ø 32.6 mm, height 5.7 mm; 19 jewels; skeletonized spinning dial with real hand-set bullet; 52-hour power reserve
Functions: hours, minutes
Case: ultralight ITR2 (Innovative Technical Resin and Revolutionary), 48 mm, height 12 mm; screw-down engraved case back; water-resistant to 3 atm
Remarks: fast spinning dial with hand-set real bullet
Band: reptile skin, buckle
Price: $17,900; limited to 20 pieces

ArtyA Son of Sound Guitar "Race"

Movement: automatic, Artya-Woodstock by Concepto; 27 jewels; 28,800 vph; 48-hour power reserve
Functions: hours, minutes, subsidiary seconds; date; patented active "tuning pegs" system for chronograph functions/date setting; 30-minute counter
Case: stainless steel, 36.62 × 52.3 mm, height 15 mm; water-resistant to 50 atm
Band: reptile skin, buckle
Price: $17,900; limited to 99 pieces

AUDEMARS PIGUET

The history of Audemars Piguet is one of the most engaging stories of Swiss watch-making folklore: Ever since their school days together in the Vallée de Joux, Jules-Louis Audemars (b. 1851) and Edward-Auguste Piguet (b. 1853) knew they would follow in the footsteps of their fathers and grandfathers and become watchmakers. They were members of the same sports association, sang in the same choir, attended the same vocational school—and both became outstandingly talented watchmakers.

The *manufacture* founded over 140 years ago by these two is still in family hands. The company was able to make extensive investments in production facilities and new movements thanks to the ongoing success of the sporty Royal Oak collection (launched in 1972) and the profits from selling off shares in Jaeger-LeCoultre in 2000. The Manufacture des Forges, designed according to the latest ecological and economical standards, opened in August 2009 in Le Brassus and is a key to the future of the brand.

The second key to the brand's enduring success was no doubt the acquisition of the atelier Renaud et Papi in 1992. APRP, as it is known, specializes in creating and executing complex complications, a skill it lets other brands share in as well. But its main task has been to continue exploring the possibilities offered by AP's phenomenally enduring Royal Oak. At the SIHH, like clockwork, François-Henry Bennahmias, the company CEO since 2012, presents a range of new models in the family with some remarkable complications, chief among them being the Supersonnerie, a minute repeater with a special architecture to maximally amplify the sound. Another is the openworked Royal Oak with two balance wheels operating in opposite directions on a single shaft, a novelty from 2016, which fascinates the aficionados.

Manufacture d'Horlogerie
Audemars Piguet
Route de France 16
CH-1348 Le Brassus
Switzerland

Tel.:
+41-21-642-3900

E-mail:
info@audemarspiguet.com

Website:
www.audemarspiguet.com

Founded:
1875

Number of employees:
approx. 1,300

Annual production:
40,000 watches

U.S. distributor:
Audemars Piguet (North America) Inc.
Service Center of the Americas
3040 Gulf to Bay Boulevard
Clearwater, FL 33759

Most important collection/price range:
Royal Oak / from approx. $17,800; Millenary / from approx. $28,400; special concept watches

Royal Oak Offshore Tourbillon Chronograph

Reference number: 26407BA.OO.A002CA.01
Movement: manually wound, AP Caliber 2943; ø 29.4 mm, height 5.5 mm; 28 jewels; 21,600 vph; 1-minute tourbillon, skeletonized movement; 72-hour power reserve
Functions: hours, minutes, subsidiary seconds; chronograph
Case: yellow gold, ø 44 mm, height 14.43 mm; bezel screwed to case back with 8 screws; sapphire crystal; transparent case back; ceramic pushers and crown, screw-in crown; water-resistant to 10 atm
Band: rubber, folding clasp
Price: $270,000

Royal Oak Tourbillon Extra-Thin

Reference number: 26510IP.OO.1220IP.01
Movement: manually wound, AP Caliber 2924; ø 31.5 mm, height 4.46 mm; 25 jewels; 21,600 vph; 1-minute tourbillon; 70-hour power reserve
Functions: hours, minutes
Case: titanium, ø 41 mm, height 8.95 mm; bezel screwed to case back with 8 screws; sapphire crystal; transparent case back; water-resistant to 5 atm
Band: titanium with platinum, folding clasp
Price: $145,000

Royal Oak Double Balance Wheel Openworked

Reference number: 15407OR.OO.1220OR.01
Movement: automatic, AP Caliber 3132; ø 26.59 mm, height 5.57 mm; 38 jewels; 21,600 vph; double balance wheel with two opposing hairsprings; skeletonized movement; 45-hour power reserve
Functions: hours, minutes, sweep seconds
Case: rose gold, ø 41 mm, height 9.9 mm; bezel screwed to case back with 8 screws; sapphire crystal; transparent case back; water-resistant to 5 atm
Band: rose gold, folding clasp
Remarks: skeletonized dial
Price: $76,800
Variations: stainless steel ($43,100)

Royal Oak Concept Supersonnerie

Reference number: 26577TI.OO.D002CA.01
Movement: manually wound, AP Caliber 2937;
ø 29.9 mm, height 8.28 mm; 43 jewels; 21,600 vph;
1-minute tourbillon; 42-hour power reserve
Functions: hours, minutes; minute repeater;
chronograph
Case: titanium, ø 44 mm; bezel screwed to case
back with 8 screws; sapphire crystal; ceramic pushers
and crown
Band: rubber, folding clasp
Remarks: case with resonating back/lateral
openings for sound emission
Price: on request

Jules Audemars Minute Repeater

Reference number: 26590PT.OO.D028CR.01
Movement: manually wound, AP Caliber 2944;
ø 30 mm, height 6 mm; 35 jewels; 21,600 vph;
72-hour power reserve
Functions: hours, minutes, subsidiary seconds;
minute repeater
Case: platinum, ø 43 mm, height 13.15 mm;
sapphire crystal; transparent case back
Band: reptile skin, folding clasp
Remarks: enamel dial
Price: $325,500

Royal Oak Perpetual Calendar

Reference number: 26579CE.OO.1225CE.01
Movement: automatic, AP Caliber 5134; ø 29 mm,
height 4.31 mm; 38 jewels; 19,800 vph; 40-hour
power reserve
Functions: hours, minutes; perpetual calendar with
date, weekday, weeks of the year, month, moon
phase, leap year
Case: ceramic, ø 41 mm, height 9.5 mm; bezel
screwed to case back with 8 screws; sapphire crystal;
transparent case back; screw-in crown
Band: ceramic, folding clasp
Price: $93,900

Royal Oak Offshore Chronograph

Reference number: 26400IO.OO.A002CA.01
Movement: automatic, AP Caliber 3126/3840;
ø 29.92 mm, height 7.16 mm; 59 jewels;
21,600 vph; 50-hour power reserve
Functions: hours, minutes, subsidiary seconds;
chronograph; date
Case: titanium, ø 44 mm, height 14.4 mm; ceramic
bezel screwed through to case back with 8 screws;
sapphire crystal; transparent case back; ceramic
pushers and crown, screw-in crown; water-resistant
to 10 atm
Band: rubber, buckle
Price: $30,400
Variations: various bands, cases, and dials

Royal Oak Offshore Chronograph

Reference number: 26405CE.OO.A002CA.02
Movement: automatic, AP Caliber 3126/3840;
ø 29.92 mm, height 7.16 mm; 59 jewels;
21,600 vph; 50-hour power reserve
Functions: hours, minutes, subsidiary seconds;
chronograph; date
Case: ceramic, ø 44 mm, height 14.4 mm; bezel
screwed to case back with 8 screws; sapphire crystal;
transparent case back; water-resistant to 10 atm
Band: rubber, buckle
Price: $32,100
Variations: various bands, cases, and dials

Royal Oak Offshore Chronograph

Reference number: 26401RO.OO.A002CA.02
Movement: automatic, AP Caliber 3126/3840;
ø 29.92 mm, height 7.16 mm; 59 jewels;
21,600 vph; 50-hour power reserve
Functions: hours, minutes, subsidiary seconds;
chronograph; date
Case: rose gold, ø 44 mm, height 14.4 mm; ceramic
bezel screwed through to case back with 8 screws;
sapphire crystal; transparent case back; ceramic
pushers and crown, screw-in crown; water-resistant
to 10 atm
Band: rubber, buckle
Price: $45,900
Variations: various bands, cases, and dials

Royal Oak Offshore Chronograph

Reference number: 26470BA.OO.1000BA.01
Movement: automatic, AP Caliber 3126/3840; ø 29.92 mm, height 7.16 mm; 59 jewels; 21,600 vph; 50-hour power reserve
Functions: hours, minutes, subsidiary seconds; chronograph; date
Case: yellow gold, ø 42 mm, height 14.54 mm; bezel screwed to case back with 8 screws; sapphire crystal; transparent case back; ceramic pushers and crown, screw-in crown; water-resistant to 10 atm
Band: yellow gold, folding clasp
Price: $75,700
Variations: various bands, cases, and dials

Royal Oak Offshore Diver

Reference number: 15710ST.OO.A051CA.01
Movement: automatic, AP Caliber 3120; ø 26.6 mm, height 4.26 mm; 40 jewels; 21,600 vph; movement entirely hand-decorated; 60-hour power reserve
Functions: hours, minutes, sweep seconds; date
Case: stainless steel, ø 42 mm, height 14.1 mm; bezel screwed to case back with 8 screws; crown adjustable scale ring with 0-60 scale; sapphire crystal; screw-in crown; water-resistant to 30 atm
Band: rubber, buckle
Price: $19,900

Royal Oak Chronograph

Reference number: 26331ST.OO.1220ST.03
Movement: automatic, AP Caliber 2385; ø 26.2 mm, height 5.5 mm; 37 jewels; 21,600 vph; movement entirely hand-decorated; 40-hour power reserve
Functions: hours, minutes, subsidiary seconds; chronograph; date
Case: stainless steel, ø 41 mm, height 10.8 mm; bezel screwed to case with 8 white gold screws; sapphire crystal; screw-in crown and pusher; water-resistant to 5 atm
Band: stainless steel, folding clasp
Price: $24,300

Royal Oak Automatic Bicolor

Reference number: 15400ST.OO.1220ST.01
Movement: automatic, AP Caliber 3120; ø 26.6 mm, height 4.26 mm; 40 jewels; 21,600 vph; movement entirely hand-decorated; 60-hour power reserve
Functions: hours, minutes, sweep seconds; date
Case: stainless steel, ø 41 mm, height 9.8 mm; rose gold bezel, bezel screwed to case with 8 white gold screws; sapphire crystal; transparent case back; screw-in crown, in pink gold; water-resistant to 5 atm
Band: stainless steel with rose gold elements, folding clasp
Price: $17,800
Variations: various bands and dials

Royal Oak Automatic

Reference number: 15450ST.OO.1256ST.02
Movement: automatic, AP Caliber 3120; ø 26.6 mm, height 4.25 mm; 40 jewels; 21,600 vph; movement entirely hand-decorated; 60-hour power reserve
Functions: hours, minutes, sweep seconds; date
Case: stainless steel, ø 37 mm, height 9.8 mm; bezel screwed to case with 8 white gold screws; sapphire crystal; transparent case back; water-resistant to 5 atm
Band: stainless steel, folding clasp
Price: $16,500

Ladies Millenary

Reference number: 77247OR.ZZ.A812CR.01
Movement: manually wound, AP Caliber 5201 × 32.74 × 28.59 mm, height 4.16 mm; 19 jewels; 21,600 vph; inverted movement design with balance and escapement on dial side; 54-hour power reserve
Functions: hours, minutes, subsidiary seconds
Case: white gold, 39.5 × 35.4 mm; sapphire crystal; transparent case back
Band: reptile skin, buckle
Remarks: dials with mother-of-pearl and diamonds, case set with 116 diamonds
Price: $28,400

Caliber 2885

Automatic; single spring barrel, 45-hour power reserve

Functions: hours, minutes; minute repeater; split-second chronograph; perpetual calendar with date, weekday, month, moon phase, leap year
Diameter: 31.6 mm
Height: 8.55 mm
Jewels: 52
Frequency: 19,800 vph
Shock protection: Kif Elastor
Remarks: skeletonized rotor; 648 components

Caliber 2908

Manually wound; inverted movement design with dial-side balance wheel and escapement; double mainspring barrel, 90-hour power reserve; COSC-certified chronometer

Functions: hours, minutes, subsidiary seconds; power reserve indicator
Diameter: 39.8 mm
Height: 8.11 mm
Jewels: 33
Balance: with variable inertia
Frequency: 43,200 vph
Remarks: all components decorated by hand, 267 components

Caliber 2913

Manually wound; 1-minute tourbillon; bridges of black anodized aluminum; selection button for hand position and winding; single spring barrel, 237-hour power reserve

Functions: hours, minutes; additional 12-hour display (second time zone)
Diameter: 35.6 mm
Height: 9.9 mm
Jewels: 29
Balance: screw balance
Frequency: 21,600 vph
Remarks: movement for Royal Oak concept watch; beveled and polished steel parts, matte mainplate, straight-grain polished bridges; 291 components

Caliber 3132

Automatic; single spring barrel, 45-hour power reserve

Functions: hours, minutes, sweep seconds
Diameter: 26.59 mm
Height: 5.57 mm
Jewels: 38
Balance: double balance wheel
Frequency: 21,600 vph
Balance spring: two hairsprings wound in opposite directions
Remarks: fully skeletonized movement

Caliber 5134

Automatic; flying spring barrel; single spring barrel, 40-hour power reserve

Functions: hours, minutes; perpetual calendar with date, weekday, weeks of the year, month, moon phase, leap year
Diameter: 29 mm
Height: 4.31 mm
Jewels: 38
Balance: with adjustable inertia
Frequency: 19,800 vph
Balance spring: flat hairspring
Remarks: finely finished movement; gold rotor; 374 components

Caliber 5201

Manually wound; inverted movement design with balance and escapement on dial side; single spring barrel, 49-hour power reserve

Functions: hours, minutes, subsidiary seconds
Measurements: 32.74 × 28.59 mm
Height: 4.16 mm
Jewels: 19
Balance: with variable inertia
Frequency: 21,600 vph
Shock protection: Kif Elastor
Remarks: all components decorated by hand, dial side of mainplate decorated with horizontal côtes de Genève and perlage on movement side; 157 components

AZIMUTH

Creativity can take on all forms and accept all forms as well. It's the philosophy behind Azimuth, a brand that has managed, perhaps like no other, to surprise, to amaze, to attract the watch-loving public with amazing designs, some of which, like the Mr. Roboto, have achieved cult status. Remaining fresh and interesting is key to the Neuchâtel-based brand, so in 2015 it invited the Swiss watchmaker Giuseppe Picchi to become CEO and technical director of Azimuth.

Picchi holds a diploma in High Watchmaking, and has worked for almost 30 years with some of the most esteemed names in the industry. Picchi is currently in the driver's seat as Azimuth seeks new adventures in innovative, state-of-the-art watchmaking.

"I am thrilled by the opportunity to push the envelope on avant-garde watchmaking with Azimuth," says Picchi. "The brand founders and I share the same vision of taking contemporary watchmaking as far as possible." As Azimuth's new master watchmaker, Picchi has been working on creating and prototyping new timepieces, as well as the development of base movements to support Azimuth's complicated and semi-complicated modules. These are used in such out-of-the-box watches as the King Casino (with a game) and the wrist-robot Mr. Roboto.

The automotive world is also an inspiration to the brand and, true to style, the resulting watches are special: Twin Turbo, Crazy Rider, and, planned for 2018, a new Gran Turismo (GT), a timepiece that oozes contemporary charm while paying tribute to the iconic four-wheelers of yesteryear.

Like genuine artists, though, the creative heads at Azimuth are also capable of doing a "watch for the watch's sake." There's the Back In Time, a traditional regulator with date, or the complicated Spaceship Predator, which, when coming with a full set of diamonds, will raise quite a few eyebrows, which is definitely a big benefit these days.

Azimuth Watch Co. Sàrl
Rue des Draizes 5
CH-2000 Neuchâtel
Switzerland

Tel.:
+41-79-765-1466

E-mail:
gpi@azimuthwatch.com
sales@azimuthwatch.com

Website:
www.azimuthwatch.com

Founded:
2004

Number of employees:
6

U.S. distributor:
About Time Luxury Group
210 Bellevue Avenue
Newport RI 02840
401-952-4684

Most important collections/price range:
SP-1 / from $3,800

Back In Time Beige

Reference number: RN.BT.SS.D007
Movement: automatic, in-house modified (base ETA/Sellita); 21,600/28,800 vph; ø 34.4 mm, height 4.5 mm
Functions: single hand in counterclockwise motion; date
Case: stainless steel, ø 42 mm, height 14.4 mm; domed sapphire crystal; water-resistant to 3 atm
Band: calfskin, buckle
Price: $1,900
Variations: silver, black, blue, anthracite dial colors

SP-1 Spaceship Predator Full Pave

Reference number: SP.SS.SS.N004
Movement: manual winding, AZM 768 modified and skeletonized; 18,000 vph; ø 36.6 mm, height 4.5 mm
Functions: jumping hours, minutes, seconds
Case: stainless steel, ø 48 mm; set with diamonds; domed sapphire crystal; water-resistant to 3 atm
Band: reptile skin, folding clasp
Remarks: 3D titanium minute hand
Price: $28,500

SP-1 Landship

Reference number: SP.LS.TI.L001
Movement: automatic, in-house modified (base ETA); 21,600/28,800 vph; diameter 32.5 mm, height 6.4 mm
Functions: wandering hour, retrograde minutes
Case: titanium, 55 × 40 mm; water-resistant to 3 atm
Band: rubber, folding clasp
Price: $7,300
Variations: case in hand-painted military camouflage

SP-1 Twin Turbo

Reference number: SP.SS.TT.N002
Movement: manual winding, ETA 2512-1;
21,600 vph; ø 17.2 mm, height 2.85 mm
Functions: hours, minutes; 2 time zones
Case: stainless steel and aluminum, 51 × 50 mm;
water-resistant to 3 atm
Band: calfskin strap, folding clasp
Remarks: vintage movement
Price: $6,000; limited to 88 pieces
Variations: top hood in silver, yellow, red (red
limited to 50 pieces)

SP-1 Gran Turismo

Reference number: SP.SS.GT.L003
Movement: automatic winding, ETA 2671;
28,800 vph; ø 17.2 mm, height 4.80 mm
Functions: hours, minutes; seconds
Case: stainless steel with gold plating, 50 × 45 mm;
water-resistant to 3 atm
Band: calfskin, folding clasp
Price: $4,850; limited to 100 pieces
Variations: top in steel polished, black PVD coating
or blue PVD coating

SP-1 Crazy Rider

Reference number: SP.SS.CR.N003
Movement: automatic, in-house modified,
28,800 vph; length 47.7 mm, height 4.35 mm
Functions: 24-hour chain drive hour system,
minutes
Case: stainless steel, forged carbon bezel, 55 ×
36 mm; sapphirè crystal; water-resistant to 3 atm
Band: calfskin, folding clasp
Price: $5,450

SP-1 Twin Barrel Tourbillon

Reference number: SP.TB.TI.L001
Movement: manual winding tourbillon; in-
house modified; 5-day power reserve; twin barrels;
28,800 vph; 36.3 × 32.0 mm, height 6.4 mm
Functions: jumping hours, minutes; specially
modified twin-disk jumping hour system on
3-dimensional minute hand
Case: titanium with carbon fiber side inserts, 45 ×
50 mm, height 18 mm; domed sapphire crystal;
water-resistant to 5 atm
Band: calfskin, folding clasp
Price: $90,000; limited to 25 pieces

SP-1 Mr. Roboto R2

Reference number: SP.SS.ROT.N001
Movement: automatic, in-house modified, sapphire
rotor; 28,800 vph; ø 32.5 mm, height 6.7 mm
Functions: regulator hours, retrograde minutes,
GMT
Case: stainless steel; 47 × 55 mm; sapphire crystal;
water-resistant to 3 atm
Band: calfskin, folding clasp
Price: $6,000
Variations: center case in forged carbon

SP-1 King Casino

Reference number: SP.KC.SS.N001
Movement: automatic, in-house modified (base
ETA); 21,600 vph; ø 25.6 mm, height 6.0 mm
Functions: casino game function via crown; hours,
minutes, seconds
Case: stainless steel, 45 × 45 mm; domed sapphire
crystal; water-resistant to 3 atm
Band: calfskin, folding clasp
Remarks: roulette and baccarat game functions
Price: $3,650
Variations: chocolate color plated or yellow gold
plated

BALL WATCH CO.

BALL Watch Company SA
Rue du Châtelot 21
CH-2300 La Chaux-de-Fonds
Switzerland

Tel.:
+41-32-724-53-00

Fax:
+41-32-724-53-01

E-mail:
info@ballwatch.ch

Website:
www.ballwatch.com

Founded:
1891

U.S. distributor:
BALL Watch USA
1920 Dr. Martin Luther King Jr. St N
Suite D
St. Petersburg, FL 33704
727-896-4278

Most important collections/price range:
Engineer, Fireman, Trainmaster, Conductor /
$1,300 to $6,500

The "RR" at the tail end of Ball Watch Co. second hands stands for "railroad," an industry that is intimately linked with the company's origins in the glorious age when trains puffing smoke and steam crisscrossed America. Back then, the pocket watch was a necessity to maintain precise rail schedules. By 1893, many companies had adopted the General Railroads Timepiece Standards, which included such norms as regulation in at least five positions, precision to within thirty seconds per week, Breguet balance springs, and so on. One of the chief players in developing the standards was Webster Clay Ball. This farmboy-turned-watchmaker from Fredericktown, Ohio, decided to leave the homestead for a more lucrative occupation. He apprenticed as a watchmaker, became a salesperson for Dueber watch cases, and finally opened the Webb C. Ball Company in Cleveland. In 1891, he added the position of chief inspector of the Lake Shore Lines to his CV. When a hogshead's watch stopped, resulting in an accident, Ball decided to establish quality benchmarks for watches that included antimagnetic technology, and he set up an inspection system for the timepieces.

For those with a strong affinity for technical gadgetry on the wrist, Ball watches have a lot to offer. Readability in dark places, for instance, is guaranteed by the use of tritium gas in tiny tubes to light up dials, markers, and hands. The chronograph pushers have been made water-resistant in compliance with the requirements of the U.S. Navy. At an even higher technical level, Ball has devised highly effective shock-absorbing technology (Amortizer® and the SpringLOCK® systems) to protect its watches, a plus for active people. The A-PROOF® system has also allowed the company to furnish its watches with a water-resistant transparent case back. And finally, there's the innovative case material that protects the watches from magnetic fields of up to 80,000 A/m.

Engineer Hydrocarbon AeroGMT

Reference number: DG2016A-SCJ-BK
Movement: automatic, BALL Caliber RR1201-C; ø 25.6 mm, height 4.1 mm; 21 jewels; 28,800 vph; 42-hour power reserve; COSC-certified chronometer
Functions: hours, minutes, sweep seconds; date; 2nd time zone indication
Case: stainless steel, ø 42 mm, height 13.85 mm; sapphire bidirectional bezel with micro gas tube illumination; sapphire crystal; crown protection system; water-resistant to 30 atm
Band: stainless steel, folding clasp with extension
Remarks: micro gas tube illumination; shock-resistant; antimagnetic
Price: $3,499
Variations: rubber strap

Engineer Hydrocarbon Airborne

Reference number: DM2076C-S1CAJ-BK
Movement: automatic, BALL Caliber RR1102-CSL; ø 25.6 mm, height 5.05 mm; 25 or 26 jewels; 28,800 vph; 38-hour power reserve; COSC-certified chronometer; SpringLOCK® anti-shock system
Functions: hours, minutes, sweep seconds; day, date
Case: stainless steel, ø 42 mm, height 13.85 mm; ceramic unidirectional bezel; sapphire crystal; crown protection system; water-resistant to 12 atm
Band: stainless steel, folding clasp with extension
Remarks: micro gas tube illumination; shock-resistant; antimagnetic
Price: $4,399

Engineer Hydrocarbon NEDU

Reference number: DC3026A-SC-BK
Movement: automatic, BALL Caliber RR1402-C; ø 30 mm, height 7.9 mm; 25 jewels; 28,800 vph; 48-hour power reserve; COSC-certified chronometer
Functions: hours, minutes, subsidiary seconds; day, date; 12-hour chronograph operable underwater
Case: stainless steel, ø 42 mm, height 17.30 mm; patented helium system; ceramic unidirectional bezel; sapphire crystal; crown protection system; water-resistant to 60 atm
Band: titanium/stainless steel, folding clasp with extension
Remarks: micro gas tube illumination; shock-resistant; antimagnetic
Price: $5,099
Variations: blue dial; rubber strap

Engineer Hydrocarbon DEVGRU

Reference number: NM3200C-SJ-BK
Movement: automatic, BALL Caliber RR1102-SL;
ø 25.6 mm, height 5.05 mm; 25 or 26 jewels;
28,800 vph; 38-hour power reserve; SpringLOCK®
antishock system; patented regulator antishock system
Functions: hours, minutes, sweep seconds; day,
date; power reserve indication
Case: stainless steel, ø 42 mm, height 13.4 mm;
patented shock absorption system; sapphire crystal
with outer protective flange; patented crown
protection; water-resistant to 10 atm
Band: stainless steel, folding clasp with extension
Remarks: micro gas tube illumination; shock-
resistant; antimagnetic
Price: $2,299
Variations: blue dial; rubber strap

Engineer Master II Diver

Reference number: DM3020A-SAJ-BK
Movement: automatic, BALL Caliber RR1102;
ø 25.6 mm, height 5.05 mm; 25 or 26 jewels;
28,800 vph; 38-hour power reserve
Functions: hours, minutes, sweep seconds; day, date
Case: stainless steel, ø 42 mm, height 14.55 mm;
inner bezel with micro gas tube illumination;
sapphire crystal; screw-in crown; water-resistant to
30 atm
Band: stainless steel, folding clasp
Remarks: micro gas tube illumination; shock-
resistant; antimagnetic
Price: $2,499
Variations: rubber strap

Engineer Master II Diver Worldtime

Reference number: DG2022A-S3AJ-BK
Movement: automatic, BALL Caliber RR1501;
ø 31.4 mm, height 6.95 mm; 25 jewels; 28,800 vph;
38-hour power reserve
Functions: hours, minutes, sweep seconds; day,
date; world time display
Case: stainless steel, ø 45 mm, height 15.4 mm;
luminous bidirectional rotating inner bezel; sapphire
crystal; screw-in crown; water-resistant to 30 atm
Band: stainless steel bracelet, folding buckle
Remarks: micro gas tube illumination; shock-
resistant; antimagnetic
Price: $2,999
Variations: rubber strap

Engineer Master II Skindiver II

Reference number: DM3108A-SCJ-BK
Movement: automatic, BALL Caliber RR1103-C;
ø 25.6 mm, height 4.6 mm; 25 or 26 jewels;
28,800 vph; 38-hour power reserve; COSC-certified
chronometer
Functions: hours, minutes, sweep seconds; date
Case: stainless steel, ø 43 mm, height 14 mm;
ceramic unidirectional bezel; helium valve; sapphire
crystal; screw-in crown; water-resistant to 50 atm
Band: stainless steel, folding buckle
Remarks: micro gas tube illumination; shock-
resistant; antimagnetic
Price: $2,799
Variations: rubber strap

Engineer Master II Aviator

Reference number: NM1080C-L14A-BK
Movement: automatic, BALL Caliber RR1102;
ø 25.6 mm, height 5.05 mm; 25 or 26 jewels;
28,800 vph; 38-hour power reserve
Functions: hours, minutes, sweep seconds; day, date
Case: stainless steel, ø 46 mm, height 11.55 mm;
mumetal shield; antireflective convex sapphire
crystal; screw-in crown; water-resistant to 10 atm
Band: calfskin, buckle
Remarks: micro gas tube illumination; shock-
resistant; antimagnetic
Price: $1,999
Variations: stainless steel bracelet; rubber strap

Engineer II Genesis

Reference number: NM2028C-S7J-BE
Movement: automatic, BALL Caliber RR1102;
ø 25.6 mm, height 5.05 mm; 25 or 26 jewels;
28,800 vph; 38-hour power reserve
Functions: hours, minutes, sweep seconds; day, date
Case: stainless steel, ø 43 mm, height 13.55 mm;
sapphire crystal; screw-in crown; water-resistant to
10 atm
Band: stainless steel bracelet, folding clasp
Remarks: micro gas tube illumination; shock-
resistant; antimagnetic
Price: $1,599
Variations: ø 40 mm dial; black dial; nubuck strap

Engineer II Volcano

Reference number: NM3060C-PCJ-GY
Movement: automatic, BALL Caliber RR1102-C;
ø 25.6 mm, height 5.05 mm; 25 or 26 jewels;
28,800 vph; 38-hour power reserve; COSC-certified
chronometer
Functions: hours, minutes, sweep seconds; day, date
Case: patented mumetal and carbide composite,
ø 45 mm, height 12.4 mm; sapphire crystal; screw-in
crown; water-resistant to 10 atm
Band: rubber, buckle
Remarks: micro gas tube illumination; shock-
resistant; antimagnetic
Price: $3,499
Variations: canvas NATO strap

Engineer II PowerLIGHT 72

Reference number: NM2126C-S1C-BK
Movement: automatic, BALL Caliber RR1107-C;
ø 25.6 mm, height 3.6 mm; 25 jewels; 21,600 vph;
72-hour power reserve; COSC-certified chronometer
Functions: hours, minutes, sweep seconds;
magnified date
Case: stainless steel, ø 40 mm, height 11.55 mm;
mumetal shield; sapphire crystal; screw-in crown;
water-resistant to 10 atm
Band: stainless steel bracelet, folding clasp
Remarks: micro gas tube illumination; shock-
resistant; antimagnetic
Price: $2,799

Engineer II Magneto S

Reference number: NM3022C-N1CJ-BK
Movement: automatic, BALL Caliber RR1103-
CSL; ø 25.6 mm, height 4.6 mm; 25 or 26 jewels;
28,800 vph; 38-hour power reserve; COSC-certified
chronometer; SpringLOCK® antishock system;
Functions: hours, minutes, sweep seconds; date
Case: stainless steel, ø 42 mm, height 12.9 mm;
A-PROOF® antimagnetic system; sapphire crystal;
screw-in crown; transparent case back; water-
resistant to 10 atm
Band: cordura fabrics, buckle
Remarks: micro gas tube illumination; shock-
resistant
Price: $3,399

Trainmaster Eternity

Reference number: NM2080D-S1J-BE
Movement: automatic, BALL Caliber RR1102;
ø 25.6 mm, height 5.05 mm; 25 or 26 jewels;
28,800 vph; 38-hour power reserve
Functions: hours, minutes, sweep seconds; day, date
Case: stainless steel, ø 39.5 mm, height 11.8 mm;
sapphire crystal; screw-in crown; transparent case
back; water-resistant to 3 atm
Band: stainless steel bracelet, folding clasp
Remarks: micro gas tube illumination; shock-
resistant;
Price: $2,299
Variations: black dial; reptile skin strap

Trainmaster Kelvin

Reference number: NT3888D-LL1J-GYF
Movement: automatic, BALL Caliber RR1601;
ø 25.6 mm, height 5.1 mm; 21 jewels; 28,800 vph;
42-hour power reserve
Functions: hours, minutes, sweep seconds; date;
patented mechanical thermometric indication
Case: stainless steel, ø 39.5 mm, height 11.8 mm;
sapphire crystal; transparent case back; water-
resistant to 3 atm
Band: reptile skin strap, folding clasp
Remarks: micro gas tube illumination; shock-
resistant
Price: $3,599
Variations: silver dial; stainless steel bracelet; TMT
Celsius scale

Trainmaster Manufacture

Reference number: NM1888D-pg-LLJ-WH
Movement: automatic, BALL Manufacture Caliber
RRM1101; ø 32 mm, height 3.6 mm; 25 jewels;
21,600 vph; 38-hour power reserve
Functions: hours, minutes; date
Case: 18k/750 rose gold, ø 40 mm, height 10 mm;
sapphire crystal; transparent case back; water-
resistant to 3 atm
Band: reptile skin strap, gold buckle
Remarks: micro gas tube illumination; shock-
resistant
Price: $8,999; limited to 125 pieces

Trainmaster Worldtime

Reference number: GM2020D-S1CJ-SL
Movement: automatic, BALL Caliber RR1501-C;
ø 31.4 mm, height 6.95 mm; 25 jewels; 28,800 vph;
38-hour power reserve; COSC-certified chronometer
Functions: hours, minutes, sweep seconds; day,
date; world time display
Case: stainless steel, ø 41 mm, height 12.5 mm;
sapphire crystal; transparent case back; screw-in
crown; water-resistant to 5 atm
Band: stainless steel bracelet, folding clasp
Remarks: micro gas tube illumination; shock-
resistant; antimagnetic
Price: $2,699
Variations: black dial; reptile skin strap

Trainmaster Worldtime Chronograph

Reference number: CM2052D-LL1J-SLBE
Movement: automatic, BALL Caliber RR1502;
ø 30 mm, height 7.9 mm; 25 jewels; 28,800 vph;
48-hour power reserve
Functions: hours, minutes, subsidiary seconds; day,
date; chronograph with accumulated measurement
up to 12 hours; world time display
Case: stainless steel, ø 42 mm, height 13.7 mm;
sapphire crystal; transparent case back; screw-in
crown; water-resistant to 5 atm
Band: reptile skin strap, buckle
Remarks: micro gas tube illumination; shock-resistant
Price: $,399
Variations: black with red dial, silver with red dial;
stainless steel bracelet

Fireman Storm Chaser Pro

Reference number: CM3090C-L1J-BK
Movement: automatic, BALL Caliber RR1402;
ø 30 mm, height 7.9 mm; 25 jewels; 28,800 vph;
48-hour power reserve
Functions: hours, minutes, subsidiary seconds; day,
date; 12-hour chronograph; telemeter
Case: stainless steel, ø 42 mm, height 15.65 mm;
aluminum bezel; sapphire crystal; screw-in crown;
transparent case back; water-resistant to 10 atm
Band: calfskin, buckle
Remarks: micro gas tube illumination; shock-
resistant
Price: $3,399
Variations: gray or white dial; stainless steel
bracelet

Fireman NECC

Reference number: DM3090A-P4J-BK
Movement: automatic, BALL Caliber RR1103;
ø 25.6 mm, height 4.6 mm; 25 or 26 jewels;
28,800 vph; 38-hour power reserve
Functions: hours, minutes, sweep seconds;
magnified date
Case: stainless steel with titanium carbide coating,
ø 42 mm, height 13.2 mm; stainless steel carbide
rotating bezel; sapphire crystal; transparent case
back; screw-in crown; water-resistant to 30 atm
Band: rubber strap, buckle
Remarks: micro gas tube illumination; shock-
resistant; antimagnetic
Price: $1,599
Variations: white or blue dial; stainless steel case;
stainless steel bracelet

Fireman Enterprise

Reference number: NM2188C-S5J-BK
Movement: automatic, BALL Caliber RR1103;
ø 25.6 mm, height 4.6 mm; 25 or 26 jewels;
28,800 vph; 38-hour power reserve
Functions: hours, minutes, sweep seconds;
magnified date
Case: stainless steel, ø 40 mm, height 11.3 mm;
sapphire crystal; screw-in crown; water-resistant to
10 atm
Band: stainless steel bracelet, buckle
Remarks: micro gas tube illumination; shock-
resistant
Price: $1,199
Variations: white dial; NATO strap

Engineer III Bronze

Reference number: NM2186C-L3J-BK
Movement: automatic, BALL Caliber RR1102-SL;
ø 25.6 mm, height 5.05 mm; 25 or 26 jewels;
28,800 vph; 38-hour power reserve; SpringLOCK®
antishock system
Functions: hours, minutes, sweep seconds; day, date
Case: bronze, ø 43 mm, height 13.45 mm; mumetal
shield; sapphire crystal; screw-in crown; water-
resistant to 10 atm
Band: calfskin, buckle
Remarks: micro gas tube illumination; shock-
resistant; antimagnetic
Price: $2,300

BAUME & MERCIER

Baume & Mercier and its elite watchmaking peers Cartier and Piaget make up the quality timepiece nucleus in the Richemont Group's impressive portfolio. The tradition-rich brand counts among the most accessible and most affordable watches of the Genevan luxury brands. In the past decade, it has created a number of remarkable—and often copied—classics. The twelve-sided Riviera and the Catwalk have had to step off the stage, but the classic rectangular Hampton continues to evolve. In recent years, the company has worked hard to gain acceptance in the men's market for its Classima Executives line and to build on watchmaking glory of days gone by, when Baume & Mercier was celebrated as a chronograph specialist.

Though the brand has taken up residence in Geneva, most of the watches are produced in a reassembly center built a few years ago in Les Brenets near Le Locle. Individual parts are made by specialized suppliers according to the strictest of quality guidelines. Some of these manufacturers are sister companies within the Richemont Group.

Keeping the brand abreast of trends in both male and female fashions is key to its design strategy and is ensured by the brand's integrated design studio within the Richemont Luxury Group in Geneva. The newly interpreted, iconic Classima is very much in tune with the modern zeitgeist, a touch minimalistic perhaps. In 2016, the brand presented more luxurious versions, one with a window on the balance wheel, the other with a second time zone. But the company cleverly extended this popular line with some models in the lower price segment. And aiming at a younger age group is the new Petite Promesse line, which falls somewhere between being jewelry and simultaneously being a timekeeper, thanks to the graceful, double-looped strap, which comes in bright blue, orange, or a fine stainless steel.

Baume & Mercier
chemin de la Chênaie 50
CH-1293 Bellevue
Switzerland

Tel.:
+41-022-999-5151

Fax:
+41-44-972-2086

Website:
www.baume-et-mercier.com
register on the website to contact via e-mail

Founded:
1830

U.S. distributor:
Baume & Mercier
Richemont North America
New York, NY 10022
800-MERCIER

Most important collections/price range:
Clifton (men) / $2,700 to $13,950; Capeland (men) / $4,350 to $19,990; Hampton (men and women) / $3,450 to $15,000; Linea (women) / $1,950 to $15,750; Classima / $1,750 to $5,950; Petite Promesse (women) / $2,450 to $3,300

Clifton Club

Reference number: 10338
Movement: automatic, Sellita Caliber SW200-1; ø 25.6 mm, height 4.6 mm; 26 jewels; 28,800 vph; 48-hour power reserve
Functions: hours, minutes, sweep seconds; date
Case: stainless steel, ø 42 mm, height 10.3 mm; unidirectional bezel with 0-60 scale; sapphire crystal; screw-in crown; water-resistant to 10 atm
Band: calfskin, triple folding clasp
Price: $2,250
Variations: blue dial; stainless steel bracelet ($2,100)

Clifton Club

Reference number: 10378
Movement: automatic, Sellita Caliber SW200-1; ø 25.6 mm, height 4.6 mm; 26 jewels; 28,800 vph; 48-hour power reserve
Functions: hours, minutes, sweep seconds; date
Case: stainless steel, ø 42 mm, height 10.3 mm; unidirectional bezel with 0-60 scale; sapphire crystal; screw-in crown; water-resistant to 10 atm
Band: stainless steel, triple folding clasp
Price: $2,100
Variations: white or black dial; calfskin band ($1,950)

Clifton Club Shelby Cobra

Reference number: 10343
Movement: automatic, ETA Caliber 7750; ø 30 mm, height 7.9 mm; 25 jewels; 28,800 vph; skeletonized rotor; 48-hour power reserve
Functions: hours, minutes, subsidiary seconds; chronograph; date, weekday
Case: stainless steel, ø 44 mm, height 14.95 mm; sapphire crystal; transparent case back; water-resistant to 5 atm
Band: calfskin, triple folding clasp
Price: $4,450; limited to 1,964 pieces
Variations: white dial

Clifton Perpetual Calendar

Reference number: 10306
Movement: automatic, Vaucher Caliber 5401 with a Dubois Dépraz 5100 module; ø 30.6 mm; 29 jewels; 21,600 vph; bridges with perlage, côtes de Genève; 48-hour power reserve
Functions: hours, minutes, subsidiary seconds; perpetual calendar with date, weekday, month, moon phase, leap year
Case: pink gold, ø 42 mm, height 11.2 mm; sapphire crystal; transparent case back; water-resistant to 5 atm
Band: reptile skin, buckle
Price: $22,900

Clifton GMT

Reference number: 10316
Movement: automatic, Soprod Caliber 9035; ø 26.2 mm, height 5.1 mm; 28 jewels; 28,800 vph; with côtes de Genève, decorated rotor; 42-hour power reserve
Functions: hours, minutes, sweep seconds; second 24-hour display (second time zone), power reserve indicator; date
Case: stainless steel, ø 43 mm, height 12.05 mm; sapphire crystal; water-resistant to 5 atm
Band: reptile skin, triple folding clasp
Price: $3,690

Classima

Reference number: 10332
Movement: automatic, Sellita Caliber SW200-1; ø 25.6 mm, height 4.6 mm; 26 jewels; 28,800 vph; 38-hour power reserve
Functions: hours, minutes, sweep seconds; date
Case: stainless steel, ø 42 mm, height 8.85 mm; sapphire crystal; water-resistant to 5 atm
Band: calfskin, buckle
Remarks: comes with additional textile strap
Price: $1,490

Classique Chronograph

Reference number: 10331
Movement: automatic, ETA Caliber 7750; ø 30 mm, height 7.9 mm; 25 jewels; 28,800 vph; 48-hour power reserve
Functions: hours, minutes, subsidiary seconds; chronograph; date
Case: stainless steel, ø 42 mm, height 13.1 mm; sapphire crystal; transparent case back; water-resistant to 5 atm
Band: stainless steel, triple folding clasp
Price: $3,150

Classima

Reference number: 10324
Movement: quartz
Functions: hours, minutes; date
Case: stainless steel, ø 40 mm, height 5.95 mm; sapphire crystal; water-resistant to 5 atm
Band: calfskin, buckle
Price: $990

Classique Moon Phase

Reference number: 10329
Movement: quartz
Functions: hours, minutes, sweep seconds; date, moon phase
Case: stainless steel, ø 31 mm, height 7.1 mm; sapphire crystal; water-resistant to 5 atm
Band: reptile skin, buckle
Remarks: dial set with 8 diamonds
Price: $1,490

BELL & ROSS

If there is such a class as "military chic," Bell & Ross is undoubtedly one of the leaders. The Paris-headquartered brand develops, manufactures, assembles, and regulates its timepieces in a modern factory in La Chaux-de-Fonds in the Jura mountains of Switzerland. The early models had a certain stringency that one might associate with soldierly life, but in the past years, working with outside specialists, the company has ventured into even more complicated watches such as tourbillons and wristwatches with uncommon shapes. This kind of ambitious innovation has only been possible since perfume and fashion specialist Chanel—which also maintains a successful watch line in its own right—became a significant Bell & Ross shareholder and brought the watchmaker access to the production facilities where designers Bruno Belamich and team can create more complicated, more interesting designs for their esthetically unusual "instrument" watches. And to prove perhaps that watchmakers are not riding the coattails (or fenders) of iconic cars, in 2016 Belamich and his team presented the AeroGT at the Geneva International Auto Show, a super–sports car that can stand on its own next to a series of same-class Italians.

Belamich continues to prove his skills where technical features and artful proportions are concerned, and what sets Bell & Ross timepieces apart from those of other, more traditional professional luxury makers is their special, roguish look—a delicate balance between striking, martial, and poetic. And it is this beauty for the eye to behold that makes the company's wares popular with style-conscious "civilians" as well as with the pilots, divers, astronauts, sappers, and other hard-riding professionals drawn to Bell & Ross timepieces for their superior functionality. And the brand is also capable of producing more feminine timepieces as well, or at least objects that will stimulate the inner warrior that slumbers in everyone.

Bell & Ross Ltd.
8 rue Copernic
F-75116 Paris
France

Tel.:
+33-1-73-73-93-00

Fax:
+33-1-73-73-93-01

E-mail:
sav@bellross.com

Website:
www.bellross.com

Founded:
1992

U.S. distributor:
Bell & Ross, Inc.
605 Lincoln Road, Suite 300
Miami Beach, FL 33139
888-307-7887; 305-672-3840 (fax)
information@bellross.com
www.bellross.com

Most important collections/price range:
Instrument BR-X1, BR 01, and BR 03 / approx.
$3,100 to $200,000

BR 03-92 Horolum

Reference number: BR0392-GR-ST/SCA
Movement: automatic, Caliber BR-CAL.302 (base ETA 2824-2); ø 25.6 mm, height 4.6 mm; 25 jewels; 28,800 vph; 38-hour power reserve
Functions: hours, minutes, sweep seconds; date
Case: stainless steel, 42 × 42 mm, height 9.65 mm; bezel screwed to monocoque case with 4 screws; sapphire crystal; water-resistant to 10 atm
Band: calfskin, buckle
Remarks: sandwich dial with luminous mass underlay
Price: $3,400

BR 03-92 Diver

Reference number: BR0392-D-BL-ST/SRB
Movement: automatic, Caliber BR-CAL.302 (base ETA 2824-2); ø 25.6 mm, height 4.6 mm; 25 jewels; 28,800 vph; 38-hour power reserve
Functions: hours, minutes, sweep seconds; date
Case: stainless steel, 42 × 42 mm, height 12.3 mm; unidirectional bezel with 0-60 scale, screwed to monocoque case with 4 screws; sapphire crystal; screw-in crown; water-resistant to 30 atm
Band: rubber, buckle
Price: $3,700

BR 03 GMT 24H

Reference number: BR0393-GMT-ST/SCA
Movement: automatic, Caliber BR-CAL.303 (base ETA 2893-2); ø 25.6 mm, height 4.1 mm; 21 jewels; 28,800 vph; 42-hour power reserve
Functions: hours, minutes, sweep seconds; second 24-hour display (second time zone); date
Case: stainless steel, 42 × 42 mm, height 10.3 mm; bezel screwed to monocoque case with 4 screws; sapphire crystal; water-resistant to 10 atm
Band: calfskin, buckle
Price: $3,700

BRS Rose Gold

Reference number: BRS92-BL-pg/SCR
Movement: automatic, Caliber BR-CAL.302 (base ETA caliber 2892-A2); ø 25.6 mm, height 3.6 mm; 21 jewels; 28,800 vph; 38-hour power reserve
Functions: hours, minutes, sweep seconds; date
Case: pink gold, 39 × 39 mm, height 10.5 mm; bezel screwed to monocoque case with 4 screws; sapphire crystal; water-resistant to 10 atm
Band: reptile skin, buckle
Price: $13,900

BR-X1 RS17

Reference number: BRX1-RS17
Movement: automatic, Caliber BR-CAL.313 (base ETA Caliber 2894-2); ø 28.6 mm, height 6.1 mm; 37 jewels; 28,800 vph; skeletonized movement; 42-hour power reserve
Functions: hours, minutes, subsidiary seconds; chronograph; date
Case: carbon fiber, 45 × 45 mm, height 15.4 mm; bezel screwed to monocoque case with 4 screws; sapphire crystal; transparent case back; water-resistant to 10 atm
Band: rubber, with carbon fiber insert, buckle
Remarks: color coding like that of a Formula One steering wheel
Price: $24,200; limited to 500 pieces

BR-X2 Tourbillon Micro-Rotor

Reference number: BRX2-MRTB-ST
Movement: automatic, Caliber BR-CAL.380; flying 1-minute tourbillon, microrotor
Functions: hours, minutes
Case: stainless steel, 45 × 45 mm, height 13 mm; bezel screwed to monocoque case with 4 screws; sapphire crystal; transparent case back; water-resistant to 5 atm
Band: reptile skin, buckle
Price: $64,900

BR-X1 Tourbillon Skeleton Sapphire

Movement: automatic, Caliber BR-CAL.288; 20 jewels; 21,600 vph; flying 1-minute tourbillon; 100-hour power reserve
Functions: hours, minutes
Case: sapphire crystal, 45 × 45 mm, height 13.9 mm; bezel screwed to monocoque case with 4 screws; sapphire crystal; transparent case back; water-resistant to 3 atm
Band: rubber, with Kevlar insert, buckle
Price: $495,000; limited to 8 pieces

BR V1-92 Black Steel

Reference number: BRV1-92-BL-ST/SCA
Movement: automatic, Caliber BR-CAL.302 (base ETA 2824-2); ø 25.6 mm, height 4.6 mm; 25 jewels; 28,800 vph; 38-hour power reserve
Functions: hours, minutes, sweep seconds; date
Case: stainless steel, ø 38.5 mm, height 10 mm; sapphire crystal; water-resistant to 10 atm
Band: calfskin, buckle
Price: $1,990

BR V2-94 Black Steel

Reference number: BRV2-94-BL-ST/SST
Movement: automatic, Caliber BR-CAL.301 (base ETA 2892); ø 28.6 mm, height 6.1 mm; 37 jewels; 28,800 vph; 42-hour power reserve
Functions: hours, minutes, subsidiary seconds; chronograph; date
Case: stainless steel, ø 41 mm, height 14.2 mm; bezel with aluminum inlay; sapphire crystal; transparent case back; screw-in crown and pusher; water-resistant to 10 atm
Band: stainless steel, folding clasp
Price: $4,600

BLANCPAIN

Blancpain SA
Le Rocher 12
CH-1348 Le Brassus
Switzerland

Tel.:
+41-21-796-3636

Website:
www.blancpain.com

Founded:
1735

U.S. distributor:
Blancpain
The Swatch Group (U.S.), Inc.
1200 Harbor Boulevard
Weehawken, NJ 07086
201-271-4680

Most important collections/price range:
L'Evolution, Villeret, Fifty Fathoms, Le Brassus,
Women / $9,800 to $400,000

In its advertising, the Blancpain watch brand has always proudly declared that, since 1735, the company has never made quartz watches and never will. Indeed, Blancpain is Switzerland's oldest watchmaker, and by sticking to its ideals, the company was put out of business by the "quartz boom" of the 1970s.

The Blancpain brand we know today came into being in the mid-eighties, when Jean-Claude Biver and Jacques Piguet purchased the venerable name. The company was subsequently moved to the Frédéric Piguet watch factory in Le Brassus, where it quickly became largely responsible for the renaissance of the mechanical wristwatch. This success caught the attention of the Swatch Group—known at that time as SMH. In 1992, it swooped in and purchased both companies to add to its portfolio. Movement fabrication and watch production were melded to form the Blancpain Manufacture in mid-2010.

But being quartzless does not mean being old-fashioned. Over the past several years, Blancpain president Marc A. Hayek has put a great deal of energy into developing the company's technical originality. He is frank about the fact that making new calibers did harness most of Blancpain's creative potential, leaving little to apply to its existing collection of watches. Still, in terms of complications, Blancpain watches have always been in a class of their own. Furthermore, the farsighted move now means that other brands in the family have outstanding movements at their disposal, notably Harry Winston, which used one in its Z9.

And now even more models are being introduced, watches that feature the company's own basic movement and a choice of manual or automatic winding, like the new collection, the Fifty Fathoms Bathyscaphe, a modern interpretation of the classic diver's watch of 1953. As part of the planned consolidation of the entire collection, the other major families—the Villeret, Le Brassus, L'Evolution, and Sport—are being reworked over time.

Le Brassus Carrousel Répétition Minutes

Reference number: 00235-3631-55B
Movement: automatic, Blancpain Caliber 235; ø 32.8 mm, height 9.1 mm; 54 jewels; 21,600 vph; escapement with 1-minute flying carrousel
Functions: hours, minutes; minute repeater
Case: pink gold, ø 45 mm, height 15.35 mm; sapphire crystal; transparent case back
Band: reptile skin, folding clasp
Remarks: enamel dial
Price: $412,100

Le Brassus Tourbillon Carrousel

Reference number: 2322-3631-55B
Movement: manually wound, Blancpain Caliber 2322; ø 35.3 mm, height 5.85 mm; 70 jewels; 21,600 vph; escapement system with flying 1-minute tourbillon and 1-minute carrousel with differential compensation; 3 spring barrels, 168-hour power reserve
Functions: hours, minutes; power reserve indicator (on the rear); date
Case: pink gold, ø 44.6 mm, height 11.94 mm; sapphire crystal; transparent case back; water-resistant to 3 atm
Band: reptile skin, folding clasp
Remarks: enamel dial
Price: $319,000

Villeret Tourbillon Volant Une Minute 12 Jours

Reference number: 66240-3431-55B
Movement: automatic, Blancpain Caliber 242; ø 30.6 mm, height 6.1 mm; 43 jewels; 28,800 vph; flying 1-minute tourbillon; 288-hour power reserve
Functions: hours, minutes; power reserve indicator (on the rear)
Case: platinum, ø 42 mm, height 11.65 mm; sapphire crystal; transparent case back; water-resistant to 3 atm
Band: reptile skin, folding clasp
Remarks: enamel dial
Price: $148,800; limited to 188 pieces
Variations: pink gold ($127,400)

Villeret Carrousel Phases de Lune

Reference number: 6622L-3631-55B
Movement: automatic, Blancpain Caliber 225L; ø 31.9 mm, height 6.86 mm; 40 jewels; 28,800 vph; flying 1-minute carrousel; 120-hour power reserve
Functions: hours, minutes; date, moon phase
Case: pink gold, ø 42 mm, height 12.74 mm; sapphire crystal; transparent case back; water-resistant to 3 atm
Band: reptile skin, folding clasp
Remarks: enamel dial
Price: $129,600
Variations: platinum (limited to 88 pieces, $151,000)

Villeret Quantième Perpétuel 8 Jours

Reference number: 6659-3631-55B
Movement: automatic, Blancpain Caliber 5939A; ø 32 mm, height 7.25 mm; 42 jewels; 28,800 vph; 192-hour power reserve
Functions: hours, minutes, subsidiary seconds; perpetual calendar with date, weekday, month, moon phase, leap year
Case: pink gold, ø 42 mm, height 13.5 mm; sapphire crystal; transparent case back; water-resistant to 3 atm
Band: reptile skin, folding clasp
Remarks: enamel dial
Price: $58,900
Variations: pink gold Milanese bracelet ($78,200)

Villeret Semainier Grande Date 8 Jours

Reference number: 6637-3631-55
Movement: automatic, Blancpain Caliber 3738G2; ø 32 mm, height 7.85 mm; 44 jewels; 28,800 vph; 192-hour power reserve
Functions: hours, minutes, sweep seconds; full calendar with large date, weekday, weeks of the year
Case: pink gold, ø 42 mm, height 13.4 mm; sapphire crystal; transparent case back; water-resistant to 3 atm
Band: reptile skin, buckle
Price: $34,500

Villeret Quantième Complet 8 Days

Reference number: 6639A-3631-55B
Movement: automatic, Blancpain Caliber 6639; ø 32 mm, height 7.6 mm; 35 jewels; 28,800 vph; 192-hour power reserve
Functions: hours, minutes, subsidiary seconds; full calendar with date, weekday, month, moon phase
Case: pink gold, ø 42 mm, height 13.03 mm; sapphire crystal; transparent case back; water-resistant to 3 atm
Band: reptile skin, folding clasp
Remarks: enamel dial
Price: $41,900
Variations: pink gold Milanese bracelet ($61,200)

Villeret Jour Date

Reference number: 6652-1127-55B
Movement: automatic, Blancpain Caliber 1160DD; ø 34 mm, height 4.6 mm; 34 jewels; 28,800 vph; 72-hour power reserve
Functions: hours, minutes, subsidiary seconds; date, weekday
Case: stainless steel, ø 40 mm, height 10.4 mm; sapphire crystal; transparent case back; water-resistant to 3 atm
Band: reptile skin, buckle
Price: $10,900

Fifty Fathoms Automatique

Reference number: 5015-12B40-O52A
Movement: automatic, Blancpain Caliber 1315; ø 30.6 mm, height 5.65 mm; 35 jewels; 28,800 vph; silicon spring; 120-hour power reserve
Functions: hours, minutes, sweep seconds; date
Case: titanium, ø 45 mm, height 15.4 mm; unidirectional bezel with sapphire crystal inlay, with 0-60 scale; sapphire crystal; transparent case back; water-resistant to 30 atm
Band: textile, buckle
Price: $15,700

Fifty Fathoms Bathyscaphe

Reference number: 5100-1127-NAVA
Movement: automatic, Blancpain Caliber 1150;
ø 26.2 mm, height 3.25 mm; 28 jewels; 28,800 vph;
silicon hairspring; 100-hour power reserve
Functions: hours, minutes, sweep seconds; date
Case: stainless steel, ø 38 mm, height 10.77 mm;
unidirectional bezel with ceramic insert and 0-60
scale; sapphire crystal; transparent case back;
screw-in crown; water-resistant to 30 atm
Band: textile, buckle
Price: $9,500
Variations: various strap colors

Fifty Fathoms Bathyscaphe Chronograph Flyback

Reference number: 5200-0130-NABA
Movement: automatic, Blancpain Caliber F385;
ø 31.8 mm, height 6.65 mm; 37 jewels; 36,000 vph;
silicon hairspring; 50-hour power reserve
Functions: hours, minutes, subsidiary seconds;
flyback chronograph; date
Case: ceramic, ø 43.6 mm, height 15.25 mm;
unidirectional bezel with 0-60 scale; sapphire crystal;
water-resistant to 30 atm
Band: textile, buckle
Price: $17,200
Variations: sailcloth strap ($17,200, same price as
NATO)

Fifty Fathoms Tribute to Fifty Fathoms

Reference number: 5008-1130-NABA
Movement: automatic, Blancpain Caliber 1151;
ø 27.4 mm, height 3.25 mm; 28 jewels; 28,800 vph;
silicon hairspring; 96-hour power reserve
Functions: hours, minutes, sweep seconds; water-
resistance indicator; date
Case: stainless steel, ø 40.3 mm, height 13.23 mm;
unidirectional bezel with sapphire crystal insert, with
0-60 scale; sapphire crystal; transparent case back;
water-resistant to 30 atm
Band: textile, folding clasp
Remarks: disk on dial changes color if humidity
penetrates watch
Price: $14,100; limited to 500 pieces

X Fathoms

Reference number: 5018-1230-64A
Movement: automatic, Blancpain Caliber 9918B
(base Blancpain 1315); ø 36 mm, height 13 mm;
48 jewels; 28,800 vph; 3 barrels, 120-hour power
reserve
Functions: hours, minutes, sweep seconds;
mechanical depth gauge (two-part scale) with
maximum depth indicator, 5-minute short-time
counter (countdown)
Case: titanium, ø 55.65 mm, height 24 mm;
unidirectional bezel with 0-60 scale; sapphire crystal;
helium valve; water-resistant to 30 atm
Band: rubber, buckle
Price: $40,700

L'Evolution Tourbillon Carrousel

Reference number: 92322-34B39-55B
Movement: manually wound, Blancpain Caliber
2322V2; ø 35.3 mm, height 5.85 mm; 70 jewels;
21,600 vph; escapement system with flying 1-minute
tourbillon and 1-minute carrousel with differential
compensation; 3 spring barrels, 168-hour power
reserve
Functions: hours, minutes; power reserve indicator
(on the rear)
Case: platinum, ø 47.4 mm, height 11.66 mm;
sapphire crystal; transparent case back; water-
resistant to 3 atm
Band: reptile skin, folding clasp
Remarks: skeletonized mainplate and dial
Price: $373,130; limited to 50 pieces

Villeret Women's Quantième Moon Phase

Reference number: 6106-1127-55A
Movement: automatic, Blancpain Caliber 913QL;
ø 23.7 mm, height 4.5 mm; 20 jewels; 28,800 vph;
40-hour power reserve
Functions: hours, minutes, sweep seconds; date,
moon phase
Case: stainless steel, ø 29.2 mm, height 10.36 mm;
sapphire crystal; transparent case back; water-
resistant to 3 atm
Band: reptile skin, buckle
Price: $10,500

Caliber F385

Automatic; column wheel control of chronograph functions; single spring barrel, 50-hour power reserve
Functions: hours, minutes, subsidiary seconds; flyback chronograph; date
Diameter: 31.8 mm
Height: 6.65 mm
Jewels: 37
Balance: silicon
Frequency: 36,000 vph
Balance spring: flat hairspring
Shock protection: Kif
Remarks: finely finished movement, bridges with côtes de Genève

Caliber 2358

Automatic; escapement with a 1-minute carrousel; single spring barrel, 65-hour power reserve
Functions: hours, minutes; minute repeater with cathedral gong; flyback chronograph with 30-minute sweep counter
Diameter: 32.8 mm
Height: 11.7 mm
Jewels: 59
Balance: glucydur with gold regulating screws
Frequency: 28,800 vph
Balance spring: flat hairspring
Shock protection: Kif
Remarks: hand-engraved bridges and rotor; 546 components

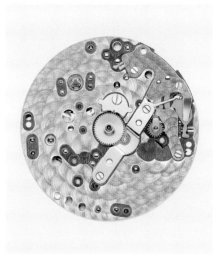

Caliber 913

Automatic; single spring barrel, 40-hour power reserve
Functions: hours, minutes, sweep seconds
Diameter: 21 mm
Height: 3.28 mm
Jewels: 20
Balance: glucydur
Frequency: 28,800 vph
Remarks: 174 components

Caliber 152B

Manually wound; inverted movement structure with time display on case back, bridges with black ceramic insert; single spring barrel, 40-hour power reserve
Functions: hours, minutes
Diameter: 35.64 mm
Height: 2.95 mm
Jewels: 21
Balance: screw balance
Frequency: 21,600 vph
Balance spring: flat hairspring
Shock protection: Kif

Caliber 225L

Automatic; flying 1-minute carrousel, two separate gearworks; single spring barrel, 120-hour power reserve
Functions: hours, minutes; date, moon phase
Diameter: 31.9 mm
Height: 6.86 mm
Jewels: 40
Balance: glucydur with weighted screws
Frequency: 28,800 vph
Balance spring: silicon
Shock protection: Kif
Remarks: 281 components

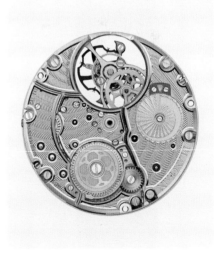

Caliber 242

Automatic; flying 1-minute tourbillon with silicon balance and pallet fork horns; peripheral rotor at edge of movement; quadruple spring barrel, 288-hour power reserve
Functions: hours, minutes; power reserve indicator (on rear)
Diameter: 30.6 mm
Height: 6.1 mm
Jewels: 43
Balance: silicon
Frequency: 21,600 vph
Remarks: very fine finishing of movement, hand-guilloché bridges; 243 components

BORGWARD

BORGWARD
Zeitmanufaktur GmbH & Co. KG
Markgrafenstrasse 16
D-79588 Efringen-Kirchen
Germany

Tel.:
+49-7628-805-7840

Fax:
+49-7628-805-7841

E-mail:
manufaktur@borgward.ag

Website:
www.borgward.ag

Founded:
2010

Number of employees:
3

Annual production:
approx. 180

Distribution:
Please contact Borgward directly for enquiries.

Most important collections:
P100, B2300, and B57

It is not unusual for prospective watch brand founders to search for the name of a dormant or even defunct horological company to connect their business with a glorious past. Watchmaker Jürgen Betz looked elsewhere when he launched a series of watches under the name Borgward. This former automobile company had a reputation for outstanding quality, reliability, and durability. For connoisseurs and fans, Borgward meant technical prowess, perfect styling, and precision engineering.

Carl F. Borgward began his career as an automobile designer in 1924, when he built a small three-wheeled van. In the early 1930s, his budding company took over the Hansa-Lloyd automobile factory and went on to conquer a global market with the Lloyd, Goliath, and Borgward brands. The real Borgward legend, however, began in the 1950s with the "Goddess," the famed Isabella Coupé, whose elegant lines and state-of-the-art technology literally heralded a new era in automotive design in Germany. In 1961, the company went bankrupt due to poor management. But the legend lives on and became the inspiration for Betz when building his Borgward watch B511. Support came from his friend Eric Borgward, grandson of Carl, who confirmed: "My grandfather would have liked it." Since the Borgward Zeitmanufaktur was founded in July 2010, it has produced three collections: the B511 limited to 511 pieces, the P100 limited to 1,890 pieces, and the B2300 limited to 1,942 pieces. They are all "made in Germany" but based on Swiss technology. At the heart of each watch is either an ETA 2824 with three hands and calendar or the famous ETA 7750 Valjoux chronograph automatic. The decoration of the movements with various stripes and perlage is the bailiwick of Betz himself. For production, Borgward relies on space in the northern city of Bremen.

Jürgen Betz also has some special offers for watch enthusiasts: a workshop in the pretty town of Efringen-Kirchen just north of Basel, where participants learn how to finish a mainplate, take apart and reassemble a watch, and print the dial.

Big Fiftyseven

Reference number: BIG57.CL.07 Heliotrop
Movement: automatic, ETA Caliber 7750; ø 30 mm, height 7.9 mm; 25 jewels; 28,800 vph; perlage on mainplate bridges with côtes de Genève, partially skeletonized and galvano-black oscillating weight; 42-hour power reserve
Functions: hours, minutes; chronograph; date, weekday
Case: stainless steel, ø 44 mm, height 15.9 mm; sapphire crystal; transparent case back; water-resistant to 5 atm
Band: calfskin, buckle
Price: $2,950
Variations: stainless steel Milanese bracelet ($3,165)

B611 Heritage

Reference number: B611.AL.SG Mattschwarz/ Grau
Movement: automatic, ETA Caliber 2824-2; ø 25.6 mm, height 4.6 mm; 25 jewels; 28,800 vph; finely finished with côtes de Genève, galvanos-black oscillating weight; 42-hour power reserve
Functions: hours, minutes, sweep seconds; date
Case: stainless steel, ø 38 mm, height 8.7 mm; sapphire crystal; transparent case back; water-resistant to 5 atm
Band: calfskin, buckle
Price: $1,655; limited to 198 pieces
Variations: stainless steel Milanese bracelet ($1,870)

C.F.W. 125 Automatic

Reference number: CFW.AL.03 Sterlingsilber
Movement: automatic, ETA Caliber 2824-2; ø 25.6 mm, height 4.6 mm; 25 jewels; 28,800 vph; finely finished with côtes de Genève, galvano-black oscillating weight; 42-hour power reserve
Functions: hours, minutes, sweep seconds; date
Case: stainless steel, ø 40 mm, height 10 mm; sapphire crystal; transparent case back; water-resistant to 5 atm
Band: calfskin, buckle
Price: $1,655
Variations: stainless steel Milanese bracelet ($1,870)

Bovet Fleurier S.A.
109 Pont-du-Centenaire
CP109
CH-1228 Plan-les-Ouates
Switzerland

Tel.:
+41-22-731-4638

Fax:
+41-22-884-1450

E-mail:
info@bovet.com

Website:
www.bovet.com

Founded:
1822

Annual production:
2,500 timepieces

U.S. distributor:
Bovet LLC USA
3363 NE 163rd Street, Suite 703
North Miami Beach, FL 33160
888-909-1822

Most important collections/price range:
Amadeo Fleurier, Dimier, Pininfarina, Sportster /
$18,500 to $1,000,000

BOVET

If any brand can claim real connections to China, it is Bovet, founded by Swiss business-man Edouard Bovet. Bovet emigrated to Canton, China, in 1818 and sold four watches of his own design there. On his return to Switzerland in 1822, he set up a company for shipping his Fleurier-made watches to China. The company name, pronounced "Bo Wei" in Mandarin, became a synonym for "watch" in Asia and at one point had offices in Canton. For more than eighty years, Bovet and his successors supplied the Chinese ruling class with valuable timepieces.

In 2001, the brand was bought by entrepreneur Pascal Raffy. He ensured the company's industrial independence by acquiring several other companies as well, notably the high-end watchmaker Swiss Time Technology (STT) in Tramelan, which he renamed Dimier 1738. In addition to creating its own line of watches, this *manufacture* produces complex technical components such as tourbillons for Bovet watches. Assembly of Bovet creations takes place at the headquarters in the thirteenth-century Castle of Môtiers in Val-de-Travers not far from Fleurier.

Bovet watches have several distinctive features—undoubtedly a reason for their growing fame. The first is intricate dial work, featuring not only complex architecture, but also very fine enameling. The second is the lugs and crown at 12 o'clock, recalling Bovet's tasteful pocket watches of the nineteenth century. On some models, the wristbands are made to be easily removed so the watch can be worn on a chain or cord. Other watches convert to table clocks.

A considerable part of Bovet's output comes from a collaboration launched in 2010 between the brand's technical staff and the Italian design firm Pininfarina, which is known for many iconic automobiles. The latest in the collection is the Tourbillon OttantaSei, a spectacular, skeletonized watch with an openworked case that makes it look as if the movement were floating in thin air.

Amadeo Fleurier Virtuoso VIII

Reference number: T10GD003
Movement: manually wound, Bovet Caliber 17BM03-GD; ø 38.3 mm, 18,000 vph; 1-minute tourbillon; 10-day power reserve
Functions: hours, minutes, seconds (on tourbillon cage); big date; power reserve indicator
Case: pink gold, ø 44 mm, height 13.45 mm; sapphire crystal; transparent case back; water-resistant to 3 atm
Band: reptile skin, buckle
Remarks: flexible lugs to turn watch into table watch or pocket watch
Price: $199,800; limited to 39 pieces
Variations: white gold ($209,800, limited to 39 pieces)

Château de Motiers 40

Reference number: HMS5048-SD12
Movement: automatic, Bovet Caliber 11BA15; ø 25.94 mm, height 5.09 mm; 28,800 vph; 42-hour power reserve
Functions: hours, minutes
Case: red gold, ø 40 mm, height 8.43 mm; bezel set with 109 diamonds; sapphire crystal; transparent case back; water-resistant to 3 atm
Band: reptile skin, buckle
Remarks: dial with miniature painting of butterfly using special luminescent material and paint
Price: $49,000
Variations: with miniature painting of luminescent roses on dial

Pininfarina OttantaSei

Reference number: TPINS002
Movement: manually wound, Bovet Caliber 17BM03MM; ø 37.2 mm, 18,000 vph; flying 1-minute tourbillon; 240-hour power reserve
Functions: hours, minutes, (off-center); power reserve indicator
Case: pink gold, ø 44 mm, height 12 mm; sapphire crystal; transparent case back; water-resistant to 3 atm
Band: rubber, folding clasp
Remarks: limited to 86 pieces for anniversary of Italian car designer company
Price: $189,000
Variations: titanium; titanium with black DLC coating

BREGUET

We never quite lose that attachment to the era in which we were born and grew up, nor do some brands. Abraham-Louis Breguet (1747–1823), who hailed from Switzerland, brought his craft to Paris in the *Sturm und Drang* atmosphere of the late eighteenth century. It was fertile ground for one of the most inventive watchmakers in the history of horology, and his products soon found favor with the highest levels of society.

Little has changed two centuries later. After a few years of drifting, in 1999 the brand carrying this illustrious name became the prize possession of the Swatch Group and came under the personal management of Nicolas G. Hayek, CEO. Hayek worked assiduously to restore the brand's roots, going as far as rebuilding the legendary Marie Antoinette pocket watch and contributing to the restoration of the Petit Trianon at Versailles.

Breguet is a full-fledged *manufacture*, and this has allowed it to forge ahead uncompromisingly with upscale watches and even jewelry. In modern facilities on the shores of Lake Joux, traditional craftsmanship still plays a significant role in the production of its fine watches, but at the same time, Breguet is one of the few brands to work with modern materials for its movements. This is not just a PR trick, but rather a sincere attempt to improve quality and rate precision. Many innovations have debuted at Breguet, for instance pallet levers and balance wheels made of silicon, the first Breguet hairspring with the arched terminal curve made of this glassy material, or even a mechanical high-frequency balance beating at 72,000 vph. Other innovations include the electromagnetic regulation of a minute repeater or the use of two micro-magnets to achieve contactless anchoring of a balance wheel staff.

Breguet, now under the auspices of Nicolas G. Hayek's grandson, Marc A. Hayek, continues to explore the edges of the technologically possible in watchmaking, while maintaining the brand's particular connection to traditional processes and esthetic codes. Even when creating a sports watch, like the new Type XXI Flyback, Breguets always give off a scent of luxury.

Montres Breguet SA
CH-1344 L'Abbaye
Switzerland

Tel.:
+41-21-841-9090

Fax:
+41-21-841-9084

Website:
www.breguet.com

Founded:
1775 (Swatch Group since 1999)

U.S. distributor:
Breguet
The Swatch Group (U.S.), Inc.
1200 Harbor Boulevard, 7th Floor
Weehawken, NJ 07087
201-271-1400

Most important collections:
Classique, Tradition, Héritage, Marine, Reine de Naples, Type XX, Type XXI, Type XXII

Classique Phase de Lune Dame
Reference number: 9088BB 29 964 DD0D
Movement: automatic, Breguet Caliber 537L; ø 20 mm; 26 jewels; 25.200 vph; silicon hairspring and escapement; 45-hour power reserve
Functions: hours, minutes, subsidiary seconds; moon phase
Case: white gold, ø 30 mm, height 9.8 mm; bezel and lugs set with 66 diamonds; sapphire crystal; transparent case back; water-resistant to 3 atm
Band: reptile skin, buckle
Price: $28,700
Variations: rose gold ($28,200)

Classique Hora Mundi
Reference number: 5727BB 12 9ZU
Movement: automatic, Breguet Caliber 77F0; ø 36 mm, height 6.15 mm; 39 jewels; 28,800 vph; silicon pallet lever, escape wheel and hairspring; 55-hour power reserve
Functions: hours, minutes, sweep seconds; world time display, day/night indicator; date
Case: white gold, ø 43 mm, height 13.55 mm; sapphire crystal; transparent case back; screw-in crown; water-resistant to 3 atm
Band: reptile skin, folding clasp
Price: $69,100
Variations: rose gold ($68,600)

Marine Équation Marchante
Reference number: 5887PT Y2 9WV
Movement: automatic, Breguet Caliber 581DPE; ø 37.2 mm; 57 jewels; 28,800 vph; 1-minute tourbillon; silicon pallet lever, escape wheel and hairspring; 80-hour power reserve
Functions: hours, minutes, subsidiary seconds (on tourbillon cage), running equation of time; perpetual calendar with date (retrograde), weekday, month
Case: platinum, ø 43.9 mm, height 11.75 mm; sapphire crystal; transparent case back; water-resistant to 10 atm
Band: reptile skin, folding clasp
Price: $230,400
Variations: rose gold ($215,000)

Classique

Reference number: 7147BB 29 9WU
Movement: automatic, Breguet Caliber 502.3SD;
35 jewels; 21,600 vph; silicon pallet lever and
hairspring; 45-hour power reserve
Functions: hours, minutes, subsidiary seconds
Case: white gold, ø 40 mm, height 6.47 mm;
sapphire crystal; transparent case back; water-
resistant to 3 atm
Band: reptile skin, buckle
Remarks: enamel dial
Price: $21,500
Variations: rose gold ($21,000)

Classique "La Musicale"

Reference number: 7800BR AA 9Y V02
Movement: automatic, Breguet Caliber 900;
ø 38.9 mm, height 8.7 mm; 59 jewels; 28,800 vph;
music box with peg disk/gong strips, liquid metal
membrane, magnetic striking regulator; 45-hour
power reserve
Functions: hours, minutes, sweep seconds; power
reserve indicator; alarm with melody and function
indication
Case: rose gold, ø 48 mm, height 16.3 mm; sapphire
crystal; water-resistant to 3 atm
Band: reptile skin, folding clasp
Remarks: hand-guillochéed, platinum-plated gold
dial rotates as melody is played
Price: $89,600

Classique Grande Complication Tourbillon Perpetual Calendar

Reference number: 3797BR 1E 9WU
Movement: manually wound, Breguet Caliber 558
QP2; 21 jewels; 18,000 vph; 1-minute tourbillon,
Breguet hairspring, balance with gold weight screws;
50-hour power reserve
Functions: hours, minutes (off-center), subsidiary
seconds (on tourbillon cage); perpetual calendar with
date (retrograde), weekday, month, leap year
Case: rose gold, ø 41 mm, height 11.6 mm; sapphire
crystal; transparent case back; water-resistant to
3 atm
Band: reptile skin, double folding clasp
Price: $164,900
Variations: platinum ($179,200)

Classique Grande Complication Tourbillon Extra-Thin

Reference number: 5377PT 12 9WU
Movement: automatic, Breguet Caliber 581 DR;
ø 36 mm, height 3 mm; 42 jewels; 28,800 vph;
1-minute tourbillon in a titanium frame, silicon
hairspring; hubless peripheral rotor at edge of
movement; 80-hour power reserve
Functions: hours, minutes, subsidiary seconds (on
tourbillon cage); power reserve indicator
Case: platinum, ø 42 mm, height 7 mm; sapphire
crystal; transparent case back; water-resistant to
3 atm
Band: reptile skin, double folding clasp
Price: $163,800
Variations: rose gold ($149,500)

Classique Chronométrie

Reference number: 7727BR 12 9WU
Movement: manually wound, Breguet Caliber
574 DR; ø 31.6 mm, height 3.5 mm; 45 jewels;
72,000 vph; 2 spring barrels, double hairspring,
silicon pallet lever and escape wheel; balance pivot
held by a magnet; 60-hour power reserve
Functions: hours, minutes, subsidiary seconds
(display of tenth of seconds); power reserve indicator
Case: rose gold, ø 41 mm, height 9.65 mm; sapphire
crystal; transparent case back; water-resistant to
3 atm
Band: reptile skin, folding clasp
Price: $40,000
Variations: white gold ($40,500)

Tradition Seconde Rétrograde

Reference number: 7097BB G1 9WU
Movement: automatic, Breguet Caliber 505 SR1;
ø 33 mm; 38 jewels; 21,600 vph; Breguet hairspring,
silicon pallets; 50-hour power reserve
Functions: hours, minutes (off-center), subsidiary
seconds (retrograde)
Case: white gold, ø 40 mm, height 11.65 mm;
sapphire crystal; transparent case back; water-
resistant to 3 atm
Band: reptile skin, folding clasp
Price: $33,500
Variations: rose gold ($32,700)

Tradition Tourbillon Fusée

Reference number: 7047PT 11 9ZU
Movement: manually wound, Breguet Caliber 569; ø 35.7 mm, height 10.82 mm; 43 jewels; 18,000 vph; Breguet silicon spring, torque regulator with chain and worm screw; 1-minute tourbillon; 50-hour power reserve
Functions: hours, minutes; power reserve indicator (on movement side)
Case: platinum, ø 41 mm, height 15.95 mm; sapphire crystal; transparent case back; water-resistant to 3 atm
Band: reptile skin, folding clasp
Price: $189,700
Variations: rose gold ($175,600)

Tradition Dame

Reference number: 7038BR 18 9V6 D00D
Movement: automatic, Breguet Caliber 505 SR; ø 33 mm; 38 jewels; 21,600 vph; silicon Breguet hairspring and pallet fork horns; 50-hour power reserve
Functions: hours, minutes (off-center), subsidiary seconds (retrograde)
Case: rose gold, ø 37 mm, height 11.85 mm; bezel set with 68 diamonds; sapphire crystal; transparent case back; crown with a ruby; water-resistant to 3 atm
Band: reptile skin, folding clasp
Price: $38,100
Variations: white gold ($38,900)

Héritage Phases de Lune Retrograde

Reference number: 8861BR 11 386 D000
Movement: manually wound, Breguet Caliber 586L; ø 20 mm; 38 jewels; 21,600 vph; Breguet hairspring, silicon anchor and anchor escape wheel; 36-hour power reserve
Functions: hours, minutes; moon phase
Case: pink gold, 25 × 35 mm, height 9.75 mm; bezel set with 140 diamonds; sapphire crystal; water-resistant to 3 atm
Band: calfskin, folding clasp
Price: $33,300
Variations: rose gold bracelet ($51,700); white gold ($54,800)

Héritage Grande Date

Reference number: 5410BR 12 9VV
Movement: automatic, Breguet Caliber 516 GG; ø 26 mm; 30 jewels; 28,800 vph; silicon hairspring and escapement; 65-hour power reserve
Functions: hours, minutes, subsidiary seconds; large date
Case: pink gold, 35 × 42 mm, height 12.9 mm; sapphire crystal; transparent case back; water-resistant to 3 atm
Band: calfskin, buckle
Price: $27,700
Variations: white gold ($28,700)

Type XXI Chrono Cadran Vintage

Reference number: 3817ST X2 3ZU
Movement: automatic, Breguet Caliber 584 Q/2; ø 30 mm; 26 jewels; 28,800 vph; silicon hairspring and escapement, central minute totalizer; 48-hour power reserve
Functions: hours, minutes, subsidiary seconds; second 24-hour display (second time zone); flyback chronograph; date
Case: stainless steel, ø 42 mm, height 15.2 mm; unidirectional bezel with 0-60 scale; sapphire crystal; transparent case back; water-resistant to 10 atm
Band: calfskin ($13,900)

Type XXII

Reference number: 3880BR Z2 9XV
Movement: automatic, Breguet Caliber 589F; ø 30 mm, height 8.3 mm; 28 jewels; 72,000 vph; high-frequency silicon escapement, sweep minute counter; 40-hour power reserve
Functions: hours, minutes, subsidiary seconds; second 24-hour display (second time zone); flyback chronograph; date
Case: rose gold, ø 44 mm, height 18.05 mm; bidirectional bezel with 0-60 scale; sapphire crystal; transparent case back; screw-in crown; water-resistant to 10 atm
Band: reptile skin, folding clasp
Price: $35,500
Variations: rose gold bracelet ($55,500); stainless steel ($21,600)

Marine Chronograph

Reference number: 5827BR 12 5ZU
Movement: automatic, Breguet Caliber 583 Q/1;
ø 30 mm; 24 jewels; 28,800 vph; hand-guillochéed
oscillating weight in rose gold, finely finished
movement with côtes de Genève; 48-hour power
reserve
Functions: hours, minutes, subsidiary seconds;
chronograph; date
Case: rose gold, ø 42 mm, height 14.1 mm; sapphire
crystal; transparent case back; screw-in crown; water-
resistant to 10 atm
Band: rubber, folding clasp
Price: $31,500
Variations: rose gold bracelet ($51,500)

Marine Large Date

Reference number: 5817ST 92 5V8
Movement: automatic, Breguet Caliber 517 GG;
ø 25.6 mm; 35 jewels; 28,800 vph; 65-hour power
reserve
Functions: hours, minutes, sweep seconds; large
date
Case: stainless steel, ø 39 mm, height 11.82 mm;
sapphire crystal; transparent case back; screw-in
crown; water-resistant to 10 atm
Band: rubber, folding clasp
Price: $15,500
Variations: stainless steel bracelet ($18,100)

Perles Impériales

Reference number: GJ29BB 8924 5D58
Movement: automatic, Breguet Caliber 586/1;
ø 15 mm; 29 jewels; 21,600 vph; silicon hairspring;
38-hour power reserve
Functions: hours, minutes
Case: white gold, set with diamonds and Akoya
pearls, 28.7 × 34.4 mm; sapphire crystal; crown with
a diamond; water-resistant to 3 atm
Band: satin, folding clasp
Remarks: mother-of-pearl dial
Price: $113,700
Variations: rose gold ($112,600)

Reine de Naples "Jour Nuit"

Reference number: 8999BB 8D 874 DD0D
Movement: automatic, Breguet Caliber 78CS;
45 jewels; 25,200 vph; silicon hairspring; 57-hour
power reserve
Functions: hours, minutes; day/night indicator via
rotating titanium disk
Case: white gold, 34 × 42.5 mm, height 10.8 mm;
dial and flange set with 73 diamonds; sapphire
crystal; transparent case back; crown with diamond
cabochon
Band: satin, folding clasp set with 26 diamonds
Price: $225,200

Reine de Naples Mini

Reference number: 8928BR 5W 844 DD0D
Movement: automatic, Breguet Caliber 586/1;
ø 15 mm; 29 jewels; 21,600 vph; silicon hairspring;
38-hour power reserve
Functions: hours, minutes
Case: pink gold, 24.95 × 33 mm, height 8.5 mm;
bezel, flange, and lugs set with 139 diamonds;
sapphire crystal; crown with diamond cabochon;
water-resistant to 3 atm
Band: satin, folding clasp set with 26 diamonds
Remarks: mother-of-pearl dial
Price: $35,100
Variations: rose gold bracelet ($59,700); white gold
($36,100)

Reine de Naples Princesse

Reference number: 8965BR 5W 986 DD0D
Movement: automatic, Breguet Caliber 591C;
ø 26 mm, height 2.95 mm; 25 jewels; 28,800 vph;
silicon anchor and lever escapement; 38-hour power
reserve
Functions: hours, minutes
Case: pink gold, 34.95 × 43 mm, height 9.65 mm;
bezel and lugs set with 83 diamonds; sapphire
crystal; transparent case back; crown with diamond
cabochon; water-resistant to 3 atm
Band: reptile skin, folding clasp set with
29 diamonds
Remarks: hand-guillochéed mother-of-pearl dial
Price: $37,400
Variations: rose gold bracelet ($52,300)

BREITLING

In 1884, Léon Breitling opened his workshop in St. Imier in the Jura mountains and immediately began specializing in integrated chronographs. His business strategy was to focus consistently on instrument watches with a distinctive design. High quality standards and the rise of aviation completed the picture.

Today, Breitling's relationship with air sports and commercial and military aviation is clear from its brand identity. The watch company hosts a series of aviation days, owns an aerobatics team, and sponsors several aviation associations.

The unveiling of its own, modern chronograph movement at Basel in 2009 was a major milestone in the company's history and also a return to its roots. The new design was to be "100 percent Breitling" and industrially produced in large numbers at a reasonable cost. Although Breitling's operations in Grenchen and in La Chaux-de-Fonds both boast state-of-the-art equipment, the contract for the new chronograph was awarded to a small team in Geneva. By 2006, the brand-new Caliber B01 had made the COSC grade with flying colors, and it has enjoyed great popularity ever since. For the team of designers, the innovative centering system on the reset mechanism that requires no manual adjustment was one of the great achievements. Since then, the in-house caliber has evolved. It now comes as the B04 with a second time zone, the B05 with world time, and the B06 with a 30-second chrono display for the Breitling for Bentley series.

By now, Breitling has a full portfolio of chronographs. In 2017, it launched the Navitimer Rattrapante with outstanding stop-second technology bundled into a 1.95-millimeter-high module integrated under the dial rather than at the back of the movement.

Breitling
Schlachthausstrasse 2
CH-2540 Grenchen
Switzerland

Tel.:
+41-32-654-5454

Fax:
+41-32-654-5400

E-mail:
sales@breitlingusa.com

Website:
www.breitling.com

Founded:
1884

Annual production:
700,000 (estimated)

U.S. distributor:
Breitling U.S.A. Inc.
206 Danbury Road
Wilton, CT 06897
203-762-1180
www.breitling.com

Most important collections:
Navitimer, Chronomat, Professional, Breitling for Bentley, Superocean, Avenger, Transocean

Chronomat 44

Reference number: AB011012/B967
Movement: automatic, Breitling Caliber B01; ø 30 mm, height 7.2 mm; 47 jewels; 28,800 vph; column wheel control of chronograph functions; 70-hour power reserve; COSC-certified chronometer
Functions: hours, minutes, subsidiary seconds; chronograph; date
Case: stainless steel, ø 44 mm, height 16.95 mm; unidirectional bezel with 0-60 scale; sapphire crystal; screw-in crown and pushers; water-resistant to 50 atm
Band: stainless steel, folding clasp
Price: $9,060
Variations: calfskin strap, tang-type buckle ($7,775)

Chronoliner

Reference number: R2431212/BE83
Movement: automatic, Breitling Caliber 24 (base ETA 7751); ø 30 mm, height 7.9 mm; 25 jewels; 28,800 vph; 42-hour power reserve
Functions: hours, minutes, subsidiary seconds; second 24-hour display (second time zone); chronograph; date
Case: pink gold, ø 46 mm, height 15.95 mm; bidirectional bezel with ceramic insert and 0-60 scale, with 0-24 scale; sapphire crystal; water-resistant to 10 atm
Band: rubber, folding clasp
Price: $29,920
Variations: calfskin strap ($24,130)

Chronoliner

Reference number: Y2431012/BE10
Movement: automatic, Breitling Caliber 24 (base ETA 7751); ø 30 mm, height 7.9 mm; 25 jewels; 28,800 vph; 42-hour power reserve
Functions: hours, minutes, subsidiary seconds; second 24-hour display (second time zone); chronograph; date
Case: stainless steel, ø 46 mm, height 15.95 mm; bidirectional bezel with ceramic insert and 0-60 scale, and 24-hour scale on the dial; sapphire crystal; water-resistant to 10 atm
Band: stainless steel Milanese mesh, folding clasp
Price: $7,575
Variations: rubber strap, folding clasp ($7,250)

Navitimer 01 (46 mm)
Reference number: AB012721/BD09
Movement: automatic, Breitling Caliber B01;
ø 30 mm, height 7.2 mm; 47 jewels; 28,800 vph;
column wheel control of chronograph functions;
70-hour power reserve; COSC-certified chronometer
Functions: hours, minutes, subsidiary seconds;
chronograph; date
Case: stainless steel, ø 46 mm, height 15.5 mm;
bidirectionally rotating bezel with integrated slide
rule and tachymeter scale; sapphire crystal; water-
resistant to 3 atm
Band: calfskin, buckle
Price: $8,215
Variations: stainless steel bracelet ($9,620)

Navitimer GMT
Reference number: AB044121/BD24
Movement: automatic, Breitling Caliber B04
(base B01); ø 30 mm, height 7.4 mm; 47 jewels;
28,800 vph; column wheel control of chronograph
functions; 70-hour power reserve; COSC-certified
chronometer
Functions: hours, minutes, subsidiary seconds; second
24-hour display (second time zone); chronograph; date
Case: stainless steel, ø 48 mm, height 15.8 mm;
bidirectionally rotating bezel with integrated
slide rule and tachymeter scale; sapphire crystal;
transparent case back; water-resistant to 3 atm
Band: calfskin, buckle
Price: $9,055
Variations: stainless steel bracelet ($10,460)

Navitimer Rattrapante
Reference number: AB031021/Q615
Movement: automatic, Breitling Caliber B03;
ø 30 mm, height 9.15 mm; 46 jewels; 28,800 vph;
70-hour power reserve; COSC-certified chronometer
Functions: hours, minutes, subsidiary seconds; split-
second chronograph; date
Case: stainless steel, ø 45 mm, height 15.73 mm;
bidirectionally rotating bezel with integrated slide
rule and tachymeter scale; sapphire crystal; water-
resistant to 3 atm
Band: reptile skin, buckle
Price: $10,840
Variations: stainless steel bracelet ($11,870)

Avenger Blackbird 44
Reference number: V1731110/BD74
Movement: automatic, Breitling Caliber 17 (base
ETA 2824-2); ø 25.6 mm, height 4.6 mm; 25 jewels;
28,800 vph; 40-hour power reserve; COSC-certified
chronometer
Functions: hours, minutes, sweep seconds; date
Case: titanium with black DLC coating, ø 44 mm,
height 14.2 mm; unidirectional bezel with 0-60
scale; sapphire crystal; screw-in crown; helium valve;
water-resistant to 200 atm
Band: textile, buckle
Price: $5,105

Avenger Bandit
Reference number: E1338310/M534
Movement: automatic, Breitling Caliber 13 (base
ETA 7750); ø 30 mm, height 7.9 mm; 25 jewels;
28,800 vph; 42-hour power reserve; COSC-certified
chronometer
Functions: hours, minutes, subsidiary seconds;
chronograph; date
Case: titanium, ø 45 mm; unidirectional bezel with
0-60 scale; sapphire crystal; screw-in crown; water-
resistant to 30 atm
Band: rubber, with textile overlay, folding clasp
Price: $5,875
Variations: rubber strap and buckle ($5,335)

Avenger Hurricane 12H
Reference number: XB0170E4/I533
Movement: automatic, Breitling Caliber B12
(base B01); ø 30 mm, height 7.4 mm; 47 jewels;
28,800 vph; 70-hour power reserve; COSC-certified
chronometer
Functions: hours, minutes, subsidiary seconds;
chronograph; date
Case: composite material "Breitlight," ø 50 mm;
unidirectional bezel with 0-60 scale; sapphire crystal;
screw-in crown; water-resistant to 10 atm
Band: textile, buckle
Price: $7,655
Variations: rubber strap and buckle ($7,600)

Super Avenger II

Reference number: A1337111/BC29
Movement: automatic, Breitling Caliber 13 (base ETA 7750); ø 30 mm, height 7.9 mm; 25 jewels; 28,800 vph; 42-hour power reserve; COSC-certified chronometer
Functions: hours, minutes, subsidiary seconds; chronograph; date
Case: stainless steel, ø 48 mm, height 17.75 mm; unidirectional bezel with 0-60 scale; sapphire crystal; screw-in crown; water-resistant to 30 atm
Band: rubber, folding clasp
Price: $5,635
Variations: stainless steel bracelet ($5,835)

Navitimer World Stratos Grey

Reference number: A243223A/F571
Movement: automatic, Breitling Caliber 24 (base ETA 7751); ø 30 mm, height 7.9 mm; 25 jewels; 28,800 vph; 42-hour power reserve; COSC-certified chronometer
Functions: hours, minutes, subsidiary seconds; second 24-hour display; chronograph; date
Case: stainless steel, ø 46 mm, height 15.5 mm; bidirectionally rotating bezel with integrated slide rule and tachymeter scale; sapphire crystal; water-resistant to 3 atm
Band: stainless steel, folding clasp
Remarks: limited to 300 pieces; limited to the European market
Price: on request
Variations: calfskin strap

Navitimer 01 (46 mm) Limited Edition

Reference number: AB01271A/F570
Movement: automatic, Breitling Caliber B01; ø 30 mm, height 7.2 mm; 47 jewels; 28,800 vph; column wheel control of chronograph functions; 70-hour power reserve; COSC-certified chronometer
Functions: hours, minutes, subsidiary seconds; chronograph; date
Case: stainless steel, ø 46 mm, height 15.5 mm; bidirectionally rotating bezel with integrated slide rule and tachymeter scale; sapphire crystal; water-resistant to 3 atm
Band: rubber, folding clasp
Price: $8,550; limited to 1,000 pieces
Variations: stainless steel bracelet ($9,720)

Superocean Héritage II 42

Reference number: AB201016/C960
Movement: automatic, Breitling Caliber B20 (base Tudor MT 5612); ø 31.8 mm, height 6.5 mm; 28 jewels; 28,800 vph; 70-hour power reserve; COSC-certified chronometer
Functions: hours, minutes, sweep seconds; date
Case: stainless steel, ø 42 mm, height 14.35 mm; unidirectional bezel with ceramic inlay; sapphire crystal; screw-in crown; water-resistant to 20 atm
Band: stainless steel Milanese mesh, folding clasp
Price: $4,700
Variations: rubber strap (Ocean Racer), folding clasp ($4,375)

Superocean Héritage II 46

Reference number: AB202012/BF74
Movement: automatic, Breitling Caliber B20 (base Tudor MT 5612); ø 31.8 mm, height 6.5 mm; 28 jewels; 28,800 vph; 70-hour power reserve; COSC-certified chronometer
Functions: hours, minutes, sweep seconds; date
Case: stainless steel, ø 46 mm, height 15 mm; unidirectional bezel with ceramic inlay; sapphire crystal; screw-in crown; water-resistant to 20 atm
Band: rubber (Ocean Racer), folding clasp
Price: $4,375
Variations: stainless steel bracelet ($4,700)

Superocean 44 Special

Reference number: M1739313/BE92
Movement: automatic, Breitling Caliber 17 (base ETA 2824-2); ø 25.6 mm, height 4.6 mm; 25 jewels; 28,800 vph; 40-hour power reserve; COSC-certified chronometer
Functions: hours, minutes, sweep seconds; date
Case: stainless steel with black DLC coating, ø 44 mm, height 14.2 mm; unidirectional bezel with 0-60 scale; sapphire crystal; screw-in crown; helium valve; water-resistant to 100 atm
Band: rubber (Ocean Racer II), buckle
Price: $4,980
Variations: Ocean Racer rubber with folding clasp ($5,505)

Superocean II 44

Reference number: A17392D7/BD68
Movement: automatic, Breitling Caliber 17 (base ETA 2824-2); ø 25.6 mm, height 4.6 mm; 25 jewels; 28,800 vph; 40-hour power reserve; COSC-certified chronometer
Functions: hours, minutes, sweep seconds; date
Case: stainless steel, ø 44 mm, height 14.2 mm; unidirectional bezel with 0-60 scale; sapphire crystal; screw-in crown; helium valve; water-resistant to 100 atm
Band: stainless steel, folding clasp
Price: $4,150
Variations: rubber strap (Diver Pro II) and buckle

Galactic 36 Automatic

Reference number: A3733053/A717
Movement: automatic, Breitling Caliber 37 (base ETA 2892-A2); ø 25.6 mm, height 3.6 mm; 27 jewels; 28,800 vph; 42-hour power reserve
Functions: hours, minutes, subsidiary seconds; date
Case: stainless steel, ø 36 mm, height 12.3 mm; unidirectional bezel set with diamonds; sapphire crystal
Band: calfskin, buckle
Remarks: mother-of-pearl dial with diamond indexes
Price: $9,450
Variations: stainless steel bracelet ($10,735)

Superocean Héritage II Chronograph

Reference number: A1331233/Q616
Movement: automatic, Breitling Caliber 13 (base ETA 7750); ø 30 mm, height 7.9 mm; 25 jewels; 28,800 vph; 42-hour power reserve; COSC-certified chronometer
Functions: hours, minutes, subsidiary seconds; chronograph; date
Case: stainless steel, ø 46 mm, height 16.35 mm; unidirectional bezel with ceramic inlay; sapphire crystal; screw-in crown; water-resistant to 20 atm
Band: rubber, with calfskin overlay, folding clasp
Price: $5,840
Variations: stainless steel bracelet ($6,040)

Caliber B01

Automatic; column wheel control of chronograph functions; vertical clutch; single spring barrel, 70-hour power reserve; COSC-certified chronometer
Functions: hours, minutes, subsidiary seconds; chronograph; date
Diameter: 30 mm
Height: 7.2 mm
Jewels: 47
Balance: glucydur
Frequency: 28,800 vph

Caliber B04

Automatic; column wheel control of chronograph functions; vertical clutch; single spring barrel, 70-hour power reserve; COSC-certified chronometer
Functions: hours, minutes, subsidiary seconds; second 24-hour display (second time zone); chronograph; date
Diameter: 30 mm
Height: 7.4 mm
Jewels: 47
Balance: glucydur
Frequency: 28,800 vph

Caliber B05

Automatic; column wheel control of chronograph functions; vertical clutch; time zone disk coupled with the hands mechanism using planetary transmission; single spring barrel, 70-hour power reserve; COSC-certified chronometer
Functions: hours, minutes, subsidiary seconds; crown-adjustable world-time display; chronograph; date
Diameter: 30 mm
Height: 8.1 mm
Jewels: 56
Balance: glucydur
Frequency: 28,800 vph

BRM

Is luxury on the outside or the inside? The answer to this question can tear the veil from the hype and reveal the true craftsman. For Bernard Richards, the true sign of luxury lies in "technical skills and perfection in all stages of manufacture." The exterior of the product is of course crucial, but all of BRM's major operations for making a wristwatch—such as encasing, assembling, setting, and polishing—are performed by hand in his little garage-like factory located outside Paris in Magny-sur-Vexin.

BRM is devoted to the ultra-mechanical look with the *haute-horlogerie* feel of high-end materials. His inspiration at the start came from the 1940s, when internal combustion engines meant business, the age of axle grease, pinups, real pilots, and a can-do attitude. The design: three dimensions visible to the naked eye, big mechanical landscapes. The inside: custom-designed components, fitting perfectly into Richards's automotive ideal. Gradually, though, Richards has been modernizing. Since the beginning of 2009, BRM aficionados have been able to engage in this process to an even greater degree: When visiting the BRM website, the client can now construct his or her own V12-44-BRM model.

BRM's unusual timepieces have mainly been based on the tried and trusted Valjoux 7750. But Richards has set lofty goals for himself and his young venture, for he intends to set up a true *manufacture* in his French factory. His Birotor model is thus outfitted with the Precitime, an autonomous caliber conceived and manufactured on French soil. The movement features BRM's own shock absorbers mounted on the conical springs of its so-called Isolastic system. Plates and bridges are crafted in Arcap, rotors are made of Fortale and tantalum. The twin rotors, found at 12 and 6 o'clock, are mounted on double rows of ceramic bearings that require no lubrication.

BRM
(Bernard Richards Manufacture)
2 Impasse de L'Aubette
ZA des Aulnaies
F-95420 Magny en Vexin
France

Tel.:
+33-1-61-02-00-25

Fax:
+33-1-61-02-00-14

Website:
www.brm-manufacture.com

Founded:
2003

Number of employees:
20

Annual production:
approx. 2,000 pieces

U.S. distributor:
BRM Manufacture North America
25 Highland Park Village, Suite 100-777
Dallas, TX 75205
214-231-0144
usa@brm-manufacture.com

Most important collections/price range:
$3,000 to $150,000

R12-46

Movement: automatic, ETA Valjoux Caliber 7753 modified in-house; ø 30 mm, height 7.90 mm; 27 jewels; 28,800 vph; skeletonized dial; shock absorbers connected to block; 42-hour power reserve
Functions: hours, minutes, subsidiary seconds; chronograph; date
Case: bronze, ø 46 mm, height 14 mm; stainless steel lugs and crown with black PVD; crystal sapphire; transparent case back; water-resistant to 10 atm
Band: leather, bronze buckle
Price: $13,550

BiRotor

Movement: automatic, Precitime Caliber Birotor; 24 × 32 mm; 35 jewels; 28,800 vph; 45-hour power reserve; Fortale HR and tantalum double rotors on ceramic ball bearings; patented isolastic system with 4 shock absorbers, arcap plates, bridges
Functions: hours, minutes, subsidiary seconds
Case: titanium with rose gold crown and strap lugs, 40 × 48 mm, height 9.9 mm; domed sapphire crystal; antireflective on both sides; domed sapphire crystal transparent case back; water-resistant to 30 m
Band: nomex, buckle
Price: $68,500

TriRotor

Movement: automatic, Precitime Caliber TriRotor; ø 48 mm; 29 jewels; 28,800 vph; 45-hour power reserve; Fortale HR main rotors with 3 macro rotors in Fortale HR with tantalum on ceramic ball bearings; patented isolastic system with 3 shock absorbers, arcap plates, bridges
Functions: hours, minutes, subsidiary seconds
Case: titanium with rose gold crown and strap lugs, ø 48 mm, height 9.9 mm; domed sapphire crystal; antireflective on both sides; domed sapphire crystal transparent case back; water-resistant to 10 atm
Band: nomex, buckle
Price: $47,950
Variations: rose gold; yellow, red, or orange hands

R50 MK

Movement: automatic, heavily modified ETA Caliber 2161; ø 38 mm; 35 jewels; 28,800 vph; 48-hour power reserve; patented Isolastic system with 3 shock absorbers; Fortale HR, tantalum, and aluminum rotor; hand-painted Gulf colors
Functions: hours, minutes, sweep seconds; power reserve indication
Case: makrolon with rose gold crown and strap lugs, ø 50 mm, height 13.2 mm; sapphire crystal; antireflective on both sides; exhibition case back; water-resistant to 3 atm
Band: leather, buckle
Price: $28,550; limited to 30 pieces
Variations: rose gold ($65,000)

TR1 Tourbillon

Movement: automatic, Precitime Caliber; ø 30 mm, height 7.9 mm; 26 jewels; 28,800 vph; 46-hour power reserve; 105-second tourbillon in arcap with reversed cage for visible escapement and suspended by 2 micro springs; patented Isolastic system with 4 shock absorbers; automatic assembly with ceramic ball bearings
Functions: hours, minutes, sweep seconds
Case: titanium, ø 52 mm; sapphire crystal; antireflective on both sides; transparent case back; water-resistant to 10 atm
Band: leather, buckle
Price: $145,350
Variations: 48 mm ($136,150)

R46

Movement: automatic, heavily modified ETA Caliber 2161; ø 38 mm; 35 jewels; 28,800 vph; 48-hour power reserve; patented Isolastic system with 3 shock absorbers; Fortale HR, tantalum and aluminum rotor; hand-painted Gulf colors
Functions: hours, minutes, sweep seconds; power reserve indication
Case: makrolon with rose gold crown and strap lugs, ø 46 mm, height 10 mm; sapphire crystal; antireflective on both sides; exhibition case back; water-resistant to 3 atm
Band: leather, buckle
Price: $24,750; limited to 30 pieces

DDF12-44-AR

Movement: automatic, ETA Valjoux Caliber 7753 modified in-house; ø 30 mm, height 7.90 mm; 27 jewels; 28,800 vph; skeletonized dial; shock absorbers connected to block; 42-hour power reserve
Functions: hours, minutes, subsidiary seconds; chronograph; date
Case: titanium with black PVD coating, ø 44 mm; stainless steel lugs and pushers; sapphire crystal; transparent case back; water-resistant to 10 atm
Band: leather, buckle
Remarks: skeletonized dial with red hands
Price: $12,750

Ringmaster

Movement: automatic, ETA Valjoux Caliber 7753; ø 30 mm, height 7.90 mm; 27 jewels; 28,800 vph; 42-hour power reserve
Functions: hours, minutes, subsidiary seconds; date; chronograph
Case: grade 5 titanium, black PVD, 46 mm; sapphire crystal; transparent case back; water-resistant to 10 atm
Band: seat belt material, buckle
Price: $8,950; limited to 100 pieces

MK 44 blue

Movement: automatic, ETA Valjoux Caliber 7753; ø 30 mm, height 7.90 mm; 27 jewels; 28,800 vph; 42-hour power reserve
Functions: hours, minutes, subsidiary seconds; date; chronograph
Case: makrolon (polycarbonate), ø 45 mm; pushers, lugs, crown from single titanium block; sapphire crystal; exhibition case back; water-resistant to 10 atm
Band: technical fabrics for extra lightness
Remarks: lightest automatic chronograph ever made; skeleton dial with blue hands
Price: $13,450
Variations: many options with configurator

BREMONT

Bremont Watch Company
PO Box 4741
Henley-on-Thames
RG9 9BZ
Great Britain

Tel.:
+44-845-094-0690

Fax:
+44-870-762-0475

E-mail:
info@bremont.com

Website:
www.bremont.com

Founded:
2002

Number of employees:
100+

Annual production:
several thousand watches

U.S. distributor:
Mike Pearson
1-855-BREMONT
michael@bremont.com

Most important collections/price range:
ALT1, Bremont Boeing, Bremont Jaguar, MB,
SOLO, Supermarine, U-2, and limited editions /
$3,695 to $42,495

At the 2012 Olympic Games in London, stuntman Gary Connery parachuted into the stadium wearing an outfit that made him look suspiciously like the Queen. He was also the first to jet suit out of a helicopter. On both occasions he was wearing a Bremont watch. And so do many other adventurous types, like polar explorer Ben Saunders or Levison Wood, who was the first person to walk the length of the Nile.

Bremonts are the brainchild of brothers Nick and Giles English, themselves dyed-in-the-wool pilots and restorers of vintage airplanes. They understand that flying safety relies on outstanding mechanics, so they took their time engineering their watches. Naming their brand required some thought, however. The solution came when they remembered an adventure they had had in southern France when they were forced to land their vintage biplane in a field to avoid a storm. The farmer, a former WWII pilot and just as passionate about aircraft as Nick and Giles, was more than happy to put them up. His name: Antoine Bremont.

Ever since the watches hit the market in 2007, the brand has grown sharply. These British-made timepieces use a sturdy, COSC-certified automatic movement, especially hardened steel, a patented shock-absorbing system, and a rotor whose design recalls a flight of planes. The brand has sought its inspiration from various cultural icons in British or international history, including the Spitfire, Bletchley Park (where the German codes were broken during World War II), or Jaguar sports cars and, most recently, Norton motorcycles. It also partnered with Boeing to produce an elegant range of watches on an organic polymer strap. Water sport is another area Bremont has explored, with models inspired by the legendary J-Class yachts, like the ladies' model AC I 32, and a special set devoted to the America's Cup. In 2017, Bremont became the first official timekeeper at the Henley Royal Regatta, one of Great Britain's top rowing events.

Norton V4

Movement: automatic, modified Caliber BE-50AE; ø 29.89 mm, height 16.5 mm; 28 jewels; 28,800 vph; COSC-certified chronometer; 42-hour power reserve
Functions: hours, minutes, subsidiary seconds; chronograph; date and world-time zone
Case: stainless steel, DLC-treated case barrel, ø 43 mm, height 16.5 mm; transparent case back; sapphire crystal; water-resistant to 10 atm
Band: reptile skin, rose gold buckle
Remarks: Norton VR Rim inspired rotor; silver with tachymeter dial ring
Price: $7,295

Jaguar MKI

Movement: automatic, Bremont BWC/01-10; ø 33.4 mm; 25 jewels; 28,800 vph; 50-hour power reserve
Functions: hours, minutes, subsidiary seconds; date
Case: stainless steel; ø 43 mm, height 16 mm; transparent case back; sapphire crystal; water-resistant to 10 atm
Band: calfskin, buckle
Remarks: miniaturized Jaguar E-Type steering wheel rotor with Growler emblem
Price: $11,395

Solo-32-AJ

automatic, modified Caliber BE-10AE; ø 20.3 mm; 18 jewels; 28,800 vph; 40-hour power reserve; Bremont molded and decorated rotor; COSC-certified chronometer
Functions: hours, minutes, sweep seconds; date
Case: stainless steel; ø 32 mm, height 9.65 mm; transparent screw-in case back; sapphire crystal; water-resistant to 5 atm
Band: reptile skin, buckle
Price: $3,695
Variations: various straps

U-22

Movement: automatic, modified Caliber BE-36AE; ø 28 mm, height 7.5 mm; 25 jewels; 28,800 vph; 38-hour power reserve; Bremont molded and decorated rotor; COSC-certified chronometer
Functions: hours, minutes, seconds; weekday, date
Case: stainless steel; ø 43 mm, height 16 mm; antimagnetic soft iron core; crown-adjustable bidirectional bezel; sapphire crystal; transparent case back; water-resistant to 10 atm
Band: leather strap, buckle
Remarks: optional Temple Island rubber strap
Price: $5,195

MBII-WH

Movement: automatic, modified Caliber BE-36AE; ø 28 mm, height 7.5 mm; 25 jewels; 28,800 vph; Bremont skeletonized rotor; COSC-certified; 38-hour power reserve
Functions: hours, minutes, sweep seconds; sweep 24-hour hand (2nd time zone); date
Case: stainless steel; ø 43 mm, height 14.35 mm; crown-operated bidirectional inner bezel; antimagnetic cage; screw-down case back; sapphire crystal; water-resistant to 10 atm
Band: leather, buckle
Remarks: with NATO military strap
Price: $4,995
Variations: bronze, orange, or anthracite barrel

AC-R-11

Movement: automatic, customized Caliber BE-36AE; ø 28 mm, height 7.5 mm; 25 jewels; 28,800 vph; 42-hour power reserve; rotor with America's Cup decoration; COSC-certified chronometer
Functions: hours, minutes, subsidiary seconds; date; chronograph with 15-minute regatta timer and 5-minute countdown at 12 o'clock
Case: hardened stainless steel and rose gold; ø 43 mm, height 16 mm; bidirectional bezel; DLC-treated case barrel; transparent case back; sapphire crystal; water-resistant to 10 atm
Band: rubber, titanium buckle
Price: $7,095
Variations: titanium case with black dial ($6,459) leather strap of various colors, or NATO strap

ALT1-P2/CR

Movement: automatic, modified Caliber BE-53AE; ø 29.89 mm, height 16.5 mm; 27 jewels; 28,800 vph; Bremont molded and decorated skeletonized rotor; COSC-certified chronometer; 42-hour power reserve
Functions: hours, minutes, subsidiary seconds; chronograph; date
Case: stainless steel, DLC-treated case barrel. ø 43 mm, height 16 mm; transparent case back; sapphire crystal; water-resistant to 10 atm
Band: leather with stainless steel deployment buckle and security clasp
Price: $4,995

Boeing Ti Model 247

Movement: automatic, modified Caliber BE-54AE; ø 28.04 mm, height 10.5 mm; 25 jewels; 28,800 vph; Bremont molded and decorated rotor; COSC-certified chronometer; 42-hour power reserve
Functions: hours, minutes, subsidiary seconds; 2nd time zone; world-time display; chronograph; date
Case: stainless steel, DLC-treated case barrel, ø 43 mm, height 16 mm; transparent case back; sapphire crystal; water-resistant to 10 atm
Band: leather-polymer composite (Seattle Hybrid), buckle
Price: $6,895

AC35

Movement: automatic, BWC/01-10; ø 33.4 mm; 25 jewels; 28,800 vph; 50-hour power reserve; bidirectional Bremont molded and decorated rotor; COSC-certified chronometer
Functions: hours, minutes, subsidiary seconds, date
Case: rose gold with stainless steel case barrel; ø 43 mm, height 14.1 mm; sapphire crystal; water-resistant to 200 atm
Band: rubber, buckle
Remarks: America's Cup "Auld Mug" embossing and "2017 America's Cup Bermuda"
Price: $22,495

BULGARI

Although Bulgari is one of the largest jewelry manufacturers in the world, watches have always played an important role for the brand. The purchase of Daniel Roth and Gérald Genta in the Vallée de Joux opened new perspectives for its timepieces, thanks to specialized production facilities and the watchmaking talent in the Vallée de Joux—especially where complicated timepieces are concerned. In March 2011, luxury goods giant Louis Vuitton Moët Hennessy (LVMH) secured all the Bulgari family shares in exchange for 16.5 million LVMH shares and a say in the group's future. The financial backing of the megagroup boosted the company's strategy to become fully independent.

Bulgari timepieces are timeless and elegant, with style elements that border on the abstract. But it's not just looks. The company manufactures the entire watch, including a number of outstanding calibers, like the 168 Automatic based on a Leschot design. The year 2014 saw the simple Octo built on the double-barreled Caliber 193. Manufacturing is done in a modern building in the industrial zone of La Chaux-de-Fonds, Switzerland.

In mid-2013, Jean-Christophe Babin, the man who turned TAG Heuer into a leading player in sports watches, was chosen to head the venerable brand. He had also managed to build up a manufacturing structure from scratch at TAG Heuer, which is exactly the direction Bulgari's watch division is headed in. Barring a few components and the "Velocissimo" caliber, Bulgari is now able to do everything on its own. Its latest venture has been into electronics, with an NFC chip for the Magnesium to store private data—such as passwords and credit card numbers—and even open garage doors or start your car. The company is especially proud of its in-house automatic minute repeater, which is 3.12 millimeters high, a record. It is used in the Octo Finissimo Minute Repeater, whose dial features slotted indices for better sound transmission.

Bulgari Horlogerie SA
rue de Monruz 34
CH-2000 Neuchâtel
Switzerland

Tel.:
+41-32-722-7878

Fax:
+41-32-722-7933

E-mail:
info@bulgari.com

Website:
www.bulgari.com

Founded:
1884 (Bulgari Horlogerie was founded in the early 1980s as Bulgari Time.)

U.S. distributor:
Bulgari Corporation of America
555 Madison Avenue
New York, NY 10022
212-315-9700

Most important collections/price range:
Bulgari-Bulgari / from approx. $4,700 to $30,300; Diagono / from approx. $3,200; Octo / from approx. $9,500 to $690,000 and above; Daniel Roth and Gérald Genta collections

Bulgari Bulgari

Reference number: BBP39WGLD
Movement: automatic, Bulgari Caliber BVL 191; ø 26.2 mm, height 3.8 mm; 26 jewels; 28,800 vph; finished with côtes de Genève; 42-hour power reserve
Functions: hours, minutes, sweep seconds; date
Case: rose gold, ø 39 mm; sapphire crystal; water-resistant to 5 atm
Band: reptile skin, folding clasp
Price: $19,900
Variations: stainless steel

Octo Finissimo Automatic

Reference number: BGO40C14TTXTAUTO
Movement: automatic, Bulgari Caliber BVL 138 Finissimo; ø 36 mm, height 2.23 mm; 23 jewels; 21,600 vph; platinum microrotor; finely finished with côtes de Genève; 60-hour power reserve
Functions: hours, minutes, subsidiary seconds
Case: titanium, ø 40 mm, height 5.15 mm; sapphire crystal; transparent case back
Band: titanium, folding clasp
Price: $13,900
Variations: reptile skin strap

Octo Finissimo Automatic

Reference number: BGO40C14TLXTAUTO
Movement: automatic, Bulgari Caliber BVL 138 Finissimo; ø 36 mm, height 2.23 mm; 23 jewels; 21,600 vph; platinum microrotor; finely finished with côtes de Genève; 60-hour power reserve
Functions: hours, minutes, subsidiary seconds
Case: titanium, ø 40 mm, height 5.15 mm; sapphire crystal; transparent case back
Band: reptile skin, buckle
Price: $12,800
Variations: titanium bracelet

Octo Ultranero Solotempo

Reference number: BGO41C9BSVD
Movement: automatic, Bulgari Caliber BVL 193;
ø 25.6 mm, height 3.7 mm; 28 jewels; 28,800 vph;
50-hour power reserve
Functions: hours, minutes, sweep seconds; date
Case: stainless steel titanium with black DLC
coating, ø 41 mm, height 10.5 mm; sapphire crystal
Band: rubber, buckle
Price: $6,950

Octo Ultranero Solotempo

Reference number: BGO41BBSVD/N
Movement: automatic, Bulgari Caliber BVL 193;
ø 25.6 mm, height 3.7 mm; 28 jewels; 28,800 vph;
50-hour power reserve
Functions: hours, minutes, sweep seconds; date
Case: stainless steel titanium with black DLC
coating, ø 41 mm, height 10.5 mm; sapphire crystal
Band: rubber, buckle
Price: $6,950

Octo Ultranero Velocissimo

Reference number: BGO41BBSVDCH
Movement: automatic, Bulgari Caliber Velocissimo
(base Zenith "El Primero"); ø 30 mm, height
6.62 mm; 31 jewels; 36,000 vph; column wheel
control of chronograph functions, silicon escapement;
50-hour power reserve
Functions: hours, minutes, subsidiary seconds;
chronograph; date
Case: stainless steel with black DLC coating,
ø 41 mm, height 13 mm; sapphire crystal;
transparent case back; screw-in crown, pink gold
Band: rubber, buckle
Price: $10,600

Octo Ultranero Velocissimo

Reference number: BGO41BBSPGVDCH
Movement: automatic, Bulgari Caliber Velocissimo
(base Zenith "El Primero"); ø 30 mm, height
6.62 mm; 31 jewels; 36,000 vph; column wheel
control of chronograph functions, silicon escapement;
50-hour power reserve
Functions: hours, minutes, subsidiary seconds;
chronograph; date
Case: stainless steel with black DLC coating,
ø 41 mm, height 13 mm; pink gold bezel; sapphire
crystal; transparent case back; screw-in crown, pink
gold
Band: rubber, buckle
Price: $13,400

Octo Finissimo Ultranero
Squelette

Reference number: BGO40BBSPGLXT/SK
Movement: manually wound, Bulgari Caliber BVL
128SK; ø 36 mm, height 2.35 mm; 28,800 vph;
skeletonized bridges and plates; 65-hour power
reserve
Functions: hours, minutes, subsidiary seconds;
power reserve indicator
Case: stainless steel with black DLC coating,
ø 40 mm, height 5.37 mm; rose gold bezel; sapphire
crystal; transparent case back; screw-in crown, pink
gold; water-resistant to 3 atm
Band: reptile skin, buckle
Remarks: skeletonized dial
Price: $26,600

Octo Finissimo Tourbillon
Ultranero

Reference number: BGO40BTLTBXT
Movement: manually wound, Bulgari Caliber
BVL 268 Finissimo Tourbillon; ø 32.6 mm, height
1.95 mm; 26 jewels; 21,600 vph; flying 1-minute
tourbillon; finely finished movement; 52-hour power
reserve
Functions: hours, minutes
Case: titanium with black DLC coating, ø 40 mm,
height 5 mm; sapphire crystal; transparent case back;
screw-in crown, pink gold; water-resistant to 3 atm
Band: reptile skin, buckle
Price: on request

Octo Finissimo Minute Repeater

Reference number: BGO40BTLMRXT
Movement: manually wound, Bulgari Caliber BVL 362; ø 28.5 mm, height 3.12 mm; 21,600 vph; finely hand-finished movement; 42-hour power reserve
Functions: hours, minutes, subsidiary seconds; minute repeater
Case: titanium, ø 40 mm, height 6.85 mm; sapphire crystal; transparent case back; water-resistant to 3 atm
Band: reptile skin, double folding clasp
Remarks: resonance dial with slit indices
Price: on request; limited to 50 pieces

Papillon Voyageur

Reference number: BRRP46C14GLGMTP
Movement: automatic, Daniel Roth Caliber DR 1307; ø 25.6 mm, height 6.78 mm; 26 jewels; 28,800 vph; 45-hour power reserve
Functions: hours (digital, jumping), minutes (retrograde), subsidiary seconds (segment display with double hand); second 24-hour display (second time zone)
Case: pink gold, 43 × 46 mm, height 15.2 mm; sapphire crystal; transparent case back; pusher to advance 24-hour display; water-resistant to 3 atm
Band: reptile skin, double folding clasp
Price: $51,000

Octo Finissimo Skeleton

Reference number: BGO40TLXTSK
Movement: manually wound, Bulgari Caliber BVL 128SK; ø 36 mm, height 2.35 mm; 28,800 vph; skeletonized bridges and plates; 65-hour power reserve
Functions: hours, minutes, subsidiary seconds; power reserve indicator
Case: stainless steel, ø 40 mm, height 5.37 mm; sapphire crystal; transparent case back; screw-in crown; water-resistant to 3 atm
Band: reptile skin, buckle
Price: $21,500

Ammiraglio del Tempo

Reference number: BRRP50BGLDEMR
Movement: manually wound, Daniel Roth Caliber 7301; ø 38 mm, height 9.38 mm; 56 jewels; 14,400 vph; chronometer escapement; Westminster chimes, 4 hammers and gongs, constant force mechanism, cylindrical balance spring, triple shock-absorbing system; 48-hour power reserve
Functions: hours, minutes; minute repeater
Case: pink gold, 45.75 × 50 mm, height 14.9 mm; sapphire crystal; transparent case back
Remarks: mobile lug at 7 o'clock to activate chimes
Band: reptile skin, double folding clasp
Price: $359,000
Variations: white gold

Tourbillon Sapphire Ultranero

Reference number: BGG53BTLTBSK/UN
Movement: manually wound, Gérald Genta Caliber GG 8000; ø 32.6 mm, height 7.85 mm; 19 jewels; 21,600 vph; 1-minute tourbillon, skeletonized movement; 70-hour power reserve
Functions: hours, minutes
Case: white gold, case sides of sapphire crystal, ø 53 mm, height 14.89 mm; bezel with black PVD coating; sapphire crystal; transparent case back; water-resistant to 3 atm
Band: reptile skin, double folding clasp
Price: $198,000; limited to 25 pieces

Octo Tourbillon Sapphire

Reference number: BGO44C4TLTBSK
Movement: manually wound, Bulgari Caliber BVL 206; ø 34 mm, height 5 mm; 21,600 vph; flying 1-minute tourbillon; bridges with black DLC coating; 64-hour power reserve
Functions: hours, minutes
Case: titanium with black DLC coating, ø 44 mm, height 12.45 mm; sapphire crystal; transparent case back; water-resistant to 5 atm
Band: reptile skin, buckle
Price: $60,000

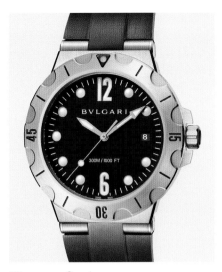

Octo Roma

Reference number: OC41C1SLD
Movement: automatic, Bulgari Caliber BVL 191; ø 26.2 mm, height 3.8 mm; 26 jewels; 28,800 vph; finely finished with côtes de Genève; 42-hour power reserve
Functions: hours, minutes, sweep seconds; date
Case: stainless steel, ø 41 mm, height 10.5 mm; sapphire crystal; transparent case back; water-resistant to 10 atm
Band: reptile skin, buckle
Price: $5,950

Octo Finissimo Tourbillon Skeleton

Reference number: BGO40PLTBXTSK
Movement: manually wound, Bulgari Caliber BVL 268 Finissimo Squelette; ø 32.6 mm, height 1.95 mm; 26 jewels; 21,600 vph; flying 1-minute tourbillon; skeletonized and finely finished movement; 62-hour power reserve
Functions: hours, minutes
Case: platinum, ø 40 mm, height 5 mm; sapphire crystal; transparent case back; water-resistant to 3 atm
Band: reptile skin, buckle
Price: on request

Diagono Scuba

Reference number: DP41C3SVSD
Movement: automatic, Bulgari Caliber BVL 191; ø 26.2 mm, height 3.8 mm; 26 jewels; 28,800 vph; finished with cótes de Genève; 42-hour power reserve
Functions: hours, minutes, sweep seconds; date
Case: stainless steel, ø 41 mm, height 11.5 mm; unidirectional bezel with 0-60 scale; sapphire crystal; screw-in crown; water-resistant to 30 atm
Band: rubber, buckle
Price: $6,550

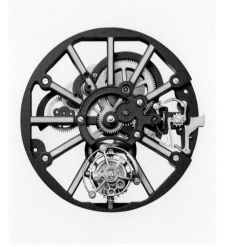

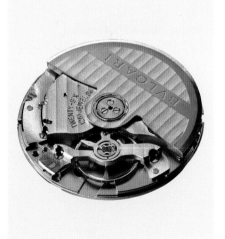

Caliber BVL 138 Finissimo

Automatic; flying platinum microrotor; flying single spring barrel, 60-hour power reserve
Functions: hours, minutes, subsidiary seconds; date
Diameter: 36 mm
Height: 2.23 mm
Jewels: 23
Balance: glucydur
Frequency: 21,600 vph
Balance spring: flat hairspring index for fine adjustment
Shock protection: Incabloc
Remarks: finely finished with cótes de Genève

Caliber BVL 206

Manually wound; flying 1-minute tourbillon; skeletonized mainplate; single spring barrel, 64-hour power reserve
Functions: hours, minutes
Diameter: 34 mm
Height: 5 mm
Frequency: 21,600 vph
Remarks: bridges with black DLC coating with green luminescent bars as hour indices

Caliber BVL 191

Automatic; single spring barrel, 42-hour power reserve
Functions: hours, minutes, sweep seconds; date
Diameter: 26.2 mm
Height: 3.8 mm
Jewels: 26
Balance: glucydur
Frequency: 28,800 vph
Balance spring: flat hairspring index for fine adjustment
Shock protection: Incabloc
Remarks: plate and bridges with perlage, polished steel parts and screw heads

CARL F. BUCHERER

Bucherer AG
Carl F. Bucherer
Langensandstrasse 27
CH-6002 Lucerne
Switzerland

Tel.:
+41-41-369-7070

Fax:
+41-41-369-7072

E-mail:
info@carl-f-bucherer.com

Website:
www.carl-f-bucherer.com

Founded:
1919, repositioned under the name Carl F.
Bucherer in 2001

Number of employees:
approx. 200

Annual production:
approx. 30,000 watches

U.S. distributor:
Carl F. Bucherer North America
1805 South Metro Parkway
Dayton, OH 45459
937-291-4366
info@cfbna.com; www.carl-f-bucherer.com

Most important collections/price range:
Patravi, Manero, Alacria and Pathos / core price
segment $5,000 to $30,000

While luxury watch brand Carl F. Bucherer is still rather young, the Lucerne-based Bucherer jewelry dynasty behind it draws its vast know-how from more than ninety years of experience in the conception and design of fine wristwatches.

The summer of 2005 ushered in a new age for the watch brand: Company decision makers chose to develop and manufacture an in-house mechanical movement. Together with Bucherer's longtime, Sainte-Croix-headquartered cooperative partner, Techniques Horlogères Appliquées SA (THA), an ambitious plan was hatched. When it became clear that such sophisticated construction could not be realized using outside suppliers, the next logical step was to purchase its partner's renowned atelier in the Jura mountains.

THA was integrated into the Bucherer Group and the watch company renamed Carl F. Bucherer Technologies SA (CFBT). The Sainte-Croix operation is led by technical director Dr. Albrecht Haake, who oversees a staff of about twenty. Dr. Haake is currently focusing much of his energy on furthering the capacities at the workshop. "Industrialization is not a question of cost, but rather a question of quality," says Haake.

The Swiss company also expanded its Lengnau location to create a competence center that can focus on manufacturing its own movements as well as in-house watches. The automatic caliber with the peripheral rotor went through a thorough revamping process with the idea of industrializing it. The general goal is to use it for new models that will consolidate the young brand's status as a manufacture.

Manero FlyBack
Reference number: 0010919.03.43.01
Movement: automatic, Caliber CFB 1970;
ø 30.4 mm, height 7.9 mm; 25 jewels; 28,800 vph;
42-hour power reserve
Functions: hours, minutes, subsidiary seconds;
flyback chronograph; date
Case: rose gold, ø 43 mm, height 14.45 mm;
sapphire crystal; transparent case back; water-resistant to 3 atm
Band: reptile skin, rose gold buckle
Price: $18,000

Manero FlyBack
Reference number: 00.10919.08.93.01
Movement: automatic, Caliber CFB 1970;
ø 30.4 mm, height 7.9 mm; 25 jewels; 28,800 vph;
42-hour power reserve
Functions: hours, minutes, subsidiary seconds;
flyback chronograph; date
Case: stainless steel, ø 43 mm, height 14.45 mm;
sapphire crystal; transparent case back; water-resistant to 3 atm
Band: reptile skin, folding buckle
Price: $6,900

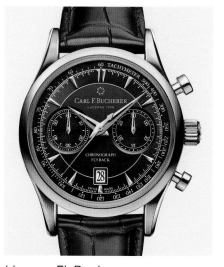

Manero FlyBack
Reference number: 00.10919.03.33.01
Movement: automatic, Caliber CFB 1970;
ø 30.4 mm, height 7.9 mm; 25 jewels; 28,800 vph;
42-hour power reserve
Functions: hours, minutes, subsidiary seconds;
flyback chronograph; date
Case: rose gold, ø 43 mm, height 14.45 mm;
sapphire crystal; transparent case back; water-resistant to 3 atm
Band: reptile skin, buckle
Price: $18,000

Manero Peripheral

Reference number: 00.10917.03.33.01
Movement: automatic, Caliber CFB A2050;
ø 30.6 mm, height 5.28 mm; 33 jewels; 28,800 vph;
peripheral rotor with tungsten oscillating mass;
55-hour power reserve; COSC-certified chronometer
Functions: hours, minutes, subsidiary seconds; date
Case: rose gold, ø 40.6 mm, height 11.2 mm;
sapphire crystal; transparent case back; water-
resistant to 3 atm
Band: reptile skin, buckle
Price: $17,800

Manero Peripheral

Reference number: 00.10917.08.23.01
Movement: automatic, Caliber CFB A2050;
ø 30.6 mm, height 5.28 mm; 33 jewels; 28,800 vph;
peripheral rotor with tungsten oscillating mass;
55-hour power reserve; COSC-certified chronometer
Functions: hours, minutes, subsidiary seconds; date
Case: stainless steel, ø 40.6 mm, height 11.2 mm;
sapphire crystal; transparent case back; water-
resistant to 3 atm
Band: reptile skin, folding buckle
Price: $7,200
Variations: black dial and band ($7,200), in pink
gold ($17,800)

Manero Peripheral Ladies

Reference number: 00.10917.08.83.11
Movement: automatic, Caliber CFB A2050;
ø 30.6 mm, height 5.28 mm; 33 jewels; 28,800 vph;
peripheral rotor with tungsten oscillating mass;
55-hour power reserve
Functions: hours, minutes, subsidiary seconds; date
Case: stainless steel, ø 40.6 mm, height 11.2 mm;
bezel set with 60 brilliant-cut diamonds; sapphire
crystal; transparent case back; water-resistant to
3 atm
Band: reptile skin, folding clasp
Remarks: mother-of-pearl dial
Price: $9,800

Manero Peripheral

Reference number: 00.10917.08.73.11
Movement: automatic, Caliber CFB A2050;
ø 30.6 mm, height 5.28 mm; 33 jewels; 28,800 vph;
peripheral rotor with tungsten oscillating mass;
55-hour power reserve
Functions: hours, minutes, subsidiary seconds; date
Case: stainless steel, ø 40.6 mm, height 11.2 mm;
bezel set with 60 brilliant-cut diamonds; sapphire
crystal; transparent case back; water-resistant to
3 atm
Band: reptile skin, folding clasp
Remarks: mother-of-pearl dial
Price: $9,800

Manero PowerReserve

Reference number: 00.10912.08.53.01
Movement: automatic, Caliber CFB A1011;
ø 32 mm, height 6.3 mm; 33 jewels; 21,600 vph;
peripheral rotor with tungsten oscillating mass;
55-hour power reserve
Functions: hours, minutes, subsidiary seconds;
power reserve indicator; large date, weekday
Case: stainless steel, ø 42.5 mm, height 12.54 mm;
sapphire crystal; transparent case back; screw-in
crown; water-resistant to 3 atm
Band: calfskin, folding clasp
Price: $11,000; limited to 188 pieces

Manero PowerReserve

Reference number: 00.10912.08.93.01
Movement: automatic, Caliber CFB A1011;
ø 32 mm, height 6.3 mm; 33 jewels; 21,600 vph;
peripheral rotor with tungsten oscillating mass;
55-hour power reserve
Functions: hours, minutes, subsidiary seconds;
power reserve indicator; large date, weekday
Case: stainless steel, ø 42.5 mm, height 12.54 mm;
sapphire crystal; transparent case back; screw-in
crown; water-resistant to 3 atm
Band: calfskin, folding clasp
Price: $11,000; limited to 188 pieces

Manero Tourbillon Limited Edition 2016

Reference number: 00.10918.02.33.99
Movement: manually wound, Caliber CFB T1001;
ø 33 mm, height 6.2 mm; 35 jewels; 21,600 vph;
1-minute tourbillon; 70-hour power reserve
Functions: hours, minutes, subsidiary seconds (on
tourbillon cage); second 24-hour display (second
time zone); power reserve indicator; date
Case: white gold, ø 41.8 mm, height 12.58 mm;
sapphire crystal; transparent case back; water-
resistant to 3 atm
Band: reptile skin, white gold folding clasp
Price: $108,000; limited to 188 pieces

Patravi TravelTec Black

Reference number: 00.10620.12.33.01
Movement: automatic, Caliber CFB 1901.1;
ø 28.6 mm, height 7.3 mm; 39 jewels; 28,800 vph;
42-hour power reserve; COSC-certified chronometer
Functions: hours, minutes, subsidiary seconds; three
time zone display; chronograph; date
Case: stainless steel with black DLC coating,
ø 46.6 mm, height 15.5 mm; pusher-activated
bidirectional inner bezel with 24-hour division (third
time zone); sapphire crystal; screw-in crown; water-
resistant to 5 atm
Band: rubber, folding clasp
Price: $13,600

Patravi ScubaTec

Reference number: 00.10632.22.53.01
Movement: automatic, Caliber CFB 1950.1;
ø 26.2 mm, height 4.8 mm; 25 jewels; 28,800 vph;
38-hour power reserve; COSC-certified chronometer
Functions: hours, minutes, sweep seconds; date
Case: pink gold, ø 44.6 mm, height 13.45 mm;
unidirectional bezel with ceramic insert and 0-60
scale; sapphire crystal; screw-in crown; automatic
helium valve and crown protection in black titanium;
water-resistant to 50 atm
Band: rubber, rose gold folding clasp with extension link
Price: $25,900
Variations: stainless steel with stainless steel bracelet
($6,800); stainless steel with rubber strap ($6,400);
rose gold and stainless steel with rubber strap ($9,800)

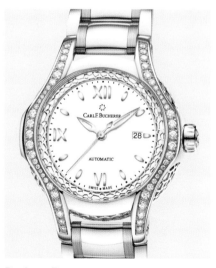

Pathos Diva

Reference number: 00.10580.08.25.31.01
Movement: automatic, Caliber CFB 1963; ø 20 mm,
height 4.8 mm; 25 jewels; 28,800 vph; 38-hour
power reserve
Functions: hours, minutes, sweep seconds; date
Case: stainless steel, ø 34 mm, height 9.65 mm;
sapphire crystal; transparent case back; water-
resistant to 3 atm
Band: stainless steel, folding clasp
Remarks: case set with 54 brilliants
Price: $10,000
Variations: rose gold ($29,300)

Pathos Diva

Reference number: 00.10580.03.75.31.01
Movement: automatic, Caliber CFB 1963; ø 20 mm,
height 4.8 mm; 25 jewels; 28,800 vph; 38-hour
power reserve
Functions: hours, minutes, sweep seconds; date
Case: rose gold, ø 34 mm, height 9.65 mm; sapphire
crystal; transparent case back; water-resistant to
3 atm
Band: rose gold, folding clasp
Remarks: case set with 54 brilliants
Price: $29,300
Variations: stainless steel ($10,000)

CFB A2050

Automatic; bidirectionally winding peripheral rotor
of tungsten on spring-based support ball bearings;
precision fine-adjustment system; single spring
barrel, 55-hour power reserve
Base caliber: CFB A2000
Functions: hours, minutes, subsidiary seconds; date
Diameter: 30.6 mm
Height: 5.28 mm
Jewels: 33
Balance: glucydur
Frequency: 28,800 vph
Balance spring: flat hairspring
Shock protection: Kif (for balance wheel), Incabloc
(for automatic module)

Cartier Joaillerie
Branch of Richemont Intl. SA
Rue André-De-Garrini 3
CH-1217 Meyrin
Switzerland

Tel:
+41-22-808-2500

Fax:
+41-22-808-2502

E-mail:
info@cartier.ch

Website:
www.cartier.ch

Founded:
1847

Number of employees:
approx. 1,300 (watch manufacturing)

U.S. distributor:
Cartier North America
645 Fifth Avenue
New York, NY 10022
1-800-CARTIER
www.cartier.us

Most important collections:
Ballon Bleu, Calibre, Clé, Drive, Pasha, Rotonde
de Cartier, Santos, Tank

CARTIER

Since the Richemont Group's founding, Cartier has played an important role in the luxury concern as its premier brand and instigator of turnover. Although it took a while for Cartier to find its footing and convince the male market of its masculinity, any concerns about Cartier's seriousness and potential are being dispelled by facts. "We aimed to become a key player in *haute horlogerie*, and we succeeded," said CEO Bernard Fornas at a July 2012 press conference at the company's main manufacturing site in La Chaux-de-Fonds. The company is growing by leaps and bounds—a components manufacturing site employing 400 people is being built at the expanding Richemont campus in Meyrin (Geneva).

It was Richemont Group's purchase of the Roger Dubuis *manufacture* in Geneva a few years ago that paved the way to the brand's independence and vertical integration. Under its brilliant head of fine watchmaking, Carole Forestier-Kasapi, Cartier has become a serious producer of movements, among them the 1904, which made its debut in the Calibre model. With a diameter of 42 mm, this strikingly designed men's watch is also well positioned in the segment. The designation 1904 MC is a reference to the year in which Louis Cartier developed the first wristwatch made for men—a pilot's watch custom designed for his friend and early pioneer of aviation, Alberto Santos-Dumont.

The automatic movement is a largely unadorned, yet efficient machine, powered by twin barrels. The central rotor sits on ceramic ball bearings, and the adjustment of the conventional escapement is by excenter screw. It is available for chronographs or diver's watches. But mainly, it has positioned Cartier as one of the most serious and effective makers of high-end watches in a very competitive industry.

Drive de Cartier Moon Phases

Reference number: WSNM0008
Movement: automatic, Cartier Caliber 1904-LU MC; ø 25 mm, height 5.2 mm; 25 jewels; 28,800 vph
Functions: hours, minutes; moon phase
Case: stainless steel, 40 × 41 mm, height 12 mm; sapphire crystal
Band: reptile skin, double folding clasp
Price: $7,850
Variations: pink gold ($19,500)

Drive de Cartier Extra-Thin

Reference number: WGNM0007
Movement: manually wound, Cartier Caliber 430 MC; ø 20 mm, height 2.15 mm; 18 jewels; 21,600 vph
Functions: hours, minutes
Case: white gold, 38 × 39 mm, height 6.6 mm; sapphire crystal; water-resistant to 3 atm
Band: reptile skin, buckle
Price: $15,300; limited to 200 pieces
Variations: pink gold ($14,300)

Drive de Cartier

Reference number: WSNM0004
Movement: automatic, Cartier Caliber 1904-PS MC; ø 24.9 mm, height 4.5 mm; 27 jewels; 28,800 vph; 48-hour power reserve
Functions: hours, minutes, subsidiary seconds; date
Case: stainless steel, 40 × 41 mm, height 11.3 mm; sapphire crystal; water-resistant to 3 atm
Band: reptile skin, double folding clasp
Price: $6,250
Variations: black dial; pink gold ($17,700)

Drive de Cartier Second Time Zone

Reference number: WSNM0005
Movement: automatic, Cartier Caliber 1904-FU MC; ø 25 mm, height 5.2 mm; 28 jewels; 28,800 vph; finely finished with côtes de Genève; 48-hour power reserve
Functions: hours, minutes, subsidiary seconds; additional 12-hour display (second time zone, retrograde), day/night indicator; large date
Case: stainless steel, 40 × 41 mm, height 12.63 mm; sapphire crystal; water-resistant to 3 atm
Band: reptile skin, double folding clasp
Price: $8,750
Variations: pink gold ($20,900)

Drive de Cartier Flying Tourbillon

Reference number: W4100013
Movement: manually wound, Cartier Caliber 9452 MC; ø 24.9 mm, height 4.5 mm; 19 jewels; 21,600 vph; flying 1-minute tourbillon; 52-hour power reserve
Functions: hours, minutes, subsidiary seconds (on tourbillon cage)
Case: pink gold, 40 × 41 mm, height 11.3 mm; sapphire crystal; transparent case back; water-resistant to 3 atm
Band: reptile skin, double folding clasp
Price: $78,500

Rotonde de Cartier Minute Repeater Double Tourbillon Mystérieux

Reference number: WHRO0023
Movement: manually wound, Cartier Caliber 9407 MC; ø 39 mm, height 6.05 mm; 45 jewels; 21,600 vph; double flying tourbillon between two sapphire disks; 84-hour power reserve; Geneva Seal
Functions: hours, minutes; minute repeater
Case: titanium, ø 45 mm, height 11.15 mm; sapphire crystal; transparent case back; water-resistant to 3 atm
Band: reptile skin, double folding clasp
Price: $471,000; limited to 50 pieces

Rotonde de Cartier Grande Complication Squelette

Reference number: W1556251
Movement: automatic, Cartier Caliber 9406 MC; ø 35 mm, height 5.49 mm; 47 jewels; 21,600 vph; flying 1-minute tourbillon, microrotor; extra-thin construction; 50-hour power reserve; Geneva Seal
Functions: hours, minutes; minute repeater; perpetual calendar with date, weekday, month
Case: platinum, ø 45 mm, height 12.6 mm; sapphire crystal; transparent case back; crown with sapphire cabochon; water-resistant to 3 atm
Band: reptile skin, double folding clasp
Remarks: skeletonized white gold dial
Price: $630,000

Rotonde de Cartier Astrotourbillon Skeleton

Reference number: W1556250
Movement: manually wound, Cartier Caliber 9461 MC; ø 38 mm, height 8.89 mm; 21,600 vph; skeletonized movement construction with integrated Roman hour numerals; 1-minute tourbillon; 48-hour power reserve
Functions: hours, minutes, sweep seconds (on tourbillon cage)
Case: white gold, ø 47 mm, height 15.5 mm; sapphire crystal; transparent case back; crown with sapphire cabochon
Band: reptile skin, double folding clasp
Price: $162,000

Rotonde de Cartier Double Tourbillon Mystérieux

Reference number: W1556210
Movement: manually wound, Cartier Caliber 9454 MC; ø 35 mm, height 5 mm; 25 jewels; 21,600 vph; double flying tourbillon between two sapphire disks; 52-hour power reserve; Geneva Seal
Functions: hours, minutes (off-center)
Case: platinum, ø 45 mm, height 12.4 mm; sapphire crystal; transparent case back; crown with sapphire cabochon
Band: reptile skin, double folding clasp
Price: $160,000

Rotonde de Cartier Annual Calendar

Reference number: WHRO0003
Movement: automatic, Cartier Caliber 9908 MC; ø 30 mm, height 5.9 mm; 32 jewels; 28,800 vph; 48-hour power reserve
Functions: hours, minutes; full calendar with large date, weekday, month
Case: white gold, ø 40 mm, height 13.26 mm; sapphire crystal; crown with sapphire cabochon; water-resistant to 3 atm
Band: reptile skin, double folding clasp
Price: $33,400
Variations: pink gold ($31,200)

Drive de Cartier Second Time Zone

Reference number: W1556368
Movement: automatic, Cartier Caliber 1904-FU MC; ø 25.6 mm; 28,800 vph; 48-hour power reserve
Functions: hours, minutes, subsidiary seconds; additional retrograde 12-hour display (second time zone), day/night indicator; large date
Case: stainless steel, ø 42 mm, height 11.96 mm; sapphire crystal; transparent case back; water-resistant to 3 atm
Band: reptile skin, folding clasp
Price: $9,300
Variations: pink gold ($23,100)

Rotonde de Cartier Power Reserve

Reference number: W1556369
Movement: manually wound, Cartier Caliber 9753 MC; ø 20.79 mm; 20 jewels; 21,600 vph; 40-hour power reserve
Functions: hours, minutes; power reserve indicator; date
Case: stainless steel, ø 40 mm, height 8.94 mm; sapphire crystal
Band: reptile skin, folding clasp
Price: $8,350
Variations: pink gold ($19,800)

Rotonde de Cartier Chronograph

Reference number: WSRO0002
Movement: automatic, Cartier Caliber 1904-CH MC; ø 25.6 mm, height 572 mm; 35 jewels; 28,800 vph; 2 spring barrels, 48-hour power reserve
Functions: hours, minutes; chronograph; date
Case: stainless steel, ø 40 mm, height 12.15 mm; sapphire crystal; transparent case back; water-resistant to 3 atm
Band: reptile skin, folding clasp
Price: $9,050
Variations: pink gold ($21,700); white gold ($23,300)

Rotonde de Cartier l'Heure Mystérieuse Squelette

Reference number: WHRO0014
Movement: manually wound, Cartier Caliber 9983 MC; ø 33 mm, height 6.15 mm; 27 jewels; 28,800 vph; hour and minute hands between two sapphire crystal disks; skeletonized movement construction with integrated Roman hour numerals; 48-hour power reserve
Functions: hours, minutes
Case: palladium, ø 42 mm, height 11 mm; sapphire crystal; transparent case back; crown with sapphire cabochon
Band: reptile skin, double folding clasp
Price: $65,500

Calibre de Cartier Diver Blue

Reference number: WGCA0009
Movement: automatic, Cartier Caliber 1904-PS MC; ø 25.6 mm, height 4 mm; 27 jewels; 28,800 vph; 2 spring barrels, 48-hour power reserve
Functions: hours, minutes, subsidiary seconds; date
Case: pink gold, ø 42 mm, height 11 mm; unidirectional bezel with ceramic insert and 0-60 scale; sapphire crystal; screw-in crown; water-resistant to 30 atm
Band: calfskin with rubber overlay, buckle
Price: $25,000
Variations: stainless steel ($7,900); stainless steel with pink gold bezel ($10,200)

Calibre de Cartier Diver Blue

Reference number: WSCA0011
Movement: automatic, Cartier Caliber 1904-PS MC; ø 25.6 mm, height 4 mm; 27 jewels; 28,800 vph; 2 spring barrels, 48-hour power reserve
Functions: hours, minutes, subsidiary seconds; date
Case: stainless steel, ø 42 mm, height 11 mm; bezel with ceramic insert, with 0-60 scale; sapphire crystal; screw-in crown; water-resistant to 30 atm
Band: calfskin with rubber overlay, buckle
Price: $7,900
Variations: black DLC coating ($7,900)

Calibre de Cartier Diver

Reference number: W7100056
Movement: automatic, Cartier Caliber 1904 MC; ø 25.6 mm, height 4 mm; 27 jewels; 28,800 vph; 2 spring barrels, 48-hour power reserve
Functions: hours, minutes, subsidiary seconds; date
Case: stainless steel, ø 42 mm, height 11 mm; bezel with black DLC coating, unidirectional, with 0-60 scale; sapphire crystal; screw-in crown; water-resistant to 30 atm
Band: rubber, buckle
Price: $7,900

Calibre de Cartier Diver

Reference number: W2CA0004
Movement: automatic, Cartier Caliber 1904-PS MC; ø 25.6 mm, height 4 mm; 27 jewels; 28,800 vph; 2 spring barrels, 48-hour power reserve
Functions: hours, minutes, subsidiary seconds; date
Case: stainless steel with black DLC coating, ø 42 mm, height 11 mm; unidirectional pink gold bezel with black numeral ring with 0-60 scale; sapphire crystal; screw-in crown; water-resistant to 30 atm
Band: rubber, buckle
Price: $10,200

Santos 100 Skeleton

Reference number: W2020018
Movement: manually wound, Cartier Caliber 9611 MC 28.6 × 28.6 mm, height 3.97 mm; 20 jewels; 21,600 vph; skeletonized movement with integrated Roman hour numerals; 2 spring barrels, 72-hour power reserve
Functions: hours, minutes
Case: palladium, 38.7 × 47.4 mm, height 16.5 mm; bezel with 8 screws; sapphire crystal; transparent case back; crown with sapphire cabochon; water-resistant to 3 atm
Band: reptile skin, folding clasp
Price: $53,500

Tank MC

Reference number: WSTA0010
Movement: automatic, Cartier Caliber 1904-PS MC; ø 25.6 mm, height 4 mm; 27 jewels; 28,800 vph; 2 spring barrels, 48-hour power reserve
Functions: hours, minutes, subsidiary seconds; date
Case: stainless steel, 34.3 × 44 mm, height 9.5 mm; sapphire crystal; transparent case back; water-resistant to 3 atm
Band: reptile skin, folding clasp
Price: $7,000
Variations: white dial; pink gold ($20,200)

Tank Louis Cartier Skeleton

Reference number: W5310012
Movement: manually wound, Cartier Caliber 9616 MC; 26 × 26.3 mm, height 3.6 mm; 21 jewels; 28,800 vph; skeletonized movement; 72-hour power reserve
Functions: 1-minute tourbillon
Case: white gold, 30 × 39.2 mm, height 7.45 mm; sapphire crystal; transparent case back; crown with sapphire cabochon; water-resistant to 3 atm
Band: reptile skin, folding clasp
Price: $44,600
Variations: pink gold ($44,600)

Caliber 9621 MC

Automatic; skeletonized movement construction with integrated Roman hour numerals; fully skeletonized winding rotor; double mainspring barrel, 72-hour power reserve
Functions: 1-minute tourbillon
Diameter: 31 mm
Height: 5.66 mm
Jewels: 28
Balance: glucydur
Frequency: 28,800 vph
Balance spring: flat hairspring

Caliber 9407 MC

Manually wound; double flying tourbillon between two sapphire disks; single spring barrel, 84-hour power reserve; Geneva Seal
Functions: hours, minutes; minute repeater; perpetual calendar with date, weekday, month
Diameter: 39.3 mm
Height: 6.05 mm
Jewels: 45
Balance: glucydur
Frequency: 21,600 vph
Balance spring: flat hairspring
Remarks: 448 components

Caliber 9983 MC

Manually wound; skeletonized movement construction with integrated Roman hour numerals; single spring barrel, 48-hour power reserve
Functions: 1-minute tourbillon (mysterious display between two sapphire disks with hidden drive)
Diameter: 36.7 mm
Height: 6.15 mm
Jewels: 27
Balance: glucydur
Frequency: 28,800 vph
Balance spring: flat hairspring
Remarks: 192 components

Caliber 1904-PS MC

Automatic; double mainspring barrel, 48-hour power reserve
Functions: hours, minutes, subsidiary seconds; date
Diameter: 25.6 mm
Height: 4 mm
Jewels: 27
Balance: glucydur
Frequency: 28,800 vph
Balance spring: flat hairspring
Remarks: finely finished with côtes de Genève

Caliber 1904-FU MC

Automatic; double mainspring barrel, 48-hour power reserve
Functions: hours, minutes, subsidiary seconds; additional 12-hour display (second time zone), day/night indicator; large date
Diameter: 25 mm
Height: 5.2 mm
Jewels: 28
Balance: glucydur
Frequency: 28,800 vph
Balance spring: flat hairspring
Remarks: finely finished with côtes de Genève

Caliber 9406 MC

Automatic; flying 1-minute tourbillon, microrotor; extra-thin construction; single spring barrel, 50-hour power reserve; Geneva Seal
Functions: hours, minutes; minute repeater; perpetual calendar with date, weekday, month
Diameter: 39.3 mm
Height: 5.49 mm
Jewels: 47
Balance: glucydur
Frequency: 21,600 vph
Balance spring: flat hairspring
Remarks: first "grande complication" designed and made in-house by Cartier Manufacture; 578 components

CHANEL

After putting the occasional jewelry watch onto the market earlier, the family-owned Chanel opened its own horology division in 1987, a move that gave the brand instant access to the world of watchmaking art. Chanel boasts its own studio and logistics center, both in La Chaux-de-Fonds. While the brand's first collections were directed exclusively at its female clientele, it was actually with the rather simple and masculine J12 that Chanel finally achieved a breakthrough. Designer Jacques Helleu says he designed the unpretentious ceramic watch mainly for himself. "I wanted a timeless watch in glossy black," shares the likable eccentric. Indeed, it's not hard to imagine that the J12 will still look modern a number of years down the road—especially given the fact that the watch now comes in white and shiny polished titanium/ceramic as well.

The J12 collection showpiece, the Rétrograde Mystérieuse, was a stroke of genius—courtesy of the innovative think tank Renaud et Papi. It instantly propelled Chanel into the world of *haute horlogerie*. And the brand has not been resting on any laurels. Lately, it entirely redid the ladies' watch Première, even though the change is not obvious at first glance. The octagonal shape of Place Vendôme in Paris (home of the brand) and the famous Chanel No. 5 bottle stopper are still there, and the simple 1980s style, but with a narrower bezel and adapted hands.

Chanel has started steering toward a younger, dynamic crowd with two collections that suggest a rapprochement between the sexes: The "Vendôme" rectangular Boy. Friend marries a feeling of subdued luxury and asceticism. Same for Monsieur de Chanel, a purist, 40-mm watch with jumping hour and retrograde minutes driven by the Caliber 1. The new Première Camélia, driven by the Caliber 2, continues in this vein, with a movement skeletonized to form a camellia. The watch comes in three versions bearing various amounts of diamonds.

Chanel
135, avenue Charles de Gaulle
F-92521 Neuilly-sur-Seine Cedex
France

Tel.:
+33-1-41-92-08-33

Website:
www.chanel.com

Founded:
1914

Distribution:
retail and 200 Chanel boutiques worldwide

U.S. distributor:
Chanel Fine Jewelry and Watches
600 Madison Avenue, 19th Floor
New York, NY 10022
212-715-4741
212-715-4155 (fax)
www.chanel.com

Most important collections:
J12, Première, Boy.Friend, Monsieur de Chanel

Monsieur de Chanel
Reference number: H4800
Movement: manually wound, Chanel Caliber I; ø 32 mm, height 5.5 mm; 30 jewels; 28,800 vph; 2 spring barrels; plate/bridges with perlage; 72-hour power reserve
Functions: hours (digital, jumping), minutes (retrograde), subsidiary seconds
Case: beige gold, ø 40 mm, height 10.4 mm; sapphire crystal; transparent back; water-resistant to 3 atm
Band: reptile skin, buckle
Remarks: opaline dial
Price: $34,500
Variations: white gold ($36,000)

Première Camélia Skeleton
Reference number: H5251
Movement: manually wound, Chanel Caliber 2; ø 32 mm, height 5.5 mm; 21 jewels; 28,800 vph; 1 barrel spring; skeletonized movement shaped like a camellia; 48-hour power reserve
Functions: hours, minutes
Case: white gold, ø 37 mm × 28.5 × 10.6 mm; set with 47 diamonds, bezel set with 94 diamonds; crown set with 11 diamonds; sapphire crystal; transparent back; water-resistant to 3 atm
Band: satin, double folding clasp
Remarks: movement set with 246 diamonds
Price: $34,500
Variations: bezel, hands, and crown set with diamonds and dial only set with diamonds ($183,500); bracelet, bezel, movement, crown set with diamonds ($444,200)

J12 Collector Mirror
Reference number: H4862
Movement: automatic, ETA Caliber 2824-2; ø 25.6 mm, height 4.6 mm; 25 jewels; 28,800 vph; 42-hour power reserve
Functions: hours, minutes, sweep seconds; date
Case: ceramic, ø 38 mm, height 13 mm; white gold bezel with ceramic inserts, unidirectional bezel with 60-minute division; sapphire crystal; screw-in crown; water-resistant to 20 atm
Band: ceramic, double folding clasp
Price: $5,400; limited to 1,200 pieces
Variations: various colors with 33-mm case

Chopard & Cie. SA
8, rue de Veyrot
CH-1217 Meyrin (Geneva)
Switzerland

Tel.:
+41-22-719-3131

E-mail:
info@chopard.ch

Website:
www.chopard.ch

Founded:
1860

Distribution:
160 boutiques

U.S. distributor:
Chopard USA
75 Valencia Ave, Suite 1200
Coral Gables, FL 33134
1-800-CHOPARD
www.us.chopard.com

Most important collections/price range:
Superfast / $9,230 to $33,190; L.U.C / $7,860
to $250,000; Imperiale / $4,390 to $250,000;
Classic Racing / $5,070 to $43,880; Happy
Sport / $5,040 to $250,000

CHOPARD

The Chopard *manufacture* was founded by Louis-Ulysse Chopard in 1860 in the tiny village of Sonvillier in the Jura mountains of Switzerland. In 1963, it was purchased by Karl Scheufele, a goldsmith from Pforzheim, Germany, and revived as a producer of fine watches and jewelry.

The past seventeen years have seen a breathtaking development, when Karl Scheufele's son, Karl-Friedrich, and his sister, Caroline, decided to create watches with in-house movements, thus restoring the old business launched by Louis-Ulysse back in the nineteenth century.

In the 1990s, literally out of nowhere, Chopard opened up its watchmaking *manufacture* in the sleepy town of Fleurier in the Val-de-Travers, which had not yet experienced the revival of the mechanical watch. Karl-Friedrich Scheufele was convinced that the future of the industry lay in producing high-end timepieces, in spite of what many competitors were saying. The success of the L.U.C models with their own calibers silenced the doubters, even more so when ETA began restricting its sales of base calibers to the industry. Over twenty years later, Chopard's own Fleurier Ebauches SA has restored Fleurier's tradition as a hub of *ébauche* (movement kits) production. Chopard now has a line-up of eleven calibers, ranging from simple three-hander automatics to a tourbillon, a perpetual calendar, chronographs, an ultra-high-frequency chronometer, and a minute repeater.

The company also continues to support the Geneva Watchmaking School with special *ébauches* for the students, a demonstration of its commitment to the industry. With its wide range of *manufacture* watch models and over 160 boutiques worldwide, the brand enjoys firm footing in the rarified air of *haute horlogerie*.

Mille Miglia 2017 Race Edition
Reference number: 168571-3002
Movement: automatic, ETA Caliber 7750;
ø 30.4 mm, height 7.9 mm; 25 jewels; 28,800 vph;
48-hour power reserve; COSC-certified chronometer
Functions: hours, minutes, subsidiary seconds;
chronograph; date
Case: stainless steel, ø 44 mm, height 13.79 mm;
sapphire crystal; water-resistant to 10 atm
Band: rubber, folding clasp
Price: $6,840; limited to 1,000 pieces

Mille Miglia Classic Chronograph
Reference number: 168589-3002
Movement: automatic, ETA Caliber 2894-2;
ø 28.6 mm, height 6.1 mm; 37 jewels; 28,800 vph;
42-hour power reserve; COSC-certified chronometer
Functions: hours, minutes, subsidiary seconds;
chronograph; date
Case: stainless steel, ø 42 mm, height 12.67 mm;
sapphire crystal; transparent case back; water-
resistant to 5 atm
Band: rubber, buckle
Price: $5,000

Mille Miglia Classic XL
90th Anniversary Limited Edition
Reference number: 161299-5001
Movement: automatic, L.U.C Caliber 03.07-L;
ø 28.6 mm, height 7.6 mm; 38 jewels; 28,800 vph;
balance cock of German silver; 60-hour power
reserve; Geneva Seal, COSC-certified chronometer
Functions: hours, minutes, subsidiary seconds;
flyback chronograph
Case: rose gold, ø 46 mm, height 13.12 mm;
sapphire crystal; transparent case back; water-
resistant to 5 atm
Band: calfskin, folding clasp
Price: $43,880; limited to 90 pieces

Mille Miglia GTS Power Control

Reference number: 168566-3001
Movement: automatic, Chopard Manufacture
Caliber 01.08-C; ø 28.8 mm, height 4.95 mm;
40 jewels; 28,800 vph; 60-hour power reserve;
COSC-certified chronometer
Functions: hours, minutes, sweep seconds; power
reserve indicator; date
Case: stainless steel, ø 43 mm, height 11.43 mm;
sapphire crystal; transparent case back; screw-in
crown; water-resistant to 10 atm
Band: rubber, folding clasp
Price: $6,020
Variations: stainless steel bracelet ($7,480); rose
gold ($20,300)

Mille Miglia GT XL Chrono

Reference number: 161293-5001
Movement: automatic, ETA Caliber 7750;
ø 30.4 mm, height 7.9 mm; 25 jewels; 28,800 vph;
48-hour power reserve; COSC-certified chronometer
Functions: hours, minutes, subsidiary seconds;
chronograph; date
Case: rose gold, ø 44 mm, height 13.79 mm;
sapphire crystal; screw-in crown; water-resistant to
10 atm
Band: rubber, folding clasp
Price: $21,420
Variations: stainless steel ($6,740)

Classic Racing Porsche 919 Edition

Reference number: 168535-3002
Movement: automatic, Chopard Manufacture
Caliber 03.05-M; ø 28.8 mm, height 7.6 mm;
45 jewels; 28,800 vph; 60-hour power reserve;
COSC-certified chronometer
Functions: hours, minutes, subsidiary seconds;
flyback chronograph; date
Case: stainless steel, ø 45 mm, height 15.18 mm;
sapphire crystal; transparent case back; screw-in
crown; water-resistant to 10 atm
Band: rubber, folding clasp
Price: $11,680; limited to 919 pieces

L.U.C Time Traveller One

Reference number: 161942-9001
Movement: automatic, L.U.C Caliber 01.05-L;
ø 35.3 mm, height 6.52 mm; 39 jewels; 28,800 vph;
60-hour power reserve; COSC-certified chronometer
Functions: hours, minutes, sweep seconds; world
time indicator (second time zone); date
Case: platinum, ø 42 mm, height 12.09 mm; crown-
adjustable inner bezel with reference city names;
sapphire crystal; transparent case back; water-
resistant to 5 atm
Band: reptile skin, buckle
Price: $35,910

L.U.C Perpetual Chrono

Reference number: 161973-9001
Movement: manually wound, L.U.C Caliber
03.10-L; ø 33 mm, height 8.32 mm; 42 jewels;
28,800 vph; mainplate and balance cock of German
silver; 60-hour power reserve; Geneva Seal, COSC-
certified chronometer
Functions: hours, minutes, sweep seconds; day/
night indicator; flyback chronograph; perpetual
calendar with large date, weekday, month, moon
phase, leap year
Case: platinum, ø 45 mm, height 15.06 mm; sapphire
crystal; transparent case back; water-resistant to 3 atm
Band: reptile skin, folding clasp
Price: on request; limited to 20 pieces

L.U.C Perpetual Twin

Reference number: 168561-3001
Movement: automatic, L.U.C Caliber 96.51-L;
ø 33 mm, height 6 mm; 32 jewels; 28,800 vph;
2 barrel springs, gold microrotor with côtes de
Genève; 58-hour power reserve; COSC-certified
chronometer
Functions: hours, minutes, subsidiary seconds;
perpetual calendar with large date, weekday, month,
leap year
Case: stainless steel, ø 43 mm, height 11.47 mm;
sapphire crystal; transparent case back; water-
resistant to 3 atm
Band: reptile skin, buckle
Price: $23,350

L.U.C Lunar One

Reference number: 161927-5001
Movement: automatic, L.U.C Caliber 96.13-L;
ø 33 mm, height 6 mm; 32 jewels; 28,800 vph;
65-hour power reserve; Geneva Seal, COSC-certified
chronometer
Functions: hours, minutes, subsidiary seconds;
second 24-hour display (second time zone);
perpetual calendar with large date, weekday, month,
orbital moon phase display, leap year
Case: rose gold, ø 43 mm, height 11.47 mm; sapphire
crystal; transparent case back; water-resistant to 5 atm
Band: reptile skin, folding clasp
Price: $57,670
Variations: diamond bezel ($89,360); white gold
($57,670)

L.U.C Lunar Big Date

Reference number: 161969-1001
Movement: automatic, L.U.C Caliber 96.20-L;
ø 33 mm, height 5.25 mm; 33 jewels; 28,800 vph;
with côtes de Genève; 65-hour power reserve; COSC-
certified chronometer
Functions: hours, minutes, subsidiary seconds; large
date, moon phase
Case: white gold, ø 42 mm, height 11.04 mm;
sapphire crystal; transparent case back; water-
resistant to 5 atm
Band: reptile skin, buckle
Price: $28,770
Variations: rose gold ($28,770)

L.U.C Quattro

Reference number: 161926-5001
Movement: manually wound, L.U.C Caliber
98.01-L; ø 28.6 mm, height 3.7 mm; 39 jewels;
28,800 vph; 4 barrel springs, swan-neck fine
regulation, gold rotor; 216-hour power reserve;
Geneva Seal, COSC-certified chronometer
Functions: hours, minutes, subsidiary seconds;
power reserve indicator; date
Case: rose gold, ø 43 mm, height 8.84 mm; sapphire
crystal; transparent case back; water-resistant to
5 atm
Band: reptile skin, buckle
Price: $24,040
Variations: white gold ($24,040); platinum
($29,580)

L.U.C Tourbillon Qualité Fleurier Fairmined Gold

Reference number: 161929-5006
Movement: manually wound, L.U.C Caliber
02.13-L; ø 29.7 mm, height 6.1 mm; 33 jewels;
28,800 vph; 1-minute tourbillon, bridges with côtes
de Genève; 216-hour power reserve; COSC-certified
chronometer, Qualité Fleurier
Functions: hours, minutes, subsidiary seconds;
power reserve indicator
Case: rose gold, ø 43 mm, height 11.15 mm; sapphire
crystal; transparent case back; water-resistant to 5 atm
Band: reptile skin, buckle
Remarks: case manufactured of fair-traded certified
gold
Price: on request; limited to 25 pieces

L.U.C 1963 Tourbillon

Reference number: 161970-5001
Movement: manually wound, L.U.C Caliber
02.19-L; ø 29.7 mm, height 6.25 mm; 33 jewels;
28,800 vph; 1-minute tourbillon; 216-hour power
reserve; Geneva Seal, COSC-certified chronometer
Functions: hours, minutes, subsidiary seconds;
power reserve indicator
Case: pink gold, ø 40 mm, height 10.6 mm; sapphire
crystal; transparent case back; water-resistant to
5 atm
Band: reptile skin, buckle
Price: on request; limited to 100 pieces

L.U.C Perpetual T

Reference number: 161940-9001
Movement: manually wound, L.U.C Caliber
02.15-L; ø 33 mm, height 9.35 mm; 31 jewels;
28,800 vph; 1-minute tourbillon, 4 barrel springs,
216-hour power reserve; Geneva Seal, COSC-
certified chronometer
Functions: hours, minutes, subsidiary seconds;
second 24-hour display (second time zone), power
reserve indicator (on the case back); perpetual
calendar with large date, weekday, month, leap year
Case: platinum, ø 43 mm, height 14.9 mm; sapphire
crystal; transparent case back; water-resistant to 3 atm
Band: reptile skin, folding clasp
Price: on request; limited to 25 pieces
Variations: rose gold (on request)

L.U.C GMT One

Reference number: 168579-3001
Movement: automatic, L.U.C Caliber 01.10-L;
ø 31.9 mm, height 5.95 mm; 31 jewels; 28,800 vph;
bridges with côtes de Genève; 60-hour power
reserve; COSC-certified chronometer
Functions: hours, minutes, sweep seconds; second
24-hour display (second time zone); date
Case: stainless steel, ø 42 mm, height 11.71 mm;
sapphire crystal; transparent case back; water-
resistant to 5 atm
Band: reptile skin, buckle
Price: $9,690
Variations: rose gold ($19,590)

L.U.C XPS Twist QF Fairmined

Reference number: 161945-5001
Movement: automatic, L.U.C Caliber 96-09-L;
ø 27.4 mm, height 3.3 mm; 29 jewels; 28,800 vph;
2 barrel springs, gold microrotor; 65-hour power
reserve; COSC-certified chronometer, Qualité Fleurier
Functions: hours, minutes, subsidiary seconds
Case: rose gold, ø 40 mm, height 7.2 mm; sapphire
crystal; transparent case back; screw-in crown; water-
resistant to 3 atm
Band: reptile skin, buckle
Remarks: case manufactured of Fairmined certified
gold
Price: $18,850; limited to 250 pieces

L.U.C Regulator

Reference number: 161971-5001
Movement: manually wound, L.U.C Caliber
98.02-L; ø 30.4 mm, height 4.9 mm; 39 jewels;
28,800 vph; 4 barrel springs, bridges with côtes
de Genève; 216-hour power reserve; Geneva Seal,
COSC-certified chronometer
Functions: hours (off-center), minutes, subsidiary
seconds; second 24-hour display (second time zone),
power reserve indicator; date
Case: rose gold, ø 43 mm, height 9.78 mm; sapphire
crystal; transparent case back; water-resistant to
3 atm
Band: reptile skin, buckle
Price: $30,400

L.U.C XPS

Reference number: 161920-5001
Movement: automatic, L.U.C Caliber 96.12-L;
ø 27.4 mm, height 3.3 mm; 29 jewels; 28,800 vph;
gold rotor, bridges with côtes de Genève; 65-hour
power reserve; COSC-certified chronometer
Functions: hours, minutes, subsidiary seconds
Case: rose gold, ø 39.5 mm, height 7.13 mm;
sapphire crystal; transparent case back; water-
resistant to 3 atm
Band: reptile skin, buckle
Price: $16,780
Variations: white gold ($16,780)

L.U.C XPS 1860 Edition

Reference number: 168583-3001
Movement: automatic, L.U.C Caliber 96.03-L;
ø 27.4 mm, height 3.3 mm; 29 jewels; 28,800 vph;
2 barrel springs, 65-hour power reserve; COSC-
certified chronometer
Functions: hours, minutes, subsidiary seconds; date
Case: stainless steel, ø 40 mm, height 7.2 mm;
sapphire crystal; transparent case back; water-
resistant to 3 atm
Band: reptile skin, buckle
Price: $8,580
Variations: rose gold ($20,660)

L.U.C XPS 1860 Edition

Reference number: 161946-5001
Movement: automatic, L.U.C Caliber 96.01-L;
ø 27.4 mm, height 3.3 mm; 29 jewels; 28,800 vph;
2 barrel springs, gold rotor; 65-hour power reserve;
Geneva Seal, COSC-certified chronometer
Functions: hours, minutes, subsidiary seconds; date
Case: rose gold, ø 40 mm, height 7.2 mm; sapphire
crystal; transparent case back; water-resistant to
3 atm
Band: reptile skin, buckle
Price: $20,660; limited to 250 pieces
Variations: in stainless steel ($8,580)

Caliber L.U.C 01.10-L

Automatic; single spring barrel, 60-hour power reserve; COSC-certified chronometer
Functions: hours, minutes, sweep seconds; second 24-hour display (second time zone); date
Diameter: 31.9 mm
Height: 5.95 mm
Jewels: 31
Balance: glucydur
Frequency: 28,800 vph
Balance spring: flat hairspring, Nivarox 1
Remarks: 291 components

Caliber L.U.C 03.10-L

Manually wound; mainplate and balance cock of German silver; single spring barrel, 60-hour power reserve; Geneva Seal, COSC-certified chronometer
Functions: hours, minutes, sweep seconds; day/night indicator; flyback chronograph; perpetual calendar with large date, weekday, month, moon phase, leap year
Diameter: 33 mm
Height: 8.32 mm
Jewels: 42
Balance: Variner with 4 weighted screws
Frequency: 28,800 vph
Balance spring: flat hairspring

Caliber L.U.C 96.01-L

Automatic; gold microrotor; double spring barrel, 65-hour power reserve; Geneva Seal, COSC-certified chronometer
Functions: hours, minutes, subsidiary seconds; date
Diameter: 27.4 mm
Height: 3.3 mm
Jewels: 29
Balance: glucydur
Frequency: 28,800 vph
Balance spring: flat hairspring, Nivarox 1

Caliber L.U.C 98.01-L

Manually wound; swan-neck fine regulation; quadruple spring barrel running in twin series barrel springs, 216-hour power reserve; Geneva Seal, COSC-certified chronometer
Functions: hours, minutes, subsidiary seconds; power reserve indicator; date
Diameter: 28.6 mm
Height: 3.7 mm
Jewels: 39
Frequency: 28,800 vph
Balance spring: Breguet hairspring

Caliber L.U.C 02.13-L

Manually wound; 1-minute tourbillon; quadruple spring barrel, 216-hour power reserve; Geneva Seal, COSC-certified chronometer, Qualité Fleurier
Functions: hours, minutes, subsidiary seconds (on tourbillon cage); power reserve indicator
Diameter: 29.7 mm
Height: 6.1 mm
Jewels: 33
Frequency: 28,800 vph
Balance spring: flat hairspring

Caliber L.U.C 03.07-L

Manually wound; column wheel control of chronograph functions, vertical chronograph clutch; single spring barrel, 60-hour power reserve; Geneva Seal, COSC-certified chronometer
Functions: hours, minutes, subsidiary seconds; date
Diameter: 28.8 mm
Height: 5.62 mm
Jewels: 38
Balance: Variner with 4 weighted screws
Frequency: 28,800 vph
Balance spring: flat hairspring
Remarks: perlage on plate, bridges beveled and with with côtes de Genève, polished steel parts and screw heads

CHRISTIAAN VAN DER KLAAUW

Christiaan van der Klaauw
Astronomical Watches
8447 SL Heerenveen
The Netherlands

Tel.:
+31-513-624-906

E-mail:
info@klaauw.com

Website:
www.klaauw.com

Founded:
1974

Annual production:
200–300 watches

U.S. distributor:
Tourneau
510 Madison Avenue
New York, NY 10022
212-758-5830

Most important collections:
astronomical watches

Christiaan van der Klaauw was one of the earliest members of the famous AHCI, the Académie Horlogère des Créateurs Indépendents (Horological Academy of Independent Creators), in Switzerland. His main focus since 1976 has been on astronomical watches. He did not have to search long for a role model: The most obvious choice was Christiaan Huygens. The famous physicist and mathematician built the first pendulum clock. Like van der Klaauw, he too came from the Netherlands. And so did the astronomer Eise Eisinga, who set up a model of the solar system in his living room in 1774 to prove to people that the moon, Mars, Jupiter, Mercury, and Venus would not collide with our own planet.

During his studies of microengineering, van der Klaauw worked in the world's oldest observatory (founded by J. H. Oort in 1633) and had already begun building astrolabes, planetaria, and complicated calendar watches.

The astronomical watch he completed in 1990 turned out to be his passport to the AHCI. From then on, van der Klaauw drove the watch world forward with his many elaborate creations. A new era began in 2009 for Christiaan van der Klaauw: A partnership with the Dutch designer Daniel Reintjes evolved into a full-fledged investment model with two other partners. The very modest master watchmaker could then concentrate on what he likes to do best: designing, inventing, tinkering. The brand's portfolio of astronomical watches has grown steadily. Van der Klaauw has also put time and talent into developing modern interpretations of astronomical displays for other brands, such as the complex planetarium module for Van Cleef & Arpels.

Supernova
Reference number: CKSN3326
Movement: automatic, Caliber CK7760 (base ETA 7751); ø 30 mm, height 7.9 mm; 25 jewels; 28,800 vph; 48-hour power reserve
Functions: hours, minutes, sweep seconds; full calendar with date, weekday, month, Luminova moon phase
Case: stainless steel, ø 44 mm, height 13 mm; sapphire crystal; transparent case back
Band: reptile skin, folding clasp
Price: $8,262

Orion
Reference number: CKOR3326
Movement: automatic, Caliber CK1072 (base Soprod A10); ø 25.6 mm, height 3.6 mm; 25 jewels; 28,800 vph; planisphere turns counterclockwise once per sidereal day (23 hours, 56 minutes, 4 seconds); 42-hour power reserve
Functions: hours, minutes, sweep seconds; planisphere (map of skies) with zodiac
Case: stainless steel, ø 40 mm, height 13.5 mm; sapphire crystal; transparent case back
Band: reptile skin, buckle folding clasp
Price: $16,728
Variations: rose gold ($33,558)

Real Moon 1980
Reference number: CKRL1124
Movement: automatic, Caliber CK7384 (base TT 738); ø 30 mm, height 4.35 mm; 35 jewels; 28,800 vph; double spring barrel, hand-engraved gold rotor; 96-hour power reserve
Functions: hours, minutes; annual calendar with date, month, 3D moon phase, declination of the sun, solar and lunar eclipse indicator
Case: rose gold, ø 40 mm, height 13 mm; sapphire crystal; transparent case back
Band: reptile skin, buckle
Remarks: sculptural spherical moon; homage to 1980 astronomical clock made by Christiaan van der Klaauw
Price: $65,229

Christophe Claret SA
Route du Soleil d'Or 2
CH-2400 Le Locle
Switzerland

Tel.:
+41-32-933-0000

Fax:
+41-32-933-8081

E-mail:
info@christopheclaret.com

Website:
www.christopheclaret.com

Founded:
manufacture 1989, brand 2010

Number of employees:
100

Distribution:
Contact the *manufacture* directly.

Most important collections:
Traditional complications (Allegro/Aventicum/
Maestoso/Kantharos/Soprano), Extreme line
(X-TREM-1/DualTow), gaming watches (Poker/
Baccara/Blackjack), and ladies' complications
line (Margot)

CHRISTOPHE CLARET

Individuals like Christophe Claret are authentic horological engineers who eat, drink, and breathe watchmaking and have developed careers based on pushing the envelope to the very edge of what's possible. By the age of twenty-three, the Lyon-born Claret was in Basel alongside Journe, Calabrese, and other independents. The late Rolf Schnyder of Ulysse Nardin commissioned him to make a minute repeater with jacquemarts. In 1989, he opened his *manufacture*, a nineteenth-century mansion tastefully extended with a state-of-the-art machining area. Claret embraces wholeheartedly the potential in modern tools to create the precise pieces needed to give physical expression to exceedingly complex ideas. In 2004, he came out with the Harry Winston Opus IV, a reversible moon phase with tourbillon and minute repeater.

Twenty years after establishing his business, Claret finally launched his own complex watches: models like the DualTow, with its hours and minutes on two tracks, minute repeater, and complete view of the great ballet of arms and levers inside. Then came the Adagio, again a minute repeater, with a clear dial that manages a second time zone and large date. In 2011, Claret wowed the watch world with a humorous, on-the-wrist gambling machine telling time and playing blackjack, craps, or roulette. It was followed by the stunning X-TREM-1, a turbocharged DualTow with two spheres controlled by magnets hovering along the numeral tracks to tell the time, plus a tourbillon. Whatever he produces—the Margot, for women; the art-laden Aventicum; or the latest minute repeater, the Allegro—the Claret signature is always present: a total dedication to power mechanics and an infallible sense of style. The winding rotor of the Marguerite, a high-end mechanical ladies' watch, features rubies that will point to "He loves me" or "He loves me not" engraved on the case back and separated by a little heart.

Maestro

Reference number: MTR.DMC16.000-088
Movement: manually wound, Christophe Claret Caliber DMC16; ø 36.25 mm, height 10.5 mm; 33 jewels; 21,600 vph; inverted movement design with dial-side escapement; 168-hour power reserve
Functions: hours, minutes, manually controlled memo display; large date (double-digit) on pyramid base
Case: rose gold, ø 42 mm, height 16 mm; sapphire crystal; transparent case back
Band: reptile skin, folding clasp
Price: $76,000; limited to 88 pieces
Variations: titanium, limited to 88 pieces ($68,000)

X-Trem-1 StingHD

Reference number: MTR.FLY11.160-168
Movement: manually wound, Christophe Claret Caliber FLY11 × 26.6 × 46.4 mm, height 11.94 mm; 66 jewels; 21,600 vph; 2 separate spring barrels for movement and time indication; flying tourbillon on ball bearing, with 30° tilt
Functions: hours, minutes (linear display using steel beads hovering in lateral meshed tubes)
Case: titanium with black PVD coating, 40.8 × 56.8 mm, height 15 mm; sapphire crystal
Band: galuchat, folding clasp
Remarks: comes with personalized strap and strap with StingHD jewels; chrome-plated aluminum skull motif with rubies by StingHD on tourbillon cage; blowing on sapphire crystal makes skull appear
Price: $278,000; limited to 8 pieces

Marguerite

Reference number: MTR.MT115.200-230
Movement: automatic, Christophe Claret Caliber MT115; ø 35.7 mm, height 9.67 mm; 36 jewels; 28,800 vph; 2 spring barrels, 72-hour power reserve
Functions: hours, minutes (with butterfly hands); dial-side text can be called up by pusher, alternating with numerals (customizable)
Case: pink gold, ø 42.5 mm, height 12 mm; bezel and lugs set with 609 diamonds; sapphire crystal; transparent case back
Remarks: "He loves me, he loves me not . . ." engraved on winding rotor to indicate yes/no
Price: $88,000; limited to 30 pieces
Variations: white gold ($69,000)

CHRONOSWISS

Chronoswiss has been assembling its signature watches—which boast such features as coin edge bezels and onion crowns—since 1983. Founder Gerd-Rüdiger Lang loved to joke about having "the only Swiss watch factory in Germany," as the brand has always adhered closely to the qualities of the Swiss watch industry while still contributing a great deal to reviving mechanical watches from its facilities in Karlsfeld near Munich, with concepts and designs "made in Germany."

There was more. Lang also created regulator watches in the 1980s, a pioneering idea that found many fans of new ways to tell the time. This is also part of the brand's history and DNA, a remarkable feat, and somewhat anachronistic back then. Chronoswiss has always been a little on the edge of the industry in terms of style and technical developments. It created the enduring *manufacture* caliber C.122—based on an old Enicar automatic movement with a patented rattrapante mechanism—and its Chronoscope chronograph has earned a solid reputation for technical prowess. The Pacific and Sirius models, additions to the classic collection, point the company in a new stylistic direction designed to help win new buyers and the attention of the international market.

In March 2012, a Swiss couple, Oliver and Eva Ebstein, purchased Chronoswiss and soon afterward moved the company headquarters to Lucerne, Switzerland. The Ebsteins are watch enthusiasts and intended from the start to keep Chronoswiss as an independent family-run company, though now with a direct connection to Switzerland. There were to be no great shake-ups.

Recent models reveal the brand to be faithful to its regulator and coin edges, and the large crown, though the dial has acquired a three-dimensional design. The Flying Regulator and the Regulator Jumping Hour find the minute hand hovering freely over the dial, with the hours and seconds on bridges. The name "Atelier Lucerne" appears on the dial, a hint of the new premises, but the trusty C.122 beats inside many of these new models.

Chronoswiss AG
Löwenstrasse 16a
CH-6004 Lucerne
Switzerland

Tel.:
+41-41-552-2100

Fax:
+41-41-552-2109

E-mail:
mail@chronoswiss.com

Website:
www.chronoswiss.com

Founded:
1983

Number of employees:
approx. 30

Annual production:
up to 5,000 wristwatches

U.S. distributor:
Chronoswiss US Service Office
Shami Fine Watchmaking
Adam Shami
155 Willowbrook Blvd.
Suite 320
Wayne, NJ 07470
Tel.: 973-785-0004
Fax.: 973-785-0055

Most important collections/price range:
approx. 30 models including Sirius Regulator, Sirius Triple Date, Sirius Perpetual Calendar, Sirius Artist, Timemaster Big Date, Timemaster Chronograph GMT / approx. $3,550 to $47,000

Flying Grand Regulator Skeleton

Reference number: CH-6723S-BKRE
Movement: manually wound, Chronoswiss Caliber C.677S; ø 37.2 mm, height 4.5 mm; 17 jewels; 18,000 vph; screw balance, swan-neck fine regulation, skeletonized mainplate, bridges, and gearwheels; finely finished movement; 46-hour power reserve
Functions: hours (off-center), minutes, subsidiary seconds
Case: stainless steel, ø 44 mm, height 12.48 mm; sapphire crystal; transparent case back; water-resistant to 3 atm
Band: reptile skin, folding clasp
Price: $10,540; limited to 30 pieces
Variations: pink gold ($22,530; limited to 10 pieces)

Flying Grand Regulator

Reference number: CH-6723-BLBL
Movement: manually wound, Chronoswiss Caliber C.678; ø 37.2 mm, height 4.5 mm; 17 jewels; 18,000 vph; screw balance, swan-neck fine regulation; finely finished movement; 46-hour power reserve
Functions: hours (off-center), minutes, subsidiary seconds
Case: stainless steel, ø 44 mm, height 12.48 mm; sapphire crystal; transparent case back; water-resistant to 3 atm
Band: reptile skin, folding clasp
Price: $9,090

Flying Regulator

Reference number: CH-1243.3-BLBL
Movement: automatic, Chronoswiss Caliber C.122; ø 26.8 mm, height 5.3 mm; 30 jewels; 21,600 vph; skeletonized rotor; finely finished movement; 45-hour power reserve
Functions: hours (off-center), minutes, subsidiary seconds
Case: stainless steel, ø 40 mm, height 12 mm; sapphire crystal; transparent case back; water-resistant to 3 atm
Band: reptile skin, buckle
Price: $8,190
Variations: black DLC coating ($8,850); pink gold ($19,380)

Flying Regulator

Reference number: CH-1242.3-BLBL
Movement: automatic, Chronoswiss Caliber C.122;
ø 26.8 mm, height 5.3 mm; 30 jewels; 21,600 vph;
skeletonized rotor; finely finished movement; 45-hour
power reserve
Functions: hours (off-center), minutes, subsidiary
seconds
Case: stainless steel, ø 40 mm, height 11.8 mm;
pink gold bezel; sapphire crystal; transparent case
back; water-resistant to 3 atm
Band: reptile skin, buckle
Price: $10,680
Variations: stainless steel ($6,960); pink gold
($16,440)

Flying Regulator

Reference number: CH-1241.3R-SISI
Movement: automatic, Chronoswiss Caliber C.122;
ø 26.8 mm, height 5.3 mm; 30 jewels; 21,600 vph;
skeletonized rotor; finely finished movement; 45-hour
power reserve
Functions: hours (off-center), minutes, subsidiary
seconds
Case: pink gold, ø 40 mm, height 11.8 mm; sapphire
crystal; transparent case back; water-resistant to
3 atm
Band: reptile skin, buckle
Price: $19,380
Variations: stainless steel ($8,190); stainless steel
with black DLC coating ($8,850)

Flying Regulator Jumping Hour

Reference number: CH-8321R-BKBK
Movement: automatic, Chronoswiss Caliber C.283;
ø 30 mm, height 5.35 mm; 27 jewels; 28,800 vph;
skeletonized rotor; finely finished movement; 42-hour
power reserve
Functions: hours (digital, jumping), minutes (off-
center), subsidiary seconds
Case: pink gold, ø 40 mm, height 11.85 mm;
sapphire crystal; transparent case back; water-
resistant to 3 atm
Band: reptile skin, buckle
Price: $19,970
Variations: stainless steel ($8,800); stainless steel
with black DLC coating ($9,400)

Flying Regulator Jumping Hour

Reference number: CH-8323-GRGR
Movement: automatic, Chronoswiss Caliber C.283;
ø 30 mm, height 5.35 mm; 27 jewels; 28,800 vph;
skeletonized rotor; finely finished movement; 42-hour
power reserve
Functions: hours (digital, jumping), minutes (off-
center), subsidiary seconds
Case: stainless steel, ø 40 mm, height 12 mm;
sapphire crystal; transparent case back; water-
resistant to 3 atm
Band: reptile skin, buckle
Price: $8,800
Variations: black DLC coating ($9,400); pink gold
($19,970)

Flying Regulator Jumping Hour

Reference number: CH-8323-BLOR
Movement: automatic, Chronoswiss Caliber C.283;
ø 30 mm, height 5.35 mm; 27 jewels; 28,800 vph;
skeletonized rotor; finely finished movement; 42-hour
power reserve
Functions: hours (digital, jumping), minutes (off-
center), subsidiary seconds
Case: stainless steel, ø 40 mm, height 12 mm;
sapphire crystal; transparent case back; water-
resistant to 3 atm
Band: reptile skin, buckle
Price: $8,800
Variations: black DLC coating ($9,400); pink gold
($19,970)

Regulator Classic

Reference number: CH-8723-BK-RALLYE
Movement: automatic, Chronoswiss Caliber C.291;
ø 30 mm, height 6.35 mm; 30 jewels; 28,800 vph;
38-hour power reserve
Functions: hours (off-center), minutes, subsidiary
seconds
Case: stainless steel, ø 40 mm, height 10.45 mm;
sapphire crystal; transparent case back; water-
resistant to 3 atm
Band: calfskin, buckle
Price: $4,550
Variations: light dial

Regulator Classic Date

Reference number: CH-8723-BLBK
Movement: automatic, Chronoswiss Caliber C.292; ø 30 mm, height 6.35 mm; 30 jewels; 28,800 vph; finely finished movement; 38-hour power reserve
Functions: hours (off-center), minutes, subsidiary seconds; date
Case: stainless steel, ø 41 mm, height 12.93 mm; sapphire crystal; transparent case back; water-resistant to 10 atm
Band: reptile skin, folding clasp
Price: $4,550
Variations: galvanic black or silver dial

Regulator Classic Date

Reference number: CH-8723-SI
Movement: automatic, Chronoswiss Caliber C.292; ø 30 mm, height 6.35 mm; 30 jewels; 28,800 vph; finely finished movement; 38-hour power reserve
Functions: hours (off-center), minutes, subsidiary seconds; date
Case: stainless steel, ø 41 mm, height 12.93 mm; sapphire crystal; transparent case back; water-resistant to 10 atm
Band: reptile skin, folding clasp
Price: $4,550
Variations: galvanic black or blue dial

Artist Regulator Jumping Hour

Reference number: CH-8323E-BL
Movement: automatic, Chronoswiss Caliber C.283; ø 29.4 mm, height 5.35 mm; 27 jewels; 28,800 vph; rotor skeletonized with guilloché, finely finished movement partially guillochéed by hand; 42-hour power reserve
Functions: hours (digital, jumping), minutes (off-center), subsidiary seconds
Case: stainless steel, ø 40 mm, height 9.75 mm; sapphire crystal; transparent case back; water-resistant to 3 atm
Band: reptile skin, buckle
Price: $11,800
Variations: pink gold ($22,570)

Sirius Big Date Small Seconds

Reference number: CH-8423
Movement: automatic, Chronoswiss Caliber C.284; ø 29.4 mm, height 5.35 mm; 26 jewels; 28,800 vph; perlage on bridges and plates, skeletonized rotor with côtes de Genève; 42-hour power reserve
Functions: hours, minutes, subsidiary seconds; large date
Case: stainless steel, ø 40 mm, height 9.75 mm; sapphire crystal; transparent case back; water-resistant to 3 atm
Band: reptile skin, buckle
Remarks: sterling silver dial
Price: $6,540
Variations: pink gold ($16,820)

Sirius Chronograph Moon Phase

Reference number: CH-7541-LR
Movement: automatic, Chronoswiss Caliber C.755 (base ETA 7750); ø 30 mm, height 7.9 mm; 25 jewels; 28,800 vph; côtes de Genève, movement with perlage; skeletonized rotor; 46-hour power reserve
Functions: hours, minutes, subsidiary seconds; chronograph; date, moon phase
Case: pink gold, ø 42 mm, height 15.45 mm; sapphire crystal; transparent case back; water-resistant to 3 atm
Band: reptile skin, buckle
Price: $21,930
Variations: stainless steel ($8,020)

Sirius Chronograph Skeleton

Reference number: CH-7543S
Movement: automatic, Chronoswiss Caliber C.741S (base ETA 7750); ø 30 mm, height 7.9 mm; 25 jewels; 28,800 vph; movement entirely skeletonized and decorated with côtes de Genève; 46-hour power reserve
Functions: hours, minutes, subsidiary seconds; chronograph; date
Case: stainless steel, ø 42 mm, height 15.45 mm; sapphire crystal; transparent case back; water-resistant to 3 atm
Band: reptile skin, buckle
Remarks: skeletonized dial
Price: $11,930
Variations: pink gold ($26,320)

Caliber C.111

Manually wound; single spring barrel, 46-hour power reserve
Base caliber: Marvin 700
Functions: hours, minutes, subsidiary seconds
Diameter: 29.4 mm
Height: 3.3 mm
Jewels: 17
Balance: glucydur, three-legged
Frequency: 21,600 vph
Balance spring: Nivarox 1
Shock protection: Incabloc
Remarks: polished pallet lever, escape wheel and screws, bridges with côtes de Genève

Caliber C.122

Automatic; skeletonized and gold-plated rotor with côtes de Genève, on ball bearings; single spring barrel, about 40-hour power reserve
Functions: hours, minutes, subsidiary seconds
Diameter: 26.8 mm
Height: 5.3 mm
Jewels: 30
Balance: glucydur, three-legged
Frequency: 21,600 vph
Balance spring: Nivarox 1
Shock protection: Incabloc
Remarks: polished pallet lever, escape wheel and screws, perlage on plate, bridges with côtes de Genève, individually numbered

Caliber C.126

Automatic; chime module E 94 (Dubois Dépraz) with all-or-nothing strike train and 2 gongs; skeletonized and gold-plated rotor with côtes de Genève, on ball bearings; single spring barrel, about 35-hour power reserve
Functions: hours, minutes, subsidiary seconds; quarter-hour repeater
Diameter: 28 mm
Height: 8.35 mm
Jewels: 38
Balance: glucydur, three-legged
Frequency: 21,600 vph
Balance spring: Nivarox 1
Shock protection: Incabloc

Caliber C.127

Automatic; calendar module with moon phase on left; skeletonized and gold-plated rotor with côtes de Genève, on ball bearings; single spring barrel, about 40-hour power reserve
Functions: hours, minutes, sweep seconds; perpetual calendar with date, weekday, month, moon phase, leap year
Diameter: 26.8 mm
Height: 8.79 mm
Jewels: 30
Balance: glucydur, three-legged
Frequency: 21,600 vph
Balance spring: Nivarox 1
Shock protection: Incabloc

Caliber C.673

Manually wound; single spring barrel, about 46-hour power reserve
Base caliber: ETA 6498
Functions: hours (off-center), minutes, subsidiary seconds
Diameter: 37.2 mm
Height: 4.5 mm
Jewels: 17
Balance: glucydur screw balance with stop-second
Frequency: 18,000 vph
Balance spring: Nivarox 1
Shock protection: Incabloc
Remarks: polished pallet lever, escape wheel and screws, hand perlage and côtes de Genève on balance cock and bridges

Caliber C.741 S

Automatic; completely skeletonized; skeletonized and gold-plated rotor with côtes de Genève, on ball bearings; single spring barrel, about 46-hour power reserve
Functions: hours, minutes, subsidiary seconds; chronograph; date
Diameter: 30 mm
Height: 7.9 mm
Jewels: 25
Balance: glucydur, three-legged
Frequency: 28,800 vph
Balance spring: Nivarox 1
Shock protection: Incabloc
Remarks: polished pallet lever, escape wheel and screws, plate with perlage, skeletonized, polished and beveled levers and wheels

CORUM

Founded in 1955, Switzerland's youngest luxury watch brand, Corum, celebrated sixty years of unusual—and sometimes outlandish—case and dial designs in 2015. The brand has had quite a busy history, but still by and large remains true to the collections launched by founders Gaston Ries and his nephew René Bannwart: the Admiral's Cup, Bridges, and Heritage. Among Corum's most iconic pieces is the legendary Golden Bridge baguette movement, which has received a complete makeover in recent years with the use of modern materials and complicated mechanisms. The development of these extraordinary movements required great watchmaking craftsmanship and expansion and modernization of the product development department.

The Bridges collection has always been an eye-catcher with its unusual movement, originally the brainchild of the great watchmaker Vincent Calabrese. Its introduction was a milestone in watchmaking history. And the Golden Bridge recently acquired a new highlight: in the Golden Bridge Tourbillon Panoramique with all components appearing to float in thin air.

To secure its financial future, Corum was sold to China Haidian Group (now Citychamp Watch & Jewellery Group) for over $90 million in April 2013. Calce welcomed the move not only for the financial independence it was to bring, but also for the access it allows to the crucial Chinese market.

Today, the sporty Admiral's Cup collection is divided into two families: Legend, in classical and elegant style, and AC-One 45, which is for active use. The colorful nautical number flags have returned to the Admiral's Cup dials. For the brand's sixtieth birthday in 2015, it produced a Legend with a flying tourbillon and revived the remarkable Bubble in a limited series. It earned its moniker from the domed shape of the crystal. Success breeds iterations. Davide Traxler, the new head of Corum, decided on a bold strategy to refresh the brand by boosting the culty Bubble, which now comes in many different shapes and sizes. In September 2017, Jérôme Briard took over for Traxler, but will undoubtedly continue with the successful and hip Bubbles.

Montres Corum Sàrl
Rue du Petit-Château 1
Case postale 374
CH-2301 La Chaux-de-Fonds
Switzerland

Tel.:
+41-32-967-0670

Fax:
+41-32-967-0800

E-mail:
info@corum.ch

Website:
www.corum.ch

Founded:
1955

Number of employees:
160 worldwide

Annual production:
16,000 watches

U.S. distributor:
Montres Corum USA
CWJ BRANDS
1551 Sawgrass Corporate Parkway
Suite 109
Sunrise, FL 33323
954-279-1220; 954-279-1780 (fax)
www.corum.ch

Most important collections/price range:
Admiral's Cup, Golden Bridge, Bubble, and Heritage, Romvlvs and Artisan, 150 models in total / approx. $1,500 to over $1,000,000

Golden Bridge Rectangle

Reference number: B113/03044
Movement: manually wound, Caliber CO 113; 4.9 × 34 mm, height 3 mm; 19 jewels; 28,800 vph; baguette movement, gold bridges and plate, hand-engraved
Functions: hours, minutes
Case: pink gold, 29.5 × 42.2 mm, height 9.3 mm; sapphire crystal; transparent case back; water-resistant to 3 atm
Band: reptile skin, triple folding clasp
Remarks: baguette movement surrounded by three-dimensional structures shaped like Roman numerals
Price: $36,900

Golden Bridge Stream

Reference number: B313/03296
Movement: automatic, Caliber CO 313; 11.25 × 33.18 mm; 26 jewels; 28,800 vph; variable inertia balance, baguette movement with gold bridges and plates, linear winding with sliding platinum weight
Functions: hours, minutes
Case: pink gold, 31 × 42.2 mm, height 14.7 mm; sapphire crystal; transparent case back; water-resistant to 3 atm
Band: reptile skin, triple folding clasp
Remarks: baguette movement with linear winding with sliding platinum weight flanked by three-dimensional microstructures reminiscent of the Golden Gate Bridge
Price: $60,000

Golden Bridge Round

Reference number: B113/03010
Movement: manually wound, Caliber CO 113; 4.9 × 34 mm, height 3 mm; 19 jewels; 28,800 vph; baguette movement, gold bridges and plate, hand-engraved
Functions: hours, minutes
Case: pink gold, ø 43 mm, height 8.8 mm; sapphire crystal; transparent case back; water-resistant to 3 atm
Band: reptile skin, triple folding clasp
Remarks: baguette movement flanked by three-dimensional microstructures
Price: $41,700
Variations: diamond bezel ($48,700)

Admiral AC-One 45mm

Reference number: A082/03209
Movement: automatic, Caliber CO 082 ø 25.6 mm;
21 jewels; 28,800 vph; skeletonized mainplate and
rotor; 42-hour power reserve
Functions: hours, minutes, sweep seconds; date
Case: titanium, ø 45 mm, height 13.3 mm; sapphire
crystal; transparent case back; water-resistant to
10 atm
Band: calfskin, triple folding clasp
Remarks: wooden dial
Price: $5,450

Admiral AC-One 45 Skeleton

Reference number: A082/03211
Movement: automatic, Caliber CO 082; ø 25.6 mm;
21 jewels; 28,800 vph; skeletonized mainplate,
bridges and rotor; 42-hour power reserve
Functions: hours, minutes, sweep seconds; date
Case: titanium, ø 45 mm, height 13.3 mm; sapphire
crystal; transparent case back; water-resistant to
30 atm
Band: calfskin, triple folding clasp
Remarks: real wood dial flange with nautical flags
Price: $9,150

Admiral AC-One 45 Chronograph

Reference number: A116/02599
Movement: automatic, Caliber CO 116 (base Sellita
2892-A2 with Dubois Dépraz module); ø 28.6 mm,
height 6.1 mm; 39 jewels; 28,800 vph; rotor with
black PVD coating; 42-hour power reserve
Functions: hours, minutes, subsidiary seconds;
chronograph; date
Case: titanium, ø 45 mm, height 14.3 mm; sapphire
crystal; transparent case back; water-resistant to
30 atm
Band: calfskin, folding clasp
Remarks: wood dial
Price: $7,700

Admiral Legend 42

Reference number: A395/03154
Movement: automatic, Caliber CO 395 (base ETA
2892-2); ø 25.9 mm; 27 jewels; 28,800 vph; 42-hour
power reserve
Functions: hours, minutes, subsidiary seconds; date
Case: stainless steel, ø 42 mm, height 9.5 mm;
sapphire crystal; transparent case back; water-
resistant to 5 atm
Band: rubber, triple folding clasp
Price: $3,600
Variations: silver-colored dial

Admiral AC-One 42 Chronograph

Reference number: A984/03178
Movement: automatic, Caliber CO 984 (base
ETA 2892-2); ø 32 mm, height 6.1 mm; 37 jewels;
28,800 vph; 42-hour power reserve
Functions: hours, minutes, subsidiary seconds;
chronograph; date
Case: stainless steel, ø 42 mm, height 11.6 mm;
sapphire crystal; transparent case back; water-
resistant to 3 atm
Band: rubber, triple folding clasp
Price: $4,950
Variations: blue dial

Admiral Legend 38

Reference number: A082/03262
Movement: automatic, Caliber CO 082; ø 25.6 mm;
21 jewels; 28,800 vph; skeletonized plate, bridges
and rotor; 42-hour power reserve
Functions: hours, minutes, sweep seconds; date
Case: stainless steel, ø 38 mm, height 9.3 mm;
sapphire crystal; transparent case back; water-
resistant to 5 atm
Band: stainless steel, triple folding clasp
Price: $3,850
Variations: rubber strap ($3,650)

Heritage Coin Watch

Reference number: C082/03059
Movement: automatic, Caliber CO 082; ø 25.6 mm; 21 jewels; 28,800 vph; 42-hour power reserve
Functions: hours, minutes
Case: silver, ø 43 mm, height 7.4 mm; sapphire crystal; water-resistant to 3 atm
Band: reptile skin, buckle
Remarks: dial and case back manufactured of a silver dollar
Price: $13,800

Heritage Coin Watch

Reference number: C082/03167
Movement: automatic, Caliber CO 082; ø 25.6 mm; 21 jewels; 28,800 vph; 42-hour power reserve
Functions: hours, minutes
Case: yellow gold, ø 43 mm, height 7.6 mm; sapphire crystal
Band: reptile skin, buckle
Remarks: dial and case back made of a "Double Eagle" gold dollar
Price: $23,000

Bubble 47 Skeleton

Reference number: L082/03162
Movement: automatic, Caliber CO 082; ø 25.94 mm; 26 jewels; 28,800 vph; 42-hour power reserve
Functions: hours, minutes, sweep seconds
Case: stainless steel, ø 47 mm, height 18.8 mm; sapphire crystal; transparent case back; water-resistant to 10 atm
Band: rubber, buckle
Remarks: high-domed sapphire crystal; skeletonized dial
Price: $6,000

Bubble 47 Pirate

Reference number: L082/03264
Movement: automatic, Caliber CO 082; ø 25.94 mm; 21 jewels; 28,800 vph; 42-hour power reserve
Functions: hours, minutes, sweep seconds; date
Case: stainless steel with black PVD coating, ø 47 mm, height 18.5 mm; sapphire crystal; transparent case back; water-resistant to 10 atm
Band: rubber, buckle
Remarks: high-domed sapphire crystal
Price: $4,200; limited to 187 pieces

Bubble Game 47 Poker

Reference number: L082/03243
Movement: automatic, Caliber CO 082; ø 25.94 mm; 21 jewels; 28,800 vph; 42-hour power reserve
Functions: hours, minutes, sweep seconds; date
Case: stainless steel with black PVD coating, ø 47 mm, height 18.5 mm; sapphire crystal; transparent case back; water-resistant to 10 atm
Band: rubber, buckle
Remarks: high-domed sapphire crystal
Price: $5,200; limited to 87 pieces

Bubble 47 Disconnected

Reference number: L405/03346
Movement: quartz
Functions: digital hours, minutes, seconds, date
Case: stainless steel with black PVD coating, ø 47 mm, height 18.5 mm; sapphire crystal; water-resistant to 10 atm
Band: rubber, buckle
Remarks: high-domed sapphire crystal
Price: $1,500

Cuervo y Sobrinos Habana SA
Via Carlo Maderno 54
CH-6825 Capolago
Switzerland

Tel.:
+41-91-921-2773

Fax:
+41-91-921-2775

E-mail:
info@cuervoysobrinos.com

Website:
www.cuervoysobrinos.com

Founded:
1882

Annual production:
3,500 watches

U.S. distributor:
Cuervo y Sobrinos Swiss Watches
P.O. Box 347890
Coral Gables, FL 33234
214-704-3000

Most important collections/price range:
Esplendido, Historiador, Prominente, Torpedo,
Robusto / $3,200 to $16,000; higher for
perpetual calendars and tourbillon models

CUERVO Y SOBRINOS

Cuba means a lot of things to different people. Today it seems to be the last bastion of genuine retro in an age of frenzied technology. However, turn the clock back to the early twentieth century and you find that Ramón Rio y Cuervo and his sister's sons kept a watchmaking workshop and an elegant store on Quinto Avenida, where they sold fine Swiss pocket watches—and more modest American models as well. As the country shed its Spanish occupiers, a new invader came in the form of tourists from the coast of Florida. The Cuervo business thrived thanks to the family's own wristwatches, whose dials Don Ramón soon had printed with Cuervo y Sobrinos—Cuervo and Nephews.

An Italian watch enthusiast and a Spanish businessman got together to resuscitate Cuervo y Sobrinos in 2002 and started manufacturing in the Italian-speaking region of Switzerland and in cooperation with various Swiss workshops. The tagline "Latin soul, Swiss brand" says it all.

These timepieces epitomize—or even romanticize—the island's heyday as a playground for foreign visitors. The colors hint at cigar leaves and old sepia photos in frames of distressed gold. The lines are at times elegant and sober, like the Esplendido, or radiate the ease of those who still have time on their hands, like the Prominente. Playfulness is also a Cuervo y Sobrinos quality: The Piratas have buttons shaped like the muzzle of a blunderbuss, a cannonball crown, and a porthole flange. The Robustos, named after the almost-five-inch cigar, are a grab bag of shapes and styles, like the boldly vintage Churchill, with its dial of fake cracked enamel (in reality, it's of white ceramic with gray "cracks"). To celebrate the original brand's 135th anniversary, Cuervo y Sobrinos came out with several special limited edition models, like one in the Prominente family, which comes with a CyS writing tool, for the times you write a postcard home from La Havana.

Prominente 135 Aniversario

Reference number: 1015.1135
Movement: automatic, Sellita SW-300; ø 25.6 mm, height 3.6 mm; 25 jewels; 28,800 vph; 42-hour power reserve; rotor with fan decoration and CyS engraving
Functions: hours, minutes, sweep seconds; date
Case: stainless steel, 32 × 43 mm, height 8.6 mm; sapphire crystal; transparent case back with mineral glass; water-resistant to 3 atm
Band: reptile skin, folding clasp
Remarks: comes with CyS writing implement
Price: $3,900; limited to 135 pieces

Robusto Day-Date Churchill

Reference number: 2810.1C17
Movement: automatic, Sellita Caliber SW 240; ø 29 mm, height 5.05 mm; 26 jewels; 28,800 vph; 38-hour power reserve
Functions: hours, minutes, sweep seconds; date, weekday
Case: stainless steel, ø 43 mm, height 12.45 mm; sapphire crystal; integrated and protected key winding crown; water-resistant to 3 atm
Band: reptile skin, folding clasp
Remarks: lacquered "cracked" ceramic dial; number printed on dial
Price: $3,900; limited to 200 pieces
Variations: stainless steel bracelet $4,340

Torpedo Pirata Chrono Day-Date

Reference number: 3051.1NDD
Movement: automatic, Caliber Valjoux 7750; ø 30 mm, height 7.9 mm; 25 jewels; 28,800 vph, 48-hour power reserve
Functions: hours, minutes, subsidiary seconds; chronograph; day, date
Case: stainless steel and titanium, black DLC-coating, ø 45 mm, height 15.5 mm; sapphire crystal; screwed see-through case back with unique "Pirata" logo engraving; water-resistant to 3 atm
Band: reptile skin, buckle
Remarks: "Pirata de el Tiempo de la vida" on bezel
Price: $7,400

CVSTOS

Today's big buzzword is "disruption," which usually has nasty connotations for legacy industries and esthetics. In the microworld of watches, though, disruption is often attractive to watch lovers seeking something out of the ordinary. The target of disruption at Cvstos (pronounced coo-stos, and meaning "guardian" in Latin) is the dial. Technology rules the roost at the brand, and thus these extroverted, stately timepieces show, quite literally, what they're made of, thanks to extensive skeletonization. The dials are nevertheless busy, maximalistic, with a complex look cultivated throughout the collection. It's definitely *haute horlogerie*, but targets a clientele that doesn't necessarily need elements such as *côtes de Genève*, gold, and guilloché to fulfill their watchmaking ideal.

Although it may not seem so at first sight, a great deal of watchmaking know-how goes into the making of a Cvstos, and that is no surprise for a brand that is the spiritual child of Sassoun Sirmakes, son of Vartan Sirmakes, the man who led Genevan watchmaker Franck Muller to world fame. Under the tutelage of his father, the cofounder of the Watchland *manufacture* in Genthod, young Sassoun was introduced to the hands-on side of watchmaking. In 2005, fate brought him together with designer and watchmaker Antonio Terranova, who had made a name for himself in the Swiss watch industry with the timepieces he designed and produced for leading brands. Even though he had freelanced for some of the more staid brands, Terranova had the heart of an avant-gardist willing to break free of the constraints of traditional forms—he collaborated on some of the early Richard Mille pieces, for example. So a Cvstos has all the thrilling complications, GMT, tourbillons, perpetual calendars, and more, but expect some technoid materials and high engineering art.

Cvstos
2, rue Albert Richard
CH-1201 Geneva
Switzerland

Tel.:
+41-22-989-1010

Fax:
+41-22-989-1019

E-mail:
info@cvstos.com

Website:
www.cvstos.com

Founded:
2005

U.S. distributor:
Cvstos USA, Inc.
207 W. 25th Street, 8th Floor
New York, NY 10001
212-463-8898

Most important collections/price range:
Challenge, Challenge-R, Concept-S, Sea Liner, High Fidelity / $10,000 to $315,000

Challenge Chrono II Eric Kuster Limited Edition

Movement: automatic, Caliber CVS-577; ø 30.4 mm, height 7.9 mm; 25 jewels; 28,800 vph; special black finishing; skeletonized; 42-hour power reserve
Functions: hours, minutes, subsidiary seconds; power reserve indicator; chronograph; date
Case: titanium and aluminum, 41 × 53.7 mm, height 13.35 mm; sapphire crystal; transparent case back; water-resistant to 10 atm
Band: rubber, folding clasp
Remarks: in cooperation with Dutch interior decorator Eric Kuster
Price: $16,500; limited to 14 pieces

Challenge Chrono II Brancard

Movement: automatic, Caliber CVS-577; ø 30.4 mm, height 7.9 mm; 25 jewels; 28,800 vph; special black finishing; skeletonized; 42-hour power reserve
Functions: hours, minutes, subsidiary seconds; power reserve indicator; chronograph; date
Case: titanium and pink gold, 41 × 53.7 mm, height 13.35 mm; sapphire crystal; transparent case back; water-resistant to 10 atm
Band: rubber, folding clasp
Price: $23,000

Challenge Jetliner II Brancard

Movement: automatic, Caliber CVS-350; ø 25.6 mm, height 4.6 mm; 21 jewels; 28,800 vph; special finishing; partially skeletonized; winding rotor with titanium and tungsten oscillating mass; 42-hour power reserve
Functions: hours, minutes, sweep seconds; date
Case: titanium and pink gold, 41 × 53.7 mm, height 16 mm; sapphire crystal; transparent case back; water-resistant to 10 atm
Band: reptile skin, folding clasp
Price: $17,000

Czapek & Cie.
Rue Saint-Léger 2
CH-1205 Genève
Switzerland

Tel.:
+41-76-815-1845

E-mail:
info@czapek.com

Website:
www.czapek.com

Founded:
2015

U.S. distributor:
Horology Works
11 Flagg Road
West Hartford, CT 06117
860-986-9676
info@horologyworks.com

Most important collections/price range:
Quai des Bergues men's and ladies' watches, up to $27,000; Place Vendôme up to $100,000

CZAPEK & CIE.

When entrepreneur, art specialist, and occasional watch collector Harry Guhl came across some of the pocket watches by the quasi-unknown Frantiszek Czapek (1811–18??), he immediately fell in love. It was not only the unusual design of the man's pocket watches, but also the mysteries surrounding his life.

In short: Czapek, born in Bohemia (Czech Republic today), was a Polish emigré in Geneva who fought in the failed Polish insurrection of 1832 against Russia. In 1839, he joined fellow Pole Jean de Patek. When the contract expired in 1845, Patek decided on a partnership with Philippe, inventor of the keyless watch. Czapek went on to become purveyor of watches to Emperor Napoleon III and author of a book on watches. Then he vanished without a trace.

Harry Guhl bought the name and brought together a management team. They chose as a model Czapek's No. 3430, an intriguing piece with elongated roman numerals and superbly cut fleur-de-lys hands. The piece also had two oddly placed subdials at 7:30 and 4:30, one for small seconds, the other featuring a clever double hand for the seven-day power reserve and days of the week. It would serve as a model for the new brand's portfolio.

The team sought out some of the best suppliers in Switzerland, including Jean-François Mojon for the in-house calibers (double barrel spring, open ratchets), Donzé for the grand-feu dials with the secret signature, and Aurélien Bouchet for the fine fleur-de-lys hands. Funding came from subscribers over the crowd equity sites Raizers and Crowd for Angels.

The first collection, the Quai des Bergues, was announced in November 2015. A year later, the model with the name No. 33bis picked up the Public Prize of the Grand Prix d'Horlogerie de Genève. For their next evolutions, Czapek & Cie decided on a ladies' version, with diamonds. At Baselworld 2017, the young brand presented the Place Vendôme collection in homage to the great square in Paris where Czapek actually had a boutique. The two famous subdials contain an unusual suspended tourbillon and a second time zone, respectively.

Quai des Bergues No. 31

Movement: manually wound, Czapek Caliber SXH1; ø 32 mm, height 4.75 mm; 21,600 vph; 2 barrel springs, double open ratchets; 168-hour power reserve
Functions: hours, minutes, subsidiary seconds; power reserve indicator; weekdays
Case: rose gold, ø 42.5 mm, height 11.9 mm; sapphire crystal; transparent case back; grand-feu enamel dial; water-resistant to 3 atm
Band: reptile skin, buckle
Price: $25,900
Variations: various case materials and dial colors

Quai des Bergues Lady No. 7

Movement: manually wound, Czapek Caliber SXH1; ø 32 mm, height 4.75 mm; 21,600 vph; 2 barrel springs, double open ratchets; 168-hour power reserve
Functions: hours, minutes, subsidiary seconds; power reserve
Case: white gold, ø 38 mm, height 10.8 mm; sapphire crystal; transparent case back; grand-feu enamel dial; water-resistant to 3 atm
Band: reptile skin, buckle
Remarks: fleur-de-lys hands; mother-of-pearl dial set with diamonds
Price: $23,500
Variations: various case materials and bands

Place Vendôme

Movement: manually wound, Czapek Caliber SXH2; ø 34.8 mm, height 9.8 mm; 21,600 vph; 1-minute tourbillon (off-center); open ratchet; finely decorated bridges and mainplate; 60-hour power reserve
Functions: hours, minutes, subsidiary seconds (on tourbillon cage); second time zone; day/night indicator; power reserve indicator
Case: platinum, ø 43.5 mm, height 14.6 mm; sapphire crystal; transparent case back; grand-feu enamel dial; water-resistant to 3 atm
Band: reptile skin, rose gold buckle
Remarks: fleur-de-lys hands
Price: $100,000
Variations: rose gold ($88,000)

DAVOSA

One of the more important brands occupying the lower segment of the market is Davosa, which offers pilot watches, quality divers (with helium valve), dress watches, and ladies' watches, all at very affordable prices. The company uses solid Swiss movements, which it occasionally modifies for its own designs, or it experiments with special coatings like the "gun" PVD coating on the latest Argonautics, which is dark green.

To create a broad portfolio requires experience, and that is something Davosa has in spades. The company was founded in 1891. Back then, farmer Abel Frédéric Hasler spent the long winter months in Tramelan, in Switzerland's Jura mountains, making silver pocket watch cases. Later, two of his brothers ventured out to the city of Geneva and opened a watch factory. The third brother also opted to engage with the watch industry and moved to Biel. The entire next generation of Haslers went into watchmaking as well.

The name Hasler & Co. appeared on the occasional package mailed in Switzerland or overseas. Playing the role of unassuming private-label watchmakers, the Haslers remained in the background and let their customers in Europe and the United States run away with the show. It wasn't until after World War II that brothers Paul and David Hasler dared produce their own timepieces.

The long experience with watchmaking and watches culminated in 1987 with the brothers developing their own line of watches under the brand name Davosa. The sustained development of the brand began in 1993, when the Haslers signed a partnership with the German distributor Bohle. In Germany, mechanical watches were experiencing a boom, so the brand was able to evolve quickly. In 2000, Corinna Bohle took over as manager of strategic development. Davosa now reaches well beyond Switzerland's borders and has become an integral part of the world of mechanical watches.

Hasler & Co. SA
CH-2543 Lengnau
Switzerland

E-mail:
info@davosa.com

Website:
www.davosa.com

Founded:
1881

U.S. distributor:
D. Freemont Inc.
P.O. Box 417
232 Karda Drive
Hollidaysburg, PA 16648
877-236-9248
david@freemontwatches.com
www.davosawatches.com

Most important collections/price range:
Apnea Diver, Argonautic, Classic, Military, Titanium, Gentleman, Pilot, Ternos / $500 to $2,000

Apnea Diver Automatic
Reference number: 161.568.55
Movement: automatic, Sellita Caliber SW200-1; ø 25.6 mm, height 4.6 mm; 25 jewels; 28,800 vph; 38-hour power reserve
Functions: hours, minutes, sweep seconds
Case: stainless steel, ø 46 mm, height 12.5 mm; unidirectional bezel with ceramic insert and 0-60 scale; sapphire crystal; screw-in crown; water-resistant to 20 atm
Band: rubber, buckle
Remarks: case middle can be extracted for upright positioning during breathing exercises, comes with additional rubber strap
Price: $998
Variations: partial or complete black PVD coating ($1,048 and $1,098)

Neoteric Pilot Automatic
Reference number: 161.565.46
Movement: automatic, Sellita Caliber SW200-1; ø 25.6 mm, height 4.6 mm; 25 jewels; 28,800 vph; 38-hour power reserve
Functions: hours, minutes, sweep seconds; date
Case: stainless steel, ø 42 mm, height 11.5 mm; sapphire crystal; transparent case back; water-resistant to 5 atm
Band: calfskin, buckle
Price: $748
Variations: black/red or gray/orange variants

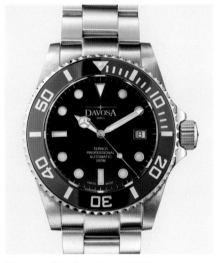

Ternos Professional TT Automatic
Reference number: 161.559.45
Movement: automatic, Sellita Caliber SW200-1; ø 25.6 mm, height 4.6 mm; 25 jewels; 28,800 vph; 38-hour power reserve
Functions: hours, minutes, sweep seconds; date
Case: stainless steel, ø 42 mm, height 15.5 mm; unidirectional bezel with ceramic insert and 0-60 scale; sapphire crystal; screw-in crown; helium valve; water-resistant to 50 atm
Band: stainless steel, folding clasp, with safety lock and extension link
Price: $848
Variations: various colors

Gentleman Automatic

Reference number: 161.566.94
Movement: automatic, Sellita Caliber SW300-1; ø 25.6 mm, height 3.6 mm; 21 jewels; 28,800 vph; 42-hour power reserve
Functions: hours, minutes, sweep seconds; date
Case: stainless steel, ø 40 mm, height 9.8 mm; sapphire crystal; transparent case back; water-resistant to 5 atm
Band: calfskin, buckle
Remarks: comes with additional leather strap
Price: $998
Variations: various dial colors; rose gold–colored PVD coating ($1,098)

Titanium Automatic

Reference number: 161.562.55
Movement: automatic, ETA Caliber 2824-2; ø 25.6 mm, height 4.6 mm; 25 jewels; 28,800 vph; 38-hour power reserve
Functions: hours, minutes, sweep seconds; date
Case: titanium with black PVD coating, ø 46 mm, height 13.9 mm; sapphire crystal; transparent case back; screw-in crown; water-resistant to 10 atm
Band: rubber, buckle
Remarks: carbon dial; comes with additional leather strap
Price: $998
Variations: without PVD coating and blue/white dial ($948); bicolor variation with partial PVD coating ($978)

Pontus All Stars Small Second Limited Edition

Reference number: 160.500.66
Movement: manually wound, DAV Caliber 6498 (base ETA 6498); ø 36.6 mm, height 5.6 mm; 17 jewels; 21,600 vph; 38-hour power reserve
Functions: hours, minutes, subsidiary seconds
Case: stainless steel, ø 44 mm, height 12.9 mm; sapphire crystal; transparent case back; water-resistant to 5 atm
Band: horse leather, buckle
Price: $998; limited to 300 pieces
Variations: large date ($1,548); as regulator ($1,548); power reserve display ($1,648)

Argonautic Lumis Color Automatic

Reference number: 161.520.40
Movement: automatic, ETA Caliber 2824-2; ø 25.6 mm, height 4.6 mm; 25 jewels; 28,800 vph; 38-hour power reserve
Functions: hours, minutes, sweep seconds; date
Case: stainless steel, ø 42 mm, height 14 mm; unidirectional bezel with ceramic insert and 0-60 scale; sapphire crystal; screw-in crown; helium valve; water-resistant to 30 atm
Band: stainless steel, Milanese mesh folding clasp with safety lock
Remarks: hands and hour markers with tritium gas tubes
Price: $848
Variations: various bands and colors

Evo 1908 Automatic

Reference number: 161.575.36
Movement: automatic, Sellita Caliber SW260; ø 25.6 mm, height 5.6 mm; 31 jewels; 28,800 vph; 38-hour power reserve
Functions: hours, minutes, subsidiary seconds; date
Case: stainless steel, 39.5 × 36 mm, height 12.0 mm; sapphire crystal; transparent case back; water-resistant to 5 atm
Band: calfskin, buckle
Price: $998
Variations: various dials

Argonautic Lumis Chronograph

Reference number: 161.508.80
Movement: automatic, ETA Caliber 7750; ø 30.0 mm, height 7.9 mm; 25 jewels; 28,800 vph; 42-hour power reserve
Functions: hours, minutes, subsidiary seconds; chronograph, date
Case: stainless steel, ø 42.5 mm, height 17.5 mm; unidirectional bezel with ceramic insert and 0-60 scale; sapphire crystal; screw-in crown; helium valve; water-resistant to 30 atm
Band: stainless steel, folding clasp with safety lock
Remarks: hands and hour markers with tritium gas tubes
Price: $1,698
Variations: without PVD plating ($1,598), regular automatic ($838)

DEEP BLUE

As far as anyone can tell, the fish do not care what you are wearing on your wrist. For the diver, it has to be accurate, genuinely water-resistant, and readable in less-than-ideal conditions. Those are the basics—or should be—of any real diver's watch. The rest is in the eye of the beholder. And it seems that New York–based Deep Blue does not wander too far off home plate, as it were. Founder Stan Betesh launched his company with the idea of providing divers with an array of tough watches that do the job and have the look and feel of a professional-quality diver's watch at a fraction of what you might expect to pay.

Little did he know in 2007—that is, ten years ago—that his watches would achieve cult status among divers. Deep Blue watches are accurate, robust, and ready for life in the open and underwater. There's no need to hide them in a safe, and getting banged up a little does them no harm—it's called patina, and it gives these timepieces the look and feel of a real tool watch . . . which is what they are.

The collection includes all sorts of models for every type of diving. The power is supplied by Miyota or ETA calibers, occasionally quartz movements. Some have special features like ceramic bezels, some are water-resistant to as much as 3,000 meters, like the Depthmaster, whose dimensions (ø 49 mm, height 19.5) and weight (300 g) will certainly contribute to the speed of the diver's descent.

For its tenth anniversary, the brand launched the Master 2000 Diver, which offers the buyer a variety of dial colors, from black to bright orange. Lots of care is given to lighting the dial, with generous application of Superluminova and the occasional use of autoluminescent tritium tubes, which may well attract some interesting fish. The second commemorative watch features this special technology: the DayNight Recon T-100 Tritium Diver 1 in a 45-mm stainless steel case with a ceramic 120-click unidirectional rotating bezel.

Deep Blue
Deep Blue Watches
1616 Coney Island Avenue
Suite 3r
Brooklyn, NY 11230

Tel.:
718-484-7717

E-mail:
info@deepbluewatches.com

Website:
www.deepbluewatches.com

Founded:
2007

Number of employees:
70

Annual production:
not specified

Distribution:
retail

Most important collections/price range:
Master collection $800 to $2,000; Daynight collection $600 to $1,000; Alpha collection $700 to $1,500; Marine collection $700 to $1,500; Ocean collection $700 to $1,500; Blue Water collection $600 to $1,400

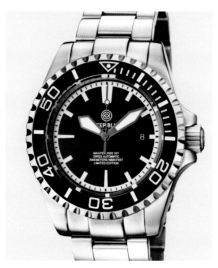

Master 2000 Swiss Automatic Diver 10 Year Limited Edition

Reference number: M2K10YBLU
Movement: automatic, ETA Caliber 2824-2; ø 25.6 mm, height 4.6 mm; 25 jewels; 28,800 vph; antimagnetic to 70,000 A/m
Functions: hours, minutes, sweep seconds; date
Case: stainless steel, ø 45 mm, height 15 mm; unidirectional bezel with countdown, ceramic lumed bezel and hour markers; sapphire crystal; steel case back; water-resistant to 200 atm
Band: stainless steel, folding clasp
Remarks: blue and white luminescent hands; luminescent ring on dial
Price: $1,199

Daynight Recon Tritium T-100 10 Year Anniversary Edition

Reference number: DNRECONT100
Movement: automatic, ETA Caliber 2824-2; ø 25.6 mm, height 4.6 mm; 25 jewels; 28,800 vph
Functions: hours, minutes, sweep seconds; date
Case: stainless steel, ø 45 mm, height 16.5 mm; unidirectional bezel with 0-120 scale; transparent case back; sapphire crystal; water-resistant to 50 atm
Band: stainless steel bracelet with wetsuit extension
Remarks: blue wave dial with tritium gas–filled tube illumination on hands and hour markers
Price: $1,449; limited edition of 200 pieces
Variations: black dial

Daynight Recon Tritium Valjoux T100

Reference number: DNT100DVR7750
Movement: automatic, ETA Valjoux 7750; ø 30 mm, height 7.9 mm; 25 jewels; 28,800 vph
Functions: hours, minutes, subsidiary seconds; chronograph; weekday, date
Case: stainless steel, ø 45 mm, height 16.5 mm; screw-down case back; screw-in crown; unidirectional bezel with 0-120 scale; sapphire crystal; water-resistant to 50 atm
Band: stainless steel bracelet
Remarks: tritium gas–filled tube illumination on hands and hour markers
Price: $2,499
Variations: blue

Detroit Watch Company, LLC
P.O. Box 60
Birmingham, MI 48012

Tel:
248-321-5601

E-mail:
info@detroitwatchco.com

Founded:
2013

Number of employees:
3

Annual production:
500 watches

Distribution:
Direct sales only

Most important collections/price range:
1701 power reserve and multifunction; 1701
Pontchartrain, 1701 L'Horloge; M1-Woodward,
B24 Liberator; M1 Moonphase; 1701 GMT /
$845 to $2,350

DETROIT WATCH COMPANY

Detroit Watch Company debuted their new brand of limited automatic timepieces a mere three years ago and in such a short period of time have not only introduced ten models to their evolving collection but continue to grow the brand at an impressive rate, most recently with the release of the B24 Liberator Aviator.

Founders Patrick Ayoub and Amy Ayoub launched Detroit Watch Company in 2013 markedly with the first and only mechanical timepieces designed and assembled in Detroit, Michigan. Patrick, a car designer, and Amy, an interior designer, share a passion for original design and timepieces and have worked hard to develop their brand, which draws inspiration from the rich history of the City of Détroit. Their introductory timepiece, the 1701, commemorates Antoine de la Mothe Cadillac, Knight of St. Louis, who, with his company of colonists, arrived at Détroit on July 24, 1701, and on that day, under the patronage of Louis XIV and protected by the flag of France, the City of Détroit, then called Fort Pontchartrain, was founded.

The Detroit Watch Company timepieces are beautifully designed and hand-assembled in-house, and may be purchased directly through the Detroit Watch Company website. Detroit Watch Company has gained the respect of serious watch aficionados and has achieved extraordinary word-of-mouth recognition for their discerning attention to detail and exceptional personalized service, along with numerous endorsements and testimonials. Detroit means a lot of things to different people, and because the history of the people and places have shaped the city, Detroit's stories are also part of the Detroit Watch Company's collective story, which deserves to be told.

M1 Woodward
Reference number: DWC M1W-BLK
Movement: automatic, ETA Caliber 7750 Valjoux; ø 30 mm, height 7.90 mm; 25 jewels; 28,800 vph; 48-hour power reserve
Functions: hours, minutes, subsidiary seconds; chronograph; day, date
Case: stainless steel, ø 44 mm, height 14.5 mm; sapphire crystal with antireflective coating, screw-down case back with engraving; water-resistant to 5 atm
Band: calfskin, folding clasp
Price: $1,850
Variations: black dial with silver subdial, silver dial with blue subdial, gray sunburst dial with transparent caseback and decorated movement with perlage, blued screws and côtes de Genève (up to $2,050)

1701 L'Horloge
Reference number: DWC 1701HDG-S1
Movement: automatic, ETA Caliber 2824 or Sellita SW200 Valjoux; ø 26.6 mm, height 4.60 mm; 26 jewels; 28,800 vph; 38-hour power reserve
Functions: hours, minutes, subsidiary seconds; date
Case: stainless steel, brushed finish, ø 39 mm, height 11.5 mm; sapphire crystal with antireflective coating, screw-down case back with engraving; water-resistant to 5 atm
Band: calfskin, buckle
Price: $1,100
Variations: light gray dial

1701 GMT
Reference number: DWC 1701GMT-S1
Movement: automatic, ETA Caliber 2893-2; ø 25.6 mm, height 4.1 mm; 21 jewels; 28,800 vph; 42-hour power reserve
Functions: hours, minutes, subsidiary seconds; second time zone, date
Case: stainless steel, ø 42 mm, height 9.4 mm; sapphire crystal with antireflective coating, screw-down case back with engraving; water-resistant to 5 atm
Band: calfskin, buckle
Price: $1,350
Variations: transparent case back

D. DORNBLÜTH & SOHN

D. Dornblüth & Sohn is a two-generation team of master watchmakers. Their workshop in Kalbe, near Magdeburg in eastern Germany, turns out remarkable wristwatches with large manual winding mechanisms, three-quarter plates, screw balances, swan-neck fine adjustments, and a clever power reserve indicator.

The history of the "Dornblüth Caliber" goes back to the 1960s in the Erz mountains in East Germany. Dieter Dornblüth, the father in this father-and-son team, had sketched the first outlines for his own movement. But he only managed to complete the work in 1999 with the assistance of his son Dirk, and by that time Germany had already been reunified.

The strength of the tiny *manufacture* lies in the high level of skill that goes into producing these classical, manually wound watches in the old-fashioned way—that is, without any CNC machines.

The 99 series is based on the reliable ETA Unitas 6497 pocket watch movement. Dirk redesigns about one-half of it by putting in a three-quarter plate and other elements. The dials are created in-house, using the 250-year-old "filled engraving" technique. They are then given a lustrous frosted layer of matte silver plating to complement the traditional *grainage* look.

The brand's fiftieth anniversary in 2012 saw the birth of the Q-2010, which features a special Maltese cross drive that reduces linear torque between two serially positioned barrel springs. The movement drives the latest models, like the Auf & Ab and Klassik. The 99.0 collection has a new model, too: the 99.9, which fits into the simple three-handed Central Second watch. The movement was also modified to create an attractive regulator watch with subsidiary hours. And in 2017, Dornblüth joined in the trend of creating a mechanical watch for women.

D. Dornblüth & Sohn
Westpromenade 7
D-39624 Kalbe/Milde
Germany

Tel.:
+49-39080-3206

Fax:
+49-39080-72796

E-mail:
info@dornblueth.com

Website:
www.dornblueth.com

Founded:
1962

Number of employees:
5

Annual production:
approx. 120 watches

U.S. distributor:
Dornblüth & Sohn
WatchBuys
888-333-4895
www.watchbuys.com

Most important collections/price range:
Various watches based on in-house between
$3,000 and $24,000

Regulator

Reference number: Regulator (GR) ST
Movement: manually wound, Dornblüth Caliber Regulator (base ETA 6498); ø 37 mm, height 5.4 mm; 20 jewels; 18,000 vph; off-center second wheel indirectly drives sweep seconds, screw balance, swan-neck fine regulation, finely finished movement
Functions: hours (off-center), minutes, sweep seconds; power reserve indicator
Case: stainless steel, ø 42 mm, height 12.5 mm; sapphire crystal; transparent case back
Band: reptile skin, buckle
Remarks: engraved and silver-plated dial
Price: $8,475
Variations: rose gold ($15,800)

Central Second

Reference number: Centersecond(1) ST
Movement: manually wound, Dornblüth Caliber Centersecond (base ETA 6498); ø 37 mm, height 5.4 mm; 20 jewels; 18,000 vph; off-center second wheel indirectly drives sweep seconds, screw balance, swan-neck fine adjustment
Functions: subsidiary hours, minutes, sweep seconds
Case: stainless steel, ø 42 mm, height 12.5 mm; sapphire crystal; transparent case back
Band: reptile skin, buckle
Price: $4,950
Variations: rose gold ($11,750)

Ladies' Watch

Reference number: Caliber 2016 (1) ST
Movement: manually wound, Dornblüth manufacture movement; ø 26 mm; 18 jewels; 18,000 vph; screw balance, Breguet hairspring; 38-hour power reserve
Functions: hours, minutes, subsidiary seconds
Case: stainless steel, ø 31 mm, height 8.5 mm; sapphire crystal; transparent case back
Band: reptile skin, buckle
Price: $4,950
Variations: various dials; rose gold ($10,950)

Doxa Watches USA
5847 San Felipe, 17th Floor
Houston, TX 77057

Tel.:
877-255-5017

Fax:
866-230-2922

E-mail:
customersupport@doxawatches.com

Website:
www.doxawatches.com

Founded:
1889

Number of employees:
48

Distribution:
Retail and direct sales

Most important collections/price range:
Doxa SUB dive watch collection / $1,500 to
$3,500

DOXA

Watch aficionados who have visited the world-famous museum in Le Locle will know that the little castle in which it is housed once belonged to Georges Ducommun, the founder of Doxa. The *manufacture* was launched as a backyard operation in 1889 and originally produced pocket watches. Quality products and good salesmanship quickly put Doxa on the map, but the company's real game-changer came in 1967 with the uncompromising SUB 300, a heavy, bold diver's watch. It featured a unidirectional bezel with the official U.S. dive table engraved on it. The bright orange dial was notable for offering the best legibility under water. It also marked the beginning of a trend for colorful dials.

Doxa continued to develop successful diver's watches in the 1970s in collaboration with U.S. Divers, Spirotechnique, and Aqualung. Their popularity increased with the commercialization of diving. Thriller writer Clive Cussler, chairman and founder of the National Underwater and Marine Agency, NUMA, even chose a Doxa as gear for his action hero Dirk Pitt.

Doxa makes watches for other occasions as well. The Ultraspeed and Régulateur are just two examples combining a classic look, fine workmanship, and an affordable price. Today, the brand has also resurrected some of the older designs from the late sixties, but with improved technology, enabling divers to go down to 1,500 meters and still read the time.

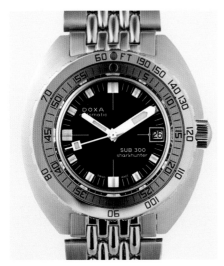

SUB 300 "Sharkhunter" 50th Anniversary Edition
Reference number: 820.10.101.10
Movement: automatic, COSC ETA Caliber 2824-2; ø 25.6 mm, height 4.6 mm; 25 jewels; 28,800 vph; 42-hour power reserve
Functions: hours, minutes, sweep seconds; date
Case: stainless steel, ø 42.5 mm, height 13.4 mm; unidirectional bezel with engraved decompression scale; sapphire crystal; screw-in crown; helium valve; water-resistant to 30 atm
Band: stainless steel, folding clasp with extension link
Remarks: Re-edition of the 1967 original; with rubber strap
Price: $2,490
Variations: "Professional"/orange dial ($2,490); "Searambler"/silver dial ($2,490)

SUB 300T-Graph "Sharkhunter"
Reference number: 877.10.101.10
Movement: automatic, ETA Caliber 2894-2; ø 28.6 mm, height 6.1 mm; 37 jewels; 28,800 vph; 42-hour power reserve
Functions: hours, minutes, subsidiary seconds; chronograph; date
Case: stainless steel, ø 47 mm, height 19 mm; unidirectional bezel with 60-minute divisions; sapphire crystal; screw-in crown; water-resistant to 30 atm
Band: stainless steel, folding clasp with safety lock and extension link
Price: $2,990; limited to 250 pieces
Variations: orange dial ($2,990); rubber strap ($2,790)

SUB 300 "Professional" Aqualung Edition
Reference number: 820.10.101.10
Movement: automatic, COSC ETA Caliber 2824-2; ø 25.6 mm, height 4.6 mm; 25 jewels; 28,800 vph; 42-hour power reserve
Functions: hours, minutes, sweep seconds; date
Case: stainless steel, ø 42.5 mm, height 13.4 mm; unidirectional bezel with engraved decompression scale; sapphire crystal; screw-in crown; helium valve; water-resistant to 30 atm
Band: stainless steel, folding clasp with extension link
Remarks: re-edition of the 1967 original; with rubber strap
Price: $2,590

SUB 4000T "Professional"

Reference number: 875.10.351.10
Movement: automatic, ETA Caliber 2897-2;
ø 25.6 mm, height 4.85 mm; 21 jewels; 28,800 vph;
42-hour power reserve
Functions: hours, minutes, sweep seconds; date;
power reserve indicator
Case: stainless steel, ø 47 mm, height 16 mm;
unidirectional bezel with 60-minute divisions;
sapphire crystal; screw-in crown; helium valve; water-
resistant to 120 atm
Band: stainless steel, folding clasp with extension
link
Price: $2,590
Variations: orange dial ($2,590); "Sharkhunter"/
black dial ($2,590)

SUB 800Ti

Reference number: 880.10.101N-WH
Movement: automatic, ETA Caliber 2824-2;
ø 25.6 mm, height 4.6 mm; 25 jewels; 28,800 vph
Functions: hours, minutes, sweep seconds; date
Case: titanium, ø 44.7 mm, height 15 mm;
unidirectional bezel, with engraved decompression
table; sapphire crystal; screw-in crown; water-
resistant to 80 atm
Band: titanium, folding clasp with extension link
Remarks: reissue of 1969 original; comes with
orange NATO fabric strap
Price: $2,790; limited to 1,000 pieces
Variations: "Sharkhunter"/black dial ($2,790);
Professional with orange hands ($2,790)

SUB MISSION 31

Reference number: 801.50.351-WH
Movement: automatic, ETA Caliber 2824-2;
ø 25.6 mm, height 4.6 mm; 25 jewels; 28,800 vph
Functions: hours, minutes, sweep seconds; date
Case: titanium, ø 44 mm, height 15 mm;
unidirectional bezel, with engraved decompression
table; sapphire crystal; screw-in crown; water-
resistant to 100 atm
Band: BOR titanium, folding clasp with extension
link
Remarks: reissue of 1969 original; comes with
orange NATO fabric strap
Price: $2,890; limited to 331 pieces

SUB 5000T Military Sharkhunter Black Ed.

Reference number: 880.30.101N.11
Movement: automatic, ETA Caliber 2892-2;
ø 25.6 mm, height 4.85 mm; 21 jewels; 28,800 vph
Functions: hours, minutes, sweep seconds; date
Case: stainless steel, ø 45 mm; helium valve;
unidirectional bezel, with engraved decompression
table; sapphire crystal; screw-in crown; water-
resistant to 150 atm
Band: stainless steel, folding clasp with extension
link
Price: $2,490
Variations: "Sharkhunter"/orange dial ($2,490);
Caribbean with blue dial ($2,490)

DOXA SUB 200T

Reference number: 802.10.021.10
Movement: automatic, ETA Caliber 2671;
ø 17.2 mm, height 4.8 mm; 25 jewels; 28,800 vph
Functions: hours, minutes, sweep seconds
Case: stainless steel, ø 35 mm, height 9 mm;
unidirectional rotating bezel with engraved
decompression table (patented); sapphire crystal;
screw-in crown; water-resistant to 20 atm
Band: stainless steel, folding clasp
Price: $1,649
Variations: "Seamaid"/black dial ($1,649)

SUB 1200T "Searambler"

Reference number: 872.10.021.10
Movement: automatic, ETA Caliber 2824-2;
ø 25.6 mm, height 4.6 mm; 25 jewels; 28,800 vph;
42-hour power reserve
Functions: hours, minutes, sweep seconds; date
Case: stainless steel, ø 42 mm, height 14 mm;
unidirectional bezel with engraved decompression
scale; sapphire crystal; screw-in crown; helium valve;
water-resistant to 120 atm
Band: stainless steel, folding clasp with extension
link
Remarks: new of 1969 original; with rubber strap
Price: $1,990
Variations: "Sharkhunter"/black dial ($1,990);
"Professional"/orange dial ($1,990)

Montres duManège Sàrl
Rue du manège 16
CH-2300 La Chaux-de-Fonds

Tel.:
+41-32-913-32-33

E-mail:
info@dumanege.com

Website:
www.dumanege.com

Founded:
2011

Number of employees:
4

Annual production:
approx. 300 watches

U.S. distributors:
Brands Consutling, LLC
Thierry Chaunu
Wells Fargo Bank, N.A.
420 Montgomery
San Francisco, CA 94104
thierrychaunu@gmail.com

Most important collections/price range:
DM Exploration / $7,526 to $18,828; Heritage /
$3,175 to $9,996; Heritage Art / $12,348 plus

DUMANÈGE

Strictly speaking, the term "Swiss-made" is something of a misnomer when applied to watches. With a few exceptions, the horological hotbed of the country is, in fact, the narrow French-speaking region in the west of the country. Geneva is only one of the hubs here, of course, the real forge for Swiss-watches being located in the stark Jura mountains, especially La-Chaux-de-Fonds and neighboring Le Locle, joint members of the UNESCO World Heritage club.

But the names of these towns never appear on a watch, oddly—until 2014, when a young *chaudefonnier*, Julien Fleury, decided to put the name of his native city on a dial. As a graphic designer with training in jewelry, he had a clear idea of what his watches were meant to look like. And he had a vision for developing his brand.

He called upon family and friends, pulled out all the stops with contacts, and managed to get a collection of large, sportive watches onto the market, which he sold by subscription. He called it DM Exploration, the initials standing for his brand's name, duManège, a reference to the magnificent nineteenth-century riding school in La-Chaux-de-Fonds, which was later used for low-cost cooperative living.

Inside the watch, a trusty Technotime movement. Today, the Exploration comes as a monopusher chronograph with a Valjoux engine. On the dial, "La-Chaux-de-Fonds."

Would he make it? Fleury is a marathon runner. He paced himself and looked to the future.

After Exploration came the Heritage line, a three-hander with date exuding the charm of a classic Swiss watch. Its main line features an ivory-white dial. The Heritage's sparsely populated dial allowed Fleury not only to exercise his talents as a jeweler, but also to explore a number of decorative crafts, from miniature painting (for bespoke commissioned pieces) to grand-feu enameling. A special piece is the Heritage Sapin, exhibiting stylized firs in champlevé enameling. Firs are ubiquitous in the bracing air of the upper Jura, and they were popularized as a local art-nouveau decoration by, among others, La-Chaux-de-Fonds' other great son, Charles Jeanneret, better known to the world of architecture as Le Corbusier.

DM Exploration

Reference number: DM.E.CMP-A.TI.45.100-1
Movement: automatic, Valjoux 7750; ø 30 mm, height 7.9 mm; 29 jewels; 28,800 vph; special black duManège treatment on bridges; 48-hour power reserve
Functions: hours, minutes, subsidiary seconds; monopusher chronograph
Case: titanium, ø 45.5 mm, height 14 mm; sapphire crystal; bezel with black DLC treatment; transparent case back; water-resistant to 5 atm
Band: reptile skin, buckle
Price: $8,702
Variations: steel ($7,526); titanium with black DLC ($10,819); pink gold ($18,828)

Heritage

Reference number: DM.H.Q-A.RG.42.122-2
Movement: manually wound, ETA Caliber 2892-2; ø 25.6 mm, height 3.6 mm; 21 jewels; 28,800 vph; 42-hour power reserve
Functions: hours, minutes, sweep seconds; date
Case: pink gold, ø 42 mm, height 9.5 mm; sapphire crystal; water-resistant to 3 atm
Band: reptile skin, folding clasp
Remarks: grand feu enamel dial
Price: $9,996
Variations: white gold ($9,996); stainless steel ($3,175); stainless steel with Swiss tennis star Conny Perrin signature ($3,175)

Heritage Sapin

Reference number: DM.H.Q-A.WG-S.42.152-1
Movement: manually wound, ETA Caliber 2892-2; ø 25.6 mm, height 3.6 mm; 21 jewels; 28,800 vph; 42-hour power reserve
Functions: hours, minutes, sweep seconds
Case: "extra" white gold, ø 42 mm, height 9.5 mm; bezel set with 70 diamonds; sapphire crystal; water-resistant to 3 atm
Band: reptile skin, folding clasp
Remarks: champlevé enamel dial depicting fir trees
Price: $26,460
Variations: dials using different crafts; watch can be customized with miniature painting

EBERHARD & CO.

Chronographs weren't always the main focus of the Eberhard & Co. brand. In 1887, Georges-Emile Eberhard rented a workshop in La Chaux-de-Fonds to produce a small series of pocket watches, but it was the unstoppable advancement of the automotive industry that gave the young company its inevitable direction. By the 1920s, Eberhard was producing timekeepers for the first auto races. In Italy, Eberhard & Co. functioned well into the 1930s as the official timekeeper for all important events relating to motor sports. And the Italian air force later commissioned some split-second chronographs from the company, one of which went for 56,000 euros at auction.

Eberhard & Co. is still doing well, thanks to the late Massimo Monti. In the 1990s, he associated the brand with legendary racer Tazio Nuvolari. The company dedicated a chronograph collection to Nuvolari and sponsored the annual Gran Premio Nuvolari oldtimer rally in his hometown of Mantua.

With the launch of its four-counter chronograph, this most Italian of Swiss watchmakers underscored its expertise and ambitions where short time/sports time measurement is concerned. Indeed, Eberhard & Co.'s Chrono 4 chronograph, featuring four little counters all in a row, has brought new life to the chronograph in general. CEO Mario Peserico has continued to develop it, putting out versions with new colors and slightly altered looks.

The brand is pure vintage, so it will come as no surprise that it regularly reissues and updates some of its older, popular models, like the two-totalizer Contograph chrono from the 1960s, which originally allowed the user to calculate phone units exactly (*conto* = bill). In 2016, it relaunched the venerable 1950s Scafograph, a very clean diver with streamlined hands and a ceramic bezel. And 2017 brought a crop of special editions of the brand's most iconic model, the Chrono 4.

Eberhard & Co.
5, rue du Manège
CH-2502 Biel/Bienne
Switzerland

Tel.:
+41-32-342-5141

Fax:
+41-32-341-0294

E-mail:
info@eberhard-co-watches.ch

Website:
www.eberhard-co-watches.ch

Founded:
1887

Distribution:
Contact main office for information on
U.S. distribution

Most important collections:
Chrono 4; 8 Jours, Tazio Nuvolari; Extra-fort;
Gilda; Contograf; Scafograf
(Prices are in Swiss francs. Use daily exchange
rate for calculations.)

Scafograf GMT

Reference number: 41038
Movement: automatic, ETA Caliber 2893-2; ø 25.6 mm, height 4.1 mm; 21 jewels; 28,800 vph; 42-hour power reserve
Functions: hours, minutes, sweep seconds; second 24-hour display (second time zone); date
Case: stainless steel, ø 43 mm, height 11.8 mm; bidirectional rotating bezel with ceramic insert and 24-hour scale; sapphire crystal; screw-in crown; water-resistant to 10 atm
Band: stainless steel, folding clasp
Price: $4,700
Variations: blue dial; rubber strap ($3,880)

Chrono 4 "130" Limited Edition

Reference number: 31130
Movement: automatic, Eberhard Caliber EB 251-12 1/2 (base ETA 2894-2); ø 33 mm, height 7.5 mm; 53 jewels; 28,800 vph; 4 counters in a row; rhodium-plated movement with perlage, blued screws, engraved rotor with côtes de Genève
Functions: hours, minutes, subsidiary seconds; second 24-hour display; chronograph; date
Case: stainless steel, ø 42 mm, height 13.3 mm; sapphire crystal; transparent case back; screw-in crown; water-resistant to 5 atm
Band: rubberized reptile skin, buckle
Remarks: sapphire crystal dial
Price: $10,640; limited to 130 pieces
Variations: black dial

8 Jours Grande Taille

Reference number: 21027
Movement: manually wound, Eberhard Caliber EB 896 (base ETA 7001); ø 34 mm, height 5 mm; 25 jewels; 21,600 vph; 2 spring barrels, 8-day power reserve (patented)
Functions: hours, minutes, subsidiary seconds; power reserve indicator
Case: stainless steel, ø 41 mm, height 10.85 mm; sapphire crystal; transparent case back; water-resistant to 30 m
Band: reptile skin, buckle
Price: $5,350
Variations: black dial

Scafograf 300

Reference number: 41034
Movement: automatic, ETA Caliber 2824-2;
ø 25.6 mm, height 4.6 mm; 25 jewels; 28,800 vph;
42-hour power reserve
Functions: hours, minutes, sweep seconds; date
Case: stainless steel, ø 43 mm, height 12.6 mm;
unidirectional bezel with ceramic insert and 0-60
scale; sapphire crystal; screw-in crown; helium valve;
water-resistant to 300 m
Band: rubber, buckle
Price: $3,260
Variations: blue indices; stainless steel bracelet
($4,070)

Champion V Grande Date

Reference number: 31064.2
Movement: automatic, ETA Caliber 7750; ø 30 mm,
height 7.9 mm; 25 jewels; 28,800 vph; 42-hour
power reserve
Functions: hours, minutes, subsidiary seconds;
chronograph; large date
Case: stainless steel, ø 42.8 mm, height 14.45 mm;
sapphire crystal; screw-in crown; water-resistant to
50 m
Band: calfskin, buckle
Price: $4,565
Variation: stainless steel bracelet ($5,357)

Chrono 4 "130"

Reference number: 31129
Movement: automatic, Eberhard Caliber EB
251-12 1/2 (base ETA 2894-2); ø 33 mm, height
7.5 mm; 53 jewels; 28,800 vph; 4 counters in a row.
(Patented—Registered Design)
Functions: hours, minutes, subsidiary seconds;
second 24-hour display; chronograph; date
Case: stainless steel, ø 42 mm, height 13.3 mm;
sapphire crystal; transparent case back; screw-in
crown; water-resistant to 50 m
Band: rubberized reptile skin, buckle
Price: $6,600
Variations: various dials

Extra-Fort Automatic

Reference number: 41029
Movement: automatic, Sellita Caliber SW200-1;
ø 35.6 mm, height 4.6 mm; 26 jewels; 28,800 vph;
42-hour power reserve
Functions: hours, minutes, sweep seconds; date
Case: stainless steel, ø 40 mm, height 10.07 mm;
sapphire crystal; screw-in crown; water-resistant to
50 m
Band: reptile skin, buckle
Price: $3,300
Variations: white or black dial; stainless steel
bracelet ($4,200)

Tazio Nuvolari Gold Car

Reference number: 31038.5
Movement: automatic, ETA Caliber 7750; ø 30 mm,
height 7.9 mm; 25 jewels; 28,800 vph; 42-hour
power reserve
Functions: hours, minutes; chronograph
Case: stainless steel, ø 43 mm, height 13 mm;
sapphire crystal; transparent case back; screw-in
crown; water-resistant to 30 m
Band: reptile skin, buckle
Remarks: gold, stylized Alfa Romeo on rotor
Price: $5,530
Variation: stainless steel bracelet ($6,270)

Tazio Nuvolari Data

Reference number: 31066
Movement: automatic, ETA Caliber 7750; ø 30 mm,
height 7.9 mm; 25 jewels; 28,800 vph; 42-hour
power reserve
Functions: hours, minutes; chronograph; date
Case: stainless steel, ø 43 mm, height 13 mm;
sapphire crystal; screw-in crown; water-resistant to
30 m
Band: reptile skin, buckle
Price: $5,170
Variation: stainless steel bracelet ($5,910)

ERNST BENZ

Necessity is really the mother of creativity and then invention. Ernst Benz was an engineer by trade, an inventor by design, and a multitalented person who dabbled in many technologies including record player styluses. And as a passionate flier, he needed solid, reliable, and readable watches that could be used in the cockpits of small aircraft and gliders, so he gradually slipped into making timepieces. Size and clarity were determining factors, hence his clean dials and 47 mm diameters. Reliability is guaranteed by a no-nonsense Valjoux 7750. These elements save pilots' lives. At first, Benz made what he called the Great Circle Chronograph and later the ChronoScope just for fellow aviators. He also engineered other aviation instruments now standard in many small aircraft.

In 2005, the brand was bought by the Khankins, a watchmaking family with generations of experience in complicated horology. Leonid Khankin has spent a lifetime in the hands-on side of the business—starting right at the bottom, cleaning out cases in a small workshop. That's why he makes sure that the sapphire crystals are flush with the bezel, for instance, and will not get chipped accidentally. The family vigorously expanded the brand both geographically and by creating exciting new models. The ChronoScope received black PVC coating and was retooled as the ChronoDiver for those attracted to water rather than air. They were also quick to adopt ultra-hard DLC coating.

Khankin, who knows every nook and cranny of the horological world, is taking the brand places. He uses the broad dial of these distinct timepieces as a platform for adding thrilling design elements. On the style side, Ernst Benz has collaborated with fashion designer John Varvatos and Food Network chef Mario Batali on a series with distinct hands and color schemes.

Ernst Benz
7 Route de Crassier
CH-1262 Eysins
Switzerland

E-mail:
info@ernstbenz.com

Website:
www.ernstbenz.com

Founded:
early 1960s

U.S. distributor:
Ernst Benz North America
177 S. Old Woodward
Birmingham, MI 48009
248-203-2323; 248-203-6633 (fax)

Most important collections:
Great Circle, ChronoScope, ChronoLunar, ChronoRacer

ChronoScope ChronoRacer CR3

Reference number: GC10100/CR3
Movement: automatic, Valjoux Caliber 7750; ø 30 mm, height 7.9 mm; 25 jewels; 28,800 vph
Functions: hours, minutes, subsidiary seconds; day/date; chronograph
Case: stainless steel, ø 47 mm, height 16 mm; sapphire crystal; screwed-down transparent case back; double O-ring sealed crown; water-resistant to 5 atm
Band: reptile skin, buckle
Price: $5,700; limited to 50 pieces, individually numbered dials

ChronoLunar Traditional DLC

Reference number: GC10318-DLC
Movement: automatic, Valjoux 7751; ø 30 mm, height 7.9 mm; 25 jewels; 28,800 vph
Functions: hours, minutes, subsidiary seconds; day/date, month, moon phase; 24-hour display; chronograph
Case: black DLC-coated stainless steel, ø 47 mm, height 16 mm; sapphire crystal; screw-down transparent case back; double O-ring sealed crown; water-resistant to 5 atm
Band: reptile skin, buckle
Price: $8,175
Variations: 44-mm case ($7,575)

ChronoScope Heritage of Jamaica

Reference number: GC10100/JA-DLC
Movement: automatic, Valjoux Caliber 7750; ø 30 mm, height 7.9 mm; 25 jewels; 28,800 vph
Functions: hours, minutes, subsidiary seconds; day/date; chronograph
Case: stainless steel with black DLC, ø 47 mm, height 16 mm; sapphire crystal; screw-down transparent case back; double O-ring sealed crown; water-resistant to 5 atm
Band: reptile skin, buckle
Price: $6,800; limited to 25 pieces

ChronoSport 18th Degree

Reference number: GC10200/18D2
Movement: automatic, automatic ETA 2836-2;
ø 30 mm, height 5.05 mm; 25 jewels; 28,800 vph;
38-hour power reserve
Functions: hours, minutes, sweep seconds; day/date
Case: stainless steel, ø 47 mm, height 16 mm;
sapphire crystal; screw-down transparent case back;
double O-ring sealed crown; water-resistant to 5 atm
Band: reptile skin, buckle
Price: $3,925
Variations: 44 mm, brushed stainless steel ($3,325)

ChronoScope Heritage of Mexico

Reference number: GC10100/HM2
Movement: automatic, Valjoux Caliber 7750;
ø 30 mm, height 7.9 mm; 25 jewels; 28,800 vph
Functions: hours, minutes, sweep seconds; day/
date; chronograph
Case: stainless steel, ø 47 mm, height 16 mm;
sapphire crystal; screw-down transparent case back;
double O-ring sealed crown; water-resistant to 5 atm
Band: reptile skin, buckle
Price: $6,500

ChronoLunar Officer DLC

Reference number: GC10383-DLC
Movement: automatic, Valjoux 7751; ø 30 mm,
height 7.9 mm; 25 jewels; 28,800 vph
Functions: hours, minutes, subsidiary seconds;
day/date, month, moon phase; 24-hour display;
chronograph
Case: black DLC-coated polished stainless steel,
ø 47 mm, height 16 mm; water-resistant to 5 atm
Band: reptile skin, buckle
Price: $8,575
Variations: 44-mm case ($7,975)

ChronoLunar Officer

Reference number: GC10386
Movement: automatic, Valjoux 7751; ø 30 mm,
height 7.9 mm; 25 jewels; 28,800 vph
Functions: hours, minutes, subsidiary seconds;
day/date, month, moon phase; 24-hour display;
chronograph
Case: polished stainless steel, ø 47 mm, height
16 mm; sapphire crystal; screw-down transparent
case back; double O-ring sealed crown; water-
resistant to 5 atm
Band: reptile skin, buckle
Price: $7,625

EBZ by John Varvatos ChronoScope

Reference number: GC10410/JV4
Movement: automatic, Valjoux Caliber 7750;
ø 30 mm, height 7.9 mm; 25 jewels; 28,800 vph
Functions: hours, minutes, subsidiary seconds; day/
date; chronograph
Case: stainless steel, ø 47 mm, height 16 mm;
sapphire crystal; screw-down transparent case back;
double O-ring sealed crown; water-resistant to 5 atm
Band: reptile skin, buckle
Price: $6,500; limited to 250 pieces, individually
numbered dials

ChronoSport Officer

Reference number: GC10281
Movement: automatic, automatic ETA 2836-2;
ø 30 mm, height 5.05 mm; 25 jewels; 28,800 vph;
38-hour power reserve
Functions: hours, minutes, sweep seconds; day/date
Case: stainless steel, ø 47 mm, height 16 mm;
angled/polished bezel, sapphire crystal; screw-down
transparent case back; double O-ring sealed crown;
water-resistant to 5 atm
Band: reptile skin, buckle
Price: $3,725
Variations: 44-mm case ($3,125)

ETERNA

Eterna is a milestone in watchmaking. Founded in 1856 in what was then a village, Grenchen, the company, named Dr. Girard & Schild, became a *manufacture*, producing pocket watches under Urs Schild in 1870. Among its earliest claims to fame was the first wristwatch with an alarm, released in 1908, by which time the company had taken on the name Eterna. Forty years later came the legendary Eterna-matic, featuring micro ball bearings for an automatic winding rotor. At the slightest movement of the watch, the rotor began to turn and set in motion what was another newly developed system of two ratchet wheels, which, independent of the rotational direction, lifted the mainspring over the automatic gears. Today, the five micro ball bearings used to cushion that rotor are the inspiration for Eterna's stylized pentagon-shaped logo. The invention itself is now standard in millions of watch movements.

In 2007, the company launched its Caliber 39 project to serve as a base for various iterations. Modules for additional indicators or functions could be affixed with just a few screws or connected by way of a bridge. The Royal KonTiki Two Time Zones is the first model making use of this base caliber. Thanks to the famous ball bearing–mounted Spherodrive winding mechanism, the movement has a power reserve of sixty-eight hours.

In 1995, Eterna was acquired by F.A. Porsche Beteiligungen GmbH and started manufacturing for Porsche Design. But in 2011, International Volant Ltd., a wholly owned subsidiary of Citychamp, bought up the Porsche-owned shares in Eterna, opening many opportunities in Asia through its chain of retailers. In March 2014, Eterna and Porsche finally separated, freeing up Eterna's technical and financial resources to focus on its growth. Older models were brought out to celebrate the company's 160th anniversary in 2016. Among the novelties were a re-release of the Super KonTiki Chronograph, a flyback equipped with the 31916A in-house caliber, and a new interpretation of the original Super KonTiki (no chronograph). For 2017, the KonTiki has been released as a three-hander in a classic bronze case, connecting through the metal with its maritime origins.

Eterna SA
Schützenstrasse 40
CH-2540 Grenchen
Switzerland

Tel.:
+41-32-654-7211

Website:
www.eterna.com

Founded:
1856

Number of employees:
approx. 80

U.S. distributor:
CWJ Brands
1551 Sawgrass Blvd. Unit 109
Sunrise, FL 33323
954-279-1220

Most important collections:
KonTiki, Eternity, 1948

KonTiki Bronze Manufacture

Reference number: 1291.78.49.1422
Movement: automatic, Eterna Caliber 3902A; ø 30.4 mm, height 5.6 mm; 30 jewels; 28,800 vph; 65-hour power reserve
Functions: hours, minutes, sweep seconds
Case: bronze, ø 44 mm, height 14.05 mm; unidirectional bezel with ceramic insert and 0-60 scale; sapphire crystal; transparent case back; water-resistant to 20 atm
Band: calfskin, buckle
Price: $2,950; limited to 300 pieces

1940 Telemeter Chronograph Flyback Bronze Manufacture

Reference number: 7950.78.54.1416
Movement: automatic, Eterna Caliber 3916A; ø 30.4 mm, height 7.9 mm; 35 jewels; 28,800 vph; 60-hour power reserve
Functions: hours, minutes, subsidiary seconds; flyback chronograph; date
Case: bronze, ø 42 mm, height 14.1 mm; sapphire crystal; transparent case back; water-resistant to 5 atm
Band: calfskin, buckle
Price: $5,100; limited to 100 pieces

KonTiki Diver Gent

Reference number: 1290.41.89.1418
Movement: automatic, Sellita Caliber SW200-1; ø 25.6 mm, height 4.6 mm; 26 jewels; 28,800 vph; 38-hour power reserve
Functions: hours, minutes, sweep seconds; date
Case: stainless steel, ø 44 mm, height 12.2 mm; unidirectional bezel with ceramic insert and 0-60 scale; sapphire crystal; water-resistant to 20 atm
Band: rubber, folding clasp
Price: $1,800

Skeleton

Reference number: 7000.41.14.1409
Movement: automatic, Eterna Caliber 3902M; ø 30.4 mm, height 4.95 mm; 20 jewels; 28,800 vph; skeletonized movement; 65-hour power reserve
Functions: hours, minutes sweep seconds
Case: stainless steel, ø 42 mm, height 103 mm; sapphire crystal; transparent case back; water-resistant to 5 atm
Band: calfskin, buckle
Price: $5,000; limited to 160 pieces

Lady Diver

Reference number: 1282.64.69.1420
Movement: quartz ETA 956.412
Functions: hours, minutes, sweep seconds; date
Case: stainless steel with rose gold–colored PVD coating, ø 36 mm, height 11.35 mm; unidirectional bezel with ceramic insert and 0-60 scale; sapphire crystal; water-resistant to 20 atm
Band: calfskin, buckle
Price: $1,200

Lady Diver

Reference number: 1282.41.66.1419
Movement: quartz ETA 956.412
Functions: hours, minutes, sweep seconds; date
Case: stainless steel, ø 36 mm, height 11.35 mm; unidirectional bezel with ceramic insert and 0-60 scale; sapphire crystal; water-resistant to 20 atm
Band: calfskin, buckle
Price: $1,100

Caliber 3916A

Automatic: rotor on ball bearings; single spring barrel, 65-hour power reserve
Functions: hours, minutes, subsidiary seconds, flyback chronograph, date
Diameter: 30.4 mm
Height: 7.9 mm
Jewels: 35
Balance: glucydur
Frequency: 28,800 vph
Balance spring: flat hairspring
Shock protection: Incabloc

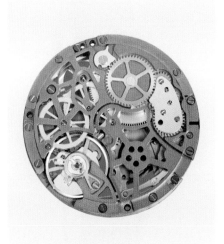

Caliber 3902M

Manually wound completely skeletonized with matte finish; single spring barrel, 65-hour power reserve
Functions: hours, minutes, sweep seconds
Diameter: 30.4 mm
Height: 4.95 mm
Jewels: 20
Balance: glucydur
Frequency: 28,800 vph
Balance spring: flat hairspring
Shock protection: Incabloc

Caliber 3902A

Automatic; rotor on ball bearings; single spring barrel, 65-hour power reserve
Functions: hours, minutes, sweep seconds
Diameter: 30.4 mm
Height: 5.6 mm
Jewels: 30
Balance: glucydur
Frequency: 28,800 vph
Balance spring: flat hairspring
Shock protection: Incabloc

FABERGÉ

Peter Carl Fabergé (1846–1920), son of a St. Petersburg jeweler of French Protestant stock, was one of those who achieved legendary status in that nebulous frontier zone where jewelry, art, and luxury meet. In 1885, he was commissioned by Tsar Alexander III to produce a special Easter egg for the tsarina. He did so, employing the best crafts-people of the time, and in the process became a supplier to the Romanovs. This also meant exile when the Bolsheviks took over in 1918.

His sons set up a business in Paris. After being sold several times during the twentieth century, the name Fabergé finally ended up being owned by Pallinghurst, a holding company with investments in mining that include the famous Gemfields, a specialist in colored stones.

In 2013, brand president and COO Robert Benvenuto decided to launch a new portfolio of watches. Utilizing colored stones and platinum was a foregone conclusion. Victor Mayer, a former licensee, took on the enamel guilloché dials of the Lady Fabergé core collection, which received a Vaucher movement. For the men's watch, Renaud & Papi produced a subtly modern tourbillon with a geometrically openworked dial. But the pièce de résistance, the Lady Compliquée, was assigned to Jean-Marc Wiederrecht of Agenhor, who created a movement driving a retrograde peacock's tail (Peacock) or a wave of frost (Winter) to display the minutes, while the hours circle the dial in the opposite direction. It won a prize at the prestigious Grand Prix d'Horlogerie de Genève.

Sourcing quality continues to pay up for Fabergé with a new crop of outstanding watches, like the iteration of the Visionnaire DTZ, which features an almost invisible rotor oscillating just on the edge of the dial. The new chronograph with three hands ingeniously stacked atop each other in the middle of the dial required an entirely new module, which was again developed by the brilliant Wiederrecht. For the latest Lady Libertine, which was to exhibit sapphires and rubies, the company resorted to the skills of the Scottish artist and watch designer Fiona Krüger, who is better known perhaps for her captivating skull-shaped watches. Together with enamel specialist Anita Porchet, she created a splendid dial where a blue, white-capped sea meets a reddish beach.

Fabergé
23 King Street
London SW1Y 6QY
Great Britain

Tel.:
+44-20-7518-7297

E-mail:
information@faberge.com

Website:
www.faberge.com

Founded:
1842, current watch department relaunched 2013

Annual production:
approx. 350 watches

U.S. distributor:
694 Madison Avenue
New York, NY 10065
646-559-8848
sales@faberge.com

Most important collections:
Lady Fabergé; Summer in the Provence; Fabergé Lady Compliquée; Fabergé Visionnaire DTZ; Fabergé Altruist

Lady Compliquée Peacock Ruby

Movement: manually wound, Caliber AGH6901 exclusive for Fabergé; ø 32.7 mm, height 3.58 mm; 38 jewels; 21,600 vph; 50-hour power reserve
Functions: hours (on disk at crown), minutes (retrograde)
Case: platinum, 38 mm, height 12.90 mm; 54 diamonds on bezel; transparent back; sapphire crystal; water-resistant to 3 atm
Band: reptile skin, platinum buckle
Remarks: after 1908 Fabergé Peacock Egg; dial set with rubies and diamonds, hand-engraved peacock on dial
Price: $89,000

Fabergé Flirt 39 mm

Movement: automatic, Vaucher Caliber 3000; ø 23.3 mm, height 3.9 mm; 28 jewels; 28,800 vph; white gold rotor; 50-hour power reserve
Functions: hours, minutes
Case: white gold, ø 39 mm; bezel set with 51 diamonds, crown with moonstone; transparent case back; sapphire crystal; water-resistant to 3 atm
Remarks: green enamel guilloché dial
Band: reptile skin, buckle
Price: $34,500
Variations: different dial colors; 36-mm case

Lady Compliquée Peacock Black

Movement: manually wound, Caliber AGH 6901 exclusive for Fabergé; ø 32.7 mm, height 3.58 mm; 38 jewels; 21,600 vph; 50-hour power reserve
Functions: hours (on disk at crown), minutes (retrograde)
Case: white gold, 38 mm; transparent back; sapphire crystal; water-resistant to 3 atm
Band: reptile skin, white gold buckle
Remarks: black lacquer dial, black painted mother-of-pearl hour ring
Price: $34,500

Fabergé Lady Libertine

Movement: manually wound, Caliber AGH 6911 exclusive for Fabergé; ø 30 mm, height 3.2 mm; 15 jewels; 21,600 vph; bridges with côtes de Genève; 50-hour power reserve
Functions: hours, minutes
Case: rose gold, 36 mm; sapphire crystal; transparent case back; bezel set with diamonds; water-resistant to 1 atm
Remarks: circular central space with representation of terrain in Zambia where emeralds for dial are mined; stylized arrowheads to point to hours and minutes
Band: reptile skin, rose gold buckle
Price: on request

Fabergé Lady Libertine II

Movement: manually wound, Caliber AGH 6911 exclusive for Fabergé; ø 30 mm, height 3.2 mm; 15 jewels; 21,600 vph; bridges with côtes de Genève; 50-hour power reserve
Functions: hours, minutes
Case: white gold, 36 mm; sapphire crystal; transparent case back; bezel set with diamonds; water-resistant to 1 atm
Remarks: circular central space with representation of terrain in Zambia where emeralds for dial are mined; stylized arrowheads to point to hours and minutes
Band: reptile skin, white gold buckle
Price: on request

Fabergé Lady Libertine III

Movement: manually wound, Caliber AGH 6911 exclusive for Fabergé; ø 30 mm, height 3.2 mm; 15 jewels; 21,600 vph; bridges with côtes de Genève; 50-hour power reserve
Functions: hours, minutes
Case: white gold, 36 mm; sapphire crystal; transparent case back; bezel set with diamonds; water-resistant to 1 atm
Remarks: dial of Mozambique rubies and sapphires and enamel arrangement depicting oceanside; stylized wave-shaped hands point to hours and minutes
Band: reptile skin, white gold buckle
Price: on request

Fabergé Visionnaire DTZ

Movement: automatic, Caliber AGH 6924 exclusive for Fabergé; ø 34.8, height 8.3 mm; 30 jewels; 21,600 vph; mainplate, bridges with côtes de Genève; 50-hour power reserve
Functions: hours, minutes; central dual time zone (24-hour indication)
Case: rose gold and titanium, ø 43 mm; sapphire crystal; transparent case back; water-resistant to 5 atm
Remarks: opaline dial with mysterious rotor on dial side and TC1 luminescent coating
Band: reptile skin, rose gold and titanium folding clasp
Price: $29,500
Variations: white gold and titanium ($29,500)

Fabergé Visionnaire Chronograph Black Ceramic

Movement: automatic, Caliber AGH 6361; ø 34.40, height 7.17 mm; 67 jewels; 21,600 vph; 60-hour power reserve; mainplate, bridges with côtes de Genève; 50-hour power reserve
Functions: hours, minutes; central chronograph
Case: black ceramic and dark gray DLC treated titanium, ø 43 mm, height 14.34 mm; sapphire crystal; transparent case back; water-resistant to 5 atm
Remarks: black dial with mysterious rotor on dial side; TC1 luminescent coating
Band: reptile skin, folding clasp
Price: $34,500
Variations: rose gold and titanium with opaline dial ($39,500)

Fabergé Altruist

Movement: automatic, Vaucher Caliber 3000; ø 23.3 mm, height 3.9 mm; 28 jewels; 28,800 vph; white gold rotor; 50-hour power reserve
Functions: hours, minutes, sweep seconds
Case: white gold, ø 41 mm; transparent case back; sapphire crystal
Band: reptile skin, white gold buckle
Remarks: blue enamel and guilloché dial
Price: $21,000
Variations: rose gold without enamel dial ($17,500)

FORTIS

Fortis Uhren AG
Lindenstrasse 45
CH-2540 Grenchen
Switzerland

Tel.:
+41-32-653-3361

Fax:
+41-32-652-5942

E-mail:
info@fortis-watches.com

Website:
www.fortis-watches.com

Founded:
1912

U.S. distributor:
Watchbuys
888-333-4895
www.watchbuys.com

Most important collections/price range:
Flieger, Official Cosmonauts, Marinemaster,
Stratoliner, Art Edition / $1,400 to $9,500

From March to September 2012, anyone visiting the Museum of Cultural History in Grenchen, Switzerland, could have enjoyed an in-depth look at one century's worth of Fortis. The exhibition was appropriately called "From Grenchen into Space." And knowing Grenchen, that is quite a step.

The 102-year history of the Fortis brand has been marked by many memorable events. The biggest milestone dates to the 1920s, when the company began the first serial production of wristwatches with automatic winding.

The word *Fortis* comes from the Latin term for "strong." With its striking and sturdy watches, the brand itself has always enjoyed a reputation for reliability and consistency. But perhaps its greatest claim to fame comes from the clients it serves: These days, if you say "Fortis," the first thing that springs to mind is aeronautics and space travel. For almost two decades, Fortis has been collaborating with specialists from the European space agency to test how the company's first generation of space chronographs would hold up in truly extreme conditions. This resulted in approval for use aboard the Russian space station *Mir*. Since then, Fortis chronographs have become part of the official equipment of the Russian space program and, from there, on the *International Space Station*.

The competencies acquired from work in space continue to flow back into the company's traditional pilot's watches, which have long served as the role models for modern cockpit wristwatches. It's hardly astonishing that many international squadrons wear Fortis watches. Aside from such high-performance, space-traveling timepieces, Fortis also regularly enjoys creating limited edition art and design timepieces in collaboration with artists to satisfy collectors. But new management in the Grenchen headquarters has slowly begun changing the range of models by adding a few more conventional everyday watches for the user.

Marinemaster Chronograph Blue

Reference number: 671.15.45 LP01
Movement: automatic, ETA Caliber 7750; ø 30 mm, height 7.9 mm; 25 jewels; 28,800 vph; 42-hour power reserve
Functions: hours, minutes, subsidiary seconds; chronograph; date, weekday
Case: stainless steel, ø 42 mm, height 13 mm; unidirectional bezel, with 0-60 scale; sapphire crystal; water-resistant to 20 atm
Band: calfskin, buckle
Price: $2,980
Variations: black or yellow bezel; stainless steel bracelet ($3,250); rubber strap ($3,200); as Day/Date ($1,500)

Monolith Chronograph

Reference number: 638.18.31 M
Movement: automatic, ETA Caliber 7750; ø 30 mm, height 7.9 mm; 25 jewels; 28,800 vph; 42-hour power reserve
Functions: hours, minutes, subsidiary seconds; chronograph; date, weekday
Case: stainless steel with black PVD coating, ø 42 mm, height 13 mm; unidirectional bezel, with 0-60 scale; sapphire crystal; water-resistant to 20 atm
Band: stainless steel with black PVD coating, folding clasp with safety lock
Price: $3,780
Variations: various bands; as Day/Date ($1,730)

Daybreaker Chronograph Alarm GMT Certified Chronometer

Reference number: 703.10.11 LC01
Movement: automatic, Fortis Caliber F-2012 (Base ETA 7750); ø 30 mm, height 7.9 mm; 39 jewels; 28,800 vph; COSC-certified chronometer
Functions: hours, minutes, subsidiary seconds; second 24-hour display (second time zone), double power reserve display, alarm; chronograph; date, day/ night indicator
Case: stainless steel, ø 43 mm, height 16.3 mm; sapphire crystal; water-resistant to 5 atm
Band: reptile skin, folding clasp
Price: $14,615; limited to 100 pieces
Variations: stainless steel bracelet ($14,710)

Cockpit Two

Reference number: 704.21.19 L01
Movement: automatic, ETA Caliber 2836-N;
ø 25.6 mm, height 5.05 mm; 25 jewels; 28,800 vph;
38-hour power reserve
Functions: hours, minutes, sweep seconds; date,
weekday
Case: stainless steel, ø 41 mm, height 12.5 mm;
sapphire crystal; water-resistant to 10 atm
Band: calfskin, buckle
Price: $1,360
Variations: stainless steel bracelet ($1,640); as
Chronograph ($2,780)

Flieger Professional Chronograph

Reference number: 705.21.11 L01
Movement: automatic, ETA Caliber 7750; ø 30 mm,
height 7.9 mm; 25 jewels; 28,800 vph; 42-hour
power reserve
Functions: hours, minutes, subsidiary seconds;
chronograph; date, weekday
Case: stainless steel, ø 43 mm, height 12.5 mm;
sapphire crystal; water-resistant to 10 atm
Band: calfskin, folding clasp
Price: $2,590
Variations: stainless steel bracelet ($2,800); as Day/
Date ($1,330)

Pilot Classic Chronograph

Reference number: 904.21.41 L 01
Movement: automatic, Dubois Dépraz Caliber 2020
(base ETA 2892 with a module); ø 30 mm, height
7.5 mm; 47 jewels; 28,800 vph; 48-hour power
reserve
Functions: hours, minutes, subsidiary seconds;
chronograph
Case: stainless steel, ø 41 mm, height 13.5 mm;
sapphire crystal; transparent case back; water-
resistant to 5 atm
Band: calfskin, buckle
Price: $2,820
Variations: as Date ($1,460); as small second
($1,630)

Official Cosmonauts Chronograph

Reference number: 638.10.11 M
Movement: automatic, ETA Caliber 7750; ø 30 mm,
height 7.9 mm; 25 jewels; 28,800 vph; 42-hour
power reserve
Functions: hours, minutes, subsidiary seconds;
chronograph; date, weekday
Case: stainless steel, ø 42 mm, height 13 mm;
unidirectional bezel, with 0-60 scale; sapphire crystal;
water-resistant to 20 atm
Band: stainless steel, folding clasp
Price: $3,170
Variations: various bands; as Day/Date ($1,760)

Classic Cosmonauts Ceramic p.m.

Reference number: 401.26.11 L 01
Movement: automatic, ETA Caliber 7750 W;
ø 30 mm, height 7.9 mm; 25 jewels; 28,800 vph;
42-hour power reserve
Functions: hours, minutes, subsidiary seconds;
chronograph; date, weekday
Case: stainless steel, ø 42 mm, height 15 mm;
ceramic bezel; sapphire crystal; transparent case
back; screw-in crown and pushers; water-resistant
to 10 atm
Band: calfskin, buckle
Price: $3,680
Variations: various bands; white dial; stainless steel
bezel

Spacematic Steel

Reference number: 623.10.71
Movement: automatic, ETA Caliber 2836-2;
ø 25.6 mm, height 4.1 mm; 25 jewels; 28,800 vph;
42-hour power reserve
Functions: hours, minutes, sweep seconds; date,
weekday
Case: stainless steel, ø 40 mm, height 13 mm;
sapphire crystal; stainless steel case back; water-
resistant to 10 atm
Band: stainless steel, folding clasp
Price: $1,290
Variations: various bands; with PVD coating

F.P. JOURNE

Born in Marseilles in 1957, François-Paul Journe might have become something else had he concentrated in school. He was kicked out and went to Paris, where he completed watchmaking school before going to work for his watchmaking uncle. And he has never looked back. By the age of twenty he had made his first tourbillon and soon was producing watches for connoisseurs.

He then moved to Switzerland, where he started out with handmade creations for a limited clientele and developing the most creative and complicated timekeepers for other brands before taking the plunge and founding his own in the heart of Geneva. The timepieces he basically single-handedly and certainly single-mindedly—hence his tagline *invenit et fecit*—conceives and produces are of such extreme complexity that it is no wonder that they leave his workshop in relatively small quantities. Journe has won numerous top awards, some several times over. He particularly values the Prix de la Fondation de la Vocation Bleustein-Blanchet, since it came from his peers.

His collection is divided into two pillars: the automatic Octa line with its more readily understandable complications and the manually wound Souveraine line, containing horological treasures that can't be found anywhere else. The latter includes a *grande sonnerie*, a minute repeater, a constant force tourbillon with deadbeat seconds, and even a timepiece with two escapements beating in resonance—and providing chronometer-precise timekeeping. The recent Centigraphe uses the movement to provide one-hundredth of a second chronograph capability with a lever rather than a pusher. Journe never stops surprising the watch world.

He even surprises while remaining true to classical codes. His women's Elégante features a microprocessor that electronically notes when the watch is immobile, stops the mechanical movement to preserve energy, and restarts it when the watch is once again in motion. The success of the watch led Journe to come out with a 48-millimeter version for men.

Montres Journe SA
17 rue de l'Arquebuse
CH-1204 Geneva
Switzerland

Tel.:
+41-22-322-09-09

Fax:
+41-22-322-09-19

E-mail:
info@fpjourne.com

Website:
www.fpjourne.com

Founded:
1999

Number of employees:
135

Annual production:
850–900 watches

U.S. distributor:
Montres Journe America
4330 NE 2nd Avenue
Miami, FL 33137
305-572-9802
phalimi@fpjourne.com

Most important collections:
Souveraine, Octa, Vagabondage, Elegante (Prices are in Swiss francs. Use daily exchange rate for calculations.)

Sonnerie Souveraine

Movement: manually wound, F.P.Journe Caliber 1505; ø 35.8 mm, height 7.8 mm; 42 jewels; 21,600 vph; rose gold plate and bridges; repeater chimes hours/quarter hours automatically, minute repeater on demand; on/off function; 422 components; 10 patents
Functions: hours, minutes (off-center), subsidiary seconds; grande sonnerie; power reserve indicator; chime indicator
Case: stainless steel, ø 42 mm, height 12.25 mm; sapphire crystal; screw-in crown and pusher; transparent case back
Band: 2 reptile skin straps, double folding clasp and 1 stainless steel bracelet
Price: CHF 771,200

Centigraphe Souverain Sport

Movement: manually wound, F.P.Journe Caliber 1506 in rose gold; ø 34.4 mm, height 5.6 mm; 26 jewels; 21,600 vph; aluminum movement; 80-hour power reserve (with chronograph off)
Functions: hours, minutes; 1-second, 20-second and 10-minute chronograph subdials at 10, 2, and 6 o'clock
Case: titanium, ø 42 mm, height 11.6 mm; sapphire crystal; transparent case back
Band: rubber strap or titanium bracelet, folding clasp
Price: CHF 45,400
Variations: gold (CHF 60,700) or platinum (CHF 64,600)

Octa Divine

Movement: automatic, F.P.Journe Caliber 1300.3 in rose gold; ø 30.8 mm, height 5.7 mm; 39 jewels; 21,600 vph; up to 120–chronometric hour power reserve; pink gold guillochéed rotor, plate, and bridges
Functions: hours, minutes, subsidiary seconds; large date; moon phase; power reserve indicator
Case: red gold, ø 42 mm, height 10.6 mm; sapphire crystal; transparent case back
Band: reptile skin, platinum buckle
Remarks: white gold dial and silver hour circle silver guilloché dial with clous de Paris
Price: CHF 49,900
Variations: platinum or red gold with 40- or 42-mm case (gold 40-mm case CHF 46,100)

Chronomètre Optimum

Movement: manually wound, F.P.Journe Caliber 1501 in rose gold; ø 34.4 mm, height 3.75 mm; 44 jewels; 21,600 vph; pink gold plate and bridges; double barrel, constant force remontoire, EPHB high-performance biaxial escapement, balance spiral with Phillips curve, deadbeat seconds on back
Functions: hours, minutes, subsidiary seconds; power reserve indicator
Case: platinum, ø 40 mm, height 10.1 mm; sapphire crystal; transparent case back
Band: reptile skin, buckle
Price: CHF 92,100
Variations: red gold (CHF 88,200)

Chronomètre à Résonance

Movement: manually wound, F.P.Journe Caliber 1499.3 in rose gold; ø 32.6 mm, height 4.2 mm; 36 jewels; 21,600 vph; unique concept of 2 escapements mutually influencing and stabilizing each other through resonance; pink gold plate and bridges
Functions: hours, minutes, subsidiary seconds; second time zone; power reserve indicator
Case: platinum, ø 40 mm, height 9 mm; sapphire crystal; transparent case back
Band: reptile skin, platinum buckle
Price: CHF 84,300
Variations: red gold (CHF 80,400)

Chronomètre Bleu

Movement: manually wound, F.P.Journe Caliber 1304 in rose gold; ø 30.4 mm, height 3.75 mm; 22 jewels; 21,600 vph; pink gold plate and bridges; chronometer balance with "invisible" connection to gear train; 2 spring barrels
Functions: hours, minutes, subsidiary seconds
Case: tantalum, ø 39 mm, height 8.6 mm; sapphire crystal; transparent case back
Band: reptile skin, tantalum buckle
Price: CHF 23,400

Tourbillon Souverain

Movement: manually wound, F.P.Journe Caliber 1403 in rose gold; ø 32.4 mm, height 7.15 mm; 26 jewels; 21,600 vph; tourbillon with constant force; balance with variable inertia; mainplate with côtes de Genève; 42-hour power reserve
Functions: hours, minutes, subsidiary deadbeat seconds; power reserve indicator
Case: platinum, ø 40 mm, height 9.9 mm; sapphire crystal; transparent case back
Band: calfskin, platinum buckle
Price: CHF 167,700
Variations: red gold case (on request)

Elégante 48 mm

Movement: electromechanical, F.P.Journe Caliber 1210; 28.5 x 28.3 mm, height 3.13 mm; 18 jewels; quartz frequency 32,000 Hz; autonomy: daily use up to 10 years, 18 years in standby mode
Functions: hours, minutes, subsidiary seconds; motion detector with inertia weight at 4:30
Case: titanium, 48 × 40 mm, height 7.35 mm; sapphire crystal; transparent case back
Band: navy blue rubber strap, titanium buckle
Remarks: standby mode after 30 minutes motionless, microprocessor keeps time, restarts automatically, sets time when watch put back on; luminescent dial
Price: CHF 11,500
Variations: in 48 mm: titanium with diamonds (CHF 24,500); various strap colors

Elégante with diamonds

Movement: electromechanical, F.P.Journe Caliber 1210; 28.5 × 28.3 mm, height 3.13 mm; 18 jewels; quartz frequency 32,000 Hz; autonomy: 100-year/18 years standby mode; pink gold
Functions: hours, minutes, subsidiary seconds; motion detector with inertia weight at 4:30
Case: platinum, 40 × 35 mm, height 7.35 mm; pave-set with diamonds and sapphires; sapphire crystal; transparent case back
Band: navy blue rubber strap, pink gold buckle
Remarks: standby mode after 30 minutes motionless, microprocessor keeps time, restarts automatically, sets time when watch put back on; black sapphire dial
Price: CHF 119,000
Variations: titanium with rubber strap (CHF 15,200); platinum with rubber or snake strap (CHF 29,200)

FRANCK MULLER

Groupe Franck Muller Watchland SA
22, route de Malagny
CH-1294 Genthod
Switzerland

Tel.:
+41-22-959-8888

Fax:
+41-22-959-8882

E-mail:
info@franckmuller.ch

Website:
www.franckmuller.com

Founded:
1997

Number of employees:
approx. 500 (estimated)

U.S. distributor:
Franck Muller USA, Inc.
207 W. 25th Street, 8th Floor
New York, NY 10001
212-463-8898
www.franckmuller.com

Most important collections:
Giga, Aeternitas, Revolution, Evolution 3-1,
Vanguard, Cintrex

Francesco "Franck" Muller has been considered one of the great creative minds in the industry ever since he designed and built his first tourbillon watch back in 1986. In fact, he never ceased amazing his colleagues and competition ever since, with his astounding timepieces combining complications in a new and fascinating manner.

Recently, the "master of complications" has been stepping away from the daily business of the brand, leaving space for the person who had paved young Muller's way to fame, Vartan Sirmakes. It was Sirmakes, previously a specialist in watch cases, who had contributed to the development of the double-domed, tonneau-shaped Cintrée Curvex case, with its elegant, 1920s retro look. The complications never stop either. Franck Muller created the Gigatourbillons, which are 20 millimeters across, and the Revolution series has a tourbillon that rises toward the crystal.

It was in 1997 that Muller and Sirmakes founded the Franck Muller Group Watchland, which now holds the majority interest in thirteen other companies, eight of which are watch brands. During the 2009 economic crisis, the company downsized somewhat, but it was only a glitch in an otherwise well-planned-out strategy to focus on developing complicated watches, like the Vanguard series, which has gone through numerous iterations, including being skeletonized. Franck Muller remains the leading brand in the Watchland portfolio. The far-reaching synergies within the Group, however, mean that the success of the leader is indeed trickling laterally to the other participants, like Barthelay, Backes & Strauss, ECW, Martin Braun, Pierre Kunz, Rodolphe, Smalto Timepieces, and Roberto Cavalli by Franck Muller.

Vanguard Skeleton

Reference number: V 45 S6 SQT
Movement: manually wound, FM Caliber 1740; 34.9 × 41.35 mm, height 5.3 mm; 19 jewels; 18,000 vph; fully skeletonized movement; 168-hour power reserve
Functions: hours, minutes, subsidiary seconds
Case: rose gold, 44 × 53.7 mm, height 12.8 mm; sapphire crystal; transparent case back
Band: rubber, with reptile skin layer, buckle
Price: $43,800
Variations: titanium ($35,800)

Vanguard Gravity Skeleton

Reference number: V 45 T GR CS SQT
Movement: manually wound, FM Caliber CS-03; 38.4 × 39.6 mm, height 8.7 mm; 25 jewels; 18,000 vph; 1-minute tourbillon, skeletonized movement; 120-hour power reserve
Functions: hours, minutes
Case: titanium with black PVD coating, 44 x 53.7 mm, height 15.1 mm; sapphire crystal; transparent case back; water-resistant to 3 atm
Band: reptile skin, buckle
Price: $130,000 (titanium version)

Vanguard Yachting Chronograph

Reference number: V 45 CC DT YACHT
Movement: automatic, FM Caliber 7000; ø 30 mm, height 7.9 mm; 27 jewels; 28,800 vph; 48-hour power reserve
Functions: hours, minutes, subsidiary seconds; chronograph; date
Case: pink gold, 44 × 53.7 mm, height 15.8 mm; sapphire crystal; transparent case back
Band: rubber, with textile overlay, buckle
Price: $25,800 (rose gold version)

Vanguard Slim Mécanique

Reference number: V 45 SLIM MECH
Movement: manually wound, FM Caliber 2250; ø 21.3 mm, height 2.6 mm; 21,600 vph; 45-hour power reserve
Functions: hours, minutes, subsidiary seconds
Case: stainless steel, 44 × 53.7 mm, height 9.5 mm; sapphire crystal
Band: rubber, with reptile skin layer, buckle
Price: $7,700 (stainless steel version)
Variations: pink gold $16,700

Vanguard Golf

Reference number: V 45 SC DT COUNTER GOLF
Movement: automatic, FM Caliber 800CGS; ø 26.2 mm, height 5.6 mm; 21 jewels; 28,800 vph; 42-hour power reserve
Functions: hours, minutes, sweep seconds; manual stroke counter
Case: titanium, 44 × 53.7 mm, height 13.7 mm; sapphire crystal; transparent case back; water-resistant to 3 atm
Band: rubber, buckle
Price: $9,000 (titanium case)
Price: $11,000 (score reset version)

Vanguard Lady Moon Phase

Reference number: V 32 SC AT FO L
Movement: automatic, FM Caliber 2671 (base ETA 2671 with FM module); ø 17.5 mm; 25 jewels; 28,800 vph; 38-hour power reserve
Functions: hours, minutes, sweep seconds; moon phase
Case: stainless steel, 32 × 42.3 mm, height 9.9 mm; sapphire crystal
Band: reptile skin, buckle
Price: $8,800

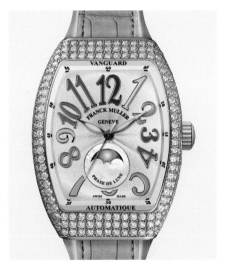

Vanguard Lady Mondphase

Reference number: V 32 SC AT FO L D
Movement: automatic, FM Caliber 2671 (base ETA 2671 with FM module); ø 17.5 mm; 25 jewels; 28,800 vph; 38-hour power reserve
Functions: hours, minutes, sweep seconds; moon phase
Case: stainless steel, set with diamonds, 32 × 42.4 mm, height 9.9 mm; sapphire crystal
Band: reptile skin, buckle
Price: $19,800 (stainless steel version with diamonds)

Cintrée Curvex Master Banker

Reference number: 8880 MB SC DT IND MAP 5N
Movement: automatic, FM Caliber 2800 MB SC; ø 25.6 mm, height 5.6 mm; 31 jewels; 21,600 vph; finely finished movement; 42-hour power reserve
Functions: hours, minutes, sweep seconds; 2 second 24-hour display (2nd and 3rd time zones); date
Case: rose gold, 43.3 × 60.5 mm, height 12.9 mm; sapphire crystal; water-resistant to 3 atm
Band: reptile skin, buckle
Price: $32,000
Variations: platinum ($48,000); stainless steel ($21,000)

Cintrée Curvex 7 Days Power Reserve Skeleton

Reference number: 8880 B S6 SQT
Movement: manually wound, FM Caliber 1740 CS; 34.9 × 41.35 mm, height 5.3 mm; 21 jewels; 18,000 vph; Breguet hairspring, double spring barrel, skeletonized mainplate and rotor, finely finished with perlage and côtes de Genève; 168-hour power reserve
Functions: hours, minutes, subsidiary seconds
Case: rose gold, 39.6 × 55.4 mm, height 13.7 mm; sapphire crystal; transparent case back
Band: reptile skin, buckle
Price: $49,800 (rose gold version)
Variations: white gold ($49,800); stainless steel ($40,800)

FRÉDÉRIQUE CONSTANT

Frédérique Constant SA
Chemin du Champ des Filles 32
CH-1228 Plan-les-Ouates (Geneva)
Switzerland

Tel.:
+41-22-860-0440

Fax:
+41-22-860-0464

E-mail:
info@frederique-constant.com

Website:
www.frederique-constant.com

Founded:
1988

Number of employees:
100

Annual production:
approx. 146,000 watches

U.S. distributor:
Alpina Frederique Constant USA
700 W. Hillsboro Blvd., Suite 2-102
Deerfield Beach, FL 33441
954-312-3600
morgane@usa.frederique-constant.com

Most important collections/price range:
Slimline Manufacture Automatic / from approx.
$2,900; Heart Beat Manufacture / from approx.
$3,600; Ladies Automatic / from approx.
$2,300; Runabout / from approx. $1,550;
Vintage Rally / from approx. $1,895; Art Deco /
approx. $1,000; Classics / from approx. $650;
Horological Smart Watch / from approx. $750
to $2,695

Peter and Aletta Stas, the Dutch couple who founded Frédérique Constant, have always sought to make high-end watches for consumers without deep pockets. So high-end, in fact, that in 2004 they went public with the brand's first movement produced entirely in-house and equipped with innovative silicon components. The move was in line with the other strategy of staying independent, and it was crowned a success. The Heart Beat calibers proved to be reliable, popular, and affordable.

Since 1991, the Dutch couple have genuinely lived up to the tagline they use for their Swiss brand: "live your passion." The watch brand, named for Aletta's great-grandmother Frédérique Schreiner and Peter's great-grandfather Constant Stas, was conceived in the late 1980s. The new company had its work cut out for it: Frédérique Constant had to compete in a watch market truly saturated with brands.

After the success of the Heart Beat *manufacture* mode, the Stases decided to invest in their own watch factory, an impressive, four-floor facility with ample room for a spacious atelier, administrative offices, conference rooms, a fitness area, and a cafeteria, in Geneva's industrial Plan-les-Ouates. Frédérique Constant moved into its new home in 2006, joined shortly after by sister brand Alpina. The Heart Beat collection continues to make waves, but the brand is growing in other directions as well, seeking to bridge the gap between fans of fine watchmaking and users of electronic nannies. The Horological Smartwatch, equipped with a quartz movement, connects with mobile phones and other electronic devices and can display data on its analog dial.

In 2016, much to the surprise of the watch world, the Stases decided it was time to find an investor to carry on their work. Frédérique Constant and Alpina were sold to Citizen. The two founders agreed to stay on as CEOs for four years.

Slimline Perpetual Calendar Manufacture

Reference number: FC-775V4S4
Movement: automatic, Caliber FC-775; ø 30 mm, height 6.38 mm; 26 jewels; 28,800 vph; finely finished with côtes de Genève; 38-hour power reserve
Functions: hours, minutes; perpetual calendar with date, weekday, month, moon phase, leap year
Case: stainless steel rose gold–plated, ø 42 mm, height 12.4 mm; sapphire crystal; transparent case back; water-resistant to 3 atm
Band: reptile skin, folding clasp
Price: $8,995

Flyback Chronograph Manufacture

Reference number: FC-760V4H4
Movement: automatic, Caliber FC-760; ø 30 mm, height 7.9 mm; 32 jewels; 28,800 vph; finely finished with côtes de Genève; 38-hour power reserve
Functions: hours, minutes, subsidiary seconds; flyback chronograph; date
Case: stainless steel rose gold–plated, ø 42 mm, height 14.6 mm; sapphire crystal; transparent case back; water-resistant to 5 atm
Band: reptile skin, folding clasp
Price: $4,295

Slimline Moonphase Manufacture

Reference number: FC-702S3S6
Movement: automatic, Caliber FC-702; ø 27.5 mm, height 6.2 mm; 26 jewels; 28,800 vph; finely finished with côtes de Genève; 42-hour power reserve
Functions: hours, minutes; date, moon phase
Case: stainless steel, ø 38.8 mm, height 11.17 mm; sapphire crystal; transparent case back; water-resistant to 3 atm
Band: reptile skin, folding clasp
Price: $2,895

Runabout GMT

Reference number: FC-350RMG5B6
Movement: automatic, Caliber FC-350; ø 26 mm, height 6.1 mm; 26 jewels; 28,800 vph; 38-hour power reserve
Functions: hours, minutes, sweep seconds; second 24-hour display (second time zone); date
Case: stainless steel, ø 42 mm, height 12.45 mm; sapphire crystal; transparent case back; water-resistant to 5 atm
Band: calfskin, folding clasp
Remarks: limited to 2,888 pieces
Price: $1,795

Horological Smartwatch Notify

Reference number: FC-282AS5B6
Movement: quartz
Functions: hours, minutes; electronic motion detection and sleep monitoring; date
Case: stainless steel, ø 42 mm, height 13.35 mm; sapphire crystal; water-resistant to 5 atm
Band: calfskin, buckle
Price: $795

Classics Automatic GMT

Reference number: FC-350MC5B4
Movement: automatic, Caliber FC-350; ø 26 mm, height 6.1 mm; 26 jewels; 28,800 vph; 38-hour power reserve
Functions: hours, minutes, sweep seconds; second 24-hour display (second time zone); date
Case: stainless steel rose gold–plated, ø 42 mm, height 13.75 mm; sapphire crystal; transparent case back; water-resistant to 5 atm
Band: calfskin, buckle
Price: $1,895

Slimline Moonphase Manufacture

Reference number: FC-705WR4S4
Movement: automatic, Caliber FC-705; ø 30 mm, height 6.2 mm; 26 jewels; 28,800 vph; finely finished with côtes de Genève; 42-hour power reserve
Functions: hours, minutes; date, moon phase
Case: stainless steel rose gold–plated, ø 42 mm, height 11.3 mm; sapphire crystal; transparent case back; water-resistant to 3 atm
Band: reptile skin, folding clasp
Price: $3,395

Horological Smartwatch Delight

Reference number: FC-281WHD3ER2B
Movement: quartz
Functions: hours, minutes; electronic motion detection and sleep monitoring; date
Case: stainless steel, ø 34 mm, height 11.04 mm; rose gold–plated bezel; sapphire crystal; water-resistant to 3 atm
Band: stainless steel with rose gold–plated elements, folding clasp
Price: $1,295

Caliber FC-775

Automatic; single spring barrel, 38-hour power reserve
Functions: hours, minutes; perpetual calendar with date, weekday, month, moon phase, leap year
Diameter: 30.5 mm
Height: 6.67 mm
Jewels: 26
Frequency: 28,800 vph
Balance spring: flat hairspring with fine regulation
Shock protection: Incabloc II
Remarks: 191 components

GIRARD-PERREGAUX

Girard-Perregaux
1, Place Girardet
CH-2300 La Chaux-de-Fonds
Switzerland

Tel.:
+41-32-911-3333

Fax:
+41-32-913-0480

Website:
www.girard-perregaux.com

Founded:
1791

Number of employees:
280

Annual production:
approx. 12,000 watches

U.S. distributor:
Girard-Perregaux
Tradema of America, Inc.
7900 Glades Road, Suite 200
Boca Raton, FL 33434
833-GPWATCH
www.girard-perregaux.com

Most important collections/price range:
Laureato / Vintage 1945 / approx. $7,500 to
$625,000; ww.tc / $12,300 to $23,800; GP
1966 / $7,500 to $291,000

When Girard-Perregaux CEO Luigi ("Gino") Macaluso died in 2010, the former minority partner of Sowind Group, PPR (Pinault, Printemps, Redoute), increased its equity stake to 51 percent. Under the leadership of Michele Sofisti since 2011, the brand has been charting a rather bold course that includes some technically sharp developments with the support of a strong development team and an excellently equipped production department. Under his guidance, the company has reduced its multitude of references but continues treading the fine line between fashionable watches and technical miracles. The various combinations of tourbillons and the gold bridges remain the company specialty. The most dazzling talking piece lately has undoubtedly been the Constant Escapement, a new concept that stores energy by buckling an ultrathin silicon blade and then releasing it to the balance wheel. Like many sophisticated systems, it was born of the banal: inventor Nicolas Déhon was absentmindedly bending a train ticket one day when he was suddenly struck by the simple thought. As the ticket bent, it collected energy that was released in even bursts when it straightened out.

In 2015, Antonio Calce of Eterna and Corum fame became the company CEO and launched a freshening-up program, which included its marketing strategies. The Vintage 1945 and the elegant GP 1966 are still the mainstays of the brand, together with the Competizione chronographs. But Calce has also decided to put the ladies' Cat's Eye collection in the limelight and given a serious face-lift to the Three Bridges tourbillon.

In addition, in 2016, Girard-Perregaux celebrated its 225th anniversary with a set of exclusive watches that aimed to highlight the company's most important milestones, the Gyromatic HF from 1966, and the legendary Esmeralda, which won first prize at the Universal Exhibition in Paris in 1889 and will now continue its cycle as a wristwatch. The company also revived the much coveted Laureato from the 1970s, making it something of a leading line for the 2017 cycle.

Laureato 42mm Automatic
Reference number: 81010-11-431-11A
Movement: automatic, GP Caliber 01800-0013; ø 30 mm, height 3.97 mm; 28 jewels; 28,800 vph; 54-hour power reserve
Functions: hours, minutes, sweep seconds; date
Case: stainless steel, ø 42 mm, height 10.88 mm; sapphire crystal; transparent case back; water-resistant to 10 atm
Band: stainless steel, double folding clasp
Price: $11,000
Variations: silver or gray dial; reptile skin strap ($10,300)

Laureato 42mm Automatic
Reference number: 81010-11-131-BB6A
Movement: automatic, GP Caliber 01800-0008; ø 30 mm, height 3.97 mm; 28 jewels; 28,800 vph; 54-hour power reserve
Functions: hours, minutes, sweep seconds; date
Case: stainless steel, ø 42 mm, height 10.88 mm; sapphire crystal; transparent case back; water-resistant to 10 atm
Band: reptile skin, double folding clasp
Remarks: additional rubber strap
Price: $10,300
Variations: stainless steel bracelet ($11,000); titanium with rose gold bezel on leather strap ($15,200)

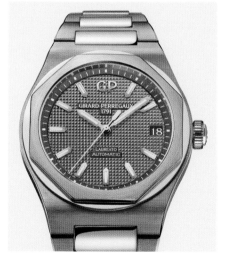

Laureato 42mm Automatic
Reference number: 81010-26-232-26A
Movement: automatic, GP Caliber 01800-0013; ø 30 mm, height 3.97 mm; 28 jewels; 28,800 vph; 54-hour power reserve
Functions: hours, minutes, sweep seconds; date
Case: titanium, ø 42 mm, height 10.88 mm; rose gold bezel; sapphire crystal; transparent case back; rose gold crown; water-resistant to 10 atm
Band: titanium with rose gold elements, double folding clasp
Remarks: additional rubber strap
Price: $22,600
Variations: reptile skin strap ($15,200)

Laureato 38mm Automatic

Reference number: 81005-52-232-52A
Movement: automatic, GP Caliber 03300-0130/
0129; ø 25.6 mm, height 3.36 mm; 27 jewels;
28,800 vph; 46-hour power reserve
Functions: hours, minutes, sweep seconds; date
Case: rose gold, ø 38 mm, height 10.02 mm;
sapphire crystal; transparent case back; water-
resistant to 10 atm
Band: pink gold, double folding clasp
Price: $34,300
Variations: stainless steel ($10,400)

Laureato 38mm Automatic

Reference number: 81005-11-431-BB6A
Movement: automatic, GP Caliber 03300-0132;
ø 25.6 mm, height 3.36 mm; 27 jewels; 28,800 vph;
46-hour power reserve
Functions: hours, minutes, sweep seconds; date
Case: stainless steel, ø 38 mm, height 10.02 mm;
sapphire crystal; transparent case back; water-
resistant to 10 atm
Band: reptile skin, double folding clasp
Remarks: additional rubber strap
Price: $9,700
Variations: rose gold with rose gold bracelet
($34,300)

Laureato Tourbillon

Reference number: 99105-26-231-BB6A
Movement: automatic, GP Caliber 09510-0001;
ø 36.6 mm, height 6.05 mm; 33 jewels; 21,600 vph;
1-minute tourbillon; microrotor in gold; 49-hour
power reserve
Functions: hours, minutes
Case: titanium, ø 45 mm, height 11.96 mm; rose
gold bezel; sapphire crystal; rose gold crown; water-
resistant to 3 atm
Band: reptile skin, double folding clasp
Price: $93,700
Variations: titanium and white gold ($98,400)

GP 1966 Large Date and Moon Phase

Reference number: 49556-52-131-BB6C
Movement: automatic, GP Caliber 03300-0110;
ø 25.6 mm, height 4.9 mm; 32 jewels; 28,800 vph;
46-hour power reserve
Functions: hours, minutes, subsidiary seconds; large
date, moon phase
Case: rose gold, ø 40 mm, height 10.7 mm; sapphire
crystal; transparent case back; water-resistant to
3 atm
Band: reptile skin, buckle
Price: $20,500
Variations: white gold ($22,200)

GP 1966 Full Calendar

Reference number: 49535-11-131-BB60
Movement: automatic, GP Caliber 03300-0118;
ø 25.6 mm, height 4.8 mm; 27 jewels; 28,800 vph;
46-hour power reserve
Functions: hours, minutes, sweep seconds; full
calendar with date, weekday, month, moon phase
Case: stainless steel, ø 40 mm, height 10.8 mm;
sapphire crystal; transparent case back; water-
resistant to 3 atm
Band: reptile skin, buckle
Price: $10,600
Variations: stainless steel bracelet ($11,300)

GP 1966

Reference number: 49555-11-131-BB60
Movement: automatic, GP Caliber 03300-0030;
ø 25.6 mm; 27 jewels; 28,800 vph; 46-hour power
reserve
Functions: hours, minutes, sweep seconds; date
Case: stainless steel, ø 40 mm, height 8.9 mm;
sapphire crystal; transparent case back; water-
resistant to 3 atm
Band: reptile skin, buckle
Price: $7,500
Variations: stainless steel bracelet ($8,200)

GP 1966 ww.tc

Reference number: 49557-11-132-11A
Movement: automatic, GP Caliber 03300-0022;
ø 25.6 mm, height 5.71 mm; 32 jewels; 28,800 vph;
46-hour power reserve
Functions: hours, minutes, subsidiary seconds;
world time display, day/night indicator (second time
zone)
Case: stainless steel, ø 40 mm, height 11 mm;
crown-adjustable inner bezel with reference city
names; sapphire crystal; transparent case back;
water-resistant to 3 atm
Band: stainless steel, double folding clasp
Price: $13,000

GP 1966 ww.tc

Reference number: 49557-52-131-BB6C
Movement: automatic, GP Caliber 03300-0022;
ø 25.6 mm, height 5.71 mm; 32 jewels; 28,800 vph;
46-hour power reserve
Functions: hours, minutes, subsidiary seconds;
world time display, day/night indicator (second time
zone)
Case: rose gold, ø 40 mm, height 12 mm; crown-
adjustable inner bezel with reference city names;
sapphire crystal; transparent case back; water-
resistant to 3 atm
Band: reptile skin, buckle
Price: $23,800

Planetarium Tri-Axial

Reference number: 99290-52-151-BA6A
Movement: manually wound, GP Caliber 09310-
0001; ø 36.1 mm, height 16.87 mm; 42 jewels;
21,600 vph; triple-axis tourbillon that turns on each
axis in 30, 60, and 120 seconds; 60-hour power
reserve
Functions: hours, minutes (off-center); day/night
indicator with 3-D globe; moon phase
Case: rose gold, ø 48 mm, height 21.52 mm;
sapphire crystal; transparent case back; water-
resistant to 3 atm
Band: reptile skin, double folding clasp
Price: $291,000

Neo Bridges

Reference number: 84000-21-001-BB6A
Movement: automatic, GP Caliber 08400;
ø 32 mm, height 5.45 mm; 29 jewels; 21,600 vph;
symmetrical skeletonized construction; NAC-coated
mainplate, PVD-coated bridges; microrotor; 48-hour
power reserve
Functions: hours, minutes
Case: titanium, ø 45 mm, height 12.18 mm;
sapphire crystal; transparent case back; water-
resistant to 3 atm
Band: reptile skin, buckle
Price: $24,000

Constant Escapement L.M.

Reference number: 93505-52-233-BA6F
Movement: manually wound, GP Caliber 09100-
0002; ø 39.2 mm, height 8.05 mm; 28 jewels;
21,600 vph; escapement with constant force, two
escape wheels and flat silicon blade spring to provide
impulses; 2 spring barrels, 144-hour power reserve
Functions: hours, minutes (off-center), sweep
seconds; linear power reserve indicator
Case: rose gold, ø 46 mm, height 14.84 mm;
sapphire crystal; transparent case back; water-
resistant to 3 atm
Band: reptile skin, folding clasp
Remarks: dedicated to late head of brand, Luigi
("Gino") Macaluso
Price: $113,000

Constant Escapement L.M.

Reference number: 93505-39-633-BA6J
Movement: manually wound, GP Caliber 09100-
0004; ø 39.2 mm, height 8.05 mm; 28 jewels;
21,600 vph; escapement with constant force, two
escape wheels and flat silicon blade spring to provide
impulses; 2 spring barrels, 144-hour power reserve
Functions: hours, minutes (off-center), sweep
seconds; linear power reserve indicator
Case: composite material (titanium and carbon
fiber), ø 46 mm, height 14.84 mm; sapphire crystal;
transparent case back; water-resistant to 3 atm
Band: reptile skin, folding clasp
Remarks: dedicated to late head of brand, Luigi
("Gino") Macaluso
Price: $98,100

Caliber GP01800-0008

Automatic; single spring barrel, 54-hour power reserve
Functions: hours, minutes, sweep seconds; date
Diameter: 30 mm
Height: 3.97 mm
Jewels: 28
Frequency: 28,800 vph

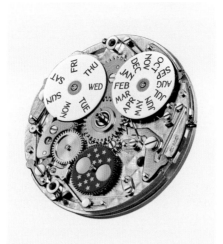

Caliber GP3300-009

Automatic; rotor with ceramic ball bearing, stop-seconds; single spring barrel, 46-hour power reserve
Functions: hours, minutes, sweep seconds; full calendar with date, weekday, month, moon phase
Diameter: 25.6 mm
Height: 3.2 mm
Jewels: 27
Balance: glucydur
Frequency: 28,800 vph
Balance spring: flat hairspring, fine adjustment
Shock protection: Kif
Remarks: 295 components

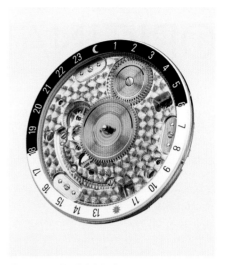

Caliber GP3300-0027

Automatic; rotor with ceramic ball bearing, stop-seconds; single spring barrel, 46-hour power reserve
Functions: hours, minutes, subsidiary seconds; world time display, day/night indicator; date
Diameter: 25.6 mm
Height: 5.71 mm
Jewels: 32
Balance: glucydur
Frequency: 28,800 vph
Balance spring: flat hairspring, fine adjustment
Shock protection: Kif
Remarks: 248 components

Caliber GP3200

Automatic; rotor with ceramic ball bearing, stop-seconds; single spring barrel, 42-hour power reserve
Functions: hours, minutes, sweep seconds or subsidiary seconds at 9 o'clock; date
Diameter: 23.3 mm
Height: 3.2 mm
Jewels: 27
Balance: glucydur
Frequency: 28,800 vph
Balance spring: flat hairspring, fine adjustment
Shock protection: Kif
Remarks: 185 components

Caliber GP09400

Automatic; 1-minute tourbillon, bidirectionally winding microrotor; tourbillon bridges of PVD-coated titanium; single spring barrel, 60-hour power reserve
Functions: hours, minutes, subsidiary seconds (on tourbillon cage)
Diameter: 36.6 mm
Height: 8.21 mm
Jewels: 27
Balance: screw balance
Frequency: 21,600 vph
Remarks: modern version of classic tourbillon under 3 gold bridges

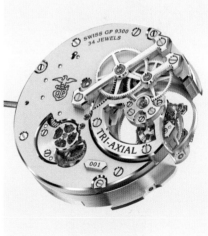

Caliber GP09300

Manually wound; 1-minute tourbillon held in 2 cages positioned at 90° with 30-second and 2-minute rotation speed; minutes; single spring barrel, 52-hour power reserve
Functions: hours, minutes; power reserve indicator
Diameter: 36.1 mm
Height: 16.83 mm
Jewels: 34
Balance: screw balance
Frequency: 21,600 vph

GLASHÜTTE ORIGINAL

Is there a little nostalgia creeping into the designers at Glashütte Original? Or is it just understated ecstasy for older looks? The retro touches that started appearing again a few years ago with the Sixties Square Tourbillon are still in vogue as the company delves into its own past for inspiration, such as the use of a special silver treatment on dials.

Glashütte Original *manufacture* roots go back to the mid-nineteenth century, though the name itself came later. The company, which had a sterling reputation for precision watches, became subsumed in the VEB Glashütter Uhrenbetriebe, a group of Glashütte watchmakers and suppliers who were collectivized as part of the former East German system. After reunification, the company took up its old moniker of Glashütte Original, and in 1995, the *manufacture* released an entirely new collection. Later, it purchased Union Glashütte. In 2000, the *manufacture* was sold to the Swiss Swatch Group, which invested a sizable amount in production space expansion at Glashütte Original headquarters.

Manufacturing depth has reached 95 percent. All movements are designed by a team of experienced in-house engineers, while the components comprising them such as plates, screws, pinions, wheels, levers, spring barrels, balance wheels, and tourbillon cages are manufactured in the upgraded production areas. These parts are lavishly finished by hand before assembly by a group of talented watchmakers. Even dials are in-house, ever since the purchase of a dial maker in Pforzheim, Germany, in 2012.

The large and elegant Senator Chronometer is a highlight of recent years with its classic design. It also boasts second and minute hands that automatically jump to zero when the crown is pulled, allowing for extremely accurate time setting. And to prove that the company is not just about tradition, it has even created a Senator-based app.

Glashütter Uhrenbetrieb GmbH
Altenberger Strasse 1
D-01768 Glashütte
Germany

Tel.:
+49-350-53-460

Fax:
+49-350-53-46-10999

E-mail:
info@glashuette-original.com

Website:
www.glashuette-original.com

Founded:
1951 (as VEB Glashütter Uhrenbetriebe)

Annual production:
N/A

U.S. distributor:
Glashütte Original
The Swatch Group (U.S.), Inc.
1200 Harbor Boulevard
Weehawken, NJ 07087
201-271-1400

Most important collections/price range:
Senator, Pano, Vintage, Ladies / $4,900 to $118,600

Grande Cosmopolite Tourbillon

Reference number: 1-89-01-03-03-04
Movement: manually wound, Glashütte Original Caliber 89-01; ø 39.2 mm, height 7.5 mm; 70 jewels and 2 diamond endstones; 21,600 vph; flying 1-minute tourbillon; 72-hour power reserve
Functions: hours, minutes, subsidiary seconds (on the tourbillon cage); world time display with 37 time zones, day/night indicator, power reserve indicator (dial side); perpetual calendar with panorama date, weekday, month, leap year
Case: platinum, ø 48 mm, height 16 mm; sapphire crystal; transparent case back; water-resistant to 5 atm
Band: reptile skin, folding clasp
Price: on request; limited to 25 pieces

PanoLunarTourbillon

Reference number: 1-93-02-05-05-04
Movement: automatic, Glashütte Original Caliber 93-02; ø 39.2 mm, height 7.65 mm; 48 jewels; 21,600 vph; flying 1-minute tourbillon, screw balance with 18 weighted screws, blued screws, skeletonized rotor with gold oscillating weight; 48-hour power reserve
Functions: hours, minutes (off-center), subsidiary seconds (on tourbillon cage); panorama date, moon phase
Case: pink gold, ø 40 mm, height 13.1 mm; sapphire crystal; transparent case back; water-resistant to 5 atm
Band: reptile skin, folding clasp
Price: $117,400
Variations: buckle ($115,400)

Senator Cosmopolite

Reference number: 1-89-02-01-04-30
Movement: automatic, Glashütte Original Caliber 89-02; ø 39.2 mm, height 8 mm; 63 jewels; 28,800 vph; Glashütte three-quarter plate, swan-neck spring to regulate rate, hand-engraved balance cock, finely finished movement; 72-hour power reserve
Functions: hours, minutes, subsidiary seconds; additional 12-hour display (second time zone), world time display with 37 time zones, day/night indicator, power reserve indicator; panorama date
Case: white gold, ø 44 mm, height 14 mm; sapphire crystal; transparent case back; water-resistant to 5 atm
Band: reptile skin, folding clasp
Price: $45,300
Variations: buckle ($42,900); pink gold ($43,500)

PanoMaticLunar

Reference number: 1-90-02-42-32-05
Movement: automatic, Glashütte Original Caliber 90-02; ø 32.6 mm, height 7 mm; 47 jewels; 28,800 vph; screw balance with 18 weighted screws, duplex-swan-neck fine regulation, three-quarter plate with Glashütte ribbing; 42-hour power reserve
Functions: hours, minutes (off-center), subsidiary seconds; panorama date, moon phase
Case: stainless steel, ø 40 mm, height 12.7 mm; sapphire crystal; transparent case back; water-resistant to 5 atm
Band: reptile skin, folding clasp
Price: $11,500
Variations: buckle ($11,200); stainless steel bracelet ($12,800); blue or gray dial ($11,500); pink gold ($23,900)

PanoReserve

Reference number: 1-65-01-26-12-35
Movement: manually wound, Glashütte Original Caliber 65-01; ø 32.2 mm, height 6.1 mm; 48 jewels; 28,800 vph; Glashütte three-quarter plate, duplex-swan-neck fine regulation; 42-hour power reserve
Functions: hours, minutes (off-center), subsidiary seconds; power reserve indicator; panorama date
Case: stainless steel, ø 40 mm, height 11.7 mm; sapphire crystal; transparent case back; water-resistant to 5 atm
Band: reptile skin, folding clasp
Price: $11,500
Variations: buckle ($11,200); stainless steel bracelet ($12,800); silver or gray dial ($11,500); pink gold with black or silver dial ($23,900)

PanoMaticInverse

Reference number: 1-91-02-01-05-30
Movement: automatic, Glashütte Original Caliber 91-02; ø 38.2 mm, height 7.1 mm; 49 jewels; 28,800 vph; Glashütte three-quarter plate, duplex-swan-neck fine regulation; inverted movement construction, hand-engraved balance cock, skeletonized rotor with gold oscillating weight; 42-hour power reserve
Functions: hours, minutes (off-center), subsidiary seconds; panorama date
Case: pink gold, ø 42 mm, height 12.3 mm; sapphire crystal; transparent case back; water-resistant to 5 atm
Band: reptile skin, folding clasp
Price: $29,700
Variations: stainless steel ($14,900)

Senator Chronograph Panorama Date

Reference number: 1-37-01-03-02-35
Movement: automatic, Glashütte Original Caliber 37-01; ø 31.6 mm, height 8 mm; 65 jewels; 28,800 vph; swan-neck spring to regulate rate; skeletonized rotor; 70-hour power reserve
Functions: hours, minutes, subsidiary seconds; power reserve indicator; flyback chronograph; panorama date
Case: stainless steel, ø 42 mm, height 14.6 mm; sapphire crystal; transparent case back; screw-in crown; water-resistant to 10 atm
Band: calfskin, folding clasp
Price: $14,900
Variations: rubber strap ($14,900); stainless steel bracelet ($16,400); pink gold with silver dial ($31,500); platinum with silver dial ($55,600)

Senator Chronometer

Reference number: 1-58-01-05-34-30
Movement: manually wound, Glashütte Original Caliber 58-01; ø 35 mm, height 6.47 mm; 58 jewels; 28,800 vph; Glashütte three-quarter plate, second reset when crown is pulled allowing precise setting of the minutes hand; DIN certified chronometer
Functions: hours, minutes, subsidiary seconds; day/ night indicator, power reserve indicator; panorama date
Case: white gold, ø 42 mm, height 12.47 mm; sapphire crystal; transparent case back; water-resistant to 5 atm
Band: reptile skin, folding clasp
Price: $32,200
Variations: buckle ($29,800); rose gold with silver dial ($30,300)

Senator Moon Phase Skeletonized Edition

Reference number: 1-49-13-15-04-30
Movement: manually wound, Glashütte Original Caliber 49-13; ø 35 mm, height 5.8 mm; 35 jewels; 28,800 vph; screw balance with 18 weighted screws, 5 gold chatons, swan-neck fine regulation; hand-skeletonized plate, bridges and cock, finely finished movement; 40-hour power reserve
Functions: hours, minutes, subsidiary seconds; power reserve indicator, moon phase
Case: white gold, ø 42 mm, height 11.2 mm; sapphire crystal; transparent case back; water-resistant to 3 atm
Band: reptile skin, folding clasp
Price: $45,000
Variations: buckle ($42,600)

Senator Observer

Reference number: 100-14-07-02-30
Movement: automatic, Glashütte Original Caliber 100-14; ø 31.15 mm, height 6.5 mm; 60 jewels; 28,800 vph; screw balance, swan-neck fine regulation; divided three-quarter plate, skeletonized rotor with gold oscillating weight, finely finished movement; 55-hour power reserve
Functions: hours, minutes, subsidiary seconds; power reserve indicator; panorama date
Case: stainless steel, ø 44 mm, height 12 mm; sapphire crystal; transparent case back; water-resistant to 5 atm
Band: calfskin, folding clasp
Price: $11,800
Variations: buckle ($11,500); silver or gray dial ($11,800); stainless steel bracelet ($13,300)

Senator Excellence

Reference number: 1-36-01-02-05-01
Movement: automatic, Glashütte Original Caliber 36-01; ø 32.2 mm, height 4.45 mm; 27 jewels; 28,800 vph; silicon hairspring, screw balance, three-quarter plate with stripe finishing, blued screws, skeletonized rotor with gold oscillating weight, finely finished movement; 100-hour power reserve
Functions: hours, minutes, sweep seconds
Case: pink gold, ø 40 mm, height 10 mm; sapphire crystal; transparent case back; water-resistant to 5 atm
Band: reptile skin, buckle
Price: $17,700
Variations: folding clasp ($19,700); stainless steel ($9,700)

Senator Excellence

Reference number: 1-36-01-03-02-01
Movement: automatic, Glashütte Original Caliber 36-01; ø 32.2 mm, height 4.45 mm; 27 jewels; 28,800 vph; silicon hairspring, screw balance, three-quarter plate with stripe finishing, blued screws, skeletonized rotor with gold oscillating weight; 100-hour power reserve
Functions: hours, minutes, sweep seconds
Case: stainless steel, ø 40 mm, height 10 mm; sapphire crystal; transparent case back; water-resistant to 5 atm
Band: calfskin, buckle
Price: $9,700
Variations: folding clasp ($10,000)

Senator Excellence Perpetual Calendar

Reference number: 1-36-02-02-05-30
Movement: automatic, Glashütte Original Caliber 36-02; ø 32.2 mm, height 7.35 mm; 49 jewels; 28,800 vph; silicon hairspring, screw balance, swan-neck fine regulation, three-quarter plate with Glashütte ribbing; 100-hour power reserve
Functions: hours, minutes, sweep seconds; perpetual calendar with panorama date, weekday, month, moon phase, leap year
Case: pink gold, ø 42 mm, height 12.8 mm; sapphire crystal; transparent case back; water-resistant to 5 atm
Band: reptile skin, folding clasp
Price: $37,100
Variations: buckle ($35,100); stainless steel ($22,300)

Senator Excellence Panorama Date Moon Phase

Reference number: 1-36-04-01-02-30
Movement: automatic, Glashütte Original Caliber 36-04; ø 32.2 mm, height 6.7 mm; 43 jewels; 28,800 vph; silicon hairspring, screw balance, three-quarter plate with Glashütte ribbing; 100-hour power reserve
Functions: hours, minutes, sweep seconds; panorama date, moon phase
Case: stainless steel, ø 40 mm, height 12.2 mm; sapphire crystal; transparent case back; water-resistant to 5 atm
Band: reptile skin, folding clasp
Price: $11,700
Variations: buckle ($11,400); stainless steel bracelet ($12,900); pink gold ($23,900)

Senator Excellence Panorama Date

Reference number: 1-36-03-02-05-30
Movement: automatic, Glashütte Original Caliber 36-03; ø 32.2 mm, height 6.7 mm; 41 jewels; 28,800 vph; silicon hairspring, screw balance, three-quarter plate with Glashütte ribbing; skeletonized rotor with gold oscillating weight; 100-hour power reserve
Functions: hours, minutes, sweep seconds; panorama date
Case: pink gold, ø 40 mm, height 12.2 mm; sapphire crystal; transparent case back; water-resistant to 5 atm
Band: reptile skin, folding clasp
Price: $22,900
Variations: buckle ($20,900); stainless steel ($10,700)

Seventies Chronograph Panorama Date

Reference number: 1-37-02-03-02-30
Movement: automatic, Glashütte Original Caliber 37-02; ø 31.6 mm, height 8 mm; 65 jewels; 28,800 vph; finely finished movement; 70-hour power reserve
Functions: hours, minutes, subsidiary seconds; power reserve indicator; flyback chronograph; panorama date
Case: stainless steel, 40 × 40 mm, height 13.5 mm; sapphire crystal; transparent case back; screw-in crown; water-resistant to 10 atm
Band: reptile skin, folding clasp
Price: $14,900
Variations: gray or silver dial ($14,900); rubber strap ($14,900); stainless steel bracelet ($16,400)

Seventies Panorama Date

Reference number: 2-39-47-12-12-14
Movement: automatic, Glashütte Original Caliber 39-47; ø 30.95 mm, height 5.9 mm; 39 jewels; 28,800 vph; swan-neck fine adjustment, three-quarter plate with Glashütte ribbing; 40-hour power reserve
Functions: hours, minutes, sweep seconds; panorama date
Case: stainless steel, 40 × 40 mm, height 11.5 mm; sapphire crystal; transparent case back; screw-in crown; water-resistant to 10 atm
Band: stainless steel, folding clasp
Price: $11,600
Variations: blue or silver dial ($11,600); reptile skin or rubber strap ($10,100)

Sixties Panorama Date

Reference number: 2-39-47-06-02-04
Movement: automatic, Glashütte Original Caliber 39-47; ø 30.95 mm, height 5.9 mm; 39 jewels; 28,800 vph; swan-neck fine adjustment, three-quarter plate with stripe finishing, skeletonized rotor with gold oscillating weight; finely finished movement; 40-hour power reserve
Functions: hours, minutes, sweep seconds; panorama date
Case: stainless steel, ø 42 mm, height 12.4 mm; sapphire crystal; transparent case back; water-resistant to 3 atm
Band: reptile skin, buckle
Price: $9,300
Variations: silver or black dial ($9,300); rose gold with silver or black dial ($19,200)

Lady Serenade

Reference number: 1-39-22-09-06-04
Movement: automatic, Glashütte Original Caliber 39-22; ø 26 mm, height 4.3 mm; 25 jewels; 28,800 vph; swan-neck fine adjustment, three-quarter plate with stripe finishing, skeletonized rotor with gold oscillating weight; finely finished movement; 40-hour power reserve
Functions: hours, minutes, sweep seconds; date
Case: stainless steel, ø 36 mm, height 10.2 mm; rose gold bezel; sapphire crystal; transparent case back; rose gold crown, set with a diamond; rose gold water-resistant to 5 atm
Band: reptile skin, buckle
Remarks: mother-of-pearl dial
Price: $10,000
Variations: various cases, bands, and dials

PanoMatic Luna

Reference number: 1-90-12-03-12-02
Movement: automatic, Glashütte Original Caliber 90-12; ø 32.6 mm, height 7 mm; 47 jewels; 28,800 vph; duplex swan-neck fine regulation, three-quarter plate with Glashütte ribbing; 42-hour power reserve
Functions: hours, minutes, subsidiary seconds; panorama date, moon phase
Case: stainless steel, ø 39.4 mm, height 12 mm; bezel set with 64 brilliant-cut diamonds; sapphire crystal; transparent case back; water-resistant to 3 atm
Band: reptile skin, buckle
Remarks: mother-of-pearl dial
Price: $20,400
Variations: white or dark mother-of-pearl dial ($20,400)

Pavonina

Reference number: 1-03-02-05-05-31
Movement: quartz
Functions: hours, minutes
Case: pink gold, 31 × 31 mm, height 7.5 mm; sapphire crystal; crown set with a diamond; water-resistant to 5 atm
Band: reptile skin, folding clasp
Remarks: mother-of-pearl dial
Price: $16,000
Variations: various cases, bands, and dials

Caliber 36

Automatic; single spring barrel, 100-hour power reserve
Functions: hours, minutes, sweep seconds
Diameter: 32.2 mm
Height: 4.45 mm
Jewels: 27
Balance: screw balance with 4 gold weight screws
Frequency: 28,800 vph
Balance spring: silicon
Shock protection: Incabloc
Related calibers: 36-02 (perpetual calendar), 36-03 (panorama date), 36-04 (panorama date, moon phase)

Caliber 37

Automatic; single spring barrel, 70-hour power reserve
Functions: hours, minutes, subsidiary seconds; power reserve indicator; flyback chronograph; panorama date
Diameter: 31.6 mm
Height: 8 mm
Jewels: 65
Balance: screw balance with 4 gold regulating screws
Frequency: 28,800 vph
Balance spring: flat hairspring, swan-neck fine regulation for rate
Remarks: finely finished movement, beveled edges, polished steel parts, blued screws, three-quarter plate with Glashütte ribbing, skeletonized rotor with 21-kt gold oscillating mass

Caliber 39

Automatic; single spring barrel, 40-hour power reserve
Functions: hours, minutes, sweep seconds (base caliber)
Diameter: 26.2 mm
Height: 4.3 mm
Jewels: 25
Balance: glucydur
Frequency: 28,800 vph
Balance spring: flat hairspring, swan-neck fine adjustment
Shock protection: Incabloc
Related calibers: 39-55 (GMT, 40 jewels), 38-52 (automatic, 25 jewels), 39-50 (perpetual calendar, 48 jewels), 38-41/39-42 (panorama date, 44 jewels), 39-31 (chronograph, 51 jewels), 39-21/39-22 (date, 25 jewels)

Caliber 58-01

Manually wound; second reset when crown is pulled allowing precise setting of minutes hand; single spring barrel, 44-hour power reserve
Functions: hours, minutes, subsidiary seconds; day/night indicator, power reserve indicator with planetary drive; panorama date
Diameter: 35 mm
Height: 6.5 mm
Jewels: 58
Balance: screw balance with 18 weighted screws
Frequency: 28,800 vph
Balance spring: flat hairspring, swan-neck fine adjustment
Remarks: three-quarter plate with Glashütte ribbing, hand-engraved balance cock

Caliber 61

Manually wound; single spring barrel, 42-hour power reserve
Functions: hours, minutes (off-center), subsidiary seconds; flyback chronograph; panorama date
Diameter: 32.2 mm
Height: 7.2 mm
Jewels: 41
Balance: screw balance with 18 weighted screws
Frequency: 28,800 vph
Balance spring: flat hairspring, swan-neck fine adjustment
Remarks: finely finished movement, beveled edges, polished steel parts, screw-mounted gold chatons, blued screws, bridges and balance cock with côtes de Genève, hand-engraved balance cock

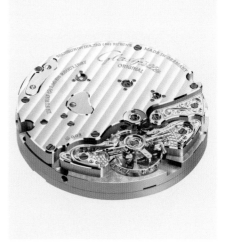

Caliber 65

Manually wound; single spring barrel, 42-hour power reserve
Functions: hours, minutes (off-center), subsidiary seconds; power reserve indicator; panorama date
Diameter: 32.2 mm
Height: 6.1 mm
Jewels: 48
Balance: screw balance with 18 weighted screws
Frequency: 28,800 vph
Balance spring: flat hairspring, duplex swan-neck fine regulation for rate and beat
Shock protection: Incabloc
Remarks: finely finished movement, three-quarter plate with Glashütte ribbing, hand-engraved balance bridge

Caliber 89-02

Automatic; single spring barrel, 72-hour power reserve
Functions: hours, minutes, subsidiary seconds; second time zone, world time with 37 time zones, day/night indicator, power reserve indicator; panorama date
Diameter: 39.2 mm
Height: 8 mm
Jewels: 63
Balance: screw balance with 4 gold regulating screws
Frequency: 28,800 vph
Balance spring: flat hairspring, duplex swan-neck fine regulation for rate and beat
Shock protection: Incabloc
Remarks: winding gears with double sun brushing, three-quarter plate with Glashütte ribbing, hand-engraved balance bridge

Caliber 90

Automatic; single spring barrel, 42-hour power reserve
Functions: hours, minutes (off-center), subsidiary seconds; panorama date, moon phase
Diameter: 32.6 mm
Height: 5.4 mm
Jewels: 28
Balance: screw balance with 18 weighted screws
Frequency: 28,800 vph
Balance spring: flat hairspring, duplex swan-neck fine regulation for rate and beat
Shock protection: Incabloc
Remarks: eccentric, skeletonized, 21-kt gold oscillating weight, hand-engraved balance bridge

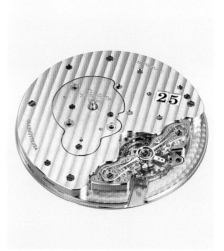

Caliber 91-02

Automatic; inverted movement with rate regulator on dial side; single spring barrel, 42-hour power reserve
Functions: hours, minutes (off-center), subsidiary seconds; panorama date
Diameter: 38.2 mm
Height: 7.1 mm
Jewels: 49
Balance: screw balance with 18 weighted screws
Frequency: 28,800 vph
Balance spring: flat hairspring, duplex swan-neck fine regulation for rate and beat
Shock protection: Incabloc
Remarks: finely finished movement, three-quarter plate with Glashütte ribbing

Caliber 94-03

Automatic; flying tourbillon; single spring barrel, 48-hour power reserve
Functions: hours, minutes, subsidiary seconds (on tourbillon cage); panorama date
Diameter: 32.2 mm
Height: 7.65 mm
Jewels: 50
Balance: screw balance with 18 weighted screws in rotating frame
Frequency: 21,600 vph
Balance spring: flat hairspring
Remarks: finely finished movement, beveled edges, polished steel parts, three-quarter plate with Glashütte ribbing, blued screws, eccentric, skeletonized, 21-kt gold oscillating weight

Caliber 96-01

Automatic; twin spring barrel, bidirectional winding in two speeds via stepped reduction gear, 42-hour power reserve
Functions: hours, minutes (off-center), subsidiary seconds; two-digit counter (pusher-controlled, forward and backward); flyback chronograph; panorama date
Diameter: 32.2 mm
Height: 8.9 mm
Jewels: 72
Balance: screw balance with 18 weighted screws
Frequency: 28,800 vph
Balance spring: flat hairspring, swan-neck fine adjustment
Remarks: separate wheel bridges for winding and chronograph, finely finished movement

Caliber 100

Automatic; single spring barrel, 55-hour power reserve
Functions: hours, minutes, sweep seconds; 0-reset mechanism for second hand activated by case pusher; panorama date
Diameter: 31.15 mm
Height: 7.1 mm
Jewels: 59
Balance: screw balance with 18 weighted screws
Frequency: 28,800 vph
Balance spring: flat hairspring, swan-neck fine adjustment
Related calibers: 100-01 (power reserve indicator), 100-02 (perpetual calendar), 100-03 (panorama date), 100-04 (moon phases), 100-05 (53 calendar weeks), 100-06 (full calendar)

GLYCINE

Founded in 1914 by Eugène Meylan, Glycine evolved into one of the industry's most innovative companies. It was already known early on for very large wristwatches, for instance. The venerable company also managed to weather the main crises of the twentieth century well, notably the Great Depression and World War II. In 1953, it came up with one of its iconic lines: 24-hour watches conceived for commercial pilots and swept up by early jet-setters. The collection is still the brand's flagship and available in both modern and newly produced retro versions.

In 1984, Hans Brechbühler took over a Glycine floundering during the quartz crisis and managed to save it from bankruptcy. Together with his youngest daughter, Katherina, he rebuilt the brand and positioned it as a specialist in robust pilot's and sports watches, which continued to be larger than those of the competition. In 2005, Katherina Brechbühler became CEO and added striking watches with an almost military look to the repertoire.

Over a century after the first Glycine watches hit the market, this dynamic company is forging ahead on a very independent path, with timekeepers that are always a little unconventional. Stephan Lack, who took over as CEO in 2011, presided over the 100th anniversary celebrations of this very traditional Swiss company.

Glycine Watch SA
Eckweg 8
CH-2500 Biel
Switzerland

Tel.:
+41-32-341-2213

Fax:
+41-32-341-2216

Web:
www.glycine-watch.ch

E-mail:
glycine@glycine-watch.ch

Founded:
1914

Number of employees:
8

Annual production:
not specified

U.S. distribution:
DKSH Luxury & Lifestyle North America, Inc
103 Carnegie Center, Suite 300
Princeton, NJ 08540
609-750-8800, 609-751-9370 (fax)
usc@glycine.us

Most important collections/price range:
Airman, Incursore, Combat, Aquarius /
mechanical watches between $1,250 and
$4,950

Combat Sub Aquarius

Reference number: GL0040
Movement: automatic, Caliber GL224 (base ETA 2824-2); ø 25.6 mm, height 4.6 mm; 25 jewels; 28,800 vph; 38-hour power reserve
Functions: hours, minutes, sweep seconds; date
Case: stainless steel, ø 46 mm, height 18.8 mm; unidirectional ceramic bezel with 0-60 scale; sapphire crystal; screw-in crown; helium valve; water-resistant to 50 atm
Band: rubber, folding clasp
Price: $1,950
Variations: various colors

Combat Sub Stealth 48

Reference number: GL0098
Movement: automatic, Caliber GL224 (base ETA 2824-2); ø 25.6 mm, height 4.6 mm; 25 jewels; 28,800 vph; 38-hour power reserve
Functions: hours, minutes, sweep seconds; date
Case: stainless steel with black PVD coating, ø 48 mm, height 11.3 mm; unidirectional bezel with aluminum inlay, with 0-60 scale; sapphire crystal; screw-in crown; water-resistant to 20 atm
Band: textile, folding clasp
Price: $990

Airman "Airfighter"

Reference number: GL0050
Movement: automatic, Caliber GL754 (base ETA 7754); ø 30 mm, height 7.9 mm; 25 jewels; 28,800 vph; finely finished movement; 48-hour power reserve
Functions: hours (24), minutes, subsidiary seconds; second 24-hour display (second time zone); chronograph; date
Case: stainless steel with black PVD coating, ø 46 mm, height 17.1 mm; bidirectional bezel, with 0-24 scale and safety screws; sapphire crystal; transparent case back; water-resistant to 20 atm
Band: calfskin, buckle
Price: $2,990
Remarks: chronograph function control with slider on left side

Graham
Boulevard des Eplatures 38
CH-2300 La Chaux-de-Fonds
Switzerland

Tel.:
+41-32-910-9888

Fax:
+41-32-910-9889

E-mail:
info@graham1695.com

Website:
www.graham1695.com

Founded:
1995

Number of employees:
approx. 30

Annual production:
5,000–7,000 watches

U.S. distributor:
Graham Watches USA
261 Madison Avenue, 9th Floor
New York, NY 10016
516-526-9092

Most important collections:
Geo.Graham, Chronofighter, Silverstone,
Swordfish

GRAHAM

In the mid-1990s, unusual creations gave an old English name in watchmaking a brand-new life. In the eighteenth century, George Graham perfected the cylinder escapement and the dead-beat escapement as well as inventing the chronograph. For these contributions and more, Graham certainly earned the right to be considered one of the big wheels in watchmaking history.

Despite his merits in the development of precision timekeeping, it was the mechanism he invented to measure short times—the chronograph—that became the trademark of his wristwatch company. To this day, the fundamental principle of the chronograph hasn't changed at all: A second set of hands can be engaged to or disengaged from the constant flow of energy of the movement. Given the British Masters' aim to honor this English inventor, it is certainly no surprise that the Graham collection includes quite a number of fascinating chronograph variations.

In 2000, the company released the Chronofighter, with its striking thumb-controlled lever mechanism—a modern twist on a function designed for WWII British fighter pilots, who couldn't activate the crown button of their flight chronographs with their thick gloves on. To enhance the retro look and feel, the brand decided to release several models bearing famous World War II pinups. The company has also started a special series to "give back," as it were. Made of a special carbon, this US Navy SEAL Chronofighter also features a special camo look designed to help hide soldiers from satellite cameras. A part of the sales of these watches will go the nonprofit Navy SEAL Foundation.

In recent years, Graham has also added comparatively conventionally designed watches to its collection. For lovers of special pieces, there are the models of the Geo. Graham series. It was the name used by the brilliant watchmaker-inventor The Tourbillon "Orrery" developed in collaboration with Christophe Claret, is a perfect exemplar of the line featuring a beautifully finished flying tourbillon with a miniaturized 3D view of the solar system.

Chronofighter Vintage GMT
Reference number: 2CVBC.G01A
Movement: automatic, Graham Caliber G1733 (base ETA 7750); ø 30 mm, height 8.4 mm; 28 jewels; 28,800 vph; 48-hour power reserve
Functions: hours, minutes, subsidiary seconds; second 24-hour display (2nd time zone); chronograph; large date
Case: stainless steel, ø 44 mm; unidirectional ceramic bezel with 0-24 scale; sapphire crystal; transparent case back; crown and pusher with finger lever on left side; water-resistant to 10 atm
Band: calfskin, buckle
Price: $6,950

Chronofighter Vintage Nose Art Ltd.
Reference number: 2CVAS.B21A
Movement: automatic, Graham Caliber G1747; ø 30 mm, height 8 mm; 25 jewels; 28,800 vph; 48-hour power reserve
Functions: hours, minutes, subsidiary seconds; chronograph; date, weekday
Case: stainless steel, ø 44 mm; sapphire crystal; transparent case back; crown and pusher with finger lever on left side; water-resistant to 10 atm
Band: calfskin, buckle
Price: $5,450; limited to 100 pieces

Chronofighter Vintage Aircraft Ltd.
Reference number: 2CVAV.B17A
Movement: automatic, Graham Caliber G1747; ø 30 mm, height 8 mm; 25 jewels; 28,800 vph; 48-hour power reserve
Functions: hours, minutes, subsidiary seconds; chronograph; date, weekday
Case: stainless steel with gray PVD coating, ø 44 mm; ceramic bezel; sapphire crystal; crown and pusher with finger lever on left side; water-resistant to 10 atm
Band: textile, buckle
Price: $5,450; limited to 250 pieces

Chronofighter Vintage Pulsometer Ltd.

Reference number: 2CVCS.B20A
Movement: automatic, Graham Caliber G1718; ø 30 mm, height 8 mm; 25 jewels; 28,800 vph; 48-hour power reserve
Functions: hours, minutes, subsidiary seconds; chronograph; date, weekday
Case: stainless steel, ø 44 mm; sapphire crystal; transparent case back; crown and pusher with finger lever on left side; water-resistant to 10 atm
Band: calfskin, buckle
Remarks: pulsometer scale on dial
Price: $4,450; limited to 250 pieces

Chronofighter Target

Reference number: 2CCAC.B33A
Movement: automatic, Graham Caliber G1747; ø 30 mm, height 8 mm; 25 jewels; 28,800 vph; 48-hour power reserve
Functions: hours, minutes, subsidiary seconds; chronograph; date, weekday
Case: stainless steel, ø 47 mm; ceramic bezel; sapphire crystal; transparent case back; crown and pusher and carbon finger lever on left side; water-resistant to 10 atm
Band: calfskin, buckle
Price: $6,900

Chronofighter Target

Reference number: 2CCAU.B32A
Movement: automatic, Graham Caliber G1747; ø 30 mm, height 8 mm; 25 jewels; 28,800 vph; 48-hour power reserve
Functions: hours, minutes, subsidiary seconds; chronograph; date, weekday
Case: stainless steel with black PVD coating, ø 47 mm; ceramic bezel; sapphire crystal; transparent case back; crown and pusher and carbon finger lever on left side; water-resistant to 10 atm
Band: calfskin, buckle
Price: $6,900

Chronofighter Superlight Carbon

Reference number: 2CCBK.B30A
Movement: automatic, Graham Caliber G1747; ø 30 mm, height 8 mm; 25 jewels; 28,800 vph; 48-hour power reserve
Functions: hours, minutes, subsidiary seconds; chronograph; date
Case: carbon fiber, ø 47 mm, height 15 mm; sapphire crystal; transparent case back; crown and pusher with finger lever on left side; water-resistant to 10 atm
Band: rubber, buckle
Price: $9,900

Silverstone RS Racing

Reference number: 2STEA.B16A
Movement: automatic, Graham Caliber G1749 (base ETA 7750); ø 30 mm, height 7.9 mm; 25 jewels; 28,800 vph; 48-hour power reserve
Functions: hours, minutes, subsidiary seconds; chronograph; date, weekday
Case: stainless steel, ø 46 mm, height 16.1 mm; sapphire crystal; transparent case back; water-resistant to 10 atm
Band: rubber, folding clasp
Price: $5,200

Geo.Graham Orrery Tourbillon

Reference number: 2GGAP.U01A
Movement: manually wound, Graham Caliber G1800 (base Christophe Claret); ø 39 mm, height 10.5 mm; 35 jewels; 21,600 vph; 1-minute tourbillon, mechanical model of solar system with 3D planet display, two spring barrels, with côtes de Genève; 72-hour power reserve
Functions: hours, minutes (off-center); 100-year calendar with date, month, zodiac signs and year (case back); 3D Earth, moon, and Mars
Case: pink gold, ø 48 mm, height 17.6 mm; sapphire crystal; transparent case back; water-resistant to 5 atm
Band: reptile skin, folding clasp
Price: on request; limited to 8 pieces

Seiko Holdings
Ginza, Chuo, Tokyo
Japan

Website:
www.seikowatches.com

Founded:
1881

Number of employees:
90,000 (for the entire holding)

U.S. distributor:
Seiko Corporation of America
1111 Macarthur Boulevard
Mahwah, NJ 07430
201-529-5730
custserv@seikousa.com
www.seikousa.com

Most important collections/price range:
Grand Seiko / approx. $5,000 to $55,000

GRAND SEIKO

In the hustle and bustle of Baselworld 2017, the news may have been somewhat muffled, but it was a big step for the traditional brand Seiko: Shinji Hattori, president of the Seiko Watch Company, announced that the Grand Seiko line had become a separate manufacture brand. The Grand Seiko watches always had their own dedicated personality, he said, and their design required a separate approach to building the movements.

Indeed, the models released in this line always existed in a segment of their own and had become something of a focus for collectors. For the brand's fiftieth anniversary in 2010, the Grand Seiko collection was given a host of new models and started being sold on the European market.

What makes the Grand Seiko collection special is the "Spring Drive" technology, a technology invented by a Seiko engineer that took twenty-eight years to perfect and, according to the company, six hundred prototypes. Essentially, it consists of a complex combination of mostly mechanical parts with a small but crucial electronic regulating element to tame the energy from the mainspring. These watches also boast some classical mechanical hijinks, such as the "High-Beat" balance with 36,000 vibrations per hour. It's no surprise that classic watch fans have welcomed the Grand Seikos into their midst. The range of models has been widened with a number of sportive divers' watches that are giving established Swiss brands some stiff competition when it comes to price and amenities. In terms of segments, the Seiko Watch Corporation also covers the highest end of the spectrum with its brand Credor, which, however, is not sold outside of Japan.

Spring Drive Chronograph
Reference number: SBGC205
Movement: manually wound, Seiko Caliber 9R86; ø 30 mm, height 7.6 mm; 50 jewels; electromagnetical Tri-Synchro Regulator escapement system with sliding wheel column, wheel control of chronograph functions/vertical clutch; 72-hour power reserve
Functions: hours, minutes, subsidiary seconds; second 24-hour display (second time zone), power reserve indicator; chronograph; date
Case: titanium, ø 43.5 mm, height 16 mm; sapphire crystal; transparent case back; screw-in crown; water-resistant to 10 atm
Band: titanium, folding clasp
Price: $9,600

Spring Drive
Reference number: SBGA211
Movement: manually wound, Seiko Caliber 9R65; ø 30 mm, height 5.1 mm; 30 jewels; electromagnetic Tri-Synchro Regulator escapement system with sliding wheel; 72-hour power reserve
Functions: hours, minutes, sweep seconds; power reserve indicator; date
Case: titanium, ø 41 mm, height 12.5 mm; sapphire crystal; transparent case back; screw-in crown; water-resistant to 10 atm
Band: titanium, folding clasp
Price: $5,800

Spring Drive 8 Day Power Reserve
Reference number: SBGD201
Movement: manually wound, Seiko Caliber 9R01; ø 37 mm, height 7.1 mm; 56 jewels; electromagnetic Tri-Synchro Regulator escapement system with sliding wheel; 192-hour power reserve
Functions: hours, minutes, sweep seconds
Case: platinum, ø 43 mm, height 13.2 mm; sapphire crystal; transparent case back; water-resistant to 10 atm
Band: reptile skin, folding clasp
Price: $55,000

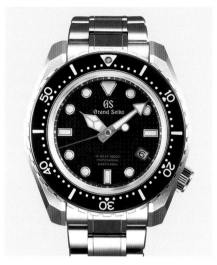

Hi-Beat Professional Diver's
Reference number: SBGH255
Movement: automatic, Seiko Caliber 9S85;
ø 28.4 mm, height 5.9 mm; 37 jewels; 36,000 vph;
antimagnetic up to 16,000 A/m; 55-hour power
reserve
Functions: hours, minutes, sweep seconds; date
Case: titanium, ø 46.9 mm, height 17 mm;
unidirectional bezel, with 0-60 scale; sapphire crystal;
screw-in crown; water-resistant to 60 atm
Band: titanium, folding clasp with safety lock and
extension link
Price: $9,600

Hi-Beat 36,000 GMT
Reference number: SBGJ203
Movement: automatic, Seiko Caliber 9S86;
ø 28.4 mm, height 5.9 mm; 37 jewels; 36,000 vph;
antimagnetic up to 4,800 A/m; 55-hour power
reserve
Functions: hours, minutes, sweep seconds; second
24-hour display (second time zone); date
Case: stainless steel, ø 40 mm, height 14 mm;
sapphire crystal; transparent case back; screw-in
crown; water-resistant to 10 atm
Band: stainless steel, folding clasp
Price: $6,300

Automatic
Reference number: SBGR261
Movement: automatic, Seiko Caliber 9S65;
ø 28.4 mm, height 6 mm; 35 jewels; 28,800 vph;
antimagnetic up to 4,800 A/m; 72-hour power
reserve
Functions: hours, minutes, sweep seconds; date
Case: stainless steel, ø 39.5 mm, height 13.1 mm;
sapphire crystal; transparent case back; water-
resistant to 3 atm
Band: reptile skin, folding clasp
Price: $4,300

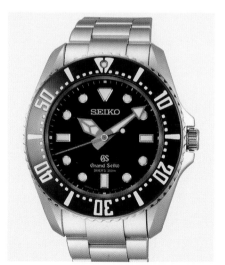

High-Precision Quartz Diver's
Reference number: SBGX117
Movement: quartz, Seiko Caliber 9F61; twin pulse
control motor, antimagnetic up to 16,000 A/m
Functions: hours, minutes, sweep seconds
Case: stainless steel, ø 40 mm, height 13 mm;
unidirectional bezel, with 0-60 scale; sapphire crystal;
water-resistant to 20 atm
Band: stainless steel, folding clasp, with safety lock
and extension link
Price: $4,100

High-Precision Quartz
Reference number: SBGV205
Movement: quartz, Seiko Caliber 9F82; twin pulse
control motor, antimagnetic up to 4,800 A/m
Functions: hours, minutes, sweep seconds; date
Case: stainless steel, ø 40 mm, height 10.4 mm;
sapphire crystal; water-resistant to 10 atm
Band: stainless steel, folding clasp
Price: $3,100

High-Precision Quartz
Reference number: SBGX259
Movement: quartz, Seiko Caliber 9F82; twin pulse
control motor, antimagnetic up to 4,800 A/m
Functions: hours, minutes, sweep seconds; date
Case: stainless steel, ø 37 mm, height 10 mm;
sapphire crystal; water-resistant to 10 atm
Band: stainless steel, folding clasp
Price: $2,200

Greubel Forsey SA
Eplatures-Grise 16
CH-2301 La Chaux-de-Fonds
Switzerland

Tel.:
+41-32-925-4545

Fax:
+41-32-925-4502

E-mail:
info@greubelforsey.com
press@greubelforsey.com

Website:
www.greubelforsey.com

Founded:
2004

Number of employees:
approx. 100

Annual production:
approx. 100 watches

U.S. distributor:
Time Art Distribution
550 Fifth Avenue
New York, NY 10036
212-221-8041
info@timeartdistribution.com

Remarks:
Prices given only in Swiss francs (before taxes).
Use daily exchange rate for conversion.

GREUBEL FORSEY

Each year, at the SIHH, the journalists visit brands. But they congregate at the Greubel Forsey booth to take part in something close to a religious experience, an initiation into the esoteric art of *ultra-haute horlogerie*.

In 2004, when Alsatian Robert Greubel and Englishman Stephen Forsey presented a new movement at Baselworld, eyes snapped open: Their watch featured not one but *two* tourbillon carriages working at a 30° incline. In their design, not only did Forsey and Greubel take up the basic Abraham-Louis Breguet idea of canceling out the deviations of the balance by the continuous rotation of the tourbillon cage, but they went further, creating a quadruple tourbillon.

In 2010, Greubel Forsey moved into new facilities at a renovated farmhouse between Le Locle and La Chaux-de-Fonds and a brand-new modern building. After capturing an Aiguille D'Or for the magical Double Tourbillon 30° and the Grand Prix d'Horlogerie in Geneva, these two specialists snatched up the top prize at the International Chronometry Competition in Le Locle for the Double Tourbillon 30°.

Greubel and Forsey continue to stun the highest-end fans with some spectacular pieces, like the Quadruple Tourbillon Secret, which shows the complex play of the tourbillons through the case back, and the Greubel Forsey GMT with the names of world cities and a huge floating globe. Their first Art Piece came out in 2013, a most natural collaboration with British miniaturist Willard Wigan, who can sculpt the head of a pin.

Having founded and nursed a strong ultra-technical brand, Greubel and Forsey decided to let other watchmakers use their resources to actualize their own vision of watchmaking. The Signature series started with a remarkably simple three hand watch (on two dials) by the company's own Didier J.G. Cretin.

Signature 1 Platinum

Reference number: P370
Movement: manually wound, Caliber GFS1; ø 34.4 mm, height 7.4 mm; 21 jewels; 18,000 vph; large balance wheel with variable inertia (ø 12.6 mm), Phillips end curve, mainplate of German silver with black PVD coating; 54-hour power reserve
Functions: hours, minutes, subsidiary seconds
Case: platinum, ø 41.4 mm, height 11.7 mm; sapphire crystal; transparent case back; water-resistant to 3 atm
Band: reptile skin, buckle
Remarks: exclusive design developed in cooperation with watchmaker Didier J. Crétin
Price: CHF 190,000; limited to 33 pieces
Variations: platinum (limited to 11 pieces); white gold (limited to 11 pieces); pink gold (limited to 11 pieces)

Tourbillon 24 Seconds Vision Platinum

Reference number: P160
Movement: manually wound, Caliber GF 01r; ø 36.4 mm, height 7.09 mm; 41 jewels; 21,600 vph; 24-second tourbillon cage containing variable inertia balance inclined at 25°; Phillips end curve; 2 spring barrels, plate and bridges of German silver; 72-hour power reserve
Functions: hours, minutes, subsidiary seconds; power reserve indicator (on movement side)
Case: platinum, ø 43.5 mm, height 13.65 mm; sapphire crystal; transparent case back; water-resistant to 3 atm
Band: reptile skin, folding clasp
Price: CHF 310,000

Grande Sonnerie

Reference number: P048
Movement: manually wound ø 36.4 mm, height 11.13 mm; 85 jewels; 21,600 vph; 24-second tourbillon, large balance with 6 regulating screws, Phillips end curve; 2 spring barrels; large and small striking mechanism on demand; 72-hour power reserve
Functions: hours, minutes, subsidiary seconds; displays (for movement and chimes); minute repeater
Case: titanium, ø 43.5 mm, height 16.13 mm; sapphire crystal; transparent case back; pushers in white gold; water-resistant to 3 atm
Band: reptile skin, folding clasp
Price: CHF 1,150,000

H. MOSER & CIE.

H. Moser & Cie has been making a name for itself in the industry as a serious watchmaker, though not averse to flashes of humor, like the Swiss Mad (sic) Watch made of Vacherin Mont d'Or cheese it presented at the SIHH 2017 (the cheese for the case is mixed with a hardening resin). And there's the Swiss Alp watch, made to look like an Apple Watch, but with all the essential Moser codes.

The company was founded by one Heinrich Moser (1805–1874) from Schaffhausen, where he served as "city watchmaker." He moved to Le Locle and, in 1825, founded his company at age twenty-one. Soon after, he moved to Saint Petersburg, Russia, where ambitious watchmakers were enjoying a good market. In 1828, H. Moser & Cie. was brought to life—a brand resuscitated in modern times by a group of investors and watch experts together with Moser's great-grandson, Roger Nicholas Balsiger.

Under the technical leadership of Dr. Jürgen Lange, H. Moser & Cie. has focused on the fundamentals. The company has made movements that contain a separate, removable escapement module supporting the pallet lever, escape wheel, and balance. The latter is fitted with the Straumann spring, made by Precision Engineering, another one of the Moser Group companies.

This small company has considerable technical know-how, which is probably what attracted MELB Holding, owners of Hautlence, and now majority owners of H. Moser shares. Edouard Meylan became CEO of the brand in May 2013 and set out to streamline and refocus its energy on the core look and feel: understatement, soft tones, and subtle technicity. They have been divided over three core collections named Endeavour, Venturer, and Pioneer, all with deceptively simple esthetics. The dials are kept "clean," in solid colors and with a minimum of distractions. The month on the Endeavour, for instance, is a small sweep hand ending in an arrowhead that points to the hours, which double as the months.

H. Moser & Cie.
Rundbuckstrasse 10
CH-8212 Neuhausen am Rheinfall
Switzerland

Tel.:
+41-52-674-0050

Fax:
+41-52-674-0055

E-mail:
info@h-moser.com

Website:
www.h-moser.com

Founded:
1828

Number of employees:
55

Annual production:
approx. 1,200 watches

U.S. distributor:
H. Moser & Cie. distributor:
Horology Works LLC
11 Flagg Road
West Hartford, CT 06117
M. +1-860-986-9676
mmargolis@horologyworks.com
For authorized retailers, please see
www.h-moser.com.

Most important collections/price range:
Endeavour / approx. $17,200 to $77,000;
Pioneer / approx. $11,900 to $49,900;
Venturer / approx. $19,500 to $100,000

Endeavour Perpetual Calendar
Reference number: 1341-0207
Movement: manually wound, Moser Caliber HMC 341; ø 34 mm, height 5.8 mm; 28 jewels; 18,000 vph; interchangeable escapement with Straumann hairspring, "flash calendar" functions correctable forward and backward; 168-hour power reserve
Functions: hours, minutes, subsidiary seconds; power reserve indicator; perpetual calendar with large date and small month display in middle, leap year (dial side)
Case: white gold, ø 40.8 mm, height 11.05 mm; sapphire crystal; transparent case back
Band: reptile skin, folding clasp
Price: $60,000
Variations: rose gold ($60,000)

Venturer Tourbillon Dual Time
Reference number: 2802-0202
Movement: automatic, Moser Caliber HMC 802; ø 34 mm, height 6.5 mm; 33 jewels; 21,600 vph; interchangeable escapement with 1-minute tourbillon, Straumann double hairspring; 72-hour power reserve
Functions: hours, minutes; additional 12-hour display (second time zone) on request
Case: white gold, ø 41.5 mm, height 14.3 mm; sapphire crystal; transparent case back
Band: reptile skin, folding clasp
Price: $99,500
Variations: various dials

Venturer Small Seconds XL
Reference number: 2327-0203
Movement: manually wound, Moser Caliber HMC 327; ø 32 mm, height 4.4 mm; 28 jewels; 18,000 vph; escapement with Straumann hairspring; 72-hour power reserve
Functions: hours, minutes, subsidiary seconds; power reserve indicator (on movement side)
Case: white gold, ø 43 mm, height 12.6 mm; sapphire crystal; transparent case back
Band: antelope leather, buckle
Price: $23,800

Endeavour Centre Seconds Concept Cosmic Green

Reference number: 1343-0110
Movement: manually wound, Moser Caliber HMC 343; ø 34 mm, height 5.8 mm; 28 jewels; 18,000 vph; interchangeable escapement with Straumann hairspring; 168-hour power reserve
Functions: hours, minutes, sweep seconds; power reserve indicator (on movement side)
Case: rose gold, ø 40.8 mm, height 10.9 mm; sapphire crystal; transparent case back
Band: reptile skin, buckle
Price: $26,500; limited to 20 pieces
Variations: white gold (limited to 20 pieces)

Venturer Big Date

Reference number: 2100-0200
Movement: manually wound, Moser Caliber HMC 100; ø 34 mm, height 6.3 mm; 31 jewels; 18,000 vph; interchangeable escapement with Straumann hairspring "flash calendar" functions correctable forward and backward; 168-hour power reserve
Functions: hours, minutes, subsidiary seconds; power reserve indicator (on movement side); large date
Case: white gold, ø 41.5 mm, height 14.5 mm; sapphire crystal; transparent case back
Band: reptile skin, buckle
Price: $29,900
Variations: blue dial

Swiss Alp Watch S

Reference number: 5324-0201
Movement: manually wound, Moser Caliber HMC 324; 32.6 × 36.6 mm, height 4.8 mm; 27 jewels; 18,000 vph; interchangeable escape with Straumann double balance spring, white gold pallet fork and escapement wheel; 96-hour power reserve
Functions: hours, minutes, subsidiary seconds
Case: white gold, 38.2 × 44 mm, height 10.3 mm; sapphire crystal; transparent case back
Band: reptile skin, buckle
Price: $24,900

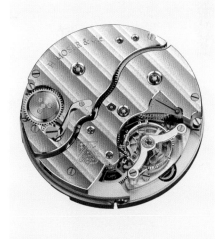

Caliber HMC 341

Manually wound; exchangeable escape with beveled wheels, hardened gold pallet fork and escapement wheel; screw mounted gold chatons; double spring barrel, 168-hour power reserve
Functions: hours, minutes, subsidiary seconds; power reserve indicator; perpetual calendar with large date and small sweep month hand, leap year (dial side)
Diameter: 34 mm
Height: 5.8 mm
Jewels: 28
Balance: glucydur with white gold screws
Frequency: 18,000 vph
Balance spring: Straumann with Breguet endcurve
Shock protection: Incabloc
Remarks: double-pull crown mechanism for easy switching of crown position

Caliber HMC 802

Automatic; exchangeable 1-minute tourbillon, double hairspring; single spring barrel, 72-hour power reserve
Functions: hours, minutes; additional 12-hour display (second time zone, display on request)
Diameter: 34 mm
Height: 6.5 mm
Jewels: 33
Balance: glucydur with white gold screws
Frequency: 21,600 vph
Balance spring: Straumann double hairspring
Shock protection: Incabloc
Remarks: rotor with gold oscillating weight

Caliber HMC 100

Manually wound; exchangeable escapement, gold pallet fork and escapement wheel; double mainspring barrel, 168-hour power reserve
Functions: hours, minutes, subsidiary seconds; power reserve indicator (on movement side); large date
Diameter: 34 mm
Height: 6.3 mm
Jewels: 31
Balance: glucydur with white gold screws
Frequency: 18,000 vph
Balance spring: Straumann with Breguet endcurve
Shock protection: Incabloc
Remarks: double-pull crown mechanism for easy switching of crown position

HABRING²

Fine mechanical works of art are created with smaller and larger complications in a small workshop in Austria's Völkermarkt, where the name Habring² stands for an unusual joint project. "We only come in a set," Maria Kristina Habring jokes. Her husband, Richard, adds with a grin, "You get double for your money here." The couple's first watch labeled with their own name came out in 2004: a simple, congenial three-handed watch based on a refined and unostentatiously decorated ETA pocket watch movement, the Unitas 6498-1. In connoisseur circles the news spread like wildfire that exceptional quality down to the smallest detail was hidden behind its inconspicuous specifications.

Since then, they have put their efforts into such projects as completely revamping the Time Only, powered by brand-new base movement Caliber A09. All the little details that differentiate this caliber are either especially commissioned or are made in-house. Caliber A09 is available both as a manually wound movement (A09M) and a bidirectionally wound automatic with an exclusive gear system. Its sporty version drives a pilot's watch. Also more or less in-house are the components of the Seconde Foudroyante. Because the drive needs a lot of energy, the foudroyante mechanism has been given its own spring barrel. In the Caliber AO7F, the eighth of a second is driven by a gear train directly coupled with the movement without surrendering any reliability, power reserve, or amplitude.

For the twentieth anniversary of the IWC double chronograph, Habring² has built a limited, improved edition. The movement, based on the ETA 7750 "Valjoux," was conceived in 1991/1992 with an additional module between the chronograph and automatic winder. With new processes like deep reacting ion etching allowing many brands to create their own escapements, Habring² still remains true to traditional materials like steel. "Being able to make a pallet lever is not only having command of a key technology," says Maria, "it's the best way to remain competitive in an unevenly distributed field."

Habring Uhrentechnik OG
Hauptplatz 16
A-9100 Völkermarkt
Austria

Tel.:
+43-4232-51-300

Fax:
+43-4232-51-300-4

E-mail:
info@habring.com

Website:
www.habring2.com; www.habring.com

Founded:
1997

Number of employees:
4

Annual production:
180 watches

U.S. retailers:
Martin Pulli (USA-East)
215-508-4610
www.martinpulli.com
Passion Fine Jewelry (USA-West)
858-794-8000
www.passionfinejewelry.com

Most important collections/price range:
Felix / from $5,100; Jumping Second / from $6,150; Doppel 3 / from $7,550; Chrono COS / from $6,900

Felix
Movement: manually wound, Habring Caliber A11B; ø 30 mm, height 4.2 mm; 18 jewels; 28,800 vph; Triovis fine adjustment, finely finished movement; 48-hour power reserve
Functions: hours, minutes, subsidiary seconds
Case: stainless steel, ø 38.5 mm, height 7 mm; sapphire crystal; transparent case back; water-resistant to 3 atm
Band: calfskin, buckle
Price: $5,000

Felix
Movement: manually wound, Habring Caliber A11B; ø 30 mm, height 4.2 mm; 18 jewels; 28,800 vph; Triovis fine adjustment, finely finished movement; 48-hour power reserve
Functions: hours, minutes, subsidiary seconds
Case: stainless steel, ø 38.5 mm, height 7 mm; sapphire crystal; transparent case back; water-resistant to 3 atm
Band: calfskin, buckle
Price: $5,000

Felix
Movement: manually wound, Habring Caliber A11B; ø 30 mm, height 4.2 mm; 18 jewels; 28,800 vph; Triovis fine adjustment, finely finished movement; 48-hour power reserve
Functions: hours, minutes, subsidiary seconds
Case: stainless steel, ø 38.5 mm, height 7 mm; sapphire crystal; transparent case back; water-resistant to 3 atm
Band: calfskin, buckle
Price: $5,000

Erwin

Movement: manually wound, Habring Caliber A11MS; ø 30 mm, height 5.3 mm; 21 jewels; 28,800 vph; Triovis fine adjustment, finely finished movement; 48-hour power reserve
Functions: hours, minutes, sweep seconds (jumping)
Case: stainless steel, ø 38.5 mm, height 9 mm; sapphire crystal; transparent case back; water-resistant to 3 atm
Band: calfskin, buckle
Price: $6,150

Repetition

Movement: manually wound, Habring Caliber 11B (base with Dubois Dépraz D90 module); ø 36 mm, height 7.85 mm; 18 jewels; 28,800 vph; Triovis fine adjustment, finely finished movement; 48-hour power reserve
Functions: hours, minutes, subsidiary seconds; 5-minute repeater
Case: titanium, ø 42 mm, height 13.5 mm; sapphire crystal; transparent case back
Band: calfskin, buckle
Price: $20,000
Variations: stainless steel

Jumping Second Pilot

Movement: manually wound, Habring Caliber A11MS; ø 36.6 mm, height 7 mm; 20 jewels; 28,800 vph; Triovis fine adjustment
Functions: hours, minutes, sweep seconds (jumping)
Case: stainless steel, ø 42 mm, height 13 mm; sapphire crystal; transparent case back
Band: calfskin, buckle
Price: $5,950
Variations: automatic winding ($6,300); various dials

Foudroyante

Movement: manually wound, Habring Caliber A11MF; ø 30 mm, height 7 mm; 20 jewels; 28,800 vph; Triovis fine adjustment
Functions: hours, minutes, sweep seconds (jumping); eighth of a second display (flashing second or "foudroyante")
Case: stainless steel, ø 42 mm, height 13 mm; sapphire crystal; transparent case back; water-resistant to 5 atm
Band: calfskin, buckle
Price: $7,100
Variations: automatic winding ($7,450); various dials

Chrono COS

Movement: automatic, Habring Caliber A08COS; ø 30 mm, height 7.9 mm; 25 jewels; 28,800 vph; Triovis fine adjustment, crown-control of all chronograph functions ("Crown Operation System")
Functions: hours, minutes, subsidiary seconds; chronograph
Case: stainless steel, ø 42 mm, height 13 mm; sapphire crystal; transparent case back; water-resistant to 5 atm
Band: calfskin, buckle
Price: $6,650
Variations: titanium ($7,750); hand-wound ($6,900); various dials

Doppel 3

Movement: manually wound, Habring Caliber A08MR-MONO; ø 30 mm, height 8.4 mm; 23 jewels; 28,800 vph; Triovis fine adjustment; 48-hour power reserve
Functions: hours, minutes, subsidiary seconds; split-second chronograph
Case: stainless steel, ø 42 mm, height 13 mm; sapphire crystal; transparent case back; water-resistant to 5 atm
Band: calfskin, buckle
Price: $7,650; limited to 20 pieces per year
Variations: various dial designs

HAGER WATCHES

Keeping it simple and smart is a Hager specialty. The company, owned and operated by American service veteran Pierre "Pete" Brown, is named after the town where the company was started in 2009. The business model is equally streamlined: create high-quality and affordable automatic watches accessible to those who have never experienced the joy of owning a mechanical watch. The look: rugged and refined, for individuals with a bit of adventure in their bones.

The timepieces are designed by Brown and his small team in Hagerstown. All the cues are there for the watch connoisseur, the brushed and polished cases with beveled edges, two-tiered stadium dial, brass markers and hands outlined in black and coated with Superluminova, domed sapphire crystal. Also enhanced with Superluminova are 120-click and 24-click GMT ceramic bezels. The cases are rated a sporty 20 atm, meaning the timepieces are good for more than just washing the dishes. Inside them beats one of a variety of automatic winding Swiss and Japanese mechanical movements that are both installed and regulated in the United States. The goal is to balance quality and affordability. "Although we assemble on-site, we use components from third-parties suppliers," says Brown. "We have several suppliers that we work with in Switzerland and Hong Kong that supply us with the best components that I'm seeking." The spirit of elegant adventure is in each of the collections, be it the tough-looking Commando Professional, the Traveler GMT with ceramic inserts and DLC coating, or the classic Flieger (pilot's watch).

Brown is well aware of the foibles of the watch industry, one major complaint being customer service. His personal boast since launching the company, is that Hager has never charged a customer for a repair yet, even when it's clear that the customer is at fault. "We aren't just selling watches," says Brown, "we are selling the experience of owning a luxury timepiece. That's not to say that at some point we may have to reverse this because of overall costs, but it's been a hallmark of our brand and it builds brand loyalty."

Hager Watches
36 South Potomac Street
Suite 204
Hagerstown, MD 21740

Tel.:
240-329-0071

E-mail:
info@hagerwatches.com

Website:
www.hagerwatches.com

Founded:
2009

Number of employees:
2

Annual production:
500–1,000 watches

Most important collections/price range:
Commando Professional, GMT Traveler, Skymaster, Flieger / $350 to $3,525

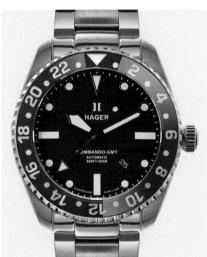

GMT Traveler Blue Insert

Reference number: 16738
Movement: automatic, HGR 60 (base ETA 2836); ø 25.6 mm; height 5.67 mm; 26 jewels; 28,800 vph; 40-hour power reserve
Functions: hours, minutes, sweep seconds; date; 2nd time zone
Case: stainless steel with DLC coating, ø 42 mm, height 14.5 mm; screw-in crown; bidirectional bezel with black ceramic insert; sapphire crystal; screwed-down case back; water-resistant to 20 atm
Band: stainless steel, buckle
Price: $700
Variations: black ceramic insert ($700); DLC with black ceramic insert ($800); DLC with blue ceramic insert ($800)

Skymaster

Reference number: A120771
Movement: Dubois Dépraz; ø 25.6 mm; height 7.9 mm; 62 jewels; 28,800 vph; quick correction of day-date; 40-hour power reserve
Functions: hours, minutes, tachymeter hand as second hand; chronograph; date
Case: stainless steel, ø 44 mm, height 16 mm; sapphire crystal; screwed-down case back; water-resistant to 10 atm
Band: stainless steel, buckle
Price: $3,250

Aquamariner

Reference number: 6203M
Movement: automatic, HGR 50 (base Miyota 8215), ø 26 mm; height 5.67 mm; 21 jewels; 21,600 vph; 40-hour power reserve
Functions: hours, minutes, sweep seconds; date
Case: stainless steel ø 41 mm, height 13 mm; screw-in crown; unilateral bezel with black stainless steel insert; sapphire crystal; screwed-down case back; water-resistant to 30 atm
Band: stainless steel, folding clasp with slide lock extension
Price: $350
Variations: stainless steel with midnight blue stainless steel insert; stainless steel with red stainless steel insert

Hamilton International Ltd.
Mattenstrasse 149
CH-2503 Biel/Bienne
Switzerland

Tel.:
+41-32-343-4004

Fax:
+41-32-343-4006

E-mail:
info@hamiltonwatch.com

Website:
www.hamiltonwatch.com
https://shop.hamiltonwatch.com/

Founded:
1892

U.S. distributor:
Hamilton
Swatch Group (US), Inc.
703 Waterford Way, Suite 450
Miami, FL 33126
201-394-4000
lrelys.martinez@swatchgroup.com

Price range:
between approx. $500 and $2,500

HAMILTON

The Hamilton Watch Co. was founded in 1892 in Lancaster, Pennsylvania, and, within a very brief period, grew into one of the world's largest *manufactures*. Around the turn of the twentieth century, every second railway employee in the United States was carrying a Hamilton watch in his pocket, not only to make sure the trains were running punctually, but also to assist in coordinating them and organizing schedules. And during World War II, the American army officers' kits included a service Hamilton.

Hamilton is the sole survivor of the large U.S. watchmakers—if only as a brand within the Swiss Swatch Group. At one time, Hamilton had itself owned a piece of the Swiss watchmaking industry in the form of the Büren brand in the 1960s and 1970s. As part of a joint venture with Heuer-Leonidas, Breitling, and Dubois Dépraz, Hamilton-Büren also made a significant contribution to the development of the automatic chronograph. Just prior in its history, the tuning fork watch pioneer was all the rage when it took the new movement technology and housed it in a modern case created by renowned industrial designer Richard Arbib. The triangular Ventura hit the watch-world ground running in 1957, in what was truly a frenzy of innovation that benefited the brand, especially in the U.S. market. The American spirit of freedom and belief in progress this model embodies, something evoked in Hamilton's current marketing, are taken quite seriously by its designers—even those working in Biel, Switzerland. Today's collections are more inspired by adventure and aviator watches. The brand also continues to focus on revamped remakes of its classics, and prices have come down a bit as a reaction to the unstable markets.

Khaki Pilot

Reference number: H64715145
Movement: automatic, Hamilton Caliber H-30 (base ETA 2834-2); ø 25.6 mm, height 5.05 mm; 25 jewels; 21,600 vph; 80-hour power reserve
Functions: hours, minutes, sweep seconds; date, weekday
Case: stainless steel, ø 46 mm, height 12 mm; sapphire crystal; water-resistant to 20 atm
Band: stainless steel, folding clasp
Price: $1,045

Khaki X-Wind Auto Chrono

Reference number: H77736733
Movement: automatic, Hamilton Caliber H-21 (base ETA 7750); ø 30 mm, height 7.9 mm; 25 jewels; 28,800 vph; 60-hour power reserve
Functions: hours, minutes, subsidiary seconds; chronograph; date, weekday
Case: stainless steel with black PVD coating, ø 45 mm, height 14.85 mm; crown-controlled scale ring, with slide rule to calculate drift angle with side winds; sapphire crystal; transparent case back; screw-in crown; water-resistant to 10 atm
Band: calfskin, buckle
Price: $2,195

Khaki X-Wind Day Date

Reference number: H77755533
Movement: automatic, Hamilton Caliber H-30 (base ETA 2834-2); ø 25.6 mm, height 5.05 mm; 25 jewels; 21,600 vph; 80-hour power reserve
Functions: hours, minutes, sweep seconds; date, weekday
Case: stainless steel, ø 45 mm, height 12.8 mm; sapphire crystal; transparent case back; water-resistant to 10 atm
Band: calfskin, buckle
Price: $1,095

HAMILTON

Intra-Matic 68

Reference number: H38716731
Movement: automatic, Hamilton Caliber H-31 (base ETA 7753); ø 30 mm, height 7.9 mm; 27 jewels; 28,800 vph; 60-hour power reserve
Functions: hours, minutes, subsidiary seconds; chronograph; date
Case: stainless steel, ø 42 mm, height 14.6 mm; sapphire crystal; water-resistant to 10 atm
Band: calfskin, buckle
Price: $2,195; limited to 1,968 pieces

Ventura Skeleton

Reference number: H24555181
Movement: automatic, Hamilton Caliber H-10 (base ETA 2824-2); ø 25.6 mm, height 4.6 mm; 25 jewels; 21,600 vph; movement partially skeletonized; 80-hour power reserve
Functions: hours, minutes, sweep seconds
Case: stainless steel, 42.5 × 4.4.6 mm, height 11.38 mm; sapphire crystal; transparent case back; water-resistant to 5 atm
Band: stainless steel, folding clasp
Price: $1,745

ODC X-03

Reference number: H51598990
Movement: automatic, ETA 2671; ø 17.2 mm, height 4.8 mm; 25 jewels; 21,600 vph; two additional quartz movements (ETA 901.001) for second and third time zone; 80-hour power reserve
Functions: hours, minutes, sweep seconds; second and third time zone (additional 12-hour display)
Case: titanium with black PVD coating, 49 × 52 mm, height 13 mm; sapphire crystal; transparent case back; water-resistant to 10 atm
Band: textile with calfskin layer, buckle
Price: $3,500; limited to 999 pieces

Jazzmaster Power Reserve

Reference number: H32635781
Movement: automatic, Hamilton Caliber H-13 (base ETA 2834-2); ø 25.6 mm, height 5.05 mm; 25 jewels; 21,600 vph; 80-hour power reserve
Functions: hours, minutes, sweep seconds; power reserve indicator; date
Case: stainless steel, ø 42 mm, height 12.64 mm; sapphire crystal; transparent case back; water-resistant to 5 atm
Band: calfskin, buckle
Price: $1,245

Jazzmaster Open Heart

Reference number: H32705541
Movement: automatic, Hamilton Caliber H-10 (base ETA 2824-2); ø 25.6 mm, height 4.6 mm; 25 jewels; 21,600 vph; skeletonized movement; 80-hour power reserve
Functions: hours, minutes, sweep seconds
Case: stainless steel, ø 42 mm, height 11.44 mm; sapphire crystal; transparent case back; water-resistant to 5 atm
Band: calfskin, buckle
Price: $995

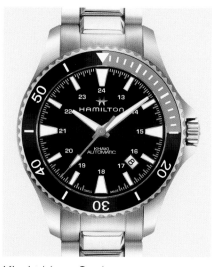

Khaki Navy Scuba

Reference number: H82305131
Movement: automatic, Hamilton Caliber H-10 (base ETA 2824-2); ø 25.6 mm, height 4.6 mm; 25 jewels; 21,600 vph; 80-hour power reserve
Functions: hours, minutes, sweep seconds; date
Case: stainless steel, ø 40 mm, height 12.95 mm; unidirectional bezel, with 0-60 scale; sapphire crystal; transparent case back; screw-in crown; water-resistant to 10 atm
Band: stainless steel, folding clasp
Price: $745

Hanhart 1882 GmbH
Hauptstrasse 33
D-78148 Gütenbach
Germany

Tel.:
+49-7723-93-44-0

Fax:
+49-7723-93-44-40

E-mail:
info@hanhart.com

Website:
www.hanhart.com

Founded:
1882 in Diessenhofen, Switzerland;
in Germany since 1902

Number of employees:
15

Annual production:
approx. 1,000 chronographs and 30,000
stopwatches

U.S. distributor:
BluePointe, LLC
207 W. Millbrook Road
Raleigh, NC 27609
888-333-4895

Most important collections/price range:
Mechanical stopwatches / from approx. $600;
Pioneer / from approx. $1,090; Primus / from
approx. $2,600

HANHART

The reputation and of this rather special company really goes back to the twenties and thirties. At the time, the brand manufactured affordable and robust stopwatches, pocket watches, and chronograph wristwatches. These core timepieces were what the fans of instrument watches wanted, and so they were thrilled as the company slowly abandoned its quartz dabbling of the eighties and reset its sights on the brand's rich and honorable tradition. A new collection was in the wings, raising expectations of great things to come. Support by the shareholding Gaydoul Group provided the financial backbone to get things moving.

Hanhart managed to rebuild a name for itself with a foot in Switzerland and the other in Germany, but it began to drift after the 2009 recession. Following bankruptcy, the company reorganized under the name Hanhart 1822 GmbH and moved everything to its German hometown. It has also returned to its stylistic roots: the characteristic red start/stop pusher grace the new collections, even on the bi-compax chronos of the Racemasters, which come with a smooth bezel. Pilots' chronographs have never lost any of their charm, either, and Hanhart was already making them in the 1930s, notably the Caliber 41 and the Tachy Tele, with assymetrical pushers and the typical red pusher. These timepieces have to survive extreme conditions, like shocks and severe temperature fluctuations. Obviously, the company has supported a number of personalities in power sports, people like Artur Kielak, the world's number one aerobatic pilot, who flies with an XtremeAir XA41. And since 2014, Hanhart has been backing Stephan Schott and Holm Schmidt, two Dakar Rally drivers, who were present at the Abu Dhabi Desert Challenge.

Primus Desert Pilot

Reference number: 740.250-372
Movement: automatic, Caliber HAN3809 (base ETA 7750); ø 30 mm, height 10.4 mm; 28 jewels; 28,800 vph; 42-hour power reserve
Functions: hours, minutes, subsidiary seconds; chronograph; date
Case: stainless steel, ø 44 mm, height 15 mm; sapphire crystal; transparent case back; screw-in crown; water-resistant to 10 atm
Band: textile, folding clasp
Remarks: movable lugs
Price: $2,970
Variations: various bands and dials

Pioneer MonoScope

Reference number: 733.220-011
Movement: automatic, Caliber HAN4212 (base ETA 7750); ø 30 mm, height 11.4 mm; 31 jewels; 28,800 vph; rebuilt for single pusher activation, rotor with skeletonized brand logo; 42-hour power reserve
Functions: hours, minutes, subsidiary seconds; chronograph
Case: stainless steel, ø 45 mm, height 16 mm; bidirectional bezel with reference markers; sapphire crystal; water-resistant to 10 atm
Band: calfskin, buckle
Price: $3,130
Variations: black dial; various bands; stainless steel bracelet; smooth bezel

Pioneer Preventor9

Reference number: 752.210-6428
Movement: automatic, Hanhart Caliber HAN4112 (base Sellita SW200-1); ø 25.6 mm, height 7.99 mm; 30 jewels; 28,800 vph; 38-hour power reserve
Functions: hours, minutes, subsidiary seconds
Case: stainless steel, ø 40 mm, height 12.15 mm; sapphire crystal; water-resistant to 10 atm
Band: stainless steel, folding clasp
Price: $1,310
Variations: white dial; various leather bands

HERMÈS

La Montre Hermès
Erlenstrasse 31A
CH-2555 Brügg
Switzerland

Tel.:
+41-32-366-7100

Fax:
+41-32-366-7101

E-mail:
info@montre-hermes.ch

Website:
www.hermes.ch

Founded:
1978

Number of employees:
150

Annual production:
not specified

U.S. distributor:
Hermès of Paris, Inc.
55 East 59th Street
New York, NY 10022
800-441-4488
www.hermes.com

Most important collections/price range:
Arceau, Cape Cod, Clipper, Dressage, Faubourg,
Heure H, Kelly, Medor, Slim / $2,400 to
$500,000

Thierry Hermès's timing was just right. When he founded his saddlery in Paris in 1837, France's middle class was booming and spending money on beautiful things and activities like horseback riding. Hermès became a household name and a symbol of good taste—not too flashy, not trendy, useful. The advent of the automobile gave rise to luggage, bags, headgear, and soon Hermès, still in family hands today, diversified its range of products— foulards, fashion, porcelain, glass, perfume, and gold jewelry are active parts of its portfolio.

Watches were a natural, especially with the advent of the wristwatch in the years prior to World War I. Hermès even had a timepiece that could be worn on a belt. But some time passed before the company engaged in "real" watchmaking. In 1978, La Montre Hermès opened its watch manufactory in Biel.

Rather than just produce fluffy lifestyle timepieces, Hermès has gone to the trouble to get an in-depth grip on the business. "Our philosophy is all about the quality of time," says Laurent Dordet, who took over as CEO from Luc Perramond in March 2015. "It's about imagination; we want people to dream." "Poetic complications" is what allowed the company to navigate between classy but plain watches and muscular tool timepieces bristling with complications. On the one hand, there was the esthetics: the lively leaning numerals of the Arceau series or the bridoon recalling the company's equine roots at 12 o'clock for holding the strap. As for in-house complications, they are produced in collaboration with external designers, notably Jean-Marc Wiederrecht and his company, Agenhor. In the Slim line, one finds a thin perpetual calendar with modern numerals that raise it above the standard retro watch. The clever "Temps Suspendu" lets the wearer stop time for a moment. The "Heure Masquée" hides the hour hand behind hand movements with varying speeds, an option to "suspend" time for a moment, or one to hide time.

To ensure its independence, Hermès invested close to 25 million Swiss francs for 25 percent of the Vaucher Manufacture's stock. Movements not being everything, the company also wisely picked up shares in dial maker Natéber and case maker Joseph Erard. The bracelets, understated, elegant pieces that require two hours' work to complete by hand, are made in Biel.

Slim d'Hermès L'Heure Impatiente

Reference number: CA4.870.220/MM7K
Movement: automatic, Hermès Caliber H1912 (base caliber with "L'heure Impatiente" module); ø 31.96 mm, height 5.9 mm; 36 jewels; 28,800 vph; mainplate and bridges with snail and côtes de Genève decoration; 42-hour power reserve
Functions: hours, minutes; "Heure Impatiente" alarm function with 60-minute countdown
Case: rose gold, ø 40.5 mm, height 10.67 mm; sapphire crystal; transparent case back; water-resistant to 3 atm
Band: reptile skin, buckle
Price: $39,900

Slim d'Hermès Quantième Perpétuel

Reference number: CA3.865.630/MM7K
Movement: automatic, Hermès Caliber H1950 with Agenhor module; ø 30 mm, height 4 mm; 32 jewels; 21,600 vph; microrotor; 42-hour power reserve
Functions: hours, minutes; additional 12-hour display (second time zone); perpetual calendar with date, month, moon phase, leap year
Case: platinum, ø 39.5 mm, height 9.06 mm; sapphire crystal; transparent case back; water-resistant to 3 atm
Band: reptile skin, buckle
Price: $42,500

Cape Cod TGM Automatic

Reference number: CD7.810.630/MM76
Movement: automatic, Hermès Caliber H1912; ø 23.3 mm, height 3.9 mm; 28 jewels; 28,800 vph; 50-hour power reserve
Functions: hours, minutes, sweep seconds; date
Case: stainless steel, 33 × 33 mm; sapphire crystal; transparent case back; water-resistant to 3 atm
Band: reptile skin, buckle
Price: $6,200

Dressage "L'Heure Masquée"

Reference number: DR5.870.221/MHA
Movement: automatic, Hermès Caliber H1925;
ø 26 mm, height 3.7 mm; 28 + 18 jewels;
28,800 vph; activating a pusher lets hour hand
emerge from behind minute hand; 45-hour power
reserve
Functions: hours (on request), minutes; second
24-hour display (second time zone, appears when
pusher-activated)
Case: rose gold, ø 40.5 mm, height 8.4 mm;
sapphire crystal; water-resistant to 5 atm
Band: reptile skin, buckle
Price: $45,900

Arceau "Le Temps Suspendu"

Reference number: AR8.910.220/MHA
Movement: automatic, ETA Caliber 2892
(modified); ø 26 mm, height 5.6 mm; 28,800 vph;
hands can be parked at 12:30 and started again
at current time with pusher, double spring barrel,
42-hour power reserve
Functions: hours, minutes; date (retrograde)
Case: stainless steel, ø 43 mm; sapphire crystal;
water-resistant to 3 atm
Band: reptile skin, folding clasp
Price: $21,750

Slim d'Hermès

Reference number: CA2.810.220/MHA
Movement: automatic, Hermès Caliber H1950;
ø 30 mm, height 2.6 mm; 29 jewels; 21,600 vph;
microrotor; 42-hour power reserve
Functions: hours, minutes, subsidiary seconds
Case: stainless steel, ø 39.5 mm, height 8.11 mm;
sapphire crystal; transparent case back; water-
resistant to 3 atm
Band: reptile skin, buckle
Price: $7,650

Cape Cod TGM

Reference number: CC1.810.223/VBA4
Movement: quartz
Functions: hours, minutes, sweep seconds; date
Case: stainless steel, 33 × 33 mm; sapphire crystal;
water-resistant to 3 atm
Band: reptile skin, buckle
Price: $3,400

Cape Cod Shadow

Reference number: CC3.711.331/VBN8-I
Movement: quartz
Functions: hours, minutes
Case: stainless steel with black DLC coating, 29 ×
29 mm, height 8 mm; sapphire crystal; transparent
case back; water-resistant to 3 atm
Band: calfskin, buckle
Price: $4,300

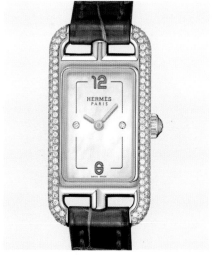

Nantucket TPM

Reference number: NA2.171.290/ZZ8C
Movement: quartz
Functions: hours, minutes
Case: rose gold, 17 × 23 mm, height 7.8 mm bezel
set with 186 diamonds; sapphire crystal; water-
resistant to 3 atm
Band: reptile skin, buckle
Price: $16,100

HUBLOT

Ever since Hublot moved into a new, modern, spacious factory building in Nyon, near Geneva—in the midst of a recession, no less—the brand has evolved with stunning speed. The growth has been such that Hublot has even built a second factory, which is even bigger than the first. The ground-breaking ceremony took place on March 3, 2014, and the man holding the spade was Hublot chairman Jean-Claude Biver, who is also head of LVMH's Watch Division.

It was together with current CEO Ricardo Guadalupe that Biver developed the idea of fusing different and at times incompatible materials in a watch: carbon composite and gold, ceramic and steel, denim and diamonds. In 2011, the brand introduced the first scratchproof precious metal, an alloy of gold and ceramic named "Magic Gold." In 2014, Hublot came out with a watch whose dial is made of osmium, one of the world's rarest metals. Using a new patented process, Hublot has also implemented a unique concept of cutting wafer-thin bits of glass that are set in the open spaces of a skeletonized movement plate.

The "art of fusion" tagline drove the brand into all sorts of technical and scientific partnerships and created a phenomenal buzz that is ongoing, apparently, regardless of the economic environment. Even fashion house Sartoria Rubinacci was picked up by the Hublot radar for a Classic Fusion Chronograph with a hound's-tooth pattern. And during the past decade, Hublot also managed to verticalize. Most of the brand's models are now run on the in-house Unico movements.

Hublot's communication concept also needs mentioning. It consists in being everywhere, including on soccer pitches, a sport that was considered too popular for an industry that prides itself on exclusiveness. This particular love affair began in 2006, when the brand sponsored the Swiss national team. It has since signed on numerous other clubs, including the FC Bayern München, Manchester United, and even the lesser-known San Lorenzo de Almagro in Argentina. The world's fastest man, Usain Bolt, is also a brand ambassador. The company does move quickly.

Hublot SA
Chemin de la Vuarpillière 33
CH-1260 Nyon
Switzerland

Tel.:
+41-22-990-9900

E-mail:
info@hublot.ch

Website:
www.hublot.com

Founded:
1980

Number of employees:
approx. 450

Annual production:
approx. 40,000 watches

U.S. distributor:
Hublot of America, Inc.
The International Building, ST-402
2455 East Sunrise Blvd.
Fort Lauderdale, FL 33304
800-536-0636

Most important collections/price range:
Big Bang / $15,000 to $5,000,000; King Power / $20,000 to $200,000; Classic Fusion / $7,000 to $2,000,000; Master Piece (MP) / $275,000 to $1,500,000

Techframe Ferrari Tourbillon Chronograph PEEK Carbon

Reference number: 408.QU.0123.RX
Movement: manually wound, Caliber HUB 6311; ø 34 mm, height 6.7 mm; 27 jewels; 21,600 vph; 1-minute tourbillon; single pusher for chronograph functions; mainplate and bridges with slate-colored coating; 115-hour power reserve
Functions: hours, minutes; chronograph
Case: carbon fiber, ø 45 mm, height 14.8 mm; bezel screwed to case back with 6 titanium screws; sapphire crystal; transparent case back; water-resistant to 3 atm
Band: rubber, folding clasp
Remarks: designed by Ferrari
Price: $137,000; limited to 70 pieces
Variations: titanium; rose gold

Big Bang Ferrari Titanium

Reference number: 402.NX.0123.WR
Movement: automatic, Caliber HUB 1243 "Unico"; ø 30 mm, height 9.8 mm; 38 jewels; 28,800 vph; movement plate and bridges coated black; 72-hour power reserve
Functions: hours, minutes, subsidiary seconds; flyback chronograph; date
Case: titanium, ø 45 mm, height 16.7 mm; bezel screwed to case back with 6 titanium screws; sapphire crystal; transparent case back; water-resistant to 10 atm
Band: rubber, with calfskin overlay, folding clasp
Remarks: designed by Ferrari
Price: $26,200; limited to 1,000 pieces
Variations: rose gold; carbon

Big Bang Unico GMT Titanium

Reference number: 471.NX.7112.RX
Movement: automatic, Caliber HUB 1251 "Unico"; ø 30 mm, height 8.05 mm; 41 jewels; 28,800 vph; mainplate and bridges with slate-colored coating; 72-hour power reserve
Functions: hours, minutes, sweep seconds; additional 12-hour display (second time zone), day/night indicator
Case: titanium, ø 45 mm, height 15.85 mm; bezel screwed to case back with 6 titanium screws; sapphire crystal; transparent case back; water-resistant to 10 atm
Band: rubber, folding clasp
Price: $19,900
Variations: carbon

Big Bang Unico Sang Bleu All Black

Reference number: 415.CX.1114.VR.MXM17
Movement: automatic, Caliber HUB 1213 "Unico"; ø 30 mm, height 6.8 mm; 28 jewels; 28,800 vph; 72-hour power reserve
Functions: hours, minutes, sweep seconds (disk display with index corners)
Case: ceramic, ø 45 mm, height 15.55 mm; bezel screwed to case back with 6 titanium screws; sapphire crystal; transparent case back; water-resistant to 10 atm
Band: rubber, with calfskin overlay, folding clasp
Price: $20,900; limited to 200 pieces
Variations: rose gold ($39,900); titanium set with diamonds ($37,300)

Big Bang MECA-10 Full Magic Gold

Reference number: 414.MX.1138.RX
Movement: manually wound, Caliber HUB 1201; ø 35.19 mm, height 6.8 mm; 24 jewels; 21,600 vph; bridges with black coating; 240-hour power reserve
Functions: hours, minutes, subsidiary seconds; power reserve indicator; date
Case: "Magic Gold" (alloy with ceramics), ø 45 mm, height 15.95 mm; bezel screwed to case back with 6 titanium screws; sapphire crystal; transparent case back; water-resistant to 10 atm
Band: rubber, folding clasp
Price: $34,600; limited to 200 pieces
Variations: rose gold; titanium ($19,900)

Big Bang Steel Blue

Reference number: 301.SX.7170.LR
Movement: automatic, Caliber HUB 4100 (base ETA 7750); ø 30 mm, height 8.4 mm; 27 jewels; 28,800 vph; 42-hour power reserve
Functions: hours, minutes, subsidiary seconds; chronograph; date
Case: stainless steel, ø 44 mm, height 14.6 mm; bezel screwed to case back with 6 titanium screws; sapphire crystal; transparent case back; water-resistant to 10 atm
Band: reptile skin, folding clasp
Price: $12,900
Variations: various cases

Classic Fusion Chronograph Italia Independent "Pieds-de-poule" Titanium

Reference number: 521.NX.2702.NR.ITI17
Movement: automatic, Caliber HUB 1143; ø 30 mm, height 6.9 mm; 59 jewels; 28,800 vph
Functions: hours, minutes, subsidiary seconds; chronograph; date
Case: titanium, ø 45 mm, height 13.05 mm; bezel screwed to case back with 6 titanium screws; sapphire crystal; transparent case back; water-resistant to 5 atm
Band: textile, folding clasp
Remarks: textile overlay on dial and strap with houndstooth pattern; limited to 100 pieces
Price: $15,100

Classic Fusion Chronograph Berluti Scritto King Gold

Reference number: 521.OX.0500.VR.BER17
Movement: automatic, Caliber HUB 1143; ø 30 mm, height 6.9 mm; 59 jewels; 28,800 vph; 42-hour power reserve
Functions: hours, minutes, subsidiary seconds; chronograph; date
Case: rose gold, ø 45 mm, height 13.4 mm; bezel screwed to case back with 6 titanium screws; sapphire crystal; transparent case back; water-resistant to 5 atm
Band: calfskin, folding clasp
Price: $36,700; limited to 250 pieces

Classic Fusion Integrated Bracelet King Gold Blue

Reference number: 510.OX.7180.OX
Movement: automatic, Caliber HUB 1112; ø 25.6 mm, height 4.25 mm; 25 jewels; 28,800 vph; 42-hour power reserve
Functions: hours, minutes, sweep seconds; date
Case: rose gold, ø 45 mm, height 10.95 mm; bezel screwed to case back with 6 titanium screws; sapphire crystal; transparent case back; water-resistant to 5 atm
Band: rose gold, folding clasp
Price: $37,400
Variations: titanium

Classic Fusion King Gold Racing Grey Chronograph

Reference number: 521.OX.7081.LR
Movement: automatic, Caliber HUB 1143;
ø 30 mm, height 6.9 mm; 59 jewels; 28,800 vph;
42-hour power reserve
Functions: hours, minutes, subsidiary seconds;
chronograph; date
Case: rose gold, ø 45 mm, height 13.05 mm;
bezel screwed to case back with 6 titanium screws;
sapphire crystal; transparent case back; water-
resistant to 5 atm
Band: reptile skin, folding clasp
Price: $30,800
Variations: titanium ($10,800)

Spirit of Big Bang Sapphire

Reference number: 601.JX.0120.RT
Movement: automatic, Caliber HUB 4700 (based
on the Zenith El Primero); ø 30 mm, height 6.6 mm;
31 jewels; 36,000 vph; 50-hour power reserve
Functions: hours, minutes, subsidiary seconds;
chronograph; date
Case: 45 × 51 mm, height 15.1 mm; bezel screwed
to case back with 6 titanium screws; sapphire crystal;
transparent case back; water-resistant to 5 atm
Band: transparent silicon, folding clasp
Price: $79,000; limited to 250 pieces
Variations: "Magic Gold"

Spirit of Big Bang Moonphase Titanium Dark Blue

Reference number: 647.NX.5171.LR.1201
Movement: automatic, Caliber HUB 1770;
27 jewels; 28,800 vph; 50-hour power reserve
Functions: hours, minutes, subsidiary seconds; large
date, moon phase
Case: titanium, 42 × 53 mm, height 13.8 mm; bezel
screwed to case back with 6 titanium screws and set
with 48 amethysts; sapphire crystal; transparent case
back; water-resistant to 10 atm
Band: reptile skin, folding clasp
Price: $22,400
Variations: various cases and dials

MP-09 Tourbillon Bi-Axis Titanium

Reference number: 909.NX.1120.RX
Movement: automatic, Caliber HUB 9009.H1.RA;
ø 43 mm, height 8.4 mm; 43 jewels; 21,600 vph;
double-axis tourbillon with different rotation times
(60 and 30 seconds); date with rapid correction by
lever on the case left; 120-hour power reserve
Functions: hours, minutes (off-center); power
reserve indicator; date
Case: titanium, ø 49 mm, height 17.95 mm; bezel
screwed to case back with 5 titanium screws; sapphire
crystal; transparent case back; water-resistant to 3 atm
Band: rubber, folding clasp
Price: $169,000; limited to 50 pieces
Variations: set with precious stones ($190,000);
rose gold ($211,000)

Caliber HUB 1240

Automatic; column wheel control of chronograph
functions; silicon pallet lever and escapement,
removable escapement; double-pawl automatic
winding (Pellaton system), rotor with ceramic ball
bearing; single spring barrel, 70-hour power reserve
Functions: hours, minutes, subsidiary seconds;
flyback chronograph; date
Diameter: 30.4 mm
Height: 8.05 mm
Jewels: 38
Balance: glucydur
Frequency: 28,800 vph

Caliber HUB 1201

Manually wound; skeletonized movement; silicon
pallet lever and escape wheel; double mainspring
barrel, 240-hour power reserve
Functions: hours, minutes, subsidiary seconds;
power reserve indicator; date
Diameter: 35,19 mm
Height: 6.8 mm
Jewels: 24
Balance: CuBe
Frequency: 21,600 vph

HYT SA
Route des Falaises 74
CH-2000 Neuchâtel
Switzerland

Tel.:
+41 32-323-2770

E-mail:
info@hytwatches.com

Website:
www.hytwatches.com

Founded:
2011

Number of employees:
45

Annual production:
approx. 350 wristwatches

U.S. distributor:
Westime Los Angeles
310-470-1388; 310-475-0628 (fax)
info@westime.com
Cellini
509 Madison Avenue, at 53rd Street
10022 New York, NY 10022
212-888-0505
www.cellinijewelers.com

Most important collections/price range:
Hydro mechanical wristwatches / $39,000 to
$280,000

HYT

The earliest timekeepers were water clocks, known as clepsydras. The ancient Greeks had already devised a system by which water was guided from one vessel into another through an orifice of a predetermined diameter. Time was read on a calibrated scale on the second vessel. The three founders of HYT loved this idea of displaying the passage of time with moving fluids, and so they set out to solve the many problems generated if one were to introduce a liquid into a watch.

They developed a closed system made up of a capillary tube that would serve as a time track. It had a special pump-tank at either end that could either receive or pump out liquid. The two tanks had their dedicated space at 6 o'clock. After much research, they realized that the tube needed to be filled with two liquids, not one. Their different physical properties meant they don't mix and thus create a sharp line at the point where they met, which could serve as a pointer.

As for the pump-tanks, they were based on sensors used by NASA, a piston-driven bellows made of ultrathin but robust material that bends easily, but offers a stable surface. This allows very exact amounts of liquid to be pumped from one tank into the other. The system is driven by way of an in-house mechanical movement and cams. HYT became an instant sensation when it came out with its first watch in 2012.

Most important, perhaps, the basic concept left lots of opportunities for a great variety of designs and new technological gimmicks, which accounts for the company's stunning success. HYT has introduced a number of different models that often include clever innovations, such as a miniature hand-wound generator, or attractive design elements, like luminescent liquids.

H0 Silver

Reference number: 048-TT-91-BF-RU
Movement: manually wound, HYT Caliber 101; ø 37.8 mm, height 10.1 mm; 35 jewels; 28,800 vph; module with 2 bellows and capillary tubes containing 2 immiscible fluids, separation line points to time; temperature compensation; 65-hour power reserve
Functions: minutes (off-center), hours (capillary display, retrograde), subsidiary seconds; power reserve indicator
Case: titanium, ø 48.8 mm, height 17.9 mm; sapphire crystal; screw-in crown; water-resistant to 3 atm
Band: rubber, folding clasp
Price: $39,000
Variations: H0 Black with blackened titanium case; H0 Orange with orange dial elements

H2 Tradition

Reference number: 248-TW-10-BF-AB
Movement: manually wound, HYT Caliber 210; ø 39.9 mm, height 10.67 mm; 28 jewels; 21,600 vph; module with 2 bellows and capillary tubes with 2 immiscible fluids, separation line points to time; temperature compensation; guillochéed and beveled plate; 192-hour power reserve
Functions: minutes (off-center), hours (capillary, retrograde), subsidiary seconds; power reserve indicator; crown position display
Case: titanium, ø 48.8 mm, height 17.9 mm; white gold unidirectional bezel; in white gold; sapphire crystal; screw-in crown, crown with torque limitation; water-resistant to 5 atm
Band: reptile skin, folding clasp
Price: $179,000; limited to 50 pieces

Skull Bad Boy

Reference number: 151-DL-43-NF-AS
Movement: manually wound, HYT Caliber 101; ø 37.2 mm, height 10.1 mm; 35 jewels; 28,800 vph; module with 2 bellows and capillary tubes with 2 immiscible fluids, separation line points to time; temperature compensation; 65-hour power reserve
Functions: hours (capillary display, retrograde), subsidiary seconds (in left eye); power reserve indicator (in right eye)
Case: titanium with black DLC coating, ø 51 mm, height 17.9 mm; sapphire crystal; screw-in crown; water-resistant to 5 atm
Band: reptile skin, Velcro tie
Remarks: skull of Damascus steel
Price: $95,000; limited to 50 pieces

ITAY NOY

Israeli watchmaker Itay Noy started his career as a jeweler, so it comes as no surprise that his earlier watches tended to emphasize form, while the functional aspects are left to solid Swiss movements. As a shaper, though, he reveals himself to be a pensive, philosophical storyteller making each timepiece a unique, encapsulated tale of sorts. The City Squares model, for example, gives the time on the backdrop of a map of the owner's favorite or native city, thus creating an intimate connection with, perhaps, a past moment. At Baselworld 2013, Noy showcased a square watch run on a Techno-time automatic movement with a face-like dial that changes with the movement of the hands, a reminder of how our life has become dominated by the rectangular frame of mobile gadgets. The Cityscape, square as well, represents a modern urban landscape. The skeletonization of the Point of View dial, his 2014 model, creates a harmonious collage of the world's religious symbols superimposed on the inexorable passage of time. Each year brings new ideas as Noy ratchets up his craft and begins reaching into the engineer's magic box. In 2015, he came up with a special module to create a fascinating, two-part square dial for his Part Time, dividing day and night and providing the time plus the position of the sun and the moon through little apertures. This fascination with the times of day was reiterated in 2016 with the Chrono Gears model, which essentially runs on a large invisible circular gear that drives a.m. and p.m. indicators and more. The 2017 novelty is the Time Tone, which gives the owner the choice of a colored hour that only he or she will know. The minute hand does its work in the center of the dial. It's a clever way to personalize time. It's no wonder that Noy's collections find their way into museums and special exhibitions. The Museum of Art and Design in New York showed his works in April 2016.

Itay Noy
P.O. Box 16661
Tel Aviv 6116601
Israel

Tel.:
+972-352-47-380

Fax:
+972-352-47-381

E-mail:
studio@itay-noy.com

Website:
www.itay-noy.com

Founded:
2000

Number of employees:
4

Annual production:
200–300 pieces

U.S. distributor:
Bareti, California
949-715-7084
info@bareti.com
www.bareti.com

Most important collections/price range:
Chrono Gears, Part Time, Open Mind, Time Tone, X-Ray / $2,000 to $7,500

Celestial Time

Reference number: CT.W
Movement: manually wound IN.IP13; ø 36.6 mm, height 5.5 mm; 20 jewels; 21,600 vph; 42-hour power reserve
Functions: dynamic dial with zodiac hour disk, minutes and seconds.
Case: stainless steel, ø 44 mm, height 12 mm; sapphire crystal dome; transparent case back; water-resistant to 5 atm
Band: leather, double folding clasp
Remarks: limited and numbered edition of 24 pieces
Price: $5,200
Variations: Western or Chinese zodiac signs

Time Tone

Reference number: TT.BL
Movement: manually wound IN.IP13; ø 36.6 mm, height 5.5 mm, 20 jewels; 21,600 vph; 42-hour power reserve
Functions: dynamic dial with tone color disk, minutes and seconds
Case: stainless steel, ø 44 mm, height 12 mm; sapphire crystal;, transparent case back; water-resistant to 5 atm
Band: leather, double folding clasp
Remarks: limited and numbered edition of 24 pieces
Price: $5,600
Variations: blue or black

Chrono Gears

Reference number: CG.G
Movement: manually wound, IN.IP13; ø 36.6 mm, height 5.5 mm; 20 jewels; 21,600 vph; 42-hour power reserve
Functions: chronogear hand indicator for a.m./ p.m., chronogear hand indicator for 8 time situations, central hours, minutes and seconds
Case: stainless steel, ø 44 mm, height 12 mm; sapphire crystal; transparent case back; water-resistant to 5 atm
Band: leather, double folding clasp
Remarks: limited and numbered edition of 24 pieces
Price: $5,800
Variations: blue or black

DiaLOG

Reference number: DiaLOG.Num
Movement: manually wound, ETA Caliber 6498-1; ø 36.6 mm, height 4.5 mm; 17 jewels; 21,600 vph; 38-hour power reserve
Functions: hours, minutes, subsidiary seconds
Case: stainless steel, ø 41.6 mm × 44.6 mm; height 10 mm; sapphire crystal;, screw-down case back; water-resistant to 5 atm
Band: leather, double folding clasp
Remarks: limited and numbered edition of 99 pieces
Price: $3,900

Part Time

Reference number: PT-DN.BL
Movement: manually wound, IN.DD&6498-1; ø 36.6 mm, height 5.2 mm; 17 jewels; 21,600 vph; 38-hour power reserve
Functions: hours from 6 a.m.–6 p.m., hours from 6 p.m.–6 a.m., analog hours, moon disk, sun disk, minutes, subsidiary seconds
Case: stainless steel, ø 41.6 mm × 44.6 mm, height 10.6 mm; sapphire crystal; transparent case back; water-resistant to 5 atm
Band: leather, double folding clasp
Remarks: limited and numbered edition of 24 pieces
Price: $5,800
Variations: blue or black

X-Ray

Reference number: XRAY6498
Movement: manually wound, ETA Caliber 6498-1; ø 36.6 mm, height 4.5 mm, 17 jewels; 21,600 vph; 38-hour power reserve
Functions: hours, minutes, subsidiary seconds
Case: stainless steel, 41.6 × 44.6 mm, height 10 mm; sapphire crystal; transparent case back; water-resistant to 5 atm
Band: leather, double folding clasp
Remarks: limited and numbered edition of 99 pieces
Price: $3,640
Variations: gold-plated dial ($3,900); black or brown leather band

Open Mind

Reference number: OM-S.G
Movement: manually wound skeleton 6497-1; ø 36.6 mm, height 4.5 mm; 17 jewels; 21,600 vph; 38-hour power reserve
Functions: hours, minutes, subsidiary seconds
Case: stainless steel, ø 44 mm, height 12 mm; sapphire crystal; transparent case back; water-resistant to 5 atm
Band: leather, double folding clasp
Remarks: limited and numbered edition of 99 pieces
Price: $4,400
Variations: blue or black

ID-Hebrew

Reference number: ID-HEB.G
Movement: automatic, ETA Caliber 2824-2; ø 25.6 mm, height 4.6 mm; 25 jewels; 28,800 vph; 38-hour power reserve
Functions: hours, minutes, sweep seconds; quick-set date window
Case: stainless steel, ø 42.4 mm, height 10 mm; sapphire crystal; screw-down case back; water-resistant to 5 atm
Band: leather band
Remarks: gold-plated dial; limited and numbered edition of 99 pieces
Price: $2,800
Variations: black or brown leather band

Maximalism

Reference number: MAX-DECO
Movement: automatic, ETA Caliber 2824-2; ø 25.6 mm, height 4.6 mm; 25 jewels; 28,800 vph; 38-hour power reserve
Functions: hours, minutes, sweep seconds; quick-set date window
Case: stainless steel, ø 42.4 mm, height 10 mm; sapphire crystal; screw-down case back; water-resistant to 5 atm
Band: leather, folding clasp
Remarks: limited and numbered edition of 99 pieces
Price: $2,400
Variations: black or brown leather band

IWC

It was an American who laid the cornerstone for an industrial watch factory in Schaffhausen—now environmentally state-of-the-art facilities. In 1868, Florentine Ariosto Jones, watchmaker and engineer from Boston, crossed the Atlantic to the then low-wage venue of Switzerland to open the International Watch Company Schaffhausen.

Jones was not only a savvy businessperson but also a talented designer who had a significant influence on the development of watch movements. Soon, he gave IWC its own seal of approval, the *Ingenieursmarke* (Engineer's Brand), a standard it still maintains today. IWC is synonymous with excellently crafted watches that meet high technical benchmarks. Not even a large variety of owners over the past 100 years has been able to change the company's course, though it did ultimately end up in the hands of the Richemont Group in 2000.

Technical milestones from Schaffhausen include the Jones caliber, named for the IWC founder, and the pocket watch caliber 89, introduced in 1946 as the creation of then technical director Albert Pellaton. Four years later, Pellaton created the first IWC automatic movement and, with it, a company monument. Over the years, IWC has made a name for itself with its pilot's watches. The technical highlight of the present day is no doubt the Perpetual Calendar, which is programmed to run until the year 2499.

Georges Kern, the current CEO at IWC, has pursued the development of in-house movements, such as those found in the company's Da Vinci and Ingenieur models, and of course the Portuguese, which has now passed its seventy-fifth year and is still going strong in watches that are naturally retro-styled. Lately, IWC has revisited its Aquatimer and brought out the Deep Three, with two depth gauges, one of which records how deep the diver has gone.

The careful balance between tapping into past glories to keep fans and newcomers to the brand happy continues to boost the brand. So much so that the company has started building new, ultra-modern facilities just outside its home city, Schaffhausen, in Switzerland.

International Watch Co.
Baumgartenstrasse 15
CH-8201 Schaffhausen
Switzerland

Tel.:
+41-52-635-6565

Fax:
+41-52-635-6501

E-mail:
info@iwc.com

Website:
www.iwc.com

Founded:
1868

Number of employees:
approx. 750

U.S. distributor:
IWC North America
645 Fifth Avenue, 7th Floor
New York, NY 10022
800-432-9330

Most important collections/price range:
Da Vinci, Pilot's, Portuguese, Ingenieur, Aquatimer / approx. $4,000 to $260,000

Da Vinci Tourbillon Retrograde Chronograph
Reference number: IW393101
Movement: automatic, IWC Caliber 89900; ø 30 mm; 42 jewels; 28,800 vph; flying 1-minute tourbillon with stop function, double-pawl automatic winding system; 68-hour power reserve
Functions: hours, minutes; flyback chronograph; date (retrograde)
Case: pink gold, ø 44 mm, height 17 mm; sapphire crystal; transparent case back; water-resistant to 3 atm
Band: reptile skin, folding clasp
Price: $103,000

Da Vinci Perpetual Calendar Chronograph
Reference number: IW392103
Movement: automatic, IWC Caliber 89630; ø 30 mm; 51 jewels; 28,800 vph; screw balance; gold oscillating weight; 68-hour power reserve
Functions: hours, minutes, subsidiary seconds; flyback chronograph; perpetual calendar with date, weekday, month, moon phase, year display (four digits)
Case: stainless steel, ø 43 mm, height 15.5 mm; sapphire crystal; transparent case back; water-resistant to 3 atm
Band: reptile skin, folding clasp
Price: $29,900
Variations: pink gold ($40,200)

Da Vinci Automatic 36
Reference number: IW458310
Movement: automatic, IWC Caliber 35111 (base Sellita SW300-1); ø 25.6 mm, height 3.75 mm; 25 jewels; 28,800 vph; 42-hour power reserve
Functions: hours, minutes, sweep seconds; date
Case: pink gold, ø 36 mm, height 10 mm; bezel set with 54 diamonds; sapphire crystal; water-resistant to 3 atm
Band: pink gold, double folding clasp
Price: $37,800
Variations: stainless steel with leather strap ($10,800)

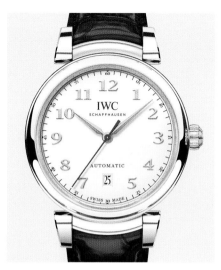

Da Vinci Automatic

Reference number: IW356601
Movement: automatic, IWC Caliber 35111 (base Sellita SW300-1); ø 25.6 mm, height 3.75 mm; 25 jewels; 28,800 vph; 42-hour power reserve
Functions: hours, minutes, sweep seconds; date
Case: stainless steel, ø 40 mm, height 10 mm; sapphire crystal; water-resistant to 3 atm
Band: reptile skin, buckle
Price: $5,400
Variations: stainless steel bracelet ($6,400)

Da Vinci Automatic 36

Reference number: IW458312
Movement: automatic, IWC Caliber 35111 (base Sellita SW300-1); ø 25.6 mm, height 3.75 mm; 25 jewels; 28,800 vph; 42-hour power reserve
Functions: hours, minutes, sweep seconds; date
Case: stainless steel, ø 36 mm, height 10 mm; sapphire crystal; water-resistant to 3 atm
Band: reptile skin, double folding clasp
Price: $5,600
Variations: pink gold with leather band ($13,800); stainless steel with stainless steel bracelet ($6,400)

Da Vinci Automatic Moon Phase 36

Reference number: IW459308
Movement: automatic, IWC Caliber 35800; ø 25.6 mm, height 5.35 mm; 25 jewels; 28,800 vph; 42-hour power reserve
Functions: hours, minutes, sweep seconds; moon phase
Case: pink gold, ø 36 mm, height 11.5 mm; sapphire crystal; water-resistant to 3 atm
Band: reptile skin, buckle
Price: $16,400
Variations: stainless steel ($8,500); stainless steel with diamond bezel leather strap ($13,900)

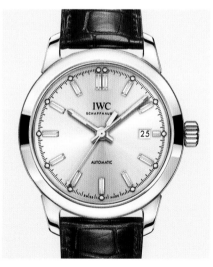

Ingenieur Automatic

Reference number: IW357001
Movement: automatic, IWC Caliber 35111 (base Sellita SW300-1); ø 25.6 mm, height 3.75 mm; 25 jewels; 28,800 vph; 42-hour power reserve
Functions: hours, minutes, sweep seconds; date
Case: stainless steel, ø 40 mm, height 10.5 mm; sapphire crystal; screw-in crown; water-resistant to 12 atm
Band: reptile skin, buckle
Price: $4,590
Variations: stainless steel bracelet ($5,500); pink gold ($13,600)

Ingenieur Chronograph

Reference number: IW380802
Movement: automatic, IWC Caliber 69375; ø 30 mm; 33 jewels; 28,800 vph
Functions: hours, minutes, subsidiary seconds; chronograph; date
Case: stainless steel, ø 42 mm, height 15 mm; sapphire crystal; transparent case back; screw-in crown; water-resistant to 12 atm
Band: stainless steel, folding clasp
Price: $7,950
Variations: white dial; pink gold numerals ($7,950)

Ingenieur Chronograph

Reference number: IW380803
Movement: automatic, IWC Caliber 69375; ø 30 mm; 33 jewels; 28,800 vph
Functions: hours, minutes, subsidiary seconds; chronograph; date
Case: pink gold, ø 42 mm, height 15 mm; sapphire crystal; transparent case back; screw-in crown; water-resistant to 12 atm
Band: reptile skin, buckle
Price: $18,200

Portuguese Chronograph Flyback Edition "Boutique Munich"

Reference number: IW371217
Movement: manually wound, IWC Caliber 76240; ø 30 mm, height 7.35 mm; 27 jewels; 28,800 vph; 44-hour power reserve
Functions: hours, minutes, subsidiary seconds; split-second chronograph
Case: stainless steel, ø 40.9 mm, height 12.3 mm; sapphire crystal; water-resistant to 3 atm
Band: reptile skin, folding clasp
Price: on request; limited to 250 pieces

Portuguese Chronograph Classic

Reference number: IW390302
Movement: automatic, IWC Caliber 89361; ø 30 mm, height 7.5 mm; 38 jewels; 28,800 vph; double-pawl automatic winding system; 68-hour power reserve
Functions: hours, minutes, subsidiary seconds; flyback chronograph; date
Case: stainless steel, ø 42 mm, height 14.25 mm; sapphire crystal; water-resistant to 3 atm
Band: reptile skin, folding clasp
Price: $12,100

Pilot's Watch Chronograph Spitfire

Reference number: IW377719
Movement: automatic, IWC Caliber 79320 (base ETA 7750); ø 30 mm, height 7.9 mm; 25 jewels; 28,800 vph; soft iron cap for antimagnetic protection; 44-hour power reserve
Functions: hours, minutes, subsidiary seconds; chronograph; date, weekday
Case: stainless steel, ø 43 mm, height 15 mm; sapphire crystal; screw-in crown; water-resistant to 6 atm
Band: stainless steel, folding clasp
Price: $5,950

Pilot's Watch Mark XVIII Edition "Antoine de Saint Exupéry"

Reference number: IW327003
Movement: automatic, IWC Caliber 30110 (base ETA 2892-A2); ø 25.6 mm, height 3.6 mm; 21 jewels; 28,800 vph; 42-hour power reserve
Functions: hours, minutes, sweep seconds; date
Case: stainless steel, ø 40 mm, height 11 mm; sapphire crystal; screw-in crown; water-resistant to 6 atm
Band: calfskin, buckle
Price: $3,950

Portugese Chronograph

Reference number: IW371480
Movement: automatic, IWC Caliber 79350 (base ETA 7750); ø 30 mm; 31 jewels; 28,800 vph; 44-hour power reserve
Functions: hours, minutes, subsidiary seconds; chronograph
Case: pink gold, ø 40.9 mm, height 12.3 mm; sapphire crystal; water-resistant to 3 atm
Band: reptile skin, buckle
Price: $16,600
Variations: stainless steel ($6,900)

Portofino Hand-Wound Moon Phase

Reference number: IW516403
Movement: manually wound, IWC Caliber 59800; ø 37.8 mm, height 7.3 mm; 30 jewels; 28,800 vph; 192-hour power reserve
Functions: hours, minutes, subsidiary seconds; power reserve indicator; date, moon phase
Case: pink gold, ø 45 mm, height 12 mm; sapphire crystal; transparent case back; water-resistant to 3 atm
Band: reptile skin, buckle
Price: $22,900

Caliber 89361

Automatic; double-pawl automatic winding (Pellaton system); column wheel control of chronograph functions; single spring barrel, 68-hour power reserve
Base caliber: 89000
Functions: hours, minutes, subsidiary seconds; flyback chronograph; date
Diameter: 30 mm
Height: 7.46 mm
Jewels: 38
Balance: glucydur variable inertia balance
Frequency: 28,800 vph
Balance spring: flat hairspring
Shock protection: Incabloc
Remarks: concentric chronograph totalizer for minutes and hours

Caliber 89900

Automatic; flying 1-minute tourbillon with stop-seconds function, pink gold oscillating mass; single spring barrel, 68-hour power reserve
Functions: hours, minutes; flyback chronograph; date
Diameter: 30 mm
Jewels: 42
Balance: glucydur with fine-regulation eccentrics on balance arms

Caliber 69375

Automatic; single spring barrel, 46-hour power reserve
Base caliber: 69370
Functions: hours, minutes, subsidiary seconds; chronograph; date
Diameter: 30 mm
Height: 6.9 mm
Jewels: 36
Balance: glucydur
Frequency: 28,800 vph

Caliber 52610

Automatic; Pellaton winding; single spring barrel, 168-hour power reserve
Base caliber: 52000
Functions: hours, minutes, subsidiary seconds; power reserve indicator; perpetual calendar with date, weekday, month, moon phase
Diameter: 37.8 mm
Height: 9 mm
Jewels: 54
Balance: glucydur with weighted screws
Frequency: 28,800 vph
Balance spring: Breguet hairspring
Remarks: pink gold oscillating mass

Caliber 94800

Manually wound; 1-minute tourbillon, constant force escapement; double mainspring barrel, 96-hour power reserve
Base caliber: 94000
Functions: hours, minutes, subsidiary seconds; power reserve indicator; double moon phase display
Diameter: 37.8 mm
Height: 7.7 mm
Jewels: 43
Frequency: 18,000 vph

Caliber 98295 "Jones"

Manually wound; single spring barrel, 46-hour power reserve
Base caliber: 98000
Functions: hours, minutes, subsidiary seconds
Diameter: 38.2 mm
Height: 5.3 mm
Jewels: 18
Balance: screw balance with precision adjustment cams on the balance arms
Frequency: 18,000 vph
Balance spring: Breguet hairspring
Shock protection: Incabloc
Remarks: noticeably long regulator index; three-quarter plate of German silver, hand-engraved balance cocks

JAEGER-LECOULTRE

In 1833, Antoine LeCoultre opened his own gear wheel factory and made a fortune. So, in 1866, he had a large house built and brought together all the craftspeople needed to produce timepieces, from the watchmakers to the turners and polishers. He outfitted the workshop with the most modern machinery of the day. "La Grande Maison" was the first watch *manufacture* in the Vallée de Joux.

At the start of the twentieth century, the grandson of the company founder, Jacques-David LeCoultre, built slender, complicated watches for the Paris manufacturer Edmond Jaeger. The Frenchman was so impressed with these that, after a few years of fruitful cooperation, he engineered a merger of the two companies.

In the 1970s, the *manufacture* was taken over by the German VDO Group (later Mannesmann). Under the leadership of Günter Blümlein, Jaeger-LeCoultre weathered the quartz crisis, and during the mechanical watch renaissance in the 1980s, the company finally recouped its status as an innovative, high-performance *manufacture*.

Then, in 2000, Mannesmann's watch division (JLC, IWC, A. Lange & Söhne) sold Jaeger-LeCoultre to the Richemont Group. Given the group's strength, Jaeger-LeCoultre continued to grow. Fifty new calibers, including minute repeaters, tourbillons, and other *grandes complications*, a lubricant-free movement, and more than 400 patents tell their own story. Today, it is the largest employer in the Vallée de Joux—just as it was back in the 1860s. With all the complicated watches, though, the most enduring collection produced by the brand is the Reverso, which can swivel around to show a second watch face on the back. To celebrate the icon's eighty-fifth anniversary in 2016, Jaeger-LeCoultre came out with a whole new crop in the Tribute and Classic lines, including a number of affordable models that can be customized to a certain degree by consumers.

Manufacture Jaeger-LeCoultre
Rue de la Golisse, 8
CH-1347 Le Sentier
Switzerland

Tel.:
+41-21-852-0202

Fax:
+41-21-852-0505

E-mail:
info@jaeger-lecoultre.com

Website:
www.jaeger-lecoultre.com

Founded:
1833

Number of employees:
over 1,000

Annual production:
approx. 50,000 watches

U.S. distributor:
Jaeger-LeCoultre
645 Fifth Avenue
New York, NY 10022
800-JLC-TIME
www.jaeger-lecoultre.com

Most important collections/price range:
Atmos starting at $6,600; Duomètre starting at $5,700; Geophysic starting at $9,100; Master starting at $5,700, Rendez-Vous starting at $8,700; Reverso starting at $4,150

Geophysic True Second

Reference number: 801 81 20
Movement: automatic, JLC Caliber 770; ø 28.6 mm, height 6.57 mm; 36 jewels; 28,800 vph; jumping seconds display drive with remontoir; ringless Gyrolab balance; 40-hour power reserve
Functions: hours, minutes, sweep seconds (jumping); date
Case: stainless steel, ø 39.6 mm, height 11.81 mm; sapphire crystal; transparent case back; water-resistant to 5 atm
Band: stainless steel, folding clasp
Price: $10,500
Variations: pink gold ($16,900)

Geophysic Universal Time

Reference number: 810 81 20
Movement: automatic, JLC Caliber 772; ø 30 mm, height 7.13 mm; 36 jewels; 28,800 vph; jumping seconds display drive with remontoir; ringless Gyrolab balance; 40-hour power reserve
Functions: hours, minutes, sweep seconds (jumping); world time display (second time zone)
Case: stainless steel, ø 41.6 mm, height 11.84 mm; sapphire crystal; transparent case back; water-resistant to 5 atm
Band: stainless steel, folding clasp
Price: $15,700
Variations: reptile skin strap (stainless steel $14,000; pink gold $23,900)

Geophysic Tourbillon Universal Time

Reference number: 812 64 20
Movement: automatic, JLC Caliber 948; ø 30 mm, height 11.24 mm; 42 jewels; 28,800 vph; flying 1-minute tourbillon with ringless Gyrolab balance, rotation of world time disk once in 24 hours; 48-hour power reserve
Functions: hours, minutes, subsidiary seconds (on tourbillon cage); world time display (second time zone)
Case: platinum, ø 43.5 mm, height 14.87 mm; sapphire crystal; transparent case back; water-resistant to 5 atm
Band: reptile skin, folding clasp
Price: on request

Master Compressor Chronograph Ceramic with Pink Gold

Reference number: 205 L5 70
Movement: automatic, JLC Caliber 757; ø 25.6 mm, height 6.27 mm; 45 jewels; 28,800 vph; fine hand-finished movement; 65-hour power reserve
Functions: hours, minutes, subsidiary seconds; additional 12-hour display (second time zone), day/night indicator; chronograph; date
Case: ceramic, ø 46 mm, height 14.3 mm; sapphire crystal; pink gold crown and pushers; crown with compression key; water-resistant to 10 atm
Band: textile, buckle
Price: $15,400; limited to 300 pieces

Master Compressor Chronograph Ceramic

Reference number: 205 C5 71
Movement: automatic, JLC Caliber 757; ø 25.6 mm, height 6.26 mm; 45 jewels; 28,800 vph; fine hand-finished movement; 65-hour power reserve
Functions: hours, minutes, subsidiary seconds; additional 12-hour display (second time zone), day/night indicator; chronograph; date
Case: ceramic, ø 46 mm, height 14.3 mm; sapphire crystal; crown with compression key; water-resistant to 10 atm
Band: textile, buckle
Price: $13,000

Master Compressor Extreme LAB 2

Reference number: 203 S5 40
Movement: automatic, JLC Caliber 780; ø 33.8 mm, height 9.08 mm; 70 jewels; 28,800 vph; crown function selector; segmented power reserve indicator on dial edge, 60-hour power reserve
Functions: hours, minutes, sweep seconds; second 24-hour display (second time zone), power reserve indicator; chronograph with digital minutes totalizer; date
Case: pink gold, ø 46.8 mm, height 16.5 mm; bezel with black PVD coating; sapphire crystal; transparent case back; screw-in crown; water-resistant to 10 atm
Band: reptile skin, buckle
Price: $50,500

Duomètre Quantième Lunaire

Reference number: 604 34 20
Movement: manually wound, JLC Caliber 381; ø 33.7 mm, height 7.25 mm; 40 jewels; 21,600 vph; 2 spring barrels and 2 separate gear trains for watch and foudroyante mechanism; 50-hour power reserve
Functions: hours, minutes (off-center), sweep seconds, foudroyante sixth-second counter; double power reserve indicator; date, moon phase and age
Case: white gold, ø 40.5 mm, height 13.5 mm; sapphire crystal; transparent case back; water-resistant to 5 atm
Band: reptile skin, folding clasp
Price: $41,700
Variations: pink gold ($35,200 to $39,100)

Reverso Tribute Gyrotourbillon

Reference number: 394 64 20
Movement: manually wound, JLC Caliber 179 × 26.2 × 41 mm, height 5.97 mm; 52 jewels; 21,600 vph; double-axis spherical tourbillon with different rotation times (60 and 12.6 seconds), Gyrolab balance with hemispheric hairspring; certified chronometer according to the German industrial norm (DIN)
Functions: hours, minutes, subsidiary seconds (on the tourbillon cage); additional 12-hour display (second time zone) and day/night indicator on rear
Case: platinum, 31 × 51.2 mm, height 12.4 mm; sapphire crystal; water-resistant to 3 atm
Band: reptile skin, double folding clasp
Remarks: case can be turned and rotated 180°
Price: on request; limited to 75 pieces

Reverso Tribute Calendar

Reference number: 391 24 20
Movement: manually wound, JLC Caliber 853; 17.2 × 22 mm, height 5.15 mm; 19 jewels; 21,600 vph; 42-hour power reserve
Functions: hours, minutes; additional 12-hour display (second time zone) and day/night indicator on rear; full calendar with date, weekday, month, moon phase
Case: pink gold, 29.9 × 49.4 mm, height 10.9 mm; sapphire crystal; water-resistant to 3 atm
Band: reptile skin, folding clasp
Remarks: case turns and swivels 180°
Price: $23,900

Reverso Classic Medium Small Second

Reference number: 243 85 20
Movement: manually wound, JLC Caliber 822/2; height 2.94 mm; 19 jewels; 21,600 vph; 42-hour power reserve
Functions: hours, minutes, subsidiary seconds
Case: stainless steel, 25.5 × 42.9 mm; sapphire crystal; water-resistant to 3 atm
Band: reptile skin, buckle
Remarks: case turns and swivels 180°
Price: $5,900

Reverso Classic Medium Duetto

Reference number: 258 81 20
Movement: manually wound, JLC Caliber 854B/2; height 3.43 mm; 19 jewels; 21,600 vph; 42-hour power reserve
Functions: hours, minutes (front and back)
Case: stainless steel, 24 × 40 mm, height 9.5 mm; sapphire crystal; water-resistant to 3 atm
Band: stainless steel, folding clasp
Remarks: case turns and swivels 180°
Price: $9,150

Reverso Classic Medium Duoface Small Second

Reference number: 245 84 20
Movement: manually wound, JLC Caliber 854B/2; 17.2 × 22 mm, height 3.8 mm; 19 jewels; 21,600 vph; 42-hour power reserve
Functions: hours, minutes, subsidiary seconds; additional 12-hour display (second time zone) and day/night indicator on rear
Case: stainless steel, 25.5 × 42.9 mm, height 9.2 mm; sapphire crystal; water-resistant to 3 atm
Band: reptile skin, folding clasp
Remarks: case turns and swivels 180°
Price: $8,300

Reverso Classic Large Duoface Small Second

Reference number: 384 84 20
Movement: manually wound, JLC Caliber 8241/2; height 3.8 mm; 19 jewels; 21,600 vph; 42-hour power reserve
Functions: hours, minutes, subsidiary seconds; second 24-hour display (second time zone) on rear
Case: stainless steel, 28.3 × 47 mm, height 10.3 mm; sapphire crystal; water-resistant to 3 atm
Band: reptile skin, folding clasp
Remarks: case turns and swivels 180°
Price: $8,400

Reverso Tribute Duoface

Reference number: 390 24 20
Movement: manually wound, JLC Caliber 854A/2; 17.2 × 22 mm, height 3.8 mm; 19 jewels; 21,600 vph; 42-hour power reserve
Functions: hours, minutes, subsidiary seconds; second 24-hour display (second time zone) on rear
Case: pink gold, 25.5 × 42.9 mm, height 9.2 mm; sapphire crystal; water-resistant to 3 atm
Band: reptile skin, folding clasp
Price: $19,100

Reverso Tribute Moon

Reference number: 395 84 20
Movement: manually wound, JLC Caliber 853A; 17.2 × 22 mm, height 5.15 mm; 19 jewels; 21,600 vph; 42-hour power reserve
Functions: hours, minutes; additional 12-hour display (second time zone) and day/night indicator on rear; date, moon phase
Case: stainless steel, 29.9 × 49.4 mm, height 10.9 mm; sapphire crystal; water-resistant to 3 atm
Band: reptile skin, folding clasp
Price: $12,700

Master Ultra Thin Small Second

Reference number: 135 84 80
Movement: automatic, JLC Caliber 896/1;
ø 26 mm, height 3.98 mm; 32 jewels; 28,800 vph;
43-hour power reserve
Functions: hours, minutes, subsidiary seconds
Case: stainless steel, ø 40 mm, height 7.58 mm;
sapphire crystal; transparent case back; water-
resistant to 5 atm
Band: reptile skin, folding clasp
Price: $7,350

Master Ultra Thin Réserve de Marche

Reference number: 137 84 80
Movement: automatic, JLC Caliber 938/1;
ø 26 mm, height 4.9 mm; 41 jewels; 28,800 vph;
43-hour power reserve
Functions: hours, minutes, subsidiary seconds;
power reserve indicator; date
Case: stainless steel, ø 39 mm, height 9.85 mm;
sapphire crystal; transparent case back; water-
resistant to 5 atm
Band: reptile skin, folding clasp
Price: $8,650

Master Ultra-Thin Moon

Reference number: 136 35 40
Movement: automatic, JLC Caliber 925/1;
ø 26 mm, height 4.9 mm; 30 jewels; 28,800 vph;
38-hour power reserve
Functions: hours, minutes, sweep seconds; date,
moon phase
Case: white gold, ø 39 mm, height 9.9 mm; sapphire
crystal; transparent case back; water-resistant to
5 atm
Band: reptile skin, folding clasp
Price: $18,800

Master Control Date

Reference number: 154 85 30
Movement: automatic, JLC Caliber 899/1;
ø 26 mm, height 3.3 mm; 32 jewels; 28,800 vph;
38-hour power reserve
Functions: hours, minutes, sweep seconds; date
Case: stainless steel, ø 39 mm, height 8.5 mm;
sapphire crystal; transparent case back; water-
resistant to 5 atm
Band: reptile skin, buckle
Price: $5,700

Master Chronograph

Reference number: 153 85 30
Movement: automatic, JLC Caliber 751G;
ø 25.6 mm, height 5.72 mm; 37 jewels; 28,800 vph;
2 spring barrels, 65-hour power reserve
Functions: hours, minutes; chronograph
Case: stainless steel, ø 40 mm, height 11.7 mm;
sapphire crystal; water-resistant to 5 atm
Band: reptile skin, buckle
Price: $8,000

Master Geographic

Reference number: 142 85 30
Movement: automatic, JLC Caliber 809/1; height
5.9 mm; 23 mm; 31 jewels; 28,800 vph
Functions: hours, minutes, sweep seconds; second
24-hour display (second time zone) with reference
city markings
Case: stainless steel, ø 39 mm, height 11.77 mm;
sapphire crystal; transparent case back; water-
resistant to 5 atm
Band: reptile skin, buckle
Price: $9,400

Caliber 844

Manually wound; single spring barrel, 38-hour power reserve

Functions: hours, minutes (twice, on front and back)
Measurements: 13 × 21 mm
Height: 3.45 mm
Jewels: 18
Balance: glucydur
Frequency: 21,600 vph
Remarks: 100 components

Caliber 362

Automatic; ultrathin construction; 1-minute flying tourbillon with flying (i.e., one-sided) mounted balance; hubless peripheral winding rotor; repeater mechanism with lowered wait times; single spring barrel, 45-hour power reserve

Functions: hours, minutes; hours, quarter hour, and minute repeater
Diameter: 33.3 mm
Height: 4.8 mm
Jewels: 68
Balance: glucydur
Frequency: 21,600 vph
Balance spring: glucydur
Remarks: 471 components

Caliber 383

Manually wound; 2 separate spring barrels and 2 separate gear works for the two time displays; pull crown to reset second hand; double mainspring barrel, 50-hour power reserve

Functions: hours, minutes (off-center), sweep seconds; second time zone (digital, jumping hours, minutes), world time indicator, separate power reserve indicator for each spring barrel
Diameter: 34.3 mm
Height: 7.25 mm
Jewels: 54
Balance: glucydur
Frequency: 28,800 vph

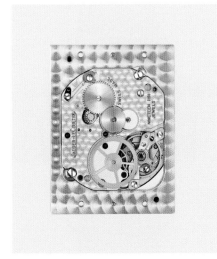

Caliber 986

Manually wound; single spring barrel, 48-hour power reserve

Functions: hours, minutes, subsidiary seconds; second 24-hour display (second time zone); date
Measurements: 22.6 × 25.6 mm
Height: 4.15 mm
Jewels: 19
Balance: glucydur with smooth ring
Frequency: 28,800 vph
Balance spring: flat hairspring
Shock protection: Kif
Remarks: perlage on plate

Caliber 995

Automatic; flying 1-minute tourbillon; single spring barrel

Functions: hours, minutes, subsidiary seconds (on tourbillon cage)
Diameter: 34.7 mm
Height: 6.5 mm
Jewels: 31
Frequency: 28,800 vph
Balance spring: cylindrical
Remarks: 275 components

Caliber 770

Automatic; jumping seconds display drive with remontoir; ringless Gyrolab balance; single spring barrel, 40-hour power reserve

Functions: hours, minutes, sweep deadbeat seconds (jumping); hour hand can be switched back and forth in 1-hour steps; date
Diameter: 28.6 mm
Height: 6.57 mm
Jewels: 36
Balance: Gyrolab
Frequency: 28,800 vph
Remarks: 275 components

Caliber 757

Automatic; column wheel control of chronograph functions; double mainspring barrel, 65-hour power reserve
Functions: hours, minutes, subsidiary seconds; additional 12-hour display (second time zone), day/night indicator; chronograph; date
Diameter: 28 mm
Height: 6.26 mm
Jewels: 45
Balance: glucydur 4 regulating screws
Frequency: 28,800 vph
Balance spring: flat hairspring
Shock protection: Kif

Caliber 849

Manually wound; single spring barrel, 35-hour power reserve
Functions: hours, minutes
Diameter: 26 mm
Height: 1.85 mm
Jewels: 19
Balance: glucydur
Frequency: 21,600 vph
Balance spring: flat hairspring
Shock protection: Kif
Remarks: finely finished movement, bridges with côtes de Genève; 123 components

Caliber 898A

Automatic; single spring barrel, 43-hour power reserve
Functions: hours, minutes, sweep seconds; day/night indicator
Diameter: 26 mm
Height: 3.3 mm
Jewels: 30
Balance: glucydur, 4 regulating screws
Frequency: 28,800 vph
Balance spring: flat hairspring
Shock protection: Kif

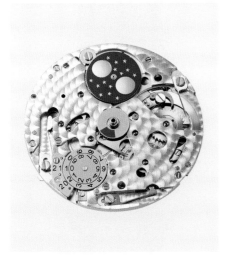

Caliber 868

Automatic; single spring barrel, 38-hour power reserve
Functions: hours, minutes, sweep seconds; perpetual calendar with date, weekday, month, moon phase, year display (four digits)
Diameter: 27.8 mm
Height: 4.72 mm
Jewels: 46
Balance: glucydur
Frequency: 28,800 vph
Remarks: 336 components

Caliber 866

Automatic; single spring barrel, 43-hour power reserve
Functions: hours, minutes, subsidiary seconds; full calendar with date, weekday, month, moon phase
Diameter: 26 mm
Height: 5.65 mm
Jewels: 32
Balance: glucydur
Frequency: 28,800 vph
Remarks: 305 components

Caliber 982

Automatic; 1-minutes tourbillon; full gold rotor; single spring barrel, 48-hour power reserve
Functions: hours, minutes, subsidiary seconds (on tourbillon cage)
Diameter: 30 mm
Height: 6.4 mm
Jewels: 33
Balance: glucydur with weighted screws
Frequency: 28,800 vph
Balance spring: Breguet hairspring
Shock protection: Kif
Remarks: perlage on mainplate bridges with côtes de Genève

JAQUET DROZ

Though this watch brand first gained real notice when it was bought by the Swatch Group in 2001, Jaquet Droz looks back on a long tradition. Pierre Jaquet-Droz (1721–1790) was actually supposed to be a pastor, but instead followed the call to become a mechanic and a watchmaker. In the mid-eighteenth century, he began to push the limits of micromechanics, and his enthusiasm for it quickly led him to work on watch mechanisms and more complicated movements, which he attempted to operate through purely mechanical means.

Jaquet-Droz became famous in Europe for his automatons. More than once, he had to answer to religious institutions, whose guardians of public morals suspected there might be some devil's work and witchcraft behind his mechanical children, scribes, and organists. He even designed prostheses. A small enterprise in La Chaux-de-Fonds still produces items of this applied art, proof that the name Jaquet-Droz is still alive and well in the Jura mountains, and its watches combined with automatons continue to thrill collectors and enthusiasts alike.

The Swatch Group has developed an esthetically and technically sophisticated collection based on an outstanding Frédéric Piguet movement. In recent years, the classically beautiful watch dials have taken on a slightly modern look without losing any of their identity. The spirit of the maverick founder of the brand still hovers about. Among the leading items in the current portfolio are automatons featuring twittering birds, an ancient technique revived and perfected by the brand. This focus on quality and inventiveness has made Jaquet Droz a top representative in the Swatch Group's portfolio. Its CEO is Marc A. Hayek, who is also CEO of Breguet and Blancpain.

Montres Jaquet Droz SA
CH-2300 La Chaux-de-Fonds
Switzerland

Tel.:
+41-32-924-2888

Fax:
+41-32-924-2882

E-mail:
info@jaquet-droz.com

Website:
www.jaquet-droz.com

Founded:
1738

U.S. distribution:
The Swatch Group (U.S.), Inc.
1200 Harbor Boulevard
Weehawken, NJ 07086
201-271-1400
www.swatchgroup.com

Most important collections:
Les Ateliers d'Art, Grande Seconde, Grande Seconde SW, Astrale Collection, Petite Heure Minute, Lady 8

Grande Seconde Moon Ivory Enamel

Reference number: J007533200
Movement: automatic, Jaquet Droz Caliber 2660QL3; ø 26.2 mm; 30 jewels; 28,800 vph; double spring barrel, silicon balance spring and pallet horns; pink gold oscillating mass; 68-hour power reserve
Functions: hours, minutes (off-center), subsidiary seconds; date, moon phase
Case: red gold, ø 43 mm, height 13.23 mm; sapphire crystal; water-resistant to 3 atm
Band: reptile skin, buckle
Remarks: enamel dial
Price: $28,900

Loving Butterfly Automaton

Reference number: J032533270
Movement: automatic, Jaquet Droz Caliber 2653.ATI; ø 26.2 mm, height 4.47 mm; 57 jewels; 28,800 vph; silicon balance spring and pallet horns; double spring barrel, hand-engraved pink gold oscillating mass; 68-hour power reserve
Functions: hours, minutes (off-center)
Case: red gold, ø 43 mm, height 16.63 mm; sapphire crystal; water-resistant to 3 atm
Band: reptile skin, buckle
Remarks: black onyx dial, hand-engraved 18-kt red gold appliques; limited to 28 pieces
Price: $126,000

Grande Seconde Quantième Satin-Brushed Anthracite

Reference number: J007030248
Movement: automatic, Jaquet Droz Caliber 2660Q2.P; ø 26.2 mm; 30 jewels; 28,800 vph; double spring barrel, silicon balance spring and pallet horns; 68-hour power reserve
Functions: hours, minutes (off-center), subsidiary seconds; date
Case: stainless steel, ø 43 mm, height 12.13 mm; sapphire crystal; water-resistant to 3 atm
Band: reptile skin, folding clasp
Price: $9,500

Jörg Schauer
c/o Stowa GmbH & Co. KG
Gewerbepark 16
D-75331 Engelsbrand
Germany

Tel.:
+49-7082-9306-0

Fax:
+49-7082-9306-2

E-mail:
info@schauer-germany.com

Website:
www.schauer-germany.com

Founded:
1990

Number of employees:
20

Annual production:
approx. 500 watches

Distribution:
direct sales; please contact the address in
Germany

JÖRG SCHAUER

Jörg Schauer's watches are first and foremost cool. The cases have been carefully worked, the look is planned to draw the eye. After all, he is a perfectionist and leaves nothing to chance. He works on every single case himself, polishing and performing his own brand of magic for as long as it takes to display his personal touch. This time-consuming process is one that Schauer believes is absolutely necessary. "I do this because I place a great deal of value on the fact that my cases are absolutely perfect," he explains. "I can do it better than anyone, and I would never let anyone else do it for me."

Schauer, a goldsmith by training, has been making watches since 1990. He began by doing one-off pieces in precious metals for collectors and then opened his business and simultaneously moved to stainless steel. His style is to produce functional, angular cases with visibly screwed-down bezels and straightforward dials in plain black or white. Forget finding any watch close to current trends in his collection; Schauer only builds timepieces that he genuinely likes.

Purchasing a Schauer is not that easy. He has chosen a strategy of genuine quality over quantity and produces only about 500 watches annually. This includes special watches like the One-Hand Durowe, with a movement from one of Germany's movement manufacturers, Durowe, which Schauer acquired in 2002. His production structure is a vital part of his success and includes prototyping, movement modification, finishing, case production, dial painting and printing—all done in Schauer's own workshop in Engelsbrand. Any support he needs from the outside he prefers to search out among regional specialists.

Schauer Analog Reminder

Reference number: AnalogReminder
Movement: automatic, ETA Caliber A07.171; ø 36.6 mm, height 7.9 mm; 24 jewels; 28,800 vph; exclusive "Schauer" rotor with engraving; 46-hour power reserve
Functions: hours, minutes, sweep seconds; laser-engraved dial disk with "reminder" function
Case: titanium, ø 46 mm, height 16 mm; stainless steel bezel, fixed with 12 screws, with Superluminova inserts; sapphire crystal; transparent case back; water-resistant to 20 atm
Band: calfskin, double folding clasp
Price: $5,440
Variations: rubber strap ($5,440)

Edition 10

Reference number: Ed10
Movement: automatic, ETA Caliber 7753; ø 30 mm, height 7.9 mm; 27 jewels; 28,800 vph; finished with ornamental stripes and blued screws, exclusive engraved "Schauer" rotor; 48-hour power reserve
Functions: hours, minutes, subsidiary seconds; chronograph
Case: stainless steel, ø 42 mm, height 15 mm; bezel fixed with 12 screws; sapphire crystal; transparent case back; water-resistant to 5 atm
Band: calfskin, double folding clasp
Price: $3,350
Variations: stainless steel bracelet ($3,612); reptile skin strap ($3,305); hand-wound ($3,693)

Edition 12

Reference number: Ed12
Movement: automatic, ETA Caliber 7753; ø 30 mm, height 7.9 mm; 27 jewels; 28,800 vph; finished with ornamental stripes and blued screws, exclusive engraved "Schauer" rotor; 48-hour power reserve
Functions: hours, minutes, subsidiary seconds; chronograph
Case: stainless steel, ø 41 mm, height 15 mm; bezel fixed with 12 screws; sapphire crystal; transparent case back; water-resistant to 5 atm
Band: calfskin, double folding clasp
Price: $3,423
Variations: stainless steel bracelet ($3,702)

JUNGHANS

The Erz Mountains in eastern Germany, home of Glashütte, is not the only place to have produced watches in the country. Another success story was written on the other side of the country, in the Black Forest. To be precise, in Schramberg, a recondite town crouching in a valley squeezed between wooded slopes on the old trade route leading from Strasbourg in Alsace south to Lake Constance. It's here that Erhard Junghans founded a watchmaking factory in 1861.

Around the turn of the century, his son Arthur developed it into a large-scale production site built on American models. And so Schramberg became the hub of the watchmaking world. Nearly three thousand men and women worked at that factory and made nine thousand wall clocks and alarm clocks daily.

In the boom years following World War II, the company, with its logo featuring a star, manufactured wristwatches. The company went on to ring in modern times with its own solar and radio-controlled watches. Junghans was twice the official timekeeper at the Olympic Games, and for a long time it maintained its position as the largest chronometer maker in the world.

When quality became less of an issue in consumer consciousness, things started quieting down in the Black Forest factory. Nevertheless, wristwatches made their comeback in the 1990s, which is when many people remembered the precision timekeepers from the Black Forest. Among them was Dr. Hans-Jochem Steim, a successful entrepreneur from Schramberg, who decided to boost the rebirth of the Schramberg brand.

Together with his son, Hannes Steim, he purchased the company and decided to take the financing of the necessary structural measures in themselves. Just in time for the company's 150th anniversary (2011), Junghans devised a new production and distribution schedule. Today, the brand is proud of its extensive collection of high-quality wristwatches, ranging from genuine icons of design to major classics, and all the way to sporty chronographs. Junghans's success is also driving the growth of a number of suppliers. And Schramberg is once again a big name in the region, its fame even spreading throughout Germany and beyond.

Uhrenfabrik Junghans
GmbH & Co. KG
Geisshaldenstrasse 49
D-78713 Schramberg

Tel.:
+49-742-218-0

Fax:
+49-742-218-665

E-mail:
info@junghans.de

Website:
www.junghans.de

Founded:
1861

Number of employees:
127

Annual production:
approx. 60,000 watches

Distributor:
All About Time, Inc.
Junghans Watches USA
P.O. Box 24550
Cleveland, OH 44124
877-589-8463
https://www.junghanswatchesusa.net/

Most important collections/price range:
Erhard Junghans; Junghans Meister; Max Bill by Junghans; Junghans Performance; from approx. $750 to $2,500, special pieces up to $14,000

Meister Driver Automatic
Reference number: 027/7710
Movement: automatic, Caliber J800.1 (base ETA 2824-2 or Sellita SW200-1); ø 25.6 mm, height 4.6 mm; 25 or 26 jewels; 28,800 vph; blued screws, rhodium-plated movement, with diamond polish; rotor with côtes de Genève; 38-hour power reserve
Functions: hours, minutes, sweep seconds; date
Case: stainless steel with rose gold–colored PVD coating, ø 38.4 mm, height 9.9 mm; hard-coated Plexiglas crystal; transparent case back; water-resistant to 3 atm
Band: calfskin, buckle
Price: $1,199
Variations: green strap; various models without PVD coating ($1,199)

Meister Driver Day Date
Reference number: 027/4721
Movement: automatic, Caliber J800.4 (base ETA 2836-2); ø 25.6 mm, height 5.05 mm; 25 jewels; 28,800 vph; blued screws, rhodium-plated and finely finished movement with diamond polish and côtes de Genève; 38-hour power reserve
Functions: hours, minutes, sweep seconds; date, weekday
Case: stainless steel, ø 40.4 mm, height 11.2 mm; hard-coated Plexiglas crystal; transparent case back; water-resistant to 3 atm
Band: calfskin, buckle
Price: $1,419
Variations: with sand-colored dial and gray band

Meister Agenda
Reference number: 027/4364
Movement: automatic, Caliber J810.5 (base ETA 2892 with Soprod 9075 module); ø 25.6 mm, height 5.1 mm; 28 jewels; 28,800 vph; rhodium-plated movement, blued screws; rotor with côtes de Genève; 42-hour power reserve
Functions: hours, minutes, sweep seconds; power reserve indicator; full calendar with date, weekday, weeks of the year
Case: stainless steel, ø 40.4 mm, height 12.2 mm; hard-coated Plexiglas crystal; transparent case back
Band: horse leather, buckle
Price: $2,190
Variations: stainless steel bracelet ($2,300)

Meister Driver Day Date

Reference number: 027/4722.44
Movement: automatic, Caliber J800.4 (base ETA 2836-2); ø 25.6 mm, height 5.05 mm; 25 jewels; 28,800 vph; blued screws, finely finished movement with diamond polish and côtes de Genève; 38-hour power reserve
Functions: hours, minutes, sweep seconds; date, weekday
Case: stainless steel, ø 40.4 mm, height 11.2 mm; hard-coated Plexiglas crystal; transparent case back; water-resistant to 3 atm
Band: stainless steel, folding clasp
Price: $1,529

Meister Pilot

Reference number: 027/3594
Movement: automatic, Caliber J880.4 (base ETA 2824-2 with Dubois Dépraz module); ø 30 mm, height 7.6 mm; 49 jewels; 28,800 vph; rhodium-plated movement; rotor with côtes de Genève; 38-hour power reserve
Functions: hours, minutes, subsidiary seconds; chronograph
Case: stainless steel with DLC coating, ø 43.3 mm, height 14.4 mm; sapphire crystal; water-resistant to 10 atm
Band: calfskin, buckle
Price: $2,684
Variations: gray dial and band

Form A

Reference number: 027/4734
Movement: automatic, Caliber J800.2 (base ETA 2824-2 or Sellita SW200-1); ø 25.6 mm, height 4.6 mm; 25 or 26 jewels; 28,800 vph; 38-hour power reserve
Functions: hours, minutes, sweep seconds; date
Case: stainless steel, ø 39.1 mm, height 9.5 mm; sapphire crystal; transparent case back; water-resistant to 5 atm
Band: calfskin, buckle
Price: $924
Variations: various bands and dials; chronograph quartz movement ($493)

Form A

Reference number: 027/4735
Movement: automatic, Caliber J800.2 (base ETA 2824-2 or Sellita SW200-1); ø 25.6 mm, height 4.6 mm; 25 or 26 jewels; 28,800 vph; 38-hour power reserve
Functions: hours, minutes, sweep seconds; date
Case: stainless steel, ø 39.1 mm, height 9.5 mm; sapphire crystal; transparent case back; water-resistant to 5 atm
Band: calfskin, buckle
Price: $924
Variations: various bands and dials; chronograph quartz movement ($493)

Max Bill Chronoscope

Reference number: 027/4600
Movement: automatic, Caliber J880.2 (base ETA 7750 or Sellita SW500); ø 30 mm, height 7.9 mm; 25 jewels; 28,800 vph; 42-hour power reserve
Functions: hours, minutes; chronograph; date
Case: stainless steel, ø 40 mm, height 14.4 mm; hard-coated Plexiglas crystal
Band: calfskin, buckle
Price: $1,810
Variations: black dial and Arabic numbers; stainless steel Milanese bracelet ($1,920)

Max Bill Hand-Wound

Reference number: 027/3701
Movement: manually wound, Caliber J805.1 (base ETA 2801-2); ø 25.6 mm, height 3.35 mm; 17 jewels; 28,800 vph; 42-hour power reserve
Functions: hours, minutes, sweep seconds
Case: stainless steel, ø 34 mm, height 9 mm; hard-coated Plexiglas crystal
Band: calfskin, buckle
Price: $690
Variations: various bands and dials

KOBOLD

Kobold Watch Company, LLC
1801 Parkway View Drive
Pittsburgh, PA 15205

Tel.:
724-533-3000

E-mail:
info@koboldwatch.com

Website:
www.koboldwatch.com

Founded:
1998

Number of employees:
20

Annual production:
maximum 2,500 watches

Distribution:
factory-direct, select retailers

Most important collections/price range:
Soarway / $1,950 to $35,000

Like many others in the field, Michael Kobold had already developed an interest in the watch industry in childhood. As a young man, he found a mentor in Chronoswiss founder Gerd-Rüdiger Lang, who encouraged him to start his own brand. This he did in 1998—at the age of nineteen while he was still a student at Carnegie Mellon University.

Today, Kobold Watch Company is headquartered in a big red farm in Amish country, Pennsylvania. There, it manufactures cases, movement components, dials, hands, and even straps.

The company's motto—Embrace Adventure—is reflected in the adventure-themed watches it turns out, worn by explorers such as Sir Ranulph Fiennes, whom *Guinness World Records* describes as "the world's greatest living explorer." The brand's centerpiece is the Soarway collection and the fabled Soarway case, which was originally created in 1999 by Sir Ranulph, master watchmaker and Chronoswiss founder Lang, as well as company founder Kobold, himself an avid mountain climber.

Kobold's love of the Himalayas has driven his commitment to the people of Nepal. He produces leather accessories and straps there and uses the operation to offer women vocational training. In 2015, he launched the Soarway Foundation to help Nepal in the event of earthquakes. Coincidentally, a few weeks later the first of two struck, devastating the country and the subsidiary. To help in such emergencies and others, he has started an initiative to get fire trucks to the country, hence the making of fire truck–themed watches. Kobold Nepal also works with Maiti Nepal to reintegrate trafficked women into society.

Kobold has contributed to the renaissance of American watchmaking and originally set its sights even higher, namely, on an in-house U.S.-made movement. Things have changed, though. "We make tough, rugged watches and so the case plays a more important role than the movement," says Kobold. "So for now, we're concentrating on making the toughest cases possible. One day, we'll tackle making in-house movements." The Soarway collection includes several novelties, such as the Soarway Transglobe, a watch with a second time zone that displays minutes as well as hours.

Soarway Transglobe
Reference number: KN 266853
Movement: automatic, Caliber K.793 (base ETA 2892-A2); ø 36 mm, height 4.95 mm; 26 jewels; 28,800 vph; 46-hour power reserve
Functions: hours, minutes, sweep seconds; date; 2nd time zone with hours, minutes
Case: stainless steel, ø 44 mm, height 14.3 mm; sapphire crystal; screw-down case back; water-resistant to 30 atm
Band: canvas, signed buckle
Price: $4,750

Himalaya
Reference number: KN 880121
Movement: automatic, ETA Caliber 2824-A2; ø 30.4 mm, height 10.35 mm; 25 jewels; 28,800 vph; 42-hour power reserve
Functions: hours, minutes, sweep seconds
Case: stainless steel, ø 44 mm, height 11.3 mm; antireflective sapphire crystal; screw-down case back; water-resistant to 10 atm
Band: calfskin, buckle
Price: $3,650
Variations: Arctic Blue, black or white dial

Intrepid Automatic
Reference number: KD 130852
Movement: automatic, ETA Caliber 2824-A2; ø 30.4 mm, height 10.35 mm; 25 jewels; 28,800 vph; 42-hour power reserve
Functions: hours, minutes, sweep seconds
Case: stainless steel, ø 44 mm, height 11.3 mm; antireflective sapphire crystal; screw-down case back; water-resistant to 10 atm
Band: calfskin, buckle
Price: $3,650
Variations: Arctic blue, white

Phantom Tactical Chronograph

Reference number: KD 924451
Movement: automatic, ETA Valjoux Caliber 7750; ø 30 mm, height 8.1 mm; 25 jewels; 28,800 vph; 46-hour power reserve; côtes de Genève, perlage, engraved and skeletonized gold-plated rotor
Functions: hours, minutes, subsidiary seconds; date, day; chronograph
Case: PVD-coated stainless steel, made in USA, ø 41 mm, height 15.3 mm; unidirectional bezel with 60-minute divisions; screw-in crown/buttons; sapphire crystal; screw-down back; water-resistant to 300 m
Band: PVD-coated stainless steel, folding clasp
Price: $4,250

Intrepid Firetruck Expedition Special Edition

Reference number: KN 664583
Movement: automatic, ETA Caliber 2824-A2; ø 30.4 mm, height 10.35 mm; 25 jewels; 28,800 vph; 42-hour power reserve
Functions: hours, minutes, sweep seconds
Case: stainless steel, ø 44 mm, height 11.3 mm; antireflective sapphire crystal; screw-down case back; water-resistant to 10 atm
Band: alligator, buckle
Price: $3,950; limited to 100 pieces

Seal Firetruck Expedition Special Edition

Reference number: KD 1152147
Movement: automatic, ETA Caliber 2824-A2; ø 30.4 mm, height 10.35 mm; 25 jewels; 28,800 vph; 42-hour power reserve
Functions: hours, minutes, sweep seconds
Case: stainless steel, ø 44.25 mm, height 17.5 mm; antireflective sapphire crystal; screw-down case back; water-resistant to 100 atm
Band: reptile skin, buckle
Price: $4,250; limited to 100 pieces

Soarway Gurkhas

Reference number: KD 1142164
Movement: automatic, ETA Caliber 2892-A2; ø 28 mm, height 3.6 mm; 25 jewels; 28,800 vph; 46-hour power reserve
Functions: hours, minutes, sweep seconds; date
Case: stainless steel, made in USA; ø 43.5 mm, height 15 mm; unidirectional bezel; soft iron core; antireflective sapphire crystal; screw-down case back; screw-in crown; water-resistant to 50 atm
Band: reptile skin and canvas strap, buckle
Price: $4,250
Variations: limited edition of 100 watches

Soarway Diver

Reference number: KD 212441
Movement: automatic, ETA Caliber 2892-A2; ø 28 mm, height 3.6 mm; 25 jewels; 28,800 vph; 46-hour power reserve
Functions: hours, minutes, sweep seconds; date
Case: stainless steel, made in USA; ø 43.5 mm, height 15 mm; unidirectional bezel; soft iron core; antireflective sapphire crystal; screw-down case back; screw-in crown; water-resistant to 50 atm
Band: canvas, buckle
Price: $3,850
Variations: standard, non-California dial; Arctic blue dial

SMG-2

Reference number: KD 956853
Movement: automatic, Caliber ETA 2893-A2; ø 26.2 mm, height 6.1 mm; 21 jewels; 28,800 vph; 40-hour power reserve
Functions: hours, minutes, sweep seconds; 2nd time zone; date
Case: stainless steel, made in USA; ø 43 mm, height 12.75 mm; unidirectional bezel; soft iron core; antireflective sapphire crystal; screw-down case back; screw-in crown; water-resistant to 30 atm
Band: canvas, buckle
Price: $4,250

KUDOKE

Stefan Kudoke, a watchmaker from Frankfurt/Oder, has made a name for himself as an extremely skilled and imaginative creator of timepieces. He apprenticed with two experienced watchmakers and graduated as the number one trainee in the state of Brandenburg. This earned him a stipend from a federal program promoting gifted individuals. He then moved on to one of the large *manufactures* in Glashütte, where he refined his skills in its workshop for complications and prototyping. At the age of twenty-two, with a master's diploma in his pocket, he decided to get an MBA and then devote himself to building his own company.

His guiding principle is individuality, and that is not possible to find in a serial product. So Kudoke began building unique pieces. By realizing the special wishes of customers, he manages to reflect each person's uniqueness in each watch. And he has produced some out-of-the-ordinary pieces, like the ExCentro1 and 2, whose dials are off-center and hint at a feeling for the absurd, à la Dalí.

His specialties include engraving and goldsmithing. Within his creations bridges may in fact be graceful bodies, or the fine skeletonizing of a plate fragment, a world of figures and garlands. His recent creations include a skull watch done with characteristic care, and the superbly minimalistic Open Sector Dial.

Kudoke Uhren
Tannenweg 5
D-15236 Frankfurt (Oder)
Germany

Tel.:
+49-335-280-0409

E-mail:
info@kudoke.eu

Website:
www.kudoke.eu

Founded:
2007

Number of employees:
1

Annual production:
30–50 watches

Distribution
Contact the brand directly for information

Price range:
between approx. $4,500 and $11,500

Kurt

Movement: manually wound, ETA Caliber 6498 (modified); ø 36.6 mm, height 4.5 mm; 17 jewels; 18,000 vph; movement skeletonized by hand; 46-hour power reserve
Functions: hours, minutes, subsidiary seconds
Case: stainless steel, ø 42 mm, height 10.5 mm; sapphire crystal; transparent case back
Band: calfskin, buckle
Price: $5,650

Skull

Movement: automatic, ETA Caliber 2824-2; ø 25.6 mm, height 4.6 mm; 25 jewels; 28,800 vph; hand-engraved rotor; 38-hour power reserve
Functions: hours, minutes, sweep seconds
Case: stainless steel, ø 38 mm, height 10.5 mm; sapphire crystal; transparent case back; water-resistant to 5 atm
Band: reptile skin, buckle
Remarks: hand-engraved silver dial
Price: $8,540
Variations: skull set with diamonds

Open Sector Dial

Movement: manually wound, ETA Caliber 6498 (modified); ø 36.6 mm, height 4.5 mm; 17 jewels; 18,000 vph; movement engraved and skeletonized by hand; 46-hour power reserve
Functions: hours, minutes, subsidiary seconds
Case: stainless steel, ø 42 mm, height 10.5 mm; sapphire crystal; transparent case back
Band: reptile skin, buckle
Remarks: hand-engraved and skeletonized silver dial
Price: $8,540

Laurent Ferrier
Route de Saint Julien 150
CH-1228 Plan-les-Ouates
Switzerland

Tel.:
+41-22-716-3388

E-mail:
info@laurentferrier.ch

Website:
www.laurentferrier.ch

Founded:
2010

Number of employees:
10

Annual production:
120

U.S. distributor:
Totally Worth It, LLC
76 Division Avenue
Summit, NJ 07901-2309
201-894-4710
info@totallyworthit.com

Most important collections/price range:
Variations of the Galet / from $40,000 to
$317,000

LAURENT FERRIER

A rock rolling along a riverbed or being buffeted by coastal surf will, over time, achieve a kind of perfect shape, streamlined, flowing, smooth. It will usually become a comfortable touchstone for the human hand, a beautiful pebble, or *galet* in French. And that is the name given to the watches made by Laurent Ferrier in Geneva, Switzerland. The name refers to the special look and feel of the cases, which are just one hallmark of this very unusual, yet classical, watch brand.

The metaphor of the rock in water optimizing its form in a slow but consistent process could apply to Laurent Ferrier himself. He is a real person, the offspring of a watchmaking family from the Canton of Neuchâtel, and a trained watchmaker. As a young man he had a passion for cars, too, and even raced seven times at the 24 Hours of Le Mans. In 2009, after thirty-five years of employment at Patek Philippe working on new movements, Ferrier decided he had been shaped enough by his industry. He gathered up his deep experience and founded his own enterprise. He was joined by his son, Christian Ferrier, a watchmaker in his own right, and fellow former race driver François Sérvanin.

One of the first watches was a tourbillon, and it was a winner. The geeks loved the technical wizardry of the natural escapement with the double hairspring ensuring greater accuracy (a technical idea going back to Breguet). The traditionalists found the tourbillon concealed on the movement side (as it used to be) very intriguing and effective, since it kept the dial free of clutter. Purists and estheticians understandably went for precisely that minimal dial, the spear hands, the drop markers. Ferrier had not missed a single detail.

The brand has since evolved, but the DNA is well in place. In addition to the flagship Galet Classic, there is a Galet Secret, for example, which adds a special complication that pivots two opaque crystals on the dial to reveal various scenes, a moon, a ship, a dragon, and so forth. And for women, Ferrier has the Lady Micro-Rotor F of 2017, with a decorated mother-of-pearl dial and a simple diamond at 12 o'clock as a single marker.

Galet Tourbillon Double Balance Spring

Reference number: LCF001.G1.E09
Movement: manually wound, Laurent Ferrier Caliber LF619.01; ø 31.6 mm, height 5.57 mm; 21,600 vph; 23 jewels; double balance spring; 1-minute tourbillon on movement back; Besançon Observatory chronometer certification; 80-hour power reserve
Functions: hours, minutes, subsidiary seconds
Case: white gold, ø 41 mm, height 12.5 mm; sapphire crystal; transparent case back; water-resistant to 3 atm
Band: reptile skin, buckle
Remarks: ivory-colored grand feu enamel dial
Price: $208,000

Galet Tourbillon Double Balance Spring Secret

Reference number: LCF002.G1
Movement: manually wound, Laurent Ferrier Caliber LF619.02; ø 31.6 mm, height 5.57 mm; 21,600 vph; 23 jewels; double balance spring; 1-minute tourbillon on movement back; Besançon Observatory chronometer certification; 80-hour power reserve
Functions: hours, minutes, subsidiary seconds
Case: white gold, ø 42 mm, height 12.5 mm; sapphire crystal; transparent case back; water-resistant to 3 atm
Band: reptile skin, buckle
Remarks: grand feu enamel miniature painting; pusher activated shutter opens to 240° on dial in 60 minutes
Price: $317,000; unique piece

Galet Micro-Rotor—Lady F

Reference number: LCF011 G/R
Movement: automatic, Laurent Ferrier Caliber FBN229.01; ø 31.6 mm, height 4.35 mm; 21,600 vph; 34 jewels; pawl-fitted microrotor; silicon escapement with dual direct impulse on balance; finely decorated bridges and mainplate
Functions: hours, minutes
Case: white gold, ø 39 mm, height 11.1 mm; sapphire crystal; transparent case back; water-resistant to 3 atm
Band: reptile skin, rose gold buckle
Remarks: mother-of-pearl dial, diamond at 12 o'clock
Price: $60,000
Variations: blue mother-of-pearl dial ($60,000)

LONGINES

The Longines winged hourglass logo is the world's oldest trademark, according to the World Intellectual Property Organization (WIPO). Since its founding in 1832, the brand has manufactured somewhere in the region of 35 million watches, making it one of the genuine heavyweights of the Swiss watch world. In 1983, Nicolas G. Hayek merged the two major Swiss watch manufacturing groups ASUAG and SIHH into what would later become the Swatch Group. Longines, the leading ASUAG brand, barely missed capturing the same position in the new concern; that honor went to Omega, the SIHH frontrunner. However, from a historical and technical point of view, this brand has what it takes to be at the helm of any group. Was it not Longines that equipped polar explorer Roald Amundsen and air pioneer Charles Lindbergh with their watches? It has also been the timekeeper at many Olympic Games and, since 2007, the official timekeeper for the French Open at Roland Garros. In fact, this brand is a major sponsor at many sports events, from riding to archery.

It is not surprising then to find that this venerable Jura company also has an impressive portfolio of in-house calibers in stock, from simple manual winders to complicated chronographs. This broad technological base has benefited the company. As a genuine "one-stop shop," the brand can supply the Swatch Group with anything from cheap, thin quartz watches to heavy gold chronographs and calendars with quadruple retrograde displays. Longines does have one particular specialty, besides elegant ladies' watches and modern sports watches, in that it often has the luxury of rebuilding the classics from its own long history.

Longines Watch Co.
Rue des Noyettes 8
CH-2610 St.-Imier
Switzerland

Tel.:
+41-32-942-5425

Fax:
+41-32-942-5429

E-mail:
info@longines.com

Website:
www.longines.com

Founded:
1832

Number of employees:
worldwide approx. 900

U.S. distributor:
Longines
The Swatch Group (U.S.), Inc.
1200 Harbor Boulevard
Weehawken, NJ 07087
201-271-1400
www.longines.com

Most important collections/price range:
Master Collection, DolceVita, Conquest Classic Collection, Heritage Collection / from approx. $1,350 to $6,500

HydroConquest

Reference number: L3.741.4.56.6
Movement: automatic, Caliber L888 (base ETA A31.L01); ø 25.6 mm, height 4.6 mm; 21 jewels; 25,200 vph; 64-hour power reserve
Functions: hours, minutes, sweep seconds; date
Case: stainless steel, ø 39 mm, height 11.9 mm; unidirectional bezel, with 0-60 scale; sapphire crystal; screw-in crown; water-resistant to 30 atm
Band: stainless steel, folding clasp with safety lock and extension link
Price: $1,275

HydroConquest Chronograph

Reference number: L3.744.4.96.6
Movement: automatic, Caliber L688 (Base ETA A08.L01); ø 30 mm, height 7.9 mm; 27 jewels; 28,800 vph; 54-hour power reserve
Functions: hours, minutes, subsidiary seconds; chronograph; date
Case: stainless steel, ø 41 mm, height 15.6 mm; unidirectional bezel with aluminum inlay, with 0-60 scale; sapphire crystal; screw-in crown; water-resistant to 30 atm
Band: stainless steel, folding clasp with safety lock
Price: $2,050

Conquest

Reference number: L3.277.4.76.6
Movement: quartz, Caliber L250 (Base ETA 956.112); ø 17.20 mm, height 2.5 mm; 7 jewels; 364/377 Renata battery
Functions: hours, minutes, seconds, date; E.O.L. indicator
Case: stainless steel, ø 29.5 mm, height 9.3 mm; antireflective sapphire crystal; screw-in case back; water-resistant to 30 atm
Band: stainless steel, folding clasp with safety lock
Price: $800

Conquest
Reference number: L3.676.4.99.6
Movement: automatic, Caliber L633 (Base ETA 2824-2); ø 25.6 mm, height 4.6 mm; 25 jewels; 28,800 vph; 38-hour power reserve
Functions: hours, minutes, sweep seconds; date
Case: stainless steel, ø 39 mm, height 11.8 mm; sapphire crystal; screw-in crown; water-resistant to 30 atm
Band: stainless steel, folding clasp with safety lock
Price: $1,225

Elegant Collection
Reference number: L4.910.4.11.2
Movement: automatic, Caliber L619 (base ETA 2892-A2); ø 25.6 mm, height 3.85 mm; 21 jewels; 28,800 vph; 42-hour power reserve
Functions: hours, minutes, sweep seconds; date
Case: stainless steel, ø 39 mm, height 8.6 mm; sapphire crystal; transparent case back; water-resistant to 3 atm
Band: reptile skin, buckle
Price: $1,900

Master Collection Moonphase
Reference number: L2.673.4.78.3
Movement: automatic, Caliber L678 (base ETA 7751); ø 30 mm, height 7.9 mm; 25 jewels; 28,800 vph; 48-hour power reserve
Functions: hours, minutes, subsidiary seconds; second 24-hour display; chronograph; full calendar with date, weekday, month, moon phase
Case: stainless steel, ø 40 mm, height 14.3 mm; sapphire crystal; transparent case back; water-resistant to 3 atm
Band: reptile skin, folding clasp
Price: $3,325
Variations: stainless steel bracelet

Master Collection
Reference number: L2.257.4.71.3
Movement: automatic, Caliber L592.2 (base ETA A20.L01); ø 19.4 mm, height 4.1 mm; 22 jewels; 28,800 vph; 40-hour power reserve
Functions: hours, minutes, sweep seconds; date
Case: stainless steel, ø 29 mm, height 8.5 mm; sapphire crystal; transparent case back; water-resistant to 3 atm
Band: reptile skin, double folding clasp
Price: $1,925

Record
Reference number: L2.821.4.11.6
Movement: automatic, Caliber L888.4 (base ETA A31.L11); ø 25.6 mm, height 3.85 mm; 21 jewels; 25,200 vph; 64-hour power reserve; COSC-certified chronometer
Functions: hours, minutes, sweep seconds; date
Case: stainless steel, ø 40 mm, height 10.8 mm; sapphire crystal; transparent case back; water-resistant to 3 atm
Band: stainless steel, folding clasp
Price: $2,025

Record
Reference number: L2.321.0.87.6
Movement: automatic, Caliber L592.4 (base ETA A20.L11); ø 17.9 mm, height 3.8 mm; 22 jewels; 25.200 vph; 40-hour power reserve; COSC-certified chronometer
Functions: hours, minutes, sweep seconds; date
Case: stainless steel, ø 30 mm, height 10.7 mm; bezel set with 60 diamonds; sapphire crystal; transparent case back; water-resistant to 3 atm
Band: stainless steel, folding clasp
Price: $4,325

Flagship Heritage
60th Anniversary (1954–2017)
Reference number: L4.817.4.76.2
Movement: automatic, Caliber L609 (base ETA 2895-2); ø 25.6 mm, height 4.35 mm; 27 jewels; 28,800 vph; 42-hour power reserve
Functions: hours, minutes, subsidiary seconds
Case: stainless steel, ø 38.5 mm, height 9.7 mm; sapphire crystal; water-resistant to 3 atm
Band: reptile skin, buckle
Price: $2,000; limited to 1,957 pieces
Variations: rose gold (limited to 25 pieces, $8,000); yellow gold (limited to 25 pieces, $8,000)

The Lindbergh Hour
Angle Watch—90th Anniversary
Reference number: L2.678.1.71.0
Movement: automatic, Caliber L699.2 (base ETA A07.L01); ø 36.6 mm, height 7.9 mm; 24 jewels; 28,800 vph; 46-hour power reserve
Functions: hours, minutes sweep seconds, rotatable interior dial to synchronize second hand with radio time signals
Case: titanium, ø 47.5 mm, height 14.9 mm; bezel with black PVD coating, bidirectional, with scale for synchronization of time; sapphire crystal; crown in stainless steel; water-resistant to 3 atm
Band: calfskin, buckle
Price: $5,250

Heritage 1945
Reference number: L2.813.4.66.0
Movement: automatic, Caliber L609 (base ETA 2895-2); ø 25.6 mm, height 4.35 mm; 27 jewels; 28,800 vph; 42-hour power reserve
Functions: hours, minutes, subsidiary seconds
Case: stainless steel, ø 40 mm, height 12 mm; sapphire crystal; water-resistant to 3 atm
Band: calfskin, buckle
Price: $1,800

Legend Diver Watch
Reference number: L3.674.4.50.0
Movement: automatic, Caliber L633 (base ETA 2824-2); ø 25.6 mm, height 4.6 mm; 25 jewels; 28,800 vph; 38-hour power reserve
Functions: hours, minutes, sweep seconds; date
Case: stainless steel, ø 42 mm, height 13.6 crown-controlled inner bezel with 60-minute divisions; sapphire crystal; screw-in crown; water-resistant to 30 atm
Band: textile, buckle
Price: $2,300
Variations: stainless steel bracelet ($2,400)

Heritage Military
Reference number: L2.811.4.53.0
Movement: automatic, Caliber L609 (base ETA 2895-2); ø 25.6 mm, height 4.35 mm; 27 jewels; 28,800 vph; 42-hour power reserve
Functions: hours, minutes, subsidiary seconds; date
Case: stainless steel, ø 44 mm, height 12.8 mm; water resistant to 3 atm
Band: reptile skin, buckle
Price: $2,050

Conquest Classic
Reference number: L2.785.4.56.6
Movement: automatic, Caliber L619.2 (base ETA 2892-A2); ø 25.6 mm, height 3.6 mm; 21 jewels; 28,800 vph; 42-hour power reserve
Functions: hours, minutes, sweep seconds; date
Case: stainless steel, ø 40 mm, height 10.3 mm; sapphire crystal; transparent case back; water-resistant to 5 atm
Band: stainless steel, double folding clasp
Price: $2,100
Variations: pink gold bezel and reptile skin strap, buckle ($2,950); pink gold with pink gold and stainless steel bracelet ($4,100)

Les Ateliers Louis Moinet SA
Rue du Temple 1
CH-2072 Saint-Blaise
Switzerland

Tel.:
+41-32-753-6814

E-mail:
info@louismoinet.com

Website:
www.louismoinet.com

Founded: 2005

U.S. distributor:
Fitzhenry Consulting
1029 Peachtree Parkway, #346
Peachtree City, GA 30269
561-212-6812
Don@fitzhenry.com

Most important collections:
Memoris, Sideralis, 20-second Tempograph,
Derrick Tourbillon, Mecanograph, Space Mystery

LOUIS MOINET

In the race to be the first to invent something new, Louis Moinet (1768–1853) emerged as a notable winner: In 2013, a *Compteur de tierces* from 1816 was shown to the public, a chronograph that counts one-sixtieth of a second with a frequency of 216,000 vph. It was proudly signed by Moinet. This professor at the Academy of Fine Arts in Paris and president of the Société Chronométrique was in fact one of the most inventive, multitalented men of his time. He worked with such eminent watchmakers as Breguet, Berthoud, Winnerl, Janvier, and Perrelet. Among his accomplishments is an extensive two-volume treatise on horology.

Following in such footsteps is hardly an easy task, but Jean-Marie Schaller and Micaela Bertolucci decided that their idiosyncratic creations were indeed imbued with the spirit of the great Frenchman. They work with a team of independent designers, watchmakers, movement specialists, and suppliers to produce the most unusual wristwatches filled with clever functions and surprising details. The Jules Verne chronographs have hinged levers, for example, and the second hand on the Tempograph changes direction every ten seconds.

Some watches tell industrial tales, like the Derrick Tourbillon or the Gaz Derrick. Increasingly, this independently minded brand is exploring the space-time continuum. The dial of the chronograph-watch Memoris, for the centenary of the invention of the chronograph by Louis Moinet, is dotted with stars. The epic inverted double tourbillon Sideralis, presented at Baselworld in 2016, features fragments of the famous Rosetta stone and dust from Mars and the moon on a space backdrop on the small dial, with an aventurine backdrop. And the Space Memory, besides having a miniature planet to balance out a tourbillon cage, also displays a sample of meteorite containing amino acids, the building blocks of human life, a signal, perhaps, from a distant galaxy . . .

Black Gold Derrick
Reference number: LM-43.70.03N
Movement: manually wound, Louis Moinet Caliber LM14D; ø 33.20 mm, height 6.64 mm; 27 jewels; 21,600 vph; 1-minute tourbillon; openworked bridges with black PVD; multifunctional "octopus" spring; 72-hour power reserve
Functions: hours, minutes, subsidiary seconds (on revolving barrel at 9 o'clock)
Case: white gold, ø 45.4 mm, height 13.3 mm; sapphire crystal; transparent case back; water-resistant to 3 atm
Band: reptile skin, double folding clasp
Price: $260,000; limited to 28 pieces

Metropolis
Reference number: LM-45.50.55
Movement: automatic, Louis Moinet Caliber LM45; ø 30.4 mm, height 6.7 mm; 22 jewels; 28,800 vph; 48-hour power reserve; côtes de Genève decoration
Functions: hours and minutes, subsidiary seconds
Case: rose gold, ø 43.2 mm, height 14.8 mm; sapphire crystal; screw-in transparent back; water-resistant to 5 atm
Band: reptile skin, double folding clasp
Remarks: skeletonized dial and hour markers
Price: $29,995; limited to 60 pieces
Variations: stainless steel ($12,900; limited to 60 pieces); "magic" blue dial pattern

Space Mystery
Reference number: LM-48.70G.25
Movement: manually wound, Louis Moinet Caliber LM 48; ø 37.65 mm, height 10.33 mm; 20 jewels; 21,600 vph; 72-hour power reserve; "satellite" 13.59-mm tourbillon balanced by a planet on cage
Functions: hours, minutes
Case: white gold, ø 46 mm, height 17.13 mm; hand-engraved casing with sapphire crystal; transparent case back; water-resistant to 5 atm
Remarks: "magic" blue dial; aperture at 9 o'clock for sample of meteorite containing amino acids
Band: reptile skin, double folding clasp
Price: $195,000; limited to 8 pieces
Variations: rose gold ($195,000), smooth case rose gold ($175,000), white gold ($175,000)

LOUIS VUITTON

The philosophy of this over-150-year-old brand states that any product bearing the name Louis Vuitton must be manufactured in the company's own facilities. That is why Louis Vuitton has allowed itself the luxury of building its own workshop in Switzerland, specifically in La Chaux-de-Fonds, at the technology center of LVMH (Louis Vuitton, Moët & Hennessy).

Designing is carried out in Paris at the company headquarters, and it is obvious that it would not suit an upscale watch to simply cobble together various parts supplied by outside workshops. The cases and dials with all the details and the hands are all exclusive Louis Vuitton designs, as are other components, such as the pushers and the band clasps—in other words, all that is needed to ensure a unique look. In 2011, Louis Vuitton purchased the dial maker Léman Cadran and the movement specialist Fabrique du Temps (both in Geneva), giving the company a great deal of independence vis-à-vis other brands in the group. And helping it clinch a Geneva Seal for its brand-new tourbillon, whose transparency almost makes it "mysterious."

Increasingly, Louis Vuitton has been exploring new shores. The LV Fifty Five collection, the Tambour, and the unconventional Escale world-time watch feature handpainted scale fields in the style of the monograms that Louis Vuitton uses to mark its bags. The new Tambour Moons bring together high fashion and "quartz" watchmaking. And for the incurably connected, the brand has developed the Tambour Horizon with a variety of colorful dials.

Louis Vuitton Malletier
2, rue du Pont Neuf
F-75034 Paris, Cedex 01
France

Tel.:
+33-1-55-80-41-40

Fax:
+33-1-55-80-41-40

Website:
www.vuitton.com

Founded:
1854

U.S. distributor:
Louis Vuitton
1-866-VUITTON
www.louisvuitton.com

Most important collection/price range:
Tambour / Voyage / LV Fifty Five / Escale / starting at $3,250

Flying Tourbillon Poinçon de Genève

Movement: manually wound, LV Caliber 104; ø 34.4 mm, height 4.47 mm; 17 jewels; 21,600 vph; flying 1-minute tourbillon; skeletonized baguette construction (in-house); 80-hour power reserve; Geneva Seal
Functions: hours, minutes (off-center)
Case: platinum, ø 41 mm, height 9.1 mm; sapphire crystal; transparent case back; water-resistant to 5 atm
Band: reptile skin, folding clasp
Remarks: sapphire crystal dial
Price: $243,000

Escale Worldtime Minute Repeater

Reference number: Q5EH00
Movement: manually wound, LV Caliber 235; ø 38.9 mm, height 9.01 mm; 31 jewels; 21,600 vph; 100-hour power reserve
Functions: hours, minutes; 24-zone world time display with hand-painted rotating disks; minute repeater
Case: rose gold, ø 44 mm, height 11.75 mm; sapphire crystal; transparent case back; water-resistant to 3 atm
Band: reptile skin, folding clasp
Price: $283,000

Tambour Moon Star Chronograph Black

Reference number: QAAA54
Movement: quartz; 22 jewels; 12 polished cabochons set on flange; star monogram flower on dial
Functions: hours, minutes, subsidiary seconds; chronograph; date
Case: stainless steel, ø 39.5 mm, height 10 mm; sapphire crystal; LV engraved on back; water-resistant to 5 atm
Band: reptile skin, folding clasp
Remarks: interchangeable straps
Price: $4,795

Escale Spin Time Blue

Reference number: Q5EG21
Movement: automatic, LV Caliber 77; ø 35.2 mm, height 7.2 mm; 27 jewels; 28,800 vph; 42-hour power reserve
Functions: hours (jumping) using rotating cube elements, minutes
Case: titanium, ø 41 mm, height 11.2 mm; bezel, lugs, and crown in white gold; sapphire crystal; water-resistant to 3 atm
Band: reptile skin, double folding clasp
Price: $39,500

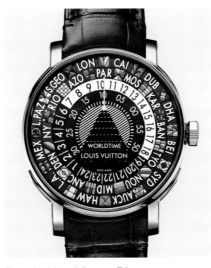

Escale Worldtime Blue

Reference number: Q5EK50
Movement: automatic, LV Caliber 106; ø 37 mm, height 6.65 mm; 26 jewels; 28,800 vph; 38-hour power reserve
Functions: hours, minutes; 24-zone world time display (second time zone) with hand-painted rotating disks
Case: titanium, ø 41 mm, height 9.75 mm; bezel, lugs, and crown in white gold; sapphire crystal; transparent case back; water-resistant to 3 atm
Band: reptile skin, folding clasp
Price: $50,500

Tambour Evolution Spin Time GMT in Black

Reference number: Q1AG00
Movement: automatic, LV Caliber 111; ø 35.2 mm; 27 jewels; 28,800 vph; 42-hour power reserve
Functions: hours, minutes; second 24-hour display (second time zone using rotating cube elements as hour markers)
Case: stainless steel with black DLC coating, ø 45 mm, height 14.17 mm; sapphire crystal; transparent case back; water-resistant to 10 atm
Band: calfskin, buckle
Price: $18,000

Voyager GMT

Reference number: Q7D311
Movement: automatic, ETA Caliber 2893-2 (modified); ø 25.6 mm, height 4.1 mm; 21 jewels; 28,800 vph; 42-hour power reserve
Functions: hours, minutes, sweep seconds; second 24-hour display (second time zone)
Case: stainless steel, ø 41.5 mm, height 10.5 mm; sapphire crystal; transparent case back; water-resistant to 5 atm
Band: stainless steel, folding clasp
Price: $5,700

Tambour Twin Chronograph

Reference number: Q1A612
Movement: automatic, ETA Caliber 2894-2; ø 28.6 mm, height 6.1 mm; 37 jewels; 28,800 vph; 42-hour power reserve
Functions: hours, minutes, subsidiary seconds; chronograph; date
Case: stainless steel, ø 46 mm, height 15.5 mm; unidirectional bezel, 0-60 scale; sapphire crystal; crown with rubber coating; water-resistant to 10 atm
Band: sailcloth, buckle
Price: $6,800

Tambour Spin Time Galaxy

Reference number: Q1EG40
Movement: automatic, LV Caliber 76; ø 35.2 mm, height 7.2 mm; 21 jewels; 28,800 vph; 40-hour power reserve
Functions: hours (jumping) using rotating cube elements, minutes
Case: white gold, ø 39.5 mm, height 10 mm; bezel and lugs set with 336 diamonds; sapphire crystal; transparent case back
Band: reptile skin, double folding clasp set with 159 diamonds
Remarks: malachite dial set with emeralds and diamonds
Price: $132,000; limited to 8 pieces

LUMINOX

Watches, as the old industry axiom goes, are jewelry for men. And some men do like watches that express masculinity in no uncertain terms, or that feel like real tools, or that recall the cockpits of fast-moving vehicles. So when Barry Cohen came across the tiny tritium gas–filled luminescent tubes made by the Swiss company mb-microtech, he spotted an opportunity. Here was a way to give sports watches the kind of illumination that would make them dependable and practical time-givers at night. The radioactive tritium, which has a half-life of 12.32 years, makes a coating on the inside of the tubes glow for up to 25 years.

Cohen and his business partner Richard Timbo called their brand Luminox, derived from the Latin "light" and "night." They created a collection of rugged-looking sports timepieces that soon found a loyal following. In 1992 came the first big breakthrough, when a Luminox watch prevailed in a tough competition to become a mission watch for Navy SEALS. The brand now established a reputation, and soon other law enforcement agencies and organizations began ordering watches, notably F-117 Nighthawk and Stealth pilots.

As the brand grew and expanded beyond American borders, it continued developing its product. A new lightweight carbon compound case with a matte finish was developed that is insensitive to outside temperatures. The latest versions of this case can withstand dives of up to 300 meters. A special mineral crystal was also developed that is highly scratch resistant.

Luminox also partnered with the Swiss company Mondaine, famous for its Railroad Watch and the Helvetica, to manufacture watches in their premises in Switzerland. A new company, called Lumondi Inc., was founded to oversee the two brands after Mondaine purchased the 50 percent of remaining shares from Barry Cohen in November 2016.

Luminox watches are unabashedly muscular and outdoorsy. Wherever extreme sports or activities are being performed, that is where Luminox finds its fans. The Scott Cassell Deep Dive Automatic, for example, was made for explorer and deep-seas diver Scott Cassell as part of his "essential gear." The watches are run either on Swiss quartz or on mechanical movements.

Lumondi Inc. (Luminox Watches)
27 W. 24th Street, Suite 804
New York, NY 10010

Tel.:
917-522-3600

E-mail:
info@luminoxusa.com

Website:
www.luminox.com
shop.luminox.com

Founded:
1989

Most important collections:
Navy SEAL 3500, Leatherback Sea, Turtle Giant, XCOR Aerospace

Scott Cassell Deep Dive Automatic
Reference number: 1523
Movement: automatic, ETA Caliber 2826-2; ø 25.6 mm, height 6.2 mm; 25 jewels; 28,800 vph; 38-hour power reserve
Functions: hours, minutes, sweep seconds; large date
Case: stainless steel, ø 44 mm, height 17 mm; unidirectional bezel with blue aluminum ring, bezel locker at 3 o'clock; sapphire crystal with antireflective coating; helium release valve; stainless steel screw-in case back; water-resistant to 50 atm
Band: rubber strap, stainless steel buckle
Remarks: constant glow for up to 25 years in any light condition
Price: $2,000
Variations: black/yellow dial with black rubber strap

XCOR Aerospace Automatic Valjoux Chronograph
Reference number: 5261
Movement: automatic, ETA Caliber 7750 Valjoux; ø 30 mm, height 7.9; 25 jewels; 28,800 vph; 42-hour power reserve
Functions: hours, minutes, chronograph; date
Case: titanium and black PVD, ø 45.5 mm, height 18 mm; sapphire crystal; titanium screw-down case back; water-resistant to 20 atm
Band: calfskin, titanium buckle
Remarks: constant glow for up to 25 years in any light condition
Price: $3,000

F-117 Nighthawk
Reference number: 6422
Movement: quartz, Ronda Caliber 515; ø 26.2 mm, height 3 mm
Functions: hours, minutes; date; 2nd time zone
Case: stainless steel IP gun metal, ø 44 mm, height 12.6 mm; bidirectional bezel; sapphire crystal; water-resistant to 20 atm
Band: stainless steel, buckle with black PVD
Remark: constant glow for up to 25 years in any light condition
Price: $1,400
Variations: Kevlar strap with black stitching, black leather lining, and black PVD buckle

Manufacture Royale SA
ZI Le Day
CH-1337 Vallorbe
Switzerland

Tel.:
+41-21-843-01-01

E-mail:
info@manufacture-royale.com

Website:
www.manufacture-royale.com

Founded:
by Voltaire in 1770, revived in 2010

Number of employees:
5

Annual production:
150 watches

Distribution:
retail and online

In the U.S.:
Café Time, LLC
917-907-1127

Most important collections/price range:
Androgyne / from $47,200; 1770 / from:
$52,800; Opera /$385,000

MANUFACTURE ROYALE

François-Marie Arouet (1694–1778), was one of the richest men in Europe, which allowed him to express his very progressive views—he opposed slavery and the death penalty. Wherever he perceived injustice, he drew his pen. In Geneva, where he had often found refuge from the French king, he went further: The local bourgeoisie refused to give political and economic rights to a class of craftsmen known as the *natifs*, who were not local. In 1770, at his estate in neighboring Ferney-Voltaire (France), Voltaire opened his "Manufacture Royale," which produced very respectable watches.

The enterprise did not survive Voltaire's death in 1778, but 132 years later, in 2010, four highly experienced and related watch executives, Gérard, David, and Alexis Gouten and Marc Guten, decided to revive the brand. Their basic idea: high-end complications, affordable prices, *manufacture* movements assembled in-house.

They set up shop in Vallorbe, in the foothills of the Jura, and soon had three respected collections on the market. The 1770 is the most classic piece, with a simple dial as backdrop to a flying tourbillon. The Androgyne, an edgy timepiece with flexible lugs, a screwed-down bezel, and a generally steampunkish look, offers insight into the movement thanks to extensive skeletonizing. Finally, there is the Opera, a minute repeater with a cleverly designed case made of sixty parts that unfolds to form a kind of shell that amplifies the sound of the chimes and looks a little like the Opera House in Sydney, Australia.

The brand has gained experience and the self-confidence to sally into more experimental realms, but without ever disturbing the fundamental classicism of the timepieces. The 1770 Haute Voltige series is definitely twenty-first century, with its second time zone cowering under the mysterious bridges that rise from the dial to hold the balance wheel over the dial. The Micromégas Revolution comes in three strong colors. As for the ADN, it cuts to the chase, with extreme skeletonization inside a redesigned, softer Androgyne case.

ADN

Reference number: ADN46.01P01.A
Movement: manually wound, Caliber MR09; ø 37.4 mm, height 7.4 mm; 1-minute flying tourbillon on ceramic ball bearings, silicon escapement wheel and pallet; 15 jewels; 21,600 vph; hand-decorated plates and bridges; 80-hour power reserve
Functions: hours (jumping), minutes, sweep seconds
Case: stainless steel, ø 46 mm, height 11.72 mm; sapphire crystal, transparent sapphire case back, water-resistant to 3 atm
Band: reptile skin, stainless steel buckle
Price: $90,300
Variations: DLC and forged carbon ($97,700); pink gold and forged carbon ($116,500); rubber bracelet

1770 Micromégas Revolution

Reference number: 1770MR45.10.BL
Movement: automatic, MR08 Caliber; ø 36 mm, height 8.7 mm; 26 jewels; 1-minute flying tourbillon (28,800 vph) and 6-second tourbillon (21,600 vph), both with silicon escapement wheel and levers; skeletonized movement; 40-hour power reserve
Functions: hours (off-center), minutes
Case: titanium, ø 45 mm, height 11.8 mm; transparent case back, water-resistant to 3 atm
Band: reptile skin, titanium buckle
Price: $149,100
Variations: pink gold ($172,200)

1770 Haute Voltige Dragon

Reference number: 1770HVT45.01.K
Movement: automatic, MR07 Caliber; 31 jewels; ø 36 mm, height 9.45 mm; 21,600 vph; 40-hour power reserve; red anodized aluminum balance wheel
Functions: hours, minutes, second time zone
Case: stainless steel, ø 45 mm, height 14 mm; khaki sunray dial, sapphire crystal; water resistant to 3 atm
Remarks: raised bridge on dial holds balance wheel over dial; raised subsidiary dial for second time zone
Band: reptile skin, buckle
Price: $36,800
Variations: blue sunray dial; black sunray dial with rose gold case

MAURICE LACROIX

Maurice Lacroix watches are found in sixty countries. The heart of the company, however, remains the production facilities in the highlands of the Jura, in Saignelégier and Montfaucon, where the brand built La Manufacture des Franches-Montagnes SA (MFM) outfitted with state-of-the-art CNC technology for the production of very specific individual parts and movement components.

The watchmaker can thank the clever interpretations of "classic" pocket watch characteristics for its steep ascent in the 1990s. Since then, the *manufacture* has redesigned the complete collection, banning every lick of Breguet-like bliss from its watch designs. In the upper segment, *manufacture* models such as the chronograph and the retrograde variations on Unitas calibers set the tone. In the lower segment, modern "little" complications outfitted with module movements based on ETA and Sellita are the kings. The brand is mainly associated with the hypnotically turning square wheel, the "roue carrée." The idea was used for the latest ladies' watch, the Power of Love, which has three turning hearts forming the word "love" at regular intervals.

Maurice Lacroix's drive to freshen up its look has earned the brand a great deal of recognition in the past years, notably eleven Red Dot awards.

In 2011, DKSH (Diethelm Keller & SiberHegner) took over the brand. This Swiss holding company specializing in international market expansions with 600 establishments throughout the world has ensured Maurice Lacroix a strong position in all major markets, with flagship stores and its own boutiques. A special partnership with the Barcelona football club is bound to have an impact on sales as well, justifying the production of 90,000 watches per year.

Maurice Lacroix SA
Rüschlistrasse 6
CH-2502 Biel/Bienne
Switzerland

Tel.:
+41-44-209-1111

E-mail:
info@mauricelacroix.com

Website:
www.mauricelacroix.com

Founded:
1975

Number of employees:
about 250 worldwide

Annual production:
approx. 90,000 watches

U.S. distributor:
DKSH Luxury & Lifestyle North America Inc.
9-D Princess Road
Lawrenceville, NJ 08648
609-750-8800

Most important collections/price range:
Aikon / $890 to $1,900; Les Classiques / $950 to $4,300; Fiaba (ladies) / $980 to $2,900; Pontos / $1,750 to $7,900; Masterpiece *manufacture* models / $6,800 to $14,900

Masterpiece Gravity

Reference number: MP6118-SS001-434-1
Movement: automatic, Caliber ML 230; ø 37.2 mm, height 9.05 mm; 35 jewels; 18,000 vph; inverted movement design with dial-side escapement; silicon anchor and anchor escape wheel; 50-hour power reserve
Functions: hours, minutes (off-center), subsidiary seconds
Case: stainless steel, ø 43 mm, height 16.2 mm; sapphire crystal; transparent case back; water-resistant to 5 atm
Band: reptile skin, folding clasp
Price: $13,900

Masterpiece Chronograph Skeleton

Reference number: MP6028-PVC01-002-1
Movement: automatic, Caliber ML 206; ø 30.4 mm, height 8.4 mm; 25 jewels; 28,800 vph; skeletonized movement, bridges with black-gold finish; 48-hour power reserve
Functions: hours, minutes, subsidiary seconds; chronograph
Case: stainless steel with blue PVD coating, ø 45 mm, height 16.4 mm; sapphire crystal; screw-in crown; water-resistant to 10 atm
Band: reptile skin, folding clasp
Price: $7,900

Masterpiece Double Retrograde

Reference number: MP6578-SS001-131-1
Movement: automatic, Caliber ML 191; ø 36.6 mm, height 8.2 mm; 74 jewels; 18,000 vph; 52-hour power reserve
Functions: hours, minutes, subsidiary seconds; 2nd 24-hour display (2nd time zone, retrograde); date (retrograde)
Case: stainless steel, ø 43 mm, height 15.4 mm; sapphire crystal; transparent case back; water-resistant to 5 atm
Band: reptile skin, folding clasp
Price: $4,500

Masterpiece Moon Retrograde

Reference number: MP6588-SS001-431-1
Movement: automatic, Caliber ML 192; ø 36.6 mm, height 8.2 mm; 59 jewels; 18,000 vph; 52-hour power reserve
Functions: hours, minutes; power reserve indicator (retrograde); full calendar with date (retrograde), weekday, moon phase
Case: stainless steel, ø 43 mm, height 15.4 mm; sapphire crystal; transparent case back; water-resistant to 5 atm
Band: reptile skin, folding clasp
Price: $5,000

Pontos Chronographe

Reference number: PT6388-SS001-430-2
Movement: automatic, Caliber ML 112 (base ETA 7750); ø 30 mm, height 7.9 mm; 25 jewels; 28,800 vph; 46-hour power reserve
Functions: hours, minutes, subsidiary seconds; chronograph; date
Case: stainless steel, ø 43 mm, height 14.9 mm; sapphire crystal; water-resistant to 10 atm
Band: calfskin, double folding clasp
Price: $2,750
Variations: various band and dial colors

Pontos Day Date

Reference number: PT6358-SS001-330-2
Movement: automatic, Caliber MB 143 (base Sellita SW220); ø 25.6 mm, height 4.6 mm; 26 jewels; 28,800 vph; 38-hour power reserve
Functions: hours, minutes, sweep seconds; date, weekday
Case: stainless steel, ø 41 mm, height 11.1 mm; sapphire crystal; transparent case back; screw-in crown; water-resistant to 10 atm
Band: calfskin, double folding clasp
Price: $1,750
Variations: various bands and dials

Aikon Chronograph

Reference number: AI1018-SS001-430-1
Movement: quartz
Functions: hours, minutes, subsidiary seconds; chronograph; date
Case: stainless steel, ø 44 mm; sapphire crystal; screw-in crown; water-resistant to 10 atm
Band: calfskin, double folding clasp
Price: $1,190

Aikon Gents

Reference number: AI1008-SS002-332-1
Movement: quartz
Functions: hours, minutes, sweep seconds; date
Case: stainless steel, ø 42 mm; sapphire crystal; screw-in crown; water-resistant to 10 atm
Band: stainless steel, double folding clasp
Price: $890

Aikon Ladies

Reference number: AI1004-PVY13-171-1
Movement: quartz
Functions: hours, minutes, sweep seconds; date
Case: stainless steel, ø 30 mm; yellow gold–plated bezel; sapphire crystal; screw-in crown; water-resistant to 10 atm
Band: stainless steel with gold-plated elements, double folding clasp
Price: $1,100

Les Classiques Chronographe
Reference number: LC6158-SS002-330
Movement: automatic, Caliber ML 112 base ETA 7750 or Sellita SW500); ø 30 mm, height 7.9 mm; 25 jewels; 28,800 vph; 46-hour power reserve
Functions: hours, minutes, subsidiary seconds; chronograph; date
Case: stainless steel, ø 41 mm, height 14.1 mm; sapphire crystal; water-resistant to 3 atm
Band: stainless steel, folding clasp
Price: $2,900

Les Classiques Date
Reference number: LC6098-SS001-130-2
Movement: automatic, Caliber ML 115 (base Sellita SW200); ø 25.6 mm, height 4.6 mm; 25 jewels; 28,800 vph; 38-hour power reserve
Functions: hours, minutes, sweep seconds; date
Case: stainless steel, ø 40 mm, height 10.5 mm; sapphire crystal; transparent case back; water-resistant to 3 atm
Band: reptile skin, folding clasp
Price: $1,480
Variations: stainless steel bracelet

Les Classiques Moonphase
Reference number: LC6168-SS001-120-1
Movement: automatic, Caliber ML 37 (base ETA 2892 with a module); ø 25.6 mm, height 5.4 mm; 21 jewels; 28,800 vph; 38-hour power reserve
Functions: hours, minutes, sweep seconds; date, moon phase
Case: stainless steel, ø 40 mm, height 12 mm; sapphire crystal
Band: reptile skin, folding clasp
Price: $2,650

Caliber ML 230
Manually wound; inverted movement design with dial-side escapement, silicon anchor and anchor escape wheel; single spring barrel, 50-hour power reserve
Functions: hours, minutes (off-center), subsidiary seconds
Diameter: 37.2 mm
Height: 9.05 mm
Jewels: 35
Balance: glucydur
Frequency: 18,000 vph

Caliber ML 191
Automatic; single spring barrel, 52-hour power reserve; COSC-certified chronometer
Functions: hours, minutes, subsidiary seconds; 2nd 24-hour display (2nd time zone), power reserve indicator; date (retrograde)
Diameter: 36.6 mm
Height: 8.2 mm
Jewels: 74
Balance: glucydur
Frequency: 18,000 vph

Caliber ML 192
Automatic; single spring barrel, 52-hour power reserve
Functions: hours, minutes; power reserve indicator; full calendar with date, weekday, moon phase
Diameter: 36.6 mm
Height: 7.9 mm
Jewels: 59
Balance: glucydur
Frequency: 18,000 vph

MB&F
Boulevard Helvétique 22
Case postale 3466
CH-1211 Geneva 3
Switzerland

Tel.:
+41-22-786-3618

Fax:
+41-22-786-3624

E-mail:
info@mbandf.com

Website:
www.mbandf.com

Founded:
2005

Number of employees:
20

Annual production:
approx. 280 watches

U.S. Distributors:
Westime Los Angeles
310-470-1388; 310-475-0628 (fax)
info@westime.com
Provident Jewelry, Florida
561-747-4449; nick@providentjewelry.com
Stephen Silver, Redwood City (California)
650-325-9500; www.shsilver.com
London Jewelers, Long Island
516-627-7475, www.LondonJewelers.com

Most important collections/price range:
Horological Machines / from $63,000; Legacy
Machines / from $64,000

MB&F

Maximilian Büsser & Friends goes beyond the standard idea of a brand. Perhaps calling it a tribe would be better: one aiming to create unique works of horology. MB&F is doing something unconventional in an industry that usually takes its innovation in small doses.

After seeing the Opus projects to fruition at Harry Winston, Büsser decided it was time to set the creators free. At MB&F he acts as initiator and coordinator. His Horological Machines are developed and realized in cooperation with highly specialized watchmakers, inventors, and designers in an "idea collective" creating unheard-of mechanical timepieces of great inventiveness, complication, and exclusivity. The composition of this collective varies as much as each machine. Number 5 ("On the Road Again") is an homage to the 1970s, when streamlining rather than brawn represented true strength. The display in the lateral window is reflected by a prism. The "top" of the watch opens to let in light to charge the Superluminova numerals on the disks. As for the Space Pirate, Number 6, it is a talking piece that makes a genial nod to sci-fi moviemakers, and all the talk was real: The model won a coveted Red Dot "Best of the Best" award in 2015. Contrasting sharply with the modern productions are the Legacy Machines, which reach into horological history and reinterpret past mechanical feats.

The spirit of Büsser is always present in each new watch, but it is now vented freely in the M.A.D. Gallery in Geneva, where "mechanical art objects" on display are beautiful, intriguing, technically impeccable, and sometimes perfectly useless. They have their own muse and serve as worthy companions to the sci-fi-inspired table clocks that MB&F produces with L'épée 1938. One is shaped like a spaceship; the other is a huge spider; the latest, Sherman, is a tank with real treads, presented at the SIHH 2016, where MB&F appeared as one of nine independent brands that shook up the routine a bit. All these pieces tell the time very accurately and mechanically.

Legacy Machine Perpetual

Reference number: 03.WL.B
Movement: manually wound, MB&F Caliber LM Perpetual; ø 36.6 mm, height 12.6 mm; 41 jewels; 18,000 vph; double spring barrel, inverted movement design with 1 balance floating over dial; finely finished with côtes de Genève; 72-hour power reserve
Functions: hours, minutes (off-center); power reserve indicator; perpetual calendar with date, weekday, month, leap year (backward counting)
Case: white gold, ø 44 mm, height 17.5 mm; sapphire crystal; transparent case back; water-resistant to 3 atm
Band: reptile skin, folding clasp
Price: $155,000

HM7 Aquapod

Reference number: 70.TSL.B
Movement: automatic, MB&F Caliber HM7; ø 31.4 mm, height 17.45 mm; 35 jewels; 18,000 vph; flying 1-minute tourbillon, 3D vertical architecture; 72-hour power reserve
Functions: hours, minutes (using spherical aluminum/titanium rings)
Case: titanium, ø 53.8 mm, height 21.3 mm; unidirectional bezel, with 0-60 scale; sapphire crystal; transparent case back; winding and time-setting crowns; water-resistant to 5 atm
Band: rubber, folding clasp
Price: $98,000; limited to 33 pieces

Legacy Machine N°2 Titanium

Reference number: 02.TL.G
Movement: manually wound, MB&F Caliber LM2; ø 36.5 mm, height 13 mm; 44 jewels; 18,000 vph; inverted movement design with 2 balances floating over dial; planetary differential transmits average value of the 2 regulators to gearwheels
Functions: hours, minutes
Case: titanium, ø 44 mm, height 19 mm; sapphire crystal; transparent case back; water-resistant to 3 atm
Band: reptile skin, buckle
Price: $138,000; limited to 18 pieces

MEISTERSINGER

In 2014, MeisterSinger completed a long process of reorientation, setting the German brand in redux mode. At Baselworld 2014, it presented a portfolio of exclusively one-hand watches, the actual core of the brand. These watches express a relaxed and self-determined approach to the perception of time apparent in the special diurnal rituals that everyone knows, young, old, in private, or at work. These rituals actually divide up and define certain moments. And it is the reiteration of these moments which leads to order, or at least avoids chaos.

Founder Martin Brassler launched his little collection of stylistically neat one-hand dials at the beginning of the new millennium. Looking at these ultimately simplified dials does tempt one to classify the one-hand watch as an archetype. The single hand simply cannot be reduced any further, and the 144 minutes for 12 hours around the dial do have a normative function of sorts. In a frenetic era when free time has become so rare, these watches slow things down a little. The most recent one-hander does provide the hour, jumping very precisely in a window under 12 o'clock—hence its Italian name Salthora, or "jumping hour."

Nevertheless, Brassler has put a few three-hand watches on the market, like the Paleograph, but the hour hand remains the dominant feature on the dials. Design, product planning, service, and management all happen in Münster, Germany. The watches, however, are Swiss made, with ETA and Sellita movements. The Circularis, however, is the brand's first model with an in-house movement, a manually wound caliber with two barrel springs developed in collaboration with the Swiss firm Synergies Horlogères.

MeisterSinger GmbH & Co. KG
Hafenweg 46
D-48155 Münster
Germany

Tel.:
+49-251-133-4860

E-mail:
info@meistersinger.de

Website:
www.meistersinger.de

Founded:
2001

Number of employees:
13

Annual production:
approx. 10,000 watches

U.S. distributor:
Duber Time
1920 Dr. MLK Jr. Street North
Suite #D
St. Petersburg, FL 33704
727-202-3262
damir@meistersingertime.com

Price range:
from approx. $1,200 to $7,000

Circularis Automatic

Reference number: CC907
Movement: automatic, MeisterSinger Caliber MSA01; ø 32.7 mm, height 6.4 mm; 29 jewels; 28,800 vph; 2 spring barrels; finely finished movement; 120-hour power reserve
Functions: hours (each graduation mark represents 5 minutes); date
Case: stainless steel, ø 43 mm, height 13.5 mm; sapphire crystal; transparent case back; water-resistant to 5 atm
Band: stainless steel Milanese mesh, folding clasp
Price: $5,545
Variations: various dial colors; gold bezel ($6,495); reptile skin strap ($5,395)

Circularis Gangreserve

Reference number: CCP317G
Movement: manually wound, MeisterSinger Caliber MSH02; ø 32.7 mm, height 5.4 mm; 27 jewels; 28,800 vph; 2 spring barrels; finely finished movement; 120-hour power reserve
Functions: hours (each graduation mark represents 5 minutes); power reserve indicator; date
Case: stainless steel, ø 43 mm, height 12.5 mm; sapphire crystal; transparent case back; water-resistant to 5 atm
Band: reptile skin, double folding clasp
Price: $5,325
Variations: various dial colors; gold bezel ($6,750); stainless steel Milanese bracelet ($5,475)

N° 01

Reference number: AM3303
Movement: manually wound, Sellita Caliber SW210; ø 25.6 mm, height 3.4 mm; 19 jewels; 28,800 vph; 42-hour power reserve
Functions: hours (each graduation mark represents 5 minutes)
Case: stainless steel, ø 43 mm, height 11.5 mm; sapphire crystal; water-resistant to 5 atm
Band: calfskin, buckle
Price: $1,595
Variations: various dial colors; reptile skin strap ($1,870); stainless steel Milanese bracelet ($2,020)

Pangaea

Reference number: PM908
Movement: automatic, ETA Caliber 2892-A2 or Sellita SW300-1; ø 25.6 mm, height 3.6 mm; 21 or 25 jewels; 28,800 vph; 42-hour power reserve
Functions: hours (each graduation mark represents 5 minutes)
Case: stainless steel, ø 40 mm, height 10.1 mm; sapphire crystal; transparent case back; water-resistant to 5 atm
Band: calfskin, buckle
Price: $2,750
Variations: various dial colors; reptile skin strap ($3,025); stainless steel Milanese bracelet ($3,175)

Phanero

Reference number: PH307G
Movement: manually wound, Sellita Caliber SW210; ø 25.6 mm, height 3.4 mm; 19 jewels; 28,800 vph; 42-hour power reserve
Functions: hours (each graduation mark represents 5 minutes)
Case: stainless steel, ø 35 mm, height 7.5 mm; sapphire crystal; transparent case back; water-resistant to 5 atm
Band: calfskin, buckle
Price: $1,595
Variations: various dial colors; reptile skin strap ($1,870); stainless steel Milanese bracelet; stainless steel bracelet

Neo Plus

Reference number: NE401
Movement: automatic, ETA 2824-2 or Sellita SW200-1; ø 25.6 mm, height 4.6 mm; 25 or 26 jewels; 28,800 vph; 38-hour power reserve
Functions: hours (each graduation mark represents 5 minutes); date
Case: stainless steel, ø 40 mm, height 10.1 mm; plexiglass; water-resistant to 3 atm
Band: calfskin, buckle
Price: $1,395
Variations: various dial colors; reptile skin strap ($1,670); stainless steel Milanese bracelet ($1,445)

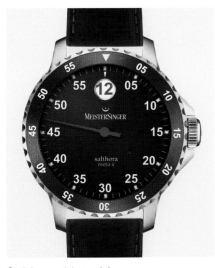

Salthora Meta X

Reference number: SAMX902
Movement: automatic, ETA Caliber 2824-2 or Sellita SW200-1 with in-house module for jumping hours; additional 24-hour display; ø 25.6 mm, height 6.9 mm; 25 or 26 jewels; 28,800 vph; with côtes de Genève; 38-hour power reserve
Functions: hours (digital, jumping), minutes
Case: stainless steel, ø 43 mm, height 14.2 mm; unidirectional ceramic bezel with 0-60 scale; sapphire crystal; screw-in crown; water-resistant to 20 atm
Band: calfskin with rubber overlay, buckle
Price: $3,350
Variations: reptile skin strap ($3,625); stainless steel Milanese bracelet ($3,775)

Pangaea Day Date

Reference number: PDD901
Movement: automatic, ETA Caliber 2836-2 or Sellita Caliber SW220-1; ø 25.6 mm, height 5.05 mm; 26 jewels; 28,800 vph; with côtes de Genève; 38-hour power reserve
Functions: hours (each graduation mark represents 5 minutes); date, weekday (disk display)
Case: stainless steel, ø 40 mm, height 10.5 mm; sapphire crystal; transparent case back; water-resistant to 5 atm
Band: calfskin, buckle
Price: $2,825
Variations: various dial colors; reptile skin strap ($3,100); stainless steel Milanese bracelet ($3,250)

N° 02

Reference number: AM6609N
Movement: manually wound, ETA Caliber 6498-1; ø 36.6 mm, height 4.5 mm; 17 jewels; 18,000 vph; 46-hour power reserve
Functions: hours (each graduation mark represents 5 minutes)
Case: stainless steel, ø 43 mm, height 11.5 mm; sapphire crystal; transparent case back; water-resistant to 5 atm
Band: calfskin, buckle
Price: $2,595
Variations: various dial colors; reptile skin strap ($2,870); stainless steel Milanese bracelet ($3,020)

MK II

If vintage and unserviceable watches had their say, they would probably be naturally attracted to Mk II for the name alone, which is a military designation for the second generation of equipment. The company, which was founded by watch enthusiast and maker Bill Yao in 2002, not only puts retired designs back into service, but also modernizes and customizes them. Before the screw-down crown, diving watches were not nearly as reliably sealed, for example. And some beautiful old pieces were made with plated brass cases or featured Bakelite components, which are either easily damaged or have aged poorly. The company substitutes not only proven modern materials, but also modern manufacturing methods and techniques to ensure a better outcome.

These are material issues that the team at Mk II handles with great care. They will not, metaphorically speaking, airbrush a Model-T. As genuine watch lovers themselves, they make sure that the final design is in the spirit of the watch itself, which still leaves a great deal of leeway for many iterations given a sufficient number of parts. In the company's output, vintage style and modern functionality are key. The watches are assembled by hand at the company's workshop in Pennsylvania—and subjected to a rigorous regime of testing. The components are individually inspected, the cases tested at least three times for water resistance, and at the end the whole watch is regulated in six positions. Looking to the future, Mk II aspires to carry its clean vintage style into the development of what it hopes will be future classics of its own.

Mk II Corporation
303 W. Lancaster Avenue, #283
Wayne, PA 19087

E-mail:
info@mkiiwatches.com

Website:
www.mkiiwatches.com

Founded:
2002

Number of employees:
3

Annual production:
800 watches

Distribution:
direct sales and select retail

Most important collections/price range:
Professional series / $1,200 to $2,000;
Specialist series / $500 to $1,345

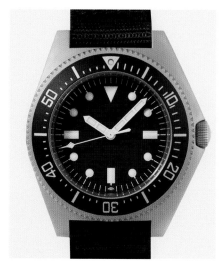

Paradive
Reference number: CD04.1-1004
Movement: automatic (hack setting), Caliber SII NE15 (Made in Japan); ø 27.4 mm, height 5.32 mm; 24 jewels; 21,600 vph; 50-hour power reserve; rotor decorated with côtes de Genève
Functions: hours, minutes, sweep seconds
Case: stainless steel, ø 41.2 mm, height 15.50 mm; 120-click unidirectional bezel; high domed sapphire crystal with antireflective coating; screw-down case back; screw-in crown; water-resistant to 20 atm
Band: nylon, buckle
Price: $895
Variations: with date, 12-hour GMT bezel

Hawkinge
Reference Number: CG05-1002S2
Movement: automatic (hack setting), Caliber SII NE15 (Made in Japan); ø 27.4 mm, height 5.32 mm; 24 jewels; 21,600 vph; 50-hour power reserve; rotor decorated with côtes de Genève
Functions: hours, minutes, sweep seconds; date
Case: stainless steel; ø 37.8 mm, height 12.75 mm; domed sapphire crystal with antireflective coating; screw-down case back; screw-in crown; water-resistant to 10 atm
Band: leather, buckle
Price: $649
Variations: nylon strap, non-date

Tornek-Rayville Series 2
Reference Number: CD02.1-2001N
Movement: automatic, Caliber Soprod A10; ø 26.2 mm, height 3.6 mm; 25 jewels; 28,800 vph; 42-hour power reserve; rhodium-plated; rotor decorated with côtes de Genève
Functions: hours, minutes, sweep seconds
Case: stainless steel, ø 42 mm, height 13.9 mm; 60-click unidirectional bezel; domed sapphire crystal with antireflective coating; luminous sapphire inlay, screw-down case back; screw-in crown; antimagnetic shielding, water-resistant to 20 atm
Band: nylon NATO-style strap
Price: $1,295
Variations: stainless steel bracelet

Montblanc Montre SA
10, chemin des Tourelles
CH-2400 Le Locle
Switzerland

Tel.:
+41-32-933-8888

Fax:
+41-32-933-8880

E-mail:
service@montblanc.com

Website:
www.montblanc.com

Founded:
1997 (1906 in Hamburg)

Number of employees:
worldwide approx. 3,000

U.S. distributor:
Montblanc North America
645 Fifth Avenue, 7th Floor
New York, New York 10022
+1-800-995-4810
+1-908-464-3722 (fax)
www.montblanc.com

Most important collections:
Heritage Chronométrie, Heritage Spirit,
Meisterstück, Star, Nicolas Rieussec, 4810,
TimeWalker, Collection Villeret, 1858 Collection

MONTBLANC

It was with great skill and cleverness that Nicolas Rieussec (1781–1866) used the invention of a special chronograph—the "Time Writer," a device that released droplets of ink onto a rotating sheet of paper—to make a name for himself. Montblanc, once famous only for its exclusive writing implements, borrowed that name on its way to becoming a distinguished watch brand. Within a few years, it had created an impressive range of chronographs driven by in-house calibers: from simple automatic stopwatches to flagship pieces with two independent spring barrels for time and "time-writing."

The Richemont Group, owner of Montblanc, has placed great trust in its "daughter" company, having put the little *manufacture* Minerva, which it purchased at the beginning of 2007, at the disposal of Montblanc. The Minerva Institute serves as a kind of think tank for the future, a place where young watchmakers can absorb the old traditions and skills, as well as the wealth of experience and mind-set of the masters.

In the summer of 2013, Jerôme Lambert from sister brand Jaeger-LeCoultre took over the presidency and focused the brand on the top and lower price segments. For its 110th birthday, in 2016, the brand came out with the Montblanc 4810 collection, bearing new manufacture movements and unconventional complications that have been attracting lots of attention. The latest extensions of the portfolio, notably the TimeWalker line and some new references, have been inspired by the field of sports, specifically motor sports.

TimeWalker Chrono RallyTimerCounter LE100

Reference number: 116103
Movement: manually wound, Montblanc Caliber MB M16.29; ø 38.4 mm, height 6.3 mm; 22 jewels; 18,000 vph; screw balance; balance spring with Phillips terminal curve; column wheel control of chronograph functions using a single pusher; 50-hour power reserve
Functions: hours, minutes, subsidiary seconds; chronograph
Case: titanium, ø 38.4 mm, height 15.2 mm; sapphire crystal; transparent case back; water-resistant to 3 atm
Band: calfskin, buckle
Remarks: movable lugs function as support for use as table clock
Price: $33,600; limited to 100 pieces

TimeWalker Chronograph UTC

Reference number: 116101
Movement: automatic, Montblanc Caliber 25.03 (base ETA 7751); ø 30 mm, height 7.9 mm; 25 jewels; 28,800 vph; 46-hour power reserve
Functions: hours, minutes, subsidiary seconds; second 24-hour display (second time zone); chronograph; date
Case: stainless steel with black DLC coating, ø 43 mm, height 15.2 mm; unidirectional ceramic bezel with 0-24 scale; sapphire crystal; transparent case back; water-resistant to 10 atm
Band: rubber, triple folding clasp
Price: $4,990

TimeWalker Date Automatic

Reference number: 116059
Movement: automatic, Montblanc Caliber 24.17 (base Sellita SW200-1); ø 25.6 mm, height 4.6 mm; 26 jewels; 28,800 vph; 38-hour power reserve
Functions: hours, minutes, sweep seconds; date
Case: stainless steel, ø 41 mm, height 11.38 mm; unidirectional ceramic bezel with 0-12 scale; sapphire crystal; transparent case back; water-resistant to 10 atm
Band: rubber, buckle
Price: $2,985

TimeWalker Chronograph 1000

Reference number: 116828
Movement: manually wound, Montblanc Caliber MB M66.26; ø 38.4 mm, height 10.6 mm; 46 jewels; 18,000 vph; independent chronograph mechanism with its own escapement system (360,000 vph) and its own power management; single pusher for chronograph functions
Functions: hours, minutes, subsidiary seconds; chronograph, with 1/100th and 1/1000th second measurement
Case: titanium with black DLC coating, ø 46.4 mm, height 17.34 mm; ceramic bezel; sapphire crystal; transparent case back; water-resistant to 3 atm
Band: reptile skin, triple folding clasp
Price: on request; limited to 18 pieces

TimeWalker Chronograph Automatic

Reference number: 117051
Movement: automatic, Montblanc Caliber 25.07 (base ETA 7750); ø 30 mm, height 7.9 mm; 25 jewels; 28,800 vph; 46-hour power reserve
Functions: hours, minutes, subsidiary seconds; chronograph; date
Case: pink gold, ø 43 mm, height 15.2 mm; unidirectional ceramic bezel with 0-12 scale; sapphire crystal; transparent case back; water-resistant to 10 atm
Band: calfskin, triple folding clasp
Price: $19,500

Heritage Chronométrie ExoTourbillon Flyback

Reference number: 115993
Movement: manually wound, Montblanc Caliber MB M16.62; ø 38.4 mm, height 12.27 mm; 36 jewels; 18,000 vph; 1-minute tourbillon with external hairspring, screw balance; column wheel control of chronograph functions; 50-hour power reserve
Functions: hours, minutes, subsidiary seconds; additional 12-hour display, day/night indicator; split-second chronograph
Case: pink gold, ø 47 mm, height 18.58 mm; sapphire crystal; transparent case back; water-resistant to 3 atm
Band: reptile skin, buckle
Price: on request; limited to 8 pieces

1858 Chronograph Tachymeter Limited Edition

Reference number: 116243
Movement: manually wound, Montblanc Caliber MB M16.29; ø 38.4 mm, height 6.3 mm; 22 jewels; 18,000 vph; screw balance; balance spring with Phillips terminal curve; column wheel control of chronograph functions using a single pusher; gold-plated gear train; finely finished movement; 50-hour power reserve
Functions: hours, minutes, subsidiary seconds; chronograph
Case: bronze, ø 44 mm, height 13.15 mm; sapphire crystal; transparent case back; water-resistant to 3 atm
Band: reptile skin, buckle
Price: $27,500; limited to 100 pieces

Bohème Collection Date Automatic

Reference number: 116498
Movement: automatic, Montblanc Caliber 24.14 (base ETA 2824-2); ø 25.6 mm, height 4.6 mm; 25 jewels; 28,800 vph; 38-hour power reserve
Functions: hours, minutes, sweep seconds; date
Case: stainless steel, ø 28 mm, height 9.35 mm; sapphire crystal; water-resistant to 3 atm
Band: stainless steel, folding clasp
Remarks: dial set with 8 diamonds
Price: $3,305

Bohème Collection ExoTourbillon

Reference number: 116494
Movement: automatic, Montblanc Caliber MB M29.24; ø 30.6 mm, height 4.5 mm; 29 jewels; 21,600 vph; 1-minute tourbillon with external hairspring; screw balance; gold microrotor double mainspring barrel; 50-hour power reserve
Functions: hours, minutes, subsidiary seconds (on tourbillon cage)
Case: stainless steel, ø 38 mm, height 9.37 mm; pink gold bezel; sapphire crystal; water-resistant to 3 atm
Band: reptile skin, buckle
Price: $27,500

Caliber MB M16.29

Manually wound; column wheel control of chronograph functions using a single pusher; single spring barrel, 55-hour power reserve
Functions: hours, minutes, subsidiary seconds; chronograph
Diameter: 38.4 mm
Height: 6.3 mm
Jewels: 22
Balance: screw balance
Frequency: 18,000 vph
Balance spring: with Phillips terminal curve
Remarks: rhodium-plated movement with perlage, bridges with côtes de Genève, gold-plated gear train

Caliber MB M66.26

Manually wound; independent chronograph mechanism with its own escapement system (360,000 vph) and its own power management; single pusher for chronograph functions, German silver plate; single spring barrel, 50-hour power reserve
Functions: hours, minutes, subsidiary seconds; chronograph (display and measurement of 1/100th and 1/1000th seconds)
Diameter: 38.4 mm
Height: 10.6 mm
Jewels: 46
Balance: screw balance
Frequency: 18,000 vph
Balance spring: flat hairspring with Phillips terminal curve
Remarks: 488 components

Caliber MB LL100

Automatic; column wheel control of the chronograph functions, horizontal clutch, sweep minutes and seconds totalizer with double flyback function; double mainspring barrel, 72-hour power reserve
Functions: hours, minutes, subsidiary seconds; second 24-hour display (second time zone); flyback chronograph; date
Diameter: 31 mm
Height: 7.9 mm
Jewels: 36
Balance: glucydur variable inertia balance
Frequency: 28,800 vph
Balance spring: flat hairspring
Shock protection: Incabloc
Remarks: perlage on mainplate bridges with côtes de Genève

Caliber MB R230

Automatic; 1-minute tourbillon with balance outside the cage (ExoTourbillon); stop-seconds system; column-wheel control using individual chronograph pushers, vertical chronograph clutch; double mainspring barrel, 50-hour power reserve
Functions: hours, minutes (off-center); chronograph; date
Diameter: 33.7 mm
Height: 8.65 mm
Jewels: 44
Balance: screw balance
Frequency: 21,600 vph
Balance spring: flat hairspring
Remarks: 296 components

Caliber MB M16.62

Manually wound; ExoTourbillon with external balance spring; single pusher for chronograph functions; German silver mainplate; single spring barrel, 50-hour power reserve
Functions: hours, minutes, subsidiary seconds; additional 12-hour display (second time zone), day/night indicator; split-second chronograph
Diameter: 38.4 mm
Height: 12.27 mm
Jewels: 36
Balance: screw balance
Balance spring: flat hairspring with Phillips terminal curve
Remarks: 432 components; finely finished with côtes de Genève

Caliber MB M29.24

Automatic; 1-minute tourbillon with external balance spring; double spring barrel, 50-hour power reserve
Functions: hours, minutes
Diameter: 30.6 mm
Height: 4.5 mm
Jewels: 29
Balance: screw balance with 18 weighted screws
Frequency: 21,600 vph
Balance spring: flat hairspring
Remarks: gold microrotor bridges with côtes de Genève

MÜHLE GLASHÜTTE

Mühle Glashütte GmbH
Nautische Instrumente und Feinmechanik
Altenberger Strasse 35
D-01768 Glashütte
Germany

Tel.:
+49-35053-3203-0

Fax:
+49-35053-3203-136

E-mail:
info@muehle-glashuette.de

Website:
www.muehle-glashuette.de

Founded:
first founding 1869; second founding 1993

Number of employees:
47

U.S. distributor:
Mühle Glashütte
Old Northeast Jewelers
1131 4th Street North
St. Petersburg, FL 33701
800-922-4377
www.muehle-glashuette.com

Most important collections/price range:
mechanical wristwatches / approx. $1,399 to
$5,400

Mühle Glashütte has survived all the ups and downs of Germany's history. The firm Rob. Mühle & Sohn was founded by its namesake in 1869. At that time, the company made precision measuring instruments for the local watch industry and the German School of Watchmaking. In the early 1920s, the firm established itself as a supplier for the automobile industry, making speedometers, automobile clocks, tachometers, and other measurement instruments.

Having manufactured instruments for the military during the war, the company was not only bombarded by the Soviet air force, but was also nationalized in 1945, as it was in the eastern part of the country. After the fall of the Iron Curtain, it was reestablished as a limited liability corporation. In 2007, Thilo Mühle took over the helm from his father, Hans-Jürgen Mühle.

The company's wristwatch business was launched in 1996 and now overshadows the nautical instruments that had made the name Mühle Glashütte famous. Its collection comprises mechanical wristwatches at entry and mid-level prices. For these, the company uses Swiss base movements that are equipped with such in-house developments as a patented woodpecker-neck regulation and the Mühle rotor. The modifications are so extensive, they have led to the calibers having their own names. A new traditional line named "R. Mühle & Sohn" was introduced in 2014 beginning with the Robert Mühle Auf/Ab and the Small Seconds equipped with the RMK 1 and RMK 2 calibers. In 2017, the company looks like it's heading for the racetrack, with a sportive Teutonia chronograph that lets the wearer check the speed of moving vehicles at a glance.

Lunova Chronograph

Reference number: M1-43-06-LB
Movement: automatic, Mühle Caliber MU 9413; ø 30 mm, height 7.9 mm; 25 jewels; 28,800 vph; woodpecker neck regulator, three-quarter Glashütte plate; carefully reworked with special Mühle finish; 48-hour power reserve
Functions: hours, minutes, subsidiary seconds; chronograph; date, weekday
Case: stainless steel, ø 42.3 mm, height 14.2 mm; sapphire crystal; transparent case back; screw-in crown; water-resistant to 10 atm
Band: reptile skin, buckle
Price: $3,499

Lunova Tag/Datum

Reference number: M1-43-26-LB
Movement: automatic, Caliber SW220-1; ø 25.6 mm, height 5.05 mm; 26 jewels; 28,800 vph; woodpecker neck regulator, Mühle rotor; carefully reworked with special Mühle finish; 38-hour power reserve
Functions: hours, minutes, sweep seconds; date, weekday
Case: stainless steel, ø 42.3 mm, height 11 mm; sapphire crystal; transparent case back; screw-in crown; water-resistant to 10 atm
Band: reptile skin, buckle
Price: $2,349

Teutonia Sport I

Reference number: M1-29-63-NB
Movement: automatic, Mühle Caliber MU 9413; ø 30 mm, height 7.9 mm; 25 jewels; 28,800 vph; woodpecker neck regulator, three-quarter Glashütte plate; carefully reworked with special Mühle finish; 48-hour power reserve
Functions: hours, minutes, subsidiary seconds; chronograph; date
Case: stainless steel, ø 42.6 mm, height 15.5 mm; bidirectionally rotating bezel with 0-60 scale; sapphire crystal; transparent case back; screw-in crown; water-resistant to 10 atm
Band: rubber, with calfskin overlay, buckle
Price: $3,899

Teutonia II Grossdatum Chronometer

Reference number: M1-33-76-LB
Movement: automatic, ETA Caliber 2892 with Jaquet module 3532; ø 25.6 mm; 21 jewels; 28,800 vph; woodpecker neck regulator, Mühle rotor; carefully reworked with special Mühle finish; 46-hour power reserve; DIN certified chronometer
Functions: hours, minutes, subsidiary seconds; large date
Case: stainless steel, ø 41 mm, height 12.7 mm; sapphire crystal; transparent case back; screw-in crown; water-resistant to 10 atm
Band: reptile skin, double folding clasp
Price: $5,299; limited to 250 pieces

Teutonia II Chronograph

Reference number: M1-30-95-LB
Movement: automatic, Mühle Caliber MU 9413; ø 30 mm, height 7.9 mm; 25 jewels; 28,800 vph; woodpecker neck regulator, three-quarter Glashütte plate; carefully reworked with special Mühle finish; 48-hour power reserve
Functions: hours, minutes, subsidiary seconds; chronograph; date, weekday
Case: stainless steel, ø 42 mm, height 15.5 mm; sapphire crystal; transparent case back; screw-in crown; water-resistant to 10 atm
Band: reptile skin, double folding clasp
Price: $4,599
Variations: stainless steel bracelet ($4,799)

29er Chronograph

Reference number: M1-25-41-LB
Movement: automatic, Mühle Caliber MU 9413; ø 30 mm, height 7.9 mm; 25 jewels; 28,800 vph; woodpecker neck regulator, three-quarter Glashütte plate; carefully reworked with special Mühle finish; 48-hour power reserve
Functions: hours, minutes, subsidiary seconds; chronograph; date
Case: stainless steel, ø 42.4 mm, height 14.2 mm; sapphire crystal; transparent case back; screw-in crown; water-resistant to 10 atm
Band: calfskin, buckle
Price: $4,099
Variations: stainless steel bracelet ($4,299)

29er Big

Reference number: M1-25-33-NB
Movement: automatic, Caliber SW200-1; ø 25.6 mm, height 4.6 mm; 26 jewels; 28,800 vph; woodpecker neck regulator, Mühle rotor; carefully reworked with special Mühle finish; 38-hour power reserve
Functions: hours, minutes, sweep seconds; date
Case: stainless steel, ø 42.4 mm, height 11.3 mm; sapphire crystal; transparent case back; screw-in crown; water-resistant to 10 atm
Band: rubber, with calfskin overlay, buckle
Price: $2,099
Variations: calfskin strap ($2,099); stainless steel bracelet ($2,199)

Terrasport I Chronograph

Reference number: M1-37-74-LB
Movement: automatic, Caliber 9413; ø 30 mm, height 7.9 mm; 25 jewels; 28,800 vph; woodpecker neck regulator, three-quarter plate, Mühle rotor; carefully reworked with special Mühle finish; 48-hour power reserve
Functions: hours, minutes, subsidiary seconds; chronograph; date
Case: stainless steel, ø 44 mm, height 13.6 mm; sapphire crystal; transparent case back; screw-in crown; water-resistant to 10 atm
Band: calfskin, buckle
Price: $4,099
Variations: stainless steel bracelet ($4,299)

Terrasport IV GMT

Reference number: M1-37-94-LB
Movement: automatic, Caliber SW330-1; ø 25.6 mm, height 4.1 mm; 21 jewels; 28,800 vph; woodpecker neck regulator, Mühle rotor; carefully reworked with special Mühle finish; 42-hour power reserve
Functions: hours, minutes, sweep seconds; second 24-hour display (second time zone); date
Case: stainless steel, ø 42 mm, height 10.2 mm; sapphire crystal; transparent case back; screw-in crown; water-resistant to 10 atm
Band: bison leather, buckle
Price: $2,299
Variations: stainless steel bracelet ($2,399)

S.A.R. Rescue-Timer

Reference number: M1-41-03-MB
Movement: automatic, Caliber SW 200-1;
ø 25.6 mm, height 4.6 mm; 26 jewels; 28,800 vph;
woodpecker neck regulator, Mühle rotor; carefully
reworked with special Mühle finish; 38-hour power
reserve
Functions: hours, minutes, sweep seconds; date
Case: stainless steel, ø 42 mm, height 13.5 mm;
bezel with rubber inlay; sapphire crystal; screw-in
crown; water-resistant to 100 atm
Band: stainless steel, folding clasp, with extension
link
Price: $2,799
Variations: rubber strap ($2,699)

S.A.R. Flieger Chronograph

Reference number: M1-41-33-KB
Movement: automatic, Caliber MU 9413; ø 30 mm,
height 7.9 mm; 25 jewels; 28,800 vph; woodpecker
neck regulator, three-quarter plate, Mühle rotor;
carefully reworked with special Mühle finish; 48-hour
power reserve
Functions: hours, minutes, subsidiary seconds;
chronograph; date
Case: stainless steel, ø 45 mm, height 16.2 mm;
bidirectional bezel with 0-60 scale; sapphire crystal;
transparent case back; screw-in crown; water-
resistant to 10 atm
Band: rubber, folding clasp with safety lock
Price: $4,699
Variations: stainless steel bracelet ($4,899)

Seebataillon GMT

Reference number: M1-28-62-KB
Movement: automatic, Caliber SW330-1;
ø 25.6 mm, height 4.1 mm; 21 jewels; 28,800 vph;
Mühle version with woodpecker neck regulation,
own rotor with typical special finish; 42-hour power
reserve
Functions: hours, minutes, sweep seconds; second
24-hour display (second time zone); date
Case: titanium, ø 45 mm, height 12.7 mm;
bidirectional bezel with 0-60 scale; sapphire crystal;
screw-in crown; water-resistant to 30 atm
Band: rubber, folding clasp
Price: $3,999

ProMare Chronograph

Reference number: M1-42-04-NB
Movement: automatic, Mühle Caliber MU 9408;
ø 30 mm, height 7.9 mm; 25 jewels; 28,800 vph;
woodpecker neck regulator, three-quarter Glashütte
plate; carefully reworked with special Mühle finish;
48-hour power reserve
Functions: hours, minutes, subsidiary seconds;
chronograph; date
Case: stainless steel, ø 44 mm, height 15.4 mm;
sapphire crystal; transparent case back; screw-in
crown; water-resistant to 30 atm
Band: rubber, with calfskin overlay, buckle
Price: $4,299
Variations: stainless steel bracelet ($4,399)

Robert Mühle Zeigerdatum

Reference number: M1-11-46-LB
Movement: manually wound, Robert Mühle Caliber
RMK 03; ø 36.6 mm, height 8.35 mm; 33 jewels;
21,600 vph; engraved balance cock with woodpecker
neck regulator three-fifth plate, Glashütte long-slot
click, 3 screw-down gold chatons; 56-hour power
reserve
Functions: hours, minutes, subsidiary seconds;
power reserve indicator; date
Case: stainless steel, ø 44 mm, height 12.56 mm;
sapphire crystal; transparent case back; water-
resistant to 10 atm
Band: reptile skin, folding clasp
Price: $8,999; limited to 100 pieces

RMK 03

Manually wound; woodpecker neck fine regulator;
single spring barrel, 56-hour power reserve
Functions: hours, minutes, subsidiary seconds;
power reserve indicator; date
Diameter: 36.6 mm
Height: 8.35 mm
Jewels: 33, including 3 screw-mounted gold
chatons
Balance: glucydur
Frequency: 21,600 vph
Balance spring: Nivarox
Remarks: three-fifth plate, Glashütte stopwork,
hand-engraved balance cock

Nivrel Uhren
Gerd Hofer GmbH
Kossmannstrasse 3
D-66119 Saarbrücken
Germany

Tel.:
+49-681-584-6576

Fax:
+49-681-584-6584

E-mail:
info@nivrel.com

Website:
www.nivrel.com

Founded:
1978

Number of employees:
10, plus external staff members

Distribution:
Please contact headquarters for inquiries.

Most important collections/price range:
mechanical watches, most with complications /
approx. $600 to $45,000

NIVREL

In 1891, master goldsmith Friedrich Jacob Kraemer founded a jewelry and watch shop in Saarbrücken that proved to be the place to go for fine craftsmanship. Gerd Hofer joined the family business in 1956, carrying it on into the fourth generation. However, his true passion was for watchmaking. In 1993, he and his wife, Gitta, bought the rights to use the Swiss name Nivrel, a brand that had been established in 1936, and integrated production of these watches into their German-based operations.

Today, Nivrel is led by the Hofers' daughter Anja, who is keeping both lineages alive. Mechanical complications with Swiss movements of the finest technical level and finishing as well as gold watches in the high-end design segment of the industry are manufactured with close attention to detail and an advanced level of craftsmanship. In addition to classic automatic watches, the brand has introduced everything from complicated chronographs and skeletonized watches to perpetual calendars and tourbillons. The movements and all the "habillage" of the watches—case, dial, crystal, crown, etc.—are made in Switzerland. Watch design, assembly, and finishing are done in Saarbrücken.

Nivrel watches are a perfect example of how quickly a watch brand incorporating a characteristic style and immaculate quality can make a respected place for itself in the industry. Affordable prices also play a significant role in this brand's success, but they do not keep the brand from innovating. Nivrel has teamed up with the Department of Metallic Materials of Saarland University to develop a special alloy for repeater springs that is softer and does not need as much energy to press.

Jubilé III
Reference number: N 121.001 AAWAS
Movement: automatic, ETA Caliber 2824-2; ø 25.6 mm, height 4.6 mm; 25 jewels; 28,800 vph; 38-hour power reserve
Functions: hours, minutes, sweep seconds; date
Case: stainless steel, ø 40 mm, height 10 mm; sapphire crystal; transparent case back; water-resistant to 5 atm
Band: calfskin, buckle
Price: $650
Variations: black dial, stainless steel Milanese bracelet ($750)

Deep Ocean Red
Reference number: N 147.001
Movement: automatic, Miyota Caliber 9015; ø 25.6 mm, height 3,9 mm; 24 jewels; 28,800 vph; 42-hour power reserve
Functions: hours, minutes, sweep seconds; date
Case: stainless steel, ø 43 mm, height 13.5 mm; unidirectionally rotating bezel with 0-60 scale; sapphire crystal; screw-in crown; water-resistant to 50 atm
Band: stainless steel, folding clasp with safety lock and extension link
Price: $690

Chronographe Réplique III
Reference number: N 512.001 AASDS
Movement: automatic, ETA Caliber 7750; ø 30 mm, height 7.9 mm; 25 jewels; 28,800 vph; finely finished, rotor with côtes de Genève; 42-hour power reserve
Functions: hours, minutes, subsidiary seconds; chronograph; date, weekday
Case: stainless steel, ø 42 mm, height 13.5 mm; sapphire crystal; transparent case back; screw-in crown; water-resistant to 5 atm
Band: calfskin, buckle
Price: $2,250

NOMOS

NOMOS Glashütte/SA
Roland Schwertner KG
Ferdinand-Adolph-Lange-Platz 2
01768 Glashütte
Germany

Tel.:
+49-35053-4040

Fax:
+49-35053-40480

E-mail:
nomos@glashuette.com

Website:
nomos-glashuette.com

Founded:
1990

Number of employees:
260

U.S. distributor:
For the U.S. market, please contact:
NOMOS Glashuette USA Inc.
347 W. 36th St., Suite 600
New York, NY 10018
212-929-2575
contact@nomos-watches.com

Most important collections/price range:
Ahoi / $3,760 to $4,660; Club / $1,550
to $3,550; Lambda / $17,000 to $20,000;
Ludwig / $1,700 to $3,780; Metro / $3,480 to
$3,780; Orion / $1,920 to $3,060; Sundial /
$185 to $310; Tangente / $1,760 to $3,500;
Tangomat / $2,980 to $4,920; Tetra / $1,980 to
$3,980; Zürich / $4,180 to $6,100

Still waters run deep, and discreet business practices at times travel far. Nomos, founded in 1990, has suddenly become a full-fledged *manufacture* with brand-new facilities and a smart policy of only so much growth as the small team gathered around the founder Roland Schwertner and his associate Uwe Ahrendt can easily absorb.

The collection is based on five or six basic models, though the number of calibers available is growing at an impressive rate, including two luxury manually wound movements with fine finishings. Over the past years the brand has invested heavily in the design and construction of an in-house escapement with a spring "made in Germany." The escapement made its debut at Baselworld 2014 under the name DUW 4401 (Deutsche Uhrenwerke Nomos Glashütte) and will gradually be used in all the movements, including the new, automatic ultrathin DUW 3001.

Between 2010 and 2017, staff more than doubled in size to around 300 people, including about 40 design and communication staff at the Berlinblau in-house design studio and in the USA, where Nomos has offices (in New York) and about fifty points of sale. The key strategy: outstanding watches at an affordable price, a simple look full of subtle details, and marketing that is bold and humorous. Nomos, visibly, is a member of the Deutscher Werkbund, precursor of the Bauhaus school, meaning pared-down industrial design, with a touch of Berlin's biting humor. The recent Ahoi (as in "ship ahoy!"), a swimmer's watch with an optional synthetic strap like those that carry locker keys at Germany's public swimming pools, has won several prizes. The latest Aqua series based in part on the Ahoi is composed of automatics in lively colors that can be worn in formal settings or, perhaps incongruously, when diving, thanks to a 20-atm water-resistance. By the same token, Nomos has been addressing the young and chic with the highly affordable Campus models.

Club 38 Campus Nacht
Reference number: 736
Movement: manually wound, Nomos Caliber Alpha; ø 23.3 mm, height 2.6 mm; 17 jewels; 21,600 vph; 43-hour power reserve
Functions: hours, minutes, subsidiary seconds
Case: stainless steel, ø 38.5 mm, height 8.25 mm; sapphire crystal; stainless steel case back; water-resistant to 10 atm
Band: suede, pin buckle
Price: $1,650

Club Campus
Reference number: 708
Movement: manually wound, Nomos Caliber Alpha; ø 23.3 mm, height 2.6 mm; 17 jewels; 21,600 vph; 43-hour power reserve
Functions: hours, minutes, subsidiary seconds
Case: stainless steel, ø 36 mm, height 8.17 mm; sapphire crystal; stainless steel case back; water-resistant to 10 atm
Band: suede, pin buckle
Price: $1,500

Tangente Neomatik Nachtblau
Reference number: 177
Movement: automatic, Nomos Caliber DUW 3001; ø 28.8 mm, height 3.2 mm; 27 jewels; 21,600 vph; 42-hour power reserve
Functions: hours, minutes, subsidiary seconds
Case: stainless steel, ø 35 mm, height 6.9 mm; sapphire crystal; transparent case back; water-resistant to 3 atm
Band: horse leather, buckle clasp
Price: $3,580

Metro Neomatik Nachtblau

Reference number: 1110
Movement: automatic, Nomos Caliber DUW 3001; ø 28.8 mm, height 3.2 mm; 27 jewels; 21,600 vph; 42-hour power reserve
Functions: hours, minutes, subsidiary seconds
Case: stainless steel, ø 35 mm, height 8.06 mm; sapphire crystal; transparent case back; water-resistant to 3 atm
Band: horse leather, buckle clasp
Price: $3,960

Minimatik

Reference number: 1203
Movement: automatic, Nomos Caliber DUW 3001; ø 28.8 mm, height 3.2 mm; 27 jewels; 21,600 vph; 42-hour power reserve
Functions: hours, minutes, subsidiary seconds
Case: stainless steel, ø 35.5 mm, height 8.86 mm; sapphire crystal; transparent case back; water-resistant to 3 atm
Band: horse leather, buckle clasp
Price: $3,680

Tetra Neomatik

Reference number: 421
Movement: automatic, Nomos Caliber DUW 3001; ø 28.8 mm, height 3.2 mm; 27 jewels; 21,600 vph; 42-hour power reserve
Functions: hours, minutes, subsidiary seconds
Case: stainless steel, 33 × 33 mm, height 7.2 mm; sapphire crystal; transparent case back; water-resistant to 3 atm
Band: horse leather, buckle clasp
Price: $3,860

Tangente Neomatik

Reference number: 175
Movement: automatic, Nomos Caliber DUW 3001; ø 28.8 mm, height 3.2 mm; 27 jewels; 21,600 vph; 42-hour power reserve
Functions: hours, minutes, subsidiary seconds
Case: stainless steel, ø 35 mm, height 6.9 mm; sapphire crystal; transparent case back; water-resistant to 3 atm
Band: horse leather, buckle clasp
Price: $3,460

Orion Neomatik Champagner

Reference number: 393
Movement: automatic, Nomos Caliber DUW 3001; ø 28.8 mm, height 3.2 mm; 27 jewels; 21,600 vph; 42-hour power reserve
Functions: hours, minutes, subsidiary seconds
Case: stainless steel, ø 36 mm, height 8.45 mm; sapphire crystal; transparent case back; water-resistant to 3 atm
Band: calfskin, buckle clasp
Price: $3,700

Ahoi Neomatik Signalrot

Reference number: 563
Movement: automatic, Nomos Caliber DUW 3001; ø 28.8 mm, height 3.2 mm; 27 jewels; 21,600 vph; 42-hour power reserve
Functions: hours, minutes, subsidiary seconds
Case: stainless steel, ø 36.3 mm, height 9.55 mm; sapphire crystal; transparent case back; screw-down crown, crown guard; water-resistant to 20 atm
Band: water-resistant textile strap, buckle clasp
Price: $4,120

NOMOS

Ahoi Atlantik

Reference number: 552
Movement: automatic, Nomos Caliber Epsilon;
ø 31 mm, height 4.3 mm; 26 jewels; 21,600 vph;
43-hour power reserve
Functions: hours, minutes, subsidiary seconds
Case: stainless steel, ø 40.3 mm, height 10.64 mm;
sapphire crystal; transparent case back; screw-down
crown, crown guard; water-resistant to 20 atm
Band: water-resistant textile strap, buckle clasp
Price: $4,060

Ahoi Datum

Reference number: 551
Movement: automatic, Nomos Caliber Zeta;
ø 31 mm, height 4.3 mm; 26 jewels; 21,600 vph;
42-hour power reserve
Functions: hours, minutes, subsidiary seconds; date
Case: stainless steel, ø 40.3 mm, height 10.64 mm;
sapphire crystal; transparent case back; screw-down
crown, crown guard; water-resistant to 20 atm
Band: water-resistant textile strap, buckle clasp
Price: $4,660

Club Neomatik Atlantik

Reference number: 741
Movement: automatic, Nomos Caliber DUW 3001;
ø 28.8 mm, height 3.2 mm; 27 jewels; 21,600 vph;
42-hour power reserve
Functions: hours, minutes, subsidiary seconds
Case: stainless steel, ø 37 mm, height 9.27 mm;
sapphire crystal; transparent case back; water-
resistant to 20 atm
Band: water-resistant textile strap, buckle clasp
Price: $3,160

Club Automat Datum Signalblau

Reference number: 777
Movement: automatic, Nomos Caliber DUW 5101;
ø 31 mm, height 4.3 mm; 26 jewels; 21,600 vph;
42-hour power reserve
Functions: hours, minutes, subsidiary seconds; date
Case: stainless steel, ø 41.5 mm, height 9.78 mm;
sapphire crystal; transparent case back; water-
resistant to 20 atm
Band: water-resistant textile strap, buckle clasp
Price: $3,550

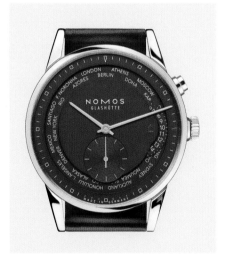

Zürich Weltzeit Nachtblau

Reference number: 807
Movement: automatic, Nomos Caliber DUW 5201;
ø 31 mm, height 5.7 mm; 26 jewels; 21,600 vph;
42-hour power reserve
Functions: hours, minutes, subsidiary seconds;
world time display (second time zone)
Case: stainless steel, ø 39.9 mm, height 10.85 mm;
sapphire crystal; transparent case back; water-
resistant to 3 atm
Band: horse leather, pin buckle
Price: $6,100

Metro Datum Gangreserve

Reference number: 1101
Movement: manually wound, Nomos Caliber
DUW 4401; ø 32.1 mm, height 2.8 mm; 23 jewels;
21,600 vph; 42-hour power reserve
Functions: hours, minutes, subsidiary seconds;
power reserve indicator; date
Case: stainless steel, ø 37 mm, height 7.65 mm;
sapphire crystal; transparent case back; water-
resistant to 3 atm
Band: horse leather, pin buckle
Price: $3,780

Metro 38 Datum Stadtschwarz

Reference number: 1103
Movement: manually wound, Nomos Caliber DUW 4101; ø 32.1 mm, height 2.8 mm; 23 jewels; 21,600 vph; 42-hour power reserve
Functions: hours, minutes, subsidiary seconds; date
Case: stainless steel, ø 38.5 mm, height 7.75 mm; sapphire crystal; transparent case back; water-resistant to 3 atm
Band: horse leather, pin buckle
Price: $3,480

Tangomat GMT

Reference number: 635
Movement: automatic, Nomos Caliber DUW 5201; ø 31 mm, height 5.7 mm; 26 jewels; 21,600 vph; 42-hour power reserve
Functions: hours, minutes, subsidiary seconds; world time display (second time zone)
Case: stainless steel, ø 40 mm, height 10.85 mm; sapphire crystal; transparent case back; water-resistant to 3 atm
Band: horse leather, pin buckle
Price: $4,920

Lambda Roségold

Reference number: 932
Movement: manually wound, Nomos Caliber DUW 1001; ø 32 mm, height 3.6 mm; 29 jewels; 21,600 vph; screw balance with swan-neck fine regulation; twin mainspring barrels; 84-hour power reserve
Functions: hours, minutes, subsidiary seconds; power reserve indicator
Case: rose gold, ø 42 mm, height 8.9 mm; sapphire crystal; transparent case back; water-resistant to 3 atm
Band: horse leather, buckle clasp
Price: $18,500

DUW 1001

Manually wound; swan-neck fine regulation; twin mainspring barrels, 84-hour power reserve
Functions: hours, minutes, subsidiary seconds; power reserve indicator
Diameter: 32 mm
Height: 3.6 mm
Jewels: 29, including 5 screw-mounted gold chatons
Balance: screw balance
Frequency: 21,600 vph
Balance spring: Nivarox 1A
Shock protection: Incabloc
Remarks: hand-engraved balance cock, beveled and polished edges, rhodium-plated movement surfaces with Glashütte sun-brushing and perlage

DUW 4401

Manually wound; single spring barrel, 42-hour power reserve
Functions: hours, minutes, subsidiary seconds; power reserve indicator; date
Diameter: 32.1 mm
Height: 2.8 mm
Jewels: 23
Balance: in-house manufacture
Frequency: 21,600 vph
Balance spring: tempered blue
Shock protection: Incabloc
Remarks: three-quarter plate, movement surfaces rhodium-plated, with Glashütte ribbing and perlage

DUW 3001

Automatic; single spring barrel, 42-hour power reserve
Functions: hours, minutes, subsidiary seconds
Diameter: 28.8 mm
Height: 3.2 mm
Jewels: 27
Balance: in-house manufacture
Frequency: 21,600 vph
Balance spring: tempered blue
Shock protection: Incabloc
Remarks: three-quarter plate, movement surfaces rhodium-plated, with Glashütte ribbing and perlage

OMEGA

Omega has played a major role in the history of the watch business in Switzerland. The brand was founded in 1848. In 1930, it merged with Tissot to form SIHH, which in turn merged with watch conglomerate ASUAG to form the Swatch Group in 1983, of which Omega was the leading brand. In the 1990s, the brand managed to expand incrementally into the Chinese market and thus established a firm foothold in Asia. This also led to a steep growth in production numbers, putting it neck and neck with Rolex.

Today Omega is back in the competition, with technology as the key. It introduced the innovative coaxial escapement to several collections, which has pushed the brand back among the technological front-runners in its market segment. Swatch Group subsidiary Nivarox-FAR has finally mastered the production of the difficult, oil-free parts of the system designed by Englishman George Daniels, although the escapement continues to include lubrication, as the long-term results of "dry" coaxial movements are less than satisfactory. Thus, the most important plus for this escapement design remains high rate stability after careful regulation. Omega has even revived the Ladymatic, adding a silicon spring and the trademark coaxial escapement.

A few years ago, Omega officially unveiled a brand-new 15,000-gauss amagnetic movement, a technological innovation that is gradually being added to all new movements. Indeed, in the past two years, Omega has presented no fewer than eight new "Master Chronometer" movements. These not only meet the stringent requirements set out by the COSC but also have to pass the tests developed by Switzerland's Federal Institute of Metrology (METAS). The testing and certification process is performed in the new production building at the entirely renovated Swatch Group premises in Bienne/Biel. After promulgating the benefits of decentralization for years, Omega appears to be returning to the good old *manufacture* system of all crafts under a single roof.

Omega SA
Jakob-Stämpfli-Strasse 96
CH-2502 Biel/Bienne
Switzerland

Tel.:
+41-32-343-9211

E-mail:
info@omegawatches.com

Website:
www.omegawatches.com

Founded:
1848

U.S. distributor:
Omega
A division of The Swatch Group (U.S.), Inc.
1200 Harbor Boulevard
Weehawken, NJ 07086
201-271-1400
www.omegawatches.com

Seamaster Aqua Terra Master Chronometer

Reference number: 220.10.41.21.01.001
Movement: automatic, Omega Caliber 8900; ø 29 mm, height 5.5 mm; 39 jewels; 25,200 vph; 2 spring barrels, coaxial escapement, silicon balance and hairspring, amagnetic to 15,000 gauss; certified chronometer (METAS); 60-hour power reserve
Functions: hours, minutes, sweep seconds; date
Case: stainless steel, ø 41 mm, height 13.2 mm; sapphire crystal; transparent case back; screw-in crown; water-resistant to 15 atm
Band: stainless steel, folding clasp
Price: $5,500
Variations: various dial colors; calfskin strap; rubber strap

Seamaster Aqua Terra Master Chronometer

Reference number: 220.13.41.21.03.002
Movement: automatic, Omega Caliber 8900; ø 29 mm, height 5.5 mm; 39 jewels; 25,200 vph; 2 spring barrels, coaxial escapement, silicon balance and hairspring, amagnetic to 15,000 gauss; certified chronometer (METAS); 60-hour power reserve
Functions: hours, minutes, sweep seconds; date
Case: stainless steel, ø 41 mm, height 13.2 mm; sapphire crystal; transparent case back; screw-in crown; water-resistant to 15 atm
Band: reptile skin, folding clasp
Price: $5,400
Variations: various dial colors; stainless steel bracelet; rubber strap

Seamaster Aqua Terra Master Chronometer

Reference number: 220.12.38.20.02.001
Movement: automatic, Omega Caliber 8800; ø 26 mm, height 4.6 mm; 35 jewels; 25,200 vph; 2 spring barrels, coaxial escapement, silicon balance and hairspring, amagnetic to 15,000 gauss; certified chronometer (METAS); 55-hour power reserve
Functions: hours, minutes, sweep seconds; date
Case: Stainless steel, ø 38 mm, height 12.26 mm; sapphire crystal; transparent case back; screw-in crown; water-resistant to 15 atm
Band: rubber, folding clasp
Price: $5,400
Variations: various dial colors; calfskin strap; stainless steel bracelet

Seamaster Aqua Terra

Reference number: 231.10.42.21.03.003
Movement: automatic, Omega Caliber 8500;
ø 29 mm, height 5.5 mm; 39 jewels; 25,200 vph;
coaxial escapement, silicon balance and hairspring,
amagnetic to 15,000 gauss; 60-hour power reserve;
COSC-certified chronometer
Functions: hours, minutes, sweep seconds; date
Case: stainless steel, ø 41.5 mm, height 12.95 mm;
sapphire crystal; water-resistant to 15 atm
Band: stainless steel, folding clasp
Price: $6,000
Variations: various dials; leather strap; pink gold
bezel; in yellow gold

Seamaster Aqua Terra Annual Calendar

Reference number: 231.10.43.22.02.003
Movement: automatic, Omega Caliber 8602;
ø 29 mm, height 6.5 mm; 39 jewels; 25,200 vph;
coaxial escapement, silicon balance and hairspring;
60-hour power reserve; COSC-certified chronometer
Functions: hours, minutes, sweep seconds; annual
calendar with date, weekday
Case: stainless steel, ø 43 mm, height 14.3 mm;
sapphire crystal; transparent case back; screw-in
crown; water-resistant to 15 atm
Band: stainless steel, folding clasp
Price: $8,600
Variations: pink gold bezel; in pink gold

Seamaster Aqua Terra GMT

Reference number: 231.13.43.22.01.001
Movement: automatic, Omega Caliber 8605;
ø 29 mm, height 6 mm; 38 jewels; 25,200 vph;
2 spring barrels, coaxial escapement, silicon balance
and balance spring, amagnetic to 15,000 gauss;
60-hour power reserve; certified chronometer (METAS)
Functions: hours, minutes, sweep seconds; second
24-hour display (second time zone); date
Case: stainless steel, ø 43 mm, height 14.15 mm;
sapphire crystal; transparent case back; screw-in
crown; water-resistant to 15 atm
Band: reptile skin, folding clasp
Price: $7,800
Variations: stainless-steel bracelet; pink gold bezel;
in pink gold

Seamaster Aqua Terra Master Chronometer

Reference number: 220.25.34.20.55.001
Movement: automatic, Omega Caliber 8800;
ø 26 mm, height 4.6 mm; 35 jewels; 25,200 vph;
coaxial escapement, silicon balance and hairspring,
amagnetic to 15,000 gauss; 55-hour power reserve;
certified chronometer (METAS)
Functions: hours, minutes, sweep seconds; date
Case: stainless steel, ø 34 mm, height 11.88 mm;
rose gold bezel, set with diamonds; sapphire crystal;
rose gold crown; water-resistant to 15 atm
Band: stainless steel with rose gold elements,
folding clasp
Remarks: mother-of-pearl dial set with 11 diamonds
Price: $17,300
Variations: stainless steel bezel without diamonds

Seamaster Aqua Terra

Reference number: 220.10.28.60.60.001
Movement: quartz
Functions: hours, minutes
Case: stainless steel, ø 28 mm, height 9.51 mm;
sapphire crystal; water-resistant to 15 atm
Band: stainless steel, folding clasp
Remarks: dial set with 4 diamonds
Price: $2,800
Variations: various dials

Seamaster Aqua Terra Railmaster

Reference number: 220.10.40.20.01.001
Movement: automatic, Omega Caliber 8806;
ø 26 mm, height 4.6 mm; 35 jewels; 25,200 vph;
coaxial escapement, silicon balance and hairspring,
amagnetic to 15,000 gauss; 55-hour power reserve;
certified chronometer (METAS)
Functions: hours, minutes, sweep seconds
Case: stainless steel, ø 40 mm, height 12.65 mm;
sapphire crystal; water-resistant to 15 atm
Band: stainless steel, folding clasp
Price: $5,000
Variations: various dials; calfskin strap; textile strap

Seamaster Planet Ocean Master Chronometer

Reference number: 215.30.44.21.01.002
Movement: automatic, Omega Caliber 8900;
ø 29 mm, height 5.5 mm; 39 jewels; 25,200 vph;
2 spring barrels, coaxial escapement, silicon balance
and hairspring, amagnetic to 15,000 gauss; 60-hour
power reserve; certified chronometer (METAS)
Functions: hours, minutes, sweep seconds; date
Case: stainless steel, ø 43.5 mm, height 16.04 mm;
unidirectional bezel with ceramic insert and 0-60
scale; sapphire crystal; transparent case back; screw-in
crown; helium valve; water-resistant to 60 atm
Band: stainless steel, folding clasp
Price: $6,550
Variations: rubber strap; reptile skin strap

Seamaster Planet Ocean Deep Black Master Chronometer

Reference number: 215.92.46.22.01.001
Movement: automatic, Omega Caliber 8906;
ø 29 mm, height 6 mm; 38 jewels; 25,200 vph;
2 spring barrels, coaxial escapement, silicon balance
and hairspring, amagnetic to 15,000 gauss; 60-hour
power reserve; certified chronometer (METAS)
Functions: hours, minutes, sweep seconds; second
24-hour display (second time zone); date
Case: ceramic, ø 43.5 mm, height 17.04 mm;
bidirectionally rotating bezel with 0-60 scale;
sapphire crystal; screw-in crown; helium valve; water-
resistant to 60 atm
Band: textile, folding clasp
Price: $11,700

Seamaster Planet Ocean Pyeong Chang 2018

Reference number: 522.32.44.21.03.001
Movement: automatic, Omega Caliber 8900;
ø 29 mm, height 5.5 mm; 39 jewels; 25,200 vph;
2 spring barrels, coaxial escapement, silicon balance
and hairspring, amagnetic to 15,000 gauss; 60-hour
power reserve; certified chronometer (METAS)
Functions: hours, minutes, sweep seconds; date
Case: stainless steel, ø 43.5 mm, height 16.04 mm;
unidirectional bezel with ceramic insert and 0-60
scale; sapphire crystal; transparent case back;
screw-in crown; helium valve; water-resistant to
60 atm
Band: rubber, folding clasp
Price: $6,950; limited to 2,018 pieces

Constellation

Reference number: 127.10.27.20.52.001
Movement: automatic, Omega Caliber 8700;
ø 20 mm, height 5.3 mm; 28 jewels; 25,200 vph;
coaxial escapement, silicon balance and hairspring,
amagnetic to 15,000 gauss; 50-hour power reserve;
certified chronometer (METAS)
Functions: hours, minutes, sweep seconds; date
Case: stainless steel, ø 27 mm, height 12.25 mm;
sapphire crystal; water-resistant to 10 atm
Band: stainless steel, folding clasp
Remarks: dial set with 11 diamonds
Price: $7,650

Globemaster Master Chronometer

Reference number: 130.33.39.21.03.001
Movement: automatic, Omega Caliber 8901;
ø 29 mm, height 5.5 mm; 39 jewels; 25,200 vph;
coaxial escapement, silicon balance and hairspring,
amagnetic to 15,000 gauss; 60-hour power reserve;
certified chronometer (METAS)
Functions: hours, minutes, sweep seconds; date
Case: stainless steel, ø 39 mm, height 12.53 mm;
sapphire crystal; water-resistant to 10 atm
Band: reptile skin, folding clasp
Price: $6,900
Variations: various dials; stainless steel bracelet;
pink gold bezel; in pink gold

De Ville Prestige

Reference number: 424.13.40.20.02.005
Movement: automatic, Omega Caliber 2500;
ø 25.6 mm, height 4.1 mm; 27 jewels; 25,200 vph;
coaxial escapement; 48-hour power reserve; COSC-
certified chronometer
Functions: hours, minutes, sweep seconds; date
Case: stainless steel, ø 39.5 mm, height 10.1 mm;
sapphire crystal; transparent case back; water-
resistant to 3 atm
Band: reptile skin, folding clasp
Price: $3,600
Variations: stainless steel bracelet; pink gold or
yellow gold bezel

Speedmaster Ladies' Co-Axial Chronometer

Reference number: 324.28.38.50.02.002
Movement: automatic, Omega Caliber 3330;
ø 30 mm, height 7.9 mm; 31 jewels; 28,800 vph;
coaxial escapement, silicon balance and hairspring;
52-hour power reserve; COSC-certified chronometer
Functions: hours, minutes, subsidiary seconds;
chronograph; date
Case: stainless steel, ø 38 mm, height 14.7 mm;
pink gold bezel set with diamonds; sapphire crystal;
transparent case back; water-resistant to 10 atm
Band: reptile skin, folding clasp
Price: $9,300
Variations: various dials

Speedmaster Ladies' Co-Axial Chronometer

Reference number: 324.30.38.50.06.001
Movement: automatic, Omega Caliber 3330;
ø 27 mm, height 7.9 mm; 31 jewels; 28,800 vph;
coaxial escapement, silicon balance and hairspring;
52-hour power reserve; COSC-certified chronometer
Functions: hours, minutes, subsidiary seconds;
chronograph; date
Case: stainless steel, ø 38 mm, height 14.7 mm;
bezel with ceramic insert; sapphire crystal;
transparent case back; water-resistant to 10 atm
Band: stainless steel, folding clasp
Price: $4,900

Speedmaster Moonphase

Reference number: 304.33.44.52.03.001
Movement: automatic, Omega Caliber 9904;
ø 32.5 mm, height 8.35 mm; 54 jewels; 28,800 vph;
2 spring barrels, coaxial escapement, silicon balance
and hairspring, amagnetic to 15,000 gauss; 60-hour
power reserve; certified chronometer (METAS)
Functions: hours, minutes, subsidiary seconds;
chronograph; date, moon phase
Case: stainless steel, ø 44.25 mm, height 16.85 mm
bezel with ceramic insert; sapphire crystal; water-
resistant to 10 atm
Band: reptile skin, folding clasp
Price: $10,600

Speedmaster Racing Master Chronometer

Reference number: 329.32.44.51.01.001
Movement: automatic, Omega Caliber 9900;
ø 32.5 mm, height 7.6 mm; 54 jewels; 28,800 vph;
2 spring barrels, coaxial escapement, silicon balance
and hairspring, amagnetic to 15,000 gauss; 60-hour
power reserve; certified chronometer (METAS)
Functions: hours, minutes, subsidiary seconds;
chronograph; date
Case: stainless steel, ø 44.25 mm, height 14.9 mm;
ceramic bezel; sapphire crystal; water-resistant to 5 atm
Band: calfskin, folding clasp
Price: $8,450
Variations: various dials; reptile skin strap; stainless
steel bracelet

Speedmaster Racing Master Chronometer

Reference number: 329.32.44.51.06.001
Movement: automatic, Omega Caliber 9900;
ø 32.5 mm, height 7.6 mm; 54 jewels; 28,800 vph;
2 spring barrels, coaxial escapement, silicon balance
and hairspring, amagnetic to 15,000 gauss; 60-hour
power reserve; certified chronometer (METAS)
Functions: hours, minutes, subsidiary seconds;
chronograph; date
Case: stainless steel, ø 44.25 mm, height 14.9 mm;
ceramic bezel; sapphire crystal; water-resistant to 5 atm
Band: calfskin, folding clasp
Price: $8,450
Variations: various dials; reptile skin strap; stainless
steel bracelet

Speedmaster '57

Reference number: 331.10.42.51.01.002
Movement: automatic, Omega Caliber 9300;
ø 32.5 mm, height 7.6 mm; 54 jewels; 28,800 vph;
coaxial escapement, silicon balance and hairspring;
60-hour power reserve; COSC-certified chronometer
Functions: hours, minutes, subsidiary seconds;
chronograph; date
Case: stainless steel, ø 41.5 mm, height 16.17 mm;
sapphire crystal; water-resistant to 10 atm
Band: stainless steel, folding clasp
Price: $9,000
Variations: various dials; calfskin strap; in pink gold,
in yellow gold

9300

Automatic; coaxial escapement; column wheel control of chronograph functions; double mainspring barrel, 60-hour power reserve; COSC-certified chronometer
Functions: hours, minutes, subsidiary seconds; chronograph; date
Diameter: 32.5 mm
Height: 7.7 mm
Jewels: 54
Balance: silicon, without regulator
Frequency: 28,800 vph
Balance spring: silicon
Shock protection: Nivachoc
Remarks: mainplate, bridges, and rotor with "arabesque" côtes de Genève, blackened balance and screws

9900

Automatic; coaxial escapement; column wheel control of chronograph functions; amagnetic to 15,000 gauss; certified chronometer (METAS); double mainspring barrel, 60-hour power reserve
Functions: hours, minutes, subsidiary seconds; chronograph; date
Diameter: 32.5 mm
Height: 7.6 mm
Jewels: 54
Balance: silicon, without regulator
Frequency: 28,800 vph
Balance spring: silicon
Shock protection: Nivachoc
Remarks: mainplate, bridges, and rotor with "arabesque" côtes de Genève, blackened balance and screws

3313

Automatic; coaxial escapement; column wheel control of chronograph functions; single spring barrel, 52-hour power reserve; COSC-certified chronometer
Functions: hours, minutes, subsidiary seconds; chronograph; date
Diameter: 27 mm
Height: 6.85 mm
Jewels: 37
Balance: without regulator
Frequency: 28,800 vph
Balance spring: freely oscillating
Remarks: perlage on plate, bridges and balance cock with côtes de Genève, gold-plated engravings; rotor hub screw of blued steel

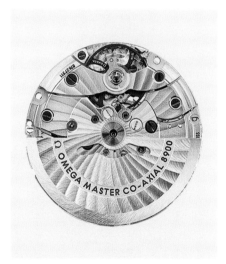

8900

Automatic; coaxial escapement; protected from magnetic fields up to 15,000 gauss, certified chronometer (METAS); double mainspring barrel, 60-hour power reserve
Functions: hours, minutes, sweep seconds; date
Diameter: 29 mm
Height: 5.5 mm
Jewels: 39
Balance: silicon, without regulator
Frequency: 25,200 vph
Balance spring: silicon
Shock protection: Nivachoc
Remarks: mainplate, bridges and rotor with "arabesque" côtes de Genève, rhodium-plated, blackened spring barrels, balance, and screws

8801

Automatic; coaxial escapement; protected from magnetic fields up to 15,000 gauss, certified chronometer (METAS); single spring barrel, 55-hour power reserve
Functions: hours, minutes, subsidiary seconds; date
Jewels: 35
Balance: silicon, without regulator
Frequency: 25,200 vph
Balance spring: silicon
Shock protection: Nivachoc
Remarks: gold rotor, gold balance wheel bridge, blackened screws

1861

Manually wound; single spring barrel, 48-hour power reserve
Base caliber: Lémania 1873
Functions: hours, minutes, subsidiary seconds; chronograph
Diameter: 27 mm
Height: 6.87 mm
Jewels: 18
Frequency: 21,600 vph
Balance spring: flat hairspring
Remarks: rhodium-plated, gold-plated engravings

Oris SA
Ribigasse 1
CH-4434 Hölstein
Switzerland

Tel.:
+41-61-956-1111

E-mail:
info@oris

Website:
www.oris.ch

Founded:
1904

Number of employees:
90

U.S. distributor:
Oris Watches USA
50 Washington Street, Suite 412
Norwalk, CT 06854
203-857-4769; 203-857-4782 (fax)

Most important collections/price range:
Diver, Big Crown, Artelier, Aquis, Williams /
approx. $1,100 to $5,500

ORIS

Oris has been producing mechanical watches in the little town of Hölstein in northwestern Switzerland, near Basel, since 1904, so 2014 was a celebratory year. The brand's strategy has always been to keep prices low and quality high, so Oris has managed to expand in a segment relinquished by other big-name competitors as they sought their fortune in the higher-end markets. The result has been growing international success for Oris, whose portfolio is divided into four "product worlds," each with its own distinct identity: aviation, motor sports, diving, and culture. In utilizing specific materials—a tungsten bezel for the divers, for example—and functions based on these types, Oris makes certain that each will fit perfectly into the world for which it was designed. Yet the heart of every watch houses a small, high-quality "high-mech" movement identifiable by the brand's standard red rotor.

The brand surprised everyone for its 110th birthday by signing off on in-house Caliber 110, an unembellished and technically efficient manually wound movement. In 2015 came the Caliber 111. These movements are special: In collaboration with the engineers from the Technical College of Le Locle, Oris developed a massive barrel spring containing a 6-foot (1.8-m) spring. With numerous trials and lots of tweaking, the unwinding of this very long spring was optimized, providing a full ten days of power of even torque. The power reserve indicator on the right of the dial does not move evenly, however, due to the transmission ratio. Toward the end, the markers are somewhat longer to give a more accurate idea of the remaining power in the spring. Following the Caliber 112 with GMT function and day/night indication, Oris added a fourth in-house caliber, 113, this time with a clever sweep hand indication of calendar weeks that also shows the month. Add to that the apertures for date and day of the week, and you have a complete calendar for businesspeople and others who need to stay dialed in to the date.

Artelier Calibre 113

Reference number: 113 7738 4031
Movement: manually wound, Oris Caliber 113; ø 34 mm, height 6.65 mm; 40 jewels; 21,600 vph; 240-hour power reserve
Functions: hours, minutes, subsidiary seconds; power reserve indicator; full calendar with date, weekday, weeks of the year
Case: stainless steel, ø 43 mm, height 13.05 mm; sapphire crystal; transparent case back; water-resistant to 5 atm
Band: reptile skin, folding clasp
Price: $6,300
Variations: anthracite-colored dial; stainless steel bracelet

Artelier Calibre 113

Reference number: 113 7738 4063
Movement: manually wound, Oris Caliber 113; ø 34 mm, height 6.65 mm; 40 jewels; 21,600 vph; 240-hour power reserve
Functions: hours, minutes, subsidiary seconds; power reserve indicator; full calendar with date, weekday, weeks of the year
Case: stainless steel, ø 43 mm, height 13.05 mm; sapphire crystal; transparent case back; water-resistant to 5 atm
Band: reptile skin, folding clasp
Price: $6,300
Variations: opal-colored dial; stainless steel bracelet

Artelier Caliber 112

Reference number: 112 7726 4055
Movement: manually wound, Oris Caliber 112; ø 34 mm, height 6.4 mm; 40 jewels; 21,600 vph; 240-hour power reserve
Functions: hours, minutes, subsidiary seconds; additional 12-hour display (second time zone), day/night indicator, power reserve indicator; date
Case: stainless steel, ø 43 mm, height 12.7 mm; sapphire crystal; transparent case back; water-resistant to 5 atm
Band: reptile skin, folding clasp
Price: $6,700
Variations: white dial; stainless steel bracelet

Big Crown 1917 Limited Edition

Reference number: 732 7736 4081
Movement: automatic, Oris Caliber 732 (base Sellita SW200-1); ø 25.6 mm, height 4.6 mm; 26 jewels; 28,800 vph; 38-hour power reserve
Functions: hours, minutes
Case: stainless steel, ø 40 mm, height 12.2 mm; sapphire crystal; water-resistant to 5 atm
Band: calfskin, buckle
Price: $2,600; limited to 1,917 pieces

Big Crown ProPilot Caliber 111

Reference number: 111 7711 4163
Movement: manually wound, Oris Caliber 111; ø 34 mm, height 6 mm; 40 jewels; 21,600 vph; 240-hour power reserve
Functions: hours, minutes, subsidiary seconds; power reserve indicator; date
Case: stainless steel, ø 44 mm, height 13.7 mm; sapphire crystal; screw-in crown; water-resistant to 10 atm
Band: reptile skin, folding clasp
Price: $5,600
Variations: stainless steel bracelet ($5,300); textile strap ($5,600)

Big Crown ProPilot Chronograph

Reference number: 774 7699 4063
Movement: automatic, Oris Caliber 774 (base Sellita SW500-1); ø 30 mm, height 7.9 mm; 25 jewels; 28,800 vph; 48-hour power reserve
Functions: hours, minutes, subsidiary seconds; chronograph; date
Case: stainless steel, ø 44 mm, height 15.5 mm; sapphire crystal; transparent case back; screw-in crown; water-resistant to 10 atm
Band: calfskin, folding clasp
Price: $3,400 on leather
Variations: textile strap ($3,400); stainless steel bracelet ($3,600)

Big Crown ProPilot GMT, Small Second

Reference number: 748 7710 4063
Movement: automatic, Oris Caliber 748 (base Sellita SW500-1); ø 32.2 mm, height 5.5 mm; 28 jewels; 28,800 vph; 38-hour power reserve
Functions: hours, minutes, subsidiary seconds; second 24-hour display (second time zone); date
Case: stainless steel, ø 45 mm, height 12.9 mm; sapphire crystal; transparent case back; screw-in crown; water-resistant to 10 atm
Band: calfskin, folding clasp
Price: $2,300 on leather
Variations: textile strap ($2,300); stainless steel bracelet ($2,500)

Divers Sixty-Five

Reference number: 733 7720 4051
Movement: automatic, Oris Caliber 733 (base Sellita SW200-1); ø 25.6 mm, height 4.6 mm; 26 jewels; 28,800 vph; 38-hour power reserve
Functions: hours, minutes, sweep seconds; date
Case: stainless steel, ø 42 mm, height 13.2 mm; unidirectional bezel, with 0-60 scale; sapphire crystal; screw-in crown; water-resistant to 10 atm
Band: calfskin, buckle
Price: $1,990
Variations: various colors; textile strap; rubber strap; stainless steel bracelet ($2,300)

Aquis Date

Reference number: 733 7730 4154
Movement: automatic, Oris Caliber 733 (base Sellita SW200-1); ø 25.6 mm, height 4.6 mm; 26 jewels; 28,800 vph; 38-hour power reserve
Functions: hours, minutes, sweep seconds; date
Case: stainless steel, ø 43.5 mm, height 12.65 mm; unidirectional bezel, with 0-60 scale; sapphire crystal; screw-in crown; water-resistant to 30 atm
Band: stainless steel, folding clasp
Price: $1,850 on leather, $2,000 on metal bracelet
Variations: rubber strap ($1,800)

Regulateur "Master Diver"

Reference number: 749 7734 7154
Movement: automatic, Oris Caliber 749 (base Sellita SW220-1); ø 25.6 mm, height 5.05 mm; 28 jewels; 28,800 vph; 38-hour power reserve
Functions: hours (off-center), minutes, subsidiary seconds; date
Case: titanium, ø 43.5 mm, height 12.65 mm; unidirectional bezel, with 0-60 scale; sapphire crystal; screw-in crown; helium valve; water-resistant to 30 atm
Band: titanium, folding clasp
Remarks: comes with additional rubber strap
Price: $3,350

Hammerhead Limited Edition

Reference number: 752 7733 4183
Movement: automatic, Oris Caliber 752; ø 32.2 mm, height 5.25 mm; 26 jewels; 28,800 vph; 38-hour power reserve
Functions: hours, minutes, sweep seconds; date, weekday
Case: stainless steel, ø 45.5 mm, height 15.25 mm; unidirectional bezel, with 0-60 scale; sapphire crystal; screw-in crown; water-resistant to 50 atm
Band: stainless steel, folding clasp
Price: $2,750; limited to 2,000 pieces
Variations: rubber strap ($2,550)

Staghorn Restoration Ltd. Edition

Reference number: 735 7734 4185
Movement: automatic, Oris Caliber 735 (base Sellita SW220-1); ø 25.6 mm, height 5.05 mm; 26 jewels; 28,800 vph; 38-hour power reserve
Functions: hours, minutes, sweep seconds; date, weekday
Case: stainless steel, ø 43.5 mm, height 12.85 mm; unidirectional ceramic bezel with 0-60 scale; sapphire crystal; water-resistant to 50 atm
Band: stainless steel, folding clasp, safety lock and extension link
Remarks: part of sales revenue goes to protection of coral reefs
Price: $2,400; limited to 2,000 pieces
Variations: rubber strap ($2,200)

Williams Engine Date

Reference number: 733 7740 4154
Movement: automatic, Oris Caliber 733 (base Sellita SW200-1); ø 25.6 mm, height 4.6 mm; 26 jewels; 28,800 vph; 38-hour power reserve
Functions: hours, minutes, sweep seconds; date
Case: stainless steel, ø 42 mm, height 11.55 mm; sapphire crystal; water-resistant to 10 atm
Band: rubber, folding clasp
Remarks: skeletonized dial
Price: $1,650
Variations: stainless steel bracelet ($1,850)

Chronoris Williams 40th Anniversary Limited Edition

Reference number: 673 7739 4084
Movement: automatic, Oris Caliber 673 (base ETA 7750); ø 30 mm, height 7.9 mm; 25 jewels; 28,800 vph; 48-hour power reserve
Functions: hours, minutes; chronograph; date
Case: stainless steel, ø 40 mm, height 15.4 mm; sapphire crystal; water-resistant to 10 atm
Band: stainless steel, folding clasp
Price: $3,950 on metal bracelet
Variations: textile strap ($3,700); rubber strap ($3,700); calfskin strap ($3,700)

Chronoris Date

Reference number: 733 7737 4053
Movement: automatic, Oris Caliber 733 (base Sellita SW200-1); ø 25.6 mm, height 4.6 mm; 26 jewels; 28,800 vph; 38-hour power reserve
Functions: hours, minutes, sweep seconds; date
Case: stainless steel, ø 39 mm, height 12.3 mm; crown-controlled scale ring, with 0-60 scale; sapphire crystal; water-resistant to 10 atm
Band: stainless steel, folding clasp
Price: $1,750
Variations: stainless steel Milanese bracelet ($1,950); textile or calfskin strap ($1,750)

PANERAI

Officine Panerai
Viale Monza, 259
I-20126 Milan
Italy

Tel.:
+39-02-363-138

Fax:
+39-02-363-13-297

Website:
www.panerai.com

Founded:
1860 in Florence, Italy

Number of employees:
approx. 250

U.S. distributor:
Panerai
645 Fifth Avenue
New York, NY 10022
877-PANERAI
concierge.usa@panerai.com; www.panerai.com

Most important collections/price range:
Luminor / $5,000 to $25,000; Luminor 1950 /
$8,000 to $30,000; Radiomir / $7,000 to
$25,000; Radiomir 1940 / $8,000 to $133,000;
special editions / $10,000 to $125,000; clocks
and instruments / $20,000 to $250,000

Officine Panerai (in English: Panerai Workshops) joined the Richemont Group in 1997. Since then, it has made an unprecedented rise from an insider niche brand to a lifestyle phenomenon. The company, founded in 1860 by Giovanni Panerai, supplied the Italian navy with precision instruments. In the 1930s, the Florentine engineers developed a series of waterproof wristwatches that could be used by commandos under especially extreme and risky conditions. After 1997, under the leadership of Angelo Bonati, the company came out with a collection of oversize wristwatches, both stylistically and technically based on these historical models.

In 2002, Panerai opened a *manufacture* in Neuchâtel, and by 2005 it was already producing its own movements (caliber family P.2000). In 2009, the new "little" Panerai *manufacture* movements (caliber family P.9000) were released. From the start, the idea behind them was to provide a competitive alternative to the base movements available until a couple of years ago. In 2014, a new *manufacture* was inaugurated in Neuchâtel to handle development, manufacturing, assembly, and quality control under one roof.

Parallel to consolidating, the brand has been steadily expanding its portfolio of new calibers. Fairly early on, it came out with an automatic chronograph with a flyback function, the P.9100. This was followed by a new caliber, the P.5000, in 2013, with an eight-day power reserve and manual winding, two features that have been with the brand ever since it received its first commissions from the Italian navy. In 2014, came caliber P.4000, with an off-center winding rotor. At 3.95 millimeters, it is very thin for Panerai, but then again, it was developed for a new set of models.

In 2016, the company updated its cases and added the P.4001 and P.4002 calibers to the P.4000 family. The new calibers featured a date function and a power reserve display. The new three-day automatic movement, P.9010, is particularly thin. It will go into a new generation of elegant Panerais with additional comfort for the wearer.

Luminor Submersible 1950 3 Days Automatic Acciaio
Reference number: PAM00682
Movement: automatic, Panerai Caliber P.9010; ø 31.1 mm, height 6 mm; 31 jewels; 28,800 vph; 72-hour power reserve
Functions: hours, minutes, subsidiary seconds; date
Case: stainless steel, ø 42 mm; unidirectional bezel with 0-60 scale; sapphire crystal; crown protector with hinged lever; water-resistant to 30 atm
Band: rubber, buckle
Price: $8,700
Variations: pink gold with ceramic bezel ($26,700)

Luminor Submersible 1950 3 Days Automatic Oro Rosso
Reference number: PAM00684
Movement: automatic, Panerai Caliber P.9010; ø 31.1 mm, height 6 mm; 31 jewels; 28,800 vph; 72-hour power reserve
Functions: hours, minutes, subsidiary seconds; date
Case: pink gold, ø 42 mm; unidirectional ceramic bezel with 0-60 scale; sapphire crystal; crown protector with hinged lever; water-resistant to 10 atm
Band: rubber, buckle
Price: $26,700
Variations: stainless steel ($8,700)

Luminor Submersible 1950 BMG-TECH 3 Days Automatic
Reference number: PAM00692
Movement: automatic, Panerai Caliber P.9010; ø 31.1 mm, height 6 mm; 31 jewels; 28,800 vph; 72-hour power reserve
Functions: hours, minutes, subsidiary seconds; date
Case: composite material, BMG technology (alloy of zirconium, copper, aluminum, titanium, nickel), ø 47 mm; unidirectional bezel, with 0-60 scale; sapphire crystal; crown protector with hinged lever; water-resistant to 30 atm
Band: rubber, buckle
Price: $10,200

LAB-ID Luminor 1950 Carbotech 3 Days

Reference number: PAM00700
Movement: manually wound, Panerai Caliber P.3001/C; ø 37.2 mm, height 6.5 mm; 21,600 vph; mainplate, bridges, and spring barrel of tantalum-ceramic-carbon nanofibers with lubricant-free bearing positions, silicon escapement; carbon nanofiber dial; 72-hour power reserve
Functions: hours, minutes, subsidiary seconds; power reserve indicator (on the rear)
Case: carbon fiber (Carbotech), ø 49 mm; sapphire crystal; transparent case back; crown protector with hinged lever; water-resistant to 10 atm
Band: calfskin, buckle
Remarks: 50-year guarantee
Price: $54,000 (est.); limited to 50 pieces

Luminor 1950 Regatta Oracle Team USA 3 Days Chrono Flyback Automatic Titanio

Reference number: PAM00726
Movement: automatic, Panerai Caliber P.9100/R; ø 31.1 mm, height 9.55 mm; 37 jewels; 28,800 vph; regatta countdown function up to 15 minutes; 2 spring barrels, 72-hour power reserve
Functions: hours, minutes, subsidiary seconds; flyback chronograph with countdown function
Case: titanium, ø 47 mm; sapphire crystal; crown protector with hinged lever; water-resistant to 10 atm
Band: calfskin, buckle
Remarks: special watch for USA Oracle team for their involvement in 35th America's Cup
Price: $8,100

Radiomir 3 Days Acciaio

Reference number: PAM00685
Movement: manually wound, Panerai Caliber P.3000; ø 37.2 mm, height 5.3 mm; 21 jewels; 21,600 vph; 2 spring barrels, 72-hour power reserve
Functions: hours, minutes
Case: stainless steel, ø 47 mm; sapphire crystal; transparent case back; water-resistant to 3 atm
Band: calfskin, buckle
Price: $9,800

Luminor 1950 Equation of Time 8 Days GMT Titanio

Reference number: PAM00670
Movement: manually wound, Panerai Caliber P.2002/E; ø 31.02 mm, height 8.35 mm; 31 jewels; 28,800 vph; 3 spring barrels, pull crown to reset second hand to zero; 192-hour power reserve
Functions: hours, minutes, subsidiary seconds; equation of time, power reserve indicator (on rear); date, month
Case: titanium, ø 47 mm; sapphire crystal; transparent case back; crown protector with hinged lever; water-resistant to 10 atm
Band: reptile skin, buckle
Price: $21,600

Radiomir Black Seal 8 Days Acciaio

Reference number: PAM00609
Movement: manually wound, Panerai Caliber P.5000; ø 34,97 mm, height 4.5 mm; 21 jewels; 21,600 vph; 2 spring barrels, screw balance; 192-hour power reserve
Functions: hours, minutes, subsidiary seconds
Case: stainless steel, ø 45 mm; sapphire crystal; transparent case back; water-resistant to 10 atm
Band: calfskin, buckle
Price: $6,000

Luminor Marina 8 Days Acciaio

Reference number: PAM00590
Movement: manually wound, Panerai Caliber P.5000; ø 34.97 mm, height 4.5 mm; 21 jewels; 21,600 vph; 2 spring barrels, screw balance; 192-hour power reserve
Functions: hours, minutes, subsidiary seconds
Case: stainless steel, ø 44 mm, height 13.6 mm; sapphire crystal; transparent case back; crown protector with hinged lever; water-resistant to 30 atm
Band: calfskin, buckle
Remarks: comes with additional bracelet
Price: $6,600

Radiomir 1940 3 Days GMT Automatic Acciaio

Reference number: PAM00657
Movement: automatic, Panerai Caliber P.4001; ø 30 mm, height 5.04 mm; 31 jewels; 28,800 vph; 2 spring barrels, microrotor; 72-hour power reserve
Functions: hours, minutes, subsidiary seconds; second 24-hour display, power reserve indicator (on case back); date
Case: stainless steel, ø 45 mm, height 13.9 mm; sapphire crystal; transparent case back; water-resistant to 10 atm
Band: calfskin, buckle
Price: $11,700

Luminor Due 3 Days Automatic Acciaio

Reference number: PAM00674
Movement: manually wound, Panerai Caliber P.4000; ø 31 mm, height 3.95 mm; 31 jewels; 28,800 vph; 2 spring barrels, 72-hour power reserve
Functions: hours, minutes, subsidiary seconds
Case: stainless steel, ø 45 mm; sapphire crystal; transparent case back; crown protector with hinged lever; water-resistant to 3 atm
Band: reptile skin, buckle
Price: $10,500
Variations: pink gold ($25,500)

Luminor Due 3 Days Oro Rosso

Reference number: PAM00677
Movement: manually wound, Panerai Caliber P.1000/10; ø 27.2 mm, height 3.85 mm; 21 jewels; 28,800 vph; 2 spring barrels, 72-hour power reserve
Functions: hours, minutes, subsidiary seconds
Case: pink gold, ø 42 mm; sapphire crystal; transparent case back; crown protector with hinged lever; water-resistant to 3 atm
Band: reptile skin, buckle
Price: $21,900
Variations: stainless steel ($7,900)

Luminor Marina 1950 3 Days Automatic Acciaio

Reference number: PAM01312
Movement: automatic, Panerai Caliber P.9010; ø 31.1 mm, height 6 mm; 31 jewels; 28,800 vph; 72-hour power reserve
Functions: hours, minutes, subsidiary seconds; date
Case: stainless steel, ø 44 mm; sapphire crystal; transparent case back; crown protector with hinged lever; water-resistant to 30 atm
Band: reptile skin, buckle
Price: $7,500

Luminor Marina 1950 3 Days Automatic Acciaio

Reference number: PAM01499
Movement: automatic, Panerai Caliber P.9010; ø 31.1 mm, height 6 mm; 31 jewels; 28,800 vph; 72-hour power reserve
Functions: hours, minutes, subsidiary seconds; date
Case: stainless steel, ø 44 mm; sapphire crystal; transparent case back; crown protector with hinged lever; water-resistant to 30 atm
Band: calfskin, buckle
Price: $7,500

Luminor Marina 1950 Carbotech 3 Days Automatic

Reference number: PAM00661
Movement: automatic, Panerai Caliber P.9010; ø 31.1 mm, height 6 mm; 31 jewels; 28,800 vph; 72-hour power reserve
Functions: hours, minutes, subsidiary seconds; date
Case: carbon fiber (Carbotech), ø 44 mm; sapphire crystal; crown protector with hinged lever; water-resistant to 30 atm
Band: calfskin, buckle
Price: $11,800

Caliber P.3001

Manually wound; 2 serially connected spring barrels, 72-hour power reserve
Functions: hours, minutes, subsidiary seconds; power reserve indicator (on rear)
Diameter: 37.2 mm
Height: 6.5 mm
Jewels: 21
Balance: glucydur
Frequency: 21,600 vph

Caliber P.4001

Automatic; 2 serially connected spring barrels, 72-hour power reserve
Functions: hours, minutes, subsidiary seconds; second 24-hour display (second time zone), power reserve indicator (on rear); date
Diameter: 30 mm
Height: 5.04 mm
Jewels: 31
Balance: glucydur
Frequency: 28,800 vph
Balance spring: flat hairspring
Shock protection: Kif
Remarks: 278 components

Caliber P.2002/E

Automatic; 3 serially connected spring barrels, 192-hour power reserve
Functions: hours, minutes, subsidiary seconds; equation of time, power reserve indicator (on rear); date, month
Diameter: 31.02 mm
Height: 8.35 mm
Jewels: 31
Balance: glucydur
Frequency: 28,800 vph
Shock protection: Kif
Remarks: pull crown to reset second hand to zero; 329 components

Caliber P.9010

Automatic; 2 serially connected spring barrels, 72-hour power reserve
Functions: hours, minutes, subsidiary seconds; date
Diameter: 31 mm
Height: 6 mm
Jewels: 31
Balance: glucydur
Frequency: 28,800 vph
Remarks: 200 components

Caliber P.9100/R

Automatic; 2 serially connected spring barrels, 72-hour power reserve
Functions: hours, minutes, subsidiary seconds; flyback chronograph with preprogrammed countdown function, precise to the minute
Diameter: 31.1 mm
Height: 9.55 mm
Jewels: 37
Balance: glucydur
Frequency: 28,800 vph
Balance spring: flat hairspring
Shock protection: Kif
Remarks: pull crown to reset second hand to zero; 328 components

Caliber P.5000

Manually wound; 2 serially connected spring barrels 192-hour power reserve
Functions: hours, minutes, subsidiary seconds
Diameter: 37.2 mm
Height: 4.5 mm
Jewels: 21
Balance: glucydur with weighted screws
Frequency: 21,600 vph
Balance spring: flat hairspring
Remarks: 127 components

PARMIGIANI

Parmigiani Fleurier SA
Rue du Temple 11
CH-2114 Fleurier
Switzerland

Tel.:
+41-32-862-6630

Fax:
+41-32-862-6631

E-mail:
info@parmigiani.ch

Website:
www.parmigiani.ch

What began as the undertaking of a single man—a gifted watchmaker and reputable restorer of complicated vintage timepieces—in the small town of Fleurier in Switzerland's Val de Travers has now grown into an empire of sorts comprising several factories and more than 400 employees.

Michel Parmigiani is in fact just doing what he has done since 1976, when he began restoring vintage works. An exceptional talent, his output soon attracted the attention of the Sandoz Family Foundation, an organization established in 1964 by a member of one of Switzerland's most famous families. The foundation bought 51 percent of Parmigiani Mesure et Art du Temps SA in 1996, turning what was practically a one-man show into a full-fledged and fully financed watch *manufacture*.

After the merger, Swiss suppliers were acquired by the partners, furthering the quest for horological autonomy. Atokalpa SA in Alle (Canton of Jura) manufactures parts such as pinions, wheels, and micro components. Bruno Affolter SA in La Chaux-de-Fonds produces precious metal cases, dials, and other specialty parts. Les Artisans Boitiers (LAB) and Quadrance et Habillage (Q&H) in La Chaux-de-Fonds manufacture cases out of precious metals and dials as well. Elwin SA in Moutier specializes in turned parts. In 2003, the movement development and production department officially separated from the rest as Vaucher Manufacture, now an autonomous entity.

Parmigiani has enjoyed great independence and, hence, strong growth, notably in the United States. The brand also set its sights on Latin America, notably Brazil, where it signed a partnership with the Confederação Brasileira de Futebol. In addition to making watches and unique pieces, like his famed Islamic clock based on a lunar calendar, Parmigiani also devotes a part of its premises to restoring ancient timepieces.

Founded:
1996

Number of employees:
520

Annual production:
approx. 4,000 watches

U.S. distributor:
Parmigiani Fleurier
Distribution Americas LLC
285 NW 26th Street
Miami, FL 33127
305-260-7770; 305-269-7770
americas@parmigiani.com

Most important collections/price range:
Kalpa, Tonda, Pershing, Toric, Bugatti / approx. $7,800 to $700,000 for *haute horlogerie* watches; no limit for unique models.

Tonda 1950
Reference number: PFC288-0000100-XA1442
Movement: automatic, Parmigiani Caliber PF702; ø 30 mm, height 2.6 mm; 21,600 vph; 48-hour power reserve
Functions: hours, minutes, subsidiary seconds
Case: stainless steel, ø 40 mm, height 8.2 mm; sapphire crystal; water-resistant to 3 atm
Band: reptile skin, folding clasp
Price: $9,500
Variations: black dial

Tonda 1950
Reference number: PFC288-0001400-XA1442
Movement: automatic, Parmigiani Caliber PF702; ø 30 mm, height 2.6 mm; 21,600 vph; 48-hour power reserve
Functions: hours, minutes, subsidiary seconds
Case: stainless steel, ø 40 mm, height 8.2 mm; sapphire crystal; water-resistant to 3 atm
Band: reptile skin, folding clasp
Price: $9,500
Variations: silver dial

Tonda Métrographe
Reference number: PFC274-0000100-XC1342
Movement: automatic, Parmigiani Caliber PF315; ø 28 mm, height 6 mm; 46 jewels; 28,800 vph; double spring barrel; finely finished with côtes de Genève; 42-hour power reserve
Functions: hours, minutes, subsidiary seconds; chronograph; date
Case: stainless steel, ø 40 mm, height 11.7 mm; sapphire crystal; transparent case back; water-resistant to 3 atm
Band: calfskin, folding clasp
Price: $11,500
Variations: black dial; stainless steel bracelet ($12,000)

Tonda Métrographe

Reference number: PFC274-0001404-B33002
Movement: automatic, Parmigiani Caliber PF315;
ø 28 mm, height 6 mm; 46 jewels; 28,800 vph;
double spring barrel; finely finished with côtes de
Genève; 42-hour power reserve
Functions: hours, minutes, subsidiary seconds;
chronograph; date
Case: stainless steel, ø 40 mm, height 11.7 mm;
sapphire crystal; transparent case back; water-
resistant to 3 atm
Band: stainless steel, folding clasp
Price: $12,000
Variations: silver dial; calfskin strap ($11,500)

Toric Chronomètre

Reference number: PFC423-1201400-HA1441
Movement: automatic, Parmigiani Caliber PF331;
ø 25.6 mm, height 3.5 mm; 28,800 vph; 55-hour
power reserve; COSC-certified chronometer
Functions: hours, minutes, sweep seconds; date
Case: white gold, ø 40.8 mm, height 9.5 mm;
sapphire crystal; water-resistant to 3 atm
Band: reptile skin, buckle
Price: $18,500
Variations: rose gold ($18,500)

Toric Chronomètre

Reference number: PFC423-1602400-HA1441
Movement: automatic, Parmigiani Caliber PF331;
ø 25.6 mm, height 3.5 mm; 28,800 vph; 55-hour
power reserve; COSC-certified chronometer
Functions: hours, minutes, sweep seconds; date
Case: rose gold, ø 40.8 mm, height 9.5 mm;
sapphire crystal; water-resistant to 3 atm
Band: reptile skin, buckle
Price: $18,500
Variations: white gold ($18,500)

Bugatti Aérolithe Performance

Reference number: PFC329-3001400-XC1442
Movement: automatic, Parmigiani Caliber PF335;
ø 30.3 mm, height 6.81 mm; 28,800 vph; 50-hour
power reserve
Functions: hours, minutes, subsidiary seconds;
flyback chronograph; date
Case: titanium, ø 41 mm, height 12.7 mm; sapphire
crystal; water-resistant to 3 atm
Band: calfskin, folding clasp
Price: $22,900

Kalpa XL Hebdomadaire Anniversaire

Reference number: PFC101-0004200-HA1442
Movement: manually wound, Parmigiani Caliber
PF110; 23.6 × 29.3 mm, height 4.9 mm; 28 jewels;
21,600 vph; double spring barrel, screw balance,
swan-neck fine regulation, mainplate and bridges in
rose gold; 192-hour power reserve
Functions: hours, minutes, subsidiary seconds;
power reserve indicator; date
Case: stainless steel, 37.2 × 44.7 mm, height
11.2 mm; sapphire crystal; transparent case back;
water-resistant to 3 atm
Band: reptile skin, folding clasp
Price: $65,000

Tonda 1950 Tourbillon

Reference number: PFH279-1000600-HA3141
Movement: automatic, Parmigiani Caliber PF517;
ø 32 mm, height 3.4 mm; 21,600 vph; 1-minute
tourbillon; 42-hour power reserve
Functions: hours, minutes, subsidiary seconds
(on tourbillon cage)
Case: rose gold, ø 40.2 mm, height 8.65 mm;
sapphire crystal; transparent case back; water-
resistant to 3 atm
Band: reptile skin, buckle
Price: $130,000
Variations: white gold ($130,000), various bands
and dials

Tonda Chronor Anniversary

Reference number: PFH282-1002400-HA4041
Movement: manually wound, Parmigiani Caliber
PF361; ø 30.6 mm, height 8.5 mm; 35 jewels;
36,000 vph; double column wheels; pink gold plate
and bridges, skeletonized; 65-hour power reserve
Functions: hours, minutes, subsidiary seconds;
split-second chronograph; large date
Case: rose gold, ø 42.1 mm, height 14.6 mm;
sapphire crystal; water-resistant to 3 atm
Band: reptile skin, buckle
Price: $135,000; limited to 25 pieces
Variations: white gold ($135,000, limited to 25
pieces)

Kalpa Donna

Reference number: PFC160-0020701-B00002
Movement: quartz
Functions: hours, minutes
Case: stainless steel, 24.8 × 34.8 mm, height
6.8 mm; sapphire crystal; water-resistant to 3 atm
Band: stainless steel; folding clasp
Remarks: case set with 43 diamonds
Price: $9,400
Variations: various dials; bracelet set with
diamonds ($17,800)

Tonda Métropolitaine

Reference number: PFC273-0000600-B00002
Movement: automatic, Parmigiani Caliber PF310;
ø 23.9 mm, height 3.9 mm; 28 jewels; 28,800 vph;
double spring barrel; finely finished with côtes de
Genève; 50-hour power reserve
Functions: hours, minutes, subsidiary seconds; date
Case: stainless steel, ø 33.1 mm, height 8.65 mm;
sapphire crystal; transparent case back; water-
resistant to 3 atm
Band: stainless steel, folding clasp
Price: $8,900
Variations: calfskin strap ($8,100); textile strap
($8,000); various dials

Tonda Métropolitaine

Reference number: PFC273-0060600-X02521
Movement: automatic, Parmigiani Caliber PF310;
ø 23.9 mm, height 3.9 mm; 28 jewels; 28,800 vph;
double spring barrel; finely finished with côtes de
Genève; 50-hour power reserve
Functions: hours, minutes, subsidiary seconds; date
Case: stainless steel, ø 33.1 mm, height 8.65 mm;
bezel set with 72 diamonds; sapphire crystal;
transparent case back; water-resistant to 3 atm
Band: textile, buckle
Price: $10,400
Variations: stainless steel band ($11,300); calfskin
strap ($10,500); various dials

Tonda 1950 Galaxy

Reference number: PFC288-1062500-HA1421
Movement: automatic, Parmigiani Caliber PF702;
ø 30 mm, height 2.6 mm; 29 jewels; 21,600 vph;
48-hour power reserve
Functions: hours, minutes
Case: rose gold, ø 39 mm, height 8.4 mm bezel set
with 84 diamonds; sapphire crystal; transparent case
back; water-resistant to 3 atm
Band: reptile skin, buckle
Remarks: aventurine dial
Price: $23,900

Tonda 1950 Poppy

Reference number: PFC267-1032001-B10002
Movement: automatic, Parmigiani Caliber PF701;
ø 30 mm, height 2.6 mm; 29 jewels; 21,600 vph;
42-hour power reserve
Functions: hours, minutes
Case: rose gold, ø 39 mm, height 8.4 mm bezel set
with 112 diamonds; sapphire crystal; transparent
case back; water-resistant to 3 atm
Band: rose gold, folding clasp
Remarks: red aventurine dial
Price: $49,500

Caliber PF361

Manually wound; control by two control wheels; skeletonized movement; pink gold plate and bridges; single spring barrel, 65-hour power reserve
Functions: hours, minutes, subsidiary seconds; split-second chronograph; large date
Diameter: 30.6 mm
Height: 8.5 mm
Jewels: 25
Frequency: 36,000 vph
Remarks: 317 components; limited edition

Caliber PF702

Automatic; platinum microrotor; single spring barrel, 48-hour power reserve
Functions: hours, minutes, subsidiary seconds
Diameter: 30 mm
Height: 2.6 mm
Jewels: 29
Frequency: 21,600 vph

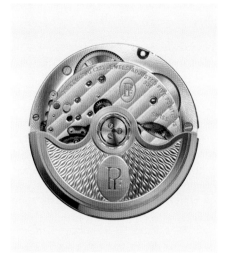

Caliber PF331

Automatic; double spring barrel, 55-hour power reserve; COSC-certified chronometer, Qualité Fleurier
Functions: hours, minutes, sweep seconds; date
Diameter: 25.6 mm
Height: 3.5 mm
Jewels: 32
Frequency: 28,800 vph

Caliber PF110

Manually wound; double mainspring barrel, 192-hour power reserve
Functions: hours, minutes, subsidiary seconds; power reserve indicator; date
Measurements: 29.3 × 23.6 mm
Height: 4.9 mm
Jewels: 28
Frequency: 21,600 vph

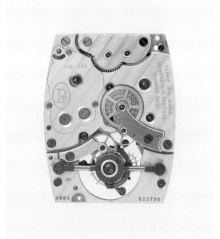

Caliber PF500

Manually wound; doubly mounted 30-second tourbillon; double mainspring barrel, 192-hour power reserve
Functions: hours, minutes, sweep seconds; power reserve indicator
Measurements: 23.6 × 29.8 mm
Height: 5.5 mm
Jewels: 28
Frequency: 21,600 vph
Remarks: perlage on plate

Caliber PF517

Automatic; flying 1-minute tourbillon, platinum microrotor; single spring barrel, 42-hour power reserve
Functions: hours, minutes, subsidiary seconds (on tourbillon cage)
Diameter: 32 mm
Height: 3.4 mm
Jewels: 29
Frequency: 21,600 vph
Remarks: 205 components

PATEK PHILIPPE

Patek Philippe SA
Chemin du pont-du-centenaire 141
CH-1228 Plan-les-Ouates
Switzerland

Tel.:
+41-22-884-20-20

Fax:
+41-22-884-20-40

Website:
www.patek.com

Founded:
1839

Number of employees:
approx. 2,000 (estimated)

Annual production:
approx. 45,000 watches worldwide per year

U.S. distributor:
Patek Philippe USA
45 Rockefeller Center, Suite 401
New York, NY 10111
212-218-1272; 212-218-1283 (fax)

Most important collections/price range:
Calatrava, Nautilus, Gondolo, Ellipse, Aquanaut /
ladies' timepieces begin at $12,135 (Twenty~4)
and men's at $19,732 (basic Calatrava)

In the Swiss watchmaking landscape, Patek Philippe has a special status as the last independent family-owned business. The company originated in 1839 with two Polish emigrés to Switzerland, Count Norbert Antoine de Patek and Frantiszek Czapek. In 1845, following the natural end of their contract, Patek sought another partner in the master watchmaker Jean Adrien Philippe, who had developed a keyless winding and time-setting mechanism. Ever since, Patek Philippe has been known for creating high-quality mechanical watches, some with extremely sophisticated complications. Even among its competition, the *manufacture* enjoys the greatest respect.

In 1932, Charles-Henri Stern took over the *manufacture*. His son Henri and grandson Philippe continued the tradition of solid leadership, steering the company through the notorious quartz crisis without ever compromising quality. The next in line, also Henri, heads the enterprise these days.

In 1997, Patek Philippe moved into new quarters, based on the most modern standards. The facility boasts the world's largest assembly of watchmakers under one roof, and yet production figures are comparatively modest. A small section of the building is reserved for restoring old watches either using parts from a large and valuable collection of components or rebuilding them from scratch.

The company recently opened a highly industrialized second branch between La Chaux-de-Fonds and Le Locle, where case components are manufactured, cases are polished, and gem setting is done. Patek Philippe's main headquarters remain in Geneva, but the *manufacture* no longer has a need for that city's famed seal: All of the company's mechanical watches now feature the "Patek Philippe Seal," the criteria for which far exceed the requirements of the *Poinçon de Genève* and include specifications for the entire watch, not just the movement. Among the most recent creations to make that grade is the World Time Chronograph, a masterful extension of the company's large range of chronographs. To make space, there is no second hand and only a thirty-minute counter. A moving city ring and twenty-four-hour ring have a place on the dial as well, and the whole piece is just over 12 millimeters high.

Perpetual Calendar with Tourbillon and Minute Repeater
Reference number: 5316P-001
Movement: manually wound, Patek Philippe Caliber R TO 27 PS QR; ø 28 mm, height 8.61 mm; 28 jewels; 21,600 vph; 1-minute tourbillon; chime with traditional gong activated by lateral slider; 38-hour power reserve
Functions: hours, minutes, subsidiary seconds; minute repeater; perpetual calendar with date (retrograde), weekday, month, moon phase, leap year
Case: platinum, ø 40.2 mm, height 13.23 mm; sapphire crystal; transparent case back
Band: reptile skin, folding clasp
Remarks: enamel dial
Price: on request

Split-Second Chronograph
Reference number: 5370P-001
Movement: manually wound, Patek Philippe Caliber 29-535 PS; ø 29.6 mm, height 7.1 mm; 34 jewels; 28,800 vph; 65-hour power reserve
Functions: hours, minutes, subsidiary seconds; split-second chronograph
Case: platinum, ø 41 mm, height 13.56 mm; sapphire crystal; transparent case back; water-resistant to 3 atm
Band: reptile skin, folding clasp
Price: $249,485

Minute Repeater
Reference number: 5078G-001
Movement: automatic, Patek Philippe Caliber R 27 PS; ø 28 mm, height 5.05 mm; 39 jewels; 21,600 vph; chime with two gongs activated by lateral slider
Functions: hours, minutes, subsidiary seconds; minute repeater
Case: white gold, ø 38 mm, height 10.2 mm; sapphire crystal; transparent case back
Band: reptile skin, folding clasp
Remarks: comes with additional white gold case back
Price: on request

Perpetual Calendar

Reference number: 5320G-001
Movement: automatic, Patek Philippe Caliber 324 S Q; ø 32 mm, height 4.97 mm; 29 jewels; 28,800 vph; gold rotor; 35-hour power reserve
Functions: hours, minutes, sweep seconds; day/night indicator; perpetual calendar with date, weekday, month, moon phase, leap year
Case: white gold, ø 40 mm, height 11.1 mm; sapphire crystal; transparent case back; water-resistant to 3 atm
Band: reptile skin, folding clasp
Remarks: comes with additional white gold case back
Price: $82,784

Perpetual Calendar

Reference number: 5940R-001
Movement: automatic, Patek Philippe Caliber 240 Q; ø 27.5 mm, height 3.88 mm; 27 jewels; 21,600 vph; 38-hour power reserve
Functions: hours, minutes; second 24-hour display (second time zone); perpetual calendar with date, weekday, month, moon phase, leap year
Case: rose gold, 37 × 44.6 mm; sapphire crystal; transparent case back; water-resistant to 3 atm
Band: reptile skin, folding clasp
Remarks: comes with additional rose gold case back
Price: $87,320

Perpetual Calendar

Reference number: 5327R-001
Movement: automatic, Patek Philippe Caliber 240 Q; ø 27.5 mm, height 3.88 mm; 27 jewels; 21,600 vph; Spiromax silicon hairspring; microrotor; 38-hour power reserve
Functions: hours, minutes; second 24-hour display; perpetual calendar with date, weekday, month, moon phase, leap year
Case: rose gold, ø 39 mm, height 9.71 mm; sapphire crystal; transparent case back; water-resistant to 3 atm
Band: reptile skin, folding clasp
Remarks: comes with additional rose gold case back
Price: $87,320
Variations: yellow gold ($85,052); white gold ($87,320)

Perpetual Calendar

Reference number: 7140G-001
Movement: automatic, Patek Philippe Caliber 240 Q; ø 27.5 mm, height 3.88 mm; 27 jewels; 21,600 vph; 38-hour power reserve
Functions: hours, minutes; second 24-hour display (second time zone); perpetual calendar with date, weekday, month, moon phase, leap year
Case: white gold, ø 35.1 mm, height 8.7 mm; bezel set with 68 diamonds; sapphire crystal; transparent case back; water-resistant to 3 atm
Band: reptile skin, buckle set with 27 diamonds
Remarks: comes with additional white gold case back
Price: $92,900

Chronograph

Reference number: 5170P-001
Movement: manually wound, Patek Philippe Caliber CH 29-535 PS; ø 29.6 mm, height 5.35 mm; 33 jewels; 28,800 vph; column wheel control of chronograph functions
Functions: hours, minutes, subsidiary seconds; chronograph
Case: platinum, ø 39.4 mm, height 10.9 mm; sapphire crystal; transparent case back; water-resistant to 3 atm
Band: reptile skin, folding clasp
Price: $96,392
Variations: rose gold ($81,083)

Annual Calendar Chronograph

Reference number: 5960/01G-001
Movement: automatic, Patek Philippe Caliber CH 28 520 IRM QA 24H; ø 33 mm, height 7.68 mm; 40 jewels; 28,800 vph; 45-hour power reserve
Functions: hours, minutes; power reserve indicator; flyback chronograph; annual calendar with date, weekday, month
Case: white gold, ø 40.5 mm, height 13.5 mm; sapphire crystal; transparent case back; water-resistant to 3 atm
Band: calfskin, buckle
Price: $65,774

Calatrava Pilot Travel Time

Reference number: 5524G-001
Movement: automatic, Patek Philippe Caliber 324 S C FUS; ø 31 mm, height 4.82 mm; 29 jewels; 28,800 vph; Spiromax silicon hairspring; 35-hour power reserve
Functions: hours, minutes, sweep seconds; additional 12-hour display (second time zone), day/night indicator; date
Case: white gold, ø 42 mm, height 10.78 mm; sapphire crystal; transparent case back; water-resistant to 6 atm
Band: calfskin, buckle
Price: $47,629

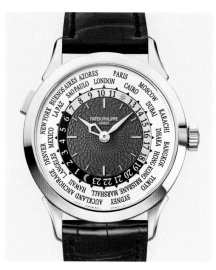

World Time

Reference number: 5230G-001
Movement: automatic, Patek Philippe Caliber 240 HU; ø 27.5 mm, height 3.88 mm; 33 jewels; 21,600 vph; Spiromax silicon hairspring; 48-hour power reserve
Functions: hours, minutes; world time display (second time zone)
Case: white gold, ø 38.5 mm, height 10.23 mm; 24 pusher-controlled time zones on scale flange with reference city names; sapphire crystal; transparent case back; water-resistant to 3 atm
Band: reptile skin, folding clasp
Price: $47,629

World Time Chronograph

Reference number: 5930G-001
Movement: automatic, Patek Philippe Caliber CH 28-520 HU; ø 33 mm, height 7.97 mm; 38 jewels; 28,800 vph; Spiromax silicon hairspring; 50-hour power reserve
Functions: hours, minutes; world time display (second time zone); chronograph
Case: white gold, ø 39.5 mm, height 12.86 mm; 24 pusher-controlled time zones on a scale flange with reference city names; sapphire crystal; transparent case back; water-resistant to 3 atm
Band: reptile skin, folding clasp
Price: $73,712

Annual Calendar

Reference number: 5396/R-014
Movement: automatic, Patek Philippe Caliber 324 S QA LU 24H/303; ø 33.3 mm, height 5.78 mm; 34 jewels; 28,800 vph; Spiromax silicon hairspring; 35-hour power reserve
Functions: hours, minutes, sweep seconds; second 24-hour display; annual calendar with date, weekday, month, moon phase
Case: rose gold, ø 38.5 mm, height 11.2 mm; sapphire crystal; transparent case back; water-resistant to 3 atm
Band: reptile skin, folding clasp
Price: $47,970
Variations: white gold ($47,970)

Annual Calendar

Reference number: 4947G-010
Movement: automatic, Patek Philippe Caliber 324 S QA LU; ø 30 mm, height 5.32 mm; 34 jewels; 28,800 vph; 35-hour power reserve
Functions: hours, minutes, sweep seconds; annual calendar with date, weekday, month, moon phase
Case: white gold, ø 38 mm, height 11 mm; bezel set with 141 diamonds; sapphire crystal; transparent case back; crown set with 14 diamonds; water-resistant to 3 atm
Band: reptile skin, buckle
Price: $49,897

Calatrava

Reference number: 6006G-001
Movement: automatic, Patek Philippe Caliber 240 PS C; ø 30 mm, height 3.43 mm; 27 jewels; 21,600 vph; microrotor in gold
Functions: hours, minutes, subsidiary seconds; date
Case: white gold, ø 39 mm, height 8.86 mm; sapphire crystal; transparent case back; water-resistant to 3 atm
Band: reptile skin, folding clasp
Price: $30,619

Calatrava

Reference number: 5180/1R-001
Movement: automatic, Patek Philippe Caliber 240 SQU/179; ø 27.5 mm, height 2.53 mm; 27 jewels; 21,600 vph; minirotor in gold; movement fully skeletonized, engraved and decorated by hand; 48-hour power reserve
Functions: hours, minutes
Case: rose gold, ø 39 mm, height 6.7 mm; sapphire crystal; transparent case back; water-resistant to 3 atm
Band: rose gold, folding clasp
Price: $98,660

Calatrava

Reference number: 7122/200R-001
Movement: manually wound, Patek Philippe Caliber 215 PS; ø 21.9 mm, height 2.55 mm; 18 jewels; 28,800 vph; Spiromax silicon hairspring; 44-hour power reserve
Functions: hours, minutes, subsidiary seconds
Case: rose gold, ø 33 mm, height 7.19 mm; bezel set with 44 diamonds; sapphire crystal; transparent case back; water-resistant to 3 atm
Band: reptile skin, buckle
Price: $27,217

Nautilus Travel Time Chronograph

Reference number: 5990/1A-001
Movement: automatic, Patek Philippe Caliber CH 28-520 C FUS; ø 31 mm, height 6.95 mm; 34 jewels; 28,800 vph; 45-hour power reserve
Functions: hours, minutes, subsidiary seconds; additional 12-hour display (second time zone), day/night indicator; flyback chronograph; date
Case: stainless steel, ø 40.5 mm, height 12.53 mm; sapphire crystal; transparent case back; screw-in crown; water-resistant to 12 atm
Band: stainless steel, folding clasp
Price: $53,299

Ladies' Nautilus

Reference number: 7118/1A-011
Movement: automatic, Patek Philippe Caliber 324 S C; ø 27 mm, height 3.3 mm; 29 jewels; 28,800 vph; 35-hour power reserve
Functions: hours, minutes, sweep seconds; date
Case: stainless steel, ø 35.2 mm, height 8.62 mm; sapphire crystal; transparent case back; screw-in crown; water-resistant to 6 atm
Band: stainless steel, folding clasp
Price: $24,836

Aquanaut

Reference number: 5168G-001
Movement: automatic, Patek Philippe Caliber 324 S C; ø 27 mm, height 3.3 mm; 29 jewels; 28,800 vph; 35-hour power reserve
Functions: hours, minutes, sweep seconds; date
Case: white gold, ø 42.2 mm, height 8.25 mm; sapphire crystal; transparent case back; screw-in crown; water-resistant to 12 atm
Band: rubber, folding clasp
Price: $38,557

Aquanaut Travel Time

Reference number: 5164R-001
Movement: automatic, Patek Philippe Caliber 324 S C FUS; ø 31 mm, height 4.82 mm; 29 jewels; 28,800 vph; Spiromax silicon hairspring; 35-hour power reserve
Functions: hours, minutes, sweep seconds; additional 12-hour display (second time zone); date
Case: rose gold, ø 40.8 mm; sapphire crystal; transparent case back; screw-in crown; water-resistant to 12 atm
Band: rubber, folding clasp
Price: $51,031

Caliber 324 S Q

Automatic; gold rotor; single spring barrel, 35-hour power reserve
Functions: hours, minutes, sweep seconds; day/night indicator; perpetual calendar with date, weekday, month, moon phase, leap year
Diameter: 32 mm
Height: 4.97 mm
Jewels: 29
Frequency: 28,800 vph
Balance spring: Spyromax silicon spring

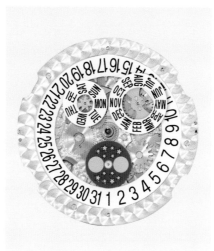

Caliber 324 S QA LU 24H-303

Automatic; 21-kt gold central rotor; single spring barrel, 45-hour power reserve
Functions: hours, minutes, sweep seconds; second 24-hour display (second time zone); annual calendar with date, weekday, month, moon phase
Diameter: 32.6 mm
Height: 5.78 mm
Jewels: 34
Balance: Gyromax
Frequency: 28,800 vph
Balance spring: Spiromax silicon spring
Remarks: silicon pallet lever, 347 components

Caliber CH 28-520 IRM QA 24H

Automatic; column wheel control of chronograph functions, 21-kt gold central rotor; single spring barrel, 55-hour power reserve
Functions: hours, minutes, sweep seconds; day/night indicator, power reserve indicator; chronograph with combined hour and minute totalizer; annual calendar with date, weekday, month, moon phase
Diameter: 33 mm
Height: 7.68 mm
Jewels: 40
Balance: Gyromax
Frequency: 28,800 vph
Balance spring: Breguet
Remarks: 456 components

Caliber CH 29-535 PS

Manually wound; column wheel control of chronograph functions; exactly jumping 30-minute counter; single spring barrel, 65-hour power reserve
Functions: hours, minutes, subsidiary seconds; split-second chronograph
Diameter: 29.6 mm
Height: 7.1 mm
Jewels: 34
Balance: Gyromax, four-armed, with four regulating weights
Frequency: 28,800 vph
Balance spring: Breguet
Shock protection: Incabloc
Remarks: 312 components

Caliber RTO 27 PS QR

Manually wound; 1-minute tourbillon; single spring barrel, 48-hour power reserve; COSC-certified chronometer
Functions: hours, minutes, subsidiary seconds; minute repeater; perpetual calendar with date (retrograde), weekday, month and leap year (in aperture), moon phase
Diameter: 28 mm
Height: 8.61 mm
Jewels: 28
Balance: Gyromax
Frequency: 21,600 vph
Balance spring: Breguet
Remarks: 336 components

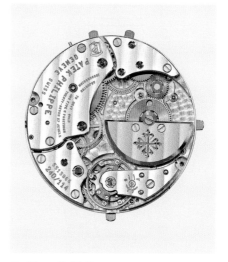

Caliber 240 Q

Automatic; microrotor in gold; single spring barrel, 48-hour power reserve
Functions: hours, minutes; second 24-hour display (second time zone); perpetual calendar with date, weekday, month, moon phase, leap year
Diameter: 30 mm
Height: 3.75 mm
Jewels: 27
Balance: Gyromax, with 8 masselotte regulating weights
Frequency: 21,600 vph
Balance spring: flat hairspring
Shock protection: Kif

Caliber R 27 PS

Automatic; microrotor in gold, chime with traditional gong activated by lateral slider; single spring barrel
Functions: hours, minutes, subsidiary seconds; minute repeater
Diameter: 28 mm
Height: 5.05 mm
Jewels: 39
Frequency: 21,600 vph

Caliber 240 SQU

Automatic; microrotor in gold; single spring barrel, 48-hour power reserve
Functions: hours, minutes
Diameter: 27.5 mm
Height: 2.53 mm
Jewels: 27
Balance: with 8 masselotte regulating weights
Frequency: 21,600 vph
Balance spring: flat hairspring
Shock protection: Kif
Remarks: movement entirely skeletonized, engraved and decorated by hand

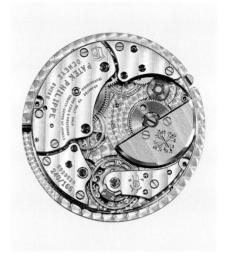

Caliber 240 PS C

Automatic; microrotor in gold; single spring barrel, 48-hour power reserve
Functions: hours, minutes, subsidiary seconds; date
Diameter: 30 mm
Height: 3.43 mm
Jewels: 27
Balance: Gyromax
Frequency: 21,600 vph
Balance spring: Spiromax silicon spring

Caliber 324 SC

Automatic; gold rotor; single spring barrel, 35-hour power reserve
Functions: hours, minutes, sweep seconds; date
Diameter: 27 mm
Height: 3.3 mm
Jewels: 29
Balance: Gyromax
Frequency: 28,800 vph
Balance spring: Breguet

Caliber 324 S QA LU

Automatic; gold rotor; single spring barrel, 35-hour power reserve
Functions: hours, minutes, sweep seconds; annual calendar with date, weekday, month, moon phase
Diameter: 30 mm
Height: 5.32 mm
Jewels: 34
Balance: Gyromax
Frequency: 28,800 vph
Balance spring: Breguet

Caliber CHR 29-535 PS

Manually wound; 2 column wheels to control chronograph functions, flyback mechanism with isolator; single spring barrel, 55-hour power reserve
Functions: hours, minutes, subsidiary seconds; split-second chronograph
Diameter: 29.6 mm
Height: 7.1 mm
Jewels: 33
Balance: Gyromax, four-armed, with four regulating weights
Frequency: 28,800 vph
Balance spring: Breguet
Remarks: 312 components

Caliber CH 28-520 HU

Automatic; single spring barrel, 50-hour power reserve

Functions: hours, minutes; world time display (second time zone); chronograph
Diameter: 33 mm
Height: 7.91 mm
Jewels: 38
Balance: Gyromax
Frequency: 28,800 vph
Balance spring: Spiromax silicon spring
Remarks: 343 components, very fine movement finishing

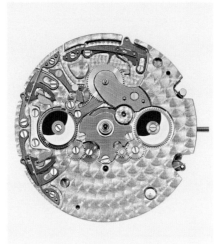

Caliber CH 28-520 C FUS

Automatic; column wheel control of chronograph functions, 21-kt gold central rotor; single spring barrel, 45-hour power reserve

Functions: hours, minutes; additional 12-hour display (second time zone), day/night indicator; flyback chronograph; date
Diameter: 31 mm
Height: 6.95 mm
Jewels: 34
Balance: Gyromax
Frequency: 28,800 vph
Balance spring: Spiromax silicon spring
Remarks: 370 components

Caliber 324 S C FUS

Automatic; gold rotor; single spring barrel, 35-hour power reserve

Functions: hours, minutes, sweep seconds; additional 12-hour display (second time zone), day/night indicator; date
Diameter: 31 mm
Height: 4.82 mm
Jewels: 29
Balance: Gyromax
Frequency: 28,800 vph
Balance spring: Spiromax silicon spring
Remarks: 294 components

Caliber 215 PS

Manually wound; single spring barrel, 44-hour power reserve

Functions: hours, minutes, subsidiary seconds
Diameter: 21.9 mm
Height: 2.55 mm
Jewels: 18
Balance: Gyromax, with 8 masselotte regulating weights
Frequency: 28,800 vph
Balance spring: flat hairspring
Shock protection: Kif
Remarks: perlage on mainplate beveled and polished bridges, with côtes de Genève, 130 components

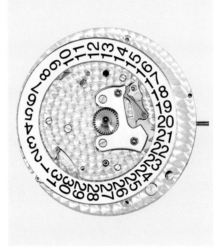

Caliber CH 28-520 C

Automatic; column wheel control of chronograph functions, 21-kt gold central rotor; single spring barrel, 55-hour power reserve

Functions: hours, minutes, sweep seconds; chronograph with combined hour and minute totalizer; date
Diameter: 30 mm
Height: 6.63 mm
Jewels: 35
Balance: Gyromax
Frequency: 28,800 vph
Balance spring: Breguet
Remarks: 327 components

Caliber 240 HU

Automatic; excenter 22-kt gold microrotor on ball-bearing, unidirectional winding; single spring barrel, 48-hour power reserve

Functions: hours, minutes; world time display (second time zone)
Diameter: 27.5 mm
Height: 3.88 mm
Jewels: 33
Balance: Gyromax
Frequency: 21,600 vph
Remarks: 239 components

QUILL & PAD

KEEPING WATCH ON TIME

Make **time** for **a unique watch experience**

Breaking Stories

Unique Photography

Interesting Angles and Subjects

Quill & Pad is an online platform combining decades of excellence and experience in watch journalism, bringing **you** original stories and photography.

Ian Skellern

Elizabeth Doerr

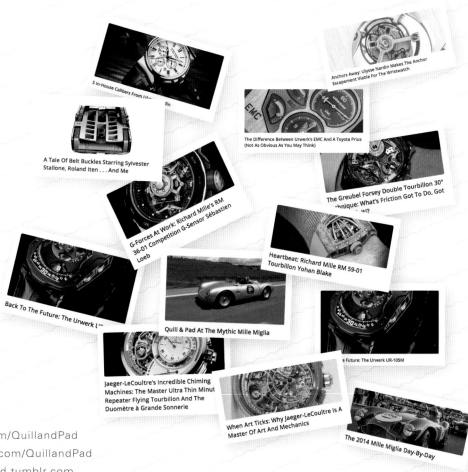

twitter.com/QuillandPad
facebook.com/QuillandPad
quillandpad.tumblr.com
instagram.com/quillandpad

www.QuillandPad.com

PAUL GERBER

Watchmaker Paul Gerber has already developed mechanisms and complications, including calendar movements, alarms, and tourbillons, for numerous renowned watchmakers over the decades. Time and again, this genial watchmaker has astonished the horological world with outrageously complicated mechanisms, which he somehow manages to create by fitting hundreds of additional tiny parts into filigree movements of watches that seem to offer not one iota of extra room. Gerber is the one who designed the complicated calendar mechanism for the otherwise minimalist MIH watch conceived by Ludwig Oechslin, curator of the International Museum of Horology (MIH) in La Chaux-de-Fonds and himself a watchmaker. Twice his work has appeared in *Guiness World Records*.

When his daily work for others lets up, Gerber gets around to building watches bearing his own name with such marvelous features as a retrograde second hand in an elegant thin case and a synchronously unidirectional rotor system with miniature oscillating weights for his self-winding Retro Twin model. Gerber's works are all limited editions.

After designing a tonneau-shaped manually wound wristwatch with a three-dimensional moon phase display, Gerber created a simple, three-hand watch with an automatic movement conceived and produced completely in-house. It features a 100-hour power reserve and is wound by three synchronically turning gold rotors. The large date can be set backward and forward. Gerber also offers the triple rotor and large date features in a watch with an ETA movement and lightweight titanium case as a classic pilot watch design or in a version with a more modern dial (the Synchron model). The Model 41 has an optional complication that switches the second hand from sweep to deadbeat motion by way of a pusher at 2 o'clock.

Gerber is allegedly retired. But a watchmaker never really does. Besides continuing to produce outstanding pieces, he occasionally gives three-day workshops for people wanting to get a real feel for the work.

Paul Gerber
Uhren-Konstruktionen
Bockhornstrasse 69
CH-8047 Zürich
Switzerland

Tel.:
+41-44-401-4569

E-mail:
info@gerber-uhren.ch

Website:
www.gerber-uhren.ch

Founded:
1976

Number of employees:
n/a

Annual production:
up to 50 watches

U.S. distributor:
Intro Swiss - Michel Schmutz
7615 Estate Circle
Niwot, CO 80503
303-652-1520
introswiss@q.com

Most important collections/price range:
mechanical watches / from approx. $4,900 to $60,000; tourbillon desk clocks / from approx. $48,000 to $70,000

Retro Twin
Reference number: 156
Movement: automatic, Gerber Caliber 15 (base ETA 7001); ø 28 mm, height 5.2 mm; 27 jewels; 21,600 vph; winding by 2 synchronously rotating platinum rotors
Functions: hours, minutes, subsidiary seconds (retrograde)
Case: rose gold, ø 36 mm, height 10.8 mm; sapphire crystal; transparent case back; water-resistant to 3 atm
Band: reptile skin, buckle
Price: $15,600
Variations: yellow or white gold ($15,600) with platinum rotors set with brilliants ($18,450)

Modell 42
Reference number: 420 DaN
Movement: automatic, Gerber Caliber 42 (base ETA 2824); ø 36 mm, height 6.1 mm; 25 jewels; 28,800 vph; winding by 3 synchronously rotating gold rotors
Functions: hours, minutes, sweep seconds; day/night indicator; date
Case: titanium, ø 42 mm, height 12 mm; sapphire crystal; transparent case back; screw-in crown; water-resistant to 10 atm
Band: calfskin, buckle
Price: $5,540
Variations: Pilot's/Synchron dial ($4,650); as Caliber 42 Pilot's/Synchron 24-hour dial ($5,490)

Modell 33
Reference number: 336
Movement: manually wound, Gerber Caliber 33; 28 × 34 × 5 mm; 20 jewels; 21,600 vph; special Gerber escapement
Functions: hours, minutes, seconds, 3D moon phase
Case: white gold, 34 × 40 × 10.2 mm; sapphire crystal; transparent case back; water-resistant to 3 atm
Band: reptile skin, gold buckle
Remarks: moon corrected for 128 years, ø 6 mm, corrected for 128 years; one hemisphere set with 54 diamonds, the other of lapis lazuli
Price: $37,670
Variations: rose gold ($37,670); platinum ($46,300)

Société des Montres
Paul Picot SA
Rue du Doubs 6
CH-2340 Le Noirmont
Switzerland

Tel.:
+41-32-911-1818

Fax:
+41-32-911-1819

E-mail:
info@paulpicot.ch

Website:
www.paulpicot.ch

Founded:
1976

U.S. distributor:
Time Innovations LLC
After Sales Services
444 Madison Avenue, Suite 601
New York, NY 10022
718-725-7509
info@timeinnovationsllc.com

Most important collections:
Atelier, C-Type, Gentleman, Technicum, Firshire,
unique pieces

PAUL PICOT

The 1976 establishment of the Société des Montres Paul Picot required a large dose of pioneering spirit on the part of its initiators. The new brand was born of the will to save the rich history of the Swiss watch industry and let its true values once again come to light. The age-old tradition of watchmaking was threatening to collapse; qualified masters of the craft were disappearing from the workplace, and the once-fascinating atmosphere of watchmakers' workshops had given way to the industrial hustle and bustle of anonymous brand names. For company founder and president Mario Boiocchi, the only chance for the survival of European watch culture was to rediscover quality and precision. While Japanese and American competitors were forcing the Swiss watch industry to make compromises in order to meet the demands of mass consumption, Paul Picot chose to walk a different path.

The market—that vague, undefinable, yet despotic entity—was calling for futuristic design and electronic technology. However, Paul Picot went in the exact opposite direction and produced fine gold cases and mechanical watch movements. In the years to follow, the collections attracted the attention of watch buyers the world over with their good balance of elegance and sportiness. This company, located in Le Noirmont in the heart of watchmaking country, is writing its own history. For a relatively small concern, it has managed to produce a very wide range of models, each with a unique look. The Firshire series comes in sober round cases or as the 1937 or 3000 Regulateur in a comfortable tonneau with a dial tightly packed with displays. It even has divers and chronographs to cap its portfolio. And while many brands have to drop their prices to attract a coveted target group, Paul Picot has already staked out this territory.

Megarotor GMT Grand Feu
Reference number: P0482.RG.2000
Movement: automatic, ETA Caliber 2892 with Dubois Dépraz module; ø 25.6 mm, height 6.2 mm; 21 jewels; 28,800 vph; crown-switchable hour hand; winding rotor with tungsten oscillating mass; 42-hour power reserve
Functions: hours, minutes, sweep seconds; world-time display (2nd time zone)
Case: rose gold, ø 42 mm, height 11.5 mm; sapphire crystal; transparent back; water-resistant to 5 atm
Band: reptile skin, folding clasp
Remarks: dial motif of champlevé enamel
Price: $28,119; limited to 88 pieces
Variations: stainless steel ($10,598; limited to 300 pieces)

Firshire Extraflat Date
Reference number: P3754.RG.5624
Movement: automatic, Caliber PP 1650 (base Lemania 8810); ø 25.6 mm, height 2.9 mm; 17 jewels; 28,800 vph; 2 spring barrels; winding rotor with côtes de Genève; 38-hour power reserve
Functions: hours, minutes; date
Case: rose gold, ø 40.5 mm, height 6.9 mm; sapphire crystal; transparent case back; water-resistant to 3 atm
Band: reptile skin, folding clasp
Price: $7,354
Variations: stainless steel ($4,434); various dial colors

Plongeur Full Black Orange
Reference number: P4118.SFB.3410
Movement: automatic, ETA Caliber 2824; ø 25.6 mm, height 4.6 mm; 25 jewels; 28,800 vph; 42-hour power reserve
Functions: hours, minutes, sweep seconds; date
Case: stainless steel, black DLC coating, ø 42 mm, height 14 mm; bezel with colored HDT-coated antifriction ring, unidirectional bezel with 60-minute divisions; sapphire crystal; screw-in crown; water-resistant to 30 atm
Band: calfskin, folding clasp
Price: $3,136
Variations: blue bezel; as chronograph ($5,299)

PERRELET

The Perrelet story will sound familiar to anyone who has read about Swiss watchmaking: Abraham-Louis Perrelet (1729–1826) was the son of a middle-class farmer from Le Locle who developed an interest in watchmaking early on in life. He was the first watchmaker in Le Locle to work on cylinder and duplex escapements, and there is a persistent rumor that he was responsible for a repeater that could be heard echoing in the mountains.

Many watchmakers later to become famous were at one time Perrelet's apprentices, and some historians even suggest that Abraham-Louis Breguet was in this illustrious group. Suffice to say, Perrelet invented a great deal, including the "perpetual" watch from around 1770, a pocket watch that wound itself utilizing the motion of the wearer.

When the brand hit the market in 1995, it came out with a double rotor and a movement, the P-181, which made waves in the industry. The Turbines soon followed featuring a kind of jet engine fan that decoratively spins over the dial, creating all sorts of effects and giving lots of potential for creative designing. It was all innovative and successful enough to attract the attention of Festina Group, which purchased the brand in 2004.

Today, the P-181 continues to power the Classic Double Rotor models and the Diamond Flowers, which balance sensual beauty with technical prowess—it was, after all, designed by a woman. And to celebrate the Double Rotor's twentieth birthday in 2015, a new caliber, the P-481, was made for the new First Class Double Rotor. It was followed in 2016 by the automatic P-411, which drives the LAB, cleverly designed to show the rotor just under a transparent dial.

Perrelet SA
Rue Bubenberg 7
CH-2502 Biel/Bienne
Switzerland

Tel.:
+41-32-346-2626

Fax:
+41-32-346-2627

E-mail:
perrelet@perrelet.com

Website:
www.perrelet.com

Founded:
1777, acquired by Festina Group in 2004

Number of employees:
10

U.S. distributor:
Perrelet USA
282 NW 25th Street
Miami, FL 33127
305-588-3628
info@perreletusa.com

Most important collections:
LAB, Turbine, First Class, Diamond Flower

First Class Double Rotor

Reference number: A1090/2
Movement: automatic, Perrelet Caliber P181-H; ø 31.6 mm, height 5.15 mm; 22 jewels; 28,800 vph; 2 coupled winding rotors on dial and movement side; 42-hour power reserve
Functions: hours, minutes, sweep seconds
Case: stainless steel, ø 42.5 mm, height 10.7 mm; sapphire crystal; transparent case back; water-resistant to 5 atm
Band: reptile skin, stainless steel buckle
Price: $3,690
Variations: white or blue dial

Turbine GMT

Reference number: A 1092/1
Movement: automatic, Perrelet Caliber P401; ø 26.2 mm, height 4.25 mm; 25 jewels; 28,800 vph; 42-hour power reserve
Functions: hours, minutes, sweep seconds; additional 24-hour display (2nd time zone)
Case: stainless steel, ø 44 mm, height 13.3 mm; sapphire crystal; transparent case back; screw-in crown; water-resistant to 5 atm
Band: rubber, buckle
Remarks: "turbine" animation on dial side (without winding function)
Price: $5,970
Variations: black PVD coating ($6,480)

LAB

Reference number: A 1100/1
Movement: automatic, Perrelet Caliber P-411; ø 34.8 mm, height 4.42 mm; 30 jewels; 28,800 vph; rhodium-plated bridges, côtes de Genève; 42-hour power reserve
Functions: hours, minutes, sweep seconds, date at 6 o'clock
Case: stainless steel, 42 × 42 mm, height 13.25 mm; sapphire crystal; transparent screwed-down back, water-resistant to 5 atm
Band: reptile skin, buckle
Remarks: circular view of oscillating weight
Price: $4,950
Variations: silver, anthracite, or black dial

Speake-Marin
Chemin en-Baffa 2
CH-1183 Bursins
Switzerland

Tel.:
+41-21-825-5069

E-mail:
info@speake-marin.com

Website:
www.speake-marin.com

Founded:
2002

Number of employees:
5

Annual production:
400 watches

U.S. distributor:
About Time Luxury Group
210 Bellevue Avenue
Newport, RI 02840
401-846-0598
Speake-marin@abouttimeluxury.com
www.abouttimeluxury.com

Most important collections:
HMS, J-Class, Resilience, Serpent Calendar,
Velsheda

PETER SPEAKE-MARIN

Peter Speake-Marin brings realism, genius, and a sense of romance to his work. As a horological innovator—he could have been a poet or adventurer—he has managed within little more than a decade to establish an outstanding reputation for originality, virtuosity, and being a very friendly and helpful colleague in a highly competitive field. He has also had his skilled fingers in a number of iconic timepieces, like the HM1 of MB&F, the Chapter One for Maîtres du Temps, and the Harry Winston Excenter Tourbillon.

Born in Essex in 1968, Speake-Marin attended Hackney College, London, and WOSTEP in Switzerland, before earning his spurs restoring antique watches at a Somlo in Piccadilly. In 1996, he moved to Le Locle, Switzerland, to work with Renaud et Papi, when he also set about making his own pieces. A dual-train tourbillon (the Foundation Watch) opened the door to the prestigious AHCI.

The recession taught him something crucial: "I was a watchmaker, not an entrepreneur," he shares. "I had to become entrepreneurial to become a watchmaker again." And so he reorganized himself as a brand with three watch families. For his flashes of creative madness, he has the grab-bag Cabinet des Mystères. The Spirit models have a military, adventurous feel. And the J-Class family recalls the discreet elegance of J-Class yachts, such as the Velsheda, launched originally in 1933 and named for Velma, Sheila, and Daphne, the three daughters of the first owner, Woolworth executive William Lawrence Stephenson.

Speake-Marin is a profoundly creative watchmaker, one willing to give a hand even to his competitors. So the 2017 announcement that he was actually leaving the brand he had given birth to and shaped for sixteen years was somewhat mitigated. In a brief letter, CEO Christelle Rosnoblet promised to continue the brand's characteristic "British elegance and sassiness." As usual, in the watch business, time will tell . . .

Resilience
Movement: automatic, Caliber Vaucher 3002; ø 26 mm, height 4.3 mm; 28 jewels; 28,800 vph; 50-hour power reserve
Functions: hours, minutes, sweep seconds
Case: pink gold, ø 38 mm, height 12 mm; sapphire crystal; transparent case back; water-resistant to 3 atm
Band: reptile skin, pink gold buckle
Remarks: enamel dial
Price: $24,800
Variations: 42 mm diameter; various dials

Spirit Seafire
Movement: automatic, ETA Caliber 7750 (modified); ø 30.4 mm, height 7.9 mm; 25 jewels; 28,800 vph; 48-hour power reserve
Functions: hours, minutes, subsidiary seconds (rosetta form); chronograph; date
Case: titanium, ø 42 mm, height 15 mm; sapphire crystal; water-resistant to 3 atm
Band: calfskin, buckle
Remarks: limited edition of 28 pieces
Price: $10,350

Serpent Calendar
Movement: automatic, Caliber Vaucher 3002; ø 26 mm, height 4.3 mm; 28 jewels; 28,800 vph; 50-hour power reserve
Functions: hours, minutes, sweep seconds; date
Case: stainless steel, ø 38 mm, height 12 mm; sapphire crystal; transparent case back; water-resistant to 3 atm
Band: reptile skin, buckle
Price: $12,100

PIAGET

One of the oldest watch manufacturers in Switzerland, Piaget began making watch movements in the secluded Jura village of La Côte-aux-Fées in 1874. For decades, those movements were delivered to other watch brands. The *manufacture* itself, strangely enough, remained in the background. It wasn't until the 1940s that the Piaget family began to offer complete watches under their own name.

Even today, Piaget, which long ago moved the business side of things to Geneva, still makes its watch movements at its main facility high in the Jura mountains.

In the late fifties, Piaget began investing in the design and manufacturing of ultrathin movements. This lends these watches the kind of understated elegance that became the company's hallmark. In 1957, Valentin Piaget presented the first ultrathin men's watch, the Altiplano, with the manual caliber 9P, which was 2 millimeters high. Shortly after, it came out with the 12P, an automatic caliber that clocked in at 2.3 millimeters.

The Altiplano has faithfully accompanied the brand for sixty years now. The movement has evolved over time. The recent 900P measures just 3.65 mm and is inverted to enable repairs, making the case back the mainplate with the dial set on the upper side. In 2015, the Chrono Altiplano equipped with the 883P caliber became the thinnest chronograph ever, at 8.25 millimeters. And for 2017, the company has produced a whole slew of special and limited editions.

Worthy of note, too, is Piaget's particular treatment of quartz watches of late. In 2016, it released a concept watch that combines mechanical and quartz technology and produced ten patents. The core energy source is still a spring barrel wound by hand or microrotor. It drives a miniature generator that turns at a constant 5.33 rpm and replaces the escapement and balance wheel. It supplies the regulating quartz with power, which in turn regulates the movement. This inverted caliber is just 5.5 millimeters high. All the basic parts are on the dial side and partly visible thanks to skeletonized plates.

Piaget SA
CH-1228 Plan-les-Ouates
Switzerland

Tel.:
+41-32-867-21-21

E-mail:
info@piaget.com

Website:
www.piaget.com

Founded:
1874

Number of employees:
900

Annual production:
watches not specified; plus about 20,000 movements for Richemont Group

U.S. distributor:
Piaget North America
645 5th Avenue, 6th Floor
New York, NY 10022
212-909-4362; 212-909-4332 (fax)
www.piaget.com

Most important collections/price range:
Altiplano / approx. $13,500 to $22,000

Altiplano 60th Anniversary

Reference number: G0A42050
Movement: automatic, Piaget Caliber 1203P; ø 30 mm, height 3 mm; 25 jewels; 21,600 vph; perlage on mainplate beveled bridges, blued screws, with côtes de Genève; gold rotor; 44-hour power reserve
Functions: hours, minutes; date
Case: white gold, ø 40 mm, height 6.36 mm; sapphire crystal; water-resistant to 3 atm
Band: reptile skin, buckle
Price: $26,000; limited to 260 pieces
Variations: rose gold ($25,000); yellow gold ($25,200)

Altiplano 60th Anniversary

Reference number: G0A42051
Movement: automatic, Piaget Caliber 1203P; ø 30 mm, height 3 mm; 25 jewels; 21,600 vph; perlage on mainplate beveled bridges, blued screws, with côtes de Genève; gold rotor; 44-hour power reserve
Functions: hours, minutes; date
Case: rose gold, ø 40 mm, height 6.36 mm; sapphire crystal; water-resistant to 3 atm
Band: reptile skin, buckle
Price: $25,200; limited to 260 pieces
Variations: white gold ($26,000); yellow gold ($25,200)

Altiplano 60th Anniversary

Reference number: G0A42107
Movement: manually wound, Piaget Caliber 430P; ø 20.5 mm, height 2.1 mm; 18 jewels; 21,600 vph; perlage on mainplate, blued screws, finely finished with côtes de Genève; 43-hour power reserve
Functions: hours, minutes
Case: white gold, ø 38 mm, height 6 mm; sapphire crystal; water-resistant to 3 atm
Band: reptile skin, buckle
Price: $17,900; limited to 460 pieces

Altiplano 900P

Reference number: G0A39110
Movement: manually wound, Piaget Caliber 900P;
ø 30.4 mm, height 3.65 mm; 20 jewels; 21,600 vph;
inverted movement construction; 48-hour power
reserve
Functions: hours, minutes
Case: rose gold, ø 38 mm, height 3.65 mm; sapphire
crystal
Band: reptile skin, buckle
Price: $24,900
Variations: white gold

Altiplano 900P

Reference number: G0A42110
Movement: manually wound, Piaget Caliber 900P;
ø 30.4 mm, height 3.65 mm; 20 jewels; 21,600 vph;
inverted movement construction; 48-hour power
reserve
Functions: hours, minutes
Case: rose gold, ø 38 mm, height 3.65 mm; sapphire
crystal
Band: reptile skin, buckle
Price: $24,900; limited to 200 pieces

Altiplano Date

Reference number: G0A38131
Movement: automatic, Piaget Caliber 1205P;
ø 29.9 mm, height 3 mm; 27 jewels; 21,600 vph;
microrotor in rose gold; côtes de Genève; 44-hour
power reserve
Functions: hours, minutes, subsidiary seconds; date
Case: rose gold, ø 40 mm, height 6.36 mm; sapphire
crystal; transparent case back; water-resistant to
3 atm
Band: reptile skin, buckle
Price: $23,800
Variations: white gold ($24,700)

Altiplano Chronograph

Reference number: G0A40030
Movement: manually wound, Piaget Caliber 883P;
ø 27 mm, height 4.65 mm; 30 jewels; 28,800 vph;
twin spring barrels; extra-thin construction; 50-hour
power reserve
Functions: hours, minutes, subsidiary seconds;
second 24-hour display (second time zone); flyback
chronograph
Case: pink gold, ø 41 mm, height 8.24 mm; sapphire
crystal; transparent case back; water-resistant to
3 atm
Band: reptile skin, buckle
Price: $28,600

Gouverneur Perpetual Calendar

Reference number: G0A40018
Movement: automatic, Piaget Caliber 855P;
ø 28.4 mm, height 5.6 mm; 38 jewels; 21,600 vph;
80-hour power reserve
Functions: hours, minutes, subsidiary seconds;
additional 12-hour display (second time zone);
day/night indicator; perpetual calendar with date,
weekday (retrograde), month, leap year
Case: pink gold, ø 43 mm, height 10.5 mm; sapphire
crystal; transparent case back; water-resistant to
3 atm
Band: reptile skin, folding clasp
Price: $55,500
Variations: white gold set with diamonds ($70,000)

Gouverneur Chronograph

Reference number: G0A37112
Movement: automatic, Piaget Caliber 882P;
ø 27 mm, height 5.6 mm; 33 jewels; 28,800 vph;
80-hour power reserve
Functions: hours, minutes; second 24-hour display
(second time zone); flyback chronograph; date
Case: pink gold, ø 43 mm, height 10.4 mm; sapphire
crystal; transparent case back; water-resistant to
3 atm
Band: reptile skin, buckle
Price: $34,200
Variations: set with diamonds ($48,500)

Polo S Automatic

Reference number: G0A41002
Movement: automatic, Piaget Caliber 1110P;
ø 25.6 mm, height 4 mm; 25 jewels; 28,800 vph;
perlage on mainplate, blued screws, finely finished
with côtes de Genève; 50-hour power reserve
Functions: hours, minutes, sweep seconds; date
Case: stainless steel, ø 42 mm, height 9.4 mm;
sapphire crystal; transparent case back; water-
resistant to 10 atm
Band: stainless steel, folding clasp
Price: $9,350
Variations: white and gray dial; rubber strap

Polo S Automatic

Reference number: G0A41002
Movement: automatic, Piaget Caliber 1110P;
ø 25.6 mm, height 4 mm; 25 jewels; 28,800 vph;
perlage on mainplate, blued screws, fine finishing
with côtes de Genève; 50-hour power reserve
Functions: hours, minutes, sweep seconds; date
Case: stainless steel, ø 42 mm, height 9.4 mm;
sapphire crystal; transparent case back; water-
resistant to 10 atm
Band: stainless steel, folding clasp
Price: $9,350
Variations: white and gray dial; rubber strap

Polo S Chronograph

Reference number: G0A41004
Movement: automatic, Piaget Caliber 1160P;
ø 25.6 mm, height 5.72 mm; 35 jewels; 28,800 vph;
perlage on mainplate, blued screws, fine finishing
with côtes de Genève; 50-hour power reserve
Functions: hours, minutes; chronograph; date
Case: stainless steel, ø 42 mm, height 11.2 mm;
sapphire crystal; transparent case back; water-
resistant to 10 atm
Band: stainless steel, folding clasp
Price: $12,400
Variations: blue and gray dial; rubber strap

Emperador Coussin XL 700P

Reference number: G0A41041
Movement: quartz, Piaget Caliber 700P;
ø 34.9 mm, height 5.5 mm; 32 jewels; hybrid
movement with a quartz regulator, internal power
generation by microgenerator, barrel spring winding
by microrotor; 42-hour power reserve
Functions: hours, minutes
Case: white gold, ø 46.5 mm, height 10.4 mm bezel
with black DLC coating; sapphire crystal; transparent
case back
Band: reptile skin, folding clasp
Price: $70,000; limited to 118 pieces

Limelight Gala

Reference number: G0A38160
Movement: quartz, Piaget Caliber 690P
Functions: hours, minutes
Case: white gold, ø 32 mm, height 7.4 mm bezel set
with 62 diamonds; sapphire crystal; water-resistant
to 3 atm
Band: satin, folding clasp
Price: $33,300
Variations: rose gold ($32,300)

Limelight Gala Milanaise

Reference number: G0A41213
Movement: quartz, Piaget Caliber 690P
Functions: hours, minutes
Case: rose gold, ø 32 mm, height 7.4 mm bezel set
with 62 diamonds; sapphire crystal; water-resistant
to 3 atm
Band: rose gold Milanese, sliding fastener
Price: $34,500
Variations: white gold ($36,000)

Caliber 883P

Manually wound; stop-seconds; double mainspring barrel, 50-hour power reserve; Geneva Seal
Functions: hours, minutes, subsidiary seconds; second 24-hour display (second time zone); flyback chronograph
Diameter: 27 mm
Height: 4.65 mm
Jewels: 30
Frequency: 28,800 vph
Shock protection: Incabloc
Remarks: world's thinnest manually wound chronograph movement currently produced

Caliber 1208P

Automatic; single spring barrel, 44-hour power reserve; Geneva Seal
Functions: hours, minutes, subsidiary seconds
Diameter: 29.9 mm
Height: 2.35 mm
Jewels: 27
Balance: glucydur
Frequency: 21,600 vph
Balance spring: flat hairspring
Shock protection: Incabloc
Remarks: world's thinnest automatic movement currently being manufactured

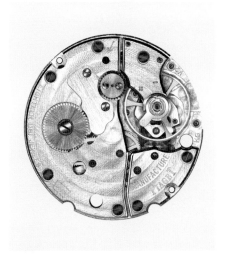

Caliber 430P

Manually wound; single spring barrel, 43-hour power reserve
Functions: hours, minutes
Diameter: 20.5 mm
Height: 2.1 mm
Jewels: 18
Balance: glucydur
Frequency: 21,600 vph
Balance spring: flat hairspring
Remarks: finely finished movement, 131 components

Caliber 1160P

Automatic; single spring barrel, 50-hour power reserve
Functions: hours, minutes; chronograph; date
Diameter: 25.58 mm
Height: 5.72 mm
Jewels: 35
Frequency: 28,800 vph
Remarks: perlage on mainplate, blued screws, fine finishing with côtes de Genève, 262 components

Caliber 1110P

Automatic; single spring barrel, 50-hour power reserve
Functions: hours, minutes, sweep seconds; date
Diameter: 25.58 mm
Height: 4 mm
Jewels: 25
Frequency: 28,800 vph
Remarks: perlage on mainplate, blued screws, fine finishing with côtes de Genève, 180 components

Caliber 700P

Quartz; hybrid movement with electromagnetic escapement with quartz-regulated micro-generator (5.33 rpm); spring drive powered by guillochéed microrotor; bridges and plates with black DLC coating; single spring barrel
Functions: hours, minutes
Diameter: 34.9 mm
Height: 5.5 mm
Jewels: 32

PIERRE DEROCHE

Pierre DeRoche SA
Le Revers 1
CH-1345 Le Lieu
Switzerland

Tel.:
+41-21-841-1169

Fax:
+41-21-841-2052

E-mail:
ca.dubois@pierrederoche.com

Website:
www.pierrederoche.com

Founded:
2004

Number of employees:
3

Annual production:
250 watches

Distribution:
retail

Most important collections/price range:
TNT Royal Retro / approx. $20,500; SplitRock
Big Numbers / approx. $11,500; GrandCliff QA /
approx. $17,600

Apples apparently, are simply destined to fall not far from the tree, no matter what they intend. Pierre Dubois was born into a family with deep roots in watchmaking and a name that reinforced that fact. Dubois Dépraz, the outstanding manufacturer of movements and special modules, was founded by his great-grandfather, and two of his brothers now head that company. He went into finance, but the horological muse set him to work for fourteen years as CFO and COO for Audemars Piguet. "It's there that the genetic makeup from the four generations of watchmakers that he comes from rose to the surface, and with it the passion for watchmaking," says his wife Carole Dubois, who developed the same passion. The couple decided to leverage family ties and create a brand of watches—chic, complicated, yet fun—produced in the Vallée de Joux, the heart of watch country.

His name, which translates as "rock from wood," was a problem. When he was a child, an old peasant once remarked to him that wood and rock don't mix and that a better name would be "rock pebble of stone": *"Pierre Caillou de Roche."* The pebble got lost, Pierre DeRoche remained.

Working with the R&D department at Dubois Dépraz has been crucial for the ten-plus years of the brand's existence. Nevertheless, the two companies remain separate. They began with complicated chronographs featuring retrograde functions, multilayered, animated dials, and solid movements. The GrandCliff collection now exists in a host of different versions, from sober-elegant to sporty-intricate. For the TNT series, they decided on genuine dance of six-second hands that deliver ten retrograde seconds each. For a slightly tamer experience, Pierre DeRoche has the SplitRock, whose large numbers and rectangular cases give it a retro art deco feel.

TNT GMT Power Reserve 43 "Atacampa"

Reference number: TNT10012ACTI2-002CAO
Movement: automatic, exclusive Dubois Dépraz caliber; ø 36.6 mm, height 6.85 mm; 21 jewels; decorated and engraved rotor; 42-hour power reserve
Functions: hours, minutes, seconds; 24-hour time zone; power reserve indicator; date hand
Case: black DLC-treated titanium, ø 43 mm, height 14.01 mm; steel lugs, bezel, crown-guard and screw-in crown; sapphire crystal; transparent case back; water-resistant to 10 atm
Band: sand-colored rubber, folding clasp
Remarks: special sand-colored dial pays tribute to the Atacampa Desert in Latin America
Price: $14,000; limited to 5 pieces

GrandCliff Pure

Reference number: GRC10009ACI0-006CRO
Movement: automatic; ø 26 mm, height 4.85 mm; 28,800 vph; 21 jewels; 40-hour power reserve
Functions: hours, minutes, seconds; date; power reserve indicator
Case: steel, ø 40 mm, height 10.40 mm; antireflective sapphire crystal; transparent case back; water-resistant to 5 atm
Band: reptile skin, folding clasp
Price: $6,320
Variations: white dial; mother-of-pearl dial ($7,220); mother-of-pearl dial and case set with diamonds

SplitRock Big Numbers Diamond-Set

Reference number: SPR30001ACI1-004CRO
Movement: exclusive Dubois Dépraz caliber; length 31.5 mm, height 6.95 mm; 39 jewels; open-worked, decorated oscillating weight; 40-hour power reserve
Functions: hours, minutes, subsidiary seconds; chronograph; power reserve indicator
Case: stainless steel, 45.5 × 31.5 mm, height 13.5 mm; set with 108 diamonds; sapphire crystal; transparent case back
Band: reptile skin, folding clasp
Price: $21,740
Variations: rose gold case (price on request), limited to 21 pieces

Porsche Design Group
Groenerstrasse 5
D-71636 Ludwigsburg
Germany

Tel.:
+49-711-911-0

E-mail:
timepieces@porsche-design.us

Website:
www.porsche-design.com

Founded:
1972

U.S. distributor:
Porsche Design of America, Inc.
Plaza Tower
600 Anton Blvd., Suite 1280
Costa Mesa, CA 92626
770-290-7500
770-290-0227 (fax)
timepieces@porsche-design.us
www.porsche-design.com

Most important collections/price range:
Chronotimer Series 1, 1919 Datetimer Eternity,
1919 Globetimer, 1919 Chronotimer, Monobloc
Actuator / $3,150 to $7,450

PORSCHE DESIGN

In watchmaking, as in many industrial fields, design without quality "inside" is nothing more than icing with no cake. Porsche Design has always made sure it was partnering with the best to manufacture its products. In 1978, it was the Schaffhausen-based brand IWC that produced watches under the name Porsche Design through a license agreement with the F.A. Porsche design firm. But when the Porsche family purchased Eterna in 1995, a new era began—for both brands. When the IWC license expired in 1998, Eterna took over manufacturing responsibilities for the designer brand. In March 2014, Eterna and Porsche Design separated. Since September of that year, all Porsche Design watches have been developed by the company subsidiary Porsche Design timepieces in Solothurn, Switzerland, in collaboration with the well-established design studio in Zell-am-See, Austria.

Porsche Design was founded by Professor Ferdinand Alexander Porsche in 1972—the fountainhead of numerous objects in daily use beyond just watches. The Professor—a title bestowed by the Austrian government—who died in April 2012, created a string of classic objects at his "Studio," but sports car fans will always remember him for the Porsche 911.

In 2003, the Professor decided to found his own company, which is separate from the carmaker. The brand is proud not only of its unusual designs, but also of its use of light metals: In the 1970s already, it was using black PVD-coated aluminum and titanium for its watches and cases. The Chronotimer collection harked back to this very avant-garde esthetic statement. The streamlined and rigorous design is also visible in the new 1919 collection, named for the foundation date of the Bauhaus movement.

Porsche Design engineers are obviously not averse to picking up ideas from the automobile industry. Not astonishingly, then, the innovative rocker arm that activates the chronograph of the new Monobloc Actuator was inspired from the valve control of high-powered race cars using tappets.

Monobloc Actuator GMT-Chronotimer
Reference number: 6030.6.02.001.02.5
Movement: automatic, ETA Caliber 7754; ø 30 mm, height 7.9 mm; 25 jewels; 28,800 vph; 48-hour power reserve
Functions: hours, minutes; rate control; 2nd 24-hour display (2nd time zone); chronograph; date
Case: titanium, ø 45.5 mm, height 15.6 mm; sapphire crystal; transparent case back; screw-in crown; water-resistant to 10 atm
Band: titanium, folding clasp
Remarks: large rocker pusher integrated into right case side
Price: $6,900

Monobloc Actuator 24H-Chronotimer
Reference number: 6030.6.01.007.05.2
Movement: automatic, ETA Caliber 7754; ø 30 mm, height 7.9 mm; 25 jewels; 28,800 vph; 48-hour power reserve
Functions: hours, minutes, rate control; 2nd 24-hour display (2nd time zone); chronograph; date
Case: titanium with black titanium carbide coating, ø 45.5 mm, height 15.6 mm; sapphire crystal; transparent case back; screw-in crown; water-resistant to 10 atm
Band: rubber, folding clasp
Remarks: large rocker pusher integrated into right case side
Price: $7,450

1919 Datetimer Eternity Blue
Reference number: 6020.3.01.005.01.2
Movement: automatic, Sellita Caliber SW200-1; ø 25.6 mm, height 4.6 mm; 26 jewels; 28,800 vph; 38-hour power reserve
Functions: hours, minutes, sweep seconds; date
Case: titanium, ø 42 mm, height 11.92 mm; sapphire crystal; screw-in crown; water-resistant to 10 atm
Band: titanium, folding clasp
Price: $3,500
Variations: rubber strap

PRAMZIUS

Whatever their political affiliations or leanings, no one can deny that Eastern Europe, the Baltic states, and Russia, in particular, exert a considerable fascination on people. It may be the extreme quality of everything that comes from that part of the world that appeals to our need for drama—the long and troubled history; the wars; the brutal leaders; the staggeringly talented people, from musicians to chess players; the brooding novels about adultery, complex love affairs, suicide, war and some peace; lucubrating students caught between guilt and the love and moral standing of a teenage prostitute. You-Tubistas are captivated by the antics of modern-day Russians caught on smartphones and dashcams. At any rate, in a large swath of land everything is bigger. And that may explain the success of Détente Group and its boisterous watches celebrating Big Mechanics—not for the limp-wristed, by any stretch.

In 2017, Craig Hester, distributor of Vostok-Europe, Sturmanskie, and other brands, parlayed over 20 years' experience in the watch business into the launch of a series of watches that would continue paying tribute to this wild, dangerous, creative, and at times sincerely eccentric part of the world. The name of the brand, Pramzius, is a reference to the Baltic Ruler of Time, an ancient and, appropriately, pagan god. Funding for the project came from a brief but successful Kickstarter campaign.

The first series of Pramzius is devoted to the renowned Trans-Siberian Railway and was inspired by a correspondingly themed pocket watch from back in the day. The modern version is, accordingly, big—48 millimeters in diameter—made of high-grade steel instead of brass. The weight is insignificant, since the watch is carried on a sportive leather strap that passes under the watch. The wide watch face makes for excellent readability even at night, when the three hands sweep the full-lume dial of Superluminova. A relief of the train appears on the case back. The machine inside is a robust Seiko NH23; it keeps time and will not break the bank.

Pramzius Watches
31 Halls Hill Road
Colchester, CT 06415

E-mail:
info@pramzius.com

Website:
www.pramzius.com

Founded:
2017

Number of employees:
4

Annual production:
2,500

Distribution:
Direct sales

Most important collections/price range:
Trans-Siberian Railroad $279 to $328; Berlin Watch (to be released end of 2017)

Trans-Siberian Railroad Blue Dial
Reference number:
Movement: automatic, Seiko Caliber NH38A; ø 27.4 mm, height 5.32 mm; 24 jewels; 21,600 vph; open-heart dial on balance; 41-hour power reserve
Functions: hours, minutes, sweep seconds
Case: stainless steel, ø 48 mm, height 14.6 mm, K1 mineral glass; 3D locomotive rendering on case back; water-resistant to 3 atm
Band: calfskin bund strap, buckle
Remarks: comes with extra leather and nylon strap
Price: $279
Variation: sapphire crystal ($328)

Trans-Siberian Antique White
Reference number:
Movement: automatic, Seiko Caliber NH38A; ø 27.4 mm, height 5.32 mm; 24 jewels; 21,600 vph; open-heart dial on balance; 41-hour power reserve
Functions: hours, minutes, sweep seconds
Case: stainless steel, ø 48 mm, height 14.6 mm, K1 mineral glass; 3D locomotive rendering on case back; water-resistant to 3 atm.
Band: calfskin bund strap, buckle
Remarks: comes with extra leather and nylon strap
Price: $279
Variation: sapphire crystal ($328)

Trans-Siberian Railroad Black
Reference number:
Movement: automatic, Seiko Caliber NH38A; ø 27.4 mm, height 5.32 mm; 24 jewels; 21,600 vph; open-heart dial on balance; 41-hour power reserve
Functions: hours, minutes, sweep seconds
Case: stainless steel, ø 48 mm, height 14.6 mm, K1 mineral glass; 3D locomotive rendering on case back; water-resistant to 3 atm.
Band: calfskin bund strap, buckle
Remarks: comes with extra leather and nylon strap
Price: $279
Variation: sapphire crystal ($328)

Ressence Watches
Meirbrug 1
2000 Antwerp
Belgium

Tel.:
+32-3-446-0060

E-mail:
hello@ressence.be

Website:
www.ressencewatches.com

Founded:
2011

U.S. distributor:
Totally Worth It, LLC
76 Division Avenue
Summit, NJ 07901-2309
201-894-4710
724-263-2286
info@totallyworthit.com

Most important collections/price range:
Type 1 / from $20,600; Type 3 / at $42,200;
Type 5 / at $35,800

RESSENCE

It's rare for anyone to cause a buzz at the great Baselworld watch and jewelry fair based on the presentation of some prototypes. But Belgian Benoit Mintiens had the luck of the newcomer. The vicious 2008–2009 recession had left space available in the Palace pavilion in Basel, one of the crucibles of innovative watchmaking, and an audience curious about novelties in the post-bling world.

He returned in 2011 with the Type 1001. It consisted of a large rotating dial carrying a hand that pointed to a minute track on the bezel. Hours, small second, and a day-night indication rotated on dedicated subsidiary dials. The ballet on the dial mesmerized those who saw it, so he sold all his fifty models off the bat.

The mechanics behind the Ressence watches—the name is a contraction of "Renaissance of the Essential"—are basically simple: a stripped-down and rebuilt ETA 2824 leaves the minute wheel as the main driver of the other wheels. Mintiens, however, was about to go further.

In 2012, came the Type 0 series, which included a few design changes. Then, in a successful bid to improve readability, he immersed the dial section in oil, giving the displays a very contemporary two-dimensional look, much like an electronic watch. The movement had to be kept separate from the oil, and was connected to the dial using magnets and a set of superconductors and a Farraday cage to protect the movement from magnetism. A series of baffles compensate for the expanding and contracting of the oil due to temperature shifts. The Type 3 also lost the crown, the only obstacle to making a perfectly smooth watch, in favor of a clever setting and winding mechanism controlled by the case back. The watch is an automatic, of course. Not surprisingly, it won the Revelation Prize at the Grand Prix d'Horlogerie in Geneva in 2013.

The latest model, the Type 5, is a divers' watch. It has a temperature gauge and a minimalistic calendar with two consecutive colored lines for a weekend of choice. The winding system has to be locked into place and provides water-resistance to 10 atm.

Type 1 Squared

Movement: automatic, ROCS 1.3 (module with ETA 2824-2 base); ø 32 mm, 40 jewels; 28,800 vph; Ressence Orbital Convex System: rotating minute dial, with rotating satellites for additional displays; winding and hand-setting using case back; 27 gear wheels, 212 components; 36-hour power reserve
Functions: minutes; hours and subsidiary seconds (eccentric, peripheral); weekday (eccentric, peripheral)
Case: stainless steel, 41 × 41 mm, height 11.5 mm; sapphire crystal
Band: reptile skin, buckle
Price: $20,600

Type 5 BB

Movement: automatic, ROCS 5 (module with ETA 2824-2 base); ø 32 mm; 41 jewels; 28,800 vph; Ressence Orbital Convex System: rotating minute dial, with rotating satellites for additional displays; winding and hand-setting using case back; 36-hour power reserve
Functions: minutes; hours and 90-second "runner," oil temperature gauge (eccentric, peripheral)
Case: titanium with black PVD coating, ø 46 mm, height 15.5 mm; sapphire crystal; water-resistant to 10 atm
Band: calfskin, buckle
Remarks: two separate, sealed case chambers; dial side chamber filled with oil; magnetic drive for display disks
Price: $42,200

Type 3

Movement: automatic, ROCS 3 (module with ETA 2824-2 base); ø 32 mm; 47 jewels; 28,800 vph; Ressence Orbital Convex System: rotating minute dial, with rotating satellites for additional displays; winding and hand-setting using case back; 36-hour power reserve
Functions: minutes; hours and 360-second "runner," oil temperature, date, weekday (eccentric, peripheral)
Case: titanium, ø 44 mm, height 15 mm; sapphire crystal
Band: calfskin, buckle
Remarks: two separate, sealed case chambers; dial side chamber filled with oil; magnetic drive for display disks
Price: $35,600

RGM

RGM Watch Company
801 W. Main Street
Mount Joy, PA 17552

Tel.:
717-653-9799

Fax:
717-653-9770

E-mail:
sales@rgmwatches.com

Founded:
1992

Number of employees:
12

Annual production:
200–300 watches

Distribution:
RGM deals directly with customers.

Most important collections/price range:
Pennsylvania Series (completely made in the
U.S.) / $2,500 to $125,000 range

If there is any part of the United States that can somehow be considered its "watch valley," it may be the state of Pennsylvania. And one of the big players there is no doubt Roland Murphy, founder of RGM. Murphy, born in Maryland, went through the watchmaker's drill, studying at the Bowman Technical School, then in Switzerland, and finally working with Swatch before launching his own business in 1992.

His first series, Signature, paid homage to local horological genius through vintage pocket watch movements developed by Hamilton. His second big project was the Caliber 801, the first "high-grade mechanical movement made in series in America since Hamilton stopped production of the 992 B in 1969," Murphy says, grinning. The next goal was to manufacture an all-American-made watch, the Pennsylvania Tourbillon.

And so, model by model, Murphy continues to expand his "Made in U.S.A." portfolio. "You cannot compare us to the big brands," says Murphy. "We are small and specialized, the needs are different. We work directly with the customer." In 2012, the brand's twentieth anniversary, RGM went retro with the 801 Aircraft. In 2015 came a baseball-themed watch. As for functionality, RGM makes a fine diver water-resistant to 70 atm, and the series 400 chronograph with a pulsometer and extra large subdials for visibility.

One of the brand's main creations is the Caliber 20, which revives an old invention once in favor for railroad watches. The motor barrel is a complex but robust system in which the watch is wound by the barrel and the barrel arbor then drives the gear train. Less friction and wear and a slimmer chance of damage to the watch if the mainspring breaks are the two main advantages. Even the finishing on components is done following research into earlier American models.

Caliber 20

Reference number: Caliber 20
Movement: manually wound, RGM motor barrel movement; 34.4 × 30.4 mm; 19 jewels; 18,000 vph; perlage and côtes de Genève; 42-hour power reserve
Functions: hours, minutes, subsidiary seconds on disk; moon phase
Case: stainless steel, 42.5 × 38.5 mm, height 9.7 mm; hands of blued steel; sapphire crystal; transparent case back
Band: reptile skin, buckle
Price: $29,500
Variations: rose gold ($42,500)

Pennsylvania Series 801

Reference number: PS 801 EE
Movement: manually wound, RGM Caliber 801; ø 37 mm; 19 jewels; lever escapement; screw balance; U.S. components: bridges, main plate, settings, 7-tooth winding click; circular côtes de Genève, silver guilloché; partially skeletonized dial; 42-hour power reserve
Functions: hours, minutes, subsidiary seconds
Case: stainless steel, ø 43.3 mm, height 12.3 mm; sapphire crystal; sapphire crystal; transparent case back; water-resistant to 5 atm
Band: reptile or ostrich skin, folding clasp
Remarks: grand feu enamel skeleton dial with Roman or Arabic numerals; guilloché
Price: $11,900
Variations: rose gold ($24,700)

Pennsylvania Tourbillon

Reference number: mm2
Movement: manual winding, American-made; ø 37.22; 19 jewels; 18,000 vph; German silver and rose gold finish with perlage and côtes de Genève; 42-hour power reserve
Functions: hours, minutes; 1-minute tourbillon
Case: stainless steel, ø 43.5 mm, height 13.5 mm; blued-steel minute and hour hands; guilloché dial; sapphire crystal; transparent case back
Band: reptile skin, buckle
Price: $95,000
Variations: rose gold ($125,000); platinum (price on request)

Enamel Corps of Engineers
Reference number: 151 COE
Movement: automatic Swiss; ø 37 mm; 23 jewels; circular côtes de Genève; in-house 14k solid gold rotor; 42-hour power reserve
Functions: hours, minutes, sweep seconds
Case: stainless steel, ø 38.5 mm, height 10.6 mm; curved sapphire crystal; transparent case back; water-resistant to 5 atm
Band: leather, buckle
Remarks: grand feu white glass enamel dial with aged luminous numbers
Price: $6,950
Variations: CP2 titanium ($7,950)

Enamel Corps of Engineers
Reference number: 801 COE
Movement: manually wound, RGM Caliber 801; ø 37 mm; 19 jewels; lever escapement; screw balance; U.S. components: bridges, main plate, settings, 7-tooth winding click; circular côtes de Genève; 42-hour power reserve
Functions: hours, minutes, subsidiary seconds
Case: stainless steel, ø 42 mm, height 10.5 mm; sapphire crystal; transparent case back; water-resistant to 5 atm
Band: leather, buckle
Remarks: grand feu white glass enamel dial with aged luminous numbers
Price: $9,700
Variations: stainless steel bracelet ($10,450)

801 Aircraft
Reference number: 801 A
Movement: manually wound, RGM Caliber 801; ø 37 mm; 19 jewels; lever escapement; screw balance; U.S. components: bridges, main plate, settings, 7-tooth winding click; circular côtes de Genève; 42-hour power reserve
Functions: hours, minutes, subsidiary seconds
Case: stainless steel, ø 42 mm, height 10.5 mm; sapphire crystal; transparent case back; water-resistant to 5 atm
Band: leather, buckle
Price: $7,450
Variations: green or red dial; stainless steel bracelet ($8,250)

Chronograph
Reference number: 400
Movement: automatic, RGM/Valgranges; ø 36.6 mm; 25 jewels; 28,800 vph; rhodium finish with perlage and côtes de Genève; 46-hour power reserve
Functions: hours, minutes, sweep second; date; chronograph, 30-minute/12-hour totalizers
Case: polished and satin brushed stainless steel, ø 42 mm, height 15.3 mm; sapphire crystal
Band: leather, buckle
Price: $3,500
Variations: black, silver, blue, or orange dial

Professional Diver
Reference number: 300-2
Movement: automatic, RGM/ETA Caliber 2892-A2; ø 25.6 mm; 21 jewels; 28,800 vph; rhodium finish with perlage and côtes de Genève; 42-hour power reserve
Functions: hours, minutes, sweep seconds; date
Case: brushed stainless steel, ø 43.5 mm, height 17 mm; sapphire crystal; unidirectional ceramic bezel insert
Band: silicon, buckle
Price: $3,700
Variations: bracelet ($4,450)

Pilot Professional
Reference number: 151 A
Movement: automatic, RGM/ETA Caliber 2892-A2; ø 25.6 mm; 21 jewels; 28,800 vph; rhodium finish with perlage and côtes de Genève; 42-hour power reserve
Functions: hours, minutes, sweep seconds; date
Case: brushed stainless steel, ø 38.5 mm, height 9.9 mm; domed sapphire crystal; transparent case back
Band: leather, buckle
Remarks: date at 4:30, two-toned technical dial with Superluminova
Price: $3,350
Variations: titanium ($4,350)

RICHARD MILLE

Mille never stops delivering the wow to the watch world with what he calls his "race cars for the wrist." He is not an engineer, however, but rather a marketing expert who earned his first paychecks in the watch division of the French defense, automobile, and aerospace concern Matra in the early 1980s. This was a time of fundamental changes in technology, and the European watch industry was being confronted with gigantic challenges. "I have no historical relationship with watchmaking whatsoever," says Mille, "and so I have no obligations either. The mechanics of my watches are geared toward technical feasibility."

In the 1990s, Mille had to go to the expert workshop of Audemars Piguet Renaud & Papi (APRP) in Le Locle to find a group of watchmakers and engineers who would take on the Mille challenge. Audemars Piguet even succumbed to the temptation of testing those scandalous innovations—materials, technologies, functions—in a Richard Mille watch before daring to use them in its own collections (Tradition d'Excellence).

Since 2007, Audemars Piguet has also become a shareholder in Richard Mille, and so the three firms are now closely bound. The assembly of the watches is done in the Franches-Montagnes region in the Jura, where Richard Mille opened the firm Horométrie.

Richard Mille timepieces have also found their way onto the wrists of elite athletes, like tennis star Rafael Nadal and sprinter Yohan Blake. To keep its fans happy, the brand never ceases to explore the lunatic fringe of the technically possible, like the collaboration with Airbus Corporate Jets, which gave rise to a case made of a lightweight titanium-aluminum alloy used in turbines. Then there is the superlight and tough material called graphene developed at the University of Manchester and used by McLaren. Mille's other side is more romantic: the Tourbillon Fleur that features a tourbillon that rises out of the opening petals of a magnolia, the Pink Lady Sapphire, or an "erotic watch" that makes naughty suggestions.

Richard Mille
c/o Horométrie SA
11, rue du Jura
CH-2345 Les Breuleux
Switzerland

Tel.:
+41-32-959-4353

Fax:
+41-32-959-4354

E-mail:
info@richardmille.ch

Website:
www.richardmille.com

Founded:
2000

Annual production:
approx. 4,000 watches

U.S. distributor:
Richard Mille Americas
8701 Wilshire Blvd.
Beverly Hills, CA 90211
310-205-5555

Tourbillon Split Seconds Chronograph Ultralight McLaren F1

Reference number: RM 50-03
Movement: manually wound, Richard Mille Caliber RM52-03 × 31.1 × 32.15 mm, height 9.92 mm; 43 jewels; 21,600 vph; 1-minute tourbillon; titanium and TPT carbon plates and bridges; 70-hour power reserve
Functions: hours, minutes, subsidiary seconds; power reserve, torque and crown position indicator; split-second chronograph
Case: composite material, Graph TPT, 44.5 × 49.65 mm, height 16.1 mm; sapphire crystal; transparent case back; crown with torque limitation
Band: textile, folding clasp
Remarks: cooperation with McLaren F1
Price: $1,000,000; limited to 75 pieces

Tourbillon Split Seconds Chronograph Jean Todt Sapphire

Reference number: RM 56-JT
Movement: manually wound, Caliber RMCC1; 32 × 36.7 mm, height 7.53 mm; 35 jewels; 21,600 vph; 1-minute tourbillon; function selector; skeletonized titanium movement; 70-hour power reserve
Functions: hours, minutes, subsidiary seconds; power reserve, torque and crown position indicator; split-second chronograph
Case: sapphire crystal, 42.7 × 50.5 mm, height 19.25 mm; sapphire crystal; transparent case back
Band: silicon, buckle
Remarks: special edition for birthday of FIA president Jean Todt
Price: $1,939,000; limited to 5 pieces

Tourbillon Split Seconds Chronograph ACJ

Reference number: RM 50-02
Movement: manually wound, Richard Mille Caliber RM52-02; 30.4 × 32 mm, height 7.87 mm; 37 jewels; 21,600 vph; 1-minute tourbillon; bridges and plate made of titanium; stainless steel; 70-hour power reserve
Functions: hours, minutes, subsidiary seconds; power reserve, torque and function display; split-second chronograph
Case: titanium-aluminum (TiAl), 42.7 × 50.1 mm, height 16.5 mm; ATZ bezel; sapphire crystal; transparent case back; crown with torque limitation
Band: rubber, folding clasp
Remarks: developed with Airbus Corporate Jets
Price: $1,050,000

Flyback Chronograph

Reference number: RM 011-03
Movement: automatic, Richard Mille Caliber RMAC3; 28.45 × 30.25 mm, height 9 mm; 68 jewels; 28,800 vph; skeletonized titanium movement; winding rotor with variable geometry; 55-hour power reserve
Functions: hours, minutes, subsidiary seconds; flyback chronograph; full calendar with large date, month
Case: red gold, 44.5 × 50 mm, height 16.15 mm; sapphire crystal; transparent case back
Band: rubber, folding clasp
Price: $161,500

Tourbillon

Reference number: RM 017-01
Movement: manually wound, Richard Mille Caliber RM017; 29.45 × 31.2 mm, height 4.65 mm; 23 jewels; 21,600 vph; 1-minute tourbillon with ceramic capstone; partially skeletonized titanium plate
Functions: hours, minutes; power reserve indicator, crown position display
Case: pink gold and ceramic, 39 × 48 mm, height 12.6 mm; sapphire crystal; transparent case back
Band: silicon, folding clasp
Price: on request (sold only in Japan)

Tourbillon Erotic

Reference number: RM 69
Movement: manually wound, Richard Mille Caliber RM69; 30.9 × 32.8 mm, height 10.26 mm; 41 jewels; 21,600 vph; 1-minute tourbillon; three pusher-activated rollers; 69-hour power reserve
Functions: hours, minutes; messages
Case: titanium, 42.7 × 50 mm, height 16.15 mm; sapphire crystal; transparent case back; crown with torque limitation; water-resistant to 3 atm
Band: rubber, folding clasp
Remarks: individualized and randomized text messages, pusher removes hands for better readability
Price: $725,500; limited to 30 pieces

Tourbillon Diamond Twister

Reference number: RM 51-02
Movement: manually wound, Richard Mille Caliber RM51-02; 28.6 × 30.2 mm, height 4.97 mm; 21 jewels; 21,600 vph; 1-minute tourbillon; black onyx movement plate; 48-hour power reserve
Functions: hours, minutes (off-center)
Case: white gold, completely set with diamonds, 39.7 × 48 mm, height 12.6 mm; sapphire crystal; transparent case back; crown with torque limitation; water-resistant to 3 atm
Band: reptile skin, folding clasp
Remarks: helical skeletonized dial set with 270 diamonds
Price: $858,500

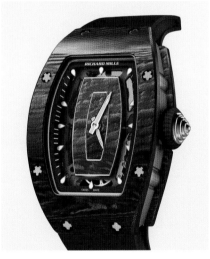

Ladies' Automatic

Reference number: RM 07-01
Movement: automatic, Richard Mille Caliber CRMA2; 22 × 29.9 mm, height 4.92 mm; 25 jewels; 28,800 vph; winding rotor with variable geometry; 50-hour power reserve
Functions: hours, minutes
Case: composite material (NTPT multilayer carbon and titanium), 31.4 × 45.6 mm, height 11.85 mm; sapphire crystal; transparent case back
Band: rubber, folding clasp
Price: $67,000

Ladies' Automatic Big Date

Reference number: RM 037
Movement: automatic, Richard Mille Caliber CRMA1; 22.9 × 28 mm, height 4.82 mm; 25 jewels; 28,800 vph; winding rotor with variable geometry; 50-hour power reserve
Functions: hours, minutes; crown function indicator; large date
Case: composite material (NTPT multilayer carbon and titanium), 34.4 × 52.6 mm, height 13 mm; sapphire crystal; transparent case back
Band: rubber, folding clasp
Price: $82,000

ROGER DUBUIS

When Richemont Group acquired a 60 percent controlling interest in the Geneva-based brand Roger Dubuis in 2008, the centerpiece of the deal was without a doubt the company's state-of-the-art workshops. Roger Dubuis, a *manufacture* fully committed to luxury and *"très haute horlogerie,"* makes some outstanding movement components—parts that, because of their quality and geographical origins, bear the coveted Seal of Geneva. Roger Dubuis credentials were also interesting to other brands in the Group, especially to Cartier, which gets its new skeletonized movements from the Roger Dubuis *manufacture*. In early 2016, Richemont went all the way and acquired the remaining 40 percent of the Genevan brand.

Roger Dubuis was founded in 1995 as SOGEM SA (Société Genevoise des Montres) by name-giver Roger Dubuis and financier Carlos Dias. These two exceptional men created a complete collection of unusual watches in no time flat—timepieces with unheard-of dimensions and incomparable complications. The meteoric development of this *manufacture* and the incredible frequency of its new introductions—even technical ones—continue to astound the traditional, rather conservative watch industry. Today, Roger Dubuis develops all of its own movements, currently numbering more than thirty different mechanical calibers. In addition, it produces just about all of its individual components in-house, from base plates to escapements and balance springs. With this heavy-duty technological know-how in its quiver, the brand has been able to build some remarkable movements, like the massive RD101, with four balance springs and all manner of differentials and gear works to drive the Excalibur Quatuor, the equivalent in horology to a monster truck. Even in their more delicate versions, like the new Brocéliande, featuring colored ivy leaves embracing the movement, Roger Dubuis watches always seem ready to jump off your wrist.

Manufacture Roger Dubuis
2, rue André-De-Garrini - CP 149
CH-1217 Meyrin 2 (Geneva)
Switzerland

Tel.:
+41-22-783-2828

Fax:
+41-22-783-2882

E-mail:
info@rogerdubuis.com

Website:
www.rogerdubuis.com

Founded:
1995

Annual production:
over 5,000 watches (estimated)

U.S. distributor:
Roger Dubuis New York
545 Madison Ave
New York, NY 10022
212-651-3773
Roger Dubuis Beverly Hills
9490 Brighton Way, Suite C
Beverly Hills, CA 90210
310-734-1855

Most important collections/price range:
Excalibur, Velvet / $12,000 to $1,100,000

Excalibur Spider Skeleton Automatic

Reference number: RDDBEX0574
Movement: automatic, Roger Dubuis Caliber RD820SQ; ø 36.1 mm, height 6.38 mm; 35 jewels; 28,800 vph; skeletonized movement, microrotor; 60-hour power reserve; Geneva Seal
Functions: hours, minutes
Case: rose gold with titanium inner case, partially rubber-coated, ø 45 mm, height 14.02 mm; sapphire crystal; transparent case back; water-resistant to 5 atm
Band: rubber, with calfskin overlay, folding clasp
Price: $87,000; limited to 88 pieces

Excalibur Spider Carbon Tourbillon

Reference number: RDDBEX0572
Movement: manually wound, Roger Dubuis Caliber RD509SQ; ø 36.1 mm, height 4.28 mm; 19 jewels; 21,600 vph; flying 1-minute tourbillon, skeletonized movement, carbon mainplate, bridges and upper tourbillon cage; 90-hour power reserve; Geneva Seal
Functions: hours, minutes, subsidiary seconds
Case: rose gold with titanium inner case, partially rubber-coated, ø 45 mm, height 14.02 mm; sapphire crystal; transparent case back; crown with rubber coating; water-resistant to 5 atm
Band: rubber, with textile overlay, folding clasp
Price: $190,000; limited to 88 pieces

Excalibur Spider Pirelli Skeleton

Reference number: RDDBEX0575
Movement: automatic, Roger Dubuis Caliber RD820SQ; ø 36.1 mm, height 6.38 mm; 35 jewels; 28,800 vph; skeletonized movement, microrotor; 60-hour power reserve; Geneva Seal
Functions: hours, minutes
Case: titanium with black DLC coating, ø 45 mm, height 14.02 mm; sapphire crystal; transparent case back; crown with rubber coating; water-resistant to 5 atm
Band: rubber, folding clasp
Remarks: strap with inserts of real, winning Formula One tires;
Price: $66,500; limited to 88 pieces
Variations: yellow or red flange

Excalibur Quatuor Cobalt MicroMelt

Reference number: RDDBEX0571
Movement: manually wound, Roger Dubuis Caliber RD101; ø 37.9 mm, height 10.6 mm; 113 jewels; 28,800 vph; four coupled escapement systems each with 4-Hz frequency; power transmission and synchronization through 3 satellite differentials; 40-hour power reserve; Geneva Seal
Functions: hours, minutes; power reserve indicator
Case: special alloy (chrome-cobalt), ø 48 mm, height 18.38 mm; sapphire crystal; transparent case back; water-resistant to 5 atm
Band: reptile skin, folding clasp
Price: $400,000; limited to 8 pieces

Excalibur Skeleton Flying Double Tourbillon

Reference number: RDDBEX0395
Movement: manually wound, Roger Dubuis Caliber RD01SQ; ø 37.8 mm, height 7.67 mm; 28 jewels; 21,600 vph; flying double tourbillon with equalizing differential, skeleton movement, galvanic black, beveled and with perlage; 48-hour power reserve; Geneva Seal
Functions: hours, minutes
Case: rose gold, ø 45 mm, height 14.7 mm; sapphire crystal; transparent case back; water-resistant to 5 atm
Band: reptile skin, folding clasp
Price: $290,000

Excalibur Skeleton Automatic

Reference number: RDDBEX0473
Movement: automatic, Roger Dubuis Caliber RD820SQ; ø 36.1 mm, height 6.38 mm; 35 jewels; 28,800 vph; skeletonized movement, microrotor; 60-hour power reserve; Geneva Seal
Functions: hours, minutes
Case: carbon fiber, ø 42 mm, height 12.14 mm; sapphire crystal; transparent case back; water-resistant to 3 atm
Band: reptile skin, folding clasp
Price: $58,000

Excalibur 45 Automatic

Reference number: RDDBEX0602
Movement: automatic, Roger Dubuis Caliber RD830; ø 29.21 mm, height 4 mm; 27 jewels; 28,800 vph; microrotor in rose gold; 48-hour power reserve
Functions: hours, minutes, subsidiary seconds; date
Case: titanium, ø 45 mm, height 14.7 mm; sapphire crystal; transparent case back; water-resistant to 3 atm
Band: rubber, folding clasp
Price: $16,600
Variations: various bands, cases, and dials

Excalibur 45 Automatic

Reference number: RDDBEX0566
Movement: automatic, Roger Dubuis Caliber RD830; ø 29.21 mm, height 4 mm; 27 jewels; 28,800 vph; microrotor in rose gold; 48-hour power reserve
Functions: hours, minutes, subsidiary seconds; date
Case: rose gold, ø 45 mm, height 14.7 mm; sapphire crystal; transparent case back; water-resistant to 3 atm
Band: reptile skin, folding clasp
Price: $30,500
Variations: various bands, cases, and dials

Excalibur 45 Automatic

Reference number: RDDBEX0567
Movement: automatic, Roger Dubuis Caliber RD830; ø 29.21 mm, height 4 mm; 27 jewels; 28,800 vph; microrotor in rose gold; 48-hour power reserve
Functions: hours, minutes, subsidiary seconds; date
Case: titanium with black DLC coating, ø 45 mm, height 14.7 mm; sapphire crystal; transparent case back; water-resistant to 3 atm
Band: rubber, folding clasp
Price: $15,800
Variations: various bands, cases, and dials

ROGER DUBUIS

Excalibur 42 Automatic

Reference number: RDDBEX0535
Movement: automatic, Roger Dubuis Caliber RD830; ø 29.21 mm, height 4 mm; 27 jewels; 28,800 vph; microrotor in rose gold; 48-hour power reserve
Functions: hours, minutes, subsidiary seconds; date
Case: stainless steel, ø 42 mm, height 10.18 mm; sapphire crystal; transparent case back; water-resistant to 3 atm
Band: reptile skin, folding clasp
Price: $12,400
Variations: various bands, cases, and dials

Excalibur 36 Automatic

Reference number: RDDBEX0587
Movement: automatic, Roger Dubuis Caliber RD830; ø 29.21 mm, height 4 mm; 27 jewels; 28,800 vph; microrotor in rose gold; 48-hour power reserve
Functions: hours, minutes, subsidiary seconds; date
Case: rose gold, ø 36 mm, height 9.8 mm; sapphire crystal; transparent case back; water-resistant to 3 atm
Band: reptile skin, folding clasp
Price: $22,100
Variations: titanium set with diamonds or sapphires ($17,400)

Excalibur 36 Automatic

Reference number: RDDBEX0588
Movement: automatic, Roger Dubuis Caliber RD830; ø 29.21 mm, height 4 mm; 27 jewels; 28,800 vph; microrotor in rose gold; 48-hour power reserve
Functions: hours, minutes, subsidiary seconds; date
Case: rose gold, ø 36 mm, height 9.8 mm; bezel set with 48 diamonds; sapphire crystal; transparent case back; water-resistant to 5 atm
Band: reptile skin, folding clasp
Remarks: mother-of-pearl dial
Price: $27,200

Velvet Automatic

Reference number: RDDBVE0069
Movement: automatic, Roger Dubuis Caliber RD830; ø 29.21 mm, height 4 mm; 27 jewels; 28,800 vph; 48-hour power reserve
Functions: hours, minutes
Case: rose gold, ø 36 mm, height 9.8 mm; sapphire crystal; transparent case back; water-resistant to 3 atm
Band: reptile skin, buckle
Remarks: dial flange set with 64 diamonds
Price: $23,600
Variations: various bands, cases, and dials

Velvet Automatic

Reference number: RDDBVE0070
Movement: automatic, Roger Dubuis Caliber RD830; ø 29.21 mm, height 4 mm; 27 jewels; 28,800 vph; 48-hour power reserve
Functions: hours, minutes
Case: white gold, ø 36 mm, height 9.8 mm; sapphire crystal; transparent case back; water-resistant to 3 atm
Band: reptile skin, buckle
Remarks: dial flange set with 64 diamonds
Price: $23,600

Velvet Automatic

Reference number: RDDBVE0073
Movement: automatic, Roger Dubuis Caliber RD830; ø 29.21 mm, height 4 mm; 27 jewels; 28,800 vph; 48-hour power reserve
Functions: hours, minutes
Case: rose gold, ø 36 mm, height 9.8 mm; bezel and lugs set with diamonds; sapphire crystal; transparent case back; water-resistant to 3 atm
Band: reptile skin, folding clasp
Remarks: mother-of-pearl dial
Price: $36,900
Variations: various bands, cases, and dials

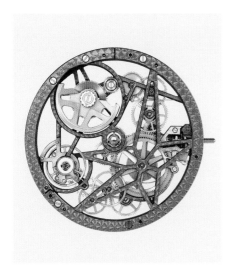

Caliber RD820SQ

Automatic; microrotor; single spring barrel, 60-hour power reserve; Geneva Seal
Functions: hours, minutes
Diameter: 36.1 mm
Height: 6.38 mm
Jewels: 35
Frequency: 28,800 vph
Remarks: skeletonized movement, rhodium-plated movement, finely finished with côtes de Genève; 167 components

Caliber RD01SQ

Manually wound; 2 flying 1-minute tourbillons with equalizing differential; skeletonized movement; single spring barrel, 48-hour power reserve; Geneva Seal, COSC certified chronometer
Functions: hours, minutes
Diameter: 37.8 mm
Height: 7.67 mm
Jewels: 28
Balance: glucydur variable inertia balance
Frequency: 21,600 vph
Remarks: 319 components

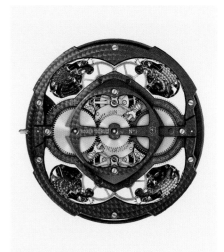

Caliber RD101

Manually wound; 4 radially mounted and inclined lever escapements, synchronized with 3 balancing differentials; planetary gears for winding and power reserve; skeletonized movement; double mainspring barrel, 40-hour power reserve; Geneva Seal
Functions: hours, minutes; power reserve indicator
Diameter: 37.9 mm
Height: 10.6 mm
Jewels: 113
Balance: glucydur (4x)
Frequency: 28,800 vph
Balance spring: flat hairspring
Remarks: galvanic blackening and beveling of frame parts, perlage; 590 components

Caliber RD640

Automatic; microrotor; single spring barrel, 52-hour power reserve; Geneva Seal
Functions: hours, minutes, subsidiary seconds; date
Diameter: 31.1 mm
Height: 4.5 mm
Jewels: 35
Balance: glucydur with smooth collar
Frequency: 28,800 vph
Balance spring: flat hairspring
Shock protection: Incabloc
Remarks: finely finished with côtes de Genève; 198 components

Caliber RD681

Automatic; column wheel control of chronograph functions, microrotor; single spring barrel, 52-hour power reserve; Geneva Seal
Functions: hours, minutes, subsidiary seconds; chronograph
Diameter: 30.6 mm
Height: 6.3 mm
Jewels: 44
Balance: glucydur
Frequency: 28,800 vph
Balance spring: flat hairspring
Remarks: finely finished with côtes de Genève; 280 components

Caliber RD830

Automatic; rose gold rotor; single spring barrel, 48-hour power reserve
Functions: hours, minutes, subsidiary seconds; date
Diameter: 29.21 mm
Height: 4 mm
Jewels: 27
Frequency: 28,800 vph
Remarks: finely finished with côtes de Genève; 183 components

ROLEX

Essentially, the Rolex formula for success has always been "what you see is what you get"—and plenty of it. For over a century now, the company has made wristwatch history without a need for *grandes complications*, perpetual calendars, tourbillons, or exotic materials. And its output in sheer quantity is phenomenal, at not quite a million watches per year. But make no mistake about it: The quality of these timepieces is legendary.

For as long as anyone can remember, this brand has held the top spot in the COSC's statistics, and year after year Rolex delivers just about half of all of the official institute's successfully tested mechanical chronometer movements. The brand has also pioneered several fundamental innovations: Rolex founder Hans Wilsdorf invented the hermetically sealed Oyster case in the 1920s, which he later outfitted with a screwed-in crown and an automatic movement wound by rotor. Shock protection, water resistance, the antimagnetic Parachrom hairspring, and automatic winding are some of the virtues that make wearing a Rolex timepiece much more comfortable and reliable. Because Wilsdorf patented his inventions for thirty years, Rolex had a head start on the competition.

Rolex watches and movements were at first produced in two different companies at two different sites. Only in 2004 did Geneva-based Rolex buy and integrate the Rolex movement factory in Biel. Then, in 2008, for its 100th birthday, the company built three gigantic new buildings with loads of steel and dark glass in the industrial suburb of Plan-les-Ouates. The automatic caliber 3255 suggests a brand still in innovation mode: It features new materials (nickel-phosphorus), special micromanufacturing technology (LIGA) to make the pallet fork and balance wheel of the Chronergy escapement, and a barrel spring that can store up more energy than ever. Meanwhile the company has built up representation in nearly 100 countries in the world, with more than 30 subsidiaries with customer service centers. The network also includes around 4,000 watchmakers trained according to Rolex standards.

Rolex SA
Rue François-Dussaud 3
CH-1211 Geneva 26
Switzerland

Website:
www.rolex.com

Founded:
1908

Number of employees:
over 2,000 (estimated)

Annual production:
approx. 1,000,000 watches (estimated)

U.S. distributor:
Rolex Watch U.S.A., Inc.
Rolex Building
665 Fifth Avenue
New York, NY 10022-5358
212-758-7700; 212-980-2166 (fax)
www.rolex.com

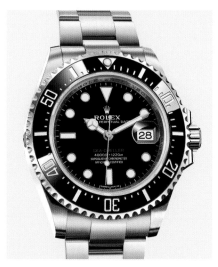

Oyster Perpetual Sea-Dweller
Reference number: 126600
Movement: automatic, Rolex Caliber 3235; ø 29.1 mm; 31 jewels; 28,800 vph; Parachrom spring, Paraflex shock absorber, Chronergy escapement, glucydur balance with microstella regulating bolts; 70-hour power reserve; COSC-certified chronometer
Functions: hours, minutes, sweep seconds; date
Case: stainless steel, ø 43 mm, height 13.8 mm; unidirectional bezel with ceramic insert and 0-60 scale; sapphire crystal; screw-in crown; helium valve; water-resistant to 122 atm
Band: Oyster stainless steel, folding clasp with extension link
Price: $11,350

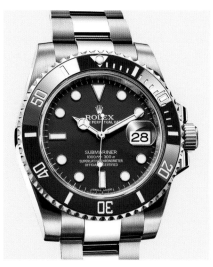

Oyster Perpetual Submariner Date
Reference number: 116619LB
Movement: automatic, Rolex Caliber 3135; ø 28.5 mm, height 6 mm; 31 jewels; 28,800 vph; Parachrom hairspring; 48-hour power reserve; COSC-certified chronometer
Functions: hours, minutes, sweep seconds; date
Case: white gold, ø 40 mm, height 12.5 mm; unidirectional bezel with ceramic insert and 0-60 scale; sapphire crystal; screw-in crown; water-resistant to 30 atm
Band: Oyster white gold, folding clasp with safety lock
Price: $36,850
Variations: stainless steel ($8,550), yellow gold bezel ($13,400); completely in yellow gold ($34,250)

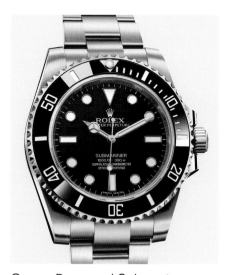

Oyster Perpetual Submariner
Reference number: 114060
Movement: automatic, Rolex Caliber 3130; ø 28.5 mm; 31 jewels; 28,800 vph; Parachrom spring, glucydur balance with microstella regulating bolts; 48-hour power reserve; COSC-certified chronometer
Functions: hours, minutes, sweep seconds
Case: stainless steel, ø 40 mm, height 12.5 mm; unidirectional bezel with ceramic insert and 0-60 scale; sapphire crystal; screw-in crown; water-resistant to 30 atm
Band: Oyster stainless steel, folding clasp with extension link
Price: $7,500

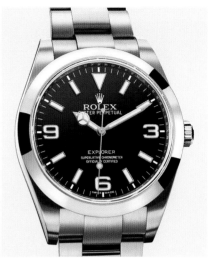

Oyster Perpetual GMT Master II

Reference number: 116710BLNR
Movement: automatic, Rolex Caliber 3186 (base Rolex Caliber 3135); ø 28.5 mm, height 6.4 mm; 31 jewels; 28,800 vph; Parachrom hairspring; 48-hour power reserve; COSC-certified chronometer
Functions: hours, minutes, sweep seconds; 2nd 24-hour display (2nd time zone); date
Case: stainless steel, ø 40 mm, height 13 mm; bidirectional bezel with ceramic insert and 0-60 scale; sapphire crystal; screw-in crown; water-resistant to 10 atm
Band: Oyster stainless steel, folding clasp with safety lock and extension link
Price: $8,950
Variations: stainless steel/yellow gold ($13,000); yellow gold ($33,250); white gold ($38,250)

Oyster Perpetual Air-King

Reference number: 116900
Movement: automatic, Rolex Caliber 3131; ø 28.5 mm; 31 jewels; 28,800 vph; Parachrom spring, glucydur balance with microstella regulating bolts; soft iron cap for antimagnetic protection; 48-hour power reserve; COSC-certified chronometer
Functions: hours, minutes, sweep seconds
Case: stainless steel, ø 40 mm; sapphire crystal; screw-in crown; water-resistant to 10 atm
Band: Oyster stainless steel, folding clasp with safety lock and extension link
Price: $6,200

Oyster Perpetual Explorer

Reference number: 214270
Movement: automatic, Rolex Caliber 3132; ø 28.5 mm; 31 jewels; 28,800 vph; Parachrom spring, Paraflex shock absorber, glucydur balance with microstella regulating bolts; 48-hour power reserve; COSC-certified chronometer
Functions: hours, minutes, sweep seconds
Case: stainless steel, ø 39 mm; sapphire crystal; screw-in crown; water-resistant to 10 atm
Band: Oyster stainless steel, folding clasp with extension link
Price: $6,550

Oyster Perpetual Cosmograph Daytona

Reference number: 116500LN
Movement: automatic, Rolex Caliber 4130; ø 30.5 mm, height 6.5 mm; 44 jewels; 28,800 vph; Parachrom spring, glucydur balance with microstella regulating bolts; 72-hour power reserve; COSC-certified chronometer
Functions: hours, minutes, subsidiary seconds; chronograph
Case: stainless steel, ø 40 mm, height 12.8 mm; Cerachrom bezel; sapphire crystal; screw-in crown and pushers; water-resistant to 10 atm
Band: Oyster stainless steel, folding clasp with safety lock and extension link
Price: $12,400

Oyster Perpetual Cosmograph Daytona

Reference number: 116500LN
Movement: automatic, Rolex Caliber 4130; ø 30.5 mm, height 6.5 mm; 44 jewels; 28,800 vph; Parachrom spring, glucydur balance with microstella regulating bolts; 72-hour power reserve; COSC-certified chronometer
Functions: hours, minutes, subsidiary seconds; chronograph
Case: stainless steel, ø 40 mm, height 12.8 mm; Cerachrom bezel; sapphire crystal; screw-in crown and pushers; water-resistant to 10 atm
Band: Oyster stainless steel, folding clasp with safety lock and extension link
Price: $12,400

Oyster Perpetual Cosmograph Daytona

Reference number: 116518LN
Movement: automatic, Rolex Caliber 4130; ø 30.5 mm, height 6.5 mm; 44 jewels; 28,800 vph; Parachrom spring; 72-hour power reserve; COSC-certified chronometer
Functions: hours, minutes, subsidiary seconds; chronograph
Case: yellow gold, ø 40 mm, height 12.8 mm; Cerachrom bezel; sapphire crystal; screw-in crown and pushers; water-resistant to 10 atm
Band: elastomer with a metal mesh, folding clasp
Price: $27,500
Variations: Everose or white gold ($28,800)

Oyster Perpetual Yacht-Master II

Reference number: 116680
Movement: automatic, Rolex Caliber 4161 (base Caliber 4130); ø 31.2 mm, height 8.05 mm; 42 jewels; 28,800 vph; Parachrom hairspring; 72-hour power reserve; COSC-certified chronometer
Functions: hours, minutes, subsidiary seconds; programmable regatta countdown with memory
Case: stainless steel, ø 44 mm, height 13.8 mm; bidirectional bezel with ceramic insert and 0-60 scale; sapphire crystal; screw-in crown; water-resistant to 10 atm
Band: Oyster stainless steel, folding clasp with safety lock and extension link
Price: $18,750
Variations: yellow gold link bracelet ($43,550); stainless steel/Everose gold ($25,150)

Oyster Perpetual Yacht-Master 40

Reference number: 116655
Movement: automatic, Rolex Caliber 3135; ø 28.5 mm, height 6 mm; 31 jewels; 28,800 vph; Parachrom hairspring, glucydur balance with microstella regulating bolts; 48-hour power reserve; COSC-certified chronometer
Functions: hours, minutes, sweep seconds; date
Case: Everose gold, ø 40 mm, height 11.7 mm; bidirectional bezel with ceramic insert and 0-60 scale; sapphire crystal; screw-in crown; water-resistant to 10 atm
Band: elastomer with a metal mesh, folding clasp
Price: $24,950

Oyster Perpetual Yacht-Master 40

Reference number: 116621
Movement: automatic, Rolex Caliber 3135; ø 28.5 mm, height 6 mm; 31 jewels; 28,800 vph; Parachrom spring, glucydur balance with microstella regulating bolts; 48-hour power reserve; COSC-certified chronometer
Functions: hours, minutes, sweep seconds; date
Case: stainless steel, ø 40 mm, height 11.7 mm; Everose gold bezel, bidirectional bezel with 60-hour scale; sapphire crystal; screw-in crown; water-resistant to 10 atm
Band: Oyster stainless steel and Everose gold, folding clasp
Price: $14,050

Oyster Perpetual Sky-Dweller

Reference number: 326934
Movement: automatic, Rolex Caliber 9001; ø 33 mm, height 8 mm; 40 jewels; 28,800 vph; Parachrom spring, Paraflex shock absorber; 72-hour power reserve; COSC-certified chronometer
Functions: hours, minutes, sweep seconds; 2nd 24-hour display (2nd time zone); annual calendar with date, month
Case: stainless steel, ø 42 mm, height 14.1 mm; bidirectional white gold bezel to control functions; sapphire crystal; screw-in crown; water-resistant to 10 atm
Band: Oyster stainless steel, folding clasp
Price: $14,400
Variations: yellow gold starting at $38,150

Oyster Perpetual Day-Date 40

Reference number: 228239
Movement: automatic, Rolex Caliber 3255; ø 29.1 mm, height 5.4 mm; 31 jewels; 28,800 vph; Parachrom spring, Paraflex shock absorber, Chronergy escapement, glucydur balance with microstella regulating bolts; 70-hour power reserve; COSC-certified chronometer
Functions: hours, minutes, sweep seconds; date, weekday
Case: white gold, ø 40 mm, height 11.6 mm; sapphire crystal; screw-in crown; water-resistant to 10 atm
Band: President white gold, folding clasp
Price: $37,500
Variations: various dials; Everose gold ($37,550); platinum ($62,500); yellow gold ($34,850)

Oyster Perpetual Datejust 41

Reference number: 126334
Movement: automatic, Rolex Caliber 3235; ø 29.1 mm; 31 jewels; 28,800 vph; Parachrom spring, Paraflex shock absorber, glucydur balance with microstella regulating bolts; 70-hour power reserve; COSC-certified chronometer
Functions: hours, minutes, sweep seconds; date
Case: stainless steel, ø 41 mm, height 11.6 mm; white gold bezel; sapphire crystal; screw-in crown; water-resistant to 10 atm
Band: Oyster stainless steel, folding clasp with extension link
Price: $9,350
Variations: stainless steel with smooth bezel ($7,350)

Oyster Perpetual Datejust 36

Reference number: 116234
Movement: automatic, Rolex Caliber 3135; ø 28.5 mm, height 6 mm; 31 jewels; 28,800 vph; Parachrom spring, glucydur balance with microstella regulating bolts; 48-hour power reserve; COSC-certified chronometer
Functions: hours, minutes, sweep seconds; date
Case: stainless steel, ø 36 mm, height 11.6 mm; white gold bezel; sapphire crystal; screw-in crown; water-resistant to 10 atm
Band: Jubilee stainless steel, folding clasp with extension link
Price: $7,950
Variations: various bands and dials

Oyster Perpetual Day-Date 36

Reference number: 118206
Movement: automatic, Rolex Caliber 3155 (base Caliber 3135); ø 28.5 mm, height 6.45 mm; 31 jewels; 28,800 vph; Parachrom spring, glucydur balance with microstella regulating bolts; COSC-certified chronometer
Functions: hours, minutes, sweep seconds; date, weekday
Case: platinum, ø 36 mm; sapphire crystal; screw-in crown; water-resistant to 10 atm
Band: President, platinum, folding clasp
Price: $57,600
Variations: Everose gold ($32,450); white gold ($32,550); yellow gold ($29,650)

Oyster Perpetual Lady-Datejust 28

Reference number: 279160
Movement: automatic, Rolex Caliber 2236; ø 20 mm, height 5.95 mm; 31 jewels; 28,800 vph; Syloxi hairspring, glucydur balance with microstella regulating bolts; 55-hour power reserve; COSC-certified chronometer
Functions: hours, minutes, sweep seconds; date
Case: stainless steel, ø 28 mm, height 10.5 mm; sapphire crystal; screw-in crown; water-resistant to 10 atm
Band: Oyster stainless steel, folding clasp with extension link
Price: $6,300
Variations: various bands and dials

Cellini Moonphase

Reference number: 50535
Movement: automatic, Rolex Caliber 3195; ø 28.5 mm; 31 jewels; 28,800 vph; Parachrom spring, Paraflex shock absorber; 48-hour power reserve; COSC-certified chronometer
Functions: hours, minutes, sweep seconds; date, moon phase
Case: Everose gold, ø 39 mm; sapphire crystal; screw-in crown; water-resistant to 5 atm
Band: reptile skin, folding clasp
Remarks: blue enameled disk at 6 o'clock showing full moon (meteorite applique) and new moon (silver ring)
Price: $26,750

Cellini Date

Reference number: 50519
Movement: automatic, Rolex Caliber 3165 (base Rolex Caliber 3187); ø 28.5 mm; 31 jewels; 28,800 vph; Parachrom hairspring; 48-hour power reserve; COSC-certified chronometer
Functions: hours, minutes, sweep seconds; date
Case: white gold, ø 39 mm; sapphire crystal; screw-in crown; water-resistant to 5 atm
Band: reptile skin, buckle
Price: $17,800
Variations: various dials; Everose gold

Cellini Dual Time

Reference number: 50525
Movement: automatic, Rolex Caliber 3180 (base Rolex Caliber 3187 with module); 28,800 vph; Parachrom spring; 48-hour power reserve; COSC-certified chronometer
Functions: hours, minutes, sweep seconds; additional 12-hour display (2nd time zone), day/night indicator
Case: Everose gold, ø 39 mm; sapphire crystal; screw-in crown; water-resistant to 5 atm
Band: reptile skin, buckle
Price: $19,400
Variations: various dials; white gold

Caliber 3255

Automatic; optimized Chronergy escapement, pallet lever and escape wheel made of nickel phosphorus using LIGA process; single spring barrel, 70-hour power reserve; COSC-certified chronometer
Functions: hours, minutes, sweep seconds; date, weekday
Diameter: 29.1 mm
Height: 5.4 mm
Jewels: 31
Balance: glucydur balance with microstella regulating bolts
Frequency: 28,800 vph
Balance spring: Parachrom hairspring
Shock protection: Paraflex
Remarks: used in the Day-Date 40

Caliber 3235

Automatic; optimized Chronergy escapement, pallet lever and escape wheel made of nickel phosphorus using LIGA process; single spring barrel, 70-hour power reserve; COSC-certified chronometer
Functions: hours, minutes, sweep seconds; date
Diameter: 28.5 mm
Height: 6 mm
Jewels: 31
Balance: glucydur with microstella regulating bolts
Frequency: 28,800 vph
Balance spring: Parachrom hairspring
Shock protection: Paraflex
Remarks: used in the Datejust 41

Caliber 2236

Automatic; single spring barrel, 55-hour power reserve; COSC-certified chronometer
Functions: hours, minutes, sweep seconds; date
Diameter: 20 mm
Height: 5.95 mm
Jewels: 31
Balance: glucydur with microstella regulating bolts
Frequency: 28,800 vph
Balance spring: Syloxi spring
Shock protection: Paraflex
Remarks: used in the Lady-Datejust 28

Caliber 4130

Automatic; single spring barrel, 72-hour power reserve; COSC-certified chronometer
Functions: hours, minutes, subsidiary seconds; chronograph
Diameter: 30.5 mm
Height: 6.5 mm
Jewels: 44
Balance: glucydur with microstella regulating bolts
Frequency: 28,800 vph
Balance spring: Parachrom hairspring
Shock protection: Kif
Remarks: used in the Daytona

Caliber 4161

Automatic; single spring barrel, 72-hour power reserve; COSC-certified chronometer
Base caliber: Caliber 4130
Functions: hours, minutes, subsidiary seconds; programmable regatta countdown with memory
Diameter: 31.2 mm
Height: 8.05 mm
Jewels: 42
Balance: glucydur with microstella regulating bolts
Frequency: 28,800 vph
Balance spring: Parachrom hairspring
Shock protection: Kif
Remarks: used in the Yacht-Master II

Caliber 9001

Automatic; single spring barrel, 72-hour power reserve; COSC-certified chronometer
Functions: hours, minutes, sweep seconds; 2nd 24-hour display (2nd time zone); annual calendar with date, month
Diameter: 33 mm
Height: 8 mm
Jewels: 40
Balance: glucydur with microstella regulating bolts
Frequency: 28,800 vph
Balance spring: Parachrom hairspring
Shock protection: Paraflex
Remarks: used in the Sky-Dweller

RJ WATCHES SA
Grand-Rue 29-31
CH-1204 Geneva
Switzerland

Tel.:
+41-22-319-29-39

Fax:
+41-22-319-29-30

E-mail:
info@romainjerome.ch

Website:
www.romainjerome.ch

Founded:
2004

Number of employees:
approx. 20

Annual production:
2,000 watches and accessories

Distribution:
Please contact RJ-Romain Jerome headquarters in Geneva, Switzerland, for any enquiries.

Most important collections/price range:
Moon-DNA, Eyjafjallajokull-DNA, Titanic-DNA, Steampunk-DNA, Collaborations / from $10,000 to approx. $300,000 for highly complicated watches

ROMAIN JEROME

Tchaikovsky once said that he always put his best ideas into his work—and took them out again when editing. This singular approach to creativity makes its own kind of sense, but in a world where the hypest is the hippest, it may not be the most successful. When the fiery Yvan Arpa took hold of the barely known Romain Jerome in 2006, he quickly transformed its products, digging up unique and strange materials that caused the kind of chatter that means business—because there is no such thing as negative feedback. Quality and design, however, followed strict rules. The watches came in historical materials that connect the wearer to the bigger picture: bits of *Apollo 11*, moon dust, fibers from the space suits worn during the *International Space Station* mission.

Under the new CEO Manuel Emch, the brand weaned itself slowly from the antics that put it on the map and started organizing its collections along sea, air, and earth lines. The oversize Moon Invader saw a shift toward a cooler techno design using the company's stock of lunar module shreds. The Steampunk Chrono won the "Couture Time Award for Watch Architecture" in Las Vegas in 2012. The transparent Skylab reflects the immaculateness of a scientific research space.

Romain Jerome has also found a way to mix some humor into all the technical wizardry. Lovers of Batman will find a collection honoring their hero on a Gotham backdrop. One watch was dedicated to Super Mario, while the eighties, notable in design circles for being less than creative, were celebrated with a rendition of Pac Man on the dial. More recently, the octopus from the Titanic series moved from its space on the case back onto the dial, where it appears at night as a silhouette thanks to a generous application of Superluminova. The eyes glow as well. Fun and games at the higher end.

Skylab 48 Speed Metal
Reference number: RJ.M.AU.030.01
Movement: manually wound, Caliber RJ004-M; ø 34.4 mm, height 5.6 mm; 21 jewels; 28,800 vph; skeletonized and black chrome finished; 48-hour power reserve
Functions: hours, minutes, subsidiary seconds
Case: steel, ø 48 mm, height 12 mm; sapphire case back; water-resistant to 3 atm
Band: reptile skin, buckle
Price: $20,950; limited to 99 pieces

RJ X Super Mario Bros.
Reference number: RJ.M.AU.IN.011.01
Movement: automatic; Caliber RJ001-A; ø 30.4 mm, height 7.9 mm; 23 jewels; 28,800 vph; 42-hour power reserve
Functions: hours, minutes
Case: black PVD-coated steel; ø 46 mm, height 16.6 mm; sapphire crystal; Super Mario Bros. medallion on case back; water-resistant to 3 atm
Band: black rubber, black PVD-coated steel folding clasp
Price: $18,950; limited to 85 pieces

Subcraft Titanium
Reference number: RJ.T.AU.SC.001.01
Movement: automatic; Caliber RJ2000-A; 36.4 × 33.26 mm, height 5.9 mm; 54 jewels; 28,800 vph; 38-hour power reserve
Functions: linear, retrograde, and jumping hour indicated by white-lacquered cursor; dragging minutes on black disk with white numerals
Case: bead-blasted titanium; 52.3 × 40.1 mm, height 17 mm; sapphire crystal; water-resistant to 3 atm
Band: calfskin, buckle
Price: $26,950; limited to 99 pieces

SCHAUMBURG WATCH

Schaumburg Watch
Lindburgh & Benson
Kirchplatz 5 and 6
D-31737 Rinteln
Germany

Tel.:
+49-5751-923-351

E-mail:
info@lindburgh-benson.com

Website:
www.schaumburgwatch.com

Founded:
1998

Number of employees:
7

Annual production:
not specified

Distribution:
retail

U.S. distributor:
Schaumburg Watch
About Time Luxury Group
210 Bellevue Avenue
Newport, RI 02840
401-846-0598
nicewatch@aol.com

Most important collections/price range:
mechanical wristwatches / approx. $1,500 to
$13,000

Frank Dilbakowski is the owner of this small watchmaking business in Rinteln, Westphalia, which has been producing very unusual yet affordable timepieces since 1998. The name Schaumburg comes from the surrounding region. The firm has gained a reputation for high-performance timepieces for rugged sports and professional use. The chronometer line Aquamatic with water resistance to 1,000 m and the Aquatitan models, secure to 2,000 m, confirm the company's maxim that form, function, and performance are inseparable from one another.

By the same token, traditional watchmaking is also high on the agenda. The Rinteln workbenches produce the plates and bridges and provide all the finishing as well (perlage, engraving, skeletonizing). Some of the bracelets, cases, and dials are even manufactured here, but the base movements come from Switzerland.

The exact stylistic strategy of the brand is not easy to nail down. Schaumburg appears at ease in many segments, from unadorned one-hand watches to outstanding creations such as a special moon phase, which, rather than simply showing a moon, has a "shadow" crossing over an immobile photo-like reproduction of the moon. The latest moon phase shows a blood moon crossing a dark sky. The effect is almost spooky. And, of course, the Schaumburg workshop also produces unique pieces that have their own share of fans.

Blood Moon Meteorite

Movement: automatic, SW Caliber 11 (basis MAB 88); ø 25.6 mm, height 3.6 mm; 25 jewels; 28,800 vph; astronomically precise moon phase
Functions: hours, minutes; date, moon phase
Case: stainless steel, ø 43 mm, height 12.4 mm; sapphire crystal; water-resistant to 5 atm
Band: reptile skin, folding clasp
Remarks: dial out of meteorite
Price: $6,000
Variations: black PVD coating ($6,100)

Marine

Movement: manually wound, SW Caliber 07 (base ETA 6498); ø 36.6 mm, height 4.5 mm; 17 jewels; 21,600 vph; movement entirely hand-decorated; 38-hour power reserve
Functions: hours, minutes, subsidiary seconds
Case: stainless steel, ø 42 mm, height 11.8 mm; sapphire crystal; water-resistant to 5 atm
Band: reptile skin, buckle
Price: $1,700

Classoco

Movement: automatic, SW Caliber 20A (base ETA 2824-2); ø 25.6 mm, height 4.6 mm; 25 jewels; 28,800 vph; 38-hour power reserve
Functions: hours, minutes, sweep seconds; date
Case: stainless steel, ø 40 mm, height 9.8 mm; sapphire crystal; transparent case back; water-resistant to 5 atm
Band: reptile skin, buckle
Price: $1,500
Variations: various cases and dials; 36-mm case

Schwarz Etienne SA
Route de L'Orée-du-Bois 5
CH-2300 La Chaux-de-Fonds
Switzerland

Tel.:
+41-32-967-9420

E-mail:
info@schwarz-etienne.ch

Website:
www.schwarz-etienne.com

Founded:
1902

Number of employees:
20

Annual production:
500

U.S. distributor:
Right Time
1485 S. Colorado Blvd.
Denver, CO 80222
877-470-TIME

Most important collections:
La Chaux-de-Fonds, Roma, Roswell

SCHWARZ ETIENNE

When Raffaello Radicchi talks about his business, you might think he was talking about a little shop he set up in Neuchâtel. Maybe it's the charming, lilting French still tinged with his mother tongue, even though he left his native Perugia decades earlier. Maybe it's the quick laugh, the smiling, vivacious eyes, the earthiness he exudes. It all seems easy. For example, ask him why he went into watchmaking, he'll answer: "I was allergic to the metal and could only wear a gold watch." Subtext: He could not afford a gold watch, so he founded a watch company.

Radicchi is a genuine maverick and a lone figure in this somewhat hermetic industry. He arrived in Switzerland at 18, a mason. Unable to continue his work, he retrained as a carpenter and started renovating homes, then buying and renovating, and soon he was earning some serious money. Easy-peasy. In the early aughts, an acquaintance bought up a watch brand in La Chaux-de-Fonds, and suggested that Radicchi buy the building that came with it. The brand, once a big name in the industry and a supplier of movements (to Chanel, among others), had been founded by Paul Schwarz and Olga Etienne.

One thing led to another, and by 2008, Radicchi owned the whole package. Even though he was not from the industry, he understood that the company needed independence to survive. Having a number of outstanding suppliers locally to partner with was a good start. But Schwarz Etienne needed movements. By 2013, he had two, and a third came in 2015. These calibers drive a series of watches, including a tourbillon, that are classical in look, yet very modern-technical, thanks to the inverted movement construction that puts the off-center microrotor on the dial.

For all its traditionalism, the brand still maintains a feeling of youthful creativity. The Roswell's case, for example, is shaped a little like a flying vessel. And if you have seven figures to spend, you can purchase a special box of seven watches honoring the days of the week, their planets, and their astrological sign.

Tourbillon Petite Seconde Rétrograde
Reference number: WCF22TSE06SS01AA
Movement: automatic, Schwarz Etienne Caliber PSR122.00; ø 30.05 mm, height 7.05 mm; 40 jewels; 21,600 vph; inverted movement, microrotor on the dial side; 1-minute tourbillon; plate/bridges sandblasted and chamfered; 72-hour power reserve
Functions: hours and minutes (off-center), seconds (retrograde)
Case: stainless steel, ø 44 mm, height 14.24 mm; sapphire crystal; transparent case back; water-resistant to 5 atm
Band: reptile skin, folding clasp
Remarks: hour, minute, and second dials of green aventurine
Price: $55,467

Roswell Voyage
Reference number: WRW20TJ40SS01AA
Movement: automatic, Schwarz Etienne Caliber ISE101.01; ø 30.05 mm, height 7.05 mm; 40 jewels; 21,600 vph; inverted movement, microrotor with Matterhorn motif on dial side; 96-hour power reserve
Functions: hours, minutes, subsidiary seconds
Case: stainless steel, ø 45 mm, height 12.24 mm; sapphire crystal; water-resistant to 5 atm
Band: reptile skin, folding clasp
Remarks: real sliver of Matterhorn rock in case back display window
Price: $13,403

Roma Manufacture GMT
Reference number: H4862
Movement: automatic, Schwarz Etienne Caliber ASE120.00; ø 30.4 mm, height 5.35 mm; 34 jewels; 21,600 vph; 96-hour power reserve
Functions: hours, minutes, subsidiary seconds; sweep GMT (24 hours)
Case: stainless steel, ø 42 mm, height 12.13 mm; sapphire crystal; transparent case back; water-resistant to 5 atm
Band: reptile skin, buckle
Price: $10,141
Variations: pink gold ($23,721); stainless steel as Power Reserve ($11,144); pink gold as Power Reserve ($22,663)

SEIKO

The Japanese watch giant is a part of the Seiko Holding Company, but the development and production of its watches are fully self-sufficient. Seiko makes every variety of portable timepiece and offers mechanical watches with both manual and automatic winding, quartz watches with battery and solar power or with the brand's own mechanical "Kinetic" power generation, as well as the groundbreaking "Spring Drive" hybrid technology. This intelligent mix of mechanical energy generation and electronic regulation is reserved for Seiko's top models.

Also in the top segment of the brand is the Grand Seiko line, a group of watches that enjoys cult status among international collectors. Only recently did the Tokyo-based company offer a large collection to the global market. Today, there are several watches with the Spring Drive technology, but most new Grand Seikos (see page 169) are conventional, mechanical hand-wound and automatic watches.

Classic Seikos are designed for tradition-conscious buyers. The Astron, however, with its automatic GPS-controlled time setting, suggests the watch of the future. In its second incarnation, the Astron is 30 percent more compact, and the energy required by the GPS system inside is supplied by a high-tech solar cell on the dial. As for the new Prospex collection, released for the 50th anniversary of the first Seiko diver's watches, it has an unmistakably modern look. The old protective case of the Marinemaster is now of ceramic instead of plastic.

Finally, Seiko has a very high-end line called Credor. In 2016, it came out with the Fugaku Tourbillon, which renders one of the famous depictions of Mount Fuji with the Great Wave off Kanagawa in the foreground, using, among others, traditional Urushi lacquering technique.

Seiko Holdings
Ginza, Chuo, Tokyo
Japan

Website:
www.seikowatches.com

Founded:
1881

U.S. distributor:
Seiko Corporation of America
1111 Macarthur Boulevard
Mahwah, NJ 07430
201-529-5730
custserv@seikousa.com
www.seikousa.com

Most important collections/price range:
Ananta / approx. $2,400 to $8,500; Astron / approx. $1,850 to $3,400; Seiko Elite (Sportura, Premier, Velatura, Arctura) / approx. $430 to $1,500; Presage / approx. $490 to $2,600; Prospex / approx. $395 to $6,000

Astron GPS Solar Chronograph

Reference number: SSE003J1
Movement: quartz, Seiko Caliber 8X82; independent energy generation using solar cells in the dial
Functions: hours, minutes, sweep seconds; world time display (second time zone), (GPS alignment of 40 time zones), flight mode, signal reception indicator, power reserve indicator, daylight savings indicator; chronograph; date
Case: titanium, ø 45 mm, height 13.5 mm; ceramic bezel; sapphire crystal; water-resistant to 10 atm
Band: titanium, folding clasp
Price: $2,300
Variations: various cases and dials

Astron GPS Solar Large Date

Reference number: SSE147J1
Movement: quartz, Seiko Caliber 8X42; independent energy generation using solar cells in the dial
Functions: hours, minutes, sweep seconds; world time indicator, power reserve indicator (second time zone), (GPS alignment of 39 time zones), flight mode, signal reception indicator, daylight savings indicator; perpetual calendar with large date
Case: stainless steel, ø 45.5 mm, height 13 mm; ceramic bezel; sapphire crystal; water-resistant to 10 atm
Band: stainless steel, folding clasp
Price: $1,600
Variations: various dials

Fugaku Tourbillon Limited Edition

Reference number: GBCC999
Movement: manually wound, Seiko Caliber 6830; ø 25.6 mm, height 3.98 mm; 22 jewels; 21,600 vph; protected from magnetic fields up to 4,800 A/m; 37-hour power reserve
Functions: hours, minutes, subsidiary seconds; chronograph; date
Case: platinum, ø 43.1 mm, height 8.8 mm; sapphire crystal; transparent case back; water-resistant to 10 atm
Band: reptile skin, folding clasp
Remarks: white gold dial, hand-painted dial in Urushi lacquer, mother of pearl, yakogai shell; Fugaku wave depicted on back
Price: $460,000; limited to 8 pieces

Prospex First Diver's Automatic Limited Edition

Reference number: SLA017
Movement: automatic, Seiko Caliber 8L35;
ø 28.4 mm, height 5.3 mm; 26 jewels; 28,800 vph;
50-hour power reserve
Functions: hours, minutes, sweep seconds; date
Case: stainless steel, ø 39.7 mm, height 14.2 mm;
unidirectional bezel, with 0-60 scale; sapphire crystal;
screw-in crown; water-resistant to 20 atm
Band: silicon, buckle
Remarks: stainless steel bracelet
Price: $3,400; limited to 2,000 pieces

Prospex Automatic Diver's

Reference number: SPB051J1
Movement: automatic, Seiko Caliber 6R15;
ø 27.4 mm, height 4.95 mm; 21,600 vph; protected
from magnetic fields up to 4,800 A/m; 50-hour
power reserve
Functions: hours, minutes, sweep seconds; date
Case: stainless steel, ø 43 mm, height 13.4 mm;
unidirectional bezel, with 0-60 scale; sapphire crystal;
screw-in crown; water-resistant to 20 atm
Band: stainless steel, folding clasp, with safety lock
and extension link
Price: $1,000

Prospex Automatic Diver's

Reference number: SRPB51K1
Movement: automatic, Seiko Caliber 4L35;
ø 27 mm, height 4.95 mm; 21,600 vph; protected
from magnetic fields up to 4,800 A/m; 41-hour
power reserve
Functions: hours, minutes, sweep seconds; date
Case: stainless steel, ø 43.8 mm, height 13.4 mm;
unidirectional bezel, with 0-60 scale; plexiglass;
screw-in crown; water-resistant to 20 atm
Band: stainless steel, folding clasp, with safety lock
and extension link
Price: $525

Presage Automatic Enamel

Reference number: SPB049J1
Movement: automatic, Seiko Caliber 6R15;
ø 27.4 mm, height 4.95 mm; 26 jewels; 21,600 vph;
protected from magnetic fields up to 4,800 A/m;
rotor with côtes de Genève; 50-hour power reserve
Functions: hours, minutes, sweep seconds; date
Case: stainless steel, ø 35.9 mm, height 12.35 mm;
sapphire crystal; transparent case back
Band: reptile skin, folding clasp
Remarks: enamel dial
Price: $1,100

Presage Automatic Multifunction

Reference number: SPB059J1
Movement: automatic, Seiko Caliber 6R27;
ø 27.4 mm, height 6 mm; 29 jewels; 28,800 vph;
protected from magnetic fields up to 4,800 A/m;
45-hour power reserve
Functions: hours, minutes, sweep seconds; power
reserve indicator; date
Dial: enamel
Case: stainless steel, ø 40.5 mm, height 13.1 mm;
sapphire crystal; transparent case back; water-
resistant to 10 atm
Band: reptile skin, folding clasp
Price: $1,100

Presage Automatic Cocktail

Reference number: SRPB43
Movement: automatic, Seiko Caliber 4R35;
ø 27.4 mm, height 6.48 mm; 23 jewels; 21,600 vph;
41-hour power reserve
Functions: hours, minutes, sweep seconds; date
Case: stainless steel, ø 40.5 mm, height 14.5 mm;
Plexiglas; transparent case back
Band: calfskin, folding clasp
Price: $425

SINN

Pilot and flight instructor Helmut Sinn began manufacturing watches in Frankfurt am Main because he thought the pilot's watches on the market were too expensive. The resulting combination of top quality, functionality, and a good price-performance ratio turned out to be an excellent sales argument. Sinn Spezialuhren zu Frankfurt am Main is a brand with origins in technology. There is hardly another source that offers watch lovers such a sophisticated and reasonable collection of sporty watches, many conceived to survive in extreme conditions by conforming to German DIN industrial norms.

In 1994, Lothar Schmidt took over the brand, and his product developers began looking for inspiration in other industries and the sciences. They did so out of a practical technical impulse without any plan for launching a trend. Research and development are consistently aimed at improving the functionality of the watches. This includes application of special Sinn technology like moisture-proofing cases by pumping in an inert gas, such as argon. Other Sinn innovations include the Diapal (a lubricant-free lever escapement), the Hydro (an oil-filled diver's watch), and tegiment processing (for hardened steel and titanium surfaces). Having noticed a lack of norms for aviator watches, Schmidt negotiated a partnership with the Aachen Technical University to create the Technischer Standard Fliegeruhren (TESTAF, or Technical Standards for Aviator Watches), which is housed at the Eurocopter headquarters.

In the spring of 2016, Sinn finalized a special project bringing together three renowned German companies from the watch industry: Sinn, the Sächsische Uhrentechnologie Glashütte (SUG), and the Uhren-Werke-Dresden (UWD). The latter produced the outstanding UWD 33.1 caliber with Sinn as chaperone. That movement was then used to drive the brand new Meisterbund I, which translates as "master alliance."

Sinn Spezialuhren GmbH
Im Füldchen 5-7
D-60489 Frankfurt / Main
Germany

Tel.:
+49-69-9784-14-200

Fax:
+49-69-9784-14-201

E-mail:
info@sinn.de

Website:
www.sinn.de

Founded:

1961

Number of employees:
approx. 100

Annual production:
approx. 12,500 watches

U.S. distributor:
WatchBuys
888-333-4895
www.watchbuys.com

Most important collections/price range:
Financial District, U-Models, Diapal / from approx. $700 to $27,500

6200 WG Meisterbund I

Reference number: 6200.020
Movement: manually wound, Caliber UWD 33.1; ø 33 mm, height 4.2 mm; 19 jewels; 21,600 vph; weighted balance; flying spring barrel, antimagnetic according to German Industrial Norm (DIN); 55-hour power reserve
Functions: hours, minutes, subsidiary seconds
Case: white gold, ø 40 mm, height 9.3 mm; sapphire crystal; transparent case back; water-resistant to 10 atm
Band: calfskin, buckle
Price: $18,340; limited to 55 pieces

910 Jubiläum

Reference number: 910.010
Movement: automatic, ETA Caliber 7750 (modified); ø 30 mm, height 8.1 mm; 31 jewels; 28,800 vph; column wheel control of chronograph functions, shockproof and antimagnetic (DIN-norm); 46-hour power reserve
Functions: hours, minutes, subsidiary seconds; split-second chronograph
Case: stainless steel, ø 41.5 mm, height 15.5 mm; sapphire crystal; transparent case back; water-resistant to 10 atm
Band: horse leather, folding clasp
Remarks: comes with stainless steel bracelet
Price: $6,860; limited to 300 pieces

EZM 12

Reference number: 112.010
Movement: automatic, ETA Caliber 2836-2; ø 25.6 mm, height 5.05 mm; 25 jewels; 28,800 vph; protected from magnetic fields up to 80,000 A/m; 38-hour power reserve
Functions: hours, minutes, sweep seconds; date, weekday
Case: tegimented stainless steel, black hard coating, ø 44 mm, height 14 mm; bidirectional bezel with 0-60 scale (counting downward); crown-activated inner ring with 0-60 scale (counting upward); sapphire crystal; water-resistant to 20 atm
Band: silicon, folding clasp with extension link
Remarks: developed for emergency medical professionals; comes with pocketknife; dehumidifying technology (protective gas)
Price: $4,120

EZM 10 TESTAF

Reference number: 950.011
Movement: automatic, Sinn Caliber SZ 01 (base ETA 7750); ø 30 mm, height 7.9 mm; 29 jewels; 28,800 vph; sweep minute counter, lubrication-free escapement (Diapal), shockproof and antimagnetic
Functions: hours, minutes, subsidiary seconds; second 24-hour display; chronograph; date
Case: tegimented titanium, ø 46.5 mm, height 15.6 mm; bidirectional bezel with 0-60 scale; sapphire crystal; screw-in crown; water-resistant to 20 atm
Band: calfskin, buckle
Remarks: certified according to Technical Standard for Flyers' Watches (TESTAF); dehumidifying technology (protective gas)
Price: $5,790

103 Ti UTC IFR

Reference number: 103.0794
Movement: automatic, ETA Caliber 7750; ø 30.4 mm, height 7.9 mm; 25 jewels; 28,800 vph; shockproof and antimagnetic (DIN-norm); 42-hour power reserve
Functions: hours, minutes, subsidiary seconds; chronograph; date
Case: pearl-blasted titanium, ø 41 mm, height 17 mm; bidirectional bezel with 0-60 scale; sapphire crystal; transparent case back; screw-in crown; water-resistant to 20 atm
Band: calfskin, buckle
Remarks: certified according to DIN 8830 for pilots' watches; dehumidifying technology (protective gas)
Price: $3,640
Variations: without UTC ($2,970)

857 UTC VFR

Reference number: 857.0401
Movement: automatic, ETA Caliber 2893-2; ø 25.6 mm, height 4.1 mm; 21 jewels; 28,800 vph; shockproof and antimagnetic (DIN-norm); 42-hour power reserve
Functions: hours, minutes, sweep seconds; second 24-hour display (second time zone); date
Case: tegimented stainless steel, ø 43 mm, height 12 mm; sapphire crystal; screw-in crown
Band: silicon, folding clasp with safety lock and extension link
Remarks: certified according to DIN 8830 for pilots' watches; dehumidifying technology (protective gas)
Price: $2,760
Variations: without DIN certification ($2,340); without UTC ($2,190)

EZM 9 TESTAF

Reference number: 949.010
Movement: automatic, Sellita Caliber SW200-1; ø 25.6 mm, height 4.6 mm; 26 jewels; 28,800 vph; shockproof and antimagnetic (DIN-norm)
Functions: hours, minutes, sweep seconds; date
Case: tegimented titanium, ø 44 mm, height 12 mm; bidirectional bezel with 0-60 scale; sapphire crystal; screw-in crown; water-resistant to 20 atm
Band: tegimented titanium, folding clasp with safety lock and extension link
Remarks: certified according to Technical Standard for Flyers' Watches (TESTAF);
Price: $4,150
Variations: leather strap ($3,780)

212 KSK

Reference number: 212.050
Movement: automatic, ETA Caliber 2893-2; ø 25.6 mm, height 4.1 mm; 21 jewels; 28,800 vph; shockproof and antimagnetic (DIN-norm); 42-hour power reserve
Functions: hours, minutes, sweep seconds; second 24-hour display (second time zone); date
Case: stainless steel, ø 47 mm, height 14.5 mm; bidirectional bezel with black hard coating, with 0-64 scale (compass function); sapphire crystal; crown D3 seal; water-resistant to 100 atm
Band: silicon, folding clasp with safety lock and extension link
Remarks: dehumidifying technology (protective gas)
Price: $3,345; limited to 300 pieces

104 St Sa I W

Reference number: 104.012
Movement: automatic, Sellita Caliber SW220-1; ø 25.6 mm, height 5.05 mm; 26 jewels; 28,800 vph; shockproof and antimagnetic (DIN-norm); 38-hour power reserve
Functions: hours, minutes, sweep seconds; date, weekday
Case: stainless steel, ø 41 mm, height 11.5 mm; bidirectional bezel with 0-60 scale; sapphire crystal; transparent case back; screw-in crown; water-resistant to 20 atm
Band: calfskin, buckle
Price: $1,380
Variations: Arabic numerals ($1,380); black dial ($1,380)

U1 S E

Reference number: 1010.023
Movement: automatic, Sellita Caliber SW200-1; ø 25.6 mm, height 4.6 mm; 26 jewels; 28,800 vph; shockproof and antimagnetic (DIN-norm)
Functions: hours, minutes, sweep seconds; date
Case: stainless steel (submarine steel), tegimented, with black hard coating, ø 44 mm, height 14 mm; unidirectional bezel, with 0-60 scale; sapphire crystal; water-resistant to 100 atm
Band: calfskin, buckle
Remarks: EU diving certified
Price: $2,380
Variations: without hard covering ($1,970); bezel with black coating ($2,070)

U1000

Reference number: 1011.010
Movement: automatic, Sinn Caliber SZ 02 (base ETA 7750); ø 30.4 mm, height 7.9 mm; 25 jewels; 28,800 vph; 60-minute totalizer; special oil lubrication
Functions: hours, minutes, subsidiary seconds; chronograph; date
Case: stainless steel (submarine steel), tegimented, ø 44 mm, height 18 mm; unidirectional bezel, with 0-60 scale; sapphire crystal; crown and pusher with D3 seal; water-resistant to 100 atm
Band: silicon, folding clasp with safety lock
Remarks: EU diving certified dehumidifying technology (protective gas)
Price: $5,080
Variations: black hard coating ($5,360)

T1 B

Reference number: 1014.011
Movement: automatic, Caliber SOP A10-2A (base Soprod A10); ø 25.6 mm, height 3.6 mm; 25 jewels; 28,800 vph; shockproof and antimagnetic (DIN-norm); 42-hour power reserve
Functions: hours, minutes, sweep seconds; date
Case: pearl-blasted titanium, ø 45 mm, height 12.5 mm; unidirectional bezel, with 0-60 scale; sapphire crystal; screw-in crown; water-resistant to 100 atm
Band: silicon, folding clasp with safety lock
Remarks: EU diving certified; dehumidifying technology (protective gas)
Price: $3,640
Variations: 41-mm case ($3,390)

240 St GZ

Reference number: 240.011
Movement: automatic, Sellita Caliber SW220-1; ø 25.6 mm, height 5.05 mm; 26 jewels; 28,800 vph; shockproof and antimagnetic (DIN-norm); 38-hour power reserve
Functions: hours, minutes, sweep seconds; date, weekday
Case: stainless steel, ø 43 mm, height 11 mm; crown-controlled inner bezel with tides indication, power reserve indicator; sapphire crystal; crown with D3 seal; water-resistant to 10 atm
Band: stainless steel, folding clasp, with safety lock and extension link
Price: $2,100
Variations: 0-60 scale ring ($2,050)

856 B-Uhr

Reference number: 856.012
Movement: automatic, Sellita Caliber SW300-1; ø 25.6 mm, height 4.1 mm; 21 jewels; 28,800 vph; shockproof and antimagnetic (DIN-norm)
Functions: hours, minutes, sweep seconds; date
Case: stainless steel, pearl-blasted, tegimented, ø 40 mm, height 11 mm; sapphire crystal; screw-in crown; water-resistant to 20 atm
Band: calfskin, buckle
Remarks: dehumidifying technology (protective gas); magnetic field protection to 80,000 A/m
Price: $1,990; limited to 856 pieces
Variations: without inner scale ring ($1,880); blackened case ($2,030); second time zone ($2,010)

900 Diapal

Reference number: 900.013
Movement: automatic, Sellita Caliber SW500; ø 30 mm, height 7.9 mm; 25 jewels; 28,800 vph; lubrication-free escapement (Diapal), shockproof and antimagnetic (DIN-norm); 48-hour power reserve
Functions: hours, minutes, subsidiary seconds; second 24-hour display (second time zone); chronograph; date
Case: stainless steel tegimented, ø 44 mm, height 15.5 mm; crown-controlled scale ring; sapphire crystal; screw-in crown; water-resistant to 20 atm
Band: calfskin, buckle
Remarks: dehumidifying technology (protective gas); magnetic field protection to 80,000 A/m
Price: $4,420

6000 Rose Gold

Reference number: 6000.040
Movement: automatic, Sellita SW500 (modified); ø 30.4 mm, height 7.9 mm; 26 jewels; 28,800 vph; lubrication-free escapement (Diapal), finely finished, shockproof and antimagnetic (DIN-norm); 42-hour power reserve
Functions: hours, minutes, subsidiary seconds; additional 12-hour display (second time zone); chronograph; date
Case: rose gold, ø 38.5 mm, height 16.5 mm; crown-controlled inner bezel with 0-12 scale; sapphire crystal; transparent case back; water-resistant to 10 atm
Band: reptile skin, buckle
Price: $15,140
Variations: stainless steel ($4,375)

6068

Reference number: 6068.010
Movement: automatic, Sellita Caliber SW300-1; ø 25.6 mm, height 3.6 mm; 25 jewels; 28,800 vph; shockproof and antimagnetic (DIN-norm); 42-hour power reserve
Functions: hours, minutes, sweep seconds; date
Case: stainless steel, ø 38.5 mm, height 12 mm; crown-adjustable inner bezel with 0-12 scale; sapphire crystal; transparent case back; water-resistant to 10 atm
Band: stainless steel, folding clasp
Remarks: comes with stainless steel bracelet
Price: $2,590

1736 St I 4N

Reference number: 1736.011
Movement: automatic, ETA Caliber 2892-A2); ø 25.6 mm, height 3.6 mm; 21 jewels; 28,800 vph; shockproof and antimagnetic (DIN-norm); 42-hour power reserve
Functions: hours, minutes
Case: stainless steel, ø 36 mm, height 9.1 mm; sapphire crystal; transparent case back; water-resistant to 10 atm
Band: calfskin, buckle
Price: $2,230

356 Sa Flieger III

Reference number: 356.0721
Movement: automatic, Sellita Caliber SW500 (modified); ø 30.4 mm, height 7.9 mm; 25 jewels; 28,800 vph; shockproof and antimagnetic (DIN-norm); finely finished movement; 42-hour power reserve
Functions: hours, minutes, subsidiary seconds; chronograph; date, weekday
Case: stainless steel, ø 38.5 mm, height 15 mm; sapphire crystal; transparent case back; water-resistant to 10 atm
Band: calfskin, buckle
Price: $2,840
Variations: black dial ($2,740); copper-colored dial ($2,790)

434 TW68 WG S

Reference number: 434.030
Movement: quartz, shockproof and antimagnetic (DIN-norm)
Functions: hours, minutes, sweep seconds
Case: stainless steel, ø 34 mm, height 7.8 mm; white gold case with white gold bezel, set with 68 diamonds; sapphire crystal; water-resistant to 10 atm
Band: calfskin, buckle
Remarks: Q technology (protection from electromagnetic impulses)
Price: $5,430
Variations: without diamonds ($870); yellow gold bezel ($1,630)

556 A

Reference number: 556.0
Movement: automatic, ETA Caliber 2824-2; ø 25.6 mm, height 4.6 mm; 25 jewels; 28,800 vph; shockproof and antimagnetic (DIN-norm); 38-hour power reserve
Functions: hours, minutes, sweep seconds; date
Case: stainless steel, ø 38.5 mm, height 11 mm; sapphire crystal; transparent case back; screw-in crown; water-resistant to 20 atm
Band: calfskin, buckle
Price: $1,130
Variations: mocha-colored dial ($1,250)

STOWA

Stowa GmbH & Co. KG
Gewerbepark 16
D-75331 Engelsbrand
Germany

Tel.:
+49-7082-9306-0

Fax:
+49-7082-9306-2

E-mail:
info@stowa.com

Website:
www.stowa.com

Founded:
1927

Number of employees:
20

Annual production:
around 4,500 watches

Distribution:
direct sales; please contact company in Germany; orders taken by phone Monday–Friday 9 a.m.–5 p.m., European time. Note: Prices are determined according to daily exchange rate.

When a watch brand organizes a museum for itself, it is usually with good reason. The firm Stowa may not be the biggest fish in the horological pond, but it has been around for more than eighty years, and its products are well worth taking a look at as expressions of German watchmaking culture. Stowa began in Pforzheim, then moved to the little industrial town of Rheinfelden, and now operates in Engelsbrand, a "suburb" of Pforzheim. After a history as a family-owned company, today the brand is headed by Jörg Schauer, who has maintained the goal and vision of original founder Walter Storz: delivering quality watches at a reasonable price.

Stowa is one of the few German brands to have operated without interruption since the start of the twentieth century, albeit with a new owner as of 1990. Besides all the political upheavals, it survived the quartz crisis of the 1970s, during which Europe was flooded with cheap watches from Asia and many traditional German watchmakers were put out of business. Storz managed to keep Stowa going, but even a quality fanatic has to pay a price during times of trouble: With huge input from his son, Werner, Storz restructured the company so that it was able to begin encasing reasonably priced quartz movements rather than being strictly an assembler of mechanical ones.

Schauer bought the brand in 1996. Spurred on by the success of his own eponymous line, he also steered Stowa back toward mechanical watches, taking inspiration from older Stowa timepieces but using Swiss ETA movements. But the way out of the retro trap was about to become apparent: In 2015, Schauer joined forces with Hartmut Esslinger to create the Rana (frog) model, with an almost ethereal case and a modern dial, whose dot markers (called DynaDots) grow larger by the hour. These new shapes are, above all, expressed in the new Flieger (pilot) watches.

Flieger without Logo

Reference number: FliegerohneLogo
Movement: automatic, ETA Caliber 2824-2; ø 25.6 mm, height 4.6 mm; 25 jewels; 28,800 vph; blued screws, hand-made rotor with engraving; 40-hour power reserve
Functions: hours, minutes, sweep seconds
Case: stainless steel, ø 40 mm, height 10.2 mm; sapphire crystal; water-resistant to 5 atm
Band: calfskin, buckle (optional folding clasp)
Price: $870
Variations: reptile skin strap ($983); stainless steel bracelet ($992)

Antea Small Seconds

Reference number: AnteaKS
Movement: manually wound, ETA Caliber 7001; ø 23.3 mm, height 2.5 mm; 17 jewels; 21,600 vph; finely finished with côtes de Genève and blued screws; 42-hour power reserve
Functions: hours, minutes, subsidiary seconds
Case: stainless steel, ø 35.5 mm, height 6.9 mm; sapphire crystal; transparent case back; water-resistant to 3 atm
Band: deerskin, buckle (optional folding clasp)
Price: $955
Variations: reptile skin strap ($1,030); stainless steel bracelet ($1,011)

Antea "Back to Bauhaus"

Reference number: Antea355b2b
Movement: manually wound, ETA Caliber 7001; ø 23.3 mm, height 2.5 mm; 17 jewels; 21,600 vph; finely finished with côtes de Genève and blued screws; 42-hour power reserve
Functions: hours, minutes, subsidiary seconds
Case: stainless steel, ø 35.5 mm, height 6.9 mm; sapphire crystal; transparent case back; water-resistant to 3 atm
Band: calfskin, buckle (optional folding clasp)
Price: $889
Variations: reptile skin strap ($945)

Marine Original

Reference number:
MarineOriginalpolweissarabisch
Movement: manually wound, ETA Caliber 6498-1;
ø 36.6 mm, height 4.5 mm; 17 jewels; 18,000 vph;
screw balance, swan-neck fine regulation, with côtes
de Genéve, blued screws; 46-hour power reserve
Functions: hours, minutes, subsidiary seconds
Case: stainless steel, ø 41 mm, height 12 mm;
sapphire crystal; transparent case back; water-
resistant to 5 atm
Band: calfskin, buckle
Price: $1,198
Variations: reptile skin strap ($1,292); stainless
steel bracelet ($1,292)

Seatime BlackForest

Reference number: SeatimeBlackForest
Movement: automatic, ETA Caliber 2836-2;
ø 25.6 mm, height 4.6 mm; 25 jewels; 28,800 vph;
fine finishing with côtes de Genève and blued
screws; 40-hour power reserve
Functions: hours, minutes, sweep seconds; date
Case: titanium, ø 42 mm, height 13.5 mm;
unidirectional bezel, with 0-60 scale; sapphire
crystal; transparent case back; screw-in crown; water-
resistant to 20 atm
Band: rubber, double folding clasp with safety lock
and extension link
Price: $1,283
Variations: buffalo leather band ($1,301)

Flieger DIN Professional

Reference number: FliegerDinProfessional
Movement: automatic, ETA Caliber 2824-2;
ø 25.6 mm, height 4.6 mm; 25 jewels; 28,800 vph;
blued screws; 40-hour power reserve
Functions: hours, minutes, sweep seconds
Case: titanium, ø 47 mm, height 13.9 mm;
bidirectional bezel with 0-60 scale; sapphire crystal;
transparent case back; water-resistant to 20 atm
Band: rubber, double folding clasp with safety lock
and extension link
Price: $2,012
Variations: buffalo leather band ($2,031)

Flieger TO2

Reference number: Flieger TO2
Movement: automatic, ETA Caliber 2824-2;
ø 25.6 mm, height 4.6 mm; 25 jewels; 28,800 vph;
fine finishing with côtes de Genève and blued
screws; 40-hour power reserve
Functions: hours, minutes, sweep seconds
Case: stainless steel, ø 43 mm, height 13 mm;
sapphire crystal; transparent case back; water-
resistant to 20 atm
Band: rubber, folding clasp with safety lock
Price: $1,189
Variations: buffalo leather band ($1,208)

Chronograph 1938 "Black"

Reference number: Chronograph1938Schwarz
Movement: automatic, ETA Caliber 7753; ø 30 mm,
height 7.9 mm; 27 jewels; 28,800 vph; 48-hour
power reserve
Functions: hours, minutes, subsidiary seconds;
chronograph; date
Case: stainless steel, ø 41 mm, height 14.7 mm;
sapphire crystal; transparent case back; water-
resistant to 5 atm
Band: calfskin, buckle
Price: $1,713
Variations: manual winding, no date ($1,994)

Partitio Manually-Wound White

Reference number: PartitioHandaufzugweiss
Movement: manually wound, ETA Caliber 2804-2;
ø 25.6 mm, height 3.35 mm; 17 jewels; 28,800 vph;
42-hour power reserve
Functions: hours, minutes, sweep seconds
Case: stainless steel, ø 37 mm, height 10.8 mm;
sapphire crystal; transparent case back; water-
resistant to 5 atm
Band: calfskin, buckle
Price: $739
Variations: black dial ($739)

TAG HEUER

Measuring speed accurately in ever greater detail was always the goal of TAG Heuer. The brand also established numerous technical milestones, including the first automatic chronograph caliber with a microrotor (created in 1969 with Hamilton-Büren, Breitling, and Dubois Dépraz). Of more recent vintage is the fascinating mechanical movement V4 with its belt-driven transmission, unveiled in a limited edition. At the same time TAG Heuer released its first chronograph with an in-house movement, Caliber 1887, the basis of which was an existing chronograph movement by Seiko. Some of the components are made by the company itself in Switzerland, while assembly is done entirely in-house.

Lately, TAG Heuer has increased its manufacturing capacities to meet the strong and growing demand and to maintain its independence. It also serves as an extended workbench for companion brands Zenith and Hublot, also part of the LVMH Group.

TAG Heuer has continued to break world speed records for mechanical escapements. The Caliber 360 combined a standard movement with a 360,000-vph (50-Hz) chronograph mechanism able to measure 100ths of a second. In 2011, the Micrograph 1/100th brought time display and measurement on a single plate. Shortly after, the Mikrotimer Flying 1000 broke the 1,000th of a second barrier. A year later, the Mikrogirder 2000 doubled the frequency using a vibrating metal strip instead of a balance wheel. The MikrotourbillonS features a separate chronograph escapement driven at a record-breaking 360,000 vph.

But these flights of fancy slowed when, at the end of 2014, the new LVMH coordinator, Jean-Claude Biver, devised a new strategy for TAG Heuer to cut back on the top end of the pricing scale. Guy Sémon, the new CEO, prescribed a return to former pricings, with a broader choice of models, including a connected watch. The new portfolio includes a tourbillon at under $16,000 in the Carrera family and a revived classic, the Autovia, which was the first chronograph by Heuer with a rotating bezel for remembering times or as a second time zone. The watch runs on the Heuer 02 Caliber.

TAG Heuer
Branch of LVMH SA
6a, rue L.-J.-Chevrolet
CH-2300 La Chaux-de-Fonds
Switzerland

Tel.:
+41-32-919-8164

Fax:
+41-32-919-9000

E-mail:
info@tagheuer.com

Website:
www.tagheuer.com

Founded:
1860

Number of employees:
1,600 employees internationally

U.S. distributor:
TAG Heuer/LVMH Watch & Jewelry USA
966 South Springfield Avenue
Springfield, NJ 07081
973-467-1890

Most important collections/price range:
TAG Heuer Formula 1, Aquaracer, Link, Carrera, Connected, Monaco, Heritage / from approx. $1,300 to $20,000

TAG Heuer Formula 1 Calibre 16

Reference number: CAZ2015.BA0876
Movement: automatic, TAG Heuer Caliber 16 (base ETA 7750); ø 30.4 mm, height 7.9 mm; 25 jewels; 28,800 vph
Functions: hours, minutes, subsidiary seconds; chronograph; date
Case: stainless steel, ø 44 mm, height 15 mm; sapphire crystal; screw-in crown; water-resistant to 20 atm
Band: stainless steel, folding clasp
Price: $2,800

Aquaracer 300M Calibre 7 GMT

Reference number: WAY201F.BA0927
Movement: automatic, TAG Heuer Caliber 7 (base ETA 2893-2); ø 26.2 mm, height 4.1 mm; 21 jewels; 28,800 vph
Functions: hours, minutes, sweep seconds; second 24-hour display (second time zone); date
Case: stainless steel, ø 43 mm; bidirectional bezel with aluminum inserts and 24-hour divisions; sapphire crystal; screw-in crown; water-resistant to 30 atm
Band: stainless steel, folding clasp
Price: $2,600

Aquaracer 300M Calibre 5

Reference number: WAY208D.FC8221
Movement: automatic, TAG Heuer Caliber 5 (base ETA 2824-2); ø 26 mm, height 4.6 mm; 25 jewels; 28,800 vph
Functions: hours, minutes, sweep seconds; date
Case: titanium with black PVD coating, ø 43 mm; unidirectional bezel with ceramic insert and 0-60 scale; sapphire crystal; screw-in crown; water-resistant to 30 atm
Band: textile, buckle
Price: $3,550

Link Calibre 5

Reference number: WBC2111.BA0603
Movement: automatic, TAG Heuer Caliber 5 (base ETA 2824-2); ø 26 mm, height 4.6 mm; 25 jewels; 28,800 vph
Functions: hours, minutes, sweep seconds; date
Case: stainless steel, ø 41 mm, height 11.05 mm; sapphire crystal; water-resistant to 10 atm
Band: stainless steel, folding clasp
Price: $2,900

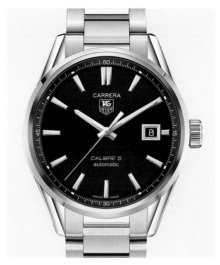

Carrera Calibre 5

Reference number: WAR211A.BA0782
Movement: automatic, TAG Heuer Caliber 5 (base ETA 2824-2); ø 26 mm, height 4.6 mm; 25 jewels; 28,800 vph
Functions: hours, minutes, sweep seconds; date
Case: stainless steel, ø 39 mm, height 12 mm; sapphire crystal; transparent case back; water-resistant to 10 atm
Band: stainless steel, folding clasp
Price: $2,400
Variations: various dial colors; reptile skin strap ($2,400)

Carrera Calibre 5 Day-Date

Reference number: WAR201E.FC6292
Movement: automatic, TAG Heuer Caliber 5 (base ETA 2836-2); ø 26 mm, height 5.05 mm; 25 jewels; 28,800 vph
Functions: hours, minutes, sweep seconds; date, weekday
Case: stainless steel, ø 41 mm, height 13 mm; sapphire crystal; transparent case back; water-resistant to 10 atm
Band: reptile skin, folding clasp
Price: $2,600
Variations: various dials; stainless steel bracelet ($2,600)

Carrera Calibre 16 Day-Date

Reference number: CV2A1AC.FC6380
Movement: automatic, TAG Heuer Caliber 16 (base ETA 7750); ø 30.4 mm, height 7.9 mm; 25 jewels; 28,800 vph
Functions: hours, minutes, subsidiary seconds; chronograph; date, weekday
Case: stainless steel, ø 43 mm, height 16.5 mm; sapphire crystal; transparent case back; water-resistant to 10 atm
Band: reptile skin, folding clasp
Price: $4,700
Variations: stainless steel bracelet ($4,700)

Carrera Calibre 16 Day-Date Black Titanium

Reference number: CV2A84.FC6394
Movement: automatic, TAG Heuer Caliber 16 (base ETA 7750); ø 30.4 mm, height 7.9 mm; 25 jewels; 28,800 vph
Functions: hours, minutes, subsidiary seconds; chronograph; date, weekday
Case: titanium with black PVD coating, ø 43 mm, height 16.5 mm; bezel with ceramic insert; sapphire crystal; transparent case back; water-resistant to 10 atm
Band: calfskin, folding clasp
Price: $5,050

Carrera Calibre Heuer 01

Reference number: CAR201U.FC6405
Movement: automatic, TAG Heuer Caliber Heuer 01; ø 29.3 mm, height 7.13 mm; 39 jewels; 28,800 vph
Functions: hours, minutes, subsidiary seconds; chronograph; date
Case: stainless steel, ø 43 mm, height 16 mm; ceramic bezel; sapphire crystal; transparent case back; water-resistant to 10 atm
Band: reptile skin, folding clasp
Price: $5,350

Carrera Calibre Heuer 01

Reference number: CAR201Z.BA0714
Movement: automatic, TAG Heuer Caliber Heuer 01; ø 29.3 mm, height 7.13 mm; 39 jewels; 28,800 vph
Functions: hours, minutes, subsidiary seconds; chronograph; date
Case: stainless steel, ø 43 mm, height 16 mm; ceramic bezel; sapphire crystal; transparent case back; water-resistant to 10 atm
Band: stainless steel, folding clasp
Price: $5,150

Carrera Calibre Heuer 01

Reference number: CAR2A1T.FT6052
Movement: automatic, TAG Heuer Caliber Heuer 01; ø 29.3 mm, height 7.13 mm; 39 jewels; 28,800 vph
Functions: hours, minutes, subsidiary seconds; chronograph; date
Case: stainless steel, ø 45 mm, height 16 mm; ceramic bezel; sapphire crystal; transparent case back; water-resistant to 10 atm
Band: rubber, folding clasp
Price: $5,300

Carrera Calibre Heuer 01

Reference number: CAR2A1W.BA0703
Movement: automatic, TAG Heuer Caliber Heuer 01; ø 29.3 mm, height 7.13 mm; 39 jewels; 28,800 vph
Functions: hours, minutes, subsidiary seconds; chronograph; date
Case: stainless steel, ø 45 mm, height 16 mm; ceramic bezel; sapphire crystal; transparent case back; water-resistant to 10 atm
Band: stainless steel, folding clasp
Price: $5,450

Carrera Calibre Heuer 01
Grey Phantom

Reference number: CAR2A90.FT6071
Movement: automatic, TAG Heuer Caliber Heuer 01; ø 29.3 mm, height 7.13 mm; 39 jewels; 28,800 vph
Functions: hours, minutes, subsidiary seconds; chronograph; date
Case: titanium, ø 45 mm, height 16 mm; ceramic bezel; sapphire crystal; transparent case back; water-resistant to 10 atm
Band: rubber, black titanium-carbide folding clasp
Price: $6,300

Carrera Calibre Heuer 01
Black Matt Ceramic

Reference number: CAR2A91.BH0742
Movement: automatic, TAG Heuer Caliber Heuer 01; ø 29.3 mm, height 7.13 mm; 39 jewels; 28,800 vph
Functions: hours, minutes, subsidiary seconds; chronograph; date
Case: ceramic, ø 45 mm, height 16 mm; ceramic bezel; sapphire crystal; transparent case back; water-resistant to 10 atm
Band: ceramic, folding clasp
Price: $6,300

Carrera Calibre Heuer 01
Special Edition Red Bull Racing

Reference number: CAR2A1N.FT6100
Movement: automatic, TAG Heuer Caliber Heuer 01; ø 29.3 mm, height 7.13 mm; 39 jewels; 28,800 vph
Functions: hours, minutes, subsidiary seconds; chronograph; date
Case: stainless steel, ø 45 mm, height 16 mm; ceramic bezel; sapphire crystal; transparent case back; water-resistant to 10 atm
Band: calfskin, folding clasp
Price: $5,850
Variations: stainless steel bracelet ($5,950)

Carrera Calibre Heuer 02 Tourbillon C.O.S.C. Black Titanium

Reference number: CAR5A8Y.FC6377
Movement: automatic, TAG Heuer Caliber 02 T; ø 31 mm, height 6.9 mm; 33 jewels; 28,800 vph; 1-minute tourbillon; COSC-certified chronometer
Functions: hours, minutes; chronograph; date
Case: titanium; titanium with black titanium carbide coating, ø 45 mm; sapphire crystal; water-resistant to 10 atm
Band: reptile skin, folding clasp
Price: $15,900

Carrera Calibre Heuer 02 Tourbillon C.O.S.C. Baguette-Cut Diamonds

Reference number: CAR5A81.FC6377
Movement: automatic, TAG Heuer Caliber 02 T; ø 31 mm, height 6.9 mm; 33 jewels; 28,800 vph; 1-minute tourbillon; COSC-certified chronometer
Functions: hours, minutes; chronograph; date
Case: titanium, ø 45 mm; bezel set with 68 baguette diamonds; sapphire crystal; water-resistant to 10 atm
Band: reptile skin, folding clasp
Price: $64,650

Carrera Calibre Heuer 02 Tourbillon C.O.S.C. Full Set Diamonds

Reference number: CAR5A1Z.BA0510
Movement: automatic, TAG Heuer Caliber 02 T; ø 31 mm, height 6.9 mm; 33 jewels; 28,800 vph; 1-minute tourbillon; COSC-certified chronometer
Functions: hours, minutes; chronograph; date
Case: stainless steel, ø 45 mm; bezel set with 154 diamonds; sapphire crystal; water-resistant to 10 atm
Band: stainless steel set with diamonds, folding clasp
Price: $53,850

Connected Modular 45

Reference number: SBF8A8019.11FT6118
Movement: quartz, Intel Core Duo microprocessor; Android OS; near-field communication with smartphone for data sharing and reciprocal function control
Functions: hours, minutes, sweep seconds; other displays and functions through smartphone connection; chronograph; date
Case: titanium, ø 45 mm, height 13.75 mm; unidirectional bezel with aluminum inlay, with 0-60 scale; sapphire crystal
Band: rubber, folding clasp
Remarks: removable smartwatch module
Price: $1,700
Variations: various colors

Monaco Calibre 11 Monaco

Reference number: CAW211P.FC6356
Movement: automatic, TAG Heuer Caliber 11 (base Sellita SW300 with Dubois Dépraz module 2006); ø 30 mm, height 7.3 mm; 59 jewels; 28,800 vph
Functions: hours, minutes, subsidiary seconds; chronograph; date
Case: stainless steel, 39 × 39 mm, height 14.5 mm; sapphire crystal; transparent case back; water-resistant to 10 atm
Band: calfskin, folding clasp
Price: $5,900

Autavia Calibre Heuer 02

Reference number: CBE2110.FC8226
Movement: automatic, TAG Heuer Caliber Heuer 02; ø 31 mm, height 6.9 mm; 33 jewels; 28,800 vph; 80-hour power reserve
Functions: hours, minutes, subsidiary seconds; chronograph; date
Case: stainless steel, ø 42 mm, height 15.5 mm; bidirectional bezel with aluminum inserts and 12-hour division; sapphire crystal; transparent case back; water-resistant to 10 atm
Band: calfskin, folding clasp
Price: $5,150
Variations: stainless steel bracelet ($5,300)

TEMPTION

Temption GmbH
Raistinger Str. 46
D-71083 Herrenberg
Germany

Tel.:
+49-7032-977-954

Fax:
+49-7032-977-955

E-mail:
ftemption@aol.com

Website:
www.temption.info

Founded:
1997

Number of employees:
4

Annual production:
700 watches

U.S. distributor:
TemptionUSA
Debby Gordon
2053 North Bridgeport Drive
Fayetteville, AR 72704
888-400-4293
temptionusa@sbcglobal.net

Most important collections/price range:
automatics (three-hand), GMT, chronographs,
and chronographs with complications / approx.
$1,900 to $4,200

Temption has been operating under the leadership of Klaus Ulbrich since 1997. Ulbrich is an engineer with special training in the construction of watches and movements, and right from the start, he intended to develop timekeepers that were modern in their esthetics but not subject to the whims of zeitgeist. Retro watches would have no place in his collections. The design behind all Temption models is inspired more by the Bauhaus or the Japanese concept of wabi sabi. Reduction to what is absolutely necessary is the golden rule here. Beauty emerges from clarity, or in other words, less is more.

Ulbrich sketches all the watches himself. Some of the components are even made in-house, but all the pieces are assembled in the company facility in Herrenberg, a town just to the east of the Black Forest. The primary functions are always easy to read, even in low light. The company logo is discreetly included on the dial.

Ulbrich works according to a model he calls the "information pyramid." Hours and minutes are at the tip, with all other functions subordinated. To maintain this hierarchy, the dials are dark, the date windows are in the same hue, and all subdials are not framed in any way. The most unimportant information for reading time comes at the end of the "pyramid"; it is shiny black on black: the logo can only be identified in lateral light.

The Cameo rectangular model is a perfect example of Ulbrich's esthetic ideas and his consistent technological approach: Because rectangular sapphire crystals can hardly be made water-resistant, the Cameo's crystal is chemically bonded to the case and water-resistant to 10 atm. The frame for the sapphire was metalized inside to hide the bonded edge. The overall look is one of stunning simplicity and elegance. With the CGK205 chronograph, Ulbrich took the concept out of the case. Whether it be the leather strap or the stainless steel bracelet, the watch's attachment is seamlessly integrated into the case, without any visible split.

CM05

Reference number: CM05A10SST
Movement: automatic, Temption Caliber T15.1 (base Soprod A10, or on request with a Caliber ETA 2892-A2); ø 25.6 mm, height 3.6 mm; 21 jewels; 28,800 vph; finely finished movement; 42-hour power reserve
Functions: hours, minutes, sweep seconds; date
Case: stainless steel, ø 42 mm, height 10.8 mm; sapphire crystal; transparent case back; screw-in crown; water-resistant to 10 atm
Band: stainless steel, double folding clasp with safety lock
Price: $2,400

Chronograph CGK205 V2

Reference number: 205V2316BSST
Movement: automatic, Temption Caliber T18.1 (base ETA 7751); ø 30 mm, height 7.8 mm; 25 jewels; 28,800 vph; finely finished movement; 42-hour power reserve
Functions: hours, minutes; second 24-hour display; chronograph; full calendar with date, weekday, month, moon phase
Case: stainless steel, ø 43 mm, height 14 mm; sapphire crystal; transparent case back; screw-down crown and pusher with colored cabochons; water-resistant to 10 atm
Band: stainless steel, double folding clasp
Remarks: comes with additional textile strap
Price: $3,540

Cameo-B

Reference number: CAMBLBFS151
Movement: automatic, Temption Caliber T15.1 (base Soprod A10); ø 25.6 mm, height 3.6 mm; 21 jewels; 28,800 vph; finely finished movement; 42-hour power reserve
Functions: hours, minutes, sweep seconds; date
Case: stainless steel, 37 × 41 mm, height 9.9 mm; sapphire crystal; transparent case back; screw-in crown; water-resistant to 10 atm
Band: calfskin, double folding clasp
Price: $1,750

TISSOT

The Swiss watchmaker Tissot was founded in 1853 in the town of Le Locle in the Jura mountains. In the century that followed, it gained international recognition for its Savonnette pocket watch. And even when the wristwatch became popular in the early twentieth century, time and again Tissot managed to attract attention to its products. To this day, the Banana Watch of 1916 and its first watches in the art deco style (1919) remain design icons of that epoch. The watchmaker has always been at the top of its technical game as well: The first antimagnetic watch (1930), the first mechanical plastic watch (Astrolon, 1971), and its touch-screen T-Touch (1999) all bear witness to Tissot's remarkable capacity for finding unusual and modern solutions.

Today, Tissot belongs to the Swatch Group and, with its wide selection of quartz and inexpensive mechanical watches, serves as the group's entry-level brand. Within this price segment, Tissot offers something special for the buyer who values traditional watchmaking, but is not of limitless financial means. The brand, which celebrated its 160th anniversary in style in 2013 with a comprehensive retrospective in Geneva, has gravitated toward the sports crowd. Tissot is timing everything from basketball to superbike racing, from ice hockey to fencing—and water sports, of course. The Sailing Touch, a watch that provides sailors with a vast array of needed information, came out in 2010. The chronograph Couturier line is outfitted with the new ETA chronograph caliber C01.211. This caliber features a number of plastic parts: another step in simplifying, and lowering the cost of, mechanical movements.

Increasingly, as well, a number of Tissot models are being equipped with silicon hairsprings, which are notorious for outstanding isochronous oscillation as well as imperviousness to magnetic fields and changes in temperature. And for the buyer, it means only a slight increase in price.

Tissot SA
Chemin des Tourelles, 17
CH-2400 Le Locle
Switzerland

Tel.:
+41-32-933-3111

Fax:
+41-32-933-3311

E-mail:
info@tissot.ch

Website:
www.tissot.ch

Founded:
1853

U.S. distributor:
Tissot
The Swatch Group (U.S.), Inc.
703 Waterford Way
Suite: 450
Miami, FL 33126
www.us.tissotshop.com

Most important collections/price range:
Ballade / from $925; T-Touch / from $575; NBA Collection / from $395; Chemin des Tourelles / from $795

Ballade Powermatic 80 COSC

Reference number: T108.408.16.057.00
Movement: automatic, Tissot Powermatic 80 (base ETA 2824-2); ø 25.6 mm, height 4.7 mm; 25 jewels; 21,600 vph; silicon hairspring; 80-hour power reserve; COSC-certified chronometer
Functions: hours, minutes, sweep seconds; date
Case: stainless steel, ø 41 mm, height 9.84 mm; sapphire crystal; transparent case back; water-resistant to 5 atm
Band: calfskin, double folding clasp
Price: $925

T-Complication Squelette

Reference number: T070.405.16.411.00
Movement: manually wound, ETA Caliber 6497-1; ø 36.6 mm, height 4.5 mm; 17 jewels; 18,000 vph; skeletonized movement; 46-hour power reserve
Functions: hours, minutes, subsidiary seconds
Case: stainless steel, ø 43 mm, height 11.99 mm; sapphire crystal; transparent case back; water-resistant to 5 atm
Band: calfskin, double folding clasp
Price: $1,950

T-Race Cycling Tour de France 2017

Reference number: T111.417.37.441.00
Movement: quartz
Functions: hours, minutes, subsidiary seconds; chronograph; date
Case: stainless steel with gray PVD coating, ø 45 mm, height 11 mm; aluminum bezel; sapphire crystal; water-resistant to 10 atm
Band: silicon, buckle
Price: $495

T-Touch Expert Solar

Reference number: T091.420.47.057.00
Movement: quartz, multifunctional movement with LCD display and solar cell for separate energy source
Functions: hours, minutes; additional 12-hour display (second time zone), barometer, altimeter and altitude difference meter, compass, regatta function, 2 alarms; chronograph with countdown timer; perpetual calendar with date, weekday, weeks of the year
Case: titanium, ø 45 mm, height 13 mm; bezel with black PVD coating; sapphire crystal; water-resistant to 10 atm
Band: silicon, folding clasp
Price: $1,150

T-Race Automatic Moto GP Ltd. Edition 2017

Reference number: T092.427.27.051.00
Movement: automatic, ETA Caliber C01.211; ø 31 mm, height 8.44 mm; 15 jewels; 21,600 vph; 45-hour power reserve
Functions: hours, minutes, subsidiary seconds; chronograph; date
Case: stainless steel with rose gold–colored PVD coating, ø 47.25 mm, height 15.98 mm; bezel with black PVD coating, unidirectional bezel with 0-60 scale; sapphire crystal; water-resistant to 10 atm
Band: silicon, folding clasp
Price: $1,295

Le Locle

Reference number: T006.407.11.033.00
Movement: automatic, Tissot Powermatic 80 (base ETA 2824-2); ø 25.6 mm, height 4.7 mm; 25 jewels; 21,600 vph; 80-hour power reserve
Functions: hours, minutes, sweep seconds; date
Case: stainless steel, ø 39.3 mm, height 9.75 mm; sapphire crystal; transparent case back; water-resistant to 3 atm
Band: stainless steel, double folding clasp
Price: $630
Variations: with black dial and calfskin band ($575)

Tradition Small Second

Reference number: T063.428.36.038.00
Movement: automatic, ETA 2825-2; ø 25.6 mm, height 6.6 mm; 25 jewels; 28,800 vph; 38-hour power reserve
Functions: hours, minutes, subsidiary seconds; date
Case: stainless steel with rose gold–colored PVD coating, ø 40 mm, height 11.16 mm; sapphire crystal; transparent case back; water-resistant to 3 atm
Band: calfskin, double folding clasp
Price: $700

Chemin des Tourelles

Reference number: T099.407.16.058.00
Movement: automatic, Tissot Powermatic 80 (base ETA 2824-2); ø 25.6 mm, height 4.7 mm; 25 jewels; 21,600 vph; 80-hour power reserve
Functions: hours, minutes, sweep seconds; date
Case: stainless steel, ø 42 mm, height 10.89 mm; sapphire crystal; transparent case back; water-resistant to 5 atm
Band: calfskin, double folding clasp
Price: $795

Bridgeport Mechanical Skeleton

Reference number: T859.405.29.273.00
Movement: manually wound, ETA Caliber 6498-1; ø 36.6 mm, height 4.5 mm; 17 jewels; 21,600 vph; skeletonized movement; 46-hour power reserve
Functions: hours, minutes, subsidiary seconds
Case: stainless steel with rose gold–colored PVD coating, ø 47.5 mm, height 14 mm; mineral glass, transparent case back; crown with rose gold–colored PVD coating; water-resistant to 3 atm
Price: $1,250

TOWSON WATCH COMPANY

Towson Watch Co.
502 Dogwood Lane
Towson, MD 21286

Tel.:
410-823-1823

Fax:
410-823-8581

E-mail:
towsonwatchco@aol.com

Website:
www.twcwatches.com

After over forty years repairing high-grade watches, repeaters, and chronographs, and making his own tourbillons, George Thomas, a master watchmaker, met Hartwig Balke, a graduate in mechanical engineering and also a talented watchmaker, by chance in a bar in Annapolis. The two men, each well on their way to retirement, decided to turn their passion into a business and, in 2000, founded the Towson Watch Company.

Thomas's first tourbillon pocket watches are displayed at the National Watch and Clock Museum in Columbia, Pennsylvania. In 1999, Balke made his first wrist chronograph, the STS-99 Mission, for a NASA astronaut and mission specialist. It was worn during the first shuttle mission in the new millennium, in the year 2000. The two also restored one of the world's oldest watches, one belonging to Philip Melanchton. In 2009, Thomas was invited to open up a pocket watch belonging to President Lincoln, and revealed a secret message engraved by a servicing watchmaker and Union supporter working in Maryland: "Jonathan Dillon April 13-1861 Fort Sumpter [sic] was attacked by the rebels on the above date J Dillon."

Towson timepieces pay tribute to local sites, like the Choptank or Potomac rivers. The timepieces are imaginative, a touch retro, a bit nostalgic perhaps, and very personal—not to mention affordable. A number of chronographs give the brand a sportive look. For the Dress Chronograph, Towson recruited the German watchmaker and dial specialist Jochen Benzinger.

Their local commitment is also shared by entrepreneur and former University of Maryland football captain Kevin Plank, who launched the technological sports apparel company Under Armour. In early 2016, the company announced it had bought a 25 percent stake in Towson, to boost its market presence and ensure its future. The two founders had been thinking of succession. Those concerns have now been laid to rest: "The brand will continue to grow and thrive for a long time to come," they told the *Baltimore Sun*.

Founded:
2000

Number of employees:
4

Annual production:
200 watches

Distribution:
retail

Most important collections/price range:
Skipjack GMT / approx. $2,950; Mission / approx. $2,500; Potomac / approx. $2,000; Choptank / approx. $4,500; Martin / approx. $3,950 / custom design / $10,000 to $35,000

14-kt Gold Potomac

Reference number: GP 001-14K
Movement: manually wound, Soprod Unitas Caliber 6497; diameter 37.2 mm; height 4.5 mm; 17 jewels; 18,000 vph; swan-neck fine adjustment; barley and solar guilloché on the dial, rhodium-plated dial; skeletonized movement
Functions: hours, minutes, subsidiary seconds
Case: rose gold; ø 42 mm, height 12.5 mm; sapphire crystal; transparent case back; water-resistant to 3 atm
Band: reptile skin, 14k rose gold buckle
Price: $23,500.

Gold Dress Watch

Reference number: TWC001-WG
Movement: manually wound, Soprod Unitas Caliber 6498; ø 37.2 mm; height 4.5 mm; 17 jewels; 18,000 vph; skeletonized, engraved and coated bridges: swan-neck fine adjustment
Functions: hours, minutes, subsidiary seconds
Case: white gold, 45 × 45 mm, height 12.5 mm; sapphire crystal, screw-down transparent case back, water-resistant to 3 atm
Band: reptile skin, white gold buckle
Price: $35,000

Potomac

Reference number: PO250-S
Movement: manually wound, Soprod Unitas Caliber 6498; ø 37.2 mm; height 4.5 mm; 17 jewels; 18,000 vph
Functions: Hour, minute, subsidiary seconds
Case: stainless steel, ø 42 mm, height 12.5 mm; domed sapphire crystal; screw-down transparent back; water-resistant to 3 atm
Band: calfskin, buckle
Price: $1,995
Variations: black dial with gold numerals and black calfskin band; stainless steel mesh bracelet ($2,345)

Martin M-130

Reference number: CC100
Movement: automatic, ETA Caliber 7750 Valjoux,
ø 30 mm; height 7.9 mm; 25 jewels; 28,800 vph;
fine finishing with côtes de Genève.
Functions: hours, minutes, subsidiary seconds,
chronograph, date
Case: stainless steel, ø 42 mm, height 13.5 mm,
sapphire crystal, screw-down back with engraving,
water-resistant to 5 atm
Band: leather, folding clasp
Price: $3,950
Variations: mesh stainless steel bracelet ($4,250)

Dress Chronograph

Reference number: BCH 25
Movement: automatic, Caliber 7750 Valjoux;
diameter ø 30 mm; height 7.9 mm; 21 jewels;
28,800 vph; finely finished with côtes de Genève
Functions: hours, minutes, subsidiary seconds;
chronograph; date
Case: stainless steel, ø 42 mm, height 15.8 mm;
sapphire crystal; screw-down transparent case back;
water-resistant to 5 atm
Band: reptile skin, folding clasp
Remarks: elaborate silver dial with guilloché by
Jochen Benzinger
Price: $8,250
Variations: mesh stainless steel bracelet ($8,600)

Mission Moon SC

Reference number: MM250-CS
Movement: automatic ETA Caliber 7751;
ø 25.6 mm, height 3.6 mm; 21 jewels; 28,800 vph;
fine finishing with côtes de Genève.
Functions: hours, minutes, subsidiary seconds;
weekday, month, date; moon phase; 24-hour display;
chronograph
Case: stainless steel, 40 mm, height 13.5 mm,
sapphire crystal, screw-down back with engraving,
water-resistant to 5 atm
Band: calfskin, orange stitching, folding clasp
Price: $4,160
Variations: stainless steel bracelet ($4,460)

Pride II

Reference number: PR250-S
Movement: Automatic Caliber ETA 2892A2;
ø 25.6 mm, height 3.6 mm; 21 jewels; 28,800 vph;
fine finish with côtes de Genève.
Functions: hours, minutes, sweep seconds; date
Case: stainless steel; shield shape; ø 39 mm ×
44 mm; sapphire crystal; screw-down back with the
engraving of Pride of Baltimore II; water-resistant to
5 atm
Band: calfskin, folding clasp
Price: $4,150
Variations: white dial and calfskin strap with
folding clasp; stainless steel mesh bracelet ($3,850)

Skipjack GMT

Reference number: SKJ100-S
Movement: Automatic Caliber ETA 2893-2;
ø 25.6 mm; height 4.1 mm; 21 jewels; 28,800 vph;
fine finish with côtes de Genève
Functions: hours, minutes, sweep seconds; date;
24-hour adjustable hand
Case: stainless steel, cannelage; ø 41.5 mm;
sapphire crystal; screw-down transparent back with
sapphire crystal; water-resistant to 5 atm
Band: calfskin, folding clasp
Price: $2,950
Variations: black dial with rhodium-plated numerals
and leather band with deployment clasp; stainless
steel bracelet ($3,250)

Choptank Moon Chrono Special

Reference number: CT025-G
Movement: automatic, ETA Caliber 7751 Valjoux;
ø 30 mm; height 7.9 mm; 25 jewels; 28,800 vph;
fine finishing with côtes de Genève
Functions: hours, minutes, subsidiary seconds;
weekday, month, date; moon phase; 24-hour display;
chronograph
Case: stainless steel; 40 mm × 44 mm; height
13.5 mm; sapphire crystal at front; transparent
screw-down back; water-resistant to 5 atm
Band: reptile skin with folding clasp
Price: $8,500
Variations: mesh stainless steel bracelet ($8,850)

TUDOR

The Tudor brand came out of the shadow cast by its "big sister" Rolex in 2007 and worked hard to develop its own personality. The strategy focuses on distinctive models that draw inspiration from the brand's rich past but remain in the "affordable quality watch segment."

Rolex founder Hans Wilsdorf started Tudor in 1946 as a second brand in order to offer the legendary reliability of his watches to a broader public at a more affordable price. To this day, Tudor still benefits from the same industrial platform as Rolex, especially in the area of cases and bracelets, assembly and quality assurance, not to mention distribution and after-sales. However, the movements themselves are usually delivered by ETA and "tudorized" according to the company's own esthetic and technical criteria.

In the era of vintage and retro, it's no wonder that the brand has started tapping into its own treasure trove of icons. Following the success of the Heritage Black Bay diver's watch, based on a 1954 model, came the turn of the blue-highlighted 1973 Chronograph Montecarlo. In 2014, Tudor completed the Heritage collection with the Ranger, a sports watch with an urban-adventurer feel, inspired by the same "tool watch" from the 1960s. In a bit of sibling rivalry, the brand has now come out with its own caliber, designed and built in-house. The MT-5621 made its debut in the simple North Flag and was built as a three-hander (MT-5612) for the Pelagos models. Two other caliber iterations are used for the new Black Bay models.

Following the release of the M5601/5602 calibers, with three hands and a date, Tudor jolted the watch watchers at Baselworld 2017 with an automatic chronograph. It achieved this feat by using Breitling's B01 Caliber in exchange for the three-hand MT5912. The advantage for both brands is independence from the large suppliers of movements.

Montres Tudor SA
Rue François-Dussaud 3-7
Case postale 1755
CH-1211 Geneva
Switzerland

Tel.:
+41-22-302-2200

Fax:
+41-22-300-2255

E-mail:
info@tudorwatch.com

Website:
www.tudorwatch.com

Founded:
1946

U.S. distributor:
Tudor Watch U.S.A., LLC
665 Fifth Avenue
New York, NY 10022
212-897-9900; 212-371-0371(fax)
www.tudorwatch.com

Most important collections/price range:
Fastrider / $4,100 to $4,925; Heritage / $2,825 to $6,075; North Flag / $3,550 to $3,675; Pelagos / $4,400; Style / $2,100 to $3,400; Glamour / $2,150 to $5,725

Heritage Black Bay Bronze

Reference number: 79250BM
Movement: automatic, Tudor Caliber MT5601; ø 33.8 mm, height 6.5 mm; 25 jewels; 28,800 vph; silicon hairspring; 70-hour power reserve; COSC-certified chronometer
Functions: hours, minutes sweep seconds
Case: bronze, ø 43 mm; unidirectional bezel, with 0-60 scale; sapphire crystal; screw-in crown; water-resistant to 20 atm
Band: textile, buckle
Remarks: comes with calfskin band
Price: $3,975

Heritage Black Bay Dark

Reference number: 79230DK
Movement: automatic, Tudor Caliber MT5602; ø 31.8 mm, height 6.5 mm; 25 jewels; 28,800 vph; silicon hairspring; 70-hour power reserve; COSC-certified chronometer
Functions: hours, minutes, sweep seconds
Case: stainless steel with black PVD coating, ø 41 mm; unidirectional bezel, with 0-60 scale; sapphire crystal; screw-in crown; water-resistant to 20 atm
Band: stainless steel with black PVD coating, folding clasp with safety lock
Price: $4,475
Variations: calfskin ($4,150)

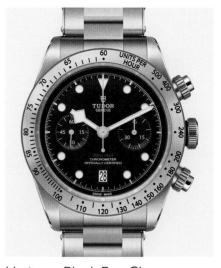

Heritage Black Bay Chrono

Reference number: 79350
Movement: automatic, Tudor Caliber MT5813; ø 30.4 mm, height 7.23 mm; 41 jewels; 28,800 vph; silicon hairspring, variable inertia balance; 70-hour power reserve; COSC-certified chronometer
Functions: hours, minutes, subsidiary seconds; chronograph; date
Case: stainless steel, ø 41 mm; sapphire crystal; screw-in crown; water-resistant to 20 atm
Band: stainless steel, folding clasp
Remarks: comes with additional textile strap
Price: $5,050
Variations: leather strap ($4,725)

Heritage Black Bay S&G

Reference number: 79733N
Movement: automatic, Tudor Caliber MT5612;
ø 31.8 mm, height 6.5 mm; 26 jewels; 28,800 vph;
silicon hairspring, variable inertia balance; 70-hour
power reserve; COSC-certified chronometer
Functions: hours, minutes, sweep seconds; date
Case: stainless steel, ø 41 mm; unidirectional yellow
gold bezel, with 0-60 scale; sapphire crystal; screw-in
crown in yellow gold; water-resistant to 20 atm
Band: stainless steel with yellow gold elements,
folding clasp with safety lock
Remarks: comes with additional textile strap
Price: $4,975
Variations: calfskin strap ($3,775)

Heritage Black Bay Steel

Reference number: 79730
Movement: automatic, Tudor Caliber MT5612;
ø 31.8 mm, height 6.5 mm; 26 jewels; 28,800 vph;
silicon hairspring, variable inertia balance; 70-hour
power reserve; COSC-certified chronometer
Functions: hours, minutes, sweep seconds; date
Case: stainless steel, ø 41 mm; unidirectional bezel,
with 0-60 scale; sapphire crystal; screw-in crown;
water-resistant to 20 atm
Band: calfskin, folding clasp with safety lock
Remarks: comes with additional textile strap
Price: $3,475
Variations: stainless steel bracelet ($3,800)

Heritage Black Bay 41

Reference number: 79540
Movement: automatic, Tudor Caliber 2824 (base
ETA 2824-2); ø 25.6 mm, height 4.6 mm; 25 jewels;
28,800 vph; 38-hour power reserve
Functions: hours, minutes, sweep seconds
Case: stainless steel, ø 41 mm; sapphire crystal;
screw-in crown; water-resistant to 20 atm
Band: textile, buckle
Remarks: comes with stainless steel bracelet
Price: $2,950
Variations: calfskin strap ($2,625)

Heritage Advisor

Reference number: 79620TC
Movement: automatic, Tudor Caliber 2892
(base ETA 2892-A2); with additional manufacture
mechanism for mechanical alarm clock; ø 25.6 mm;
21 jewels; 28,800 vph; 42-hour power reserve
Functions: hours, minutes, sweep seconds; alarm;
date
Case: stainless steel, titanium, ø 42 mm; sapphire
crystal; water-resistant to 10 atm
Band: reptile skin, folding clasp with safety lock
Remarks: comes with additional silk strap
Price: $5,850
Variations: stainless steel bracelet ($6,075)

Caliber MT5601

Automatic; single spring barrel, 70-hour power
reserve; COSC-certified chronometer
Functions: hours, minutes, sweep seconds
Diameter: 33.8 mm
Height: 6.5 mm
Jewels: 25
Balance: glucydur with weighted screws
Frequency: 28,800 vph
Balance spring: silicon
Related caliber: MT5602 (with smaller encasement
diameter of 31.8 mm)

Caliber MT5813

Automatic; single spring barrel, 70-hour power
reserve; COSC-certified chronometer
Functions: hours, minutes, subsidiary seconds;
chronograph; date
Diameter: 30.4 mm
Height: 7.23 mm
Jewels: 41
Balance: glucydur with weighted screws
Frequency: 28,800 vph
Balance spring: silicon

TUTIMA

The name Glashütte is synonymous with watches in Germany. The area, known also for precision engineering, already had quite a watchmaking industry going when World War I closed off markets, followed by the hyperinflation of the early twenties. To rebuild the local economy, a conglomerate was created to produce finished watches under the leadership of jurist Dr. Ernst Kurtz consisting of the movement manufacturer UROFA Glashütte AG and UFAG. The top watches were given the name Tutima, derived from the Latin *tutus*, meaning "whole" or "sound." Among the brand's most famous timepieces was a pilot's watch that set standards in terms of esthetics and functionality.

A few days before World War II ended, Kurtz left Glashütte and founded Uhrenfabrik Kurtz in southern Germany. A young businessman and former employee of Kurtz by the name of Dieter Delecate is credited with keeping the manufacturing facilities and the name Tutima going even as the company sailed through troubled waters. In founding Tutima Uhrenfabrik GmbH in Ganderkesee, this young, resolute entrepreneur prepared the company's strategy for the coming decades.

Delecate has had the joy of seeing Tutima return to its old home and vertically integrated operations, meaning it is once again a genuine *manufacture*. Under renowned designer Rolf Lang, it has developed an in-house minute repeater. In 2013, Tutima proudly announced a genuine made-in-Glashütte movement (at least 50 percent must be produced in the town), Caliber 617.

In addition to technically advanced and sportive watches, Tutima Glashütte has started reviving the great watchmaking crafts that have made the region world famous. There is the Hommage minute repeater and the three-hand Patria. In 2017, the brand introduced the Tempostopp, a flyback chronograph run on the Caliber 659, a replica of the legendary Urofa Caliber 59 from the 1930s with a few necessary improvements in the details.

Tutima Uhrenfabrik GmbH Ndl. Glashütte
Altenberger Strasse 6
D-01768 Glashütte
Germany

Tel.:
+49-35053-320-20

Fax:
+49-35053-320-222

E-mail:
info@tutima.com

Website:
www.tutima.com

Founded:
1927

Number of employees:
approx. 60

U.S. distributor:
Tutima USA, Inc.
P.O. Box 983
Torrance, CA 90508
1-TUTIMA-1927
info@tutimausa.com
www.tutima.com

Most important collections/price range:
Patria, Saxon One, M2, Grand Flieger, Hommage / approx. $2,600 to $22,000

Saxon One Chronograph Royal Blue

Reference number: 6420-05
Movement: automatic, Tutima Caliber 521 (base ETA 7750); ø 30 mm, height 7.9 mm; 25 jewels; 28,800 vph; sweep minute counter; rotor with gold seal; 48-hour power reserve
Functions: hours, minutes, subsidiary seconds; second 24-hour display (second time zone); chronograph; date
Case: stainless steel, ø 43 mm, height 15.7 mm; bidirectional bezel with reference markers; sapphire crystal; transparent case back; screw-in crown; water-resistant to 20 atm
Band: stainless steel, folding clasp
Price: $6,500
Variations: reptile skin, folding clasp ($6,100)

Saxon One Automatic

Reference number: 6120-03
Movement: automatic, Tutima Caliber 330 (base ETA 2836-2); ø 25.6 mm, height 5.05 mm; 25 jewels; 28,800 vph; rotor with gold seal; 38-hour power reserve
Functions: hours, minutes, sweep seconds; date, weekday
Case: stainless steel, ø 42 mm, height 13 mm; bidirectional bezel with reference markers; sapphire crystal; transparent case back; screw-in crown; water-resistant to 20 atm
Band: reptile skin, folding clasp
Price: $3,400
Variations: stainless steel bracelet ($3,800)

Saxon One Lady Diamonds

Reference number: 6701-01
Movement: automatic, Tutima Caliber 340 (base ETA 2824-2); ø 25.6 mm, height 4.6 mm; 25 jewels; 28,800 vph; rotor with gold seal; 42-hour power reserve
Functions: hours, minutes, sweep seconds; date
Case: stainless steel, ø 36 mm, height 10.7 mm; bezel set with 48 brilliant-cut diamonds; sapphire crystal; transparent case back; water-resistant to 10 atm
Band: stainless steel, folding clasp
Remarks: mother-of-pearl dial
Price: $6,500
Variations: reptile skin, folding clasp ($6,100)

M2

Reference number: 6450-03
Movement: automatic, Tutima Caliber 521 (base ETA 7750); ø 30 mm, height 7.9 mm; 25 jewels; 28,800 vph; sweep minute counter; 48-hour power reserve
Functions: hours, minutes, subsidiary seconds; second 24-hour display; chronograph; date
Case: titanium, ø 46 mm, height 15.5 mm; sapphire crystal; screw-in crown; water-resistant to 30 atm
Band: titanium, folding clasp
Remarks: magnetic field protection from soft-iron inner case
Price: $6,500
Variations: Kevlar strap ($5,900)

M2 Pioneer

Reference number: 6451-02
Movement: automatic, Tutima Caliber 521 (base ETA 7750); ø 30 mm, height 7.9 mm; 25 jewels; 28,800 vph; sweep minute counter; rotor with gold seal; 48-hour power reserve
Functions: hours, minutes, subsidiary seconds; second 24-hour display; chronograph; date
Case: titanium, ø 46.5 mm, height 16 mm; bidirectional bezel with 0-60 scale; sapphire crystal; screw-in crown; water-resistant to 30 atm
Band: Kevlar, folding clasp
Remarks: magnetic field protection from soft-iron inner case
Price: $6,100
Variations: titanium bracelet ($6,700)

M2 Seven Seas

Reference number: 6151-04
Movement: automatic, Tutima Caliber 330 (base ETA 2836-2); ø 25.6 mm, height 5.05 mm; 25 jewels; 28,800 vph; rotor with gold seal; 38-hour power reserve
Functions: hours, minutes, sweep seconds; date, weekday
Case: titanium, ø 44 mm, height 13 mm; unidirectional bezel, with 0-60 scale; sapphire crystal; screw-in crown; water-resistant to 50 atm
Band: titanium, folding clasp
Price: $2,300
Variations: Kevlar strap ($1,900)

Grand Flieger Classic Chronograph

Reference number: 6402-02
Movement: automatic, Tutima Caliber 320 (base ETA 7750); ø 30 mm, height 7.9 mm; 25 jewels; 28,800 vph; rotor with gold seal; 48-hour power reserve; DIN certified chronometer
Functions: hours, minutes, subsidiary seconds; chronograph; date
Case: stainless steel, ø 43 mm, height 16 mm; bidirectional bezel with reference markers; sapphire crystal; transparent case back; screw-in crown; water-resistant to 20 atm
Band: stainless steel, folding clasp
Price: $5,500
Variations: calfskin strap ($5,100)

Grand Flieger Airport Chronograph

Reference number: 6401-02
Movement: automatic, Tutima Caliber 320 (base ETA 7750); ø 30 mm, height 7.9 mm; 25 jewels; 28,800 vph; rotor with gold seal; 48-hour power reserve; DIN certified chronometer
Functions: hours, minutes, subsidiary seconds; chronograph; date
Case: stainless steel, ø 43 mm, height 16 mm; bidirectional bezel with 0-60 scale; sapphire crystal; transparent case back; screw-in crown; water-resistant to 20 atm
Band: stainless steel, folding clasp
Price: $5,500
Variations: calfskin strap ($5,100)

Grand Flieger Classic Automatic

Reference number: 6102-01
Movement: automatic, Tutima Caliber 330 (base ETA 2836-2); ø 25.6 mm, height 5.05 mm; 25 jewels; 28,800 vph; rotor with gold seal; 38-hour power reserve
Functions: hours, minutes, sweep seconds; date, weekday
Case: stainless steel, ø 43 mm, height 13 mm; bidirectional bezel with reference markers; sapphire crystal; transparent case back; screw-in crown; water-resistant to 20 atm
Band: calfskin, folding clasp
Price: $2,500
Variations: stainless steel bracelet ($2,900)

Patria

Reference number: 6600-02
Movement: manually wound, Tutima Caliber 617;
ø 31 mm, height 4.78 mm; 20 jewels; 21,600 vph;
screw balance with weighted screws, Breguet
hairspring; Glashütte three-quarter plate; winding
wheels with click; gold-plated and finely finished
movement; 65-hour power reserve
Functions: hours, minutes, subsidiary seconds
Case: rose gold, ø 43 mm, height 11.2 mm; sapphire
crystal; transparent case back; water-resistant to
5 atm
Band: reptile skin, buckle
Price: $17,900
Variations: Arabic numerals ($17,900)

Tempostopp

Reference number: 6650-01
Movement: manually wound, Tutima Caliber 659;
ø 33.7 mm, height 6.6 mm; 28 jewels; 21,600 vph;
screw balance with gold weighted screws, Breguet
hairspring; winding wheels with click; gold-plated
and finely finished movement; 65-hour power reserve
Functions: hours, minutes, subsidiary seconds;
flyback chronograph
Case: rose gold, ø 43 mm, height 12.95 mm;
sapphire crystal; transparent case back
Band: reptile skin, buckle
Remarks: improved replica of legendary UROFA
Caliber 59 from 1940s
Price: $29,500; limited to 90 pieces

Hommage

Reference number: 6800-02
Movement: manually wound, Tutima Caliber 800;
ø 32 mm, height 7.2 mm; 42 jewels; 21,600 vph;
screw balance with gold weighted screws, Breguet
hairspring; Glashütte three-quarter plate; winding
wheels with click; hand-engraved balance cock, gold-
plated and finely finished movement; 65-hour power
reserve
Functions: hours, minutes, subsidiary seconds;
minute repeater
Case: rose gold, ø 43 mm, height 13.4 mm; sapphire
crystal; transparent case back
Band: reptile skin, buckle
Price: on request

Caliber Tutima 617

Manually wound; 3 screw-mounted gold chatons,
Glashütte three-quarter plate, winding wheels with
click; single spring barrel, 65-hour power reserve
Functions: hours, minutes, subsidiary seconds
Diameter: 31 mm
Height: 4.78 mm
Jewels: 20
Balance: screw balance with gold weight screws
Frequency: 21,600 vph
Balance spring: Breguet hairspring
Remarks: gold-plated and finely finished movement

Caliber Tutima 659

Manually wound; column wheel control of
chronograph functions; single spring barrel, 65-hour
power reserve
Functions: hours, minutes, subsidiary seconds;
flyback chronograph
Diameter: 33.7 mm
Height: 6.6 mm
Jewels: 28
Balance: screw balance with gold weight screws
Frequency: 21,600 vph
Balance spring: Breguet hairspring
Remarks: improved replica of legendary UROFA
Caliber 659; gold-plated and finely finished
movement

Caliber Tutima 800

Manually wound; 4 screw-mounted gold chatons,
Glashütte three-quarter plate, 2 gongs, winding
wheels with click; single spring barrel, 65-hour
power reserve
Functions: hours, minutes, subsidiary seconds;
minute repeater
Diameter: 32 mm
Height: 7.2 mm
Jewels: 42
Balance: screw balance with gold weight screws
Frequency: 21,600 vph
Balance spring: Breguet hairspring
Remarks: gold-plated and finely finished movement

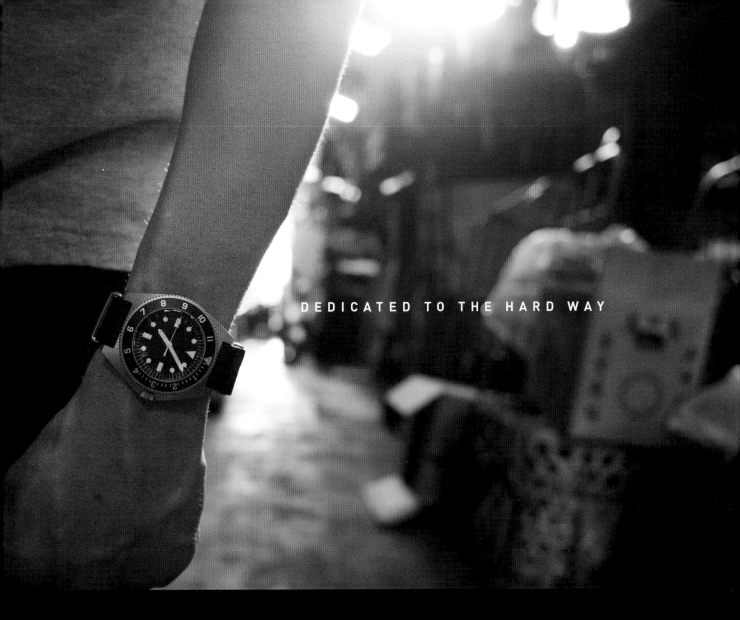

DEDICATED TO THE HARD WAY

MKII PARADIVE

- Case Width - 41.25 mm (bezel diameter)
- Case Thickness - 15.54 mm
- Case Length - 49.50 mm end to end
- Lug Width - 20.00 mm
- Crystal - Double domed sapphire crystal
- Luminous - SuperLumiNova BGW9
- Water Resistance - 20 ATMs (200 meters)

American Crafted   Swiss Assembled

ULYSSE NARDIN

Ulysse Nardin SA
3, rue du Jardin
CH-2400 Le Locle
Switzerland

Tel.:
+41-32-930-7400

Fax:
+41-32-930-7419

Website:
www.ulysse-nardin.com

Founded:
1846

U.S. distributor:
Ulysse Nardin Inc.
7900 Glades Rd., Suite 200
Boca Raton, FL 33434
561-988-8600; 561-988-0123 (fax)
usa@ulysse-nardin.com

Most important collections:
Marine chronometers and diver's watches; Dual Time (also ladies' watches); complications (alarm clocks, perpetual calendar, tourbillons, minute repeaters, jacquemarts, astronomical watches)

At the beginning of the 1980s, following the infamous quartz crisis, Rolf Schnyder revived the venerable Ulysse Nardin brand, which once upon a time had a reputation for marine chronometers and precision watches. He had the luck to meet the multitalented Dr. Ludwig Oechslin, who realized Schnyder's vision of astronomical wristwatches in the Trilogy of Time. Overnight, Ulysse Nardin became a name to be reckoned with in the world of fine watchmaking. Oechslin developed a host of innovations for Ulysse Nardin, from intelligent calendar movements to escapement systems. He was the first to use silicon and synthetic diamonds and thus gave the entire industry a great deal of food for thought. Just about every Ulysse Nardin has become famous for some spectacular technical innovation, be it the Moonstruck with its stunning moon phase accuracy or the outlandish Freak series that more or less does away with the dial.

After Schnyder's death in 2011, his wife, Chai Schnyder, was named president of the board of directors, and Patrik Hoffmann was appointed CEO. The brand developed a strategy of partnerships and acquisitions, notably of the enameler Donzé Cadrans SA, which gave rise to the Marine Chronometer Manufacture, powered by the Caliber UN-118. In 2014, Ulysse Nardin was purchased by the French luxury group Kering, which has not stopped the innovative energy, like the new blade-driven anchor escapement or the more recent regatta countdown watch with a second hand that runs counterclockwise first before running clockwise like a conventional chronograph once the race has started. Pricing, too, has seen an update, with a definite willingness to broaden its buyer segment.

Marine Grand Deck

Reference number: 6302-300/GD
Movement: manually wound, Caliber UN-630; ø 37 mm, height 11.3 mm; 48 jewels; 21,600 vph; flying 1-minute tourbillon; 48-hour power reserve
Functions: jumping hour, retrograde minutes; display with sailing boom, rope, and pulleys
Case: rose gold, ø 44 mm, height 15.9 mm; sapphire crystal; transparent case back; water-resistant to 10 atm
Band: reptile skin, folding clasp
Remarks: wood marquetry dial
Price: $280,000; limited to 18 pieces
Variations: rose gold ($270,000)

Marine Chronometer Manufacture

Reference number: 1186-126-3/43
Movement: automatic, Caliber UN-118; ø 31.0 mm, height 5.88 mm; 50 jewels; 28,800 vph; silicon escapement and hairspring; 60-hour power reserve; COSC-certified chronometer
Functions: hours, minutes, subsidiary seconds; power reserve indicator; date with forward/backward quick setting
Case: rose gold, ø 43 mm, height 14 mm; sapphire crystal; transparent case back; screw-in crown; water-resistant to 10 atm
Band: rubber, with rose-gold elements, folding clasp
Price: $31,800
Variations: stainless steel: $10,300

Freak Blue Cruiser

Reference number: 2050-131/03
Movement: manually wound, Caliber UN-205; ø 35 mm; 28 jewels; 28,800 vph; tourbillon on rotating carousel, silicon escapement and hairspring; movement components used as hands, time-setting via bezel, winding by turning case back; 7-day power reserve
Functions: hours, minutes, subsidiary seconds
Case: white gold, ø 45 mm, height 13.6 mm; bidirectional bezel to set hands; sapphire crystal; transparent case back
Band: reptile skin, folding clasp
Price: $95,000
Variations: rose gold ($89,000)

Marine Chronograph Manufacture Regatta

Reference number: 1553-155-3/43
Movement: automatic, Caliber UN-155; ø 34 mm, height 8.28 mm; 72 jewels; 28,800 vph; silicon escapement and hairspring
Functions: hours, minutes, subsidiary seconds; chronograph with integrated 10-minute countdown; date
Case: stainless steel, ø 44 mm; sapphire crystal; transparent case back; screw-in crown; water-resistant to 10 atm
Band: rubber, with titanium elements, folding clasp
Remarks: countdown totalizer can be freely set; second hand turns counterclockwise first, then changes direction at "0"
Price: $15,900
Variations: enamel dial (limited edition, $29,800)

Marine Tourbillon Manufacture

Reference number: 1283-181/E0
Movement: self-winding, Caliber UN-128; ø 31 mm, height 6.08 mm; 36 jewels; 28,800 vph; flying 1-minute tourbillon; silicon escapement and hairspring; 60-hour power reserve
Functions: hours, minutes; power reserve indicator
Case: stainless steel, ø 43 mm; sapphire crystal; transparent case back; screw-in crown; water-resistant to 10 atm
Band: reptile skin, folding clasp
Remarks: enamel dial
Price: $28,000
Variations: rubber/titanium strap ($27,900); stainless steel bracelet ($28,700)

Marine Chronometer Annual Calendar Manufacture

Reference number: 1133-210/E3
Movement: automatic, Caliber UN-113; ø 31 mm, height 6.78 mm; 55 jewels; 28,800 vph; silicon escapement and hairspring; 60-hour power reserve; Ulysse Nardin Performance Certificate
Functions: hours, minutes, subsidiary seconds; power reserve indicator; annual calendar with month, date with forward/backward quick setting
Case: stainless steel, ø 43 mm; sapphire crystal; transparent case back; screw-in crown; water-resistant to 10 atm
Band: reptile skin, folding clasp
Remarks: enamel dial
Price: $12,900
Variations: rubber/titanium strap ($12,800) or stainless steel bracelet ($13,600)

Marine Chronograph Annual Calendar Manufacture

Reference number: 1533-150/E0
Movement: automatic, Caliber UN-153; ø 31 mm, height 7.37 mm; 53 jewels; 28,800 vph; silicon escapement; 52-hour power reserve
Functions: hours, minutes, subsidiary seconds; chronograph; annual calendar with date, month
Case: stainless steel, ø 43 mm, height 15.0 mm; sapphire crystal; transparent case back; screw-in crown; water-resistant to 10 atm
Band: reptile skin, folding clasp
Remarks: enamel dial
Price: $14,500
Variations: painted dial ($11,900)

Marine 1846

Reference number: 1183-900/E0
Movement: automatic, Caliber UN-118; ø 31.0 mm, height 5.88 mm; 50 jewels; 28,800 vph; silicon escapement and hairspring; 60-hour power reserve
Functions: hours, minutes, subsidiary seconds; power reserve indicator; date
Case: stainless steel, ø 41 mm; sapphire crystal; screw-in crown; water-resistant to 10 atm
Band: reptile skin, buckle
Remarks: enamel dial
Price: $9,900

Diver Chronograph Manufacture

Reference number: 1502-151-3/93
Movement: automatic, Caliber UN-150; ø 31 mm, height 6.75 mm; 25 jewels; 28,800 vph; silicon escapement
Functions: hours, minutes, subsidiary seconds; chronograph; date
Case: rose gold, ø 44 mm, height 15.8 mm; unidirectional bezel, with 0-60 scale; sapphire crystal; transparent case back; screw-in crown; water-resistant to 30 atm
Band: rubber, with rose gold elements, folding clasp
Price: $35,000
Variations: stainless steel ($12,500)

Marine Diver

Reference number: 266-10-3/93
Movement: automatic, Caliber UN-26; ø 25.6 mm, height 5.1 mm; 28 jewels; 28,800 vph; 42-hour power reserve
Functions: hours, minutes, subsidiary seconds; power reserve indicator; date
Case: rose gold, ø 44 mm, height 13 mm; unidirectional bezel, with 0-60 scale; sapphire crystal; screw-in crown; water-resistant to 30 atm
Band: rubber, with rose gold elements, folding clasp
Price: $31,700
Variations: stainless steel with rubber/titanium strap ($8,500)

Diver Chronograph Artemis

Reference number: 353-98LE-3/ARTEMIS
Movement: automatic, Caliber UN-35; ø 30 mm, height 6.9 mm; 57 jewels; 28,800 vph; 42-hour power reserve
Functions: hours, minutes, subsidiary seconds; chronograph; date
Case: stainless steel with rubber coating, ø 46 mm, height 16 mm; unidirectional bezel, with 0-60 scale; sapphire crystal; transparent case back; water-resistant to 20 atm
Band: rubber with titanium elements, folding clasp
Price: $10,800; limited to 250 pieces

Diver Le Locle

Reference number: 3203-950
Movement: automatic, Caliber UN-320; ø 26.4 mm, height 4.6 mm; 39 jewels; 28,800 vph; silicon escapement and hairspring; 48-hour power reserve
Functions: hours, minutes, subsidiary seconds; quick forward/backward date setting
Case: stainless steel, ø 42.2 mm, height 12.7 mm; unidirectional bezel, with 0-60 scale; sapphire crystal; water-resistant to 10 atm
Band: sailcloth, buckle
Price: $9,600

Classico Small Second Manufacture

Reference number: 3203-136-2/E3
Movement: automatic, Caliber UN-320; ø 26.4 mm, height 4.6 mm; 39 jewels; 28,800 vph; silicon anchor escapement and hairspring; 48-hour power reserve
Functions: hours, minutes, subsidiary seconds; date
Case: stainless steel, ø 40 mm, height 9.75 mm; sapphire crystal; transparent case back
Band: reptile skin, buckle
Price: $8,800

Dual Time Manufacture

Reference number: 3243-132/E0
Movement: automatic, Caliber UN-324; ø 26.4 mm, height 6.15 mm; 53 jewels; 28,800 vph; silicon escapement and hairspring; 42-hour power reserve
Functions: hours, minutes, subsidiary seconds, crown position display; second 24-hour display (second time zone); large date
Case: stainless steel, ø 42 mm, height 12.8 mm; sapphire crystal; transparent case back; water-resistant to 3 atm
Band: reptile skin, folding clasp
Remarks: enamel dial
Price: $12,900

Classico Paul David Nardin

Reference number: 3203-900
Movement: automatic, Caliber UN-320; ø 26.4 mm, height 4.6 mm; 39 jewels; 28,800 vph; silicon escapement and hairspring; 48-hour power reserve
Functions: hours, minutes, subsidiary seconds; date
Case: stainless steel, ø 39 mm, height 10.8 mm; sapphire crystal; water-resistant to 3 atm
Band: calfskin, buckle
Price: $9,500

Classic Perpetual Ludwig

Reference number: 333-900
Movement: automatic, Caliber UN-33; ø 31 mm, height 6.95 mm; 34 jewels; 28,800 vph; 48-hour power reserve
Functions: hours, minutes, subsidiary seconds; perpetual calendar with large date, weekday, month, year, forward/backward date quick setting
Case: stainless steel, ø 41 mm, height 13.2 mm; sapphire crystal; transparent case back; screw-in crown; water-resistant to 3 atm
Band: reptile skin, buckle
Price: $19,800

Classic Sonata

Reference number: 673-05/90
Movement: automatic, Caliber UN-67; ø 34.2 mm, height 7.45 mm; 109 jewels; 28,800 vph; silicon escapement and hairspring; alarm with gong sets to the minute; alarm on/off function, 42-hour power reserve
Functions: hours, minutes, sweep seconds; second 24-hour display (second time zone); alarm clock; count-down display to alarm; large date
Case: stainless steel, ø 44 mm, height 14 mm; sapphire crystal; transparent case back; water-resistant to 3 atm
Band: reptile skin, folding clasp
Price: $24,800
Variations: rose gold ($42,800)

Executive Skeleton Tourbillon

Reference number: 1713-139/43
Movement: manually wound, Caliber UN-171; ø 37 mm, height 6.70 mm; 23 jewels; 18,000 vph; 1-minute tourbillon; skeletonized movement; twin spring barrels; silicon pallet lever, escape wheel and hairspring; 170-hour power reserve
Functions: hours, minutes
Case: titanium, ø 45 mm, height 12.6 mm; ceramic bezel; sapphire crystal; transparent case back; water-resistant to 3 atm
Band: calfskin with carbon structure, folding clasp
Price: $38,000

Caliber UN-155

Automatic; silicon escapement; column wheel control of chronograph functions; single spring barrel, 52-hour power reserve
Functions: hours, minutes, subsidiary seconds; chronograph with integrated 10-minute countdown function; date
Diameter: 34 mm
Height: 8.28 mm
Jewels: 67
Frequency: 28,800 vph
Balance spring: silicon
Remarks: for regatta countdown function, stop-seconds hand first runs counterclockwise and changes direction when it reaches pre-set (exact to the minute) goal time; 650 components

Caliber UN-178

Manually wound; 1-minute tourbillon, Ulysse Nardin DiamOnSil anchor escapement (anchor turns without pivots between 2 blades) with new geometry; double spring barrel, 168-hour power reserve
Functions: hours, minutes; power reserve indicator
Diameter: 37 mm
Height: 6 mm
Jewels: 29
Balance: glucydur
Frequency: 18,000 vph
Balance spring: silicon

Caliber UN-334

Automatic; silicon escapement, single spring barrel, 48-hour power reserve
Functions: hours, minutes, subsidiary seconds; additional 24-hour display (2nd time zone); large date
Jewels: 49
Balance: variable inertia balance
Frequency: 28,800 vph
Balance spring: silicon
Shock protection: Incabloc
Remarks: patented quick adjustment for 2nd time zone; perlage on plate, bridges with concentric côtes de Genève ("côtes circulaires")

URBAN JÜRGENSEN & SØNNER

For all aficionados and collectors of fine timekeepers, the name Urban Jürgensen & Sønner is synonymous with outstanding watches. The company was founded in 1773 and has always strived for the highest rungs of the horological art. Technical perfection consistently combines with imaginative cases. A lot of attention is given to dials and hands.

Today, Urban Jürgensen & Sønner—originally a Danish firm—manufactures watches in Switzerland, where a team of eight superbly qualified watchmakers do the work in three ateliers. For over a quarter century now, they have been making highly complicated unique pieces and very upmarket wristwatches in small editions of 50 to 300 pieces. The series were based mostly on *ébauches* by Frédéric Piguet. Like all keen watchmakers, those at Urban Jürgensen have also sought to make their own movements, which would meet the highest standards of precision and reliability and not require too much servicing.

In 2003, a team began collaborating with a well-known external design engineer to construct a base movement. The new UJS-P8 was conceived with both a traditional Swiss lever escapement and in a special variation featuring a pivoting chronometer escapement, available for the first time in a wristwatch.

The esthetic concept behind the brand's watches is clearly vintage. Urban Jürgensen & Sønner timepieces have the broad open face of old pocket watches and classic hands, including a Breguet-type hour hand. The lugs on the new 1741 recall the links of a watch chain.

A few years ago, Urban Jürgensen was purchased by Scandinavian investors. They put the brand into the skillful hands of CEO Søren Jenry Petersen, an industrialist and watch lover, who decided that the best strategy was to maintain the watchmaking concept. The latest crop of models, the 1140s, classical watches with a modernized eighteenth-century feel, suggests he is doing just that.

Urban Jürgensen & Sønner
Chemin Creux 18
CH-2503 Biel-Bienne
Switzerland

Tel.:
+41-32-365-1526

Fax:
+41-32-365-2266

E-mail:
info@urbanjurgensen.com

Website:
www.urbanjurgensen.com

Founded:
1773/1980

Annual production:
max. 200 watches

U.S. distributor:
Martin Pulli
4337 Main Street
Philadelphia, PA 19127
215-508-4610
martin@martinpulli.com
www.martinpulli.com

Most important collections:
high-end references with in-house movements

1741

Reference number: 1741 RT
Movement: manually wound, Urban Jürgensen Caliber P4; ø 32 mm, height 6.85 mm; 24 jewels; 21,600 vph; 2 spring barrels, 60-hour power reserve
Functions: hours, minutes, sweep seconds; perpetual calendar with date, weekday, month, moon phase, leap year
Case: platinum, ø 41 mm, height 12.3 mm; sapphire crystal; transparent case back; water-resistant to 3 atm
Band: reptile skin, buckle
Price: $98,600

1140 Lever Platinum

Reference number: 1140 L
Movement: manually wound, Urban Jürgensen Caliber UJS-P4; ø 32 mm, height 5.2 mm; 23 jewels; 21,600 vph; 2 spring barrels, 72-hour power reserve
Functions: hours, minutes, subsidiary seconds
Case: platinum, ø 40 mm, height 10.5 mm; sapphire crystal; transparent case back; water-resistant to 3 atm
Band: reptile skin, buckle
Price: $45,500

1140 PT Blue

Reference number: 1140 PT
Movement: manually wound, Urban Jürgensen Caliber UJS-P4; ø 32 mm, height 5.2 mm; 23 jewels; 21,600 vph; 2 spring barrels, 72-hour power reserve
Functions: hours, minutes, subsidiary seconds
Case: platinum, ø 40 mm, height 10.5 mm; sapphire crystal; transparent case back; water-resistant to 3 atm
Band: reptile skin, buckle
Price: $53,700; limited to 30 pieces

Urwerk SA
114, rue du Rhône
CH-1204 Geneva
Switzerland

Tel.:
+41-22-900-2027

Fax:
+41-22-900-2026

E-mail:
info@urwerk.com

Website:
www.urwerk.com

Founded:
1995

Annual production:
150 watches

U.S. distributor:
Ildico Inc.
8701 Wilshire Blvd.,
Beverly Hills, CA 90211
310-205-5555

URWERK

Felix Baumgartner and designer Martin Frei count among the living legends of innovative horology. They founded their company, Urwerk, in 1997 with a name that is a play on the words *Uhrwerk*, for movement, and *Urwerk*, meaning a sort of primal mechanism. Their specialty is inventing surprising time indicators featuring digital numerals that rotate like satellites and display the time in a relatively linear depiction on a small "dial" at the front of the flattened case, which could almost—but not quite—be described as oval. Their inspiration goes back to the so-called night clock of the eighteenth-century Campanus brothers, but the realization is purely *2001: A Space Odyssey*.

Urwerk's debut was with the Harry Winston Opus 5. Later, they created the Black Cobra, which displays time using cylinders and other clever ways to recoup energy for driving rather heavy components. The Torpedo is another example of high-tech watchmaking, again based on the satellite system of revolving and turning hands. These pieces remind one of the frenetic engineering that has transformed the planet since the eighteenth century. And with each return to the drawing board, Baumgartner and Frei find new ways to explore what has now become an unmistakable form, using high-tech materials, like aluminum titanium nitride (AlTiN), or finding new functions for the owner to play with.

In 2017, Urwerk celebrated its twentieth anniversary. For the occasion, it gathered all its creative high points into a single watch. The minute hand hovers along an arc and bears the hour indices. The "Transformator" adds a rotatable, pivotable case to the watch. If you're not interested in the time, you can turn the watch around and admire the automatic mechanism through the back.

EMC Time Hunter

Movement: manually wound, Caliber UR EMC2; 28,800 vph; integrated monitoring of rate precision with optical sensor on the escapement and comparison with referential oscillator (16,000,000 Hz), power from microgenerator with large collapsible winding handle on case side
Functions: hours, minutes, subsidiary seconds; power reserve indicator, rate precision and amplitude indication
Case: stainless steel, titanium, with green ceramic coating, 43 × 51 mm, height 15.8 mm; sapphire crystal; rate fine regulation screw on the back; water-resistant to 3 atm
Band: textile, buckle
Price: $120,000

UR-210 "Clous de Paris"

Movement: automatic, Caliber UR 7.10; 51 jewels; 28,800 vph; revolving hour cubes with retrograde minutes arc, winding system regulated by fluid dynamics decoupling and adjustable efficiency; 39-hour power reserve
Functions: hours (digital, rotating), minutes (retrograde); power reserve indicator, winding efficiency
Case: titanium and AlTin coated steel, 43.8 × 53.6 mm, height 17.8 mm; sapphire crystal
Band: textile, buckle
Remarks: hour cubes travel across semicircular minute scale, skeletonized minute hand jumps back at end of scale and "picks up" next satellite
Price: $150,000

UR-T8 Edge

Movement: automatic, Caliber UR 8.01; 28,800 vph; revolving hour satellites with Maltese Cross control and planetary transmission (all numerals always remain in vertical position), winding system regulated by fluid dynamics decoupling; 50-hour power reserve
Functions: hours (digital, rotating), minutes
Case: titanium, titanium with black PVD coating, 48.3 × 60.2 mm, height 20 mm; sapphire crystal; water-resistant to 3 atm
Band: reptile skin, buckle
Remarks: case on carrier frame can be pivoted and turned 180°
Price: $100,000

UTS

UTS Watches, Inc.
P.O. Box 6293
Los Osos, CA 93412

Tel.:
877-887-0123 or 805-528-9800

E-mail:
info@utswatches.com

Website:
www.utswatches.com

Founded:
1999

Number of employees:
2

Annual production:
fewer than 500

Distribution:
direct sales only

Most important collections/price range:
sports and diver's watches, chronographs / from
$2,500 to $7,000

UTS, or "Uhren Technik Spinner," was the natural outgrowth of a company based in Munich and manufacturing CNC tools and machines for the watch industry. Nicolaus Spinner, a mechanical engineer and aficionado in his own right, learned the nitty-gritty of watchmaking by the age-old system of taking watches apart. From there to making robust diver's watches was just a short step. The collection has grown considerably since he started production in 1999. The watches are built mainly around ETA calibers. Some, like the new 4000M, feature a unique locking bezel using a stem, a bolt, and a ceramic ball bearing system invented by Spinner. Another specialty is the 6 mm sapphire crystal, which guarantees significant water resistance. Spinner's longtime friend and business partner, Stephen Newman, is the owner of the UTS trademark in the United States. He not only has worked on product development, but has also contributed his own design ideas and handles sales and marketing for the small brand. A new watch released in 2014, the 4000M Diver, boasts an extreme depth rating even without the need for a helium escape valve and is available in a GMT version. The collection is small, but UTS has a faithful following in Germany and the United States. The key for the fan club is a unique appearance coupled with mastery of the technology. These are pure muscle watches with no steroids.

Diver 4000M

Movement: automatic, ETA Caliber 2824-2;
ø 25.6 mm, height 4.6 mm; 25 jewels; 28,800 vph;
42-hour power reserve
Functions: hours, minutes, sweep seconds; date
Case: stainless steel, ø 45 mm, height 17.5 mm;
bidirectional bezel with 60-minute scale; 6 mm
sapphire crystal, antireflective on back; screwed-
down case back; screw-in crown and buttons;
locking bezel; water-resistant to 400 atm
Band: stainless steel with diver's extension folding
clasp or rubber or leather strap
Price: $6,800

Diver 4000M GMT

Movement: automatic, ETA Caliber 2893-2;
ø 25.6 mm, height 4.6 mm; 25 jewels; 28,800 vph;
42-hour power reserve
Functions: hours, minutes, sweep seconds; date;
2nd time zone
Case: stainless steel, ø 45 mm, height 17.5 mm;
bidirectional bezel with 60-minute scale; 6 mm
sapphire crystal, antireflective on back; screwed-
down case back; screw-in crown and buttons;
locking bezel; water-resistant to 400 atm
Band: stainless steel with diver's extension folding
clasp or rubber or leather strap
Price: $6,800

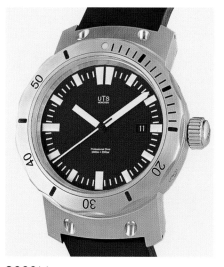

2000M

Movement: automatic, ETA Caliber 2824-2;
ø 25.6 mm, height 4.6 mm; 25 jewels; 28,800 vph;
42-hour power reserve
Functions: hours, minutes, sweep seconds; date
Case: stainless steel, ø 44 mm, height 16.5 mm;
unidirectional bezel with 60-minute scale; automatic
helium escape valve; sapphire crystal, antireflective
on back; screwed-down case back; screw-in crown
and buttons; water-resistant to 200 atm
Band: stainless steel with diver's extension folding
clasp, comes with rubber leather strap
Price: $3,950

1000M V2

Movement: automatic, ETA Caliber 2824-2;
ø 25.6 mm, height 4.6 mm; 25 jewels; 28,800 vph;
42-hour power reserve
Functions: hours, minutes, sweep seconds; date
Case: stainless steel, ø 43 mm, height 14 mm;
unidirectional bezel with 60-minute scale; sapphire
crystal, antireflective on back; screwed-down
sapphire (optional) crystal case back; screw-in crown
and buttons; water-resistant to 10 atm
Band: stainless steel with diver's extension folding
clasp or rubber or leather strap
Price: $3,390

1000 GMT

Movement: automatic, ETA Caliber ETA 2893-2;
ø 25.6 mm, height 4.1 mm; 21 jewels; 28,800 vph;
42-hour power reserve
Functions: hours, minutes, sweep seconds; 2nd time
zone; date; quick set GMT hand
Case: stainless steel, ø 43 mm, height 14 mm;
unidirectional bezel with 60-minute scale; sapphire
crystal, antireflective on back; screwed-down case
back with optional transparent back (sapphire
crystal); screw-in crown and buttons; water-resistant
to 100 atm
Band: stainless steel with diver's extension folding
clasp or rubber or leather strap
Price: $3,950

Adventure Automatic

Movement: automatic, ETA Valgranges Caliber
A07.111; ø 36.6 mm, height 7.9 mm; 24 jewels;
28,800 vph; 46-hour power reserve
Functions: hours, minutes, sweep seconds; date
Case: stainless steel, ø 46 mm, height 15.5 mm;
screw-in crown; antireflective sapphire crystal;
screwed-down sapphire crystal case back; water-
resistant to 50 atm
Band: rubber, buckle
Price: $3,950
Variations: leather strap; stainless steel bracelet
with folding clasp and diver's extension

Adventure Automatic GMT

Movement: automatic, ETA Valgranges Caliber
A07.171; ø 36.6 mm, height 7.9 mm; 24 jewels;
28,800 vph; 46-hour power reserve
Functions: hours, minutes, sweep seconds; date;
2nd time zone
Case: stainless steel, ø 46 mm, height 15.5 mm;
screw-in crown; antireflective sapphire crystal;
screwed-down sapphire crystal case back; water-
resistant to 50 atm
Band: rubber, buckle
Price: $4,550
Variations: leather strap; stainless steel bracelet
with folding clasp and diver's extension

Chrono Diver

Movement: automatic, ETA Valjoux Caliber 7750;
ø 30 mm, height 7.9 mm; 25 jewels; 28,800 vph;
45-hour power reserve
Functions: hours, minutes, subsidiary seconds; date;
chronograph
Case: stainless steel, ø 46 mm, height 16.5 mm;
unidirectional bezel with 60-minute scale; screw-in
crown and buttons; antireflective sapphire crystal;
screwed-down case back; water-resistant to 600 m
Band: stainless steel, folding clasp
Price: $4,550
Variations: leather strap

Adventure Manual Wind

Movement: manually wound, ETA Unitas Caliber
6497; ø 36.6 mm, height 5.4 mm; 18 jewels;
18,000 vph; 48-hour power reserve
Functions: hours, minutes, subsidiary seconds
Case: stainless steel, ø 46 mm, height 14 mm;
screw-in crown; antireflective sapphire crystal;
screwed-down sapphire crystal case back; water-
resistant to 50 atm
Band: leather, buckle
Price: $3,400
Variations: rubber strap

VACHERON CONSTANTIN

The origins of this oldest continuously operating watch *manufacture* can be traced back to 1755 when Jean-Marc Vacheron opened his workshop in Geneva. His highly complex watches were particularly appreciated by clients in Paris. The development of such an important outlet for horological works there had a lot to do with the emergence of a wealthy class around the powerful French court. The Revolution put an end to all the financial excesses of that market, however, and the Vacheron company suffered as well . . . until the arrival of marketing wizard François Constantin in 1819.

Fast-forward to the late twentieth century: The brand with the Maltese cross logo had evolved into a tradition-conscious keeper of *haute horlogerie* under the aegis, starting in the mid-1990s, of the Vendôme Luxury Group (today's Richemont SA). Gradually, it began creating collections that combine modern shapes with traditional patterns. The company has been expanding steadily. In 2013 it opened boutiques in the United States as well as China, and it has become a leading sponsor of the New York City Ballet.

Vacheron Constantin is one of the last luxury brands to have abandoned the traditional way of dividing up labor. Today, most of its basic movements are made in-house at the production facilities and headquarters in Plan-les-Ouates and the workshops in Le Brassus in Switzerland's Jura region, which were expanded in the summer of 2013.

What the *manufacture* is capable of was demonstrated in 2016, when it presented the world's most complicated watch, the 57260. This commissioned piece was the product of eight years of dedicated work by a team of watchmakers. It almost overshadowed the new and rejuvenated Overseas models, which continue to be successful. But high complications and métiers d'art seem to be where the brand's heart really is.

Vacheron Constantin
Chemin du Tourbillon
CH-1228 Plan-les-Ouates
Switzerland

Tel.:
+41-22-930-2005

E-mail:
info@vacheron-constantin.com

Website:
www.vacheron-constantin.com

Founded:
1755

Number of employees:
approx. 800

Annual production:
over 20,000 watches (estimated)

U.S. distributor:
Vacheron Constantin
Richemont North America
645 Fifth Avenue
New York, NY 10022
877-701-1755

Most important collections:
Harmony, Patrimony, Traditionnelle, Historiques, Metiers d'Art, Malte, Overseas, Quai de l'Ile

Les Cabinotiers Celestia Astronomica Grande Complication 3600

Reference number: 9720C/000G-B281
Movement: manually wound, Vacheron Caliber 3600; ø 36 mm, height 8.7 mm; 64 jewels; 18,000 vph; 1-minute tourbillon; 6 spring barrels, 21 days; Geneva Seal
Functions: hours, minutes, sweep seconds; power reserve indicator; perpetual calendar with date, weekday, month, moon phase, season, moon age, sunrise and sunset times; duration of day and night; solar system conjunctions; celestial map of the northern hemisphere
Case: white gold, ø 45 mm, height 13.6 mm; sapphire crystal; transparent case back; water-resistant to 3 atm
Band: reptile skin, buckle
Price: on request

Les Cabinotiers Symphonia Grande Sonnerie 1860

Reference number: 9200E/000G-B099
Movement: manually wound, Vacheron Constantin Caliber 1860; ø 37 mm, height 9.1 mm; 74 jewels; 21,600 vph; 2 spring barrels, 72-hour power reserve (20-hour power reserve for the chiming system); Geneva Seal
Functions: hours, minutes, subsidiary seconds; displays (for movement and chimes); minute repeater
Case: white gold, ø 45 mm, height 15.1 mm; bezel with pusher to select display of chiming function (grande sonnerie/petite sonnerie/silent); sapphire crystal; transparent case back
Band: reptile skin, folding clasp
Price: on request

Overseas Small Model

Reference number: 2305V-100R-B077
Movement: automatic, Vacheron Constantin Caliber 5300; ø 22.6 mm, height 4 mm; 31 jewels; 28,800 vph; gold rotor; 44-hour power reserve; Geneva Seal
Functions: hours, minutes, subsidiary seconds
Case: rose gold, ø 37 mm, height 10.8 mm; dial set with 84 diamonds; sapphire crystal; transparent case back; water-resistant to 15 atm
Band: pink gold, double folding clasp
Price: $51,800
Variations: reptile skin/rubber strap; stainless steel ($24,900)

Overseas Automatic

Reference number: 4500V-110A-B128
Movement: automatic, Vacheron Constantin Caliber 5100; ø 30.6 mm, height 4.7 mm; 37 jewels; 28,800 vph; gold rotor; 60-hour power reserve; Geneva Seal
Functions: hours, minutes, sweep seconds; date
Case: stainless steel, ø 41 mm, height 11 mm; sapphire crystal; transparent case back; water-resistant to 15 atm
Band: stainless steel, double folding clasp
Price: $20,200
Variations: reptile skin strap; rubber strap

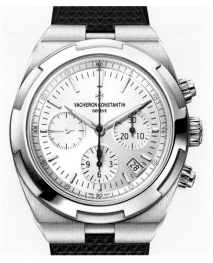

Overseas Chronograph

Reference number: 5500V-000R-B074
Movement: automatic, Vacheron Constantin Caliber 5200; ø 30.6 mm, height 6.6 mm; 54 jewels; 28,800 vph; column wheel control of chronograph functions; gold rotor; 52-hour power reserve; Geneva Seal
Functions: hours, minutes, subsidiary seconds; chronograph; date
Case: rose gold, ø 42.5 mm, height 13.7 mm; sapphire crystal; transparent case back; screw-in crown and pushers; water-resistant to 15 atm
Band: rubber, buckle
Remarks: comes with additional calfskin band
Price: $52,300

Overseas Word Time Watch

Reference number: 7700V/110A-B172
Movement: automatic, Vacheron Constantin Caliber 2460 WT; ø 36.6 mm, height 7.55 mm 27 jewels; 28,800 vph; 40-hour power reserve; Geneva Seal
Functions: hours, minutes, sweep seconds; world time display (second time zone), day/night indicator
Case: stainless steel, ø 43.5 mm, height 12.6 mm; sapphire crystal; transparent case back; screw-in crown; water-resistant to 15 atm
Band: reptile skin, buckle
Remarks: soft iron cage for antimagnetic protection comes with stainless steel bracelet
Price: $37,500

Traditionnelle Tourbillon Minute Repeater

Reference number: 6500T/000P-9949
Movement: manually wound, Vacheron Constantin Caliber 2755 TMR; ø 33.9 mm, height 6.1 mm; 40 jewels; 18,000 vph; 1-minute tourbillon; 58-hour power reserve; Geneva Seal
Functions: hours, minutes, subsidiary seconds (on tourbillon cage); power reserve indicator (on movement side); minute repeater
Case: platinum, ø 44 mm, height 12.2 mm; sapphire crystal; transparent case back; water-resistant to 3 atm
Band: reptile skin, folding clasp
Remarks: guilloché gold dial
Price: $523,300

Traditionnelle Chronograph Perpetual Calendar

Reference number: 5000T/000R-B304
Movement: manually wound, Vacheron Constantin Caliber 1142 QP; ø 27.5 mm, height 7.37 mm; 21 jewels; 21,600 vph; column wheel control of chronograph functions; 48-hour power reserve; Geneva Seal
Functions: hours, minutes, subsidiary seconds; chronograph; perpetual calendar with date, weekday, month, moon phase, leap year
Case: rose gold, ø 43 mm, height 12.94 mm; sapphire crystal; transparent case back; water-resistant to 3 atm
Band: reptile skin, folding clasp
Price: $106,800
Variations: platinum

Traditionnelle Manually Wound

Reference number: 82172/000R-9382
Movement: manually wound, Vacheron Constantin Caliber 4400; ø 28,6 mm, height 2.8 mm; 21 jewels; 28,800 vph; 65-hour power reserve; Geneva Seal
Functions: hours, minutes, subsidiary seconds
Case: rose gold, ø 38 mm, height 7.77 mm; sapphire crystal; transparent case back; water-resistant to 3 atm
Band: reptile skin, buckle
Price: $19,700
Variations: white gold; platinum

Traditionnelle World Time
Reference number: 86060/000G-8982
Movement: automatic, Vacheron Constantin Caliber 2460 WT; ø 36.6 mm, height 8.1 mm; 27 jewels; 28,800 vph
Functions: hours, minutes, sweep seconds; world time display with 37 time zones
Case: white gold, ø 42.5 mm, height 11.62 mm; sapphire crystal; transparent case back; water-resistant to 3 atm
Band: reptile skin, folding clasp
Price: $48,800
Variations: rose gold ($48,800)

Patrimony Moon Phase and Retrograde Date
Reference number: 4010U/000G-B330
Movement: automatic, Vacheron Constantin Caliber 2460 PDL; ø 27.2 mm, height 5.4 mm; 27 jewels; 28,800 vph; 40-hour power reserve; Geneva Seal
Functions: hours, minutes; date (retrograde), moon phase and age
Case: rose gold, ø 42.5 mm, height 9.7 mm; sapphire crystal; transparent case back; water-resistant to 3 atm
Band: reptile skin, buckle
Price: $40,600
Variations: white gold

Patrimony Small Model
Reference number: 85515/000R-9840
Movement: automatic, Vacheron Caliber 2450 Q6; ø 26.2 mm, height 3.6 mm; 27 jewels; 28,800 vph; 40-hour power reserve; Geneva Seal
Functions: hours, minutes, sweep seconds; date
Case: rose gold, ø 36 mm; bezel set with diamonds; sapphire crystal; transparent case back; water-resistant to 3 atm
Band: reptile skin, buckle
Price: $36,900

Patrimony Perpetual Calendar
Reference number: 43175/000R-B343
Movement: automatic, Vacheron Constantin Caliber 1120 QP; ø 29.6 mm, height 4.05 mm; 36 jewels; 19,800 vph; 40-hour power reserve; Geneva Seal
Functions: hours, minutes; perpetual calendar with date, weekday, month, moon phase, leap year
Case: rose gold, ø 41 mm, height 8.9 mm; sapphire crystal; transparent case back; water-resistant to 3 atm
Band: reptile skin, folding clasp
Price: $77,000

Historique American 1921
Reference number: 82035/000R-9359
Movement: manually wound, Vacheron Constantin Caliber 4400; ø 28.5 mm, height 2.8 mm; 21 jewels; 28,800 vph; 65-hour power reserve; Geneva Seal
Functions: hours, minutes, subsidiary seconds
Case: rose gold, ø 40 mm, height 8 mm; sapphire crystal; transparent case back; water-resistant to 3 atm
Band: reptile skin, buckle
Remarks: modeled after a vintage piece from 1921
Price: $34,300

Quai de l'Ile
Reference number: 4500S/000A-B195
Movement: automatic, Vacheron Constantin Caliber 2460 QH; ø 26.2 mm, height 5.7 mm; 27 jewels; 28,800 vph; Geneva Seal
Functions: hours, minutes, sweep seconds; date
Case: stainless steel, 41 × 50.5 mm, height 12.9 mm; sapphire crystal; transparent case back; water-resistant to 3 atm
Band: reptile skin, folding clasp
Price: $15,200
Variations: many options for personalization

Caliber 5100

Automatic; single spring barrel, 60-hour power reserve; Geneva Seal
Functions: hours, minutes sweep seconds
Diameter: 30.6 mm
Height: 4.7 mm
Jewels: 37
Balance: glucydur
Frequency: 28,800 vph
Remarks: gold rotor, 172 components

Caliber 5200

Automatic; column wheel control of chronograph functions; single spring barrel, 52-hour power reserve; Geneva Seal
Functions: hours, minutes, subsidiary seconds; chronograph; date
Diameter: 30.6 mm
Height: 6.6 mm
Jewels: 54
Balance: glucydur
Frequency: 28,800 vph
Remarks: gold rotor, 263 components

Caliber 5300

Automatic; single spring barrel, 44-hour power reserve; Geneva Seal
Functions: hours, minutes, subsidiary seconds
Diameter: 22.6 mm
Height: 4 mm
Jewels: 31
Balance: glucydur
Frequency: 28,800 vph
Remarks: gold rotor, 128 components

Caliber 1120 QP

Automatic; extra-flat construction; winding rotor with supporting ring; single spring barrel, 40-hour power reserve; Geneva Seal
Functions: hours, minutes; perpetual calendar with date, weekday, month, moon phase, leap year
Diameter: 29.6 mm
Height: 4.05 mm
Jewels: 36
Balance: glucydur
Frequency: 19,800 vph
Remarks: skeletonized rotor with gold oscillating weight, 276 components

Caliber 1731

Manually wound; single spring barrel, 65-hour power reserve; Geneva Seal
Functions: hours, minutes, subsidiary seconds; hours, quarter hour and minute repeater
Diameter: 32.8 mm
Height: 3.9 mm
Jewels: 36
Balance: glucydur
Frequency: 21,600 vph
Remarks: perlage on mainplate beveled edges, bridges with côtes de Genève

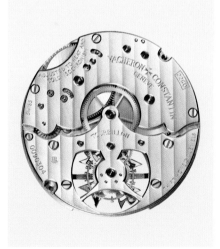

Caliber 2260

Manually wound; 1-minute tourbillon; quadruple spring barrel, 336-hour power reserve; Geneva Seal
Functions: hours, minutes, subsidiary seconds (on tourbillon cage); power reserve indicator
Diameter: 29.1 mm
Height: 6.8 mm
Jewels: 31
Balance: glucydur
Frequency: 18,000 vph
Remarks: 231 components

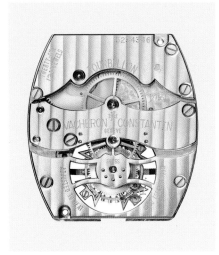

Caliber 2795

Automatic; 1-minute tourbillon; single spring barrel, 45-hour power reserve; Geneva Seal
Functions: hours, minutes, subsidiary seconds (on tourbillon cage)
Measurements: 27.37 × 29.3 mm
Height: 6.1 mm
Jewels: 27
Balance: glucydur
Frequency: 18,000 vph
Remarks: tonneau-shaped

Caliber 3500

Automatic; two control wheels to control the split-second chronograph functions, horizontal clutch; peripheral winding rotor with a gold oscillating mass; ultrathin construction; single spring barrel, 51-hour power reserve; Geneva Seal
Functions: hours, minutes, subsidiary seconds; power reserve indicator; split-second chronograph with crown pusher
Diameter: 33.4 mm
Height: 5.2 mm
Jewels: 47
Balance: glucydur
Frequency: 21,600 vph
Remarks: 459 components

Caliber 3300

Manually wound; column wheel control of chronograph functions, horizontal clutch; single spring barrel, 65-hour power reserve; Geneva Seal
Functions: hours, minutes, subsidiary seconds; power reserve indicator; chronograph with crown pusher
Diameter: 32.8 mm
Height: 6.7 mm
Jewels: 35
Balance: glucydur
Frequency: 21,600 vph
Remarks: 252 components

Caliber 2460 DT

Automatic; stop-seconds; single spring barrel, 40-hour power reserve; Geneva Seal
Functions: hours, minutes, sweep seconds; additional 12-hour display (second time zone), day/night indicator
Diameter: 28 mm
Height: 5.4 mm
Jewels: 27
Balance: glucydur
Frequency: 28,800 vph
Remarks: gold rotor, 233 components

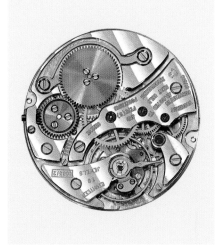

Caliber 1003

Manually wound; single spring barrel, 31-hour power reserve; Geneva Seal
Functions: hours, minutes
Diameter: 21.1 mm
Height: 1.64 mm
Jewels: 18
Balance: glucydur
Frequency: 18,000 vph
Remarks: currently the thinnest mechanical movement being produced

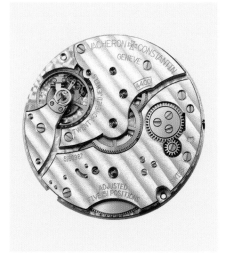

Caliber 4400

Manually wound; single spring barrel, 65-hour power reserve; Geneva Seal
Functions: hours, minutes, subsidiary seconds
Diameter: 28.5 mm
Height: 2.8 mm
Jewels: 21
Balance: glucydur
Frequency: 28,800 vph
Remarks: perlage on mainplate beveled edges, bridges with côtes de Genève

Van Cleef & Arpels
2, rue du Quatre-Septembre
F-75002 Paris
France

Tel.:
+33-1-70-70-36-56

Website:
www.vancleefarpels.com

Founded:
1906

U.S. distributor:
1-877-VAN-CLEEF

Most important collections:
Cadenas, Charms, Pierre Arpels, Poetic
Complications

VAN CLEEF & ARPELS

Surviving as a luxury concern requires a fine sense of how the market is segmented. Richemont only picks the cream of the crop. In 1999, while shopping around for more companies to add to its roster of high-end jewelers, the group struck on the idea of purchasing Van Cleef & Arpels. The venerable jewelry brand had a lot of name recognition, thanks in part to a host of internationally known customers, like Jacqueline Kennedy Onassis, whose two marriages each involved a Van Cleef & Arpels ring. It also had a reputation for the high quality of its workmanship. It was Van Cleef & Arpels that came up with the mystery setting using a special rail and cut totally hidden from the casual eye.

Van Cleef & Arpels was a family business that came to be when a young stone cutter, Alfred van Cleef, married Estelle Arpels in 1896, and ten years later opened a business on Place Vendôme in Paris with Estelle's brother Charles. More of Estelle's brothers joined the firm, which was soon booming and serving, quite literally, royalty.

Watches were always a part of the portfolio. But after joining Richemont, Van Cleef now had the support of a very complete industrial portfolio that would allow it to make stunning movements that could bring dials to life. A collaboration with Jean-Marc Wiederrecht and Agenhor produced outstanding combinations of artistry in design and crafts, with horological excellence that made the watch-loving public take notice: the double retrograde Pont des Amoureux, showing a man and a woman meeting on a bridge. For 2016, the brand relied on its own forces for two other stunners. The Ronde des Papillons uses an oval crown gear wheel to drive three butterflies in and out of clouds along minute tracks. And the Midnight Nuit Lumineuse lights up six diamonds with a pusher using a ceramic band and the phenomenon of piezoelectricity.

Lady Arpels Pont des Amoureux

Movement: manually wound, JLC846 base with exclusive Agenhor retrograde module; 34 jewels; 30-hour power reserve
Functions: retrograde hours and minutes
Case: white gold, ø 38 mm, height 11.8 mm; diamonds on white gold bezel/crown; sculpted bridge
Band: reptile skin, white gold buckle with diamonds
Remarks: grisaille enamel dial; special complication shows meeting of couple on bridge at 12
Price: $117,000
Variations: white gold bracelet with diamonds (price on request)

Lady Arpels Ronde des Papillons

Movement: automatic, Valfleurier Q020, exclusive caliber; 50 jewels; 36-hour power reserve
Functions: retrograde jumping hours (indicated by swallow's tail), minutes (indicated by 3 butterflies moving at different speeds)
Case: white gold, ø 38 mm, height 12.3 mm; white gold bezel set with diamonds; round diamond on crown; water-resistant up to 3 atm
Band: reptile skin, folding clasp
Remarks: 3 butterflies "fly" on dimensional mother-of-pearl/white gold dial with miniature painting
Price: $123,000

Midnight Nuit Lumineuse

Movement: automatic, Valfleurier Q020, exclusive caliber; 50 jewels; 40-hour power reserve
Functions: retrograde hours; minutes
Case: white gold, ø 42 mm, height 12.1 mm; white gold bezel set with diamonds; round diamond on crown; water resistant up to 3 atm
Band: reptile skin, buckle
Remarks: 6 LEDs backlight diamonds on aventurine dial to form Unicorn constellation with miniature painting
Price: on request

VOSTOK-EUROPE

Vostok-Europe is a young brand with old roots. In 2014, it celebrated its tenth anniversary. What started as a joint venture between the original Vostok company—a wholly separate entity—deep in the heart of Russia and a start-up in the newly minted European Union member nation of Lithuania, has grown into something altogether different over the years. Originally, every Vostok model had a proprietary Russian engine, a 32-jewel automatic built by Vostok in Russia. Over the years, demand and the need for alternative complications expanded the portfolio of movements to include Swiss and Japanese ones. While the heritage of the eighty-year Russian watch industry is still evident in the inspirations and designs of Vostok-Europe, the watches built today have become favorites of extreme athletes the world over.

"Real people doing real things" is the mantra that Igor Zubovskij, managing director of the company, often repeats. "We don't use models to market our watches. Only real people test our watches in many different conditions."

That community of "real people" includes cross-country drivers on the Dakar Rally, one of the most famous aerobatic pilots in the world, a team of spelunkers who literally went to the bottom of the world in the Krubera Cave, and world free-diving champions. Much of the Vostok-Europe line is of professional dive quality. For illumination, some models incorporate tritium tube technology, which offers about twenty-five years of constant lighting. The Lunokhod 2, the current flagship of the brand, incorporates vertical tubes in a "candleholder" design for full 360-degree illumination.

The watches are assembled in Vilnius, Lithuania, and Zubvoskij still personally oversees quality control operations. The Mriya, named after the world's largest cargo airplane, was the first watch in the world to carry the new Seiko NE88 column wheel chronograph movement.

Koliz Vostok Co. Ltd.
Naugarduko 41
LT-03227 Vilnius
Lithuania

Tel.:
+370-5-2106342

Fax:
+370-4-2130777

E-mail:
info@vostok-europe.com

Website:
www.vostok-europe.com

Founded:
2003

Number of employees:
24

Annual production:
30,000 watches

U.S. distributor:
Vostok-Europe
Détente Watch Group
244 Upton Road, Suite 4
Colchester, CT 06415
877-486-7865
www.detentewatches.com

Most important collections/price range:
Anchar collection / starting at $759; Mriya / starting at $649

GAZ-14 World Timer & Alarm "Tritium Gaslight"

Reference number: YM26-565B293
Movement: S. Epson YM26; ø 27 mm, height 3.7 mm
Functions: hours, minutes, subsidiary seconds; hours and minutes of second time zone, hours and minutes of sound alarm; date
Case: stainless steel with RG PVD coating, ø 45 mm, height 15 mm; K1 mineral crystal; water-resistant to 5 atm
Band: calfskin, buckle
Remarks: "Trigalight" constant tritium illumination
Price: $739

Lunokhod 2 Chrono "Tritium Gaslight"

Reference number: YM86-620A506
Movement: S. Epson YM86; ø 27 mm, height 3.7 mm; **Functions:** hours, minutes, subsidiary seconds; 24-hour chronograph; minutes and hours of sound alarm; perpetual calendar; days of the week
Case: stainless steel, ø 49 mm, height 15.5 mm; unidirectional bezel with 0-60 scale, K1 mineral glass; water-resistant to 30 atm, helium release valve
Band: silicon, buckle
Remarks: with 2nd calfskin band, screwdriver and dry box; "Trigalight" constant tritium illumination
Price: $1,119

Almaz Chrono

Reference number: 6S11-320B262
Movement: automatic, Seiko Caliber NR35; ø 34.6 mm, height 4.9 mm
Functions: hours, minutes, sweep seconds; date
Case: stainless steel, ø 47 mm, height 15.4 mm; unidirectional bezel with 0-60 scale, K1 mineral glass; water-resistant to 30 atm
Band: silicon, buckle
Remarks: with quartz Miyota 6S11 movement
Price: $599
Variations: calfskin band

Energia "Tritium Gaslight"

Reference number: NH35-5750286
Movement: automatic, Seiko Caliber NH35;
ø 26.4 mm, height 5.32 mm; 24 jewels, 21,600 vph,
40-hour power reserve
Functions: hours, minutes, sweep seconds; date
Case: bronze, ø 48 mm, height 17.3 mm;
unidirectional bezel with 0-60 scale, K1 mineral
glass; water-resistant to 30 atm, helium release valve
Band: silicon, buckle
Remarks: with 2nd calfskin band, screwdriver and
dry box; "Trigalight" constant tritium illumination
Price: $1,129

Energia Automatic "Tritium Gaslight"

Reference number: NH35-575A279
Movement: automatic, Seiko Caliber NH35;
ø 26.6 mm, height 5.32 mm; 24 jewels, 21,600 vph,
40-hour power reserve
Functions: hours, minutes, sweep seconds; date
Case: stainless steel, ø 48 mm, height 17.3 mm;
unidirectional bezel with 0-60 scale, K1 mineral
glass; water-resistant to 30 atm, helium release valve
Band: silicon, buckle
Remarks: with 2nd calfskin band, screwdriver and
dry box; "Trigalight" constant tritium illumination
Price: $1,089

Big Z Lunokhod 2 "For the World's Strongest Man"

Reference number: NH35A/6204344
Movement: automatic, Seiko Caliber NH35;
ø 26.6 mm, height 5.32 mm; 24 jewels, 21,600 vph,
40-hour power reserve
Functions: hours, minutes, sweep seconds; date
Case: stainless steel with black PVD, ø 49 mm,
height 15.5 mm; unidirectional bezel with 0-60 scale,
K1 mineral glass; water-resistant to 30 atm; helium
release valve
Band: silicon, buckle
Remarks: comes with 2nd calfskin band,
screwdriver and dry box; "Trigalight" constant tritium
illumination
Price: $979

Gaz-14 Automatic Dual Time

Reference number: 2426-5601059
Movement: automatic, Vostok Caliber 2426;
ø 24 mm, 32 jewels; 18,000 vph; blued screws;
31-hour power reserve
Functions: hours, minutes, sweep seconds;
additional 24-hour display (second time zone)
Case: stainless steel, ø 43 mm, height 13.8 mm;
K1 mineral crystal; transparent case back; water-
resistant to 5 atm
Band: calfskin, buckle
Price: $549

Gaz-14 Automatic Power Reserve Indication

Reference number: YN85-560B519
Movement: automatic, S. Epson YN85; ø 27.4 mm,
height 5.8 mm; 22 jewels; 21,600 vph; 40-hour
power reserve
Functions: hours, minutes, sweep seconds; power
reserve indicator
Case: stainless steel with RG PVD, ø 43 mm, height
13.8 mm; K1 mineral crystal; water-resistant to 5 atm
Band: calfskin, buckle
Price: $439

Ekranoplan Automatic "Tritium Gaslight"

Reference number: NH35-546H515
Movement: automatic, Seiko Caliber 35A;
ø 27.4 mm, height 5.32 mm; 24 jewels; 21,600 vph;
45-hour power reserve
Functions: hours, minutes, sweep seconds; date
Case: titanium, ø 47 mm, height 16 mm;
unidirectional bezel with 0-60 scale, K1 mineral
glass; screw-in crown; water-resistant to 20 atm
Band: calfskin, buckle
Remarks: with silicon band
Price: $899

WEMPE GLASHÜTTE

Ever since 2005, the global jewelry chain Gerhard D. Wempe KG has been putting out watches under its own name again. It was probably inevitable: Gerhard D. Wempe, who founded the company in the late nineteenth century in Oldenburg, was himself a watchmaker. And in the 1930s, the company also owned the Hamburg chronometer works that made watches for seafarers and pilots.

Today, while Wempe remains formally in Hamburg, its manufacturing is done in Glashütte. The move to the fully renovated and expanded Urania observatory in the hills above town was engineered by Eva-Kim Wempe, great-granddaughter of the founder. There, the company does all its after-sales service and tests watches according to the strict German Industrial Norm (DIN 8319), with official blessings from the Saxon and Thuringian offices for measurement and calibration and accreditation from the German Calibration Service.

The move to Glashütte coincided with a push to verticalize by creating a line of in-house movements for the exclusive Chronometerwerke models, like the very retro Chronometerwerke Power Reserve, or the eminently noticeable Tonneau Tourbillon. The calibers, bearing the initials CW, are made in partnership with companies like Nomos in Glashütte or the Swiss workshop MHVJ. In 2016, Wempe released the CW4, an automatic that had its first "outing" in a classic three-hander. It has a promising future ahead of it.

The second Wempe line is called Zeitmeister, or Master of Time. This collection uses more standard, but reworked, ETA or Sellita calibers. It meets all the requirements of the high art of watchmaking and, thanks to its accessible pricing, is attractive for budding collectors. All models are in the middle price range, which the luxury watch industry has long shunned.

Gerhard D. Wempe KG
Steinstrasse 23
D-20095 Hamburg
Germany

Tel.:
+49-40-334-480

Fax:
+49-40-331-840

E-mail:
info@wempe.de

Website:
www.wempe.de

Founded:
1878

Number of employees:
717 worldwide; 24 at Wempe Glashütte i/SA

Annual production:
5,000 watches

U.S. distributor:
Wempe Timepieces
700 Fifth Avenue
New York, NY 10019
212-397-9000
www.wempe.com

Most important collections/price range:
Wempe Zeitmeister / approx. $1,000 to $4,500;
Wempe Chronometerwerke / approx. $5,000 to $95,000

Chronometerwerke Automatic

Reference number: WG 090001
Movement: automatic, Wempe Caliber CW4; ø 32.8 mm, height 6 mm; 35 jewels; 28,800 vph; 2 spring barrels, three-quarter, hand-engraved balance cock, 6 gold chatons, tungsten microrotor finely finished, with Glashütte ribbing; 92-hour power reserve; DIN certified chronometer
Functions: hours, minutes, sweep seconds; date
Case: yellow gold, ø 41 mm, height 11.7 mm; sapphire crystal; transparent case back; water-resistant to 3 atm
Band: reptile skin, buckle
Price: $17,270
Variations: stainless steel ($8,030)

Chronometerwerke Power Reserve

Reference number: WG 080005
Movement: manually wound, Wempe Caliber CW3; ø 32 mm, height 6.1 mm; 40 jewels; 28,800 vph; three-quarter plate, 3 screw-mounted gold chatons, hand-engraved balance cock; 42-hour power reserve; DIN certified chronometer
Functions: hours, minutes, subsidiary seconds; power reserve indicator
Case: yellow gold, ø 43 mm, height 12.5 mm; sapphire crystal; transparent case back; water-resistant to 3 atm
Band: reptile skin, buckle
Price: $16,120
Variations: stainless steel ($8,500)

Chronometerwerke Small Seconds

Reference number: WG 070002
Movement: manually wound, Wempe Caliber CW3.1; ø 32.8 mm, height 6.1 mm; 40 jewels; 28,800 vph; three-quarter plate, 3 screw-mounted gold chatons, swan-neck fine regulation, hand-engraved balance cock; 42-hour power reserve; DIN certified chronometer
Functions: hours, minutes, subsidiary seconds
Case: stainless steel, ø 41 mm, height 12.5 mm; sapphire crystal; transparent case back; water-resistant to 3 atm
Band: reptile skin, buckle
Price: $6,880
Variations: yellow gold ($17,000)

Zeitmeister Annual Calendar

Reference number: WM 690003
Movement: automatic, ETA Caliber 2892-A2 with Dubois-Dépraz 5900 module; ø 25.6 mm, height 5,29 mm; 21 jewels; 28,800 vph; 42-hour power reserve; DIN certified chronometer
Functions: hours, minutes, sweep seconds; annual calendar with date, weekday, month, moon phase
Case: stainless steel, ø 42 mm, height 14.28 mm; sapphire crystal; water-resistant to 5 atm
Band: reptile skin, buckle
Price: $9,215; limited to 100 pieces

Zeitmeister Chronograph with Moon Phase and Full Calendar

Reference number: WM 530001
Movement: automatic, ETA Caliber 7751; ø 30 mm, height 7.9 mm; 25 jewels; 28,800 vph; 48-hour power reserve; DIN certified chronometer
Functions: hours, minutes, subsidiary seconds; 2nd 24-hour display; chronograph; full calendar with date, weekday, month, moon phase
Case: stainless steel, ø 42 mm, height 14.71 mm; sapphire crystal; water-resistant to 5 atm
Band: reptile skin, folding clasp
Price: $4,015

Zeitmeister Sport Diver's Chronograph Cermet

Reference number: WM 650012
Movement: automatic, Sellita SW500; ø 30 mm, height 7.9 mm; 25 jewels; 28,800 vph; modified with in-house fine regulation; 48-hour power reserve; DIN certified chronometer
Functions: hours, minutes, subsidiary seconds; chronograph; date
Case: stainless steel, ø 45 mm, height 16.5 mm; bezel with cermet insert; unidirectional bezel with 0-60 scale; sapphire crystal; screw-in crown; water-resistant to 30 atm
Band: stainless steel, folding clasp, with safety lock and extension link
Price: $4,130

Zeitmeister Sport GMT Black

Reference number: WM 650011
Movement: automatic, ETA Caliber 2893-2; ø 25.6 mm, height 4.1 mm; 21 jewels; 28,800 vph; 42-hour power reserve; DIN certified chronometer
Functions: hours, minutes, sweep seconds; 2nd 24-hour display (2nd time zone); date
Case: stainless steel, ø 42 mm, height 14.5 mm; unidirectional bezel with ceramic insert and 0-60 scale; bidirectional bezel with 0-24 hour scale; sapphire crystal; screw-in crown; water-resistant to 30 atm
Band: stainless steel, folding clasp, with safety lock and extension link
Price: $3,090
Variations: blue dial and blue bezel ($3,090)

Zeitmeister Sport Automatic

Reference number: WM 650004
Movement: automatic, ETA Caliber 2892-A2; ø 35.6 mm, height 3.6 mm; 21 jewels; 28,800 vph; 42-hour power reserve; DIN certified chronometer
Functions: hours, minutes, sweep seconds; date
Case: stainless steel, ø 40 mm; sapphire crystal; screw-in crown; water-resistant to 10 atm
Band: stainless steel, folding clasp
Price: $2,400
Variations: white dial ($2,400)

Zeitmeister Aviator Watch Chronograph XL

Reference number: WM 600005
Movement: automatic, ETA Caliber A07.211; ø 36.6 mm, height 7.9 mm; 25 jewels; 28,800 vph; 46-hour power reserve; DIN certified chronometer
Functions: hours, minutes, subsidiary seconds; chronograph; date
Case: stainless steel, ø 45 mm, height 15.45 mm; sapphire crystal; water-resistant to 5 atm
Band: horse leather, folding clasp
Price: $2,890

ZEITWINKEL

Zeitwinkel turned ten in 2016, but that is not really important for this small, independent company based in St.-Imier, one of the hubs of the watch industry in Switzerland. The key attributes of the brand, ones that many watch manufacturers aspire to endow their creations with, are "timeless, simple, and sustainable." What are ten years compared to timelessness?

The models produced by Zeitwinkel (the name means "time angle") are deceptively classical: The simplest exemplar is a two-hand watch; the most complicated, the 273°, a three-hand timepiece with power reserve display and large date. The most decoration one will find on the dials is a spangling of stylized *W*s, for *Winkel* (angle). With cases designed by Jean-François Ruchonnet (TAG Heuer V4, Cabestan), the watches look fairly "German," which comes as no surprise, because Zeitwinkel's founders, Ivica Maksimovic and Peter Nikolaus, hail from there. Some details will catch the eye, notably the extra-large subsidiary seconds dial or the large date aperture, found beside the 11 o'clock marker.

The most valuable part of the watches is their veritable *manufacture* movements, the likes of which are very rare in the business. The calibers were developed by Laurent Besse and his *artisans horlogers*, or watchmaking craftspeople. All components come courtesy of independent suppliers—Zeitwinkel balance wheels, pallets, escape wheels, and Straumann spirals, for example, are produced by Precision Engineering, a company associated with watch brand H. Moser & Cie. The 273° comes with a smoked sapphire crystal dial; the new 083° is smaller (39 millimeters) as an epitome of discreetness.

In keeping with the company's ideals, you won't find any alligator in Zeitwinkel watch bands. Choices here are exclusively rubber, calfskin, or calfskin with an alligator-like pattern. Gold cases were also once taboo for the brand, but thanks to a partnership with the Alliance for Responsible Mining, the watches now come in "fairmined" gold cases.

Zeitwinkel Montres SA
Rue Pierre-Jolissaint 35
CH-2610 Saint-Imier
Switzerland

Tel.:
+41-32-940-17-71

Fax:
+41-32-940-17-81

E-mail:
info@zeitwinkel.ch

Website:
www.zeitwinkel.ch

Founded:
2006

Annual production:
approx. 800 watches

U.S. distributor:
Tourneau
510 Madison Avenue
New York, NY 10022
212-758-5830
Right Time
7110 E. County Line Road
Highlands Ranch, CO 80126
303-862-3900; 303-862-3905 (fax)

Most important collections/price range:
mechanical wristwatches / starting at around
$7,500

082° Email Grand Feu

Reference number: 082-3.S02-01-23
Movement: automatic, Caliber ZW0102; ø 30.4 mm, height 5.7 mm; 30 jewels; 28,800 vph; German silver three-quarter plate and bridges, côtes de Genève, polished screws and edges; 72-hour power reserve
Functions: hours, minutes, sweep seconds
Case: stainless steel, ø 39 mm, height 11.6 mm; sapphire crystal; transparent case back; water-resistant to 5 atm
Band: calfskin, folding clasp
Remarks: white enamel dial, grand feu
Price: $10,500
Variations: different bands

273° Saphir Fumé

Reference number: 273-4.S01-01-21
Movement: automatic, Caliber ZW0103; ø 30.4 mm, height 8 mm; 49 jewels; 28,800 vph; German silver three-quarter plate and bridges, côtes de Genève, polished screws and edges; perlage on dial side; 72-hour power reserve
Functions: hours, minutes, subsidiary seconds; power reserve indicator; patented big date mechanism
Case: stainless steel, ø 42.5 mm, height 13.8 mm; sapphire crystal; transparent back; water-resistant to 5 atm
Band: calfskin, folding clasp
Remarks: smoky black sapphire crystal dial
Price: $15,500
Variations: various dial colors; different bands

188° Galvano-blue

Reference number: 188-23-01-23
Movement: automatic, Caliber ZW0102; ø 30.4 mm, height 5.7 mm; 28 jewels; 28,800 vph; German silver three-quarter plate and bridges, côtes de Genève, polished screws and edges; 72-hour power reserve
Functions: hours, minutes, subsidiary seconds; date
Case: stainless steel, ø 39 mm, height 11.6 mm; sapphire crystal; transparent case back; water-resistant to 5 atm
Band: calfskin, folding clasp
Price: $7,490
Variations: various dial colors

Zenith Branch
LVMH Swiss Manufactures SA
34, rue des Billodes
CH-2400 Le Locle
Switzerland

Tel.:
+41-32-930-6262

Fax:
+41-32-930-6363

Website:
www.zenith-watches.com

Founded:
1865

Number of employees:
over 330 employees worldwide

U.S. distributor:
Zenith Watches
966 South Springfield Avenue
Springfield, NJ 07081
866-675-2079
contact.zenith@lvmhwatchjewelry.com

Most important collections/price range:
Academy / from $76,100; Elite / from $4,700;
Chronomaster / from $6,700; Pilot / from
$5,700; Defy / from $9,600

ZENITH

The tall, narrow building in Le Locle, with its closely spaced high windows to let in daylight, is a testimony to Zenith's history as a self-sufficient *manufacture* in the entrepreneurial spirit of the Industrial Revolution. The company, founded in 1865 by Georges Favre-Jacot as a small watch reassembly workshop, has produced and distributed every type of watch from the simple pocket watch to the most complicated calendar. But it remains primarily linked with the El Primero caliber, the first wristwatch chronograph movement boasting automatic winding and a frequency of 36,000 vph. Only a few watch manufacturers had risked such a high oscillation frequency—and none of them with such complexity as the integrated chronograph mechanism and bilaterally winding rotor of the El Primero.

That the movement even celebrated its fortieth anniversary, though, was thanks to the mechanical watch revival. After Zenith was sold to the LVMH Group in 1999, the label was fully dusted off and modernized perhaps a little too much. Eccentric creations catapulted the dutiful watchmaker's watchmaker into the world of *haute horlogerie*.

Also being dusted off for the firm's 150th anniversary in 2015 was the historic complex in Le Locle, which was put on UNESCO's World Heritage list in 2009. Over eighty different crafts are practiced here, from watchmaking to design, from art to prototyping. Synergies with the Group companion Hublot and TAG Heuer produced the Defy 21, a complex chronograph movement based on the 36,000-vph El Primero. A second movement for the chronograph beats at 360,000 vph, allowing the hundredths of a second to be displayed.

Defy El Primero 21
Reference number: 95.9000.9004/78.R582
Movement: automatic, Zenith Caliber 9004 "El Primero"; ø 32.8 mm, height 7.9 mm; 53 jewels; 36,000 vph; independent chronograph mechanism with its own escapement system (360,000 vph) and its own power management; 50-hour power reserve; COSC-certified chronometer
Functions: hours, minutes, subsidiary seconds; power reserve indicator (for chronograph functions); chronograph with hundredths of seconds display
Case: titanium, ø 44 mm, height 14.5 mm; sapphire crystal; transparent case back; water-resistant to 10 atm
Band: rubber, with reptile skin layer, double folding clasp
Price: $10,600

Chronomaster El Primero Tourbillon Skeleton
Reference number: 18.2281.4035/98.C713
Movement: automatic, Zenith Caliber 4035B "El Primero"; ø 37 mm, height 7.65 mm; 35 jewels; 36,000 vph; 1-minute tourbillon; column wheel control of chronograph functions; 50-hour power reserve
Functions: hours, minutes; chronograph
Case: rose gold, ø 45 mm, height 14.65 mm; sapphire crystal; transparent back; water-resistant to 5 atm
Band: reptile skin, triple folding clasp
Price: $57,400; limited to 150 pieces

Chronomaster El Primero Grande Date Full Open
Reference number: 03.2530.4047/78.C813
Movement: automatic, Zenith Caliber 4047B "El Primero"; ø 30.5 mm, height 9.05 mm; 32 jewels; 36,000 vph; movement partially skeletonized; 50-hour power reserve
Functions: hours, minutes, subsidiary seconds; chronograph; large date, moon phase
Case: stainless steel, ø 45 mm, height 15.6 mm; sapphire crystal; transparent case back; water-resistant to 10 atm
Band: calfskin, triple folding clasp
Price: $10,600

Chronomaster El Primero Full Open

Reference number: 03.2081.400.78.C813
Movement: automatic, Zenith Caliber 400B "El Primero"; ø 30 mm, height 6.6 mm; 31 jewels; 36,000 vph; movement partially skeletonized; 50-hour power reserve
Functions: hours, minutes, subsidiary seconds; chronograph; date
Case: stainless steel, ø 42 mm, height 12.75 mm; sapphire crystal; transparent case back; water-resistant to 10 atm
Band: reptile skin, triple folding clasp
Price: $9,600

Chronomaster El Primero

Reference number: 03.2040.4061/69.C496
Movement: automatic, Zenith Caliber 4061 "El Primero"; ø 30 mm, height 6.6 mm; 31 jewels; 36,000 vph; partially skeletonized movement; 50-hour power reserve
Functions: hours, minutes; chronograph
Case: stainless steel, ø 42 mm, height 14.05 mm; sapphire crystal; transparent case back; water-resistant to 10 atm
Band: reptile skin, triple folding clasp
Price: $8,600
Variations: rose gold ($16,300)

Chronomaster El Primero Open

Reference number: 03.2040.4061/01.C494
Movement: automatic, Zenith Caliber 4061 "El Primero"; ø 30 mm, height 6.6 mm; 31 jewels; 36,000 vph; partially skeletonized movement; 50-hour power reserve
Functions: hours, minutes; chronograph
Case: stainless steel, ø 42 mm, height 14.05 mm; sapphire crystal; transparent case back; water-resistant to 10 atm
Band: reptile skin, triple folding clasp
Price: $8,600

Chronomaster El Primero

Reference number: 51.2080.400/69.C494
Movement: automatic, Zenith Caliber 400B "El Primero"; ø 30 mm, height 6.6 mm; 31 jewels; 36,000 vph; 50-hour power reserve
Functions: hours, minutes, subsidiary seconds; chronograph; date
Case: stainless steel, ø 42 mm, height 12.75 mm rose gold bezel; sapphire crystal; transparent case back; water-resistant to 10 atm
Band: reptile skin, triple folding clasp
Price: $8,200

El Primero 36,000 vph

Reference number: 03.2150.400/26.C714
Movement: automatic, Zenith Caliber 400 "El Primero"; ø 30 mm, height 6.6 mm; 31 jewels; 36,000 vph; 50-hour power reserve
Functions: hours, minutes, subsidiary seconds; chronograph; date
Case: stainless steel, ø 38 mm, height 12.45 mm; sapphire crystal; transparent case back; water-resistant to 10 atm
Band: reptile skin, triple folding clasp
Price: $6,700

Chronomaster El Primero Classic Cars

Reference number: 03.2046.400/25.C771
Movement: automatic, Zenith Caliber 400B "El Primero"; ø 30 mm, height 6.6 mm; 31 jewels; 36,000 vph; 50-hour power reserve
Functions: hours, minutes, subsidiary seconds; chronograph; date
Case: stainless steel, ø 42 mm, height 12.75 mm; sapphire crystal; transparent case back; water-resistant to 10 atm
Band: calfskin, triple folding clasp
Price: $6,700

Chronomaster El Primero
Reference number: 24.2041.400/21.R576
Movement: automatic, Zenith Caliber 400B "El Primero"; ø 30 mm, height 6.6 mm; 31 jewels; 36,000 vph; 50-hour power reserve
Functions: hours, minutes, subsidiary seconds; chronograph; date
Case: black ceramicized aluminum, ø 42 mm, height 12.75 mm; sapphire crystal; transparent case back; water-resistant to 10 atm
Band: rubber, triple folding clasp
Price: $8,700

Chronomaster El Primero Range Rover Velar
Reference number: 24.2042.400/27.R799
Movement: automatic, Zenith Caliber 400B "El Primero"; ø 30 mm, height 6.6 mm; 31 jewels; 36,000 vph; 50-hour power reserve
Functions: hours, minutes, subsidiary seconds; chronograph; date
Case: black ceramicized aluminum, ø 42 mm, height 12.75 mm; sapphire crystal; transparent case back; water-resistant to 10 atm
Band: rubber, with calfskin overlay, triple folding clasp
Price: $8,700; limited to 200 pieces

Chronomaster El Primero Range Rover
Reference number: 24.2040.400/27.R797
Movement: automatic, Zenith Caliber 400B "El Primero"; ø 30 mm, height 6.6 mm; 31 jewels; 36,000 vph; 50-hour power reserve
Functions: hours, minutes, subsidiary seconds; chronograph; date
Case: black ceramicized aluminum, ø 42 mm, height 12.75 mm; sapphire crystal; transparent case back; water-resistant to 10 atm
Band: rubber, with calfskin overlay, triple folding clasp
Price: $8,700

Chronomaster Heritage 146
Reference number: 03.2150.4069/51.C805
Movement: automatic, Zenith Caliber 4069 "El Primero"; ø 30 mm, height 6.6 mm; 36,000 vph; 50-hour power reserve
Functions: hours, minutes, subsidiary seconds; chronograph
Case: stainless steel, ø 38 mm, height 12.45 mm; sapphire crystal; transparent case back; water-resistant to 10 atm
Band: calfskin, buckle
Price: $6,700

Elite Chronograph Classic
Reference number: 03.2270.4069/26.C493
Movement: automatic, Zenith Caliber 4069 "El Primero"; ø 30 mm, height 6.6 mm; 31 jewels; 36,000 vph; 50-hour power reserve
Functions: hours, minutes, subsidiary seconds; chronograph
Case: stainless steel, ø 42 mm, height 11.8 mm; sapphire crystal; transparent case back; water-resistant to 5 atm
Band: reptile skin, triple folding clasp
Price: $6,700

Elite Classic
Reference number: 03.2290.679/01.C493
Movement: automatic, Zenith Caliber 679 "Elite"; ø 25.6 mm, height 3.85 mm; 27 jewels; 28,800 vph; 50-hour power reserve
Functions: hours, minutes, sweep seconds
Case: stainless steel, ø 39 mm, height 9.45 mm; sapphire crystal; transparent case back; water-resistant to 5 atm
Band: reptile skin, buckle
Price: $4,700

Pilot Type 20 Chronograph Extra Special

Reference number: 29.2430.4069/21.C800
Movement: automatic, Zenith Caliber 4069 "El Primero"; ø 30 mm, height 6.6 mm; 36,000 vph; 50-hour power reserve
Functions: hours, minutes, subsidiary seconds; chronograph
Case: bronze, ø 45 mm, height 14.25 mm; sapphire crystal; water-resistant to 10 atm
Band: calfskin, buckle
Price: $7,100

Pilot Type 20 Extra Special "Ton Up"

Reference number: 11.2430.679/21.C801
Movement: automatic, Zenith Caliber 679 "Elite"; ø 25.6 mm, height 3.9 mm; 27 jewels; 28,800 vph; 50-hour power reserve
Functions: hours, minutes, sweep seconds
Case: stainless steel, ø 45 mm, height 14.25 mm; sapphire crystal; water-resistant to 10 atm
Band: calfskin, buckle
Price: $7,100

Pilot Type 20 Extra Special

Reference number: 11.1941.679/94.C814
Movement: automatic, Zenith Caliber 679 "Elite"; ø 25.6 mm, height 3.9 mm; 27 jewels; 28,800 vph; 50-hour power reserve
Functions: hours, minutes, sweep seconds
Case: stainless steel, ø 40 mm, height 12.95 mm; sapphire crystal; water-resistant to 10 atm
Band: calfskin, buckle
Price: $5,700; limited to 250 pieces

Pilot Cronometro Tipo CP-2

Reference number: 03.2240.4069/21.C774
Movement: automatic, Zenith Caliber 4069 "El Primero"; ø 30 mm, height 6.6 mm; 35 jewels; 36,000 vph; column wheel control of chronograph functions; 50-hour power reserve
Functions: hours, minutes, subsidiary seconds; chronograph
Case: stainless steel, ø 43 mm, height 12.85 mm; unidirectional bezel, with 0-60 scale; sapphire crystal; water-resistant to 10 atm
Band: calfskin, triple folding clasp
Price: $7,700, limited to 1,000 pieces

Elite Lady Moonphase

Reference number: 18.2330.692/01.C713
Movement: automatic, Zenith Caliber 692 "Elite"; ø 25.6 mm, height 3.97 mm; 27 jewels; 28,800 vph; 50-hour power reserve
Functions: hours, minutes, subsidiary seconds; moon phase
Case: rose gold, ø 33 mm, height 9.25 mm; sapphire crystal; transparent case back; water-resistant to 5 atm
Band: reptile skin, buckle
Price: $9,600

Elite Lady Moonphase

Reference number: 16.2330.692/01.C714
Movement: automatic, Zenith Caliber 692 "Elite"; ø 25.6 mm, height 3.97 mm; 27 jewels; 28,800 vph; 50-hour power reserve
Functions: hours, minutes, subsidiary seconds; moon phase
Case: stainless steel, ø 33 mm, height 9.25 mm bezel set with 62 diamonds; sapphire crystal; transparent case back; water-resistant to 5 atm
Band: reptile skin, buckle
Price: $7,100

Caliber 9004 El Primero

Automatic; independent chronograph mechanism with its own escapement system (360,000 vph) and its own power management composite hairsprings of carbon nanotube matrix; single spring barrel, 50-hour power reserve; COSC-certified chronometer
Functions: hours, minutes, subsidiary seconds; power reserve indicator (for chronograph functions); chronograph with display of hundredths of seconds
Diameter: 32.8 mm
Height: 7.9 mm
Jewels: 53
Balance: glucydur
Frequency: 36,000 vph
Shock protection: Kif
Remarks: 203 components

Caliber 4054 El Primero

Automatic; single spring barrel, 50-hour power reserve
Functions: hours, minutes; chronograph; annual calendar with date, weekday, month
Diameter: 30 mm
Height: 8.3 mm
Jewels: 29
Balance: glucydur
Frequency: 36,000 vph
Balance spring: self-compensating flat spring
Shock protection: Kif

Caliber 410 El Primero

Automatic; single spring barrel, 50-hour power reserve
Functions: hours, minutes, subsidiary seconds; chronograph; full calendar with date, weekday, month, moon phase
Diameter: 30 mm
Height: 6.6 mm
Jewels: 31
Balance: glucydur
Frequency: 36,000 vph
Balance spring: self-compensating flat spring
Shock protection: Kif

Caliber 4057B El Primero

Automatic; chronograph hand shows 1/10th second thanks to the foudroyante complication (1 revolution every 10 seconds); single spring barrel, 50-hour power reserve
Functions: hours, minutes, subsidiary seconds; flyback chronograph; date
Diameter: 30 mm
Height: 6.6 mm
Jewels: 31
Balance: glucydur
Frequency: 36,000 vph
Balance spring: self-compensating flat spring
Shock protection: Kif

Caliber 400B El Primero

Automatic; single spring barrel, 50-hour power reserve
Functions: hours, minutes, subsidiary seconds; chronograph; date
Diameter: 30 mm
Height: 6.6 mm
Jewels: 31
Balance: glucydur
Frequency: 36,000 vph
Balance spring: self-compensating flat spring
Shock protection: Kif

Caliber 681 Elite

Automatic; single spring barrel, 50-hour power reserve
Functions: hours, minutes, subsidiary seconds
Diameter: 25.6 mm
Height: 3.81 mm
Jewels: 27
Balance: glucydur
Frequency: 28,800 vph
Balance spring: self-compensating flat spring
Shock protection: Kif

CONCEPTO

The Concepto Watch Factory, founded in 2006 in La Chaux-de-Fonds, is the successor to the family-run company Jaquet SA, which changed its name to La Joux-Perret a little while ago and then moved to a different location on the other side of the hub of watch-making. In 2008, Valérien Jaquet, son of the company founder Pierre Jaquet, began systematically building up a modern movement and watch component factory on an empty floor of the building. Today, the Concepto Watch Factory employs eighty people in various departments, such as Development/Prototyping, Decoparts (partial manufacturing using lathes, machining, or wire erosion), Artisia (production of movements and complications in large series), as well as Optimo (escapements). In addition to the standard family of calibers, the C2000 (based on the Valjoux), and the vintage chronograph movement C7000 (the evolution of the Venus Caliber), the company's product portfolio includes various tourbillon movements (Caliber C8000) and several modules for adding onto ETA movements (Caliber C1000). A brand-new caliber series, the C3000, features a retrograde calendar and seconds, a power reserve indicator, and a chronograph. The C4000 chronograph caliber with automatic winding is currently in pre-series testing.

These movements are designed according to the requirements of about forty customers and at times heavily modified. Complicated movements are assembled entirely, while others are sold as kits for assembly by the watchmakers. Annual production is somewhere between 30,000 and 40,000 units, with additional hundreds of thousands of components made for contract manufacturing.

Caliber 1053

Automatic; inverted construction with dial-side escapement; bidirectional off-center winding rotor; single spring barrel; 42-hour power reserve
Functions: hours, minutes, subsidiary seconds (all off-center)
Diameter: 33 mm
Height: 3.75 mm
Jewels: 31
Balance: glucydur
Frequency: 28,800 vph
Balance spring: flat hairspring
Remarks: black finishing on movement

Caliber 2904 (dial side)

Inverted construction with dial-side escapement; single spring barrel; 48-hour power reserve
Functions: hours, minutes, subsidiary seconds
Diameter: 30.4 mm
Height: 4.6 mm
Jewels: 31
Balance: screw balance
Frequency: 28,800 vph
Balance spring: flat hairspring

Caliber 3041 Skeleton (dial side)

Manually wound; skeletonized symmetrical construction; single spring barrel; 48-hour power reserve
Functions: hours, minutes
Diameter: 32.6 mm
Height: 5.5 mm
Jewels: 21
Balance: screw balance
Frequency: 28,800 vph
Balance spring: flat hairspring
Remarks: extensive personalization options for finishing and accessories

Caliber 2000-RAC

Automatic; column wheel control of the chronograph functions; stop-second system; single spring barrel; 48-hour power reserve
Functions: hours, minutes, subsidiary seconds; chronograph
Diameter: 30.4 mm; **Height:** 8.4 mm
Jewels: 26; **Balance:** screw balance
Frequency: 28,800 vph
Balance spring: flat hairspring
Shock protection: Incabloc
Remarks: related calibers: 2000 (without control wheel); with two or three totalizers ("tricompax") with or without date; various additional displays (moon phase, retrograde date hand, additional 24-hour sweep hand, power reserve indicator)

Caliber 8500

Manually wound; 1-minute tourbillon; column wheel control of chronograph functions; single spring barrel; 50-hour power reserve
Functions: hours, minutes, subsidiary seconds; split-seconds chronograph
Diameter: 31.3 mm
Height: 7.2 mm
Jewels: 31
Balance: screw balance
Frequency: 21,600 vph
Balance spring: flat hairspring
Remarks: very fine movement finishing

Caliber 8950-A

Automatic; 1-minute tourbillon; single spring barrel; 60-hour power reserve
Functions: hours, minutes
Diameter: 30.4 mm
Height: 6.7 mm
Jewels: 27
Balance: glucydur
Frequency: 28,800 vph
Balance spring: flat hairspring
Remarks: related caliber: 8950-M (manual winding); extensive personalization options for the finishing, accessories, and functions

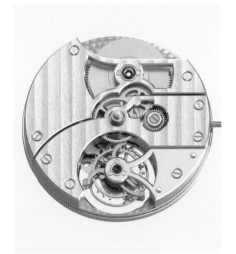

Caliber 8000 (dial side)

Manually wound; 1-minute tourbillon; single spring barrel; 72-hour power reserve
Functions: hours, minutes
Diameter: 32.6 mm
Height: 5.7 mm
Jewels: 19
Balance: screw balance
Frequency: 21,600 vph
Balance spring: flat hairspring
Remarks: extensive personalization options for the finishing, accessories, and functions

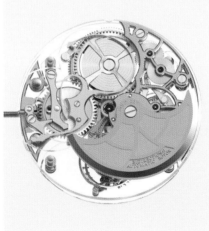

Caliber 8152

Automatic; 1-minute tourbillon; bridges and plate made of sapphire crystal; off-center, bidirectional rotor; single spring barrel; 72-hour power reserve
Functions: hours, minutes
Diameter: 32.6 mm
Height: 8.5 mm
Jewels: 25
Balance: screw balance
Frequency: 21,600 vph
Balance spring: flat hairspring
Remarks: extensive personalization options for the finishing, accessories, and functions

Caliber 8908-M (dial side)

Manually wound; flying 1-minute tourbillon; single spring barrel; 42-hour power reserve
Functions: hours, minutes
Diameter: 34.6 mm
Height: 6.6 mm
Jewels: 21
Balance: screw balance
Frequency: 28,800 vph
Balance spring: flat hairspring
Remarks: extensive personalization options for the finishing, accessories, and functions

ETA

This Swatch Group movement manufacturer produces more than five million movements a year. And after the withdrawal of Richemont's Jaeger-LeCoultre as well as Swatch Group sisters Nouvelle Lémania and Frédéric Piguet from the business of selling movements on the free market, most watch brands can hardly help but beat down the door of this full-service manufacturer.

ETA offers a broad spectrum of automatic movements in various dimensions with different functions, chronograph mechanisms in varying configurations, pocket watch classics (Calibers 6497 and 98), and manually wound calibers of days gone by (Calibers 1727 and 7001). This company truly offers everything that a manufacturer's heart could desire—not to mention the sheer variety of quartz technology from inexpensive three-hand mechanisms to highly complicated multifunctional movements and futuristic Etaquartz featuring autonomous energy creation using a rotor and generator.

The almost stereotypical accusation of ETA being "mass goods" is not justified, however, for it is a real art to manufacture filigreed micromechanical technology in consistently high quality. This is certainly one of the reasons why there have been very few movement factories in Europe that can compete with ETA, or that would want to. Since the success of Swatch—a pure ETA product—millions of Swiss francs have been invested in new development and manufacturing technologies. ETA today owns more than twenty production locales in Switzerland, France, Germany, Malaysia, and Thailand.

In 2002, ETA's management announced it would discontinue providing half-completed component kits for reassembly and/or embellishment to specialized workshops, and from 2010 only offer completely assembled and finished movements for sale. The Swiss Competition Commission, however, studied the issue, and a new deal was struck in 2013 phasing out sales to customers over a period of six years. ETA is already somewhat of a competitor of independent reassemblers such as Soprod, Sellita, La Joux-Perret, Dubois Dépraz, and others thanks to its diversification of available calibers, which has led the rest to counter by creating their own base movements.

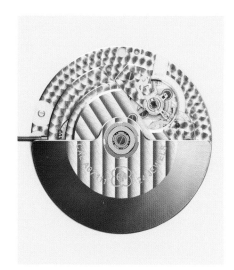  

Caliber A07.111

Automatic; ETACHRON regulating system with fine-timing device, rotor on ball bearings, stop-second system; single spring barrel; 48-hour power reserve
Functions: hours, minutes, sweep seconds
Diameter: 37.2
Height: 7.9 mm
Jewels: 24
Frequency: 28,800 vph
Balance spring: flat hairspring
Shock protection: Incabloc
Remarks: related calibers: A07.161 (with power reserve display)

Caliber A07.171 (dial side)

Automatic; ETACHRON regulating system with fine-timing device, rotor on ball bearings, stop-second system; single spring barrel; 48-hour power reserve
Functions: hours, minutes, sweep seconds; 2nd time zone, additional 24-hour display (2nd time zone); quick-set date window
Diameter: 37.2 mm
Height: 7.9 mm
Jewels: 24
Frequency: 28,800 vph
Balance spring: flat hairspring
Shock protection: Incabloc

Caliber A07.211 (dial side)

Automatic; ETACHRON regulating system with fine-timing device, rotor on ball bearings, stop-second system; single spring barrel; 48-hour power reserve
Functions: hours, minutes, subsidiary seconds; chronograph; quick-set date window
Diameter: 37.2 mm
Height: 7.9 mm
Jewels: 25
Frequency: 28,800 vph
Balance spring: flat hairspring
Shock protection: Incabloc

Caliber 2000-1

Automatic; ball bearing–mounted rotor; stop-seconds, ETACHRON regulating system; single spring barrel; 40-hour power reserve
Functions: hours, minutes, sweep seconds; quick-set date window
Diameter: 20 mm
Height: 3.6 mm
Jewels: 20
Balance: glucydur
Frequency: 28,800 vph
Balance spring: flat hairspring
Shock protection: Incabloc

Caliber 2671

Automatic; ball bearing–mounted rotor; stop-seconds, ETACHRON regulating system; single spring barrel; 38-hour power reserve
Functions: hours, minutes, sweep seconds; date window
Diameter: 17.5 mm
Height: 4.8 mm
Jewels: 25
Balance: glucydur
Frequency: 28,800 vph
Balance spring: flat hairspring
Shock protection: Incabloc
Remarks: related calibers: 2678 (additional weekday window, height 5.35 mm)

Caliber 2681 (dial side)

Automatic; ball bearing–mounted rotor; stop-seconds, ETACHRON regulating system; single spring barrel; 38-hour power reserve
Functions: hours, minutes, sweep seconds; quick-set date window
Diameter: 20 mm
Height: 4.8 mm
Jewels: 25
Balance: glucydur
Frequency: 28,800 vph
Balance spring: flat hairspring
Shock protection: Incabloc

Caliber 2801-2

Manually wound; ETACHRON regulating system; 42-hour power reserve
Functions: hours, minutes, sweep seconds
Diameter: 26 mm
Height: 3.35 mm
Jewels: 17
Frequency: 28,800 vph
Related caliber: 2804-2 (with date window and quick set)

Caliber 2824-2

Automatic; ball bearing–mounted rotor; stop-seconds, ETACHRON regulating system; 38-hour power reserve
Functions: hours, minutes, sweep seconds; quick-set date window at 3 o'clock
Diameter: 26 mm
Height: 4.6 mm
Jewels: 25
Frequency: 28,800 vph
Related calibers: 2836-2 (additional day window at 3 o'clock, height 5.05 mm); 2826-2 (with large date, height 6.2 mm)

Caliber 2834-2 (dial side)

Automatic; ball bearing–mounted rotor; stop-seconds, ETACHRON regulating system; single spring barrel; 38-hour power reserve
Functions: hours, minutes, sweep seconds; quick-set date window, quick set weekday
Diameter: 29.4 mm
Height: 5.05 mm
Jewels: 25
Balance: glucydur
Frequency: 28,800 vph
Balance spring: flat hairspring
Shock protection: Incabloc

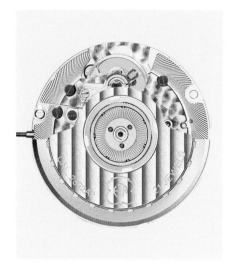

Caliber 2892-A2

Automatic; ball bearing–mounted rotor; stop-seconds, ETACHRON regulating system; single spring barrel; 42-hour power reserve
Functions: hours, minutes, sweep seconds; quick-set date window
Diameter: 26.2 mm
Height: 3.6 mm
Jewels: 21
Balance: glucydur
Frequency: 28,800 vph
Balance spring: flat hairspring
Shock protection: Incabloc

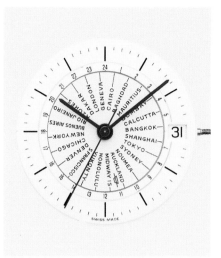

Caliber 2893-1 (dial side)

Automatic; ball bearing rotor; stop-seconds, ETACHRON regulating system; 42-hour power reserve
Functions: hours, minutes, sweep seconds; quick-set date window at 3 o'clock; world time display via central disk
Diameter: 25.6 mm
Height: 4.1 mm
Jewels: 21
Frequency: 28,800 vph
Related calibers: 2893-2 (24-hour hand; 2nd time zone instead of world time disk); 2893-3 (only world time disk without date window)

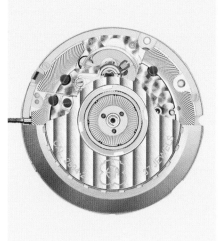

Caliber 2894-2

Automatic; ball bearing–mounted rotor; stop-seconds, ETACHRON regulating system; single spring barrel; 42-hour power reserve
Functions: hours, minutes, subsidiary seconds; chronograph; quick-set date window
Diameter: 28.6 mm
Height: 6.1 mm
Jewels: 37
Balance: glucydur
Frequency: 28,800 vph
Balance spring: flat hairspring
Shock protection: Incabloc
Related caliber: 2094 (diameter 23.9 mm, height 5.5 mm, 33 jewels)

Caliber 2895-2 (dial side)

Automatic; ball bearing–mounted rotor; stop-seconds, ETACHRON regulating system; single spring barrel; 42-hour power reserve
Functions: hours, minutes, subsidiary seconds, at 6 o'clock; quick-set date window
Diameter: 26.2 mm
Height: 4.35 mm
Jewels: 27
Balance: glucydur
Frequency: 28,800 vph
Balance spring: flat hairspring
Shock protection: Incabloc

Caliber 2896 (dial side)

Automatic; ball bearing rotor; stop-seconds, ETACHRON regulating system; 42-hour power reserve
Functions: hours, minutes, sweep seconds; power reserve display at 3 o'clock
Diameter: 25.6 mm
Height: 4.85 mm
Jewels: 21
Frequency: 28,800 vph

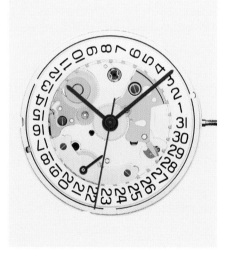

Caliber 2897 (dial side)

Automatic; ball bearing–mounted rotor; stop-seconds, ETACHRON regulating system; single spring barrel; 42-hour power reserve
Functions: hours, minutes, sweep seconds; power reserve indicator; quick-set date window
Diameter: 26.2 mm
Height: 4.85 mm
Jewels: 21
Balance: glucydur
Frequency: 28,800 vph
Balance spring: flat hairspring
Shock protection: Incabloc

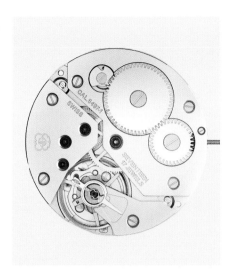

Caliber 6497-1

Manually wound; ETACHRON regulating system; single spring barrel; 46-hour power reserve
Functions: hours, minutes, subsidiary seconds
Diameter: 37.2 mm
Height: 4.5 mm
Jewels: 17
Frequency: 18,000 vph
Balance spring: flat hairspring
Remarks: pocket watch movement (Unitas model) in Lépine version with subsidiary seconds extending from the winding stem); as Caliber 6497-2 with 21,600 vph and 53-hour power reserve

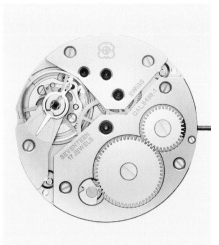

Caliber 6498-1

Manually wound; ETACHRON regulating system; single spring barrel; 46-hour power reserve
Functions: hours, minutes, subsidiary seconds
Diameter: 37.2 mm
Height: 4.5 mm
Jewels: 17
Frequency: 18,000 vph
Balance spring: flat hairspring
Remarks: pocket watch movement (Unitas model) in savonette version (subsidiary seconds at right angle to the winding stem); as Caliber 6498-2 with 21,600 vph and 53-hour power reserve)

Caliber 7001

Manually wound; ultrathin construction; single spring barrel; 42-hour power reserve
Functions: hours, minutes, subsidiary seconds
Diameter: 23.7 mm
Height: 2.5 mm
Jewels: 17
Frequency: 21,600 vph
Balance spring: flat hairspring

Caliber 7750 (dial side)

Automatic; stop-second system; single spring barrel; 42-hour power reserve
Functions: hours, minutes, subsidiary seconds; chronograph; quick-set date and weekday window
Diameter: 30.4 mm
Height: 7.9 mm
Jewels: 25
Balance: glucydur
Frequency: 28,800 vph
Balance spring: flat hairspring
Shock protection: Incabloc

Caliber 7751 (dial side)

Automatic; stop-second system; single spring barrel; 42-hour power reserve
Functions: hours, minutes, subsidiary seconds; additional 24-hour display; chronograph; full calendar with date, weekday, month, moon phase
Diameter: 30.4 mm
Height: 7.9 mm
Jewels: 25
Balance: glucydur
Frequency: 28,800 vph
Balance spring: flat hairspring
Shock protection: Incabloc
Remarks: related caliber: 7754 with sweep 24-hour hand (2nd time zone)

Caliber 7753

Automatic; stop-second system; single spring barrel; 42-hour power reserve
Functions: hours, minutes, subsidiary seconds; chronograph; quick-set date window with pusher
Diameter: 30.4
Height: 7.9 mm
Jewels: 25
Balance: glucydur
Frequency: 28,800 vph
Balance spring: flat hairspring
Shock protection: Incabloc
Remarks: variation of the Valjoux chronograph caliber with symmetrical "tricompax" ordering of the totalizers

RONDA

Ronda is a Swiss company with a long tradition. It was founded by William Mosset, born in 1909 in the village of Hölstein, a man whose gift for micro-engineering declared itself early on when he invented a way to drill thirty-two holes in a metal plate in one operation and with great accuracy. The company was founded in 1946 in Lausen, a little town in the hinterlands of German-speaking Switzerland near Basel, where the first factory was built.

In the meantime the company has turned into a group with five subsidiaries: There are two production sites in Ticino, one in the Jura mountains, one operation in Thailand, and sales offices in Hong Kong. Overall, Ronda employs around 1,800 people in Switzerland and Asia.

The shareholders of the family enterprise, which is now in its second generation, value the company's absolute independence. This is undoubtedly a key advantage for the customer, since Ronda can continue defining its own strategy and can react decisively to customer needs.

That is why the company, which had already made a name for itself with quartz movements, decided to add a portfolio of automatic mechanical movements. The first product batches arrived on the market in early 2017; in the medium term, the mechanical Ronda Caliber R150 is to be produced in batches of six figures per year.

Caliber R150

Automatic; ball bearing–mounted rotor; stop-seconds, index for fine adjustment; single spring barrel; 40-hour power reserve
Functions: hours, minutes, sweep seconds; quick set date
Diameter: 25.6 mm
Height: 4.4 mm
Jewels: 25
Frequency: 28,800 vph
Balance spring: flat hairspring
Shock protection: Incabloc

Caliber 5040.B

Quartz; 54-month power reserve; single spring barrel
Functions: hours, minutes, subsidiary seconds; chronograph, with add and split function; large date
Diameter: 28.6 mm
Height: 4.4 mm
Jewels: 13

Caliber 7004.P

Quartz; 48-month power reserve; single spring barrel
Functions: hours, minutes, subsidiary seconds; large date and weekday (retrograde)
Diameter: 34.6 mm
Height: 5.6 mm
Jewels: 6

SELLITA

Sellita, founded in 1950 by Pierre Grandjean in La Chaux-de-Fonds, is one of the biggest reassemblers and embellishers in the mechanical watch industry. On average, Sellita embellishes and finishes about one million automatic and hand-wound movements annually—a figure that represents about 25 percent of Switzerland's mechanical movement production according to Miguel García, Sellita's president.

Reassembly can be defined as the assembly and regulation of components to make a functioning movement. This is the type of work that ETA loved to give to outside companies back in the day in order to concentrate on manufacturing complete quartz movements and individual components for them.

Reassembly workshops like Sellita refine and embellish components purchased from ETA according to their customers' wishes and can even successfully fulfill smaller orders made by the company's estimated 350 clients.

When ETA announced that it would only sell *ebauches* to companies outside the Swatch Group until the end of 2010, García, who has owned Sellita since 2003, reacted immediately, deciding that his company should develop its own products.

García planned and implemented a new line of movements based on the dimensions of the most popular ETA calibers, whose patents had expired. Having expanded within a new factory on the outskirts of La Chaux-de-Fonds with 3,500 square meters of space, Sellita offers a number of movements—such as SW 200, which corresponds in all of its important dimensions to ETA Caliber 2824, and Caliber SW 300, equivalent to ETA Caliber 2892.

Another expansion project began as a joint venture with Mühle Glashütte: Gurofa in Glashütte currently makes some components for Calibers SW 220 and 240.

Caliber SW200-1

Automatic; ball bearing–mounted rotor; stop-second system; single spring barrel; 38-hour power reserve
Functions: hours, minutes, sweep seconds; quick-set date
Diameter: 25.6 mm
Height: 4.6 mm
Jewels: 26
Balance: nickel or glucydur
Frequency: 28,800 vph
Balance spring: Nivaflex
Shock protection: Novodiac or Incabloc

Caliber SW210-1

Manually wound; stop-second system; single spring barrel; 42-hour power reserve
Functions: hours, minutes, sweep seconds
Diameter: 25.6 mm
Height: 3.35 mm
Jewels: 19
Balance: nickel
Frequency: 28,800 vph
Balance spring: Nivaflex
Shock protection: Novodiac or Incabloc
Remarks: related caliber: SW215 (with window date)

Caliber SW220-1

Automatic; ball bearing–mounted rotor; stop-second system; single spring barrel; 38-hour power reserve
Functions: hours, minutes, sweep seconds; quick-set date and weekday
Diameter: 25.6 mm
Height: 5.05 mm
Jewels: 26
Balance: nickel or glucydur
Frequency: 28,800 vph
Balance spring: flat hairspring, Nivaflex
Shock protection: Novodiac or Incabloc
Remarks: related calibers: SW221-1 (with hand date); SW240-1 with larger mainplate (ø 29 mm)

Caliber SW260-1

Automatic; ball bearing–mounted rotor; stop-second system; single spring barrel; 38-hour power reserve
Functions: hours, minutes, subsidiary seconds at 6 o'clock; quick-set date
Diameter: 25.6 mm
Height: 5.6 mm
Jewels: 31
Balance: nickel or glucydur
Frequency: 28,800 vph
Balance spring: flat hairspring, Nivaflex
Shock protection: Novodiac or Incabloc
Remarks: related caliber: SW290-1 (subsidiary seconds at 9 o'clock)

Caliber SW300-1

Automatic; ball bearing–mounted rotor; stop-second system; single spring barrel; 42-hour power reserve
Functions: hours, minutes, sweep seconds; quick-set date
Diameter: 25.6 mm
Height: 3.6 mm
Jewels: 25
Balance: glucydur
Frequency: 28,800 vph
Balance spring: flat hairspring, Nivaflex
Shock protection: Incabloc
Remarks: related caliber: SW360-1 (with subsidiary seconds, height 4.35 mm, 31 jewels)

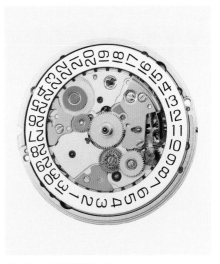

Caliber SW330-1

Automatic; ball bearing–mounted rotor; stop-second system; single spring barrel, 42-hour power reserve
Functions: hours, minutes, sweep seconds; 2nd time zone, additional 24-hour display (2nd time zone); quick-set date
Diameter: 25.6 mm
Height: 4.1 mm
Jewels: 25
Balance: glucydur
Frequency: 28,800 vph
Balance spring: flat hairspring, Nivaflex
Shock protection: Incabloc

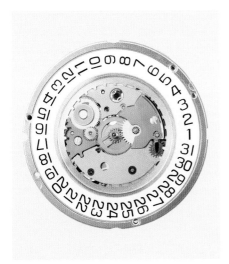

Caliber SW400-1

Automatic; ball bearing–mounted rotor; stop-second system; single spring barrel; 38-hour power reserve
Functions: hours, minutes, sweep seconds; quick-set date
Diameter: 31 mm
Height: 4.67 mm
Jewels: 26
Balance: nickel or glucydur
Frequency: 28,800 vph
Balance spring: Nivaflex
Shock protection: Novodiac or Incabloc

Caliber SW500-1

Automatic; ball bearing–mounted rotor; stop-second system; single spring barrel; 48-hour power reserve
Functions: hours, minutes, subsidiary seconds; chronograph quick-set date and weekday
Diameter: 30 mm
Height: 7.9 mm
Jewels: 25
Balance: nickel or glucydur
Frequency: 28,800 vph
Balance spring: Nivaflex
Shock protection: Incabloc

Caliber SW1000-1

Automatic; ball bearing–mounted rotor; stop-second system; single spring barrel; 38-hour power reserve
Functions: hours, minutes, sweep seconds; quick-set date
Diameter: 20 mm
Height: 3.9 mm
Jewels: 18
Balance: nickel or glucydur
Frequency: 28,800 vph
Balance spring: Nivaflex
Shock protection: Incabloc

Watch Your Watch

Mechanical watches are not only by and large more expensive and complex than quartzes, they are also a little high-maintenance, as it were. The mechanism within does need servicing occasionally—perhaps a touch of oil and an adjustment. Worse yet, the complexity of all those wheels and pinions engaged in reproducing the galaxy means that a user will occasionally do something perfectly harmless like wind his or her watch up only to find everything grinding to a halt. Here are some tips for dealing with these mechanical beauties for new watch owners and reminders for the old hands.

1. DATE CHANGES

Do not change the date manually (via the crown or pusher) on any mechanical watch—whether manual wind or automatic—when the time indicated on the dial reads between 10 and 2 o'clock. Although some better watches are protected against this horological quirk, most mechanical watches with a date indicator are engaged in the process of automatically changing the date between the hours of 10 p.m. and 2 a.m. Intervening with a forced manual change while the automatic date shift is engaged can damage the movement. Of course, you can make the adjustment between 10 a.m. and 2 p.m. in most cases—but this is just not a good habit to get into. When in doubt, roll the time past 12 o'clock and look for an automatic date change before you set the time and date. The Ulysse Nardin brand is notable, among a very few others, for in-house mechanical movements immune to this effect.

2. CHRONOGRAPH USE

On a simple chronograph, start and stop are almost always the same button. Normally located above the crown, the start/stop actuator can be pressed at will to initiate and end the interval timing. The reset button, normally below the crown, is only used for resetting the chronograph to zero, but only when the chronograph is stopped—never while engaged. Only a "flyback" chronograph allows safe resetting to zero while running. With the chronograph engaged, you simply hit the reset button and all the chronograph indicators (seconds, minutes, and hours) snap back to zero and the chronograph begins to accumulate the interval time once again. In the early days of air travel this was a valuable complication as pilots would reset their chronographs when taking on a new heading—without having to fumble about with a three-step procedure with gloved hands.

Nota bene: Don't actuate or reset your chronograph while your watch is submerged—even if you have one of those that are built for such usage, like Omega, IWC, and a few other brands. Feel free to hit the buttons before submersion and jump in and swim while they run; just don't push anything while in the water.

3. CHANGING TIME BACKWARD

Don't adjust the time on your watch in a counterclockwise direction—especially if the watch has calendar functions. A few watches can tolerate the abuse, but it's better to avoid the possibility of damage altogether. Change the dates as needed (remembering the 10 and 2 rule above).

4. SHOCKS

Almost all modern watches are equipped with some level of shock protection. Best practices for the Swiss brands allow for a three-foot fall onto a hard wood surface. But if your watch is running poorly—or even worse has stopped entirely after an impact—do not shake, wind, or bang it again to get it running; take it to an expert for service as you may do even more damage. Sports like tennis, squash, or golf can have a deleterious effect on your watch, including flattening the pivots, overbanking, or even bending or breaking a pivot.

5. OVERWINDING

Most modern watches are fitted with a mechanism that allows the mainspring to slide inside the barrel—or stops it completely once the spring is fully wound—for protection against overwinding. The best advice here is just don't force it. Over the years, a winding crown may start to get "stickier" and more difficult to turn even when unwound. That's a sure sign it is due for service.

6. JACUZZI TEMPERATURE

Don't jump into the Jacuzzi—or even a steaming hot shower—with your watch on. Better-built watches with a deeper water-resistance rating typically have no problem with this scenario. However, take a 3 or 5 atm water-resistant watch into the Jacuzzi, and there's a chance the different rates of expansion and contraction of the metals and sapphire or mineral crystals may allow moisture into the case.

Bovet's barrier to pressing the wrong pusher.

Panerai makes sure you think before touching the crown.

Do it yourself at your own risk.

7. SCREW THAT CROWN DOWN (AND THOSE PUSHERS)!

Always check and double-check to ensure a watch fitted with a screwed-down crown is closed tightly. Screwed-down pushers for a chronograph—or any other functions—deserve the same attention. This one oversight has cost quite a few owners their watches. If a screwed-down crown is not secured, water will likely get into the case and start oxidizing the metal. In time, the problem can destroy the watch.

8. MAGNETISM

If your watch is acting up, running faster or slower, it may have become magnetized. This can happen if you leave your timepiece near a computer, cell phone, or some other electronic device. Many service centers have a so-called degausser to take care of the problem. A number of brands also make watches with a soft iron core to deflect magnetic fields, though this might not work with the stronger ones.

9. TRIBOLOGY

Keeping a mechanical timepiece hidden away in a box for extended lengths of time is not the best way to care for it. Even if you don't wear a watch every day, it is a good idea to run your watch at regular intervals to keep its lubricating oils and greases viscous. Think about a can of house paint: Keep it stirred and it stays liquid almost indefinitely; leave it still for too long and a skin develops. On a smaller level the same thing can happen to the lubricants inside a mechanical watch.

10. SERVICE

Most mechanical watches call for a three- to five-year service cycle for cleaning, oiling, and maintenance. Some mechanical watches can run twice that long and have functioned within acceptable parameters, but if you're not going to have your watch serviced at regular intervals, you do run the risk of having timing issues. Always have your watch serviced by a qualified watchmaker (see box), not at the kiosk in the local mall. The best you can expect there is a quick battery change.

Gary Girdvainis is the founder of Isochron Media LLC, publishers of WristWatch *and* AboutTime *magazines.*

Glossary

ANNUAL CALENDAR

The automatic allowances for the different lengths of each month of a year in the calendar module of a watch. This type of watch usually shows the month and date, and sometimes the day of the week (like this one by Patek Philippe) and the phases of the moon.

ANTIMAGNETIC

Magnetic fields found in common everyday places affect mechanical movements, hence the use of anti- or non-magnetic components in the movement. Some companies encase movements in antimagnetic cores such as Sinn's Model 756, the Duograph, shown here.

ANTIREFLECTION

A film created by steaming the crystal to eliminate light reflection and improve legibility. Antireflection functions best when applied to both sides of the crystal, but because it scratches, some manufacturers prefer to have it only on the interior of the crystal. It is mainly used on synthetic sapphire crystals. Dubey & Schaldenbrand applies antireflection on both sides for all of the company's wristwatches, such as this Aquadyn model.

AUTOMATIC WINDING

A rotating weight set into motion by moving the wrist winds the spring barrel via the gear train of a mechanical watch movement. Automatic winding was invented during the pocket watch era in 1770, but the breakthrough automatic winding movement via rotor began with the ball bearing Eterna-Matic in the late 1940s. Today we speak of unidirectional winding and bidirectionally winding rotors, depending on the type of gear train used. Shown is IWC's automatic Caliber 50611.

BALANCE

The beating heart of a mechanical watch movement is the balance. Fed by the energy of the mainspring, a tirelessly oscillating little wheel, just a few millimeters in diameter and possessing a spiral-shaped balance spring, sets the rhythm for the escape wheel and pallets with its vibration frequency. Today the balance is usually made of one piece of antimagnetic glucydur, an alloy that expands very little when exposed to heat.

BAR OR COCK

A metal plate fastened to the base plate at one point, leaving room for a gear wheel or pinion. The balance is usually attached to a bar called the balance cock. Glashütte tradition dictates that the balance cock be decoratively engraved by hand like this one by Glashütte Original.

BEVELING

To uniformly file down the sharp edges of a plate, bridge, or bar and give it a high polish. The process is also called *anglage.* Edges are usually beveled at a 45° angle. As the picture shows, this is painstaking work that needs the skilled hands and eyes of an experienced watchmaker or *angleur.*

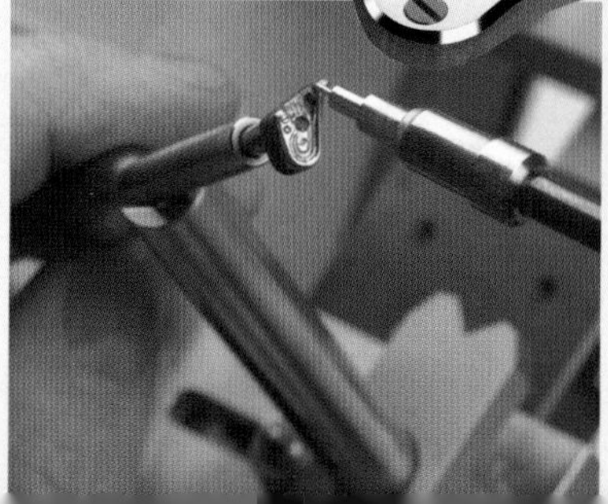

BRIDGE

A metal plate fastened to the base plate at two points leaving room for a gear wheel or pinion. This vintage Favre-Leuba movement illustrates the point with three individual bridges.

CALIBER

A term, similar to type or model, that refers to different watch movements. Pictured here is Heuer's Caliber 11, the legendary automatic chronograph caliber from 1969. This movement was a coproduction jointly researched and developed for four years by Heuer-Leonidas, Breitling, and Hamilton-Büren. Each company gave the movement a different name after serial production began.

CARBON FIBER

A very light, tough composite material, carbon fiber is composed of filaments comprised of several thousand seven-micron carbon fibers held together by resin. The arrangement of the filaments determines the quality of a component, making each unique. Carbon fiber is currently being used for dials, cases, and even movement components.

CHAMPLEVÉ

A dial decoration technique, whereby the metal is engraved, filled with enamel, and baked, as in this cockatoo on a Cartier Tortue, enhanced with mother-of-pearl slivers.

CERAMIC

An inorganic, nonmetallic material formed by the action of heat and practically unscratchable. Pioneered by Rado, ceramic is a high-tech material generally made from aluminum and zirconia oxide. Today, it is used generally for cases and bezels and now comes in many colors.

CHRONOGRAPH

From the Greek *chronos* (time) and *graphein* (to write). Originally a chronograph literally wrote, inscribing the time elapsed on a piece of paper with the help of a pencil attached to a type of hand. Today this term is used for watches that show not only the time of day, but also certain time intervals via independent hands that may be started or stopped at will. Stopwatches differ from chronographs because they do not show the time of day. This exploded illustration shows the complexity of a Breitling chronograph.

CHRONOMETER

Literally, "measurer of time." As the term is used today, a chronometer denotes an especially accurate watch (one with a deviation of no more than 5 seconds a day for mechanical movements). Chronometers are usually supplied with an official certificate from an independent testing office such as the COSC. The largest producer of chronometers in 2008 was Rolex, with 769,850 officially certified movements. Chopard came in sixth with more than 22,000 certified L.U.C mechanisms, like the 4.96 in the Pro One model shown here.

COLUMN WHEEL

The component used to control chronograph functions within a true chronograph movement. The presence of a column wheel indicates that the chronograph is fully integrated into the movement. In the modern era, modules are generally used that are attached to a base caliber movement. This particular column wheel is made of blued steel.

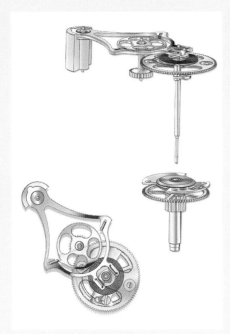

CONSTANT FORCE MECHANISM

Sometimes called a constant force escapement, it isn't really: in most cases this mechanism is "simply" an initial tension spring. It is also known in English by part of its French name, the *remontoir*, which actually means "winding mechanism." This mechanism regulates and portions the energy that is passed on through the escapement, making the rate as even and precise as possible. Shown here is the constant force escapement from A. Lange & Söhne's Lange 31—a mechanism that gets as close to its name as possible.

COSC

The Contrôle Officiel Suisse de Chronomètrage, the official Swiss testing office for chronometers. The COSC is the world's largest issuer of so-called chronometer certificates, which are only otherwise given out individually by certain observatories (such as the one in Neuchâtel, Switzerland). For a fee, the COSC tests the rate of movements that have been adjusted by watchmakers. These are usually mechanical movements, but the office also tests some high-precision quartz movements. Those that meet the specifications for being a chronometer are awarded an official certificate as shown here.

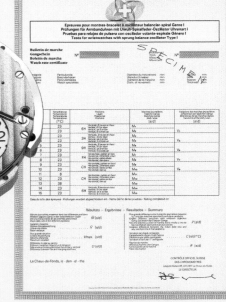

CÔTES DE GENÈVE

Also called *vagues de Genève* and Geneva stripes. This is a traditional Swiss surface decoration comprising an even pattern of parallel stripes, applied to flat movement components with a quickly rotating plastic or wooden peg. Glashütte watchmakers have devised their own version of *côtes de Genève* that is applied at a slightly different angle, called Glashütte ribbing.

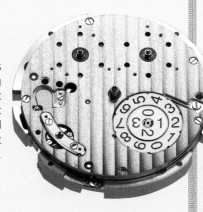

CROWN

The crown is used to wind and set a watch. A few simple turns of the crown will get an automatic movement started, while a manually wound watch is completely wound by the crown. The crown is also used for the setting of various functions, almost always including at least the hours, minutes, seconds, and date. A screwed-down crown like the one on the TAG Heuer Aquagraph pictured here can be tightened to prevent water entering the case or any mishaps while performing extreme sports such as diving.

EQUATION OF TIME

The mean time that we use to keep track of the passing of the day (24 hours evenly divided into minutes and seconds) is not equal to true solar time. The equation of time is a complication devised to show the difference between the mean time shown on one's wristwatch and the time the sun dictates. The Équation Marchante by Blancpain very distinctly indicates this difference via the golden sun-tipped hand that also rotates around the dial in a manner known to watch connoisseurs as *marchant*. Other wristwatch models, such as the Boreas by Martin Braun, display the difference on an extra scale on the dial.

ESCAPEMENT

The combination of the balance, balance spring, pallets, and escape wheel, a subgroup which divides the impulses coming from the spring barrel into small, accurately portioned doses. It guarantees that the gear train runs smoothly and efficiently. The pictured escapement is one newly invented by Parmigiani, containing pallet stones of varying colors, though they are generally red synthetic rubies. Here one of them is a colorless sapphire, or corundum, the same geological material that ruby is made of.

FLINQUÉ

A dial decoration in which a guilloché design is given a coat of enamel, softening the pattern and creating special effects, as shown here on a unique Bovet.

GEAR TRAIN

A mechanical watch's gear train transmits energy from the mainspring to the escapement. The gear train comprises the minute wheel, the third wheel, the fourth wheel, and the escape wheel.

GLUCYDUR

Glucydur is a functional alloy of copper, beryllium, and iron that has been used to make balances in watches since the 1930s. Its hardness and stability allow watchmakers to use balances that were poised at the factory and no longer required adjustment screws.

INDEX

A regulating mechanism found on the balance cock and used by the watchmaker to adjust the movement's rate. The index changes the effective length of the balance spring, thus making it move more quickly or slowly. This is the standard index found on an ETA Valjoux 7750.

FLYBACK CHRONOGRAPH

A chronograph with a special dial train switch that makes the immediate reuse of the chronograph movement possible after resetting the hands. It was developed for special timekeeping duties such as those found in aviation, which require the measurement of time intervals in quick succession. A flyback may also be called a *retour en vol*. An elegant example of this type of chronograph is Corum's Classical Flyback Large Date shown here.

GUILLOCHÉ

A surface decoration usually applied to the dial and the rotor using a grooving tool with a sharp tip, such as a rose engine, to cut an even pattern onto a level surface. The exact adjustment of the tool for each new path is controlled by a device similar to a pantograph, and the movement of the tool can be controlled either manually or mechanically. Real *guillochis* (the correct term used by a master of guilloché) are very intricate and expensive to produce, which is why most dials decorated in this fashion are produced by stamping machines. Breguet is one of the very few companies to use real guilloché on every one of its dials.

JEWEL

To minimize friction, the hardened steel tips of a movement's rotating gear wheels (called pinions) are lodged in synthetic rubies (fashioned as polished stones with a hole) and lubricated with a very thin layer of special oil. These synthetic rubies are produced in exactly the same way as sapphire crystal using the same material. During the pocket watch era, real rubies with hand-drilled holes were still used, but because of the high costs involved, they were only used in movements with especially quickly rotating gears. The jewel shown here on a bridge from A. Lange & Söhne's Double Split is additionally embedded in a gold chaton secured with three blued screws.

LIGA

The word LIGA is actually a German acronym that stands for lithography (*Lithografie*), electroplating (*Galvanisierung*), and plastic molding (*Abformung*). It is a lithographic process exposed by UV or X-ray light that literally "grows" perfect micro components made of nickel, nickel-phosphorus, or 23.5-karat gold in a plating bath. The components need no finishing or trimming after manufacture.

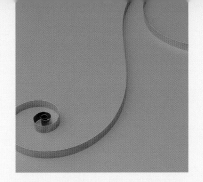

LUMINOUS SUBSTANCE

Tritium paint is a slightly radioactive substance that replaced radium as a luminous coating for hands, numerals, and hour markers on watch dials. Watches bearing tritium must be marked as such, with the letter *T* on the dial near 6 o'clock. It has now for the most part been replaced by nonradioactive materials such as Superluminova. Traser technology (as seen on these Ball timepieces) uses tritium gas enclosed in tiny silicate glass tubes coated on the inside with a phosphorescing substance. The luminescence is constant and will hold around twenty-five years.

MAINSPRING

The mainspring, located in the spring barrel, stores energy when tensioned and passes it on to the escapement via the gear train as the tension relaxes. Today, mainsprings are generally made of Nivaflex, an alloy invented by Swiss engineer Max Straumann at the beginning of the 1950s. This alloy basically comprises iron, nickel, chrome, cobalt, and beryllium.

MINUTE REPEATER

A striking mechanism with hammers and gongs for acoustically signaling the hours, quarter hours, and minutes elapsed since noon or midnight. The wearer pushes a slide, which winds the spring. Normally a repeater uses two different gongs to signal hours (low tone), quarter hours (high and low tones in succession), and minutes (high tone). Some watches have three gongs, called a carillon. The Chronoswiss Répétition à Quarts is a prominent repeating introduction of recent years.

PERPETUAL CALENDAR

The calendar module for this type of timepiece automatically makes allowances for the different lengths of each month as well as leap years until the next secular year, which will occur in 2100. A perpetual calendar usually shows the date, month, and four-year cycle, and may show the day of the week and moon phase as well, as does this one introduced by George J von Burg at Baselworld 2005. Perpetual calendars need much skill to complete.

PERLAGE

Surface decoration comprising an even pattern of partially overlapping dots, applied with a quickly rotating plastic or wooden peg, as shown here on the plates of Frédérique Constant's *manufacture* Caliber FC 910-1.

PLATE

A metal platform having several tiers for the gear train. The base plate of a movement usually incorporates the dial and carries the bearings for the primary pinions of the "first floor" of a gear train. The gear wheels are made complete by tightly fitting screwed-in bridges and bars on the back side of the plate. A specialty of the so-called Glashütte school, as opposed to the Swiss school, is the reverse completion of a movement not via different bridges and bars, but rather with a three-quarter plate. Glashütte Original's Caliber 65 (shown) displays a beautifully decorated three-quarter plate.

POWER RESERVE DISPLAY

A mechanical watch contains only a certain amount of power reserve. A fully wound modern automatic watch usually possesses between 36 and 42 hours of energy before it needs to be wound again. The power reserve display keeps the wearer informed about how much energy his or her watch still has in reserve, a function that is especially practical on manually wound watches with several days of possible reserve. The Nomos Tangente Power Reserve pictured here represents an especially creative way to illustrate the state of the mainspring's tension. On some German watches the power reserve is also displayed with the words "auf" and "ab."

PULSOMETER

A scale on the dial, flange, or bezel that, in conjunction with the second hand, may be used to measure a pulse rate. A pulsometer is always marked with a reference number—if it is marked with *gradué pour 15 pulsations*, for example, then the wearer counts fifteen pulse beats. At the last beat, the second hand will show what the pulse rate is in beats per minute on the pulsometer scale. The scale on Sinn's World Time Chronograph (shown) is marked simply with the German world *Puls* (pulse), but the function remains the same.

QUALITÉ FLEURIER

This certification of quality was established by Chopard, Parmigiani Fleurier, Vaucher, and Bovet Fleurier in 2004. Watches bearing the seal must fulfill five criteria, including COSC certification, passing several tests for robustness and precision, top-notch finishing, and being 100 percent Swiss-made (except for the raw materials). The seal appears here on the dial of the Parmigiani Fleurier Tonda 39.

RETROGRADE DISPLAY

A retrograde display shows the time linearly instead of circularly. The hand continues along an arc until it reaches the end of its scale, at which precise moment it jumps back to the beginning instantaneously. This Nienaber model not only shows the minutes in retrograde form, it is also a regulator display.

ROTOR

The rotor is the component that keeps an automatic watch wound. The kinetic motion of this part, which contains a heavy metal weight around its outer edge, winds the mainspring. It can either wind unilaterally or bilaterally (to one or both sides) depending on the caliber. The rotor from this Temption timepiece belongs to an ETA Valjoux 7750.

SCREW BALANCE

Before the invention of the perfectly weighted balance using a smooth ring, balances were fitted with weighted screws to get the exact impetus desired. Today a screw balance is a subtle sign of quality in a movement due to its costly construction and assembly utilizing minuscule weighted screws.

SAPPHIRE CRYSTAL

Synthetic sapphire crystal is known to gemologists as aluminum oxide (Al_2O_3) or corundum. It can be colorless (corundum), red (ruby), blue (sapphire), or green (emerald). It is virtually scratchproof; only a diamond is harder. The innovative Royal Blue Tourbillon by Ulysse Nardin pictured here features not only sapphire crystals on the front and back of the watch, but also actual plates made of both colorless and blue corundum within the movement.

SEAL OF GENEVA

Since 1886 the official seal of this canton has been awarded to Genevan watch *manufactures* who must follow a defined set of high-quality criteria that include the following: polished jewel bed drillings, jewels with olive drillings, polished winding wheels, quality balances and balance springs, steel levers and springs with beveling of 45 degrees and *côtes de Genève* decoration, and polished stems and pinions. The list was updated in 2012 to include the entire watch and newer components. Testing is done on the finished piece. The Seal consists of two, one on the movement, one on the case. The pictured seal was awarded to Vacheron Constantin, a traditional Genevan *manufacture*.

SILICIUM/SILICON

Silicon is an element relatively new to mechanical watches. It is currently being used in the manufacture of precision escapements. Ulysse Nardin's Freak has lubrication-free silicon wheels, and Breguet has successfully used flat silicon balance springs.

SKELETONIZATION

The technique of cutting a movement's components down to their weight-bearing basic substance. This is generally done by hand in painstaking hours of microscopic work with a small handheld saw, though machines can skeletonize parts to a certain degree, such as the version of the Valjoux 7750 that was created for Chronoswiss's Opus and Pathos models. This tourbillon created by Christophe Schaffo is additionally—and masterfully—hand-engraved.

SONNERIE

A variety of minute repeater that—like a tower clock—sounds the time not at the will of the wearer, but rather automatically *(en passant)* every hour *(petite sonnerie)* or quarter hour *(grande sonnerie)*. Gérald Genta designed the most complicated sonnerie back in the early nineties. Shown is a recent model from the front and back.

SPLIT-SECONDS CHRONOGRAPH

Also known in the watch industry by its French name, the *rattrapante* (exploded view at left). A watch with two second hands, one of which can be blocked with a special dial train lever to indicate an intermediate time while the other continues to run. When released, the split-seconds hand jumps ahead to the position of the other second hand. The PTC by Porsche Design illustrates this nicely.

SPRING BARREL

The spring barrel contains the mainspring. It turns freely on an arbor, pulled along by the toothed wheel generally doubling as its lid. This wheel interacts with the first pinion of the movement's gear train. Some movements contain two or more spring barrels for added power reserve.

SWAN-NECK FINE ADJUSTMENT

A regulating instrument used by the watchmaker to adjust the movement's rate in place of an index. The swan neck is especially prevalent in fine Swiss and Glashütte watchmaking (here, Lang & Heyne's Moritz model). Mühle Glashütte has varied the theme with its woodpecker's neck.

TACHYMETER

A scale on the dial, flange, or bezel of a chronograph that, in conjunction with the second hand, gives the speed of a moving object. A tachymeter takes a value determined in less than a minute and converts it into miles or kilometers per hour. For example, a wearer could measure the time it takes a car to pass between two mile markers on the highway. When the car passes the marker, the second hand will be pointing to the car's speed in miles per hour on the tachymetric scale.

TOURBILLON

A technical device invented by Abraham-Louis Breguet in 1801 to compensate for the influence of gravity on the balance of a pocket watch. The entire escapement is mounted on an epicyclic train in a "cage" and rotated completely on its axis over regular periods of time. This superb horological highlight is seen as a sign of technological know-how in the modern era. Harry Winston's Histoire de Tourbillon 4 is a spectacular example.

VIBRATION FREQUENCY (VPH)

The spring causes the balance to oscillate at a certain frequency measured in hertz (Hz) or vibrations per hour (vph). Most of today's wristwatches tick at 28,800 vph (4 Hz) or 21,600 vph (3 Hz). Less usual is 18,000 vph (2.5 Hz). Zenith's El Primero was the first serial movement to beat at 36,000 vph (5 Hz), and the Breguet Type XXII runs at 72,000 vph.

WATER RESISTANCE

Water resistance is an important feature of any timepiece and is usually measured in increments of one atmosphere (atm or bar, equal to 10 meters of water pressure) or meters and is often noted on the dial or case back. Watches resistant to 100 meters are best for swimming and snorkeling. Timepieces resistant to 200 meters are good for scuba diving. To deep-sea dive there are various professional timepieces available for use in depths of 200 meters or more. The Hydromax by Bell & Ross (shown) is water-resistant to a record 11,000 meters.

Editor-in-chief: Peter Braun
Editor: Marton Radkai
Production manager: Louise Kurtz
Copy editor: Virginia Carroll
Layout: Muser Medien GmbH
Composition: Madeline Brubaker
Project management: North Market Street Graphics

For more information about advertising, please contact:
Gary Girdvainis
Isochron Media, LLC
25 Gay Bower Road, Monroe, CT 06468
203-485-6276, garygeorgeg@gmail.com

For more information about book sales, please contact:
Abbeville Press, 116 West 23rd Street, New York, NY 10011 or call 1-800-Artbook.

ISBN 978-0-7892-1350-1

Twentieth edition
10 9 8 7 6 5 4 3 2 1

Library of Congress Cataloging-in-Publication Data available upon request.

For bulk and premium sales and for text adoption procedures, write to Customer Service Manager,
Abbeville Press, 116 West 23rd Street, New York, NY 10011, or call 1-800-Artbook.

Visit Abbeville Press online at www.abbeville.com.

ISBN 978-0-7892-1350-1   U.S. $39.95

53995

EAN

9 780789 213501